Disputed Truth

*To the University of Tübingen
my place of work for five decades
in great gratitude*

DISPUTED TRUTH
MEMOIRS

Hans Küng

Translated by John Bowden

continuum

Continuum International Publishing Group
Network Continuum
The Tower Building
11 York Road
SE1 7NX

80 Maiden Lane, Suite 704
New York, NY 10038

www.continuumbooks.com

First published in English in 2008

British Library Cataloguing-in-Publication Data
A catalogue record for this book is available from the British Library.

ISBN 9780826499103 (hardback)

Typeset by YHT Ltd, London
Printed and bound in the USA by Maple-Vail

Contents

CONTENTS

CONTENTS

CONTENTS

Contents

༄༅༅

List of Illustrations

Appearing between pages 496 and 497

Acknowledgements for Illustrations

Agence de Presse van Parys, Brussels,   12, 13, 14
Basle Zeitung, 24
Collegium Germanicum, Rome, 15
Deutscher Künstlerbund, Berlin, 26
Dpa Picture-Alliance GmbH, 10, 11, 16, 27
Alfred Göhner, Tübingen, 5
Manfred Grohe, Tübingen, 2, 3, 4, 20, 21, 23, 29, 30. 31, 32, 33, 34, 40, 41
New York Times and HessDesignWorks.com, 17
L'Osservatore Romano (German edition), 22
Reinhard Schmidt, Tübingen, 37
Der Spiegel,. Hamburg, 19
Anette Stuber-Rousselle, Tübingen, 38
Team editorial services, Rome, 25

All the other photographs are in the private possession of Hans Küng

ৠৄৠৄৠৄ

Prologue

'Both of us regarded this as one of the legitimate differences in theological
position that are necessary for the fruitful development of thought, and
we did not feel that our personal liking for one another or our ability to
collaborate was in any way compromised by such differences.'

Cardinal Joseph Ratzinger in 1998 on his collaboration with Hans
Küng, who was his colleague in Tübingen at that time[1]

I had always hoped to see who would be the next Pope after John Paul II. This
hope has been fulfilled, but certainly not as I and all those who had waited for a
Pope in line with John XXIII and the Second Vatican Council had wanted.

There is no doubt that the papal election in 2005 has considerably increased the
importance of these memoirs, and also my responsibility as an author. Almost all
my great comrades-in-arms in the fight for the renewal of theology and the
church since the time of the Council are dead or inactive, with one exception,
and he has become Pope. Joseph Ratzinger is Benedict XVI.

For many reasons a comparison between our two careers in the second half of
the twentieth century provides extremely illuminating analyses of the development
of Catholic theology and the Catholic Church, indeed of society generally. For a
long time it has been brought home to me that our very different reactions to the
'signs of the times' are typical of the course taken by church and theology. Readers
will often note with amazement how much Joseph Ratzinger and I have in
common, for all our differences. Of course I don't want to give the impression that
his life and mine are as it were linked together by fate or that I would see my life
reflected in Ratzinger's. Each of us is living his own life. But there is no mistaking
the fact that for around four decades our lives largely run in parallel, then make
very close contact, but once again diverge, only to keep crossing time and again.

We have been, and are, Catholic theologians in the service of the Catholic
Church. But unlike Joseph Ratzinger, in the 1960s I decided not to commit
myself to the hierarchical Roman system, which developed institutionally only in
the second millennium, and enter the service of a clerical, centralized 'world
church'; had I done so, I would in fact have restricted myself to the church world.
Rather, as a Catholic Christian and theologian with an evangelical disposition I
wanted to put myself at the service of men and women inside and outside the
Catholic Church and – *hominum confusione Dei providentia*, by human confusion

1

and divine providence – was liberated and impelled to engage intensively in the increasingly important issues of world society. Without ever giving up my roots in the Christian faith, I embarked on a life of expanding concentric circles: the unity of the churches, peace among the religions, the community of nations.

More than 'memoirs'

My career was no organic development, but rather a course of constant challenges and dangers, crises and solutions, hopes and disappointments, successes and defeats. So I am writing the history of a struggle in which I engaged in both words and actions. And at the same time I am telling a sorry story: the story of the reforms which would have been possible after the Second Vatican Council but which were stifled, both in the public arena and behind the scenes.

Readers shouldn't misunderstand what I mean when I say that the recent history of the church can be read out of my life. This is no novel centred on my inner development or even my piety. Nor is it a quasi-pietistic testimony to the faith of a theologian or a pious soul. Not least because of the danger to the continuity between the generations in Christianity, I certainly want to pass on particular experiences in which some readers may be able to recognize themselves. Insight into a human life may sometimes be able to convey wisdom to readers by involving them in it. But in this autobiography I am dealing with more than my own subjective memories; I am talking about life in the most comprehensive sense. So this book is more than memoirs. It dovetails different literary genres and has to be so long because it is written on so many levels.

Americans might possibly call such an enterprise an intellectual biography, in which the history of an individual and the history of ideas are closely interconnected. However, my memoirs are not just about intellectual matters and ideas but about existential and historical events. The history of my life, the churches, theology and the present day flow into one another, as indeed do the history of my work and how it has been received, chronicles and accounts of travels.

Insights from social history help us to understand the contexts, processes and structures in which the individual is involved; methods of social history and biography supplement each other. Distancing itself from a one-sided structuralism which is sceptical about the biographies of individuals, this second volume of memoirs, too, will make clear how time and again individuals (and not just Popes) are able to guide the course of events. And any papal election shows how structures and persons, institutions and mentalities mesh together dialectically. Constantly looking afresh at the development of church and society helps me to avoid the danger of narcissistic circularity which threatens anyone writing a first-person narrative (I think that some information about my public activity is necessary for documentary reasons; sometimes I have banished it to the notes).

In fact, despite all the social driving forces which determine its cause, history is still the drama of human beings – who by no means act rationally. Above all it is the drama of experiencing political and contemporary events, and also the drama of personal experience of life and of crises. This is the only way to correct those harmonizing historians of the churches, theology and councils who after the event and out of ignorance or conformism trivialize conflicts they have not experienced and interpret events and documents all too one-sidedly in a way which is 'friendly to the government'. I will sometimes need to make critical remarks about others involved in the drama. This is not to be seen as a personal vendetta. I understand other options and positions. But in decisive matters personal sensibilities are secondary to the need to argue freely about the truth. And that often requires a sharp pen.

Freedom and truth are and remain two core values of my spiritual and intellectual existence. In my great clash with Rome I have always defended myself against being one-sidedly assigned the role of freedom, with my opponents assigned the role of truth. However, by comparison with my first four decades, in the second half of my life the emphasis has increasingly shifted from *My Struggle for Freedom* (Volume 1) to *Disputed Truth* (Volume 2). I am convinced that the truth must be proclaimed, defended and lived out in truthfulness. I have never counted myself among the blessed possessors of the truth, who happily and proudly think that the truth is theirs. I have always counted myself more among the seekers after truth, who know that scholars, philosophers and theologians in particular must always be concerned with the truth, regardless of fashions and trends – but with all the risks often bound up with the search for it.

Of course memory is subjective and selective. It constantly needs correction. I have taken the greatest trouble to avoid as far as possible defects and caricatures and, aware of my fallibility, to check whatever I could in the sources. Much is based on indisputable public or private documents which, where necessary, have been quoted word for word. Individual chapters have been read by many contemporaries. I am particularly lucky to have in Tübingen some highly competent friends who have read the whole manuscript. I thank them at the end of this book.

So gratitude remains the basic mood in which I go on to present the second part of the account of my life. In this gratitude I hope to be able to live a little longer, boldly and cheerfully.

The historical background

The course of the world and the course of my life come together. Those who, like me, were born in 1928 (or like Joseph Ratzinger, a year earlier) will have witnessed in their lives almost all the turning points in the world during the century after the First World War, with which the nineteenth century really ended. Here I just mark out some dates in the chronicle of the world which are not without significance for the chronicle of my life.

1928: The year of my birth is the last untroubled year of the 'golden twenties', those post-war years full of a passionate desire for life and a craving for pleasure, of cultural creativity and productivity, with their shadow sides of misery and excess. They are sharply interrupted the next year by the black days on Wall Street which turn into a world economic crisis lasting for several years that also affects Europe, my Swiss homeland and politically unstable Germany. Galloping unemployment and increasing social distress form a necessary presupposition for the rise of National Socialism.

1933: Adolf Hitler seizes power and the immediate consequence is a wave of arrests, concentration camps, compulsory antisemitic measures and the establishment of a totalitarian dictatorship which takes control of everything. In Switzerland we are dramatically made aware of the Nazi rule of force that threatens the whole of Europe by the radio broadcasts from neighbouring Austria, by the Nazi coup in Vienna and the murder of Chancellor Engelbert Dolfuss on 25 July 1934. This shocks me deeply at the age of six. Hitler's invasion of Austria on 12 March 1938, which is celebrated there but poses an extreme threat to us in Switzerland, alarms us even more. It motivates me, a week before my tenth birthday, to take a passionate interest in reading the newspaper every day from then on in order to discover what is happening in the world. A free press is inconceivable in totalitarian Germany.

1939: The catastrophe of the Second World War begins with the German attack on Poland, followed the next year by the rapid occupation of Denmark and Norway and a further Blitzkrieg against Belgium, the Netherlands and Luxembourg, and finally the victory over the arch-enemy France. This is the climax of Hitler's triumphs and the threat to our own encircled island of freedom, which thus becomes susceptible to political pressure. I become an active patriot and some time later am the youngest local volunteer soldier to defend the homeland. However, Hitler spares Switzerland, nor does he invade England. Instead, in 1941 he invades the USSR. Japan's attack on Pearl Harbour provokes a declaration of war by the US against Japan and by Germany against the US. However, 1942 brings the turning point in the war: Stalingrad, the Allied landings in Africa, and later in Sicily, and the preparation of an Anglo-American invasion on the Atlantic coast. In Switzerland people are already looking forward to the end of the war.

1945: The Second World War ends. It has cost around 50 million dead and around 15 million refugees. Even before the currency reform in 1948 I can travel north across largely destroyed Germany with a group of fellow pupils to share life with German young people for two or three weeks in a tented camp, to help them in their privations and win them over to democracy. Nazism and Fascism are now finished. However, Soviet Communism outwardly seems stronger than ever, although inwardly it is already in a political, economic and social crisis because of Stalin's policies. There are hopeful beginnings of a new world order: the founding of the United Nations in San Francisco, the Bretton Woods

Agreement for a reordering of the world economy, and American economic aid for the reconstruction of Europe – rejected by Stalin for the countries under the USSR. This leads to the Iron Curtain and the division of the world into East and West. 1948 sees the proclamation of the International Declaration of Human Rights. That same year I celebrate my twentieth birthday, leave school and enter the Germanicum, the Pontifical German College in Rome, to prepare for my pastoral activity with seven years' study of philosophy and theology. In Germany, after years of deprivation in the 1950s and 1960s, times of rebuilding, social advancement, growing prosperity and consumption follow. From 1960 I am professor in Tübingen and between 1962 and 1965 take part in the Second Vatican Council as a theological expert (peritus).

1968: The politically-orientated cultural revolution of students and politicians brings their demands for emancipation, enlightenment, reform, transparency and toleration. I have described the course of my life in broad outline and in detail up to this turning point in *My Struggle for Freedom*. I now continue the narrative.

First-hand testimony: Ratzinger–Küng

Before, during and after the conclave for the 2005 papal election, no question was put to me more often than this. Why have the careers of two colleagues of like disposition drifted so far apart over time, in spite of all that they have in common? In *My Struggle for Freedom* I drew attention to the parallelism and divergence in my and Joseph Ratzinger's theological careers. However, the experiences of recent years and above all a close study of Joseph Ratzinger's own brief but full 1998 memoirs, *Milestones*, have helped me to understand many things better.

I shall be doing no more than sketch two careers in this prologue. Of course they can only be understood in the context of the historical movements and particular events against which they are set, but they are by no means exhausted by them, nor are they the product of a social stratum. In both cases we have a life which has been lived and shaped by the individual himself, on which this prologue will reflect authentically in a comparison of the two personal testimonies. Those who want more information about Joseph Ratzinger should read his *Milestones. Memoirs 1927–1977*.[2] Those who want to know more about my life between 1928 and 1968 should read *My Struggle for Freedom*, to which I often refer.

Like Joseph Ratzinger's memoirs, of course mine too have a subjective colouring, in some respects supporting my own view of things. Any history, any biography, is interpreted history. But as autobiographies, histories that we have interpreted ourselves, each has its own irreplaceable authenticity, it is first-hand testimony. Like Joseph Ratzinger, I am concerned to be as objective as possible, though this doesn't exclude personal passion – in his case concealed, in my case open. On 24 September 2005 I saw my old Tübingen colleague again for the first time after 22 years, this time as Pope Benedict XVI. It is important for the reader to know that I planned and wrote this prologue about our two careers long before our reunion in Castel Gandolfo and thus in its original version, which was considerably longer, it automatically became an intellectual preparation for our conversation.

On the same wavelength?

'In Rome I had very quickly established that we are on the same wavelength and that is the decisive thing,' I wrote in spring 1963, with reference to my possible call to Münster in Westphalia, to Joseph Ratzinger, who was already teaching there. Was I wrong? No, what we had in common at that time was unquestionably stronger than what divided us and was the result of similar backgrounds. A person's situation is not the whole story, but it shapes any career.

We both come from conservative Catholic families and from an Alpine landscape, he from Bavaria, I from Central Switzerland; we both love mountains and lakes. We are contemporaries, less than a year apart: Ratzinger was born on 16 April 1927, I on 19 March 1928. But of course the son of a policeman who grows up in a police station, who after his father's retirement lives in a modest cottage and attends a clerical boys' seminary from the age of twelve, grows up differently from a merchant's son in a hospitable middle-class home in the town square, the focal point for all the members of the extended family. This atmosphere is not a well-guarded one dominated by police or clergy, but is lively and open to the world.

For both of us, humanistic education is an ideal from the beginning, and we both go to classical grammar schools, in which Latin and Greek are the basis for all the teaching. But in the boys' seminary, a preparatory stage for the priestly seminary proper, Ratzinger leads a strictly regulated life, from which of course all girls are excluded. In the upper classes of the relatively liberal Lucerne grammar school I experience a class atmosphere to which co-education with girls (still often taboo among Catholics) has brought very positive changes, and I make lifelong friendships. Very soon Ratzinger has to do with a new generation of teachers, resolute champions of Nazism. My teachers and classmates are all strictly patriotic opponents of the Nazis. He learns what a free democracy is only many years later, and it never becomes such a strong experience for him as the hierarchical church.

Both of us are stamped by the youth movement, which for me holds precious memories of my youth, with tours of the mountains, scouting games, competitions and an open-air life, regular shared prayer and worship designed for young people: a Catholic youth movement happily free from Nazi ideas. Ratzinger evidently has no alternative to joining the state youth movement, the Hitler Youth, which has been taken over by the Nazis. His bad experiences of the last months of the war in anti-aircraft defence (a flak battery), labour service, brief military service and as an American prisoner of war correspond to those of my German fellow-students from the years 1927 and 1928 at the German College in Rome. I spend my whole youth in Switzerland, an island of peace.

In this confused time of totalitarian ideologies our roots in the Catholic Church offer us both a spiritual home, an ideological orientation and moral support. We are both enthusiastic altar servers. However, for Ratzinger the local church is represented by the traditional parish priest and the Archbishop of Munich; for me by a youth chaplain who is unconventional in appearance, dress and mentality, who proclaims the good news convincingly in his words and actions, and without whom a dozen others would never have become Catholic priests. My church is a church not so much of the old as of the young. Ratzinger doesn't need a youth chaplain to make him decide to become a priest; his priestly ideal has been traditional, static and hierarchical. Impressed by the cardinal in purple, the young man tells himself that he would like to be a cardinal too.

We both whole-heartedly celebrate the pre-conciliar liturgy and at an early stage come in contact with the beginnings of the liturgical movement. However, for Ratzinger this liturgy is full of unfathomable mysteries, a structure with nooks and crannies which it isn't always easy to find one's way around, but which precisely for that reason is wonderful and a home for him. Lectures on liturgy at the Pontifical Gregorian University (= the Gregorian) give me a precise explanation of the history of the liturgy, orientated on the historical researches of the greatest liturgical scholar of his time, Josef Andreas Jungmann, whose fundamental work *Missarum solemnia* Ratzinger never mentions. This accurate historian and advocate of the people's liturgy would have enlightened him about the original, simple and understandable celebration of the eucharist, about all the shifts in content and form, the often arbitrary additions, problematical innovations and subsequent mystifications.

We both begin by studying philosophy. And both of us are equally fascinated by Augustine's *Confessions*. However, Ratzinger cannot get on as well as I can with the rational and systematic thought of Thomas Aquinas, and for him Augustine remains the guiding figure. I am impressed by Aquinas' turn towards the creaturely and empirical, towards rational analysis and scholarly research. We both read much else as well as philosophy: the novels of Gertrud Le Fort, Elisabeth Langgässer, Georges Bernanos, Fyodor Dostoievsky, and in the sphere of philosophy and theology Romano Guardini, Josef Pieper, Theodor Häcker, Peter Wust and Theodor Steinbüchel. But at the same time I am intensively occupied with Jung's depth psychology and with modern art, Marxism–Leninism and the existential humanism of Jean-Paul Sartre.

We both then go on to an intensive study of theology, Ratzinger for three years, I for five. But right at the beginning of his university study he is thinking of turning later to academic theology; he doubts whether he is suited to practical pastoral work, especially with young people. I want to go into practical pastoral work, if possible in a city, and into youth work, for which from the beginning a comprehensive contemporary education sealed with a doctorate in theology seems to me important. He gains his doctorate in Munich in 1953 with a thesis on Augustine's doctrine of the church ('People and House of God'), I in Paris in 1957 on my famous Swiss compatriot, the Reformed theologian Karl Barth (*Justification*). Among more recent Catholic theologians he is impressed above all by de Lubac, Yves Congar and Karl Rahner.

Of course we are both particularly occupied with the exegesis of the New and Old Testaments. As a student in Rome I escape from the backward-looking exegetes of the Gregorian to the Pontifical Biblical Institute, where professors venture to correct dogmas in the light of scripture and as a result are later punished with sanctions from the Holy Office. Ratzinger also hears lectures in Munich from exegetes working with historical criticism, but he escapes from what for him is too 'liberal' exegesis into the security of dogma. While in a new immediacy and freshness I attempt to find the way from fossilized Neo-scholastic dogmatics to the original Christian message attested in the New Testament, he attempts, in precisely the opposite direction, to repel critical exegesis in obedience to dogma. For me the motive force is the biblical message discovered in a new directness, for him it is dogma.

Here a fork in the ways becomes evident which leads us as Catholic theologians in different directions. For Ratzinger's theology, historical biblical criticism is welcome only to a limited degree; it remains peripheral to his dogmatic 'construction'. But it becomes central to my systematic theology; after all, it concerns the historical truth of our Christian faith. Neither he nor I wanted a return to the old liberalism, but I didn't want a return to the old dogmatism either. Here the fundamental theological problem of the appropriate criterion is raised for both of us: Bible or dogma? Is dogma below or above scripture? Is the Christ of dogma to be understood in the light of the Jesus of history or vice versa?

Two careers cross

It's a remarkable coincidence: on 21 February 1967, the very day on which Ratzinger in Munich has his habilitation examination, for the qualification he needs to teach at a university, I complete my *leçon doctorale* in Paris at the Institut Catholique, the Catholic university, and in the afternoon the *soutenance* (defence) of my dissertation on Karl Barth's doctrine of justification, *La Justification du pécheur. La doctrine de Karl Barth et une réflexion catholique*. Everything is in French, including the discussion. It is dangerous for me (I have reported on it in *My Struggle for Freedom*, IV: A *defensio* and a little lie), because the Barth specialist Professor Henri Bouillard SJ, who is envious of the young scholar of the next generation and has still not completed his own major interpretation of Barth, withholds his researches from me and, as I hear, is thinking of making a dozen important objections. I prepare myself equally painstakingly, have a personal commendation from Karl Barth (which many theologians find sensational) and enjoy the cut and thrust of the debate. The result is that Bouillard doesn't get beyond his second objection. My doctorate wasn't a 'drama', but it was a 'battle won'.

Joseph Ratzinger's 'drama of habilitation'[3] came about because the examiner, Michael Schmaus, the famous professor of dogmatics in Munich, rejected his habilitation thesis, contrary to all expectations, 'because it did not meet the pertinent scholarly standards'. Ratzinger was 'thunderstruck' (p. 107); all his future plans seemed put in question. The dangerous subjectification of the concept of revelation diagnosed by Schmaus in Ratzinger's habilitation thesis was (and still remains) the questionable element in Ratzinger's view of revelation.[4] However, in Ratzinger's difficult situation 'an idea then came to the rescue' (p. 111), about how he could elegantly avoid making any corrections; without more ado he omitted the main sections on Bonaventure and revelation and instead developed the last part, on Bonaventure's theology of history, to which even Schmaus had no objections, into a habilitation thesis – which of course had become very short.

I get my doctorate in theology *summa cum laude* on the day of Ratzinger's habilitation; however, I am not thinking in terms of a habilitation but of a doctorate in philosophy (*doctorat ès-lettres*) at the Sorbonne, on the christology of the German philosopher Hegel. This is a topic which has fascinated me since Rome and I have already won over two important professors in Paris, Maurice de Gandillac and Jean Wahl, as sponsors for it. Both are present at my *soutenance*, along with Hans Urs von Balthasar (who has travelled there from Paris). I work with the utmost intensity on this subject after completing my theological dissertation.

I use the second year granted me by my bishop for my dissertation, but which I do not need, for lengthy periods of study in Madrid, London and Amsterdam, in order to expand my intellectual horizon and my knowledge of languages. After Germany, Italy and France I now want also to get to know Spain and the Netherlands, and also generally to improve my English. This too is an important difference: whereas the Bavarian Ratzinger loves to breathe Bavarian air and in the first decades keeps his career within the frontiers of (West) Germany, although I have deep roots in my Swiss homeland I love the air of the big wide world, the 'broad place', to quote the fine title of the memoirs of my Protestant colleague and friend Jürgen Moltmann. 'Respect everyone's fatherland but love your own'; this saying by the Swiss national poet Gottfried Keller is one of my favourites. However, for many Germans, after National Socialism, after the World War and the Holocaust, this is understandably a problem; only in the 2006 Football World Cup is it relativized by a cheerful patriotism which is not aggressive.

Before my doctorate in philosophy at the Sorbonne I want to do practical pastoral work, and between 1957 and 1959 I spend almost two happy years in the heart of Switzerland. As assistant priest at the Hofkirche in Lucerne I work in a parish in which the renewal of liturgy, preaching, pastoral care and ecumenical work is in full swing, and is considerably encouraged by the announcement of the Council. This is an experience with men and women and their needs, problems and hopes which Joseph Ratzinger, during his year as a chaplain in Munich in 1951/52 in a traditional parish and then in his move to the college in Freising, will not share in the same way. However, it is to determine my theology in a fundamental way (*My Struggle for Freedom*, V: A practical test: Lucerne). Here is another important distinction.

Hardly have I settled down in Lucerne than in October 1957 I am invited by Karl Rahner to the next meeting of the Association of German-Language Dogmatic and Fundamental Theologians in Innsbruck. There I meet for the first time not only Michael Schmaus, but also my contemporary Joseph Ratzinger – not first at the Council, as I say in *My Struggle for Freedom*. He is now professor of dogmatics in Freising and has already written an intelligent review of my dissertation which recognizes its character: '. . . for such a gift Hans Küng deserves the honest thanks of all whose prayer and work is the unity of divided Christendom'. We immediately get on well together, as is still attested in the words from 1998 put at the head of this chapter. However, I don't have a lengthy conversation with him in Innsbruck, because here am I suddenly confronted with a fundamental decision about my professional future: practical pastoral work or a university career?

During this conference of theologians Professor Heinrich Fries, formerly a fundamental theologian in Tübingen and now in Munich, tells me that after my licentiate in philosophy a doctorate in philosophy in Paris is superfluous and a theological habilitation in German is infinitely preferable. For dogmatic theology I should turn to Schmaus, Rahner or Volk. Schmaus, in Rahner's words surrounded by a 'host of worshippers', is out of the question for me. So too is Rahner, because I want to do my habilitation in Germany and not in Innsbruck. There remains Hermann Volk, at that time a highly regarded professor of dogmatics at what is then the largest faculty of Catholic theology in Germany, in Münster in Westphalia. Volk will later become Bishop of Mainz and a cardinal. I apply to him and am accepted; to give me a livelihood and to help me to develop my theology I am made an academic assistant. I work up my Hegel manuscript into a habilitation thesis and my Basle lecture on '*Ecclesia semper reformanda*' into a book for the impending Council.

Together at the Council 1962–65

As I have also indicated (*My Struggle for Freedom*, V: The way to scholarship), this time in Münster, too, is a happy time for me. But after not even a year, on the basis of my dissertation on *Justification* and my 400–page manuscript on *The Incarnation of God. The Christology of Hegel*, without a habilitation (here I resemble Karl Barth, who didn't even have a doctorate), I receive a call to the chair of fundamental theology in the University of Tübingen. In May 1960, three years after my doctorate and with only brief preparation, I take up my post as *ordinarius* professor. Now my programmatic book *The Council and Reunion. Reunion as a Call to Unity*, which the faculty also has but has held back out of well-founded concern about Roman intervention against my call, may be published. It has at the beginning a remark by the great Council Pope John XXIII, who for me is still the greatest Pope of the twentieth century. Joseph Ratzinger has also become *ordinarius* professor of fundamental theology, in the University of Bonn.

We meet again in Rome. In 1962 we two professors of fundamental theology go to the Council – he as theological peritus (expert) of the Archbishop of Cologne, Cardinal Frings, I as peritus of the Bishop of Rottenburg (Stuttgart), Carl-Joseph Leiprecht. We are the youngest theologians of the Second Vatican Council to be nominated by Pope John XXIII. Professor Schmaus, also a peritus, is annoyed at these two 'teenage theologians' who find more of a hearing than he does, and departs. The Council has no need even of his more modern kind of Neo-scholasticism. I have reported at length on our experiences at this Second Vatican Council (1962–65) in *My Struggle for Freedom*, VII-IX.

Ratzinger's call to Tübingen 1966

During the Council, in 1963, Joseph Ratzinger switched from his chair in Bonn to the chair in dogmatic theology at the University of Münster in Westphalia. I too receive a call to Münster in 1963, with Ratzinger's support. But because of the foundation of an institute for ecumenical research which I have now been promised in Tübingen, combined with a new chair for dogmatic and ecumenical theology, I refuse, and propose that Dr Walter Kasper, my sound and promising assistant who is about to do his habilitation, should take the chair in Münster in my place. As he does.

Two years later I am involved in calling Professor Joseph Ratzinger to Tübingen in two capacities – as dean and as an occupant of the parallel chair in dogmatics. In the meantime my former colleague in dogmatics, Leo Scheffczyk, has accepted a call to Munich as successor to his teacher Schmaus; as emeritus professor he later earns a cardinal's hat, not least with intensive writing directed against me. My reason for calling Ratzinger is that he is the only candidate in the German-speaking world who fulfils all the criteria that I have cited for this chair in dogmatics and the history of dogma. He may therefore be proposed to the senate and the ministry not as one among the usual list of three (*terna*) but, as is possible in exceptional cases, as the sole candidate (*unico loco*).

As I report in *My Struggle for Freedom*, before my extraordinary step I have spoken confidentially with Ratzinger on a visit to Münster at the beginning of May 1965 about a call to Tübingen and then negotiated with various colleagues. In a letter of 11 May I write to him that we could postpone the call slightly in order to make it easier for him to leave Münster. But in that case we have to know for certain that he will come. Joseph Ratzinger replies four days later: if the call can be postponed until at least Easter 1966 and we can guarantee him and his sister a convenient house by autumn 1966 at the latest, 'I will gladly give myself to the Tübingen faculty.' After a brief discussion the faculty agrees unanimously with my offer and the Greater Senate of the University endorses it soon afterwards.

What I think of Joseph Ratzinger at this time emerges clearly from the proposal that I wrote for the faculty. It ends with the words: 'The extraordinarily rich work of this scholar, who is now 38; the range, thoroughness and extent of his work, which leads us to expect yet more for the future; the independence of his line of research, which happily supplements the work of the second dogmatic theologian: all this forms the basis for the decision of the faculty to propose Joseph Ratzinger to the Senate *unico loco* as occupant of the chair for dogmatics. His call to Tübingen would also be a great gain for the university in every respect.' I stand by these words today.

Friendly co-operation

Thus in 1966 Ratzinger is called by the Minister of Education and accepts the call. I find an attractive house and garden for him and his sister to rent in Dannemannstrasse. We work together extremely well. He appreciates the lecture system proposed to him. For one semester he gives the main series of lectures on dogmatics and I give a special series of lectures; the next semester it's the other way round. We regularly see each other in faculty meetings, discuss the examination material and examine our students alternately – all without any problems. And we entertain each other to meals in our homes.

By his own confession Ratzinger has no gift for technology; he has no driving licence and prefers to make the long journey to the university by bicycle rather than on foot, but occasionally accepts a lift in my car. This is no sports car, but a compact Alfa Romeo Giulia which I chose for its advanced technology and safety; soon I replace it with a similar BMW. The contrast between us offers journalists an occasion to develop it as a pseudo-profound metaphor. After the papal election the Belgian Freddy Derwahl even writes a whole book (unfortunately partisan and theologically meagre) entitled 'The One who Rode a Bicycle and the One who Drove an Alfa' (Munich 2006). While Derwahl can utilize my and Ratzinger's memoirs and describe our early writings, his book is tolerable and sometimes amusing, though there are many errors. But when it comes to the theology of my later books he shows his ignorance; he seems to have no inkling of what I have written over the last 25 years. What he announces as an unbiased 'double portrait' increasingly becomes a caricature which idealizes the 'cyclist' and disparages the 'Alfa driver'. False contrasts, misguided comparisons, malicious insinuations; even the crucifixion of Jesus and the painful death of my poor brother who died of a brain tumour at the age of 23 have to be combined in a hair-raising way in order to distinguish my view of suffering and dying from that of Ratzinger and to devalue it. The introduction already betrays the author's prejudice: anyone who sees me a priori as 'simply a man of modern technological intellect' who 'is fascinated by machines and the explosive progress of the development of the natural sciences', a man of 'glamour', hasn't understood me at all. And anyone who by contrast wants to attribute the characteristics 'spiritual, close to nature, musical' and 'intellectual brilliance' exclusively to Ratzinger is wrong about both him and me.

But never mind. At that time Ratzinger the cyclist is grateful that his house is not on a Tübingen hill, as mine is, but down in the valley, and that now and again he can go uphill or for longer distances in my Alfa. He and I work together well for three years in Tübingen as colleagues, as can be read in *Milestones* and *My Struggle for Freedom*. There is only one occasion on which he differs not only from me but from the whole faculty: on 13 December 1968 the 'Halbfas case' is on the agenda of the faculty meeting. The academic assistants ask us to mediate with the Bishop of Rottenburg and request him not to withdraw the church's permission to teach without further investigation from the deserving but controversial Hubertus Halbfas, a religious studies teacher at the college of education in the neighbouring town of Reutlingen, who is regarded with hostility.

All the professors support such an intervention – except Joseph Ratzinger, now dean. The discussion lasts an unusually long time because he has an answer to every argument, even if his answers are often contradictory. I am amazed at his opposition to the intervention of his colleagues; this is manifestly governed by political and dogmatic factors. But the intervention with the bishop proves immaterial, because to the relief of the chancery the Catholic priest Hubertus Halbfas announces his marriage, so he is automatically dismissed from his teaching post in accordance with the Concordat. However, in a further case of conflict Joseph Ratzinger shows another, more welcome side – and I do not want to pass this over either.

Ratzinger's tolerance

Every professor has problem children among his pupils, and for me and later also for Joseph Ratzinger one of them is a particular doctoral student whom I had accepted for a dissertation on dogma and dogmatism in the Institute for Ecumenical Research, despite a moderate final theological examination, because of his great commitment. He is keen on the topic, which he had wanted, and I think it highly relevant to current theological discussion. He proves himself as a scholarly assistant who is always ready to get involved, so I encourage him in every way, and even ask him to read proofs of my manuscript and take part in academic colloquiums. He is strong in criticism, polemic and the destruction of dogmatism, and he has a whole vocabulary of appropriate condemnations in his arsenal. But he has a tendency to speculate endlessly with no solid historical foundations and produce no more than an amalgam of what he has read; he is weak in forming his ideas coherently and working them out. So despite all his justified criticism of dogmatism he has difficulty in developing a positive function for dogma, which Catholic theologians should interpret and criticize in terms of our time, and not simply throw away as useless rubbish.

After four years of fruitless starts and numerous corrections the doctoral student finally finishes his dissertation. I think his sharp criticism of dogmatism justified and his description of the fundamental importance of dogma at least sufficient. But I cannot object to what my colleague in dogmatics, Joseph Ratzinger, who as expected is appointed second examiner by the faculty, tells me in a friendly letter of 3 April 1969: difficult though it is for him, time and again he concludes 'that I simply cannot with a good conscience recommend that the faculty accept the dissertation'. So he wants to resign his position as co-examiner.

We discuss the difficult case in a friendly way. Ratzinger agrees that our pastoral theologian, Professor Günter Biemer, whom I had asked, should take his place; he receives, as I do, Ratzinger's eight pages of critical objections. I then go out on a limb for my doctoral student, saying that he is not, as Ratzinger fears, a man whose Christian faith has been shaken. Later I admire as a mark of tolerance Joseph Ratzinger's absence from the decisive session of the faculty so that he doesn't endanger the majority for my candidate. Here his painful experiences with his own habilitation have certainly had an effect; they led him 'not to agree easily to the rejection of dissertations or habilitation theses but wherever possible – and respecting the integrity of the procedure – to take the side of the weaker party' (*Milestones*, p. 113).

Thus my candidate becomes a doctor of theology and I see to it that his dissertation appears in our series Ökumenische Forschungen under the title 'Dogma in History', with a preface by me and the 'Epilegomena' called for by his two examiners to make clear his constructive intention. That's also typical of Joseph Ratzinger. Unfortunately his objections later prove to be right. A decade later, the doctoral student of that time will stab his examiner in the back at the climax of the clash with Rome over infallibility with an article in *Der Spiegel*.

Two different ways of being Catholic

Who knows how things would have gone on with Joseph Ratzinger had he not left Tübingen after three successful years? So far our careers have developed largely in parallel as the careers of two theologians who for all their similarities are very different in terms of family, cultural and national origin, but also in psychological make-up: at an early stage a very different attitude to Catholic liturgy, theology and hierarchy and especially to biblical exegesis and church history, and in the end also to revelation and dogma. Despite, or also because of, the differences, they respect and as a matter of course recognize each other as Catholic theologians, each with his own power of faith and intellect. So here, if you like, are two very different modes, forms, styles, indeed ways of being a Catholic.

Of course at the time all this was by no means as clear as it is now. There needn't have been a break. After all, as the Council showed Ratzinger, 'despite our agreement in many desires and conclusions, Karl Rahner and I lived on two different theological planets' (p. 128): in Rahner's speculative–theological Neo-scholasticism, shaped in the light of German idealism and Heidegger, 'Scripture and the Fathers did not in the end play an important role and the historical dimension was really of little significance' (ibid.).

However, over against Rahner, with Ratzinger I argue in principle for a theology governed wholly 'by Scripture and the Fathers and profoundly historical thinking' (p. 129), but with a difference that is becoming increasingly clear. Ratzinger argues for a historical–organic theology which hardly takes seriously the breaks in development and deviation from the origins, which allows criticism only in the framework of Hellenistic dogma, and instead accepts as divine revelation an oral tradition running alongside scripture (p. 59). By contrast I advocate a historical–critical theology which investigates both the Bible and the history of dogma critically and takes the original message, figure and fate of Jesus as a criterion. For Ratzinger Christianity only begins rightly when the biblical message meets up with Greek philosophy. As he explains as Pope in his 2006 Regensburg lecture, for him 'the Greek heritage, critically purged, is an essential part of the Christian faith'. It is not the church of the New Testament that primarily interests Joseph Ratzinger but always the 'church of the fathers' (of course without mothers). As is abundantly clear in his *Jesus of Nazareth* (2007), his theological concern is not concentrated on the Jesus of history, in the light of whom the later dogmas of the church are to be interpreted for our time, but on the Christ of the Hellenistic councils, whom he reads everywhere into the New Testament writings.

So our careers will increasingly diverge in the future, but cross again on important occasions. For Joseph Ratzinger, and in another way also for me, 1968 is to be a year of destiny. It is a break which allows me to end this prologue and go on first to look at the development of society and the Catholic Church after the Second Vatican Council, and then to investigate the events of 1968.

I

ᏃᏩᏨᏃᏩᏨ

Roman Provocations

*'It is not the authority of the Pope that is being put in question but
the "system" which holds him captive ... The abolition of this system
is desirable – also for the Holy Father; people have been complaining
about it for centuries without really succeeding in detaching themselves
from it and reshaping it. For even if the Popes succeed one another,
the Curia remains.'*

Cardinal Léon-Joseph Suenens, Primate of Belgium, April 1969

What would have happened had the urgent problems of an internal reform of the
Catholic Church been resolved instead of piled up after the Second Vatican
Council (1962–65)? Had they been, I could have saved myself the trouble of
analysing in detail yet again those events which have led to the present church
situation, lamented by countless of the faithful, which has also had far-reaching
effects on society as a whole. But in view of the way in which problems continue
to accumulate I feel obliged, as one who was involved in the Council, to set out
for posterity what processes took place after the Council and what persons, circles
and institutions are responsible for the conversation or restoration of a 'system
which holds the Pope (and thus the church) captive' despite all the efforts and
successes of Vatican II. This may be understood as my modest contribution to a
culture of remembrance in my church, the Catholic Church.

Pioneer of conciliar renewal: Cardinal Suenens

On 8 December 1965 the Second Vatican Council had completed its work after
four sessions (1962–65). Now the decrees were to be put into practice. A shrewd,
constructive leadership with forward impulses, like that of John XXIII, would
have held the Catholic Church together and avoided polarization. That is my
firm conviction. But in the hard core of the Roman Curia no one thought of
that. Rather, very soon there were actions, indeed provocations, on the part of
Rome which were to run counter to the implementation of the Council. There
is not a single word about all this in Joseph Ratzinger's memoirs, so I must speak
of it all the more clearly.

Provocations on the part of Paul VI and the Curia were already on the agenda

16

in the time of the Council – I have already spoken of them in *My Struggle for Freedom*. All those who took part in the Council still remember the papal interventions against the Declaration on the Jews, the Declaration on Religious Freedom and the Decree on Ecumenism, which had already been approved. There was also the prohibition of any discussion of celibacy and birth control in the Council assembly and the enforcement of a papal interpretation (*nota explicativa*) to confirm a papal primacy understood in an uncollegially absolutist way. Finally there was the proclamation of Mary as 'Mother of the church', despite its rejection by the Council's theological commission, and the traditionalistic encyclical on the eucharist, *Mysterium fidei*, which was impudently put in front of the Council assembly – not to mention all the curial tricks and intrigues over the agenda and proceedings of the Council and in the various commissions.

Certainly, not a few bishops returned to their dioceses from the Council firmly resolved on reform. Yet others would attempt to continue to rule in a pre-conciliar style with the support of Rome. The most important figure of resistance in the episcopate to the Curia's efforts at restoration was beyond question the Primate of Belgium and Archbishop of Mechelen-Brussels, Cardinal Léon-Joseph Suenens, the most influential of the four moderators at the Council. Many bishops and theologians would gladly have seen this clear-sighted, brave and shrewd man as the new Cardinal Secretary of State, but Pope Paul VI didn't want any strong supporter of conciliar renewal at his side.

Suenens was the most important strategist and orator of the Council majority, resolved on reform. That had already been shown by his famous speech towards the end of the first session of the Council, on 4 December 1962, in which he presented an overall plan for the Council which distinguished the tasks of the church '*ad intra* – inside' and '*ad extra* – outside'. Suenens was not a professional theologian and knew his limits. But he had an efficient small team of experts from the University of Louvain, though the team was also responsible for the fateful compromise in the Constitution on the Church that I analysed precisely in *My Struggle for Freedom*, between a biblically orientated communion model (chs I-II) and a pyramid model (ch. III) which despite all the concessions is still medieval and absolutist.

During the second session of the Council, on 15 October 1963, Cardinal Suenens invited me to his residence in Rome and asked me about possible topics for a speech at the Council. From my three proposals he firmly chose 'The Charisms in the Church' and asked me for a draft text in Latin. He presented this to the plenary session of the Council with very few changes, but combined it with a demand that women too should be invited to the Council, and earned thunderous applause. At his invitation, on 23 October 1963 I gave a lecture in the Belgian College and talked with him personally about the introduction of an age limit for the Pope (structurally a quite revolutionary step) and later also about the question of birth control with 'artificial' means. I got on well with a man like Suenens.

17

For Cardinal Suenens is exemplary – and this cannot by any means be said of all cardinals. In comparison with some seemingly soft eminences who are particularly 'effeminate' in their liturgical garb, the strict Archbishop of Mechelen-Brussels has an upright walk, a powerful stride and a sonorous voice which – his Latin has a slight French accent – immediately holds those taking part in the Council. He thinks clearly, likes making decisions and shows his political instinct in the Council. He feels what the great majority of people are thinking but do not dare to say, and is shrewd enough often to be the first to state it in a balanced way.

However, I must admit that initially I was somewhat mistrustful of him. As a professor and suffragan bishop, years previously he had supported the Legion of Mary, a lay organization in the service of the hierarchy which was founded by one Frank Duff in Dublin in 1921; it propagates personal sanctification and the personal apostolate on the basis of 'complete dedication to Mary'. As a student in Rome I had developed increasing suspicions, both theological and practical, of this forced form of Marian piety (cf. *My Struggle for Freedom*, III: The Marian dogma of 1950). And in the Second Vatican Council a reaction against the Marianism which had reached its climax under Pius XII with the 'infallible' definition of the Assumption of Mary had now developed among the great majority. In a declaration of war, the Council rejected a separate Council document on Mary and allowed only a chapter in the Constitution on the Church. Cardinal Suenens was emphatic in supporting this change of course. His prime concern was not Marian piety but the practical apostolate, an active pastoral concern with all men and women, above all the needy and the lonely.[1]

I maintain close relations with Cardinal Suenens after the Council. He is 24 years older than I am, but has great confidence in my theological competence. On various occasions I visit him in Brussels. The Brussels residence of the Primate of Belgium isn't large by comparison with his palace in his main seat at Mechelen, and stands in the middle of other tall buildings. A beautiful, light atrium which is also suitable for receptions displays a broad open staircase which swings up elegantly into the first storey, where the private rooms are, all linked by an open gallery, and where I am lodged in a guest room. During the day we sit comfortably opposite each other in one of the big rooms on the ground floor, he in a charcoal woollen jacket without any hierarchical signs of office. Sometimes we walk in the rectangular park which is roofed round its edges in order to protect us from the curious gaze of people in the surrounding tall houses, so that we can move round and talk peacefully. It is a joy to exchange ideas for hours into the night with a man who has a good theological education, an acute mind, courage and humour. The pros and cons of all the burning problems – from the reform of the Curia through the question of celibacy which is now especially topical in the neighbouring Netherlands to the time limit for abortion – can be considered openly.

Criticism of the Roman system

Suenens is one of the few Catholic bishops who continue to maintain and express the criticism of the Roman system current at Vatican II in the period after the Council. As early as 1968 he had campaigned in a book for shared responsibility in the church.[2] What isn't public knowledge is that several times Suenens attempted to persuade the Pope to change course, especially in spring 1968 over the planned encyclical *Humanae vitae* (which nevertheless appeared at the end of July), and then in spring 1969 over the agenda for the 'Extraordinary' Synod of Bishops on papal primacy and collegiality (planned for October 1969). All in vain. The cardinal is now convinced that only a bold new strategy will have success. He wants above all to mobilize the bishops. Close advisers warn him about the risks of a public intervention against the Curia now, after the Council. But Suenens remains convinced that this is the only way to introduce the reform of the Curia which is so urgently necessary.

A few weeks before the second Symposium of European Bishops in Chur and only a few months before the first Extraordinary Synod of Bishops in Rome in October, on 25 April 1969 Cardinal Suenens launches his programmatic reform manifesto: a well-considered interview in *Informations Catholiques Internationales* and, strategically planned, in several well-known Catholic newspapers in the Western world and also in countries under Communist rule.[3] Over many pages Cardinal Suenens subjects the central church government's practice of rule and administration to a criticism which is certainly loyal, but happily sharp, both systematic and detailed. It is so informative that some extracts also appear in the secular press.[4]

The cardinal openly criticizes the Roman system, as the words at the head of this chapter show. He clearly distinguishes two opposite pictures of the church. His analysis is perceptive; he criticizes the Roman 'perspective from the centre to the periphery': a 'tendency with a network of individual prescriptions aimed at centralization, juridical, static, bureaucratic and essentialist', which is inclined to 'regard the local churches as administrative districts, the bishops as simply delegates and executive organs of the central authority ...' Over against this he sets the perspective from the 'periphery to the centre', which he characterizes as evangelical, spiritual and sacramental: unity is to be understood as brotherly fellowship regulated by the principles of collegiality and subsidiarity which 'essentially also includes difference ... extending into the spheres of spirituality, liturgy, theology, church law and pastoral care'.

Suenens sees the 'nub of the controversy' here. In his view the great gap in the ecclesiology of the Second Vatican Council lies in a failure to develop the doctrinal statements about collegiality. The cardinal makes his plea with concrete proposals for a revaluation of the national conferences of bishops and a new understanding of the nuncios (who are not to engage in denunciations), an active participation of the clergy and the laity in the election of bishops and a less

19

authoritarian exercise of authority. Finally, he speaks out against theological repression and a Roman monopoly of orthodoxy in favour of more freedom in theological research.

This fundamental statement by the leading spokesman of the progressive majority at the Council is meant to draw the attention not only of Rome but also of the bishops to the crisis of confidence within the church after the Council. This is particularly necessary in view of the Extraordinary Synod of Bishops, at which the bishops who welcome reform are to form only a minority because of the tendentious composition arranged by the Vatican. The Latin American and African countries, where the basic structural problem is not yet felt to the same degree, have had a different agenda since the Medellín (1968) and Kampala (planned for 1970) conferences.

Suenens' interview meets with an extremely positive public response; objections come almost only from traditionalist groups. This public statement is a historic act in the framework of the cardinal's overall strategy, of which I fully approve. But the Vatican isn't used to such a bishop. The interview provokes furious public reactions from leading Curia cardinals (Delici, Tisserant, Villot and others) against Suenens. To begin with, the Pope himself is silent. Of course Suenens' thrust is noted particularly attentively in the episcopate and its substance is often endorsed. However, only Dutch and some Canadian bishops speak openly.[5] What is particularly ominous is that Suenens finds no open approval among the influential German and French bishops. The opportunist and anxious silence of many bishops, indeed the hostility to reform and to the Dutch, particularly among the bishops of north-west Germany – above all Höffner of Cologne and Hengsbach of Essen – is responsible for the collapse soon afterwards of the advance guard of renewal in Central Europe that had been evident at the Council.[6] We shall see later how Pope Paul VI reacts to Suenens' criticism and how the cardinal himself changes direction in the not too distant future.

Progressive organs of the Curia

The spirit of renewal is initially preserved in new organs of the Curia brought into being by the Council. The post-conciliar consilium for implementing the Constitution on the Liturgy, which like the Liturgical Commission of the Council has top experts as members, works most efficiently under the leadership of its knowledgeable and courageous secretary Archbishop Annibale Bugnini. The Liturgical Council is able to give life to the Constitution on the Liturgy, which is half-hearted over the vernacular, and to obtain permission from Paul VI, who before the Council had talked only of a service of the word in the vernacular, for the whole eucharist along with the prayer of thanksgiving ('canon') to be celebrated in the vernacular. I have reported in *My Struggle for Freedom* on the shock that this caused the arch-conservative Pastor Laupheimer of Tübingen.

The liturgical consilium purges many liturgical texts, eliminates certain anachronisms and inconsistencies in the rite, makes a new improved and expanded order for readings at the liturgy possible, and supports the reform of the administration of the sacraments. Those in power in the Curia (including Joseph Ratzinger) don't like this at all. They manage to have the outstanding Bugnini, who has now become Secretary of the Congregation for Worship, exiled instead of being made a cardinal. In 1976 Paul VI sends him off to Tehran as inter-nuncio – as Bugnini remarks to friends, 'beyond the Black Sea', an allusion to Ovid, Rome's most celebrated poet, whom the emperor banished to the Black Sea. He dies in Rome in 1982. Yet further progress should have been made in the reform of the liturgy. For, as Cardinal Suenens says in the interview that I have cited: 'It is not enough to translate a text into a living language to make it understandable to Christians in 1969. It must be refunctioned, transferred from one culture to another, and so on.'

The Secretariat for Unity, now under the leadership of my friend the Dutch cardinal Johannes Willebrands, also does constructive work. It makes great efforts to advance understanding between the Christian churches. 'You would certainly want to do more if you could,' I remarked to him at a lunch during the Council. He thanked me for my understanding. But what could he achieve in practice?

More than ever, all the important statements by the Secretariat for Unity have to be approved by the Holy Office, which is now called the Congregation for the Doctrine of the Faith (also referred to as the Doctrinal Congregation), but still ascribes to itself supreme authority in doctrine as the former *Suprema Congregatio Inquisitionis*. So while my Cardinal Willebrands isn't domesticated like bishops disposed to opposition or exiled as is Archbishop Bugnini, like other non-Italian Roman dignitaries he is curialized. I have discovered three different methods of bringing supporters of conciliar renewal under the control of the Curia: domestication, exile or curialization. But none of these is quite suitable for paralysing an inconvenient Tübingen theologian. What will happen to him?

There is no lack of fine declarations in the Secretariat for Unity, and numerous ecumenical visits are paid. But the central ecumenical question of the recognition of ministries and eucharistic fellowship between the churches doesn't advance a step. So I'm glad that I am not invited to join this commission or that. I am now regarded as 'radical' and 'dangerous' because I venture to tackle the real questions from the roots (Latin *radix*), formulate them clearly and without ambiguity, and don't allow myself to wriggle out of them. To work on a commission under such an authoritarian curial regime is a waste of time. Time and again I recall the remark of my American friend John Courtney Murray, who inspired the Council's Decree on Religious Freedom, 'Hans, the world has not been redeemed by a commission.' But what is to be done in the face of ever new Roman provocations?

21

Provocation I: Cementing the power structure

It seems to me, too, that the congenital defect of the Council is that despite all its positive impulses it doesn't succeed in decisively changing the institutional–personal power structure of the centralist church government in the spirit of the Christian message. Despite all the unavoidable changes, the Pope, most organs of the Curia and many bishops therefore still continue to be pre-conciliar; they also seem to have learned little from the Council. There are still people holding the reins of power in Rome, in the nunciatures and in some areas of the church who are more interested in preserving the convenient status quo and their position of power than in serious renewal. Here 'internationalization' – a demand made by the Council – is of little use. Some Germans, French and Latin Americans called to the Curia are more Roman than the Romans, indeed sometimes more dogged than they are.

The commission set up to reform the Code of Canon Law, the *Codex Iuris Canonici*, also works quietly in the Vatican. It is under the leadership of the former General Secretary of the Council, now Cardinal Pericle Felici, a member of the Curia who knows all the tricks. As in the Council, so too in the commission he ensures that nothing is decided which could decisively diminish the influence of the Roman Curia. For all the simplifications and clarifications the new code fundamentally remains the old one; it serves to safeguard the existing power structure. It does this in a quite practical way. Rome always has the law on its side; that needs to be noted for my future controversies. Precisely because in some countries such a church law is supported by the state law ('state–church law'), it prevents any breakthrough of the church renewal that is aimed at. This is happening in the widest and liveliest circles of people and clergy in the case of the most urgent problems – for example the marriage of priests and the recruitment of priests. Thus the pre-conciliar power structures can not only be preserved but also newly cemented after the Council.

It becomes increasingly clear to me that this church law, which hands down a medieval–absolutist understanding of the church, gives Rome even in a democratic age the scope to take over and administer all the churches in the world with the least possible hindrance. And the nominations of bishops all over the world are the decisive instrument for maintaining this unrestricted Roman rule. Autocratically, the Curia is highly selective in implementing the resignation of bishops at the age of 75 as prescribed by the Council. The resignation of progressive bishops who take the Council line is immediately accepted and in some cases even provoked; the resignation of important bishops who take the Curia line is rejected with an appeal to the 'special wish of the Holy Father'.

So the old Roman system of princely dispensations and privileges and a favouritism in sacral disguise continues to function. For at the same time most of the nunciatures are tested only with a questionnaire, bishops are nominated who unconditionally conform, and cardinals are created who have laid down the

Roman line in all the disputed questions from birth control to church organization and ecumenical relations, or who allow themselves to be made to toe the line before election. I know some of them. They are certainly men of good will but often have no breadth of horizon and boldness; at best they are pliant officials of headquarters in Rome. Thus they are not what the Council wanted when it emphasized the consecration of bishops as a sacrament, namely independent leaders ('shepherds') who seek to lead their dioceses in a way that accords with scripture and the present time, of course in communion with the Pope.

Since after the Council many bishops had to retire at 75, the Curia takes the opportunity over a few years to change the constellation of forces in the national (e.g. German or Dutch) or continental (e.g. Latin American) conferences of bishops in its favour. Soon in every conference there is at least a Roman fifth column which can obstruct or even block every possible decision that does not please the Vatican and at the same time can polarize the conferences. Little is left of the collaboration between bishops and even critical theologians which proved itself at the Council; court theologians are called for. And in other respects people again prefer to keep themselves to themselves; critical intelligence can only be disruptive. For me this has the inestimable advantage that I waste little time on unrealistic talk of reform and instead can concentrate on theological research, teaching and my publications.

In all this, the collegiality of church government which the Council 'in theory' fought for, in other words the collegial responsibility of Pope and bishops for the whole church, is criminally ignored and passed over. This shared responsibility, grounded in Bible and tradition, called for by the present situation and affirmed by the Council by 1808 votes to 336, may have been celebrated as a great victory for the Council. But the Curia goes on working after the Council as if collegiality had never been decided on. And the Synod of Bishops appointed by the Pope without consulting the Council soon becomes purely a debating club because it has no decision-making power. In our democratic age it is farcical that it is not the Synod of Bishops itself but the Curia that gathers the results, orders them, interprets them and finally has them proclaimed by the Pope.

I do not know of a single decisive reform resulting from this Council of Bishops. In these circumstances, of course, there is no question of the participation of the relevant clergy and laity in the election of bishops which is urgently called for by many – though this would easily be possible through priestly and pastoral councils. And no one dares to talk even at the Council about the completely obsolete medieval rules for electing the Pope. Here in particular the Roman system goes on and on. The Pope chooses those who will elect his successor solely according to his taste; with good reason he addresses the bishops not as 'brothers' but as 'sons', since they have been created simply and solely by him. They are therefore officially named 'creatures of the Pope', who will choose the next Pope – of course from their own ranks, although according to church law any baptized Catholic of the male sex can be elected.

Thus in the period after the Council the College of Cardinals is again utterly dominated by the Roman spirit, even if its members increasingly come from other nations than Italy. Those who are less faithful to the Roman line – for example the charismatic Archbishop of Recife (Brazil), Dom Helder Camara, or the eminent Apostolic Delegate in Washington, the Belgian Jean Jadot, who is responsible for the excellent nominations of several dozen bishops in the US, and also the long-time Chairman of the German Conference of Bishops, Bishop Karl Lehmann – are systematically refused promotion to cardinal. But how in the future will backward-looking cardinals who conform to the system elect a Pope who delights in renewal? This doesn't bode well for future papal elections, or for the future elections of bishops.

Exemplary: the freedom of the Swiss election of bishops

My Swiss homeland is both conservative and democratic at the same time. In the Confederation it is possible to force a popular vote on any important political bill (by initiative or referendum). Sometimes such democratic processes require a great deal of time. Only on 2 February 1971 was the right of women both to vote and to stand as candidates finally introduced for the whole of Switzerland, but with a two-thirds majority. However, with such a plebiscite the question was settled and isn't still endlessly discussed, as often happens in the Federal Republic of Germany. In Switzerland people are all the more interested in free democratic elections, and in some cantons even pastors and teachers are democratically elected by the community.

On Monday 13 February 1967, I give a lecture to a packed auditorium in the University of Fribourg on the virtue of truthfulness in the church. There is tremendous assent, but the Catholic *Freiburger Nachrichten* writes such a negative commentary that I have the last part of my lecture printed to provide objective information for readers. The result is that the Bishop of Fribourg, François Charrière, attacks me even more vigorously in his Palm Sunday sermon. I sense that here too the wind is beginning to change.

The day after the lecture I am invited to breakfast by Professor Eugen Isele of the legal faculty, the most important Catholic state–church lawyer in Switzerland. He is a friendly, understanding older man who in principle shares my views. However, he thinks (as he later makes even clearer to me in a lengthy letter of 21 March 1967) that now in the midst of the upheaval of the church – in view of the great danger to peace and unity – one must be shrewd in helping truthfulness to break through. I have nothing against shrewdness and the principle 'strong in substance, gentle in manner'. But a great deal is at stake here. Professor Isele is carrying on secret negotiations with the Roman Curia on behalf of Basle Cathedral. The free election of Swiss bishops by the cathedral chapter, which Rome has only to confirm, unique in the Catholic world, has long been a thorn in the flesh of the Roman Curia; it does not fit Rome's picture of a centrally led church.

By subtle means the Curia has already succeeded in influencing the election of bishops in the sees of Sitten, Chur and St Gallen, which go back to the first millennium. Now, after the resignation of my own Bishop of Basle, Franz von Streng, which has deliberately not yet been accepted by Rome, the situation has been exploited to abolish the freedom to elect bishops of Basle: by involving the Vatican in the information process as soon as possible, so as to guarantee candidates acceptable to Rome.

As a free Christian and a patriot I am extremely alarmed at the information Professor Isele gives me. For unlike the conservative Catholic jurist trapped in the problems of the nineteenth century, I see the freedom of the election of bishops endangered not by the free liberal state, but by an authoritarian Curia which, not unlike the Kremlin, is in process of taking over the episcopate all over the world. On returning to my lake house by the Sempachersee I investigate the legal situation thoroughly and immediately set to work on an article 'Threat to the Freedom of the Election of the Bishop of Basle?' It appears as early as March 1967, in *Civitas*, the respected monthly of the Swiss Student Association; the journal's chief editor is my bold cousin Dr Walter Gut, who is wholly in agreement with it. I adopt the pseudonym Helveticus, not out of a lack of civil courage, which hardly anyone would deny me, but in order to concentrate the debate on the subject-matter rather than the author.

My article first describes how the mode of electing the bishops of Basle rests on the Concordat (1928/29) between the Swiss cantons involved and the papal nuncio, who acts on behalf of the Pope. Any one-sided change would be an unacceptable breach of law. Accordingly the right to elect clearly lies exclusively with the senate of the cathedral of the diocese of Basle, which can carry out the election without consulting with or informing the Roman authorities, though no candidate is to be elected who is not acceptable to the cantonal governments. In the present situation these are still the only representatives of the church people concerned. Once the election has taken place, the name of the person elected is immediately to be proclaimed officially. The ceremonial consecration of the bishop can take place once the election has been confirmed by the Pope.

My argument is that any possibility of an objection from Rome *before* the election, combined with the duty of confirmation *after* the election (but still *before* the public announcement), in fact represents the possibility of a veto against candidates who are not approved of. Against such a veto is the fact that in accordance with the age-old political traditions of our free country, our bishop is democratically elected by chosen representatives of the clergy, who know our people and their needs from the inside. So bishops are not chosen from above by the proceedings of anonymous officials, for whom the report of a foreign nuncio (who very often doesn't know our language) and other 'informants' who remain secret is often of the greatest importance. In addition, the curtailing of the free election of the Bishop of Basle would go against the Second Vatican Council: its revaluation of the particular and local church, the diocese and its community, its demand for decentralization and reform of the Curia, and the limitation of the competence of the nuncios which it desires.

The election of the Bishop of Basle is an exemplary case, and I am resolved to make an example here. I refer to the history of episcopal elections; in the early Christian period it was taken for granted that a bishop was chosen by both clergy and people. After the First Ecumenical Council of Nicaea in 325 the right of confirmation and consecration does not accrue to the Roman see but to the metropolitan of the church province concerned. In the Middle Ages a clericalization then increasingly becomes established. Towards the end of the twelfth century the right to elect bishops lies with the cathedral chapter, and Innocent III makes this binding on the whole church. However, Rome increasingly uses the already existing right of confirmation to influence the choice of candidates.

History shows clearly that today the mode of election of the Bishop of Basle is in practice a unique example in the whole Western church both of what used to be universally the case and of the freedom of election by those concerned in all dioceses of the Catholic Church, something that was hoped for again after the Council. Conceivably in the future a bishop would be elected not only by the cathedral chapter but by chosen representatives of the clergy and the laity of the different deaneries, possibly also by a diocesan council made up of clergy and laity.

Successful resistance

Chief editor Dr Gut sends the proofs of my Helveticus article both to the cathedral chapter and to the cantonal governments in order to stir them up. Reactions follow quickly and sometimes vigorously. Bishop von Streng, whom we wanted to spare a departure under a cloud, is furious; on his travels, he summons Walter Gut for a discussion in the buffet of Zurich station. He has angrily corrected the proofs himself. The title is not to be 'Threat to the Freedom of the Election of the Bishop of Basle?' but 'No Threat to the Election of the Bishop of Basle'. He also deletes and changes a great deal in the article itself, as if he were the censor of the journal. But we had made provision for that. Dr Gut tells the bishop that unfortunately the corrections are too late; the issue has already been printed. In fact the whole article appears with big headlines in the *Luzerner Neueste Nachrichten* of 11 March 1967 at the same time as *Civitas*. Now the cantonal authorities are alarmed and insist on their rights. The Basle chancery attempts to deny the matter but Helveticus does a follow-up. A shorter article appears on 17 March in the Lucerne *Vaterland*, 'Unanswered Questions on the Election of the Bishop of Basle' – this time in points addressed to the Berne nunciature.

Basle's most famous citizen, the Reformed theologian Karl Barth, is particularly delighted at my intervention for the freedom of the election of the Bishop of Basle. I pay him a visit in Basle on 20 February 1967; he is also interested in these questions of church politics. That is less the case with the Catholic theologian Hans Urs von Balthasar, whom I visit the same day. He has no sense of legal and political questions and, now increasingly against the Council, moves away from the 'razing of the bastions' which he has previously called for in respect of the Roman system. In the meantime, together with Henri de Lubac and Joseph Ratzinger, supported by the conservative movement Comunione e Liberazione, he has founded a journal *Communio* to counter our international theological journal *Concilium*. It isn't interested in such questions of reform. In practice the topic of 'church and freedom', which I had already shelved personally, still occupies me intensely, for example in view of a lecture in Paris on 'L'Église et la liberté' on 6 March at the Centre Catholique des Intellectuels Français (CCIF), combined with radio conversations and a television broadcast.

While I am working on my second Helveticus article there are noises under the concrete platform of my lake house which rests on oak pillars eight metres deep; evidently a badger is dragging more and more stuff around and causing a bad smell. Three members of the hunting club whom I invite and provide with some of the Valais wine Fendant send their hunting dogs under the house; they bay wildly and race about. Evidently the badger has backed up against a wall and is defending itself with sharp teeth and claws. The first dog emerges into the daylight with a big bloody scratch in the middle of its nose and the second with an ear bitten in half; the third retreats unwounded but trembling with fear. The hunters, more intoxicated by the Fendant than by their success at hunting, depart with their sorry hounds. But our badger stops haunting me. The next night he leaves his bivouac under my lake house. See how a single militant creature, well equipped, can prevail even against a superior force of three, I think to myself.

This time we can chalk up a success, since we win on the decisive point: in the future, too, the Bishop of Basle will be chosen without giving any prior information to Rome or involving Rome. Only on one apparently incidental point has the warning of Helveticus not been heeded. Contrary to all democratic tradition the name of the bishop elected may not be announced immediately, but is given only after it has been confirmed by Rome. The cathedral canons even allow themselves to swear to a bit of undemocratic secret nonsense. The confirmation from Rome comes relatively quickly in the elections of our next bishops Anton Hänggi and later Otto Wüst, but in the case of Kurt Koch in 1996 it takes six months. As Bishop Wüst told me, he personally had given Kurt Koch the church's permission to teach as a professor, without the approval of Rome, and when I was awarded the Swiss prize for culture had delivered a fine laudation in which he called for my rehabilitation. But in the six months between election and confirmation by Rome Koch the progressive theologian was somehow made a bishop loyal to the Roman line who even assented to his consecration in St

Peter's instead of in his own cathedral in Solothurn – to the annoyance of more than the Catholic people and clergy. He is a bishop who now defends every single Roman position, and even Opus Dei, and soon also believes that he may publicly reprimand theologians such as Herbert Haag and me. But at the same time he objects to accusations that he is a 'church turncoat'. After ten years in the episcopate (2006) even his own stocktaking, like that of all the press, is for the most part negative: 'A deep gulf between bishop and people.' This too is unfortunately an exemplary 'case'.

A radical response: Charles Davis leaves the church

The credibility of the Catholic Church, which had reached a high point under John XXIII, is exposed to a severe stress test under Paul VI. Much capital of trust is squandered, much hope and joy in the church is destroyed. Pope Paul VI is a serious man of integrity; I painted a portrait of him in *My Struggle for Freedom* which tries to be fair to him. But unfortunately I also had to point out that from the third session of the Council onwards this Pope leans increasingly towards the curial right – out of growing anxiety, theological uncertainty, curial tradition and consideration for the volatile political situation in his homeland of Italy. Thus for many Catholics who are enthusiastic about the Council, after the Council the question soon arises of how to react to the vanished hope of a further renewal: resist, resign or emigrate?

Of course all over the world, in countless communities, people attempt to realize the intentions of the Council faithfully – except where this is thought undesirable, as say in Poland under the regime of Cardinal Stephan Wyszynski, Primate of Poland, and the Archbishop of Krakow, Karol Wojtyla, who keep 'Western' influence on church and theology as far away as possible, allegedly because of Communism.

In this conciliar process of renewal, questions are asked in particular of the theologians, who already at the Council often did the main intellectual work. After the Council I could immediately have abstained from church politics so as to devote myself exclusively to my lecturing activity and my publication projects. Some colleagues have retreated from current debates and enjoy a more peaceful life, for which I too often long, but resignation and unpolitical tranquillity aren't in my nature.

Nor is an exodus from ministry and church. I am still pained by an experience which comes as a shock to me. My friend Charles Davis, then the most influential Catholic theologian in England and adviser at the Council to the conservative Cardinal John Heenan of Westminster (though Heenan hardly consulted him), announces his resignation as professor of dogmatics at Heythrop College and chief editor of the important English journal *Clergy Review*, and also his resignation from the priesthood and his departure from the Catholic Church. Lengthy reasons are given in his book *A Question of Conscience,*[7] which soon follows the article. Some people undoubtedly leave the church for motives of self-interest (in Germany, for example, church tax), and these are painful for the church, but in the end they aren't politically relevant. By contrast, the departure from the church of someone like Charles Davis, a pillar of church renewal in England, inevitably resounds all over the world.

Charles Davis is protesting against the Roman system criticized by Cardinal Suenens and countless others, its lack of freedom, honesty and humanity. In particular he is protesting against a magisterium whose monopolizing of the truth he thinks to be fundamentally wrong, biblically and historically unfounded, and an obstacle to any free quest for the truth. He knows it from within just as well as I do. Of course his protest would have been even more effective had it not been combined with the announcement of his marriage to Florence, an American theological student. But the *cherchez la femme* which is always quickly produced in conservative Catholic circles is a cheap jibe. It would be just a lazy excuse if at the same time one didn't take seriously the theological and ecclesiastical reasons for a theologian to leave the church. Often it's the other way round: *cherchez l'Église* – marriage follows disappointment with the church.

The questions raised by Davis aren't specifically English but general questions to the Catholic Church which Davis was able to put with special weight. Is the present institutional church with its great claims really backed by the biblical message to which it appeals? Is it really what Jesus wanted, or merely the degenerate form of a community which originally had quite a different structure? What about the development of its doctrine, its dogmas? Is it really an organic development or a history of contradictions which has often been beautified? What is the basis for the new Marian dogmas, and do the papal claims to primacy and infallibility, cemented in dogma, have the original message of Jesus behind them? How does the church magisterium function in practice? Does it help people or sacrifice them in their specific distress (birth control, divorce) to principles it lays down itself? And what about honesty and integrity in the church? Can a theologian in the church as it is really be creatively active in freedom and intellectual honesty? Truly, these are no random questions, but get to the heart of the matter.

The stir over Davis is great, because he is identifying problems which are urgent ones for many people in the Catholic Church, even if they often don't raise them and often don't even dare to think of them. This also applies to many theologians. They are silent or adapt out of cowardice or fear of being disciplined or even of a withdrawal of love by the church authorities, but also simply out of ignorance and a lack of exegetical and historical education. At any rate I cannot fail to respect Charles Davis, a personally modest and totally committed man. He is a man of the centre, who is not to be counted among the radicals but among the moderates, a theologian with broad horizons. He continues to be true to himself and his calling in uncompromising truthfulness.

Only on one decisive point must I contradict my friend. While I endorse his criticism, for me there can be no question of leaving the church, nor will I emigrate from my homeland if I do not agree with its present government and the prevailing political system. I remain in the church community not only because of, but also despite, its hierarchy. Davis would have helped the Catholic church community most had he stayed in it. Especially in a storm, when the waves rise high and the ship, tossing and turning, is in a hopeless situation (don't forget, we're talking of men and women), it is necessary for us reform theologians to remain on deck in all truthfulness. Our slogan must not be retreat, but perseverance.

All this is now almost four decades in the past. Charles Davis was wrong in his expectation that the traditional structures of the Catholic Church would collapse and that the future would belong to new, small, church communities. But he was right in his assumption that countless men and women would tacitly or formally emigrate from this once again authoritarian church. He was also right in his assumption that many theologians and pastors would give up their priestly office, for reasons of celibacy or faith. Like Charles Davis, many have succeeded in a creative disaffiliation. They have found a new professional position – in the media, as teachers, as heads of personnel in big firms, as psychotherapists or whatever – in which they can invest their spiritual energies in a new freedom, usually in partnership with a woman. That is a tremendous loss for the Catholic Church, but despite many empty clergy houses the official church is unconcerned, at least outwardly.

Charles Davis doesn't go on to join another church but remains a committed Christian. He is active in Canadian universities (Edmonton and Montreal) and concentrates on questions such as the relationship of Christian faith to modern philosophical thought or the relationship of the uniqueness of Christ to the plurality of the world religions. But his numerous new books by no means attract the same interest as his old Catholic ones, which remarkably he no longer lists in his bibliography. Many of his readers feel that he has abandoned them and reciprocate by abandoning him, so that his publications hardly find any response in the Catholic Church.

Charles Davis, who after his retirement in 1993 returned to his beloved English homeland, died on 28 January 1999 surrounded by his family and friends after a last eucharist – on the feast of Thomas Aquinas, as his daughter Claire, who has a doctorate in theology, reports. I honour his memory. His questions to the Roman system remain. They are also questions for me, but I must go my own way – in the Catholic Church, but ecumenically open.

A fruitful research semester

Some engagements have their pitfalls; often you don't know what you've let yourself in for until the event has begun. That happened to me with a study week in Montreal under the title 'The Future of Theology' to which I had been invited by Regis College. It seemed easy enough to cope with. On the four days between 27 and 30 June three prominent theologians were to hold a free discussion before a gathering of about 150 colleagues, first among themselves and then with the audience. It was to be on major themes: the relevance of the past for theological work; reason and revelation; the new hermeneutics; theologies and cultures; new fields of theological research.

With me had been invited Professor Martin Marty, probably the best-known American historian of church and theology, from the University of Chicago, and from the same university America's most important systematic theologian and philosopher of religion, Professor Paul Tillich. But Tillich died a few months before the conference and his place was taken by Professor Harvey Cox of Harvard Divinity School, known world-wide above all for his book *The Secular City*. For me this was certainly an extremely interesting group, but also a very challenging one.

For what at first seemed easy in fact proved difficult, namely to discuss an enormous range of topics strenuously morning and afternoon, for me in English. This wasn't easy even for my two colleagues who soon became my friends, and some weeks after the end of this occasion Martin Marty wrote to me: 'By now I have begun to recover from the week at Montreal. Were you also emotionally, physically, intellectually – and maybe also spiritually – exhausted from the work-out?' But what Martin says of himself I can also say of him and Harvey: 'All in all despite everything it gave me great pleasure, and I note that I have learned a great deal from the two of you, especially in the last two days.'

In fact, as Marty himself writes, on the first two days he and Harvey Cox were a great strain on me. But, he thinks, I responded admirably. Afterwards he excuses himself to some degree for constantly pressing me to give answers, as the audience largely consisted of Catholic colleagues. Since this was the case, as soon as strictly dogmatic questions arose – from creation and virgin birth to heaven and hell – my two partners in the discussion usually said, 'That's up to Hans.' At any rate these were topics on which I felt more at home than on questions of American society and culture.

The discussion gave me one decisive stimulus, when my two colleagues asked me to answer the fundamental question, 'What is the Christian message?' I had kept referring to the Christian message as a matter of course, but had thought relatively little about how I could give a brief, prompt answer to this question. It continues to preoccupy me to such a degree that later I hold a seminar on it and also propose it as the theme for a day at the *Concilium* World Congress in Brussels in 1970.

31

After these efforts in Montreal I look forward even more to my very first research semester, though I spend the first days of it finishing my book *The Church* (I reported the completion of it on 27 August 1966 in *My Struggle for Freedom*). Then I return to the North American continent to fulfil the many invitations from there. The first of them is the crucial factor. I go to Berkeley, California, where the Pacific School of Religion wants to give me an honorary doctorate in divinity. For a Protestant institution to do this is a quite special mark of distinction for a Catholic theologian. On 8 October 1966 I fly to San Francisco and spend some stimulating days in Berkeley.

The next stop is San Francisco. There I am shown how universities in the United States are slowly but surely overtaking the conservative German universities in ecumenical matters. It has proved possible to form a union from different theological faculties, the Graduate Theological Union, which enables Catholics and members of other Christian churches to study together. I am highly delighted to be in this fascinating city once again, but just as delighted to have time to give three lectures on truthfulness to a large audience in the chapel of Stanford University; this is a particularly attractive American campus. After the lectures the president of the university gives a reception at which I can meet many interesting people from science and culture. Because of the possibility of a wider influence shouldn't I perhaps move to America, say California, or at least divide my activity between the two countries (like a colleague in German studies)?[8]

After my lecture on 1 November 1966 at the University of Hawaii I had originally intended to travel round the world from Honolulu back to Europe with my friend from Sursee and the German College, Dr Otto Wüst; plans for this had already been made. But before I leave Tübingen news reaches me that Wüst has been nominated by the Bishop of Basle as head of the priestly seminary in Solothurn, with the expectation that he would take office immediately (very soon he was to become a suffragan bishop and finally my diocesan bishop). So the plan collapses and I fly back from Hawaii to Los Angeles and Mexico City in order to spend my first peaceful weeks in the winter sunshine of Acapulco. Happily my long-time Amsterdam friends, the sculptress Inka Klinckhard and her mother, are able to stay with me in Acapulco at the peaceful Hotel Pierre Marquès outside the city. There I can relax on the beach and enjoy the surf, and at the same time read all day. For as well as a longing for peace and quiet I have a great need to fill particular gaps in my education that my Roman training had left. So I study the twelfth edition of Karl Heussi's classical compendium of church history from beginning to end, around 550 pages with more small print than large, but extremely informative. No one would have suspected that anyone in such a relaxed beach atmosphere could be preoccupied with such dry-as-dust material. But at the same time I also read *Kennedy* with the same excitement as a novel – in happy and sad memories of my meeting with him in the White House in 1963 – an 860–page biography by Ted Sorensen, personal adviser and speech-writer of the murdered president and former senator.

After the extraordinarily hectic years which lie behind me, these five weeks free of post and telephone calls, with fine weather every day, represent an incomparable physical and mental boost. On 13 December I return at last to Tübingen via New York and Amsterdam. I spend Christmas in my lake house; the celebrations are in the town house in Sursee with my family.

Of course now I am again constantly involved in theology: on 29 January 1967, the chancery of Rottenburg fortunately gives me the *imprimatur* that I need for my book *The Church*, after I have made some corrections in the manuscript. I write a lengthy article, 'Catholic Reflections on Luther's Doctrine of Justification Today', for the Festschrift for the 150th anniversary of the Tübingen Catholic Faculty 1817–1967 which takes my doctoral dissertation further.

Then comes a lecture trip to Portugal, with a lecture on the same topic, 'Church and Freedom', given first in Lisbon, then in Coimbra and finally in Porto. Here I learn at an early stage to give lectures late into the night. For in Portugal the lectures begin at a time when they normally end in Central Europe and the discussion goes on until towards midnight. Then follows the relaxing part, a glass of wine and a snack, accompanied by sad fado, songs of presumably Afro-American origin, accompanied by the guitar.

From Lisbon, on 9 April 1967 I go direct to Beirut. As I love swimming in the world's seas wherever possible, in Beirut I immediately have a short bathe in the Mediterranean in front of our hotel. Soon a second swimmer joins me and observes that it's still very cold. I reply, 'In the Atlantic, where I swam yesterday, it's very much colder!' To which he retorts, 'So you're a pilot too!' I call back, 'Yes, my job involves the heavens, but I'm a theologian!' But why did the theologian have to fly from Lisbon straight to Beirut?

A key experience for the dialogue between religions: Beirut–Jerusalem

It's a good conclusion to my research semester to be invited to Lebanon for the centenary celebrations of what at that time is the most important academic institution in the Middle East, the American University of Beirut. Muslim and Christian theologians have been asked to give ceremonial lectures, from the Christian side the General Secretary of the World Council of Churches, Dr Willem Visser 't Hooft, Cardinal Johannes Willebrands, later to become President of the Vatican Secretariat for Unity, and I, the youngest. Beirut is a city on the boundary between Christianity and Islam, and the topic of the lecture is to be 'God and Man in Today's World'. What a chance for the encounter of religions, what a unique opportunity to experience Muslim theologians directly as conversation partners! But things turn out differently.

The remarkable thing is that not a Muslim theologian is in sight as we appear, and none of us Christian theologians has an opportunity to get to know one. Why not? Because they had all been invited to speak in the previous week. When

I ask the president of the congress, Charles Malik, at that time Lebanese Foreign Minister and President of the United Nations General Assembly, why now – after the Second Vatican Council with its pioneering declarations on religious freedom and the new attitude of the church to Judaism and Christianity – Christian and Muslim theologians haven't been invited together, his answer is: '*Cher Professeur, c'est trop tôt!*', 'It's too early!' 1967 – too early? It was too late.

At that time Lebanon was still regarded as the 'Switzerland of the Middle East', a peaceful island in the midst of hard-fought-over regions and religions. But even then in Lebanon I heard off the record that the situation was explosive, that the numerical relationship and political balance between Christians and Muslims was fluid and that the Christian predominance was being endangered by the marked growth in the Muslim population. The present constitution couldn't be maintained in the long run. Would things really become as bad as that for this poor rich country? No one had any inkling then of what was to come.

I have never forgotten this Beirut experience. Later, after one of the longest and most fearsome civil wars in history, I was able to put it in context. It made me conclude – and wise Lebanese have confirmed this insight for me – that had serious religious dialogue been sought in Lebanon then it would have had the support of the faith communities, and Lebanon wouldn't have slipped into such a catastrophe. A religious understanding could have served as the basis for a reasonable and fair political solution. In this way fanatical violence, murder and destruction fed by the religions would have been mitigated. In the spirit of a Christian renunciation of power, in the early 1970s Christians could have voluntarily made those concessions to the Muslims which were later forced out of the Gemayel government in the 1980s by force of arms but which then were no longer able to pacify the country. In short, the civil war and unimaginable bloodshed could have been avoided. Instead of being a ghastly chaos, Lebanon today would be a model of ecumenical understanding.

Since this trip in 1967 I have also been convinced that, like Lebanon, the state of Israel and the city of Jerusalem can find peace and lasting existence only through religious and political dialogue between Jews and Muslims, Israelis and Palestinians. Immediately after our conference I flew from Beirut to Amman and from there on to Jerusalem. I stayed at the National Hotel. I remember this place so well because it is associated with a short but momentous conversation. While in the hotel I was accosted, somewhat nervously, by a Swiss Jewish woman from Berne: 'You're a Christian theologian. Surely you can give me an answer. Here in our city of Jerusalem one constantly comes across the name of this Jesus Christ. What kind of man was he? Why is he so tremendously important for you?'

This is the central question in the dialogue between Christianity and Judaism, which would have perplexed some Christian theologians, and also perplexes me a little. To begin here simply with the traditional answer that he was not only a human being but the Son of God, the second person of the Trinity, would certainly have brought the conversation to an abrupt end; this woman had often been given this answer, which for a Jew (or a Muslim) is completely incomprehensible. So since recently I had taken a good deal of trouble to study research into Jesus in the New Testament, I developed for her an impromptu narrative 'from below', about how his Jewish disciples had seen and experienced this Jesus of Nazareth, about the controversies over the law and the temple, and about how a conflict developed with the Jewish establishment, how Jesus was finally condemned to death by the Roman governor Pontius Pilate on the basis of Jewish accusations and was finally crucified in Jerusalem, and how the first Christians had been convinced that this Jesus had risen from the dead.

This conversation forms something like a key scene for my later book *On Being a Christian*, the practice of a 'Christianity from below'. I would have liked to have had Joseph Ratzinger with me; mightn't he perhaps have recognized that a 'christology from above' – the incarnation of the Son of God (incarnation of the Logos) – often doesn't offer a usable framework but that a 'christology from below' offers a way of speaking unpolemically about Jesus even with Jews (or Muslims)? Here I gave so to speak a more narrative answer to the question put to me in Montreal: 'What is the Christian message?' It doesn't consist in a theory or a dogma but in the quite concrete history of the Jew Jesus of Nazareth, who for Christians is the Christ, the 'anointed', the Messiah. I summed this up three years later in a statement at the *Concilium* World Congress in Brussels. It was supported – and I shall be reporting this later – on the one hand by the American exegete Raymond Brown and on the other by the dogmatic theologian Karl Rahner, who found this approach convincing. For me this is the kernel of *On Being a Christian*.

I experienced how complicated relations between Arabs and Israelis were generally when I wanted to cross from Jordan to Israeli territory at the Mandelbaum Gate. I hadn't been informed that a second visa was necessary for this. What was I to do? I returned to my hotel from the Mandelbaum Gate and made several useless taxi journeys to get the visa and a health certificate. All in vain. I couldn't enter Israel until the next day and so arrive a day late in the hotel in Haifa where I had reserved a room. To crown it all, annoyingly, my travel agent had booked my flight from Tel Aviv to Zurich on the wrong day. After an unwanted overnight stay in Rome I finally arrived in Zurich on 21 April 1967, glad to be at home again. The Six-Day War between Israel and the Arabs was to break out on 5 June 1967. Israel won the war but lost the peace. Israel's decision at that time to occupy the West Bank of the Jordan has blocked the political situation to the present day.

35

Provocation II: encyclical on celibacy

Like other bishops, my friend the Bishop of Cuernavaca (Mexico), Sergio Méndez Arceo, had been prevented by Pericle Felici, General Secretary of the Second Vatican Council, from even touching on a central structural problem, which doesn't arise only in Latin America: mandatory celibacy for the world clergy. There was no desire to attack the celibacy of members of religious orders, voluntarily chosen and lived out in communities. So after the Council mandatory celibacy for diocesan priests, which should have been resolved in collegiality, remained one of the main problems for the Pope and the episcopate. The Vatican went on as before: 'Councils and Popes come and go, but the Roman Curia remains.' Without consulting the bishops in any way, in other words with crass disregard of the collegiality which had been ceremonially decided on at the Council, on 24 June 1967 Pope Paul VI, now again on course with the Curia, published a major encyclical *Sacerdotalis caelibatus*, in favour of celibacy.[9]

After the Council, is one to accept such solitary decisions, again made in the authoritarian style of the *ancien régime*, moaning, grumbling and despairing or hoping for better times? No, after the Council the role of the theologian isn't the same as it was before. Theologians have a responsibility for their fellow men and women. But they can exercise it only by making public statements. Public opinion in the church has a right to that. At the same time a signal has to be sent to Rome that such uncollegial proceedings in the spirit of pre-conciliar Roman absolutism will not be accepted without resistance. However, no direct protest is to be expected from a conference of bishops or an individual bishop, and it is impossible to drum up a group of theologians in a short space of time. So, having been given early information on the encyclical, I resolve on a substantive statement which appears in most newspapers at the same time as a summary of the encyclical, so to speak as a commentary on it.

That earns me a summons to his palace on 12 September 1967 from the President of the German Council of Bishops, Cardinal Julius Döpfner, Archbishop of Munich. 'Why did you once again have to be the first to make a statement on the encyclical? My priests read your critical statement even before the encyclical itself,' he asks reproachfully. I reply with a smile: 'Because you didn't want to be the first: but that should have been the task of the President of the German Conference of Bishops.' In fact my statement isn't limited to a formal protest but briefly offers a theological counter-argument.

- First of all fundamental recognition and criticism: 'It is the merit of the encyclical that it openly states the difficulties regarding celibacy. However, it does not solve the problems but accentuates them by expressing them.'
- Then the counter-arguments, first and principally the Bible: 'The gospel recognizes a personal call on the part of the individual to the unmarried state in the service of fellow men and women, of the kind that was lived out by Jesus

36

and Paul in a way which is also an example for the present time. But both Jesus and Paul explicitly grant any individual complete freedom. This freedom – the unmarried state as a free charism – is contravened by a universal law of celibacy.'

- A further argument is the tradition of the first millennium: 'Peter and the apostles were and remained married even as full disciples of Jesus, and this continued to be a model for those presiding over communities for many centuries. But in later centuries what above all had its originally freely-chosen place in the monastic communities was extended as an explicit prohibition of marriage to all the clergy and in part was forced on them.'
- Finally human rights: 'In our conciliar and post-conciliar age, however, the opinion is increasingly becoming established within the Catholic Church that this unusually invasive legal intervention in personal human rights offends not only against the original free ordering of the church but also against our understanding of the freedom of the individual today.'

I have to end by drawing attention to the consequences of this unbiblical, uncatholic and outdated law: the loss of priests, amounting to tens of thousands, and the steady decline in candidates for the priesthood. My final conclusion is: 'In view of the sometimes tremendous loss of priests and the notorious aging of the clergy the question "married or unmarried?" must retreat behind the primary obligation of the church to give the communities heads.' The problem should be discussed collegially in the Synod of Bishops meeting in Rome in autumn 1967. Since it is a pure church law, the law of celibacy can also be reversed at any time.

So there is nothing against celibacy freely chosen in the spirit of the Bible, but everything against an enforced medieval law of celibacy, which should be abolished. This is a clear, well-founded demand made by the majority of Catholics in the progressive democracies. It certainly wouldn't solve all the church's problems at a stroke. But beyond question more priests would be available for pastoral care if the church contained all those who have left it because of celibacy and gained as priests those (including lay theologians) who for that reason did not seek ordination. There is no lack of priests, but a lack of those prepared for celibacy. Then comes the disappointment: as already at the Council, at the Synod of Bishops too the discussion of the law of celibacy is excluded from the agenda on the instructions of the Pope. Once again there is no collegiality.

Hardly any bishop anywhere dares to speak openly of celibacy. In a television discussion on Second German Television on 19 October 1969 the Bishop of Mainz, Hermann Volk (my boss during my years as an assistant in Münster), says to me: 'I'm not saying that celibacy must remain, I'm not supporting that at all.' To which I reply: 'I've never heard a bishop say that so clearly.' Some days later Bishop Volk retracts. He has 'never said a word nor had a thought which would put celibacy in question'. Unfortunately this is totally untrue.

A few weeks before the encyclical, on 13 May 1967, Paul VI had published his own apostolic exhortation *Signum magnum* on the veneration of Mary, though the Council had rejected a separate document on the veneration of Mary by a clear majority. And he did so on the jubilee celebrations of the appearances of Mary in Fatima in Portugal! On the 13th of each month from May to October 1917 shepherds' children there allegedly saw heavenly figures, above all the Virgin Mary. As earlier at Lourdes, she appeared without her child, in Fatima sometimes even in the form of two madonnas at the same time (*My Struggle for Freedom*, IV: Lourdes [and Fatima]). On 13 May 1967 Paul VI flew for a day to this doubtful location of an appearance of Mary. Here too we have pre-conciliar conservatism. Mary is exalted at the expense of women, who are kept down in the church, as a sexless virgin and mother, and time and again is commended to seminarians and priests for sublimation. Celibacy and Marianism supplement each other. For southern piety the Mother of God is often more important than God and Jesus, his Son. 'If God doesn't exist,' clergy in Rome have often joked, 'at least there's the Madonna.' And what do the theologians say about celibacy?

Karl Rahner and celibacy

After the first (mostly negative) press comments on the celibacy encyclical it was now up to theologians to analyse the Roman document more precisely. Already during Vatican II the brave Viennese pastoral theologian Michael Pfliegler had made available his dissertation on celibacy, which is above all a historical report, available for my series 'Theological Meditations'. It appeared at the end of the Council, in 1965. It was followed by further publications critical of celibacy, for example by Fritz Leist (1968) and Anton Antweiler (1969), and then by the standard work by the church historian Georg Denzler, 'The Papacy and Celibacy in Ministry', 2 vols, 1973/76.

It emerges from all these publications that – after some unsuccessful attempts in earlier centuries – the decisions in favour of universal compulsory celibacy were made in the eleventh century. Under the influence of the religious orders and the monk Hildebrand, later Pope Gregory VII, in a kind of comprehensive monastic ideology ('panmonasticism') Rome required of all the clergy unconditional obedience, the rejection of marriage and a life like that of the religious orders. Five years after the break with the Eastern church, the 1059 Lateran Synod prohibited the marriage of priests for the Western church; this further deepened the split with the Eastern church, which kept married priests. In the face of vigorous opposition above all from the clergy of Italy and Germany, the Second Lateran Council of 1139 drew the final line under church law: it declared the receiving of higher orders (from the subdiaconate upwards) a hindrance to marriage. This meant that the marriage of priests, hitherto prohibited but valid in law, was now a priori invalid; all wives of priests were regarded as concubines and children of priests were handed over to the church as slaves. On this issue the

New Testament says that 'the bishop shall be the husband of only one (not no!) wife' (1 Timothy 3.2). But why should the ideologists of celibacy be disturbed by the Bible?

So from this point on, in the Western church to the present day there has been a universal mandatory law of celibacy, though in practice up to the Reformation it was only partly observed even in Rome (and by the Popes) and was rejected by the Reformers for convincing reasons. Since Vatican II this mandatory celibacy has been massively put in question even in the Roman Catholic Church. But support for the celibacy encyclical comes from a completely unexpected side. The Council theologian and professor of dogmatics Karl Rahner has allowed himself to be persuaded by the President of the German Conference of Bishops, Julius Döpfner, to write an article in favour of the celibacy of secular priests in the form of an open letter to a 'dear brother'. This pathetic concoction is sent through the chanceries as a special publication in an edition of many tens of thousands of copies to all the clergy of Germany and Austria.

Many people, like me, are dismayed at this document, for several reasons. They are offended by the self-righteous, arrogant tone which without much under-standing for the concrete needs of those concerned is evidently meant to inculcate a bad conscience in any 'colleague' who holds a different view from the writer of the letter. However, for me the most important objection is that Karl Rahner, the religious, leaves out of account the decisive difference of which I was made aware for the first time by the eminent Bonn moral theologian Franz Böckle when I was chaplain at the Hofkirche in Lucerne: the difference between being unmarried as a charism (free calling to a special ministry) and as a law (an obligation which is prescribed, in some circumstances with sanctions). Franz Böckle made it clear to me that the church government has no right to make the charism ('let him who can do it, do it', Matthew 19.12) a law for all the clergy ('even if he cannot do it, he must do it'!).

The voice of Karl Rahner is too important for us to pass over. But to attack him publicly would break the common front of conciliar theology. So along with our Dutch friend Edward Schillebeeckx I resolve to speak out. Schillebeeckx declares himself ready to join me in taking Karl Rahner to task at the next session of the Foundation of *Concilium*, the theological journal in which we are all involved, in Nijmegen on 27 April 1968. This intimate conversation is serious and friendly. Of course Rahner can hardly object to the decisive argument about charism and law, since at a very early stage – though not in connection with the question of celibacy – he had published a striking monograph on charism and ministry entitled 'The Dynamic in the Church' (1958).

In retrospect, though, I have to confess that I was more nervous about this conversation with Karl Rahner which I had initiated than I realized at the time. There was already the age-difference of a generation, which was unimportant to me but certainly very important to him ('How can this young man ... ?'). And then there was above all the friendship between Karl Rahner and the writer Luise

Rinser, which was kept strictly secret from outsiders. I met her in Lucerne on 25 April 1975 for a lengthy conversation. I was very concerned that there should be a closed front of conciliar theology in times of increasing Roman conservatism. I asked Luise Rinser to persuade Karl Rahner to take part in a big *Concilium* congress held in Munich from 22 to 25 May 1975, five years after our successful congress in Brussels. However, by then Karl Rahner bore a grudge against me for my *Infallible? An Enquiry* and presumably also for my criticism of his defence of the law of celibacy. Luise Rinser understood my concern. More than once she had told Rahner, 'After all, you stand for the same thing as Küng,' but Rahner had replied, 'Yes, yes, certainly ... but not like that.' Unfortunately she couldn't convince him. Although he lived in Munich, he stayed away from the congress. I maintain links with Luise Rinser. In 1984 Walter Jens and I invite her to Tübingen for our symposium 'Theology and Literature. The State of the Dialogue'.

That Luise Rinser played a central role in Rainer's last decades became public knowledge only after Rahner's death because Luise Rinser – no longer much talked about as a writer and strongly criticized for a visit to Stalinist North Korea – couldn't resist the temptation to publish many of the letters which she had written to Karl Rahner in a book entitled 'Walking the Tightrope. Letters of Friendship to Karl Rahner 1962–1984'. Over these two decades the two of them had exchanged hundreds of love letters amounting to thousands of pages, but the Jesuit Order didn't allow the publication of Rahner's letters, which likewise are in the possession of Luise Rinser. The publication of her own love letters on the tenth anniversary of Karl Rahner's death on 30 March 1994 offended and shook many Rahner admirers. They haven't diminished my respect for Karl Rahner. But one can shelve his 'Letter to a Brother' on priestly celibacy.

Slanders

Theologians – and not just Catholic theologians – are particularly prone to being the subject of malicious and fictitious slanders. On 25 June I had sent on to Karl Rahner a letter from 'Tübingen students' which clearly slandered him; according to his assistant Dr Karl Lehmann, it had also gone to the whole Munich theological faculty, the dean of the philosophical faculty there and other professors. I could comfort Karl Rahner by telling him that I had received a similar letter – possibly by the same psychopath – three months earlier.

One morning I had received a telephone call from a lawyer friend telling me that he and several professors – it later emerged that there were between 60 and 70 of them – had received similar letters which said of me: 'He's had a bad moral effect on us. Tübingen students.' Such disgraceful communications sent to so many colleagues on the same day are extremely unpleasant. One can't give the lie to them even in a newspaper. My colleague from the law faculty urgently advised me to report it to the police immediately; should anything happen later, people could ask, 'Why didn't he report it at the time?' Walter Kasper, now a professor in Münster, wrote to me on 16 February 1967 that there too various colleagues in the theological faculty 'with abhorrence and astonishment have received quite repulsive letters' in which my name was mentioned. But what the Münster faculty thinks of me and my 'school' is best indicated by the fact that two of my habilitation pupils are on the list for the new chair of ecumenical theology, in first place Peter Lengsfeld, my friend from Roman days, though he has to undergo a further examination of his orthodoxy by the new Bishop of Münster, Joseph Heffner.

The police took the matter very seriously, and carefully investigated the typewriting in Stuttgart, discovering that it originated from a portable Olympia typewriter, model SM, Monica or SF. However, several hundred thousands of this model had been made between 1959 and 1965, so the investigation had to begin systematically in my immediate surroundings. Authors of poison-pen letters are often to be found closest to hand, since they act from personal motives such as jealousy, envy, revenge or unrequited love.

First all the typewriters in the Theological School were investigated. And because one of my colleagues in the faculty had the misfortune to live right next to the police authority, a criminal detective with the best intentions, but contrary to my express instructions, thought that he could call on him at home without advance notice to investigate his typewriter. This understandably caused bad blood. It was almost more painful for me than the painful letters themselves. I tried to explain to my colleague that the officer acted without my knowledge, but news of the incident spread very rapidly among my colleagues and provoked comment. The investigations broadened, but on 1 June 1966 the Tübingen state advocate reported to me that 'despite extensive investigations it has not proved possible to establish the author of the obscene letters sent to several professors at the university'. Investigations would be resumed only if new facts became known.

So this whole case remains unexplained. Death threats, which I sometimes also get but which I seldom take seriously, are of course worse: 'They should kill you, in former times they would have been right to burn you.' But in some circumstances perhaps such a letter should be taken seriously. So one day I am summoned by the Rector. A death threat has been received against me and is being investigated by a psychologist. I am warned that in some circumstances, if such letter-writers saw no prospect of success and I continued to present my views, they could also become physically violent. So I should be particularly careful when I go through my garden to the house at night. But nothing happens.

There is no overlooking the fact that the more I am publicly involved in the growing controversy over the form of the post-conciliar church and incur the antagonism of the Roman establishment, the more the 'hate post' increases, very often from clergy (sometimes with the closing greeting, 'we will pray for you!'), but very often anonymously. For a while I amuse myself by collecting the insults and epithets in an index; hardly one has been omitted. But it makes little sense to get excited and waste time over all this. After all, these are usually people who haven't read any of my books, but at best a press report (often taken out of context).

We also have a category 'SP' = 'Spinner' (German 'idiot') in the secretariat, which we use to describe those who have lots of bold ideas or plans to improve the world but aren't malicious. I generally reply to anything that isn't malicious, but furious insults aren't worth the postage. However, the letters of approval, often moving, indeed touching – and which are an encouragement to me – are far more numerous than the negative ones. And in general all these controversies aren't detrimental to my friendships in the faculty and university. Quite the contrary.

Friendships

One day my highly-respected colleague in economics, Professor Norbert Kloten, the first president of the Federal Government's 'Council of the Wise', which keeps an eye on economic developments in the Federal Republic, persuades me in a lengthy conversation to become a founder member of a second Rotary Club of Reutlingen-Tübingen (North). This brings a new dimension of human relations into my life. At first I refused. I didn't have time to go to a lunch every week, nor did I see any sense in such lunches, which of course aren't primarily concerned with food. Kloten argued that people would certainly understand if a heavily-burdened professor couldn't come to every meeting. But it was vitally necessary for a theologian like me to cultivate relationships and friendships outside the sphere of theology and the university.

Norbert Kloten later does me a great service in helping to form the board of trustees of our Global Ethic Foundation and attending all its discussions. Already terminally ill with cancer, he invites me to give an address at the private celebration of his eightieth birthday in his home on 12 March 2006. Sadly he can join in only from the clinic. Up to the last hours before the public celebration of his birthday on 14 March in the Festsaal of the University he works, as I had recommended, on his spiritual testament, which his daughter reads out. He is brought into the hall in a wheelchair. He dies a few weeks later, a brave death, and is buried on 13 April 2006 in the Tübingen city cemetery.

So on Kloten's advice, on 22 June 1967 I go to a founders' discussion in the Krone Hotel and am given an explanation of the meaning of Rotary: a readiness to serve in everyday life. In practice that means cultivating friendships, proving useful to others, recognizing high ethical principles in private and professional life and the value of all activities for the common good; promoting responsibility in private, business and public life; contributing with goodwill to understanding and peace among the peoples; and realizing the ideal of service in professional life.

The four critical questions which Rotarians are always to put to themselves in thought, word or deed make a special impression on me. Is it true? Am I honest?

Is it fair for all concerned? Will it promote friendship and goodwill? Of course all these are noble principles. Everything will depend on how they are realized. The founder members of my age who are invited to the new club seem to me to be progressive and some of them will in fact become friends for life. I join, and have never regretted it.

I've gained much from my four decades of membership of the Rotary Club. First, because our club combines members from two such opposite cities as the university city of Tübingen ('mind') and the nearby industrial city of Reutlingen ('money'), I make new friends from business, indeed from every possible professional group. Secondly, through the weekly meetings with lectures from the most varied spheres of professional and academic life, over the years time and again I gain new stimuli and experiences. Thirdly, for me the Rotary meetings are a seedbed for new theological ideas and notions which I can present to test their comprehensibility. Precisely because every member belongs to a different professional group, the reactions are very different. But happily there is no hierarchy here (a new president is chosen every year). Everyone speaks in the discussion after the lectures and quite generally there is that 'communication without domination' of which Jürgen Habermas has spoken in another context.

I will always be grateful to my club for letting me be the only one to be spared being elected president, vice-president or secretary because of my many commitments. Instead, I take on special tasks such as Advent celebrations, and also a lecture on 7 June 1975 in Tübingen town hall on the occasion of the 'Compass Meeting' with our partner clubs of Geneva, Grenoble and Genoa. I speak about 'The Difference between Catholic and Protestant' in three languages at the same time – German, French and Italian interwoven. My talk is also followed with great excitement even by those who don't understand all three languages. I repeat this experiment more than once for other topics. Also in the Rotary Club I speak on 'What is the Christian Message?' Of course such a lecture isn't a dogmatic lecture on a confession of faith, but an outline of the original Christian message as it is to be found in the New Testament, grounded in exegesis. Mightn't one also expect that one day from a Pope?

Provocation III: a papal creed for yesterday

One positive consequence of the Council is that the Index of Prohibited Books created in 1557 in the Counter-Reformation, of which a new edition of 492 pages was prepared in 1948, the first year of my studies in Rome, is discontinued by Pope John XXIII and abolished on 9 April 1966. The head of the Vatican Congregation for the Doctrine of the Faith, Cardinal Ottaviani, declares that it is only of 'historical value'. But the Vatican continues to be interested in the precise regulation of the faith of believers and the theories of theologians.

On 30 June 1968 Pope Paul VI, again out of the blue, publishes a creed;

however, this is not called the Pope's creed, which would be the truth, but – in the tendentious use of a term revived by the Council – the creed of 'the people of God'. This is a typical Roman gesture of identification. Without asking the people of God or even the episcopate, one declares oneself to be the people of God: '*L'église, c'est moi!*' That would of course be only half as bad were it a creed that really depicted in a contemporary way the faith of the people of God, grounded in the Bible and the great Catholic tradition. But what the Pope says in it – and this is the criticism not only of theologians – could have been said in just the same way 400 years previously, since he ignores all the fruitful thought and practice in recent years which have taken things further.

By way of introduction the Pope asserts that he is only going to sum up the Nicene Creed and extend it in accordance with 'the spiritual situation of our time'. He mentions the crisis of faith 'in some modern circles' and the 'addiction' of Catholics 'to change and renewal'. The faith must be described in a way adapted to the horizon of understanding of men and women of today, without removing anything from the substance. And that sounds like this, to quote just one section on the eucharist:

> We believe that the Mass, celebrated by the priest representing the person of Christ by virtue of the power received through the Sacrament of Orders, and offered by him in the name of Christ and the members of His Mystical Body, is the sacrifice of Calvary rendered sacramentally present on our altars. We believe that as the bread and wine consecrated by the Lord at the Last Supper were changed into His body and His blood which were to be offered for us on the cross, likewise the bread and wine consecrated by the priest are changed into the body and blood of Christ enthroned gloriously in heaven, and we believe that the mysterious presence of the Lord, under what continues to appear to our senses as before, is a true, real and substantial presence.[10]

Do such formulations of faith – relating say to transubstantiation, Adam's 'original sin', christology 'from above' or papal infallibility – correspond to the horizon of understanding of modern men and women?

A leap forward called for

'The truth is permanent, but not static,' comments the leading US Catholic journal, *The National Catholic Reporter* (10 July 1968): 'We firmly believe that it is the function of the Pope to teach the truth about the truth, but he has not fulfilled this task when he suggests, as this creed does, that the usable, relevant, living truth is preserved in a kind of Catholic Fort Knox, where it is piled up in pure gold bars, protected from any pollution.' I enjoy such witty comments.

As a Council theologian I can hardly avoid taking my own stand. On such occasions questions from radio stations and newspapers are the rule. Of course I often turn them down, above all if I haven't studied an issue thoroughly or have already made many statements on the matter. But the media are interested in statements which are at the same time competent, understandable and above all honest. And here there is a notorious problem with theologians in both churches who tend to twist and turn on inconvenient questions, whereas bishops show submission and usually keep silent in constant fear of Rome, where things always threaten to get too hot.

So in my case it isn't fanaticism about mission but a realistic awareness that calls for a statement on the creed and the people of God. Two points above all seem to me to need criticism:

1. The hierarchy of truths called for in the Council's Decree on Ecumenism is criminally disregarded. Central Christian statements of faith may not be put on the same level as peripheral statements.

2. Problematical constructs of Roman traditions are also presented as truths revealed by God. These include above all the four new Vatican dogmas, which cannot be regarded as having a foundation in scripture: the immaculate conception and bodily assumption of Mary into heaven, the Pope's primacy of rule and infallibility.

In all this Pope Paul VI disregards the admonition of his predecessor Pope John XXIII, who had said in his opening speech at the Council: 'The salient point of this Council is not ... a discussion of one article or another of Christian faith ... which is presumed to be well known and familiar to all.' What is decisive is the contemporary proclamation of faith and thus an exodus from the intellectual, terminological and religious ghetto: a leap forwards ('*un balzo inanzi*') aimed at a deepened understanding of faith and a formation of conscience – certainly true to authentic doctrine but also depicted in the formulation of modern thought. Therefore what is called for is a creed which does not confuse and split the church but enlightens and unites it, which theology is not to regiment but to provide a basis for and inspire. What is needed is a creed not for yesterday, but for today and tomorrow. But how will theology react to doctrinaire attempts at disciplining?

A world-wide demonstration for the freedom of theology

Within three years of the conclusion of the Second Vatican Council it had become clear that the freedom of theologians and theology in the service of the church which had been regained by the Council was again in danger. The 'creed of the people of God' was intended not least to discipline theologians. The Roman Inquisition, renamed the 'Congregation for the Doctrine of the Faith', still institutes inquisitional proceedings against theologians it doesn't like, and it still hasn't published an order of proceedings, though it was ordered to do so by the Pope as early as 1965. The Inquisition fears the light.

Granted, the Pope has founded an International Theological Commission. I calmly accept that the likes of me do not fit into it, but the prompt departure from it of Karl Rahner and the respected Swiss ecumenist Johannes Feiner of Chur is an alarm signal. It is clear that the Curia has paid hardly any attention to more recent conciliar and post-conciliar theology. This Theological Commission proves to be an extension of the arm of the Roman Doctrinal Congregation. At that time the post-conciliar Dutch Catechism, which is highly successful internationally but has been denounced by conservative Dutch, is being investigated for heresy. And after Pope Paul's first encyclical *Ecclesiam suam* of 1963 has attracted little enthusiasm because of its unecumenical Romanism and its lack of a biblical basis, to the annoyance of many bishops the encyclical *Mysterium fidei* on the eucharist, published immediately before the fourth session of the Council, is even more of a disappointment. Here is a Pope clearly still committed to a scholastic theology on which neither New Testament exegesis nor research into the history of dogma from recent decades nor the systematic new approaches of some theologians seem to have had any impact.

Unless we simply accept this whole development back towards traditional Neo-scholastic theology, we must begin a counter action. At the *Concilium* Foundation Meeting in Paris on 12 October 1968, under the chairmanship of its President the Dutch businessman Antoine van den Boogaard, I suggest to my colleagues Professors Yves Congar, Karl Rahner and Edward Schillebeeckx – certainly the most important representatives of post-conciliar theology – that we should compose a declaration 'On the Freedom of Theology' with concrete proposals for a fair order of procedure in the case of conflicts with the magisterium. My suggestion is discussed intensively and meets with approval, and I am given the task of working out a draft. In Tübingen I am helped with the passages which are important for church law by our eminent church lawyer Professor Johannes Neumann, who ensures that there are precise legal formulations. On 24 October I send the draft to Congar, Rahner and Schillebeeckx. They return relatively few corrections, which I incorporate. Then I send the definitive text to all the section directors through the *Concilium* secretariat. They all assent.

The fundamental statements at the beginning refer to freedom as a 'fruit and a demand of the liberating message of Jesus himself' and 'the freedom of the children of God in the Church proclaimed and defended by St Paul. Therefore it is incumbent on all the teachers in the Church to proclaim the Word *opportune importune*, in season and out of season.' Our position is clear:

> We are well aware that we theologians can commit errors in our theology. However, we are convinced that erroneous theological opinions cannot be disposed of through coercive measures. In our world they can be effectively corrected only by unrestricted, objective and scholarly discussion in which

the truth will win the day by its own resources. We affirm with conviction a teaching office of the Pope and the Bishops which stands under the word of God and in the service of the Church and its proclamation. But we also know that this pastoral ministry of proclamation ought not to constrain or impede the teaching of the theologian. Any kind of Inquisition, be it ever so subtle, damages not only the development of a healthy theology. It at the same time inflicts incalculable damage on the credibility of the entire Church in the world of today.

We also make quite concrete demands, which may be inconvenient for the Roman Curia but are extremely important for us theologians, above all this: 'The offices of the Roman Curia, especially the Congregation for the Doctrine of the Faith, will, even after a certain internationalization by Pope Paul VI, see themselves exposed to the appearance of partisanship in favour of a specific theological orientation as long as in the composition of its personnel the multiplicity of contemporary theological schools and mentalities are not clearly taken into account.'

More demands follow, especially in respect of the Congregation for the Doctrine of the Faith: 'As Consultors only outstanding and generally recognized professional people should be called' for a limited period of office and with an age limit of 75. The international commission of theologians also desired by the Synod of Bishops should 'likewise encompass the various theological directions and mentalities in a proper proportionality' (point 4). Then a 'clear and binding order of procedure' is called for, which is to be published in legal fashion (5).

Here a series of stages are proposed (written communication, professional evaluation, personal discussion), in connection with which a complete view of the records is required: 'If afterwards a personal discussion is viewed as necessary, the names of the discussion partners, the subject of the discussion, and the complete text of all existing evaluations, decrees, *relationes*, and otherwise important minutes and documents are to be communicated in sufficient time beforehand to the theologian concerned. The theologian can conduct the discussion in any language wished by him and can bring with him an expert for his support. An obligation to keep secrecy does not exist. Minutes of this discussion signed by all of the participants go to the Congregation' (6d).

The declaration ends with point 7: 'Since all faith without love is nothing, all efforts concerning the truth in the Church must be conducted according to the fundamental principles of Christian charity.'

Once all the editorial committee of *Concilium* – a group of around 40 theologians, men and women, from the most varied nations and theological disciplines – have accepted the declaration it appears (I am responsible for the publicity) on 17 December 1968 in the *Frankfurter Allgemeine Zeitung*, the *Neue Zürcher Zeitung*, the *New York Times* and other papers. At the same time it is published in the various editions of *Concilium* (German, French, English, Dutch, Italian,

Portuguese and Spanish) and the theologians of the world are asked to subscribe to it. A small miracle occurs: the declaration is signed by 1360 Catholic theologians from 53 countries and sent to the Foundation Board of the Papal Secretariat.

I should mention that Professor Joseph Ratzinger of Tübingen also signs and has never withdrawn his signature. This contrasts with his withdrawal of his signature to the statement on the time limit on bishops holding office upon his arrival in Regensburg. However, what he later writes in his *Milestones* about the Catholic theologians after the Council ('that nothing was now stable in the Church, that everything was open to revision', p. 132) verges on slander. All in all our declaration was a powerful demonstration world-wide for the freedom of theology in the church. At least it has the consequence that the Doctrinal Congregation works out the order of procedure called for by the Pope as quickly as possible and publishes it soon afterwards. But there are yet other problems.

Provocation IV: decree on mixed marriages

The proposal from the Eastern side that in the Latin Western church the more tolerant practice of the Eastern churches united with Rome should be adopted and that the remarriage of an abandoned spouse should be tolerated in certain conditions was received with applause. This is a highly uncomfortable proposal for Curia circles interested in maintaining the status quo. It finds no hearing in the Theological Commission. The moderators propose that the question should be handed over to the Pope; a large majority agrees.

At the Council, in November 1964 the question of confessionally mixed marriages, the number of which is constantly increasing, was mentioned as an urgent pastoral problem without any solution being indicated. At any rate the question of marriages between members of different confessions is discussed at the Synod of Bishops in 1967, though with no consequences.

However, on 31 March 1970 Paul VI publishes a papal decree (*motu proprio* = on his own initiative) on the question of such mixed marriages which generally causes great disappointment. I don't want to deny the Pope's good intentions and the slight improvements in proceedings (the transfer of authority for dispensations from Rome to the bishops). But once again Rome insists on positions which theologically and practically are for the most part out of date even within the Catholic Church and cannot be maintained in the long run. It clearly shows the world that behind all ecumenical assertions and gestures the Roman central administration still has a deeply unecumenical attitude, the mentality and style of which betray considerable backwardness, short-sightedness, obstinacy, arrogance and superiority.

A careful reading of the document immediately shows that this is in fact a preventative decree, in three respects. The aim is to prevent a general recognition of the validity of mixed marriages by a discriminatory practice of dispensation for all confessionally mixed couples. An ecumenical marriage based on the equal rights of the churches is not allowed. Nor is a responsible decision of the parents with respect to baptism and the bringing up of children wanted. Is one simply to put up with all this? As always, apologists are quickly in place who interpret the Roman decree as tremendous 'progress' and are little concerned with the distress caused to the marriages of those of different confessions. Again the question arises for me, What are we to do? As always, we discuss it in our institute.

A call for self-help

More and more couples from different confessions are turning away from the church: if one is already excluded from the eucharist, why keep on going to church? Our pastors sigh under the yoke of the Roman law and when faced with everyday life can only spoon out what a distant church bureaucracy offers them. They cannot expect any real help from the bishops, at best the usual excuses: this is a question for the 'whole church', in other countries it looks 'quite different', one must 'have patience and pray'.

Most theologians content themselves with criticizing and muttering, without proposing a concrete solution. So after lengthy discussion I decide on a public 'Invitation to Self-help', with a good theological grounding. This title comes from the literary editor of the *Frankfurter Allgemeine Zeitung*, which is liberal, open to critical Catholic voices and not yet infiltrated by Opus Dei. The title is an apt one, for to the question 'What is to be done?' I give the clear answer: 'Act according to your conscience, especially as this law itself attaches such great importance to conscientious responsibility! For the pastors that means exploiting as far as possible the scope opened up by the law and, if this is not enough in a special case, meeting the needs of the partners as far as possible, even contrary to the stipulations of the law' (*Frankfurter Allgemeine Zeitung*, 9 May 1970).

I go even further: 'In view of the ever more pressing problems it could come about in the German-speaking world – as is already largely customary elsewhere, especially in the United States – that the pastors no longer even seek dispensations. In this way the problem is resolved *de facto*, as was a few years ago the question of regulations about sobriety before receiving communion' (ibid.).

My language is clear and sharp for maximum effect. Here I draw a parallel to birth control: 'Self-help is not the ideal, desirable form of regulation in the question of responsible mixed marriages or in the case of responsible parenthood. But the repeated failure of the Catholic authorities over an urgent problem of today will perhaps leave no other way open' (ibid.).

The invitation has an effect

The excitement over this clear invitation simply to evade the Roman decree is tremendous. The resolute resistance of groups of priests, many individual pastors and lay people, the protest of mixed-marriage groups and the student communities, the unrest among Catholic theological students and the growing solidarity of Catholic and Protestant Christians and communities on this question all show the seriousness of the situation and the probable uselessness of disciplinary measures to preserve the status quo.

On the whole the assent to my article is tremendous. In addition there is the international response, which is brought about through its publication in *Le Monde*, *The Tablet* and *L'Europeo* and countless press reports. Of course some bishops and their advisers are extremely angry and talk of 'rebellion'. The church lawyer and Jesuit Professor J. G. Gerhartz opens up a dispute over how the decree is to be translated, which is meant to distract people from the main concern. Whether one translates the first sentence 'The church has always (*semper*) extended special concern (*sollicitudo*) to mixed marriages in accordance with its task' (as I can best justify my translation in a lengthy statement in the *Frankfurter Allgemeine Zeitung* of 16 June) – or merely a passive 'anxiety about' (thus Gerhartz) in both cases the first statement contains 'a historical untruth'. Hence my conclusion: 'Instead of being anxious about the "papal anxiety" one would do better to be anxious about the anxieties of mixed marriages!' Gerhartz's fellow Jesuit Professor Heinrich Bacht writes an admirable appeal for agreement to be reached with the Conference of Bishops.

But in his Pentecost sermon in 1970 Hermann Schäufele, Archbishop of Freiburg, a former fellow- student of the German College, accuses me by name of 'rebellion against the church authorities', indeed of 'open disobedience', as if an invitation to act in accordance with one's conscience and in serious circumstances even against specific legal stipulations was not covered by Catholic moral theology, as if such action was not even recommended by the Conference of Bishops itself in connection with the pill encyclical *Humanae vitae*.

On 19 May 1970 the President of the German Conference of Bishops, Cardinal Julius Döpfner, then unnecessarily publishes a reprimand desired by Rome which defends the Roman document without critical qualifications. It doesn't have a word of understanding and help for the distress of those in mixed marriages or the pastors concerned or in the end the honest commitment of theologians. Instead it blames me personally with sharp words and calls for strict universal observance of the legal stipulations. It refers to the 1967 Synod of Bishops, but fails to mention that a third of the bishops along with the Dutch Cardinal Bernard Alfrink had been in favour of abolishing the obstacles to the marriage of those of different confessions hitherto in force together with the promise to bring up children as Catholics, which had been unilaterally required.

My answer to the Conference of Bishops is: 'Should the German Conference of Bishops change its mind over the question of celibacy and help the freedom of the Christian conscience to break through at least by a very generous interpretation of the Roman decree (*secundum, praeter* or in some circumstances even *contra legem*), one aim of the article would have been achieved. It has been written in such sharp, though objective, language not least in order to arouse the church authorities ... It is superfluous to say that the author, who so far has expressed himself critically, will not be sparing of praise wherever the church authorities "do something bold for God's sake", as Zwingli put it, in the service of men and women' (*Publik*, 5 June 1970).

An open letter by the great theologian Yves Congar in the French Catholic newspaper *La Croix* attracts increasing attention, especially since it is addressed to a certain Tübingen theologian (3 June 1970).The French Dominican defends Paul VI, with whom he has the best personal relations, in matters of mixed marriages, birth control and celibacy. The Pope cannot stand at the spearhead of renewal, he must be cautious. He, Congar, has already told me that with regard to the renewal of the church he sees the glass half full and I see it half empty. This is the difference between someone concerned for reform and a revolutionary. I shouldn't rely too confidently on my theological charism.

Did Yves Congar write this letter '*motu proprio*, on his own initiative'? With great respect and friendliness I reply to him in the same paper on 7 August 1970. I say that long ago I described him, my friend, as a revolutionary because in our church he hadn't been content with the half-full glass when it could so easily have been filled. But I wouldn't see the difference between the revolutionary and the reformer here. Rather, the revolutionary tips over the glass, and I didn't want to do this any more than he did. And if he thought he had more 'sensitivity to the Pope', there was another perspective: 'I didn't read that Jesus showed much sensitivity to the high priests who also defended the law with some justification, and perhaps also deserved sensitivity. I know that this is a lame comparison. But remember the decisive thing that I told you: Jesus showed sensitivity to the people: "*Misereor super turbam!* I feel pity for the people." You know, dear Père Congar, that I don't want to speak for myself but for "the people" who have no voice. You also know that at least in the German-speaking and Anglo-Saxon countries the vast majority of our people and the church want a rapid solution to the question of mixed marriages of the kind that I – and so many others with me – have proposed.'[11]

All this increases the pressure on the bishops. And on 23 September 1973 the Conference of Bishops issues 'regulations for implementation' which now really usher in a turning point. Bishops need no longer be approached for dispensations; everything can be settled at a local level. Despite all the clauses the couple can decide on the form of marriage and the baptism and upbringing of their children according to their consciences, so that the emigration from the church by couples of different confessions is halted. Thus the call for self-help has become immaterial, since if not the Pope, at least the bishops have allowed our pastors this self-help.

I formally express my 'promised thanks' in a big retrospective article on the controversy: 'The bishops deserve the honest thanks of all concerned for having taken into account the distress of those in mixed marriages and pastors, for having sought better solutions with the Protestant churches in a truly ecumenical attitude and responsibility, and finally for having resolved on concrete steps which go far beyond the Roman decrees and for the future spare the couples and the pastors affected the distressed conscience caused by the church's legal order' (*Publik*, 27 November 1970). Here finally is a victory for the reformers. But what about another, no less important, question?

Provocation V: the 'pill encyclical'

Since 1930 the question of birth control has been simmering in the Catholic Church. At that time the Lambeth Conference, the conference of bishops of the world-wide Anglican Communion, resolved that birth control was morally permissible. The Vatican, as always convinced that it alone possessed the truth, didn't suspect a second Galileo case. That same year Pius XI published the encyclical *Casti connubii*, in which any form of birth control (whether by mechanical means or through the interruption of sexual intercourse) was condemned as a mortal sin. Many couples have suffered seriously under this rigoristic moral dictate, which allowed them only total abstinence or the complicated use of safe periods according to Knaus-Ogino, if they have not left the Catholic Church altogether as a result. I know this not least from hearing confessions in Lucerne before the Council.

Millions of Catholics hoped for help from Vatican II. And in fact during the third session in 1964 three prominent Council fathers on one and the same morning spoke out for opening up this question: Patriarch Maximos, Cardinal Léger of Montreal and Cardinal Suenens, in whose company I left the basilica. He revealed to me that Paul VI wanted to leave the question to a papal commission and one could count on a positive result.

But what a disappointment! The Pope forbade further discussion of the question in the plenary assembly of the Council and appointed a papal commission. There was already a heated exchange in the Council's Theological Commission: the small conservative group around Cardinal Ottaviani fought against a theology of responsible parenthood with every means at its disposal. Despite a vote of 2000 to 91, with the help of a papal intervention it achieved one of the laziest compromises of the Council. In article 50 the Council document 'On the Church in the Modern World' (*Gaudium et spes*) affirms responsible parenthood, but in article 51 it disputes it and refers to the unfortunate encyclical *Casti connubii* of 1930; at the same time a footnote refers to the last decision of the

Pope which is still to come (cf. *My Struggle for Freedom*, IX). This is to happen through an encyclical which represents an unprecedented provocation far beyond the Catholic Church.

A Pope who doubts

I myself had the chance, in a long private audience at the end of the Council (*My Struggle for Freedom*, IX: Audience with Paul VI), on 2 December 1965, to talk about birth control with Pope Paul VI, who invited me to enter 'the service of the church', on the question of birth control. I gave him a little memorandum consisting of about a dozen points which he promised to pass on to the Theological Commission. In the conversation I tried to make clear to him above all that countless couples all over the world expected an understanding statement from him on this existential question.

The Pope calmly listened to my argument but said that the papal commission would now discuss the question of birth control and – with a reference to the pile of documents in front of him – that the results would arrive on his desk. He would then have to decide, and of course it was harder to decide than to study. When I went on to object, '*Finalmente, Santità, non si tratta di una dottrina infallibile* – in the end it's not a question of an infallible doctrine', Paul VI spontaneously raised both arms, first looked up and then at me, and made clear by his doubtful face that he was by no means certain that this wasn't an infallible doctrine. At that moment I was as flabbergasted as a Western scholar in the middle of Africa who has to prove to a native that despite the boundless flat plain the earth is round. I simply said – and I had no time for more – that all leading theologians shared my view, which the Pope once again acknowledged by helplessly raising his arms.

I have already reported the friendly end to this audience. Somehow I felt pity for this Pope. How can an individual, simply because he can appeal to Peter, who was often wrong (read the discussion between Paul and Peter in the second chapter of the Letter to the Galatians), decide on such an existential question alone? The command for celibacy, which also applied to him, didn't make him competent here. Nevertheless, the Montini Pope was an intellectual who knew how to doubt where doubts were appropriate. Only later did I hear that there was an important member of the commission who had no doubts on this question, as in others, but never appeared at a commission meeting, and instead sent letters to Rome behind its back, insisting that there should be no departure from the traditional doctrine. This was Karol Wojtyla, the Archbishop of Krakow.

I have to concede after the event that during my audience with the Pope I hadn't yet recognized the heart of the problem. For that I would have had to have known the opinion of the Ottaviani group, which became known only some time after the Council as the result of an indiscretion. Then it immediately became clear to me why the Pope could nevertheless not be convinced by the progressive majority of clergy and laity in the commission, headed by Vice-President Cardinal Döpfner, who was open to a change of doctrine.

An encyclical which meets with resistance world-wide

When the opinion of the conservative minority in the papal 'pill commission' kept secret by the Vatican becomes known to me around two years after the Council – thankfully it was published in *Herder-Korrespondenz* 21 (1967, pp. 429–39) – the scales fall from my eyes. In the question of birth control the Pope isn't concerned with 'the pill', with birth control as such, but with the prestige of the church's magisterium; not with sexuality but with inerrancy, with the continuity, authority, *infallibility*, in other words with the lack of error guaranteed according to Roman doctrine by the Holy Spirit to its own magisterium.

The opinion appears in time to be analysed in my book *Truthfulness. On the Future of the Church*, under the title 'A Change of Course in Doctrine?' But it comes too late to have any influence on the encyclical which appears the next year, 1968, with the opening words *Humanae vitae*. However, the problem has now been made completely clear.

That the encyclical dated 25 July appears during the summer holidays at the beginning of August 1968 – and moreover in the middle of the Czech people's fight for freedom – is generally interpreted as Roman tactics to meet with less resistance, but was perhaps simply a consequence of the time taken to draft this delicate document, only now completed, which was to burst like a bomb on the world public. Evidently the Pope himself greatly underestimated the resistance to his teaching. He hardly expected the world to react in so negative a way. Whereas according to UNICEF information 100 million children all over the world are leading a wretched life on the streets, the Vatican has no greater concern than rigorously to tighten up the prohibition of 'artificial' methods of birth control which are unavoidable today.

In the face of the storm of rejection even within the Catholic Church, the Pope sees himself called on – uniquely – immediately after the encyclical to go to its defence and explain the subjective motives for his decision: 'The first feeling was the sense of Our own very grave responsibility ... We have never felt the weight of Our office as much as in this situation.' Why? First the Pope says: 'We had to give an answer to the Church, to the whole of mankind. We had to evaluate a traditional doctrine that was not only age-old but also recent, having been reiterated by Our three immediate predecessors.' A doctrinal tradition which manifestly cannot be erroneous in any way!

I myself receive the news of the publication in my lake house on the Sempachersee on Friday 2 August 1968, and because of the media response feel how great the stir is also among Swiss people. That leads me to telephone the management of Swiss Television in Zurich on the Sunday morning and say that I am ready to take on the much-watched 'Word on Sunday' that same evening. Of course this provokes an intense top-level discussion in Zurich, but people there agree. My Sursee friend suffragan bishop Otto Wüst later tells me that a shiver ran down his back when the change of programme was announced. He was expecting a fiery speech, but he was disappointed. Am I to pour yet more oil on the fire?

No, I am concerned to give a prudent but also unambiguous reaction to such a doctrinal dictate. Two points are particularly important to me, and I make them on television.

1. 'The key argument for the Pope was that he feels bound to the official doctrine of his predecessors and the episcopate of the first half of the century, which is presented as definitive ... That will now lead our church to a critical examination of its notions of authority, magisterium, formulation of doctrine, dogma and especially infallibility; in future must not the infallibility of the church in the light of scripture be seen less in particular doctrinal statements or doctrines than in the conviction that the church is maintained, indeed constantly renewed, by God's Spirit, *despite* all errors, *through* all errors, of Popes, bishops, theologians, pastors, men and women?' Here already my theological solution to the wretched question of infallibility is clearly formulated – without being contradicted.

2. 'We will take the conscientious decision of the Pope seriously and respect it.' But conversely this now also means: 'Those among us who after serious, mature reflection before themselves, their spouses and God arrive at the insight that to maintain their love, and for the sake of the ongoing existence and happiness of their marriage, they have to act otherwise than the encyclical envisages, are obligated, by the traditional doctrine even of Popes, to follow their conscience.' And that means that they 'will not accuse themselves of sin where they have acted in accordance with their best knowledge and conscience'. And they will continue to 'take part in the life of the church and its sacraments'.

But there is no doubt that this 'pill encyclical' in 1968 has contributed more than anything else to the critical focusing of the situation in the Catholic Church. Paul VI becomes a tragic figure and is often caricatured as 'Pill Paul'. The prohibition of 'artificial' means of contraception without exception cannot be maintained. The church's authority in moral questions destroys itself and unintentionally creates a new sphere for freedom of conscience in the church. In important sectors of the church people organize themselves, as will soon become evident: the journal *Publik*, the 'Church from Below' and 'We are Church' movements, even an unofficial Catholic counselling service for conflicts in pregnancy. Indeed a real church protest movement is developing which sees itself strengthened by the 1968 student movement.

II

꘠꘡꘢꘠꘡꘢

1968: Year of Decisions

'Our struggle for the truth will also win over the younger generation, if
we involve them in it, better than violence and angry defence, better also
than the mere preservation of authority and tradition.'

Professor Ludwig Raiser, Rector of the University of Tübingen,
on 11 October 1968

Not only the church but society as a whole needs to cultivate the culture of
remembrance, and every nation and every generation has to do this afresh in its
own way. For time and again there is the threat that the dark phases of history will
be suppressed, whether they are the First or Second World War, the Vietnam or
Iraq War, or the brown, black or red past in Europe. Therefore in these two
chapters about 1968 and the 1968ers some things must be said which might be
unwelcome or offensive, depending on one's standpoint. I can't spare myself and
others that, and will attempt to give a fair assessment of the 1968 movement,
which still has an influence today.

How the 1968 cultural revolution came about

1968 is a year that serves as a signal. To the present day it marks a decisive break
in the post-war history of Western Europe and North America, a social upheaval
which of course had begun some time previously but which exploded in 1968.
1968 is the climax of the student movement world-wide, a year of protests and
revolutions, a year in which many students and professors, but also intellectuals
and politicians, decided on a direction. To the present day the social developments which broke out in 1968 are evaluated in very different ways. Was this a
long overdue process of democratization and modernization? Or were there
ideological tensions, one-sided self-fulfilment, anti-authoritarianism, a lack of
discipline? To provide clarification, here too I want simply to recall some roots in
the history of ideology and some social background.[1]

No political programme marked the beginning but a particular feeling, an
intellectual climate which increasingly allowed provocations and breaches of
taboo, even if only to destroy a general self-satisfaction. The youth counter-
culture of the 1960s, with beat and rock music, with expressiveness and eroticism,

had been some preparation for it. But it was the politically-focused cultural revolution of the students and intellectuals which first shook a society orientated on work and achievement, indeed the whole world of ordinary people. No longer did work, achievement, income and social prestige stand at the centre of interest for the generation which was now rebelling but rather utopia and action, social criticism and hostility to convention, informality, autonomy and self-fulfilment. All sectors of society were politicized and democratized at the same time. There was fury over the US Vietnam War. 'Make love, not war' was the slogan of the hippie culture in search of alternative lifestyles.

In both the US and in Europe the social analyses of the New Left have been a preparation for this. They are sharply marked off from the old Communist Left and its discredited model, the Soviet Union, and also from the bourgeois social democratic parties, whose reformism increasingly assimilated organized labour to the middle class. There is a rebellion against both the political apathy and unwillingness for reform encouraged by the Cold War and the increasing bureaucratization of social institutions. A growing dissatisfaction is further inflamed ideologically by certain press organs and publishers, and at the end of the 1960s vents itself in a violent protest against civilization. The silence of many parents about what they had experienced and even done in the Nazi period and the shock of the Auschwitz trials in Frankfurt (1963-66) lead the German 1968ers to embittered assessments. They doubt whether the older generation is really as politically ignorant or as innocent as is often asserted, and put all authorities, both state and church, in question.

The rebellious students are soon no longer content with the 'critical theory' of the Frankfurt School of Theodor W. Adorno and Max Horkheimer, which with its negative visions of the bureaucratic–technocratic economic society had originally animated them to radical social criticism. Politically effective sanctions are called for against the hated 'establishment' which is also seen at work in the universities ('the fug of 1000 years under the gown'), and no evasion into the aesthetic realm, for which Adorno and Horkheimer stand. Instead of seeing authentic works of art as distinct from the products of the culture industry ('art as a commodity'), as documents and monuments of resistance which stand for what is morally right, the German students, like the American students before them, call for a 'new sensuality'. This abolishes the separation of art and life and dissolves the boundaries between art and triviality, between high culture and both subculture and pop culture: the literary canon is expanded with Westerns, science fiction and underground literature, and in the graphic arts too the concept of art is extended to all realms of life with the incorporation of 'happenings'.

Adorno himself also becomes a victim of the aggression that is unleashed. In the 1920s he had deliberately embarked on modernity by accepting philosophical Marxism, psychoanalysis and musically the Second Viennese School (Schoenberg), but in the post-war decades he had to note the 'fatal old age in modernity'. However, he didn't want to draw any directly revolutionary consequences for

57

society and politics from his theoretical critique of culture. The new prophet for the critical students is above all the philosopher of culture Herbert Marcuse, who as a German professor in San Diego, California, provides the link between American and German students and intellectuals. As early as May 1966 in a student gathering in Frankfurt he declares that opposition to the Vietnam War is a moral duty. He calls for a decision here and now, so that this young generation doesn't incur guilt in the same way as its parents in the time of National Socialism. Thus Marcuse advocates a new version of Marxism which is not only distinguished negatively from Communist–Stalinist Marxism but positively strives for a 'new sensitivity' and a 'new sensuality' in order to make the impulses against the culture of the establishment stronger than aggression and guilt.

The students – above all the Students for a Democratic Society (SDS) in the US and the Sozialistische Deutsche Studentenbund (also SDS) in Germany – understand themselves as catalysts of a total social change, a new 'consciousness'. In the US the students above all support the Civil Rights Movement and offer increasingly vigorous opposition to the Vietnam War and the massive bombardment of North Vietnam even with napalm bombs. For this war demands an increasingly strong US military commitment, including ground troops (525,000 in 1967) and thus the recruitment of many students to war service who have so far been spared. Thus the anti-war demonstration increasingly becomes an anti-authoritarian movement generally.

Radicalization in Germany

In Germany, after the resignation of Chancellor Ludwig Erhard in December 1966 (he has no success against the recession which threatens), a grand coalition of Christian Democrats and Social Democrats has formed under Chancellor Kurt Georg Kiesinger, whom I know personally as Prime Minister of Baden-Württemberg. He lives in Tübingen. An 'extra-parliamentary opposition', made up of students and intellectuals, forms against a state which is orderly from the outside but alleged to be internally corrupt, and its elected representatives. The opposition is headed by the SDS and its leader Rudi Dutschke and attacks above all the emergency laws planned by parliament because many students feel these to be a threat to basic democratic rights.

From 27 May to 4 June 1967 the Shah of Persia, Mohammad Reza Pahlavi, pays a state visit to the Federal Republic. At the universities and in certain cities he is greeted with protests against his authoritarian regime. On 2 June the student Benno Ohnesorg is shot at one such demonstration against the Shah in Berlin; the policeman accused of negligent killing is acquitted. This event, interpreted as a prelude to the planned emergency laws, sparks off the mobilization of students all over the country, supported by the left-wing intelligentsia. There are also mass student protests in Tübingen, of which more later. Previously 251 people had perished in Brussels during an arson attack on a department store. Four days later pamphlets from a 'Commune 1' are distributed in Berlin which compare the Brussels fire to napalm bombing in Vietnam and ask when the department stores will burn in Berlin. The commune members accused of instigating arson are acquitted on 22 March because of the allegedly 'satirical' content of the pamphlets. But in fact on 2 April 1968 two department stores are set on fire in Frankfurt. Andreas Baader, Gudrun Ensslin and two other comrades are arrested and condemned as arsonists. Hardly have they been released than they form the Red Army Fraction terrorist association, the RAF, to overturn the state and social order of the Federal Republic by urban guerrilla warfare on Latin American lines. In 1972 they are arrested and put on trial.

On 11 April 1968 the student leader Rudi Dutschke, who himself has endorsed the use of weapons in certain circumstances, is gunned down in the street by a young labourer and fatally wounded. This results in demonstrations all over Germany and bloody clashes with the police (in Munich two people are killed). For many students this attack is the result of tendentious reporting by the conservative Springer press (*Bild-Zeitung*) on the student unrest of recent months. On 30 April 1968 the German Bundestag holds a special session on the student unrest. Only a month later, despite everything it passes the controversial emergency laws with a two-thirds majority, though the laws are never implemented.

So it is relatively small minorities, initially only in the universities, which spark mass provocations and aim at a broad influence far beyond the universities. In many ways they are supported by the mass media, in which many younger editors and journalists sympathize with the protesters. But they are also supported at party conferences, in cultural life and finally also in the church and theology. Changed forms of behaviour and unconventional fashions in clothing spread, along with surprisingly new forms of action such as sit-ins, teach-ins, love-ins, and lead to new forms of life and organization: communes, anti-authoritarian children's nurseries and critical seminars.

All in all this is a true cultural revolution, which reaches a climax in 1968. In Vietnam there is the successful Tet offensive by the Communist Liberation Front which shakes the confidence of many Americans in their military and political leadership. In Berlin the International Vietnam Congress is accompanied with a big demonstration. In London there is the Vietnam Solidarity Campaign, in Rome the closure of the Città Universitaria and the 'battle in the Valle Giulia'. However, in Czechoslovakia the revolutionary 'Prague spring' – of which more later – has a different character. A no less dramatic intensification takes place in the United States, which I experience along with the radicalization in Germany.

Guest professor in New York

On Monday 12 February 1968 I conclude my lectures in Tübingen. Just two days later, on Wednesday 14 February, I begin my guest semester in New York at Union Theological Seminary. I had been invited as early as 1963, but only in 1968 can it be fitted in between the Tübingen winter and summer semesters. In New York I give my Tübingen lectures on an ecumenical theology of the sacraments, of course in English. I want to concentrate on overcoming the split in the understanding above all of the eucharist and penance. At the same time I offer a seminar on the doctrine of justification and a colloquium on the understanding of the church.

I had expected between 100 and 200 participants in this colloquium on church and truthfulness. But I have a happy and at the same time demanding surprise: 1600 participants had registered, and of course that made a 'colloquium' impossible. It had to be lectures, which Union Theological Seminary transferred to the Riverside Church, built by John D. Rockefeller, a jewel of neo-Gothic, under the title 'The Problems of the Church Today'. And I had no alternative but to work through the lectures on 'Church and Truthfulness' which I had given in Tübingen to an audience from all faculties one by one and send them to London, to be translated by my distinguished English translator Fr Edward Quinn. Thanks to his tremendous effort I was able to fly to New York on 13 February with well-prepared English translations; there I was welcomed in the *New York Times* (15 February 1968) under the headline 'Man in the News' as 'Theologian for Catholic Reform' and 'Idealist without Illusions'.

Union Theological Seminary – in Manhattan at 120th Street next to Columbia University and the Jewish Theological Seminary and adjacent to the great headquarters of the National Council of Churches – is likewise in a state of upheaval. For many years the place where great theologians such as Reinhold Niebuhr and Paul Tillich taught, it also enjoys great academic respect under its distinguished president, the social ethicist John Bennett. I truly have no complaints about the scholarly interest of my students, and contacts with colleagues and their wives are very warm and friendly. I have two very sympathetic assistants with the best academic qualifications, Karl Peters and Wesley Poorman. They not only assist me at the seminar and help me to polish the language of my lectures, but also correct written papers and sort out the numerous questions submitted in writing for my big lectures in Riverside Church.

However, I cannot overlook the fact that the interest of some students, above all coloured students, is directed less towards theological scholarship and training than towards church and social action and agitation (I remember some of the posters and notices in the elevator). In July 1967 there had been serious race riots in America; the ever more costly Vietnam War made it impossible to realize the 'great society' announced by President Lyndon B. Johnson. There had even been an assault on the Pentagon in Washington on 21 October 1967. The police were attacked, the cordon was broken and the banner of the Vietnamese liberation movement FNL hoisted on the Pentagon mast before the demonstration was broken up. There are also those who refuse war service and burn draft cards. Not least prominent Catholic clergy such as the Berrigan brothers are involved in this; both Jesuits, they are arrested, sentenced and put in prison. But by far the greater part of our students aren't prepared to go so far. After all, the war against the Communist Vietcong had long been disputed even in the American SDS, and priority had been given to social work and self-help organizations in a fight against racial discrimination and poverty which transcended the races. A US victory is becoming increasingly more improbable. A cease-fire is signed by the US government only in 1973; the war costs the lives of 56,000 Americans and more than a million Vietnamese.

I hear, see and learn a great deal when on free days after lecture engagements I explore other cities and universities: Pittsburgh, Louisville, Yale, Baton Rouge, New Orleans, Washington DC, Vassar, Marymount, Columbus, Tallahassee. I speak in the great Inter-Church Center in New York about the development in the Catholic Church after the Council; in the Goethe Institute, in German, on truthfulness in the church; and then to around 1000 women religious on the explosive question 'Jesus or Qumran?' Here I argue firmly that they shouldn't orientate themselves on the strict monastic rules of the Essenes at the time of Jesus but on the free rules of Jesus' disciples. As well as all this, in New York I go to Stravinsky's *Oedipus Rex* and Carl Orff's *Carmina Burana*, and Wagner's *Lohengrin* at the Metropolitan Opera; on Broadway I see the Don Quixote musical *Man of La Mancha* by Dale Wassermann. All in all an exciting life.

My New York secretary also has her hands full writing dozens of refusals: later I will be able to accept some invitations from major universities. But I am happy to see old friends again from my time at the Gregorian and the Council, including my fellow student in Rome, Robert Trisco, now a church historian and Vice President of the Catholic University in Washington, from which I had been 'banned' in 1963, along with three famous American theologians (*My Struggle for Freedom*, VII: A historic debate and a ban on teaching). But now I've been sent a formal invitation.

I also make many new friends. I'm thinking, for example, of William Sloane Coffin. Three years older than me and from a rich Protestant family, he took part in the Second World War and at a very early age became known all over America as the chaplain of Yale University. For him social justice stands at 'the heart of the gospel'. He became a key figure for a whole new generation of students in the campaign against the Vietnam War and in the fight for black civil rights. As such he took part in 1961 in the Freedom Ride to Montgomery, Alabama, in order to contest segregation on the buses. Now, in 1968, he is accused by the Minister of Justice in the Johnson administration of conspiracy to civil disobedience against conscription for Vietnam. He is found guilty, but is spared imprisonment because of a decision by higher authorities. From 1977 to 1987 he will be the extremely active senior minister of Riverside Church. In 1978 we shall go there for a great convocation lasting several days in honour of the famous liberal preacher Harry Emerson Fosdick (1878–1969), who is responsible for the building of Riverside Church.

William Sloane Coffin and I are invited to give ceremonial lectures to celebrate the 75th anniversary of the church in 2006, but neither of us can accept. Instead, we both answer the same five questions on the past, present and future of Christianity in television interviews. I am touched to see my friend on the screen answering the questions; he has grown very old. Only a few days after recording my own answers in Tübingen I receive the sad news that Bill died on 12 April 2006 on his estate in Strafford, Vermont, at the age of 81.

The murder of Martin Luther King

I particularly remember two events from this guest semester in New York. The first is the visit of the renowned Protestant theologian from the Free University of Berlin, Professor Helmut Gollwitzer, a pupil of Karl Barth, who gives a lecture there on 'Atheism and Theology in the Present Day' and bravely joins in discussion with the students. In connection with this he publishes an extremely moving book 'On the question of the meaning of life' in which he asks how human beings learn 'the crooked wood' (Kant's realistic picture of human beings) and the 'upright walk' (the Marxist Ernst Bloch's picture of human hope).[2] But now he identifies himself completely with the rebellious Berlin students and their protest gatherings, and in so doing advocates a theology of revolution.

I too certainly support many of the students' concerns about the delays to the reform of universities and society. But what Nietzsche calls the German 'magic of the extreme', of wherever possible taking an idea through to its ultimate, possibly hopeless conclusion, goes against my understanding of politics, which is stamped by Swiss sobriety and democratic pragmatism. And now, in the discussion group of 30 to 40 students in Union Theological Seminary in which Gollwitzer plays his political cards even more clearly, I am somewhat annoyed at the Marxist sense of mission and the ideological certainty of salvation with which he describes his experiences in Berlin. Despite all the one-sidedness these give him a certain credibility, but should we offer here and now to our American students the confusing drama of two professors from Germany arguing about the interpretation of the German student movement? Silence is better. Just as I reject any demonizing of the student rebellion and Rudi Dutschke, so too I reject any transfiguration.

The next developments come more quickly and more cruelly than I had expected. On 1 August 1968 Gollwitzer writes to me from Berlin that he spent four weeks in California and then returned via Atlanta and Washington to 'unsettled Berlin, on reading in the newspaper in Washington that Rudi Dutschke, who was living in our house, had been the victim of an assassination attempt'. Dutschke dies in 1979 of the delayed consequences of the attack and is buried by Gollwitzer.

The second event is far more serious. As well as giving my lectures on the theology of the sacraments in Union Theological Seminary as announced, I give public lectures on the problems of today's church in Riverside Church. It is 4 April 1968: I begin my lecture at 7.30 p.m. to an audience of perhaps 1500, clergy and laity from the different churches. A note is handed to me and I immediately have to announce the sad news that Martin Luther King has been murdered. The great champion of the non-violent liberation of blacks has been gunned down by a white assassin in Memphis (Tennessee) while he was speaking from the balcony of a hotel.

I confess that I stand completely stunned in the pulpit, incapable of commenting spontaneously in English on an event which seems to me to have unforeseeable consequences. After a period of silence for thought I finally continue my talk; perhaps I should have stopped it. But to send home all the audience, some of whom had made long journeys, seems to me as inappropriate as to hold a discussion which could only have ended in a highly controversial way. Shortly beforehand, the Kerner Report of the commission set up by President Johnson to investigate the causes and background of racial unrest, almost 500 pages long, had been published. It attributed the main blame for the events to the political, economic, social and human behaviour of many whites towards the coloured. So this is not a black conspiracy but an explosive mixture of discrimination, poverty, a ghetto situation and the provocative behaviour of whites (especially the police). Two years previously the Afro-American student group SNCC had turned away from Martin Luther King's non-violent strategy of direct action and supported the strategy and tactics of the anti-colonial liberation movement: this Black Power Movement is also criticized in the report because it is promoting an exodus from American society and separatism. The murder of Martin Luther King – like that of President Kennedy's brother Senator Robert Kennedy a little later on 5 June – is a tremendous setback to the American civil rights movement, whose actions hitherto have been non-violent.

The next morning confirms this. I have to go by taxi very early along 125th Street, right across Harlem, the black district of Manhattan, to La Guardia airport. There is horrifying devastation, dozens of businesses have been burnt out and plundered. After the murder of Martin Luther King, violent riots by coloured people are reported in 76 cities: 46 dead and $45 million of damage. Will that perhaps be a model for Germany, where some student groups are also hoping for unrest and toying with the idea of urban guerrilla warfare?

Charismatic Pentecostal eucharist in Paris: intercommunion

In France, too, in 1968 there is violent student unrest and a wave of strikes by the workers. It culminates in the occupation of factories, which brings France to the brink of chaos. After the closure of the Nanterre faculty and the occupation of the Sorbonne by the police there is a street battle in the Latin Quarter. There are also serious conflicts in other university cities during the following days. On 13 May the trade unions strike in solidarity with the students over the brutal police actions. By 20 May five million French are already on strike. On 24 May President de Gaulle finally intervenes and announces on the television a readiness for far-reaching social reforms and a reorganization of the universities. On 27 May there is agreement between the government and the trade unions. On 30 May parliament is dissolved by de Gaulle and new elections are announced. As 'May 68' the student unrest remains a key date for the social and political development of the country in the twentieth century and it also has a special significance for some Christians and for theology and the church.

Pentecost, 2 June 1968: 70 Catholic and Protestant Christians come together in a room in the Sorbonne – priests, pastors and lay people, some of whom are very well known – to celebrate the eucharist together.[3] 61 of them receive communion and sign an explanatory press release for their churches. Some of those taking part define this eucharistic celebration as a charismatic event which shouldn't simply be institutionalized. Subsequently the participation of Catholics in such a joint celebration of the eucharist is often connected, with praise or blame, with my view of the apostolic succession: as well as appointment to office by the laying on of hands 1 Corinthians, for example, also shows a celebration of the eucharist without apostles and appointed ministers.

The Archbishop of Paris, François Marty, reacts on 5 June with a press release. He shows understanding but declares this joint celebration of the eucharist to be 'an action of which we cannot approve'. His reason is that the eucharist is a sacrament of the unity and liturgy of the world-wide church, not an individual act, and the danger of new splits is to be avoided. But above all he cites 'the office of priest': 'The priest alone has the authority to consecrate the eucharist. This priestly authority is transferred by the bishops through the apostolic succession.' Cardinal Bea and Archbishop Willebrands of the Vatican Secretariat for Unity support the position of the Archbishop of Paris in a letter. However, the council of the Fédération protestante de France, represented by Pastors Westphal, Roux, Blanc, Bosc, Guiraud and Maury, states in its press release: 'A joint celebration of the eucharist does not pose the same problems for the churches which belong to the Federation of French Protestant Churches as it does for the Roman Catholic Church.' It recommends 'a study of the questions raised by this event'.

These events provoke an immense discussion among the wider French public. It is attested in various documents and followed with mistrust by Rome. At the request of the journal *Christianisme Social*, in July 1968 I finally make a statement which is also circulated by other organs.[4] In it I begin from the fact that such joint celebrations of the eucharist are held not only in Paris but also in other places in Europe, America and the Middle East. To many people they seem to be the expression of a newly-discovered unity between Christians of different confessions.

There seem to me to be 'no serious theological objections' to a joint celebration of the eucharist by Christians: not in the case of an individual Christian who for serious reasons, say in a marriage between members of different confessions, on some occasions takes part in the eucharistic celebration of another community. Nor – and this is the understanding of those who take part in the Paris eucharist – 'in the case of communities where the joint celebration simply imposes itself in an extraordinary situation as a charismatic event, without calling for institutionalization'.

I then turn to the rejection of such intercommunion in so far as it appeals to legally invalid church ministry or the ordination of non-Catholic pastors. This alleged invalidity rests on the one hand on a narrow mechanistic concept of the apostolic succession and on the other on a clericalist misunderstanding of the church's ministry and its authority. As a basis I refer to chapter E of my book *The Church*, where this problem is discussed over many pages on the basis of the New Testament evidence (as it also was in my *Structures of the Church*).

However, I immediately add an important qualification: 'In the present situation, nevertheless objections can be made to a regular institutionalized intercommunion of communities. Such intercommunion would suggest a unity between the separated Christian churches which unfortunately does not yet exist.' However, one mustn't be content with this, for 'Unless the pastors promote ecumenical understanding more energetically than hitherto, they will increasingly be overwhelmed by the charismatics . . . In the end, an ecumenism of words must be followed by an ecumenism of deeds.' In worship, frequent and not just exceptional joint ecumenical services of the word and greater generosity in the participation of other Christian churches in the eucharist are to be called for.

My friend the Dominican theologian Yves Congar writes to me very critically on 30 January 1969: 'I can tell you that in France and doubtless also elsewhere, you serve as a point of reference for a number of adventurous initiatives, as for example the concelebration at Pentecost 1968. I clearly see that such a situation gives rise to various assessments.' But Congar's final sentence is important to me: 'The results of an honest and serious intellectual investigation have their own value, regardless of any practical convenience or inconvenience.'

I reply to him on 14 February: 'As long as everything remains the same in Rome in essentials and above all theologically, the present crisis will not be overcome.' I tell him that I find it almost tragic that our fellow Catholic theologian, the highly-regarded Jesuit Henri de Lubac, is denounced (as I myself have been more recently), although Congar himself has suffered this fate all through his life as a theologian. Rome makes de Lubac, now in line with Rome (and later also his pupil Hans Urs von Balthasar) a cardinal, but not Congar at that time. 'Nothing would please me more than to see you nominated a cardinal, if anything were fundamentally changed in the church by that. But what decisive changes have the new cardinals made so far in the present regime? And if you should be used (in a way that the Romans loved even before the birth of Christ) simply to adorn their own Roman system, I wouldn't be able to congratulate you on it. I revere you too much for that. For me your place in the history of the theology of the century is too important.' Twenty-five years later this Roman honour is bestowed on Congar, wasting away in the hospital of Les Invalides in Paris. I visited him there on 26 June 1995, six months before his death (Balthasar had died in Basle on 26 June 1988, two days before being received into the College of Cardinals!).

French critics and Roman actions remind me of something that I hadn't forgotten in America but had put right to the back of my mind. Inquisition proceedings were still under way in Rome against my book *The Church*, which had stimulated this charismatic celebration of the eucharist. They were running their course untouched by the great world events in the *piccolo mondo chiuso* – the 'little closed world' – of the Vatican.

The quiet activity of the Roman Inquisition

The Inquisition has had its eye on me since my doctorate in theology. But Rome's mills grind slowly, and also quietly. The Inquisition fears publicity. In 1957 I had no inkling that because of my dissertation *Justification. The Doctrine of Karl Barth and a Catholic Reflection*, an Inquisition dossier had been opened on me with the file number 399/57/i (i = division of the Index of Prohibited Books). However, my teachers in Rome and Paris saved me from proceedings.

At that time the Index of Prohibited Books, first published as a weapon against the Reformers in 1559 and since then regularly brought up to date, contained the greatest names of European literature and scholarship alongside many Protestant and Catholic theologians. Since there was hardly anyone in Rome in the nineteenth century who understood 'these barbaric languages', German and English authors were often put on the Index without being examined, simply on the basis of a denunciation, or even because they had featured at the Frankfurt Book Fair. In our day theologians could sometimes simply read their condemnation in the newspaper one morning and be devastated. Any historian who studies only the acts of the Inquisition (which in 2003 were released for research at least up to 1939), opinions and counter-opinions, denunciations and censorship, agendas and minutes, can easily forget the human fates bound up with them: how the best-disposed and best-educated Catholic theologians were deeply wounded by such permanent ostracism all over the world. I heard personally from the distinguished Münster professor Helmut Dohm (put on the Index for presenting procreation and lifelong devotion as the aims of marriage, a position finally advocated even in the 'pill encyclical') and the respected Aachen pastor Dr Josef Thomé (condemned for a little book on the laity). What will happen to me?

My book *The Council and Renewal. Renewal as a Call to Unity*, written in 1960 in preparation for the Council, is preserved from sanctions – unlike the book on the Council by the Italian Jesuit Fr Riccardo Lombardi, which concentrates on reform of the Curia. This is probably because of the protective preface by Cardinal Franz König of Vienna and the preface to the French edition by Cardinal Achille Liénart of Lille. But formal proceedings are opened over my 1962 book *Structures of the Church*, and towards the end of the second session of the Council I am summoned to a session presided over by Cardinal Augustin Bea, who is well-disposed to me, in the presence of Bishops Streng of Basle and Leiprecht of Rottenburg and two professors of theology. The session isn't too bad and ends with a request first orally and later in writing to answer eight questions on the constitution of the church and church ministries, the verdict of the conscience, faith and formulations of faith, and the validity of polemical council definitions. The proceedings are stopped.

But at the beginning of the fourth session of the Council, on 14 October 1965, I am summoned in person by the feared head of the Holy Office, Cardinal Alfredo Ottaviani, for a discussion at the Palazzo of the Inquisition just to the left of St Peter's. This is because of my summing up of the third session of the Council, which is highly critical of Paul VI but correctly analysed. I also survive this interview unscathed, as is reported in *My Struggle for Freedom* (IX: Confronted with the Grand Inquisitor).

The abolition of the Index which I had called for time and again in lectures and publications even before the Council took place by decrees of the Congregation for the Doctrine of the Faith dated 14 June and 15 November 1966. But this by no means represented the abolition of the Index. That is evident when my third big book, *The Church*, appears in German in April 1967 and in Dutch a little later, and proves to be a bestseller despite its extent of 605 pages. On 29 November 1967 there is a secret session of the Congregation of Cardinals in the palace of the Holy Office, in which the senior heads of the Curia have a seat. The Congregation is concerned about the publication of the book and resolves on the following decree. The chancery of Rottenburg is to be censured for giving an imprimatur. The author is to be 'authoritatively invited' by the Bishop of Rottenburg not to disseminate the book further and not to allow it to be translated into another language 'before he has held a colloquium with men selected by this Sacred Congregation to which he will soon be invited' ('*antequam colloquium conseruerit cum viris ab hac Sacra Congregatione deligendis, ad quod quidem mox invitabitur*').

This decree is sent to Bishop Carl-Joseph Leiprecht of Rottenburg on 19 December 1967 without any substantive explanation by the Pro-Prefect Cardinal Alfredo Ottaviani (Pope Paul VI himself is the Prefect). On 27 December in

Sursee I receive the Roman decree from the chancery of Rottenburg in an express letter to my Swiss and Tübingen addresses, shortly after I have celebrated Christmas with my family, but I keep the oppressive news to myself, so as not to spoil Christmas for my parents and the rest of the family. However, the following day I telephone my publishers in Paris, London and New York in order to speed up the publication of the French, English and American editions. At the same time I inform the Spanish publisher in Barcelona through the German publisher, Herder Verlag of Freiburg. I insist that Herder must observe the conditions of my contract and keep the book in print, even if there are further attempts at intimidation. Both the English and the American editions appear soon afterwards.

In the middle of the Tübingen summer semester, on 4 May 1968, an invitation to the Vatican arrives, for 9 May. The Secretary of the Congregation for the Doctrine of the Faith, Archbishop Paul Philippe, writes in an imperative tone: 'The Congregation for the Doctrine of the Faith is examining your book *The Church*. According to the norms of the *motu proprio Integrae servandae*, a discussion with the author should be held. I ask you, Herr Professor Küng, to come to this discussion on Thursday, 9 May, at 9.30 a.m. in the Palazzo del S. Uffizio in Rome. Respectfully, Paul Philippe, Secretary.'[5]

How should I react?

I cannot simply cancel lectures and seminars in the middle of the semester. Moreover, as a free Swiss citizen and Christian I do not want to be called to account as though I were in an authoritarian regime. Even the Inquisition authorities must one day get accustomed to legal and humane forms of dealing with people. So I send a telegram to Archbishop Philippe, Città del Vaticano, with the terse communication: 'Unfortunately prevented. Letter follows.'[6]

Precisely 30 days later I send my well-considered reply, which has been examined by others, to Archbishop Philippe, and copies to the Bishop of Rottenburg and the Dean of the Catholic Faculty of the University of Tübingen, Professor Dr Joseph Ratzinger:

Dear Archbishop,
As I indicated to you by telegram on 8 May, I was unfortunately prevented from appearing at the discussion scheduled for 9 May. In the meantime, I have taken the trouble to reflect carefully on my answer to your letter and to discuss it with other competent professors and churchmen.
   I begin by stating that in principle I am prepared to participate in a conversation. I consider the invitation to a colloquium to be significant progress compared to the proceedings customary in the past. I am convinced that possible difficulties and ambiguities can all be resolved by an open and congenial exchange of views. In the post-conciliar era dialogue

among Catholics is at least as important as dialogue with other Christian churches and with the modern world. You can be assured of my co-operation.

At the same time, I cannot conceal my surprise at the way in which this invitation has been issued. Quite apart from the fact that the date for a colloquium ought to have been arranged by mutual agreement, I cannot understand how this invitation could have been issued at such short notice.

In fact I would have had only four days to get to Rome, which in any case would have been impossible because of my burden of work; at this time I had even had to decline an invitation from a Catholic university in the United States to receive an honorary doctorate. So it would surely be understood that an unplanned trip to Rome was out of the question and moreover that the conditions for a fruitful and successful colloquium had to be guaranteed beforehand. Six points seemed essential to me, of which the first was the most important.

In your letter of 30 April, as well as in earlier letters of the Congregation, you refer to your dossier 399/57/i, which evidently concerns me. If I am to participate intelligently in a colloquium, it is indispensable that I should have unrestricted access to the official documents and free use of my dossier, which, judging by its reference number, had already been started by the Index division. In my view, the colloquium cannot be fair unless I have knowledge of the official documents that concern me and am free to use them without restrictions of any kind. I hardly need to mention that in all civilized states of the West even criminals are guaranteed complete access to the dossiers that pertain to them. I therefore request a written assurance that I shall be allowed free use of the official documents relating to me.

Further points in addition to inspecting the records are: since the Congregation is evidently still 'examining' my book, the 'authoritative invitation' to renounce my right to distribute it further, which had been mentioned earlier, is unsubstantiated. Moreover I would have to be thoroughly informed beforehand about the questions to be discussed, and competent experts would have to be included in the symposium. Since my book *The Church* presupposes precise special exegetical, historical and dogmatic knowledge, it would make little sense, as I had experienced in a former colloquium, to discuss with a canon lawyer exegetical, historical and dogmatic questions with which he would not be familiar. I therefore asked for written questions and the name of my conversation partner. Moreover, German would be the appropriate language for the discussion in a colloquium of a German book by a German-speaking author. Not least, I asked for an understanding that I regarded the costs incurred by this colloquium as unreasonable and therefore requested a written assurance that all the expenses arising would be met by the Doctrinal Congregation. I said that it was also possible to hold the colloquium in Tübingen, and that I would gladly make my home available for it.[7]

No inspection of the records

'I have to say that I admire your courage and the strength which you draw from unconditional service of the truth,' writes Yves Congar to me rather later (29 August 1968), when he hears from our mutual friend the Dominican Bernard Dupuy of the conditions I have sent to the Doctrinal Congregation. He had long been persecuted by the Inquisition. 'But I have to add,' he goes on, 'that this would have been absolutely impossible under Pius XII; in two weeks at the latest you would have been driven into the blind alley of either surrendering or giving up the priesthood. That was a Stalinist regime.'

On 3 July a new decree is issued by the Doctrinal Congregation which shows a little progress; it asks the author to give dates on which he can come to Rome and guarantees that all expenses will be met. But it refuses to allow me to inspect my dossier 399/57/i.

In a letter of 27 July I declare myself ready to carry on the conversation in another modern language. At the same time I ask to be told the name of my conversation partner and the precise topics of conversation. I put aside my request to inspect the records until these questions have been clarified, but ask to be sent the new order of procedure for the Congregation ordered by the Pope. On 31 August the Congregation gives me the names of three people who have been asked to take part in the colloquium. The topics to be discussed at the colloquium will be given to me 'soon'. And although a new order of procedure has been worked out, it is only experimental and not *publici iuris*.

Meanwhile my book *The Church* is a great success. In the years 1968–70 it appears in French, Spanish, Italian and Portuguese editions and runs through several impressions. On 11 December 1968 a telegram from Chicago tells me that the Thomas More Association has awarded me the Thomas More Medal for *The Church* as 'the most outstanding contribution to Catholic literature of the year 1968'; this gives me special delight because of my admiration for Henry VIII's Lord Chancellor (cf. *My Struggle for Freedom*, V: Freedom in the world). The year before, the prize went to the 'Dutch Catechism', so I am in good company. On 4/5 June I launch the Italian edition personally, in Milan; I have a brief friendly exchange of words with Archbishop Carlo Colombo, the papal court theologian, who happens to be present. In 1970 short versions of *The Church* appear in German and in Dutch as pocket books under the title 'What is the Church?' 1970 also sees the appearance of my book *Infallible? An Enquiry*, of which more later. I continue to work intensively and so am always a step ahead of the Inquisition. In October 1968 Roger Schutz, Prior of the Taizé community, also assures me of his support: 'I want you to know that I am near you in these times of difficulty . . .

70

Next month I shall be in Rome. Do you want me to speak of the gratitude that I have for you, or would you prefer silence? You are my friend, and Christ invites us to give something of our lives (i. e. our trust) for our friends. Bound to you in true brotherhood, Yours, Frère Roger.' On 16 October I reply to him that evidently people in Rome can hardly understand my concern: 'So it would be useful if on your visit to Rome you attempted to make clear to people what my real Christian intention is.'

By February 1971 the topics still haven't been given to me. But on 5 February 1971 the Congregation publishes the new order of procedure ('Procedure for the examination of doctrines') signed by Cardinal Franjo Šeper, the new Prefect of the Congregation and former Archbishop of Zagreb, an alumnus of the German College, and the Secretary, Archbishop Philippe. Various of my demands for the provision of an 'orderly' procedure have been met, but by no means all – above all there can be no inspection of the records. However, an 'extraordinary' procedure is also provided for, according to which in some circumstances the Roman authority can proceed against an author suspected of heresy in a 'rapid judgement', avoiding the new regulations, in other words an old-style Inquisition. At the same time the Curia and its nunciatures do all they can against the book; thus the publication of a Korean edition is prevented by the apostolic nuncio in Seoul. One gets the impression that little in the Roman apparatus has been changed by the Council. The crisis is programmed. However, my 'trial' can be assessed rightly only in the wider context of church politics.

The crisis for the church after the Council – a dispute over paradigms

It is not the Council that has brought the Catholic Church to a crisis, as the conservatives assert, but betrayal of the Council; the justified hopes and expectations of by far the greater part of Catholic church people have not been fulfilled. The Catholic Church was in some respects prepared for the confrontations of 1968 by the Second Vatican Council. From 1962 to 1965 it experienced a considerable renewal. It attempted to take the concerns of the Reformation seriously: high esteem for the Bible, a popular form of worship in the vernacular, a revaluation of the laity, a reform of popular piety. It found a new attitude to the other Christian churches, to Judaism and the other world religions, indeed to the secular world generally, which calls for tolerance, freedom of religion and human rights – the great concerns of the Enlightenment. John XXIII's 1963 encyclical *Pacem in terris* was pioneering here, but Paul VI's social encyclical *Populorum progressio* of 26 March 1967 pointed in the same direction.

This represents an astonishing new orientation of the Catholic Church by comparison with its own absolutist–clerical structure as this has developed from Rome since the Gregorian reform of the eleventh century, the revolution initiated by Gregory VII 'from above'. It is important to see the historical context here: the original Jewish–Christian paradigm of primitive Christianity (Paradigm I) was overlaid at a very early stage by the early church–Hellenistic paradigm (P II), which united the Eastern and the Western churches. But in the eleventh century the specifically Roman Catholic paradigm (P III) prepared for theologically by Augustine and laboriously advanced by the bishops of Rome was definitively established, and this resulted in the split of the Western Church from the Eastern Church. In terms of this overall view of Christianity, as I analysed it later (cf. *Christianity. Its Essence and History*, 1994, ET 1995), Vatican II ventured on an epoch-making attempt at integrating the two paradigms of the Reformation (P IV) and modernity (P V). Of course this displeased those who – above all in order to keep their own power and glory – wanted to remain in the medieval Roman Catholic paradigm as consolidated in the Counter-Reformation and then rescued in anti-modernism up to the middle of the twentieth century.

However – as I had to make clear in *My Struggle for Freedom* – euphoria was inappropriate both during and after the Council. To this extent, for all my passionate commitment to the Council I was always more among the sceptics than among the enthusiasts. For what is beyond question an epoch-making renewal is only half-heartedly accomplished in most realms and suffers from pernicious compromises, especially over the contradiction, already mentioned, in the fundamental Constitution on the Church between the new biblically orientated tendencies of church as community and people of God (chs I and II) and a medieval hierarchical church (ch. III) with an intensified distinction of celibate clergy and a completely subordinate laity and unlimited papal absolutism (the result of that Gregorian 'reform'). I was often oppressed during the Council by the way in which time and again the progressive majority allowed itself to be manipulated by the small curial minority that was in complete control of the Council apparatus and brought increasingly behind it the originally progressive but anxious Pope Paul VI, who had grown up in the Curia.

It was clear to me, and not just to me, that the hard core of the Curia hadn't wanted the Council, that it was obstructing the new orientations as far as possible, and that immediately after the Council it set about repairing the 'damage' that in its view John XXIII and his Council had done. During the Council the saying went the rounds in the Curia that it would take a century to make the 'repairs'; in fact it took only a couple of decades. Instead of preparing spiritually for conciliar renewal in a new time, which would have been quite possible had others occupied the key positions, the Curia is increasingly concerned with a restoration of the Roman system and a blockage of renewal in all spheres which continues to the present day.

In a pre-conciliar way an attempt is soon also made to proceed against Catholic theologians using the methods of the Inquisition. This can give rise to a holy anger. In a letter of 19 June 1968, which I abbreviate somewhat here, I reply to the Augustinian father Dr Paulus Sladek of Zwiesel, who criticizes the passion of my language, which is sometimes quite appropriate, and sees no 'reverence' and 'love' for the church in it: 'It would be a bad thing if one could once again accuse theology of not having recognized the signs of the time or of only thinking in a quiet room about what should have been cried from the rooftops. What so many people think and want, without being able to get a hearing, must be expressed and formulated above all by theology in the public presence of the church and viewed critically and made precise in the light of the message of Jesus Christ, not out of a theological "missionary fanaticism", as some could suppose, but out of a sober awareness of the duty of a theologian and – this may be remarked for once quite unsentimentally – out of love of a church which as the itinerant people of God needs the strong, suffering and hoping love of those involved, those affected and those responsible. This is a love which need not excuse itself if it speaks the truth, but which lives by unhypocritical truth.' What is important to me is 'a love which does not exclude holy anger – as already with Moses and the prophets, but also with Jesus and Paul. This holy anger (just, not unjust, anger, grounded in personal sensibilities) needs to be rehabilitated in the church today since so many tame, lame and often opportunistic hacks could not praise gentleness enough, quite forgetting the anger with which Jesus raged, not at the poor sinners of this world but at the hypocrisy, externalized religiosity and legalistic morality, the laziness and hard-heartedness, of the religious establishment of the time. If all that is prophetical is not to depart from professors of theology, they too will have a twofold task in the church, the people of God, in which both negative and positive have be accomplished in love: "to uproot and knock down ... to build and to plant" (Jeremiah 1.10).'

After a 'Prague spring', a 'church in winter'

In autumn 1968 Pfeiffer Verlag of Munich sends me a specimen copy of the Czech edition of my *Letters to Young People*, which had appeared in 1962 (originally written for a young people's journal), under the title *Aby svet uveril* – 'That the world may believe'.[8] It's amazing how this little book has made its way further in the world than almost all my previous books. It already exists in English, American, French, Dutch, Italian, Spanish, Japanese, Danish and Portuguese editions. It's understandable that the publisher wants a further manuscript from me on the 'spiritual situation of the time', 'since even thinking young people often do not know where things are going'; for example, 'the question of ministry and authority, the courage for disobedience, i.e. for the freedom of the children of God, and for developing their own initiatives. Is it permissible for young people, students, including theological students, or chaplains to band together, "to rebel", as is sometimes already happening?' (letter from the publisher, A. Rost, of 2 December 1968). In a completely new political situation it makes sense that one of my books can at last appear in a Czech translation.

As I have already indicated, the 'rebellions' in Czechoslovakia have a different background and a different aim from the student rebellions in the US and in Western Europe that I have described. When a second wave of de-Stalinization is set off in the USSR at the beginning of the 1960s, the Communist Czechoslovakian State President Antonín Novotný sees himself compelled at the 12th Communist Party Congress in December 1962 to steer a more liberal course – the first session of Vatican II had just come to an end. Most victims of the terror trials are rehabilitated and reinstated. The discussion sparked off by intellectuals about the causes of the 'violation of social justice' quickly seizes the whole population and on 5 January 1968 the reforming wing of the Central Committee agrees on Alexander Dubček as the new head of the Czech Communist Party. Now there is also a discussion within the party of its role in state and society, along with concrete reforms and concessions to public opinion. A 'socialism with a human face' is to be realized. But there is alarm in the Moscow headquarters of world Communism. A consistent separation of state and party and acceptance of a legal opposition would endanger the leading role of the Czech Communist Party and also that of the centre of power in Moscow. The Kremlin now warns of the dangers of this 'Prague spring' with open threats.

Like everyone else, I follow these developments at the end of July and beginning of August 1968 tensely in my Swiss homeland. Under immense diplomatic and military pressure from Moscow there are difficult negotiations. The reform politician Dubček has to accept an invitation from General Secretary Leonid Brezhnev, who grew up under Stalin, to 'friendly bilateral talks' in the Moscow headquarters. But Brezhnev doesn't succeed in enforcing an immediate end to the reforms. So in the night of 20/21 August he has the Soviet army – supported by the troops of the Democratic Republic of Germany, Poland, Bulgaria and Hungary – invade Czechoslovakia in order to put a brutal end to the 'Prague spring'. There is a stop to any political, economic and cultural liberalization; a new leadership loyal to Moscow is appointed; the party is purged and critics of the regime are put on trial. But despite the reintroduction of censorship and strict ideological guidelines the political and intellectual spokesmen of the 'Prague spring' succeed in publishing a declaration of human rights, 'Charter 77', supported by more than 1000 artists, scholars and former politicians, 'for respecting civil and human rights'. Speakers are the former foreign minister Jiri Hájek, the writer Václav Havel and the sociologist Jan Patočka.

Some parallels to the development in the Catholic Church and the Vatican suggest themselves, since in that same summer of 1968 Paul VI's encyclical *Humanae vitae* against the pill sparks off discussions and disciplinary measures world-wide. Of course the 'Prague spring' can only to a limited degree be compared with the 'spring of Vatican II', although at the time of the Council people spoke of a 'spring of the Catholic Church'. However, the differences are important: Rome isn't Moscow and the Vatican isn't the Kremlin. How could one compare Curia cardinals with the red czars and their *nomenklatura*? The Roman system established in the eleventh century may be authoritarian but it isn't totalitarian. A papal encyclical may be unconditionally binding on all believers, but it can't be imposed with the same instruments of power as the Moscow ultimatum to the Czech leaders issued at the same time. Above all, the Vatican no longer has armies to discipline a people, as it did in the Middle Ages and at the time of the Counter-Reformation. And thanks to the Enlightenment dissidents can no longer be imprisoned and tortured, nor can heretics be burned (physically).

When asked about the resistance among Catholic people to the encyclical *Humanae vitae*, Cardinal Alfredo Ottaviani, head of the former Holy Office, thinks that one can speak of negative reactions in the Catholic field only 'if one means Catholics of Küng's stamp'. 'Hans Küng has a completely erroneous concept of the nature of the church. He can say what he likes, but he is far closer to the Protestants than to the Catholics' (confidential report of the Catholic News Agency, 29 August 1968). The cardinal who had come up with the election slogan '*Semper idem* – always the same' finally becomes outdated and resigns. That same year his place is taken by the moderately conservative Archbishop of Zagreb, Cardinal Franjo Šeper, whom I have already mentioned. But will things go better in this Inquisition authority which has now been named the Congregation for the Doctrine of the Faith? Many decisions are pending in 1968.

Despite all the differences, the two systems can in fact be compared. And in his book on dialectical materialism which appears the following year the former Rector of the Pontifical Russian College, Gustav A. Wetter, under whose moderation I had led a study circle on Soviet dialectical materialism in Rome in 1951, brings out the unmistakable similarities very sharply. In my lecture on 'Church and Freedom' – my topic in the US in 1963 and then in Germany in my ceremonial lecture on the foundation of the Tübingen Institute for Ecumenical Research on 12 February 1964 – I sum this up as follows: the official teaching is 'preserved, protected and expounded by the infallible magisterium of the party, by the Holy Office of the Central Committee and by the supreme infallible party secretary in person. It is not the task of the individual philosopher to enrich and increase this material but merely to teach people its application to all spheres of life and ensure that it is kept pure by unmasking heresies and deviations. The infallible magisterium of the party condemns heresies publicly. If it has spoken, the deviant heretics have to submit and renounce their heresy. If they neglect their duty, they are "excommunicated", excluded. Thus the party shows itself to be the "pillar and bastion of the truth", a bulwark of orthodoxy which is both defensive and offensive at the same time. Communism is manifestly offensive in defence of itself. As the only true message, which alone brings salvation, by nature it strives to disseminate itself all over the world with every means, and from the propaganda centre to send its missionaries everywhere. What is called for is strict organization, blind obedience, party discipline, all under the great leader, who is celebrated almost cultically with declarations of loyalty, great marches, parades and pilgrimages to his tomb.'[9]

If one compares the efficiency of this Communist system with that of Rome and for example reads the 'memoirs' of the 'Prague spring awakening' by Ota Šik,[10] the former Czech concentration camp victim, then professor of economics and finally from April to September 1968 deputy prime minister responsible for economic reform (later I shall invite him for a Tübingen series of lectures on 'Christian Europe?'), there are more parallels than a Catholic theologian would like. For in the Catholic Church, too, the government often seems to be alienated from the people; bureaucracy and regimentation take the upper hand; the efficiency of the church organization falls short of other organizations; the fundamental needs of those affected cannot be satisfied by the organization; the absence of democratic elections and controls often allows incompetent people who toe the line to rise in the system; official information conceals the truth from people; scholarship is controlled and cannot develop freely; the promises of the leadership often become empty phrases.

The 'Prague spring' – is that just a short period of hope for the Catholic Church too? Soon Karl Rahner's saying about the 'church in winter' will also be going the rounds among church people. But is there no resistance to these efforts at restoration among these church people? There certainly is, but with different degrees of strength and development in different countries.

Wave of protest at the German Katholikentag

In 1968 a young generation of Catholics calls for reform in the name of politicization and democratization and in addition for a critical social conscience, more of a say in public affairs, solidarity with the Third World, collaboration with non-Catholic Christians and non-Christians, and political activity by the church communities; to many the North–South divide seems more important than dialogue between East and West. These are all questions which will be passionately discussed in Germany at the 82nd Katholikentag in Essen between 4 and 8 September 1968 in an atmosphere pregnant with revolution.

I haven't been invited to this Katholikentag. That isn't surprising, since I have never been invited to an official commission or occasion either by Rome or by the German episcopate; my specialist knowledge isn't disputed, but people are afraid of my uncomfortable arguments. So I certainly would never have been able to speak, as Karl Rahner did, at the 'Priests' Conference' on the eve of the Katholikentag to a thousand priests about priestly life, in so doing excluding the universal priesthood of all Christians and dismissing the question of celibacy as peripheral. That too is typical of Rahner. In an ecumenical age, Protestant and Orthodox theologians, according to official Roman doctrine 'heretics' and 'schismatics', are now also being invited to a Katholikentag, but not Catholic theologians who give unambiguous and consistent expression to their criticism of the Roman system.

Besides, in any case I had sufficient possibilities of making critical public comments on the situation and on individual problems even before the Katholikentag in Essen. On 3 September 1968, the day before, my full-page article appears in the *Frankfurter Allgemeine Zeitung*, 'Realization according to the Spirit which Brings Life. Proposals for Church Reform'. In sober language I offer a comprehensive guide to everything that should have been happening in the church today but unfortunately isn't happening so far – under pressure from Rome and the failure of the bishops.

I deal with four areas of reform in detail:

- As a 'consequence of the Council' (A): implementation of the Council decrees at a national level; a renewal of theology generally; consistent implementation of liturgical reform; fundamental reform of church law.
- Then 'a renewed constitution for the church' (B): involvement of church members in local, diocesan, national and universal church bodies; the free election of heads of these bodies by representatives of the churches concerned; an examination of the traditional image of the priest; open budgeting and accountability for the use of church funds; consistent implementation of the structural and personnel reform of the Roman Curia; a more rational division of dioceses and decentralization; a new definition of the structure and tasks of the parish; a revaluation and full participation of women; reform of the religious communities.
- Further, 'ecumenical understanding' (C): unconditional mutual recognition of baptisms; regular exchanges of preachers, catechists and professors of theology; more frequent joint ecumenical services of the word and an investigation of the conditions for joint celebrations of the eucharist; more generous permission for participation in the worship of other churches; the greatest possible common use and rebuilding of churches and clergy houses; a settlement of the question of mixed marriages; promotion of joint Bible work; stronger collaboration and integration of the confessional theological faculties; investigation of the possibility of fundamental theological ecumenical studies; collaboration in public life.
- Finally, 'service in the world' (D): at a national and regional level, examination of the church's commitment in the world, purposeful unpretentious and realistic actions.

I am depressed today when I read this extremely concrete agenda for reform in the spirit of the Council. A good 40 years have passed since then, and little has been achieved. The new start at the Council – introduced by the election of John XXIII in 1958 and the convening of the Council in 1959 – had preceded the student protest movement. But in 1968 the unrest of the student movement is spilling over into the church sphere. The two movements meet at the Katholikentag in September and make the crisis of the Catholic Church glaringly evident. It is quite essentially a crisis of authority. The question of authority is now no longer just treated theoretically but addressed as an acute practical question.

For it is only six weeks since Pope Paul VI published his 'pill encyclical', after the celibacy encyclical a second document in the same spirit of church regression (in contrast to the constructive encyclical *Populorum progressio* on the development of the peoples). But an article in the *L'Osservatore Romano* which immediately before the Katholikentag attempts to make adult German Catholics passive figures who need to be given orders, pours journalistic oil on the already blazing fire of protest.

So the long-time disappointment and increasing bitterness at the Roman blockade of reforms (apart from liturgical reform) are vented in Essen. For the first time there is public protest against the Pope and the bishops at a Katholikentag and its different forums. That ushers in the downfall particularly of papal doctrinal authority within the Catholic Church, something that the American sociologist and theologian Andrew Greeley has also demonstrated statistically for the United States. The church members affected are there in person in Essen, and they rebel: against papal encyclicals and episcopal press policy, against the practice over mixed marriages, against the deprivation of women in religious orders of their rights, against the traditional image of the priest and the law of celibacy. Forum II on marriage and the family with 5000 mostly young participants ends with a statement, opposed by only a few votes, that now the demand for obedience to the decision of the Pope on questions of birth control cannot knowingly and conscientiously be followed.

As I reported in *My Struggle for Freedom*, just before the Katholikentag, on 30 August 1968 the Königstein Declaration of the German Conference of Bishops had been published, and on 3 September an extensive pastoral message. Both clearly acknowledge as the ultimate norm in matters of birth control the responsible conscientious decision of the individual and not the papal demand for obedience. All this is to the great and lasting fury of the Roman Curia, which sees its authority put in question. Over subsequent years it time and again insists – in vain – on a revision of this Königstein Declaration. As late as 1987 Pope John Paul II 'desires' the German bishops to withdraw the Königstein Declaration, again without success.

Nevertheless, the President of the Conference of Bishops, Cardinal Julius Döpfner, who in contrast to Cardinals Bengsch of Berlin and Jäger of Paderborn has fought moderately and stubbornly for the Declaration, has a hard time at the Katholikentag in Essen. Sometimes, he sighs, one might think that a bishop should stop appearing at a Katholikentag. Indeed, externally there is already a tremendous contrast between the young people in casual clothes and the hierarchs in anachronistic dress. But above all it is Döpfner's basic attitude that seems to some people too ambivalent. Beyond doubt he is recognized as a reformer in the Council and in the papal 'pill commission' and is therefore also attacked by

Marian associations as a 'great protector of heretics'. But in other respects he is criticized as an opportunistic and sometimes contradictory tactician who in human terms is sympathetic and open but nevertheless sends a devout declaration of loyalty stating his 'steadfast faithfulness and love for the Holy Father' and brusquely rejects demands from theological students. By comparison with the Curia cardinals Döpfner is progressive, but measured by the demands of the students and many other laity he is a representative of the conservative establishment. I soon have my own ambiguous experiences with him.

Representative of the rational centre

I can hardly be counted as belonging on the extreme left. Walter Jens, the writer and literary scholar, who is my colleague and friend, once asks me why, since I am on the left in the church, I am not also left-wing in politics. My answer is clear: I am not simply on the left, either in the church or in politics. So for example I do not support 'Critical Catholicism',[11] the left-wing group which sometimes acts with confused slogans, banners and pamphlets and among other things calls for a radical democratization of the Catholic student communities. I likewise resist any commandeering of Christianity for political ends, any identification of the Christian message with a party programme (right, left or centre) and the exploitation of the liturgy for controversial political propaganda actions. But on the other hand I resist the church hierarchy where it does not have the gospel behind it.

So both ecclesiastically and politically I regard myself as a representative of the rational centre, albeit with an emphasis on renewal and reform; I am 'centre-left', provided that it isn't misunderstood in party-political terms. I support the social–critical concern of the 'political theology' of Johann Baptist Metz against a privatized Christian faith, but at the same time I argue more strongly than Metz does that the criticism should also be applied to the church, for example in the doctrine of infallibility and the question of celibacy. I can largely identify with Jürgen Moltmann's 'theology of hope', but not with its radicalization into a theology of revolution. In practice that means that I am for a thorough reform of the church, the urgent need for understanding between the Christian churches, and also the reform of the university and state institutions which is now being widely discussed, but not a violent or even non-violent revolutionary overthrow. I have to take into account criticism from the left and attempts to isolate me from the right.

Later there is a further example of my exclusion by the German Conference of Bishops, which is increasingly moving to the right. In 1968 a highly professional campaign is launched for a popular interpretation of the Council in publicity inside and outside the church, by Action 365 (for all the days of the year). This renewal movement goes back to the conservative Jesuit and mass preacher Fr Johannes Leppich, but has increasingly moved towards progressive ecumenical positions. It takes up my promptings. At the end of the Council I had written a documentary final report in the journal *Epoca* under the title 'St Peter's 16 New Pillars'; in it the 16 Council decrees are presented briefly as documents of a transition in church history from the past to the future. Paul VI had received my survey benevolently, but criticized the list of unfulfilled demands as over-hasty (*My Struggle for Freedom*, IX: A surprise at Easter).

Action 365 now wants to disseminate my short versions of each of the Council documents month by month on tens of thousands of posters in churches and other forms of publicity, with newspaper advertisements and editorial contributions all over the Federal Republic of Germany. Some draft posters have already been made, for example one with the slogan 'Religious freedom must be promoted'.

On the one hand there is the 'formerly':

'Freedom of religion and tolerance were branded pernicious products of the modern spirit of the time. This is a totally erroneous view and wherever practically possible it has to be suppressed. Whereas freedom was demanded for the Catholic Church, in Catholic countries in particular other religious communities were refused the same freedom.'

On the other hand there is 'in future':

'1. Every human being has the right to freedom of religion: the dignity of the human person entails that in matters of religion human beings may act according to their consciences, privately and publicly, free from all compulsion, as individuals and in community.

2. Every religious community has the right to practise religion unhindered according to its own rules: it is to be free in respect of its worship; the selection, training and naming of its pastors; dealings with the church authorities and other communities all over the world; the erection of buildings for worship and the possession of material goods; public testimony to its faith in word and writing (unless is by dishonest means); and a share in shaping social life.

3. Freedom of religion must be protected and promoted by society, church and state: where a particular legal status is granted to a specific religious community on the basis of its historical development, at the same time the right of freedom of religion must be recognized for all citizens and faith communities. The fact that the free exercise of religion is also limited by the rights of others and the common good may not lead to the state acting arbitrarily or in a partisan way against a particular religious community. In principle, in human society there should be as much freedom as possible, as much restriction as necessary. If the church today, unlike yesterday, supports the freedom of religion, it follows the gospel of Christ.'

Some of these posters carry photographs of the two Council Popes or of German bishops who took part in the Council. Action 365 was assured that it could count on the full support of the German Conference of Bishops for this campaign, which had been planned down to the last detail and for which around DM 5,000,000 had been budgeted. But what happens? Some weeks later I hear that all these preparations are in vain: the episcopate has rejected the campaign!

Only around 25 years later am I given clear information by one of the leaders of Action 365 about what happened behind the scenes: 'Cardinal Döpfner thought the enterprise, as I presented it to him, a good thing. Following our conversation in Munich, Suffragan Bishop Tewes came to our house in Frankfurt to discuss details. Afterwards we were told that we should choose another author. We stuck to the name Küng, since we had discussed all the details in your house. Thereupon the whole project was scrapped' (21 June 1994). So a highly promising enterprise for disseminating the ideas of the Council was stopped by the bishops themselves – because of me. That too was typical of Döpfner.

Something similar happens in Germany with the much-discussed proposal for a pastoral council on the Dutch model. Only a year after the critical Essen Katholikentag the German Conference of Bishops finally decides to hold a joint synod of the German dioceses. It convenes in Würzburg – more than half a decade after the Council – on 2 January 1971, in order to 'implement the Second Vatican Council'. Many representatives of the rational centre are here. On 3 June 1971 Professor Karl Lehmann from Mainz writes to me that I am wanted as an adviser for Commission I of the Synod; he himself vigorously supports my candidature to the bishops. On 11 June the same proposal is made to the Central Committee of Bishops under Cardinal Döpfner and is rejected in a deadlock of 8 votes to 8. The matter is discussed once again in Commission I for an hour, but finally the negative decision is maintained.

Precisely the opposite was the case with Joseph Ratzinger. He had been invited to the synod, but because he was now already regarded as a man of the right wing he wasn't elected to a commission. That was painful for him. So the synod was finished as far as he was concerned; in any case its whole orientation didn't suit him. No wonder that in his *Milestones* he doesn't say a word about this great event in German Catholicism of the years 1971-75.

I ask myself why there is such great fear of a single reform theologian and come to the conclusion that, personal issues apart, this has something to do with the truth of the positions represented. People are afraid that if certain truths are expressed they will find broad assent and that the arguments could prove convincing. So in many cases attempts are being made to prohibit discussion and to make defenders of a truth as 'harmless' as possible. The same thing happens with another great publicity enterprise in which even the German bishops have invested much hope and capital, but which is blocked after a few years.

The death and resurrection of a journal: Publik

In November 1968, after long preparation, the Catholic weekly *Publik*, orientated on reform, appears for the first time, initially given massive support by the German episcopate, which is still under the influence of the Council. It is a sign of hope that criticism within the church is allowed in Germany and that conciliar renewal is going on there. As a subscriber to the left-wing liberal weekly *Die Zeit*, however, I had been sceptical from the beginning whether it would prove possible to produce a Catholic companion to *Die Zeit*, playing a major role in business and culture. The editorial forces didn't seem to me to be sufficiently strong, and above all there wasn't such a widely interested Catholic readership. Something more modest seemed to promise more success.

But of course I subscribe to *Publik*. In it on 15 August 1969 – in connection with an interview with Cardinal Suenens – I publish an article 'Petrine Service in the Church. A Portrait of the Pope after the Interview with Suenens'. It appears simultaneously in *Le Monde* ('Portrait d'un pape') and other papers and attracts marked international attention. On 2 October 1970, in connection with the *Concilium* World Congress, I follow it up with an article on 'What is the Christian Message?' Later I will also publish my theses on the revaluation of women in church and society in *Publik*.

But this reform Catholic journal is soon too critical, too uncomfortable for the bishops. Subsequently the conflict of aims of a big organization in the market of public opinion is analysed like this: it aims on the one hand to provide what in principle is a free flow of information and on the other to ensure its own domination. I can justifiably doubt whether both aims could be realized at the same time in a faith community such as the church. And when I want to give an immediate and lengthy reply to a challenging article by Karl Lehmann on infallibility (11 September 1970), I encounter incomprehensible difficulties, of the kind that I have otherwise become used to only in church journals – an ill omen.

With the election of Cardinal Joseph Höffner to succeed Cardinal Döpfner as President of the Council of Bishops, the situation with the bishops changes. A majority of them support Höffner's excuse that there isn't enough money available. In other words, funding for *Publik* is cut off. On 15 October 1971 the conference of bishops passes the death sentence on its own child. Development costs (personnel, long-term contracts) amount to DM 9,000,000. But at the same time the same bishops evidently have enough money to buy the right-wing liberal *Rheinischer Merkur,* they spend millions of Deutschemarks over coming years without being subjected to excessively sharp criticism. Of course this paper, which later buys out a Protestant journal, represents only a small segment of the Catholic public and the German public generally.

The extent of public protest at the liquidation of *Publik* surprises the bishops. The protest movement leads to a continuation of the weekly under the name *Publik-Forum*, supported by a *Publik* readers' initiative, with Harald Pawlowski as sole editor, later as chief editor and finally as publisher; he remains the pillar of this successful journalistic enterprise. Here is a 'way from below'; without support from a church, a business, a party or a bank it finances itself by subscriptions, sales through book services and a few advertisements, and thus remains independent. I gladly become a member of the advisory committee, together with the theologians Karl Rahner (as chairman), Heinrich Fries, Oswald von Nell-Breuning, and also Walter Kasper and Karl Lehmann, who are later to become bishops. The first edition of *Publik-Forum*, of 12 pages, appears on 28 January 1972, with a printing of 25,000 copies. In 2007 sales are around 40,000 copies. All in all *Publik-Forum* has about 100,000 readers and is a journal (now of around 60 pages) which must be taken seriously even by bishops, if they want to know what is happening among church people.

In time *Publik-Forum*, now fortnightly and economically independent, adopts an increasingly ecumenical course and today describes itself as a 'journal of critical Christians'; a third of its readers are Protestants. The journal analytically investigates all the prevailing positions in society regardless of the powers behind them. It also critically investigates its own positions, so that it is shaped by lively controversy.

But elsewhere, too, the press landscape of the Federal Republic is beginning to change. The originally liberal *Frankfurter Allgemeine Zeitung*, in which I published my major articles in the 1960s and early 1970s, is moving increasingly to the right in both politics and church affairs. Certainly it still addresses 'shrewd minds', but it is clearly dominated by conservative German Catholicism: later its feature articles betray the influence of Opus Dei. The more spiritually orientated *Christ in der Gegenwart*, formerly *Der christliche Sonntag*, has a very positive effect in the Catholic sphere. *Herder-Korrespondenz*, which is also published by Herder Verlag, informative and intellectual, sometimes criticizes the official church line, but on the whole is well-disposed to the hierarchy, mentions my name less and less and favours conformist theologians.

I also keenly follow developments abroad, where for me *Informations Catholiques Internationales* for France and *The Tablet* for the British Commonwealth are important. For the United States – alongside the daily *International Herald Tribune* – the weekly *National Catholic Reporter* of Kansas City is informative and critical. The debate about a contemporary form of the priesthood is now taken up in press organs orientated on reform.

Priests want a share in the decision

In its positive intentions Vatican II had been totally orientated on the bishops and left quite undetermined the new role and function of priests, who like women were not represented as such at the Council. The collegiality of the Pope with the bishops was emphasized, but that of the bishops with the priests was left in the shade. Of course the year 1968 also has an electrifying effect on the numerous groups of priests which have formed after the Council. In 1969, with the prospect of a symposium of European bishops in Chur and an 'extraordinary' synod of bishops in Rome, some priests think a striking public demonstration appropriate and necessary.

The Second Symposium of European Bishops assembles in Chur in Switzerland between 7 and 10 July 1969 to discuss 'The Priest in Today's World and Church' – without any priests! Understandably, militant representatives of priestly groups aren't invited either. Cardinal Suenens, who grasps the problem better than most other bishops, must have the credit for having attempted to build a bridge here. On Sunday 6 July 1969 he flies to Zurich and visits me in my lake house. We talk intensively that evening. The cardinal asks where he can celebrate the eucharist the next day. My answer is: either up in the hospital, which would make his visit public, or here in my house. He asks me whether I have everything necessary for the eucharist. I reply: everything that Jesus had, bread and wine. That convinces him, and next morning we celebrate the eucharist according to the customary rite at the table in our little house; he is very happy. At the same time he asks me to give him a letter which he can read out in the assembly. Of course I'm glad to accede to his wish. After the necessary modest introduction and compliments I present three observations to the bishops.

1. The crisis among our clergy is extremely serious. Many have the impression that bold and loyal dialogue has become difficult under the present conditions of leadership in our church.
2. It is no longer possible to stop this process of reflection and questioning with the means used formerly. We already have and will have a rapidly growing number of priests who are abandoning their ministry in the church.
3. It seems to me that the true dilemma for a large part of the clergy is that we are continuing the way of renewal – with the bishops or without them and consequently against them. The latter would be bad.

Hence my request to the bishops:

Help our church and especially our priests. Spare our church an even larger number of resignations, breakdowns, arbitrary and unenlightened movements. Remember those decisive years at the beginning of the Reformation when, had the bishops perceived their responsibility in time, they could perhaps still have spared us what we now so regret ... As for our priests, I am thinking particularly of the problem of celibacy, their professional status and political and social commitment.[12]

More than 100 bishops had come from 19 countries, but twice as many press, radio and television journalists and finally around 100 representatives of European priestly groups from 8 countries. At the beginning of the symposium Cardinal Döpfner speaks on the changing image of the priest in a secularized society, and at the end Cardinal Suenens speaks on the relationship of priests and bishops to the people of God, also reading out my letter. But all attempts to bring bishops and priestly groups together for a joint discussion fail. Like the Primate of Spain, Cardinal Enrique Tarancón of Toledo, the majority of bishops find the sometimes aggressive behaviour of the priestly groups unacceptable. Conversely, the priestly groups accuse the bishops of dogmatism, legalism and formulism. On Suenens' suggestion there is an informal but unsatisfactory meeting between six bishops and a larger group of priests in the presence of the press.

Suenens had previously visited Cardinal Döpfner in Munich, but noted at a meal with him how Döpfner was surrounded by clergy whose thinking was largely pre-conciliar. In the short term, no bold initiative for the continuation of post-conciliar reform in Rome could be expected from him, unless the Pope himself took it. But here time and again the central question arises: who will reform the papacy?

How the Pope could be

For me, the interview with Cardinal Suenens shortly before the symposium of bishops has so many valuable elements that I systematize them and draw from them the picture of a Pope as he could be. If one attempts to combine the various traits from the interview, the picture is quite clear.

Such a Pope would have a truly evangelical and not a juridical, formalistic and static bureaucratic view of the church. He would see the mystery of the church in the light of the gospel, in the light of the New Testament, not as a centralized administrative unit in which the bishops are merely the delegates and executive organs of the Pope, but as a church that realizes itself authentically in the local churches (the individual communities, towns, dioceses, countries), which everywhere form a community as the one church of God and thus are bound up with the Church of Rome.

This Pope would see no dangerous prelude to a possible schism in a decentralization of leadership. He would not prevent but encourage legitimate difference: in spirituality, liturgy, theology, church law and pastoral care. His aim would not be the permanent concentration of power at the centre but unpretentious service of the rich diversity of the local churches in the one church. His concern would not be the suppression of the plurality of different theologies with inquisitorial compulsion from former centuries but the promotion of their freedom and their service to the church. He would not jealously insist on powers and prerogatives and exercise the authority typical of the *ancien régime* but exercise an authority of service in the spirit of the New Testament and the needs of the present time: brotherly collaboration in partnership, dialogue, consultation and collaboration above all with the bishops and theologians of the whole church, the inclusion of those concerned in decision-making processes and an invitation to co-responsibility.

Thus this Pope would understand his function as a function of the church: a

Pope not over or outside the church but in the church, with the church, for the church. He would ensure the collaboration of the episcopate, the most capable theologians and lay people, for all important documents and actions and never subsequently disown them; he would cut back the administrative apparatus of the Curia and oppose its striving for hegemony. He would organize collaboration in accordance with the principle of subsidiarity, and change and improve the system of *ad limina* visits, the quinquennial reports of bishops, and much else.

That, sketched out briefly, is the picture of a Pope as he could be according to Cardinal Suenens (and certainly not just according to him). And no one will dispute that this view of the papacy is Catholic through and through. But how does it relate to the two Vatican Councils? That's an interesting question. This picture certainly doesn't contradict Vatican II (1962-65), for that council attached prime importance to the collegiality of the Pope, and an essential reason why Suenens went public in this way was beyond doubt that people in the Curia wanted to return to the pre-conciliar style. But how does it relate to Vatican I (1870), whose absolutist understanding of primacy had been forced on Vatican II by Paul VI with his *nota praevia* on the Constitution on the Church? If Vatican I should be found to be contradicted by Vatican II, in individual points it should be supplemented and corrected in the light of the gospel. At any rate, the legalistic categories of Vatican I are insufficient to define how a Petrine service could be understood in the light of scripture.

Whatever is to be thought of the exegetical and historical foundation of the succession of Roman bishops, I have often referred to the weak points of the traditional proof in the first centuries. But I remain convinced that a service to the whole church on the model of Peter is meaningful. However, that would have to be a primacy of service in the full biblical sense, just as the Popes after Gregory the Great call themselves *Servus servorum Dei*, indeed to the present day 'servant of the servants of God'. And what is this primacy of service to mean if the word 'service' isn't just to remain a pious phrase? At all events it must be more than a 'primacy of honour': a passive representative figure can help no one. However, it should be more than a 'primacy of jurisdiction': understood as pure authority and power, that would be a fundamental misunderstanding, for the concept says nothing about the character of service. Petrine service can only be a pastoral primacy: pastoral service of the whole church. As such its substance is backed by the New Testament and could be of great use for the whole of Christianity. John XXIII at least made pragmatically clear in outline, with firm emphases, that such a Pope would be possible.[13] But will he ever become a reality?

Counter-offensive by the Curia

Karl Rahner describes the interview with Cardinal Suenens as the programme for the next synod of bishops or even for several synods of bishops. But what does the

Roman Curia plan? Precisely the opposite. This synod is to serve to reinforce the Roman system which has been weakened by the encyclical *Humanae vitae* and other actions and to give the impression of a monolithic unity of the world episcopate. Some draw analogies with the Communist meeting taking place in Moscow at the same time which, after the repression of the 'Prague spring' on 21 August 1968 by the troops of the Warsaw Pact, is ordered by the headquarters in Moscow to strengthen the unity of the Communist bloc.

Here again reports keep circulating in the press that proceedings of the Roman Congregation for the Doctrine of the Faith are imminent against leading theologians, specifically against Chenu, Schillebeeckx and Küng. Informed circles believe that they can see in these proceedings confirmation that the 'harsh course' will again be used to achieve complete control over theology.

Meanwhile, it is interesting how the episcopate is manipulated and brought into line: in a clever way, without good reason, only an 'extraordinary' synod of bishops is convened. That means that only the presidents of the conferences of bishops are invited. What is the result? The few progressive presidents of the Central European conferences of bishops are exposed not only to the widely over-represented curial power apparatus but also to an oppressive majority of former conservative presidents. The secret document prepared by the Curia for discussion bears the ambiguous title 'Scheme worked out in accordance with the observations of the conferences of bishops'. It is entirely focused on 'unity' and culminates in the demand 'that the conferences of bishops shall duly enquire about the opinion of the Apostolic See before publishing a declaration on an important matter' ('*ut episcoporum conferentiae ante declarationem de re gravi Apostolicae Sedis mentem opportune tempore explorent*'). If this principle is established, in future Pope and Curia will have nothing to fear from critical commentaries such as that of the Central European conferences of bishops on the encyclical on birth control. Will the bishops allow themselves to be muzzled in this way?

The Zurich Jesuit Jakob David, a social expert on the churches, writes to me on 9 October 1968 about the causes of the lack of truthfulness in the church which I have enumerated in my book *Truthfulness*. Shortly beforehand he had given a bold interview to *Der Spiegel*: 'One would have to add that any court, any dictator and any authority which gets too strict necessarily encourages untruthfulness. It is terrible to see how much an obsequious attitude is once again dominant in Rome. Now you should write a second book about bravery and courage in the church, of the kind that you demonstrate so admirably.' And a few weeks later he writes about our theologians' declaration: 'This serves the cause of God and the church far more than devout and cowardly bowing. If only the bishops could understand this.'

Happily, at least one bishop has understood this, the Bishop of Basle, Dr Anton Hänggi, my own bishop. When I am 'hurtfully attacked' by the traditionalist association Una Voce through whole-page insertions in several Swiss newspapers, on 8 November 1968 the bishop issues a lengthy press release, the core sentence of which runs: 'The bishop and the chancery see themselves obliged to protect the personal honour of Professor Küng, who is one of the clergy of the diocese of Basle, and to defend themselves against these unjustified attacks.' The reaction to the events of 1968 in other regions of the Catholic Church proves very different.

Repression in the US and England

Poll findings in the United States also show that even the Catholic population for the most part rejects the encyclical *Humanae vitae*, and the younger they are, the more they are against it. In practice people don't follow the papal doctrine but the conviction of their own consciences. Time and again there is open rebellion. But the majority of bishops, who are of Irish descent and traditionally obedient to Rome, show little understanding and tolerance to protesting priests. How people now miss the Council Cardinals Meyer of Chicago and Ritter of St Louis, who were open to the world, and the long-serving President of the American Council of Bishops, Cardinal Dearden of Detroit! They have all been replaced by bishops subservient to Rome. Before the final session of the Council, on 15 May 1965, the director of the information bureau of the National Catholic Welfare Conference, Vincent Yzermans, writes to me from Washington: 'American bishops are dragging their feet on the Council. Doing nothing and seemingly most of them do not seem to care too much about it. The impression is that they would just as soon have it all over with so they can retire to the safe, secure world of the chancery.'

In England 55 priests publicly reject the encyclical *Humanae vitae*; one is immediately suspended (on a salary of £10 a week) and the others are threatened with dismissal. No one may say anything against the encyclical on the radio and in the press, but is to tell the bishop openly his attitude to it. Nevertheless, even in the Westminster diocese of Cardinal John Heenan, who inclines towards Rome, there are priests who criticize the encyclical publicly. The case of Charles Davis is still having an effect.

In the US the Cardinal of Washington, DC, Patrick O'Boyle, treats priests who take a stand against *Humanae vitae* brutally: six are immediately suspended, and strict disciplinary measures are imposed on the others. Those who are disciplined call for the resignation of the cardinal, but even the request for arbitration by the Association of Councils of Priests in the US is rejected by a suffragan bishop of Washington and ignored by the conference of bishops. Lay people and priests together engage in spectacular acts of solidarity on behalf of those disciplined: on the eve of the meeting of the conference of bishops in Washington 3500 lay people meet to protest and show their solidarity. The main speaker is the Democrat senator Eugene McCarthy, one of the most prominent Catholics in the US. During the conference itself 130 priests hold a sit-in in the conference hotel to support those who have been censured.

The bishops who control the supervisory authority also practise the same authoritarian policy of repression on the Catholic University of America in Washington, where people had hoped for the academic freedom of teaching and research customary in the United States. America's most important Catholic moral theologian, Charles Curran, a pupil of the German moral theologian the Redemptorist Bernhard Häring who is initially valued in Rome, becomes a prominent victim.

In 1967 he is refused tenure by the episcopal board of trustees of the Catholic University because of his teaching on sex, but a strike by the professors and students compels it to be given. A year later Curran is nevertheless suspended by the university authorities when he heads the opposition to Paul VI's pill encyclical. Now far fewer people support him than did the previous year. At the peak of the clashes I make a special journey from Chicago to Washington, DC to show solidarity with my friend and discuss the situation. The court called for by Curran finally decides against him. He has to leave the Catholic University – shame on it but not on him. In 1981 he occupies a chair for Christian ethics at the Southern Methodist University. His memoirs appear in 2006 under the title *Loyal Dissent. Memoir of a Catholic Theologian*. They contain his sorry yet brave history with all the background.

'How have we Catholics moved from the safe haven of 1962 into the stormy waters of 1968?', the journalist George N. Schuster asks himself in an article in the New York *Catholic News* in October 1968. He comes to the following conclusion: 'It seems as if the watershed came with the visit of Professor Hans Küng to the US. He spoke at the University of Notre Dame on 25 March 1963 ... Suddenly there was an audience of 4000, many of whom had travelled long distances to hear him ... In Notre Dame on this day it seemed as in other places where Hans Küng spoke, that what he said represented a consensus which had been achieved without difficulty.'[14]

To put it plainly: the Catholic people were ready for renewal, but the episcopate orientated on Rome had put a stop to it. The effects of this conservative system only become evident with time, above all in the paedophile scandals, the disguising of them by the American bishops and the Roman Congregation for the Doctrine of the Faith, and the payment of millions to the abused, which bankrupts several dioceses.

Resistance in the Netherlands: the Dutch Catechism

The situation in the Catholic Church in the Netherlands is quite different from that in the Anglo-Saxon countries. I have already reported how the Dutch church, which in the 1950s was still very conservative, has become the spearhead of Catholic renewal since the convening of the Second Vatican Council (cf. *My Struggle for Freedom*, IV: Amsterdam: Catholic tradition and renewal). The torch is carried by the Amsterdam student pastor Jan van Kilsdonk, who in a speech immediately before the Council vigorously criticizes the policy of the Roman Curia and speaks of the 'spiritual terrorism' of the Holy Office. Rome wants to dismiss the pastor, but his bishop resists: while he issues a *monitum* (formal admonition), he does not dismiss him. Repression in this country which had withstood the Nazi terror and has a flourishing Catholic Church caught up in the awakening around the Council is unthinkable during these years. However, a great deal of nonsense is talked, particularly in Germany, about the Catholic Church of the Netherlands. Conservatives depict Dutch Catholics as the naughty children of the world church, forgetting that nice children seldom produce anything special.

As I can spend two weeks in 1967 incognito in a small Dutch town, observing something of parish life, I feel obliged to speak out positively on developments in the Netherlands after the Council in the most important Dutch journal for Catholics, the *Volkskrant*, of 2 November 1967 – and then also in German-language journals under the title 'Holland on a Good Course': lively Sunday worship with understandable eucharistic prayers formulated in Dutch, solid preaching, participation of almost all the congregation in the eucharist, but the disappearance of confession, since 'artificial' birth control and a neglect of fasting are no longer regarded as 'mortal sins'. Instead, there is an implementation of conciliar renewal at parish level and organizational efficiency in religious work in the media, in research, in the sociology of religion, in church building and in social work.

Above all I praise the Dutch Catechism, which I have already mentioned. It appeared in October 1966 and since then has sold over 400,000 copies, more than almost any book has ever sold in the Netherlands. It's a tremendous sign of renewal when in a country such a large number of people are again interested in the Christian message and contemporary theology. The Roman difficulties with this catechism bear witness to the Neo-scholastic immobility which still prevails there. The prevention – already tolerated all too long in individual countries – of translations of this catechism, which has been approved by the whole Dutch episcopate, is deeply regrettable.

So resistance to the Roman restoration movement also has a solid basis in the Netherlands. The Dutch conference of bishops is small and united. Its spiritually most lively and influential head, Bishop Willem M. Bekkers of s'Hertogenbosch, took part in the founding session of our international journal for theology *Concilium* in Rome at the invitation of its instigator, the publisher Paul Brand of Hilversum, and in the Netherlands before everyone else argued on the television for moral permission to use contraception. Unfortunately he was already seriously ill with cancer at the Council and died in May 1966. But in Cardinal Bernard Alfrink, former professor of Old Testament and since 1955 Archbishop of Utrecht, before, at and after the Council the Dutch church has a leader whose superiority is recognized far beyond its frontiers and who if need be can be bold.

On 24 September 1968 the Schillebeeckx case makes headlines. *Le Monde* spreads the rumour that proceedings will be initiated by the Congregation for the Doctrine of the Faith against the Flemish Dominican Edward Schillebeeckx, professor at the Catholic University of Nijmegen since 1958, who has been mentioned here time and again in connection with the Council and the journal *Concilium*; evidently he is the victim of informers. The Nijmegen theological students protest in letters to Cardinal Alfrink and Cardinal Šeper, the Prefect of the Congregation for the Doctrine of the Faith, against secret proceedings on the basis of anonymous accusations. These concern a whole series of theses which are objected to, on original sin and the eucharist (transubstantiation), church ministry, celibacy and the church's magisterium, culled from a variety of publications.

But the proceedings are still at a preliminary stage, in the 'consulta' of the advisers to the Doctrinal Congregation. Theologians from universities in Rome who toe the line and are hardly known internationally sit in judgement on a man who, with an international reputation, is an expert on both classical Thomism and most recent Catholic and Protestant theology. At any rate an innovation is now introduced which the Vatican regards as a great step forward; on 8 October the Jesuit Karl Rahner, though he often doesn't follow the Roman line, is invited to the 'consulta' to defend the Dominican's theses. Schillebeeckx himself isn't informed, but learns this from the press: there are no proceedings against him – at least for the moment. Schillebeeckx continues to protest against the secret proceedings. He would have preferred a dialogue, an open debate. Of course Schillebeeckx cannot by any means be certain that the proceedings in the Doctrinal Congregation won't be started again at any time.

In Rome the Inquisition is concentrating above all on the Dutch Catechism, much of which is suspected of heresy. When negotiations in April 1967 produce no result, in the autumn a commission of cardinals and later a commission of theologians is appointed. In fact this catechism pursues quite a different method from that of the Counter-Reformation Tridentine catechism or the Roman Catechism at the beginning of the twentieth century. Instead of depicting the dogmatic truths of revelation from above downwards, it seeks answers which start from the questions of men and women today and which are based above all on Holy Scripture.

One of the key authors of the catechism is the Dutch Jesuit Piet Schoonenberg. Attempts are already made to initiate proceedings against him because of his book on original sin (*Man and Sin: A Theological View*). And in the Dutch Catechism it is above all the view of original sin that is criticized, like that of the virgin birth, the eucharist (real presence) and the nature of angels. These are specialist dogmatic questions, merely meant to conceal the real issue: more recent Dutch theology doesn't suit Rome, and there is annoyance that the Dutch Catechism is a sensational success not only in the Netherlands but also and especially in Germany. In today's situation it can no longer just be banned, as it would have been formerly. But if that is the case, Rome's will is that at least important corrections should be made. There are now endless negotiations over these between Rome and the Dutch. Finally the Dutch Catechism is translated into around 34 languages. But soon a greater conflict threatens the Dutch church.

Decisive fight over priestly celibacy: the Pastoral Council

The Netherlands is the first country to succeed in creating a church–political instrument to realize the intentions of Vatican II: the Pastoral Council. The bishops want to perform their function of leadership collegially in discussion, conversation and dialogue with the priests, religious orders and representatives of the laity. Between 1968 and 1970 six plenary assemblies are held in complete openness with major participation from the Dutch public and the world press. The basis for the discussions is a series of drafts formulated not only by theologians and priests but also by psychologists, sociologists and other experts; these are translated into practical resolutions. In the German church, subservient to the authorities, the question would be 'Is it allowed?', in the Netherlands it is, 'When do we begin?'

The bishops can hardly reject decisions made by the overwhelming majority of the Pastoral Council, but these cause indignation in Rome. In the press, in channels within the church and even in diplomatic channels an international battle for public opinion begins which doesn't shrink from slanders. Above all German and French bishops join in. This indignation turns to panic when on 7 January 1970 the plenary assembly – in the presence of 150 representatives of the mass media – calls on Rome, for the well-being of the church, also to admit married men to the priesthood. This is even reported on the front pages of world newspapers such as the *New York Times* and *Le Monde*. The Dutch bishops are in a strong position, since in a poll in the middle of 1969, 88 per cent of Catholics have expressed their trust in them. This unanimity over quite radical demands is understandable. For in the Netherlands in particular the question of the next generation is assuming dramatic forms. The Dutch bishops want to present the demand to admit married men to the priesthood both to the conferences of bishops of other countries and also to Rome itself. This is also called for in a unanimous resolution by 148 Dutch clergy.

The Primate of Belgium, Cardinal Léon Suenens, joins the Dutch. He circulates from his interview the remark which opens Chapter I of this book: 'It is not the authority of the Pope that is being put in question but the "system" which holds him captive.' But he is largely alone in his support of the Dutch. On the basis of alarming news from Rome (that people there are even thinking of excommunicating Cardinal Alfrink and the Dutch bishops), after a lengthy telephone call with Edward Schillebeeckx and in agreement with my Tübingen colleagues Norbert Greinacher and Johannes Neumann, on 3 February 1970 I formulate a declaration. Several theologians (not Rahner, who, still shy of a conflict over the question of celibacy, prefers a personal letter to Döpfner) declare their readiness to subscribe to the following public declaration on celibacy:

> The question of the law of celibacy for the Latin Church has become an extremely serious problem not only in the Netherlands but also in our countries and threatens to lead to a split in the Catholic Church. We cannot and may not look on this development without taking action. Even those who don't reject a law of celibacy outright regard the unity of the church as a greater good than the preservation of a disciplinary law which has neither applied for all time nor applies everywhere today. There are no viable reasons for refusing a conversation to clarify matters. We call on our bishops not to desert in their pastoral concerns the Dutch bishops and bishops and churchmen all over the world who are in similar difficulties. Given the present heightening of the issue, the situation outside the Netherlands is also very much more threatening than might appear at first sight. We therefore call on our bishops, in accordance with the shared responsibility of the bishops for the whole church which was endorsed again at Vatican II, as individuals and through their conferences to intercede publicly for the substantive conversation about this question in Rome which is long overdue and has often been called for.

This letter is finally signed by 84 professors of theology and presented to the conferences of bishops meeting soon afterwards in the Federal Republic, Austria and Switzerland. On 13 February 1970 it is released to the media.

On 3 February 1970 Pope Paul VI had instructed the Dutch bishops to revise their attitude on this question. Unfortunately, by 7 February he receives support – and this makes one wonder! – from the President of the German Conference of Bishops, Cardinal Julius Döpfner, who contrary to all the biblical evidence declares that mandatory priestly celibacy is a way of life founded on the Bible. Instead of forming the avant-garde in the post-conciliar implementation of the Council together with the Dutch and Belgians, the German and French bishops leave the Netherlands in the lurch in the first decisive controversy over the course of the Catholic Church after the Council, over the law of celibacy and the next generation of priests, episcopal collegiality and Roman centralism. Thus they are mainly to blame for the restoration of the authoritarian pre-conciliar Roman system by the Curia without any great resistance from the episcopate. Most prominent among those who support this restoration is Joseph Höffner, the former Bishop of Münster, who in 1969 was made Archbishop of Cologne and soon afterwards nominated a cardinal; he is to replace Döpfner earlier than expected.

Cardinal Bernard Alfrink, the Primate of the Netherlands, is summoned to Rome. For a long time I consider whether on the basis of my own experience I shouldn't telephone him and advise him to stay in the Netherlands and give a major television address to the nation there, saying that while there is no doubt of his personal loyalty and the loyalty of the Dutch church to the Pope, at the same time he is calling for an examination of the celibacy law. But I'm afraid that though I know Alfrink as well as I know Suenens, this might be regarded as presumptuous on my part. Cardinal Alfrink goes to Rome and is given no more than the assurance that the question of priesthood will be discussed at the Synod of Bishops in 1971 – as we know, an empty promise.

How Rome tames a church

On 30 November 1969 a chaplain from The Hague, Dr Adrianus J. Simonis, spokesman of the small conservative minority at the Pastoral Council, had been nominated Bishop of Rotterdam, contrary to all the proposals by the cathedral chapter and in the face of vigorous resistance in the diocese. Worse still was the appointment as Bishop of Roermond of the reactionary and incompetent Joannes Baptist Gijsen which followed soon afterwards, again in the face of vigorous resistance from the clergy and people. Along with his ultra-conservative priestly seminary, which is later involved in a sex scandal, Gijsen has to be dismissed by Rome as a total failure. The great Roman 'purge' in the Netherlands has begun, and reaches a climax in 1980. In that year the Dutch bishops are summoned to a 'special synod' in Rome – a quite extraordinary act of centralism of the kind customary in the Moscow of that time. There they are taught '*mores*', namely that in the Dutch church, too, things are to go on in the Roman way. And that means above all that the bishops, under Roman supervision, are again to act as sole rulers, without any influential experts from the priesthood and laity; the Roman guidelines are to be enough. A national Pastoral Council with permanent structures in the Netherlands has already been forbidden by Rome.

The Vatican orders an examination and thorough reordering of the system of theological education. This order is used for decades as a means of putting pressure on the theological faculties and in 2005 as a pretext for abolishing the existing faculties (Nijmegen, Tilburg and Utrecht). Only Nijmegen dares ongoing resistance. At the same time the Vatican creates facts through personnel policy. Its most effective instrument of power, also against the Dutch church, is of course the nomination of bishops in accordance with church–political Roman (instead of pastoral) standpoints. Further nominations of reactionary bishops follow after the special synod, in 1983 in Haarlem, in 1985 in Den Bosch, in 1993 in Roermond and in 1999 in Groningen.

This is the old Roman strategy of divide and rule: first international isolation of the Dutch bishops, then a fifth column collaborating with the Vatican through new nominations in the conference of bishops, then its polarization and splitting, and finally the takeover of all power. What is now initiated in the Netherlands is to be repeated throughout the Catholic Church.

Thus the resistance of this brave church is undermined from within. Many

Dutch Catholics put the blame for the catastrophic development on themselves; they fall back on the old patterns in which they had been brought up. Most intellectuals and creative minds leave the church or retreat into themselves. Over the years most of the grass-roots groups which had so enriched church life will go into decline. This mood is also transferred to the old guard of bishops, who resign, or become sick or infirm. A German friend of the Dutch reformers, the journalist Erwin Kleine, wrote to me about the Dutch bishops on 20 October 1971: 'Sometimes it seems to me as if Rome has succeeded in drawing the teeth even of these men. One can only hope with all one's heart – but without too much encouragement from the facts – that the role of the Dutch church is not yet played out in the development. And we must wait to see what consequences will follow for the progressive grass roots from the recent failure of the synod in Rome (I don't expect more, since I wasn't expecting much).' Professor Walter Goddijn, sociologist of religion and former General Secretary of the Pastoral Council, thinks a marked exodus of Catholics with a progressive attitude probable if the scales should tip one-sidedly in favour of the two bishops who have been forced on the church. He says this as a guest lecturer in Tübingen on 29 October 1975.[15] This is a blot on the German and French episcopate, which didn't come to the aid of the Dutch church.

When Cardinal Alfrink has to offer his resignation in 1975 as Archbishop of Utrecht on grounds of age it is immediately accepted, as is always the case with progressive bishops. Alfrink's successor is Curia cardinal Johannes Willebrands, to avoid Gijsen, who is favoured by the Vatican. He was highly successful as the founder of the Catholic Conference for Ecumenical Questions and then as Secretary of the Roman Secretariat for Unity under Cardinal Bea, but has little influence as primate of a church severely damaged by Rome. As early as 1983 Willebrands is replaced by Bishop (soon Cardinal) Adrianus Simonis, who maintains the Roman line. Willebrands lives for almost another 25 years; I shall have to return to him in connection with the great confrontation in the infallibility dispute.

There is now a total block on all renewal movements in the Dutch church, with devastating consequences. The number of priests drops dramatically. During 1965, the last year of the Council, only 44 priests ceased their ministries; in the years 1968 and 1969 together 533 did. Whereas in 1964 301 priests in all were ordained, in 1968 there were only 139. In 1960 there were still a good 700 candidates for the priesthood; ten years later this was around 400. Of the originally more than 50 seminaries for priests (including seminaries of religious orders) in the 1960s only 5 diocesan seminaries remain, which in 1991 are reduced to 3. At the end of 1982 314 male pastoral workers and 51 female pastoral workers are in service, but despite the dramatic loss of priests the policy of individual bishops even in the 1990s prevents the overall number ever exceeding 360. In private there is talk of 'troublemakers who are simply confusing the sacramental order'. This lack of pastoral workers cannot be balanced by the 77 deacons there are in 2004.

All this is a prelude and model for similar efforts at restoration in other countries, in order to consolidate once again the medieval ecclesiastical '*imperium Romanum*' in place of the 'Catholic commonwealth' hoped for by the Council. There is now no doubt that the Roman Curia has defeated the Catholic Church of the Netherlands and at the same time won the decisive battle over celibacy in the world church. The Roman Curia with its minions bears the main responsibility for tens of thousands of married priests not being recalled to church service. In the end tens of thousands of parishes all over the world will be without pastors, and particularly in Latin America and Africa millions of Catholics are leaving for well-cared-for Pentecostal communities. This is a Pyrrhic victory for Rome.

The voices of renewal grow weaker

The will for togetherness is still strong at the grass roots of the church. Thus in Tübingen during the Week of Prayer for Christian Unity on 22 January 1970, 1000 Protestant and Catholic Christians attend the service in the Catholic Johanneskirche, 200 more than the year before in the Protestant Stiftskirche; I preach on 1 Corinthians 3 against splits in the community, then and now.

Much is also possible in theology. I think of the collaboration of our two theological faculties or the very constructive radio discussion on Südwestfunk on 27 April 1970, in which such different Tübingen theologians as Johannes Neumann, Joseph Ratzinger, Max Seckler and I discuss four theses of Edward Schillebeeckx on 'Orthodox Belief − Criteria and Uncertainties'. Of course sometimes I am also attacked 'from below' by ultra-orthodox Catholics in their pamphlets and am called a Protestant and heretic who must be stopped. The best answer in most cases is a dignified silence.

Pope Paul VI encounters 'domestic political' difficulties, as often happens in politics generally, as a result of 'foreign political' activities: a triumphal journey to Asia and Oceania. On 26 November he stops in Teheran for a conversation with Shah Mohammad Reza Pahlavi, son of a Cossack general, who in his megalomania crowns himself 'Shah-in-Shah' ('king of kings') in succession to the old Persian Achaemenid kings, and has introduced a Pseudo-Achaemenid chronology which he has devised in place of the Islamic chronology. Neither the Shah (already warned by the demonstration in Berlin) nor the Pope suspect that a few years later the exiled Ayatollah Ruholla Khomeini will sweep away the peacock throne.

The Pope then travels on to the Philippines, where in Manila he is attacked with a knife by a man who is probably mentally disturbed. However, he is protected by his giant escort Archbishop Marcinkus, whom we shall meet later. Karl Rahner, though an apologist for papal infallibility, is well able to distinguish between papal office and the personal holder of the office. With malicious glee he later tells me that he wouldn't have been desperately sad had the attack succeeded.

Within the Roman Curia fewer and fewer dare to oppose the restoration. In November 1968 Cardinal Bea, the initiator and president of the Roman Secretariat for the Unity of Christians (since 1960), already known to me as Visitor since my first year in the German College in 1948 and the first cardinal to be invited to our Tübingen University which has been shaped by Protestantism (*My Struggle for Freedom*, VI: A Curia cardinal at the university), dies at the age of 87. Highly esteemed throughout the Christian world for his modesty, learning and ecumenical disposition, in 1966, along with the great Protestant ecumenist Dr Willem Visser 't Hooft, initiator and first General Secretary of the World Council of Churches, he had been awarded the peace prize of the German book trade. Now Cardinal Bea is dead, and I am not the only one who is sad that his successor in the Secretariat for Unity, Johannes Willebrands, doesn't find so much of a hearing as his predecessor, who is buried in his home town of Riedböhringen in Baden, an hour's drive south of Tübingen.

At the end of this eventful year 1968, another theologian has to leave us. I am more indebted to him than to anyone else for my theology and for the last 25 years I have been able to regard him as a fatherly friend who is constantly with me in spirit. Karl Barth dies on 10 December 1968 after a severe illness.

Doctor of two theologies: Karl Barth

I had visited Karl Barth on 7 August 1968, and a couple of months previously he had written to a young Catholic theologian: 'Professor Küng, whom you rightly defend against those who speak against him without having read him, is with good reason a dear friend both theologically and personally.'[16] Barth had once even said that he would best have liked the Catholic Küng as his successor in the chair of dogmatics.

It is indeed a great honour for me that on Saturday, 14 December 1968, I am allowed to evaluate Karl Barth's services in the ecumenical world from a Catholic perspective in Basle Minster at his memorial service. I speak after Dr Visser 't Hooft, Professor Josef Hromadka, the Czech President of the Christian Peace Conference, and Professor Helmut Gollwitzer of Berlin, who has recalled Barth's part in the Confessing Church against the Hitler regime. This is what I say:

There was a time which needed the *doctor utriusque iuris*, the doctor of both laws. Our time urgently needs the *doctor utriusque theologiae*, the doctor of two theologies, Protestant and Catholic. And if anyone lived that out in an exemplary way in this century, it was Karl Barth.

That may seem astonishing when we think that hardly any important theologian of our century attacked the Catholic church and Catholic theology as firmly, as angrily and in such a challenging way as Karl Barth both in his *Church Dogmatics* and in the General Assembly of the World

Council of Churches in Amsterdam. He challenged us Catholics on the right no less than his Neo-Protestant opponents on the left. And he did not always do so in the tones of Mozart, of whom he says somewhat melancholically in the *Dogmatics*, for all his love, that he does not seem to have been a particularly keen Christian and moreover was a Catholic. But despite all the polemic his challenge was governed by what he so praised in Mozart: a passionate, great, free championing of a cause. And the cause for which he wanted to get a hearing, a loud hearing, was the Christian message.

It was in the light of the gospel that he thought that he had to speak so sharply, that he had to protest against us. So to many of us he seemed to be the embodiment of Protestant theology. But this was because he was not only protesting *against* something but also protesting *for* something, for which it is still perhaps worth protesting even today: for the living God who is wholly other, whom a shallow Protestant theology thinks it can commandeer completely for its human system. He protested for the ever-topical word of God in scripture, which could be very difficult to perceive even in the church, because of merely pious and clever, all too human words, spoken and written. He protested for the one Jesus Christ, alongside whom people in the churches time and again want to put other political or spiritual leaders or even simply human beings themselves; for the fellowship of believers which time and again in church history is threatened either by institutions which have become too powerful or by arrogant enthusiasts.

With this positive protest, his great evangelical intentions, which must be maintained however one regards the Barthian system, Karl Barth has again made Protestant theology a serious evangelical discussion partner even for us Catholics. And with this protest he has at the same time aroused many of us Catholics. His word, which is prophetic even in the *Dogmatics*, has also been heard in our church and he himself was amazed how well it was heard. Precisely as a fundamentally Protestant theologian, by his influence on the Catholic Church Karl Barth has become one of the spiritual fathers of Catholic renewal in connection with the Second Vatican Council – very indirectly yet very effectively, it can be said without exaggeration. This is a renewal which made him sometimes ask in recent years in a sorrowful–joyful way whether today the spirit of God is not more alive in the Catholic Church than in his own.

Now this theologian who could point to an incomparable theological *oeuvre* has returned to his God. And I remember the moving moment when he told me that if he ever had to go before his God he would not refer to his many 'works', nor even to his 'good faith', but simply say, 'God, be merciful to me, a poor sinner.' I do not doubt for a moment that he has been received graciously.

In his last years he was sometimes rather anxious that I might neglect the truth in my struggle for more truthfulness in the church. But of course there can be no question of that. However, unlike him, the Protestant theologian, as a Catholic I now have to do with an authority which infallibly claims the truth for the most important decisions in questions of life and morality. So the great dispute over the truth has already quite clearly focused on the question: is there anyone who with an appeal to God may a priori inerrantly claim to possess the truth?

The one who drove the Alfa: for Ratzinger's free semester

A couple of days before the demise of Cardinal Bea, on 5 November 1968, the government of the canton of Basle City resolves to make the Catholic professor of theology Hans Küng a temporary occupant of the second chair of systematic theology in the Faculty of Protestant Theology in the University of Basle. This news evokes joy in Switzerland but unrest in Tübingen, so that the *Schwäbisches Tagblatt* issues a denial under the headline: 'Küng Remains Here'.

In August, negotiations with me had brought the dean of the faculty, Professor Max Geiger to my lake house in Sursee. The head of the Basle education department thereupon wrote on 25 November 1968 to the Minister of Education of the state of Baden-Württemberg: 'This appointment of a Catholic theologian to collaborate in the teaching of a faculty of Protestant theology is, as far as we know, unique in Europe. However, we thought it a significant opportunity for the ecumenical aims in a faculty's teaching and research to be expressed in this way. The public has reacted attentively and positively to the decision of the ruling council. This letter has been sent simultaneously to the Rector and the Dean of the Faculty of Catholic Theology of the University of Tübingen. We ask the authorities to do all they can to make this guest professorship possible.'

However, implementing the proposal proves far more difficult than had first been assumed. That is above all because of the present dean of the faculty of Catholic theology, Joseph Ratzinger. In his reply to the professors of the various Basle faculties who support my guest professorship and to the expert group of theologians he writes on 11 December 1968: 'Since I understand all your reasons so well, it is particularly difficult for me to have to tell you that the main difficulty for a positive solution in this case lies in my person, or, rather, in the agreements made between Herr Küng and me at the beginning of my activity here.'

After his call to the Tübingen faculty, despite serious objections to my request, Joseph Ratzinger had been ready to divide the summer semester of 1966 between Tübingen and Münster in order to relieve me during the closing phase of my book *The Church*. Because of my free research semester which followed, for the winter semester of 1966/67 the burden of both chairs fell on him. In return I had promised that I would stand in for him over his research semester in this summer of 1969. Ratzinger had also had to serve as dean since April 1968. I immediately understand my colleague's situation and ask him to keep to the plan of his research semester regardless. But how can I hold my professorship in Tübingen and be guest professor in Basle at the same time?

There is no good train link between Tübingen and Basle. So as soon as he welcomed me for our conversation in Castel Gandolfo in September 2005, my former colleague, now the Pope, with a smile put to me the rhetorical question whether Tübingen was still the only university city without an express train connection. People in Basle suggest flying, but taxis to Stuttgart airport are very expensive. And the small airfield of the Tübingen firm Braun and Kemmler can be used only by day and in good weather. If I am to be able to have my guest semester in Basle, there is no alternative to driving.

'The one who rode a bicycle' (see the Prologue) couldn't in fact have done that. But 'the one who drove the Alfa' was willing and able to take on himself the extraordinary strain of this travelling to and fro – as yet without an autobahn. How glad I am that in my little modest Alfa I have a car which holds the road well and has good acceleration. The summer semester begins on 21 April in both Tübingen and Basle. So my travel and lecture plan can look like this: Friday evening a faculty meeting, Saturday morning at 4 a.m. my alarm goes off, at 5 a.m. I set off by car for Basle and arrive at 7.15 to give a two-hour lecture on the sacraments at 8.15. Then I have a two-hour colloquium with Professors Max Geiger and Heinrich Ott, after which I usually go to my lake house. On Monday morning there are another two hours of lecturing, after which I immediately go back from Basle to Tübingen, to fulfil my obligations here on Tuesday and Wednesday.

Eventually this toing and froing with all its burdens results in chronic headaches so, mindful of my brother's brain tumour, on 28 May I have a neurological examination. Happily the result is negative, but I am told to spend some days quietly in order to recover. I'm glad to have this summer semester behind me – with many additional lectures and trips to Cologne, Amsterdam and Milan.

For me the semester in Basle was an enjoyable experience in every respect. I was invited by both the Protestant Reformed church council and the Catholic dean's office and council of priests to a reception, to conversations, and to give lectures. I had close contact not only with my sister Hildegard and her husband Willi Klarer, with whom I could relax, but also with friends from my class living in Basle, whose company I still enjoy. In every way conditions in Swiss Basle are incomparably more peaceful than in Germany, and especially in Tübingen. Here things are coming to a head.

III

Tübingen in Restless Times

'I myself have seen the rightful face of this atheistic piety unveiled, its psychological terror, the abandon with which every moral consideration could be thrown overboard as a bourgeois residue when the ideological goal was at stake. All of this is alarming enough in itself; but it becomes an unrelenting challenge to the theologian when the Church is used as its instrument.'

Cardinal Joseph Ratzinger in 1998 on his last semester in Tübingen, 1968/69[1]

Today Tübingen is one of the youngest cities in Germany, with an average age of under 40. That is because around 24,000 of the 83,000 inhabitants are students. The waves of student revolts which came from the university cities of Berkeley, Paris and Berlin had not of course stopped at the gates of our peaceful little university city. Certainly in our university, which at that time was almost 500 years old, things weren't as violent as in Berlin and Frankfurt, but we too had acts of violence. And there is no question that both for Joseph Ratzinger and for me 1968 became a year of decision.

Calm before the storm

On Easter Monday, 15 April 1968, I have returned happily from an exciting guest semester in New York to my old Tübingen. The first faculty meeting of the summer semester is on 18 April, and I greet my colleagues warmly after a lengthy absence. On the Sunday, in St Johannes church I preach the sermon for the beginning of the semester. This summer semester 1968 starts well for me – under ecumenical auspices. I give the main series of lectures on the doctrine of grace and justification and offer a seminar on Luther's *On the Babylonian Captivity of the Church*, his famous polemic against the captivity of the papal church and the seven sacraments.

I also make arrangements with Professor Peter Beyerhaus, the new Director of the Institute for Ecumenism and Missionary Science at the Protestant Faculty, for an ecumenical society, a working group which meets weekly. It is my first attempt to tackle with a notoriously conservative Lutheran theologian questions with which I have been involved for years. Beyerhaus is an evangelical with high-church leanings and a former missionary, whose views on the relationship between Christianity and the world religions interest me. The topic is 'Presence and Dialogue'. However, it soon becomes clear that Beyerhaus will have nothing to do with dialogue with the world religions. His views, like those of most Protestant theologians at that time – not least under the influence of the early Karl Barth – largely coincide with the pre-conciliar 'Catholic denigration' of the non-Christian religions. Later one of my doctoral students, also a Protestant theologian, Joachim Zehner, wrote his dissertation on the way in which Catholic and Protestant theology treat the development of the world religions.

Joseph Ratzinger is now dean of the Catholic faculty and this semester gives only a special series of lectures, on eschatology, the one topic on which, after his doctoral dissertation, habilitation and Tübingen *Introduction to Christianity*, as professor and bishop he has published an academic theological book. He too becomes ecumenically involved in Tübingen; together with the Dutch Reformed Reformation historian Heiko Oberman he gives a graduate seminar on Luther and the 1519 Leipzig dissertation. He also maintains close contact with Professor Beyerhaus, the likewise 'Catholicizing' Protestant patrologist and Mariologist Ulrich Wickert, and the head of the Tübingen Disciples Institute, Scott Barchy, who comes from America. Indeed – does Pope Benedict still recall this? – with these Protestants he celebrates the eucharist in the Disciples Institute in Wilhelmstrasse.

But how far Ratzinger really appreciates the basic concern of the Reformation is another matter. Thomas Riplinger, one of my doctoral students and at that time still an American Dominican, takes part in Ratzinger's graduate seminar and gives an introductory paper on Luther's development from his indulgence theses to the Leipzig disputation and its effects, above all the bull of excommunication. In his paper Riplinger sharply criticizes the tactics of Luther's main opponents Prierias, Eck and Cajetan, pure Thomists. With no understanding for Luther's existential concern, Riplinger argues, these had disputed with him on a purely rational scholastic level and had hardly noted Luther's biblical and historical arguments. Their insistence on the formal authority of magisterial decisions, above all those relating to the Bohemian Reformer John Hus, who was condemned at the Council of Constance and burned at the stake contrary to all the assurances he had been given, drove Luther to despair and slowly aroused in him the suspicion, which at first he accepted only with horror, that the whole papal system could be corrupt and the papacy even be the prophesied Antichrist.

However, Ratzinger shows little understanding for Riplinger's analysis. He is interested only in the intellectual and doctrinal elements in the controversy with Luther. But the Reformation was primarily an existential and emotional, though by no means irrational, reaction to a rigid unbiblical church system and a scholastic theology remote from history and life. Can anyone who doesn't take note of this ever understand the concerns of Reformation theology?

Ecumenical research in practice

Of course our Institute for Ecumenical Research is totally committed to dialogue with Protestant theology, indeed I have a Protestant theologian, Dr Friedhelm Krüger, as assistant. A series of doctoral students are working on classical ecumenical topics relating to churches and church order, grace and justification and sacraments and worship. I regularly hold colloquiums and weekend seminars with them.

In the meantime the work of documentation goes on in the Institute. My studies abroad have convinced me that theology today should no longer be carried on within narrow confessional and national boundaries. In order to gain an overview of multi-confessional research world-wide since 1945, I found the International Catalogue of Ecumenical Research with three sections for biblical studies, church history and the history of theology, and systematic theology (including all branches of practical theology). I would very much have liked to have made the catalogue electronically, but the technology wasn't yet there, so we content ourselves with a conventional card catalogue. With laborious detailed work I had produced a basic plan extending over 60 pages to construct it systematically; this could also serve as the basis of a systematic theology.

Many assistants work on this research catalogue over the years under the direction of Dr Hermann Häring, from 1980 under Dr Urs Baumann, with the growing support of Thomas Riplinger, who gains his doctorate on Catholic theology in 1975 and is our link with the university library. Over the years the catalogue grows to more than 300,000 entries, so that by the end of the 1970s we already have space problems. In order to rescue the core area, in 1981 we stop the biblical part – in any case biblical contributions on topics of systematic theology were duplicated in the systematic part – and reduce the increasingly extensive historical part to the history of theology. The scheme is brought up to date and through computer technology is provided with an alphabetical index in order to make it easier to find individual topics in systematic theology. A further cut is made in 1987. Since meanwhile the books have been comprehensively documented in the systematic catalogue of the university library, in the research catalogue we limit ourselves exclusively to the articles, for which at the time there is no corresponding documentation. We put them on the computer but print out cards to insert into the catalogue.

The catalogue was carried on in this form until my retirement in 1996. After we gave up the accomodation in Nauklerstrasse, the research catalogue was finally put in the joint library of the Theological School, in a prominent place accessible to all, and remains a unique tool for bibliographical documentation for the period between 1945 and 1995. Meanwhile the plan of the research catalogue has been developed further in the university library, now in the form of modern data banks on the internet which are available all over the world, free of charge and very much up to date. The books are listed in the Online Public Access Catalogue

(OPAC), the articles from journals and composite works in the *Index theologicus*. The content of both kinds of documents can be accessed with key words from the keyword files; usually these cover only German-speaking areas, but in the *Index theologicus* they are also in English translation.

Since the foundation of the Institute for Ecumenical Research in 1964 I have made it a principle not to become involved in any of the necessary administrative work but to carry on personal research. Each of my three scholarly colleagues is to use about half his working time for his own academic work (doctorate or habilitation thesis). However, in 1968 our Institute, too, is now drawn into the controversies over university reform.

Disputed university reform

In 1968 no one can seriously dispute that the German university, of which we had long been so proud, is in need of reform. Reform is urgently necessary, simply because of the tremendous rise in student numbers. When I began in Tübingen in 1960 there were already around 8000 students at the university, which was designed for 3000, and in 1968 there are around 12,000. Tübingen is the city in Germany with the largest percentage of students in its population. In 1964 the new *ordinarius* professor of sociology, Ralf Dahrendorf, who follows me in being the youngest member of the Greater Senate, had given an admirably documented, disturbing speech on the under-representation of the children of workers at the university. After it, entrance to the university was made considerably easier, but the requirements at grammar schools were also relaxed. However, the shortage of lecture rooms and the lack of lodgings in the city couldn't be remedied overnight.

More and more professors also see that the curricula must be reformed, studies abbreviated and the rigid hierarchy at the university dismantled. The head of the dental clinic, Professor Eugen Fröhlich, the first member of the medical faculty with whom I had become friends, had insisted on four chairs when the dental clinic was reorganized, to the annoyance of some colleagues who also had to provide for several chairs. A rotation of directors, all with primarily administrative duties, is envisaged for the large scientific institutes of physics, chemistry and biology. Because I turn down the call to Münster, in our faculty of Catholic theology the chair of dogmatics is duplicated (a course previously taboo to my colleagues because of a 'division of power'), so Joseph Ratzinger and I can work side by side. As dean I present a planning paper to the faculty which instead of splitting the faculty into all too many specialist areas (missiology, welfare-work studies, biblical archaeology, etc.) as other universities are already doing, aims at a duplication of core disciplines (Old and New Testaments, dogmatics, ethics, church history, practical theology).

As dean I also experience how difficult it is to implement reforms if the issue is the occupation of individual chairs. The excessive number of examinations is to be reduced in order to cut down the length of studies. Unusually, a senior ministerial official from Stuttgart visits me in my home; he thinks that as a young dean I would have the necessary energy to implement these reforms. But even the young representative of the faculty of canon law, who otherwise delights in reform, fights against the curtailment of examination material in canon law – 'truly just as important'. So in our faculty, too, people are prepared to accept only a lazy compromise, which in fact makes it even more difficult for the students to know precisely what will be required in the examinations.

I find more assent to a rational reordering of the process of awarding doctorates which is meant to make it easier for foreign students and also – after intensive debate – women to gain a doctorate in Catholic theology in Tübingen. Thus I can supervise the doctorates of, in 1965, the first Indian, Patrick Dias (on the diversity of the church); in 1972, the first African, Jean Amougou-Atangana (on Spirit and confirmation); and in 1971, Christa Hempel, the first woman – she too produces an interesting and solid dissertation (on the discussion of justification). Indeed finally, in 1992, under my leadership at the Institute for Ecumenical Research, Johannes Rehm can even become the first Protestant theologian to gain a doctorate in Catholic theology (on what eucharistic fellowship is possible today) – this too has now become possible by a change in the regulations for doctorates.

Encouragingly, in general the collaboration between the Catholic and Protestant faculties develops in a welcome way. Very soon after the Council, on the proposal of the Protestant New Testament scholar Ernst Käsemann, the theological study group of the Protestant theological faculty which discusses topical theological questions is in principle opened up to Catholics and established as an ecumenical working group. Previously the New Testament scholar Karl Hermann Schelkle and I had been the only Catholics to take part. Special mention must be made of the Protestant systematic theologian Jürgen Moltmann, in whom since 1967 I have had a congenial and highly-qualified conversation partner. In the winter semester of 1968/69 he holds a joint ecumenical session with me on christological questions of the present and with me heads a committee of both faculties which supports the integration of the two big theological libraries in the new Theological School and achieves reciprocal recognition of certain seminar certificates of the sister faculty. From 1 January 1971, for a good 25 years with Jürgen Moltmann I head the ecumenical working group of the two theological faculties; collaboration with him is always smooth and friendly.

Unfortunately the efforts at integration largely come to a halt when student unrest hits Tübingen and the radical left becomes active not only among students of politics, sociology and psychology but also among Protestant students of theology – always more open to innovation on the basis of Protestant tradition than their somewhat 'boring', traditionally conservative, Catholic fellow-students. In the Catholic faculty there is now a concern that certain Protestant

demagogues among the academic assistants and students might put the whole
structure of the faculty in question. I emphatically support demands such as the
abolition of the 'faculty secret', which allows every possible intrigue, and also the
legal improvement of the status of academic assistants and lecturers and their
integration. But the abolition of successful institutes and the politicizing of
scholarship, indeed the questioning of democratic institutions, is another matter.

Tübingen was ahead of other universities in its assimilation of the Nazi Socialist
past which is bitterly necessary. As early as the winter semester of 1964/1965
Tübingen professors had given a cycle of lectures on 'German Intellectual Life
and National Socialism' in which they discussed the relationship of the various
disciplines to National Socialism. Rolf Hochhuth's 1963 play *The Representative*,
on the silence of Pius XII over the Holocaust, and the Auschwitz trial (1963-65),
are intensively discussed by both professors and students. But now the situation
comes to a head.

Student rebellions

On 5 December 1966 the refusal of a lecture room to the Communist star
advocate Friedrich Karl Kaul of East Berlin leads to a demonstration of students in
front of the university and in the late evening – still with 250 students – in front
of the private house of the Rector, Gottfried Möllenstedt. In 1967 the lecture
takes place in the Festsaal and disappoints even the sympathizers. But now there is
a growing sensitivity of the students to foreign politics in connection with the
rule of the colonels in Greece and above all the visit of the Shah to our university
city and a more international focus.

I have already reported the radical democratic eruption after the shooting of
the Berlin student Benno Ohnesorg on Friday, 2 June 1967, in Berlin. In
Tübingen, too, the college–political circle SDS is now changing into a mass
organization. At noon on the following Monday, 5 July, more than 2000 students
gather in front of the main university building. In the evening there is an
emotional and controversial exchange of information in the packed Festsaal. On
Friday, the day of Benno Ohnesorg's funeral, again 2000 Tübingen students walk
in a silent march in the pouring rain from the university to the castle gate. The
Rector recommends that all lectures should be cancelled on this day, but only a
few professors take part in the silent march.

The coalition between teachers and learners begins to break up, but so too does
the common ground between the moderate students, who are calling for a reform
of studies and democratization of the university, and the radicals, who want a
revolution in society and are now constantly trying out new forms of action – first
of all the more harmless teach-in, then the more definite sit-in, and finally the
highly irresponsible occupation of premises. In autumn 1967 the 'political
mandate' of students is now also being discussed everywhere in Tübingen, and in

the university the Senate resolves to include representatives of the assistants and students as active members of the various university bodies. This is a very reasonable decision. To begin with, lectures go on unhindered.

Thus on 7/8 December 1967 the faculty of Catholic theology can peacefully celebrate in splendour the 150 years of its existence (as a new foundation alongside the older faculty, which has become Protestant) with an academic festival and a ceremonial service. All the professors once again wear their ceremonial university gowns. Great scholars are given honorary doctorates: the most important French theologian, Yves Congar; the Swiss pioneer of ecumenical theology, Otto Karrer; and the Louvain historian Roger Aubert, author of a history of Pius IX and the First Vatican Council, who also gives the ceremonial address on 'The Difficult Awakening of Catholic Theology in the Age of Restoration. An Evaluation of the Catholic Tübingen School'. It is to be the last academic festival of a traditional kind.

At this time the public is also presented with an imposing Festschrift, the title and theme of which is proposed by me as dean: 'Changing Theology'. Thirty-five theologians associated with our faculty as teachers or former pupils attempt in the spirit of the Catholic Tübingen school to give an account of the state of theology in the different specialist areas against the background of history in a completely changed situation of the church and Christians in the world. It has become an extremely informative work of 850 pages, but for reasons of time (my research semester) I had handed over the editing to my colleagues Joseph Ratzinger and Johannes Neumann.[2]

Joseph Ratzinger has contributed his programmatic Tübingen inaugural lecture on 'Salvation History and Eschatology' and I have contributed a 'Catholic Reflection on Luther's Doctrine of Justification Today'. A month previously, on 11 November 1967, I had spoken on this topic in Geneva at the invitation of the Protestant faculty there. This too is a sign that a real change of confessional theologies in an ecumenical direction has taken place; on the 450th anniversary of the University of Geneva, founded by Calvin, a Catholic theologian speaks, to great applause, not about Calvin's but about Luther's understanding of justification! This is a small challenge, in full view of the great monument to the Reformation in Geneva with its four statues of great Reformers, from whom Martin Luther in particular is absent; his name (like that of Zwingli) can be read only modestly on a memorial tablet!

For the academic year 1967/68 it should have been the turn of the Catholic faculty to appoint the Rector, and we were unanimous that our Professor of Old Testament, Herbert Haag, should be the candidate. He has great prestige in the Senate and would certainly have been elected in a secret vote. But it is known that the state government in Stuttgart wants to pursue a more restrictive financial course and that serious clashes are to be expected with the education and finance ministries. So the science and medical faculties agree in secret – the only intrigue against the faculty of Catholic theology in the Senate (which was completely unnecessary) – to elect the serving Rector, Gottfried Möllenstedt, a forceful physicist, for a second year, on the grounds that he would be better at presenting the demands of the university to Stuttgart than the admirable, calm Haag, whose steadfastness and ability to assert himself are largely underestimated. So instead of Haag, once again Möllenstedt is elected.

I am told after my return that had I been in Tübingen in December 1966 and not on the other side of the globe, I might possibly have been elected. Happily this cup passed me by. For the front on which the new (old) Rector fights is not, as expected, the Stuttgart ministry of education but the revolutionary students. And faced with them, the physicist Möllenstedt proves to be both helpless and clumsy. I attempt to comfort my Swiss friend Herbert Haag by saying that in this completely new situation he too (like me) would hardly have passed the test of dealing with the new forms of protest in the right way. The university was by no means prepared for the vehement confrontation with its own students.

Violent actions and ideological exaggerations

The rebellious students, an extremely active minority with a Marxist orientation, are very soon concerned with more than just a reform of studies and the structure of the teaching body. They object to the stagnation of German politics (above all towards the East) and the absence of a strong parliamentary opposition during the Great Coalition – a favourable climate for revolutionaries and an 'extra-parliamentary opposition' to flourish. They are therefore concerned to make the university an instrument in the fight over political opinion and power.

In their fight against a technocratic restructuring of the institutions of tertiary education in the service of business and for their democratization through the participation of lecturers, assistants and students with equal rights, the radical students see themselves in a great alliance with liberation movements and women's movements all over the world. They claim a 'political mandate' for this. So there are protests, often violent, against the Vietnam War, but also against the wretched situation in the Third World, in Africa, Central and South America. At the same time the students make violent attempts to change the existing structure of the university. Much can be justified with slogans such as 'Fight against the University of the Professors', 'Demolish Authoritarian Structures', 'Not just Co-determination but Self-determination for Students', especially if Marxist vocabulary is used. The professors, the 'non-professorial teaching staff' (assistants and academic advisers) and students are seen as three groups with a conflict of material interests which is understood as a kind of class warfare.

In all this the radicals stand for a 'political concept of scholarship': specialist scholars are not to work in ivory towers but to justify the extent to which their scholarship contributes to political action and social change. Of course that is far more difficult for experts in medieval German literature, Iranian philology,

Egyptology, numismatics or other – as they are now called contemptuously – 'orchid disciplines' than for political scientists, sociologists and psychologists. People claim in a quite general way not least in education to be 'anti-author-itarian', indeed militant, even ready to use force, if not against persons then against things. Posters and banners in the lecture rooms often replace arguments and information. Lectures by unpopular teachers are 'disrupted', 'refunctioned', become the object of strikes. No wonder that some members of the teaching body have remembered this situation as 'catastrophic'. It is a blow to their whole academic activity from which some of them never recover. Even left–wing liberal papers complain about 'student terrorism'.[3]

The political agitation of the rebellious students reaches its climax in 'hot May 1968', in the fight against the emergency laws by which the state organs are authorized to use extraordinary measures not only for external but also for internal emergencies. The lawyer Ludwig Raiser follows Möllenstedt as Rector; he is a civil lawyer, well-tried in debate, highly regarded as president of the German advisory council for institutions of tertiary education and Praeses of the Evangelical Church in Germany (his son Konrad studies theology in Tübingen and one day will become General Secretary of the World Council of Churches). By his prudence he draws criticism upon himself from some colleagues for giving way too much to the students.

But the university authorities are on the defensive. For fear of demonstrations and disruptions of all kinds, the Rector and Lesser Senate cancel the *Dies aca-demicus* with the public celebration of the appointment of the Rector planned for 7 May 1968; the university also has to reflect on the way in which it presents itself. To this end Rector Raiser wants to speak on the situation of the university and open up a discussion on 15 May at a public meeting in the Festsaal. In fact such occasions are less like a democratic parliament and more like a turbulent revolutionary assembly. There isn't a trace of dialogue with opponents. On 16 May 1968, during the second reading of the emergency laws in the German Bundestag, there are also massive student protests, disruptions and the blocking of teaching in Tübingen. On 25 May some 300 students invade the town hall in Tübingen in order to force permission to use a loudspeaker van in their demonstrations.

Things get worse on 29 May, the day of the third reading; as in most other German institutions of tertiary education, students go on 'strike' for several days. This is in fact a boycott of lectures. Whole institutions and faculties are paralysed. Access to the university is closed by 'strikers', sometimes with chains, in order to keep lecturers and students who want to learn away from teaching institutions. It isn't a good thing to get into hand–to–hand fighting with students. On 30 May there is another big demonstration in the market place in front of the town hall. But the same day the emergency laws are passed by the German Bundestag at a third reading, and in the evening towards midnight 3000 students in the Festsaal and other lecture rooms resolve to end the strike.

However, the occupations, disruptions of lectures, dissolutions of the constitutional assembly and sessions of the senate don't stop. Later, on 28 November 1968, the public celebration of the award of the Montaigne prize to the important, albeit anti-Marxist, French sociologist and political theorist Raymond Aron also has to be cancelled because, according to Rector Raiser, 'he cannot expect the guests of the university to expose themselves to the disturbances which have become customary'; the award takes place under police protection before a small group in the Biological Institute, far from the centre of the university.

Disruptions and their consequences: Eschenburg and Adorno

Those engaged in German and Romance studies, politics and sociology show particular revolutionary zeal. The rebels, who include Protestant but hardly any Catholic theologians, like to disrupt the lectures of professors who have a degree of prominence, are noted for their openness to some student concerns and thus can easily be shown up and mocked as 'bloody liberals'. In Catholic theology above all Joseph Ratzinger and I belong in this category.

However, things are by no means so bad for Ratzinger and me as they are for our colleague Theodor Eschenburg, the doyen of political science in Germany. He occupies the first chair of political science in Germany and is the founder of the Tübingen Institute of Political Science. Between the two world wars he was the closest collaborator with the most successful Democrat foreign minister and Nobel prize-winner, Gustav Stresemann. He had to watch the new democratic structures and institutions of the first German republic founded in Weimar being destroyed by extremists on the right and the left, and the consequent preparation for Adolf Hitler's rise to power. As Rector of the university from 1961 to 1963, in the face of my hesitant faculty he enthusiastically supports my invitation to Cardinal Bea to address the university. He also sets out to 'buck up' the university a bit against the resistance of conservative professors to unusual appointments: those of Walter Jens, originally a philologist, who has made a name as a critic and literary figure, to a new chair in rhetoric, and of Ernst Bloch who, because he has fallen out of favour in the German Democratic Republic for his unorthodox interpretation of Marxism, is given a permanent guest professorship – and this although Eschenburg does not agree with the political views of either of them.[4] As a man of great political experience (he also takes part in the foundation of the south-west state made up of Baden and Württemberg), a scholar with great historical knowledge and a constant critical commentator on politics in the young Federal Republic, he is so to speak a one-man institution for practising German democracy.

But in 1968 this scholar, highly respected throughout the Republic, who argues for lively democratic institutions, clear democratic rules and procedures and a politics committed to the common good, who campaigns for a strong state

110

in the face of an insatiable claim to power by parties and associations, becomes the big bogeyman of the left because he speaks out against a political mandate for the students. His understanding of the state and of authority is radically put in question. His lectures to a large audience of interested students are disrupted, and he himself is prevented from speaking. He describes these disruptions as a 'kind of bloodless running of the gauntlet'. Indeed, one day Eschenburg's Institute of Political Science is 'occupied' by revolutionary students. When he, the Director, arrives there, he finds himself literally shut out and has to return home.

Yet even that is a gracious fate compared with that of the sociologist and philosopher Theodor W. Adorno, the spiritual father of many generations of left-wing students, but who, as I have reported, shows an antipathy to direct political action. So in the winter semester of 1968/69 his Frankfurt Institute for Social Research is occupied. Adorno calls the police and lays charges against his doctoral student, the student leader Hans-Jürgen Krahl, for disturbing the peace. At the beginning of the summer semester of 1969 there is a call by a grass-roots sociology group dominated by the Socialist German Student Federation (SDS) to engage in disruptions in order to force Adorno to engage in self-criticism. The slogan is, 'Victory for Adorno, a long life for capitalism'. Hardly has Adorno, who like Eschenburg always dresses very correctly, got to his lecturing desk than he is hustled by three bare-breasted women students. He rushes from the lecture room and cancels his lectures. Psychosomatically very disturbed, in July he retreats to Zermatt, in his beloved Swiss mountains, but is plagued by heart problems and on 6 August 1969 falls victim to a heart attack in the hospital of Visp, at the entry to the Mattertal.

Theodor Eschenburg, who is to retire in 1973 at the age of 68, devotes himself to his publications and above all to his memoirs, which hardly mention any of these events. This ugly scene of the Tübingen student revolt is never mentioned in the eulogies before and after Eschenburg's death. Because of my personal relationship to their father, I was asked by Eschenburg's daughters to help in arranging his Protestant funeral on 16 July 1999, even though I am a Catholic priest. I speak of the practitioner of power who was also a preserver of the law, indeed a guardian of ethics: 'You're right,' I was told in a discussion about a global ethic by this noble and modest man, who was often a guest in our house, 'a minimum ethic is part of any constitutional state.'

Rebellious theological students

The 'fundamental democratization' of the student movement aims at discrediting any authority, especially that of the hated police and legal system, but also of the family, business and the church. As a professor I too come to feel this in my seminar in the Institute for Ecumenical Research in the summer semester of 1968.

Perhaps I've engaged in too many monologues during the introduction in the first session, thinking that the students, whose knowledge often proves to be very sparse, are primarily interested in information and not discussion; a rational discussion presupposes a minimum of information. Be this as it may, in the second session a student who had had 1968er experiences in Bochum and a Swabian fellow-student from the Protestant faculty ask very cheekily for the seminar to be led alternately by students. These students and doctoral students, committed to an anti-authoritarian form of education, argue that in 'communication free of domination' a 'group dynamic process' would develop in which ideas would simply bubble up. I am sceptical but agree, knowing full well how difficult it is to lead a seminar skilfully and effectively even with solid academic knowledge; so the two rebellious speakers may begin and lead the next session of the seminar. They do so – and fail lamentably. After their introduction they invite a 'discussion', but despite repeated invitations not a single student joins in. Neither of them has any idea of how to get a discussion going. I deliberately ignore their helpless looks at the group and finally at me. Only after a long and painful pause do I finally raise a substantive theological question, but no student can answer it, nor can the two 'chairpersons'.

The consequence is that no students declare themselves ready to lead the third session of the seminar and now the 'ringleaders of the rebellion' ask me once again to lead the seminar in person, a task which I accept with friendly reserve. I learn from these events to reflect on my teaching, which is in general too didactic and goal-orientated, and give the students more opportunity for discussion. And some students very soon change. The 'revolutionary' from Bochum establishes himself in our Institute, proves himself, and soon becomes my best academic assistant. His name is Karl-Josef Kuschel and I will soon be describing his interesting future. His 'comrade', Christel Hildebrand, becomes an eminent Protestant pastor and journalist and I am still in touch with her today.

The situation is quite different if students who don't belong to the faculty and aren't members of the seminar invade it against the regulations and seek to force a political discussion instead of a substantive one. Even the Ecumenical Society with the Protestant missionary theologian Peter Beyerhaus is disrupted on 26 June 1969 by SDS students who make their way in by force, although it takes place between 8 p.m. and 10 p.m. in a private house rented by the university. It is to be 'refunctioned' for a political discussion on the emergency laws. But with the agreement of Beyerhaus I break off the seminar. One of the student revolutionaries asks me why I don't join in, because I am regarded as open: 'Since I've fought against right-wing Fascism all my life, I may also defend myself against left-wing Fascism.' Along with many others, Jürgen Habermas also used the term Fascism when Rudi Dutschke proposed that the ban on demonstrations imposed in Berlin should be met with direct action.

Of course there are also colleagues who attempt to come to peaceful agreements with revolutionary students. In our Catholic theological faculty the only

Professor in Tübingen from 1960

Student revolts: Rector Ludwig Raiser in his Rectorate occupied by students
(13 January 1969)

Two pillars of the University of Tübingen: jurist Ludwig Raiser
and political theorist Theodor Eschenburg

150 years of the Tübingen Faculty of Catholic Theology (7/8 December 1967):
Bishop Leiprecht (Rottenburg) with honorary doctor Professor Roger Aubert (Louvain)

Jubilee exhibition. From the right: dogmatic theologian Joseph Ratzinger, moral theologian
Alfons Auer; from the left: standing church lawyer Johannes Neumann,
bending forward Old Testament scholar Herbert Haag

1970

Influential books

1973

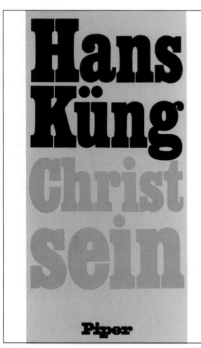

1974

1978

World trip 1971: Buddhist temple site of Borobodur (with Indonesian Jesuits)

Relaxation: diving on the Île des Pins (Polynesia)

Um nichts
als die

WAHR HEIT

Deutsche Bischofskonferenz
contra Hans Küng

Eine Dokumentation
herausgegeben
und eingeleitet von
Walter Jens

Piper

1978

Struggle for the Truth

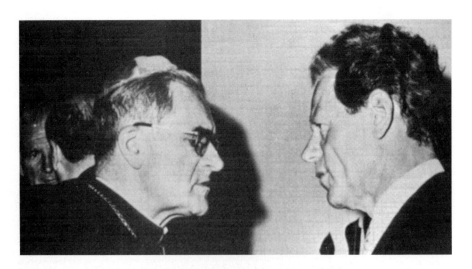

With the President of the German Conference of Bishops, Cardinal Julius Döpfner

In dispute over the church: Cardinal Léon Suenens and Pope Paul VI

Concilium World Congress, Brussels, September 1970. From the right: General Secretary Vanhengel, President van den Boogaard, Cardinal Suenens, Publisher Paul Brand, Mrs van den Boogaard

The *Concilium* Foundation. From the left: Yves Congar, Hans Küng,
Edward Schillebeeckx, Karl Rahner

Disappointed friendship: Karl Rahner

Paul VI in the German College: with Jesuit General Pedro Arrupe
and Cardinal Döpfner (10 October 1973)

Paul VI with Cardinal Franjo Šeper, Prefect of the Congregation for the Doctrine of the Faith

The focus of the international press (1975)

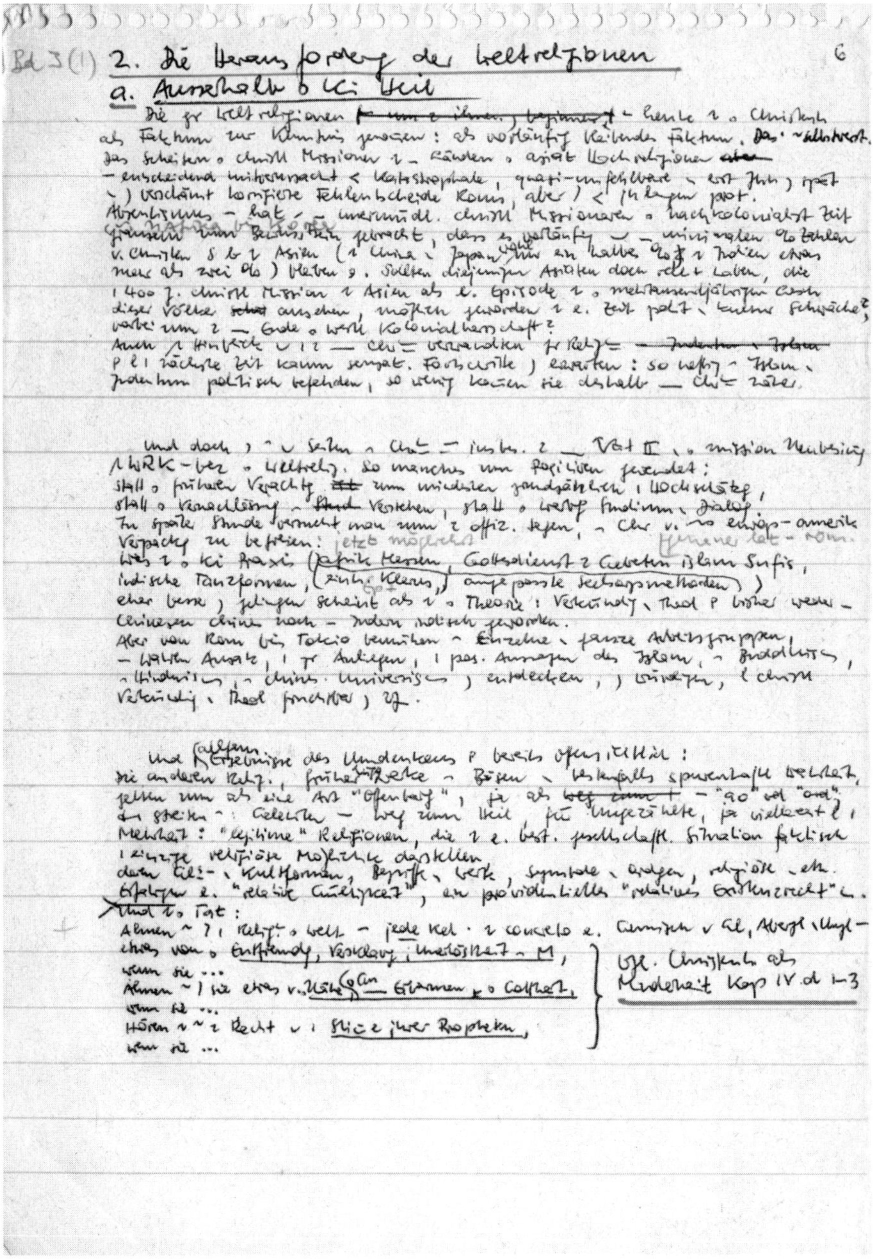

2. Die Herausforderung der Weltreligionen

a. Außerhalb... Heil

(handwritten manuscript notes — largely illegible cursive)

Manuscript page of *On Being a Christian*

SPIEGEL
BESTSELLER

BELLETRISTIK	SACHBÜCHER
1. Palmer: **Dicke Lilli-gutes Kind** Droemer; 29,50 Mark	**1.** Solschenizyn: **Der Archipel Gulag II** Scherz; 19,80 Mark
2. Kishon: **Kein Öl, Moses?** Langen-Müller; 19,80 Mark	**2.** Küng: **Christ sein** Piper; 38 Mark
3. Böll: Die verlorene Ehre der Katharina Blum k & w; 19,80 Mark	**3.** Däniken: Erscheinungen Econ; 25 Mark

An unexpected success

With Hermann Häring and Karl-Josef Kuschel,
colleagues in the 1970s, friends ever since

500 years of the University of Tübingen: ceremonial speech in the Stiftskirche (8 October 1977)

In the Opus Dei Centre, Rome: Cardinals Joseph Höffner and Karol Wojtyla
(published in *L'Osservatore Romano*, 20 October 1978)

Companion on the China visits: Professor Julia Ching (Toronto)

Cartoon coverage of the symposium in the Academy of Social Sciences, Peking (27 August 1979)

Pope John Paul I (Albino Luciani) and his successor Cardinal Karol Wojtyla
(September 1978)

German Federation of Artists: ceremonial lecture in Stuttgart (29 September 1979).
Second row from the left: Bishop Georg Moser, sculptor O. H. Hajek,
Minister of Science and Art Helmut Engler, Lord Mayor Manfred Rommel

Karol Wojtyla:
from 1978 Pope John Paul II,
with Joseph Ratzinger,
from 1977 Archbishop of Munich
and Cardinal

Main opponents in the great confrontation 1979/1980

Joseph Höffner,
from 1976 President of the
German Conference of Bishops

First public statement on 18 December 1979 after the withdrawal of the church's permission to teach

First appearance at the university after the withdrawal of the church's permission to teach,
in the Festsaal, 19 December 1979

Torchlight demonstration through the city of Tübingen on the evening of 19 December 1979

Show of solidarity in front of the Tübingen Stiftskirche
at the speech by Professor Norbert Greinacher

Caught by the photographer after the secret conversation on 23 December 1979

Bishop Georg Moser

Gaining strength in Lech am Arlberg

Protest demonstration in Switzerland in front of the Hofkirche, Lucerne, 22 December 1979

After the betrayal by the Seven,
at Professor Herbert Haag's
farewell lecture, 4 February 1980

Ecumenical round table. From the left: Professor Jürgen Moltmann,
Dr Elisabeth Moltmann-Wendel, Marianne Saur, Professor Eberhard Jüngel

Neighbours and friends: Professors Theodor Eschenburg and Walter Jens

Press conference after the 'Tübingen compromise' on 10 April 1980
with University President Adolf Theis (right) and Südwestfunk studio director Hubert Locher

Despite everything: still a priest

Survived!
Crete, May 1980

one is the practical theologian Norbert Greinacher, who has never concealed his sympathy for socialism. In the Protestant theological faculty Jürgen Moltmann, who has made use of the Marxist philosophy of Ernst Bloch for his theology, now temporarily advocates a theology of revolution, but one reads remarkably little about the events of 1968 in his autobiography, except that in 1969 he gave a speech against the emergency laws in the market place in Tübingen. Perhaps he thought that self-critical reflection on the political and theological judgements and positions of the time wouldn't interest his readers.

Ernst Käsemann, who was imprisoned by the Gestapo during the Nazi period and had to deal with Lutheran bishops who piously respected the state, thinks that big theological lectures no longer make sense in this new university. Student pamphlets entitled 'Do Lectures make Sense?' have also put in question the classical form of the lecture, at which Käsemann was a master. In his lectures he now allows the students themselves to present different interpretations of passages of Paul's letter to the Romans, but this is asking too much of them. To the end of his life he laments the 'good old' university, which has gone for ever. Even I couldn't persuade him to give a big lecture – for example in the wide-ranging *Studium Generale*. He also suffers a personal tragedy. In May 1977 his daughter Elisabeth, who had gone to Buenos Aires as a left-leaning student and had become socially and politically involved under the rule of the military junta, was kidnapped, brutally tortured and murdered by members of the military.

Euphoria over reform and perplexity in the faculty

An unparalleled zeal for reform erupts, with countless meetings and the production of tons of papers: more and more circular letters and draft reforms. Our archives swell, as does the university administration; everything becomes more complicated and impersonal. Requests to the university administration which used to be in duplicate or triplicate now have to be made in eight or even twelve copies. It's all a tremendous waste of time at the expense of research. Bureaucracy increases and the level of scholarship declines.

It is now better not to use the term 'élite' unless one wants to be decried as a reactionary. There is mass instead of quality, a lowering of academic requirements, and the appointment of lecturers who are often more 'politically correct' than eminent in their scholarship. Here one can hardly contradict the political theorist Eschenburg when in a conversation he argues that the quality of personnel, whether in scholarship, business or politics, can be compared with a pyramid in which the highly intelligent are a rarity and one must normally be content with good mediocrity; indeed the selection is often made not so much by achievement as by orientation (the man may be eminent but his direction isn't right, so it's better to select someone weaker but of the right tendency).

The animosity against élites isn't limited to the university. Although the

113

university has been Tübingen's great renown for five centuries and is still the biggest employer in the city, in the 1980s a mayor who has been given a doctorate in law by our university will replace the honorary title 'university city' of Tübingen with 'city' of Tübingen; at no small cost all the coats of arms and letterheads are changed. Only in 1998 will the shields be changed back to 'university city' under Mayor Brigitte Russ-Scherer, who is well disposed to the university, and in the new millennium it becomes fashionable to understand oneself as an 'élite university' and to strive for 'excellence'.

Elections of professors, assistants and students to the Greater Senate and 'conferences of specialist disciplines' take place at great expense, but only a relatively small number of students play an active part in them: now the university is not their home and commonwealth. The demands for participation and democratization have strange results. Some journalists and politicians, seized by the spirit of the time, adopt senseless demands for reform such as three-way parity (professors, assistants and students) in the composition of all academic bodies – a legal regulation also introduced in Baden-Württemberg, according to which students and assistants (non-professorial staff) have twice as many votes as professors.

This reordering makes it possible for Gotthold Hasenhüttl, a university lecturer who gained his habilitation in the Catholic theological faculty in 1969 with the casting vote of the dean, to be elected dean for the academic year 1973/74 by assistants and students against the votes of almost all the professors. It leads to a unnecessary polarization and a long-lasting dispute between Norbert Greinacher, who had voted with the students, and the other professors, including me, though I had emphatically supported both Greinacher's call to the chair of practical theology and Hasenhüttl's habilitation. After a few unpleasant months, in the summer semester of 1974 Dean Hasenhüttl throws in the towel, gives the key to his secretary and goes off by night, without saying goodbye to anyone, to the University of Saarbrücken, to which he has received a call.

Peace is restored in the faculty only two years later, on the basis of a compromise which I negotiate for the election of a new dean: for the academic year 1975/76 the practical theologian Norbert Greinacher is elected dean. To everyone's delight he performs his office extremely efficiently with regular consultations and even organizes a faculty trip to Hungary. As agreed, the church historian Rudolf Reinhardt, who is regarded as conservative, follows him for the academic year 1976/77 and also does a good job. The three-way parity is later withdrawn on the basis of a judgement by the Federal Court, and the legal competence of student bodies is limited to student affairs. They are excluded from discussions of internal or external policy.

Threat to the Institute for Ecumenical Research

Since the beginning of the 1970s a struggle for power has been going on in the university bodies, above all over the new 'basic order' that is to be decided on. Giving way to the pressure for equality, the Protestant theological faculty has downgraded all its institutes (which are administratively and financially independent) to seminar divisions (special spheres of work), rightly so for some not particularly efficient institutes, but wrongly for others, such as the famous Institutum Judaicum or the Institute for the Late Middle Ages and Reformation.

In the Catholic theological faculty there is only our Institute for Ecumenical Research, known internationally for a long time, and this is now being drawn into the turmoil of university reform. At a meeting of professors in Haag's house on Ascension Day (20 May) 1971, every possible attempt is made to convince me to give up the status of an institute. In this situation of all against one it is of course difficult for me to make a stand, but is this to happen after all the undisputed achievements of our Institute? That is out of the question.

On 24 May, like all the other directors of institutes, I am summoned to a 'hearing' before the Senate committee (made up of professors, assistants and students), chaired not by a professor (who could be prejudiced) but by a representative of the non-professorial staff (academic council). It's a waste of time. I have to defend myself energetically against the unreasonable request that the supervision of our Institute, too, should be handed over to directors rotating annually. This would literally have cost the Institute its head, and a head is needed in this kind of research. Some faculty colleagues, not noted for ecumenical contributions, would gladly see themselves as directors of the Institute (and me disempowered as director). Here beyond question envy plays a major role.

But I make it clear that while a change of directors in the administration of a big scientific institute or a medical clinic with dozens of staff may make sense, in the case of a small institute engaged in intensive research, where the 'head' has to bear the main burden of research, it is nonsensical. Our Institute, in which the head is at the same time the head of research, is known to work efficiently. It has a transparent structure, an administratively simple organization and very little personal or financial expense. As Director of the Institute, a 'pioneer' who doesn't spare himself, I may also ask much of my colleagues. When in this 'hearing' the chief caretaker, who represents the university staff on the commission and likes to present himself as a representative of the 'people' (= the students), asks what would happen if 'a professor went senile', I immediately retort, 'It would be the same as if a senior caretaker went "senile".' Laughter ends this debate.

But will my substantive arguments be passed on convincingly to the bodies responsible? I think it necessary laboriously to produce an extensive memorandum (9 June 1971) to the effect that the autonomy of the Institute should be guaranteed within the discipline of Catholic theology and with it the continuity of its directorate and sufficient staff and resources. This involves the training of doctoral students as carried on hitherto, the continuation of the documentation work, the name of the Institute (which has 'market value'), and finally the international relations that have been built up. We are solid in our defence. The memorandum is also signed by my academic colleagues Dr Hermann Häring, Dr Friedrich Krüger, Dr Margret Gentner and the Institute secretary Annegret Dinkel.

What will also be important for future controversies (with the church) apart from our professional competence is my strongest trump: the legal status of the Institute. Because I turned down the call to the University of Münster in 1963, the state of Baden-Württemberg established a new chair of dogmatics and ecumenical theology for me on the basis of a personal contract. The foundation and leadership of the new Institute for Ecumenical Research was legally associated with this. On the basis of this promise of tenure, safeguarded by contract, at that time I remained in Tübingen. My clear conclusion now is that 'He (the Director of the Institute for Ecumenical Research) would have to regard a one-sided change in the legal status as a breach of law which would be particularly serious for him as a Swiss citizen and which he is not prepared to accept.'

Clearly people don't now want to risk a legal dispute. In a letter of 16 July 1972 I also present my objections to the threatened breach of law directly to the education ministry of Baden-Württemberg. Later, a representative of my colleagues on the faculty asks me personally to agree to a 'new order'. Again I refuse, and since then no one has dared to attack the autonomy of our Institute. And because in any case relations in our Institute are very warm and we regularly have our parties and stimulating expeditions (to Strasbourg, to the Isenheim altar in Colmar, to Ronchamp and to Basle, to the Chagall exhibition in Zurich, to the Zugspitze and the Wieskirche), my colleagues haven't the slightest desire to agonize over a new and totally superfluous 'order for the Institute' and waste their time in useless meetings. This has been going on for a whole year in the Institute for Reformation History in the Protestant faculty, under the direction of the Dutch professor Heiko Oberman, and the Institute has become excessively large. Dr Krüger, called to the University of Münster that same year, writes to me: 'I haven't found it easy to settle down here. I came from an Institute which was very free and under personal leadership and had to fit into an anonymous faculty' (7 December 1971).

Very unpleasant and barren hours and days were wasted here. In these circumstances it was a delight a little later to travel to the most important industrial and commercial city in Scotland. On 23 June 1971 I was made a Doctor of Divinity by the University of Glasgow in a splendid academic ceremony of a traditional kind; a cap in the style of the Scottish Reformer John Knox was placed on my head. I am grateful to Allan Galloway, the dean of the divinity faculty, for emphasizing in his laudation my merits as a theological scholar: 'Hans Küng is a "troubler of Israel". But any theologian who is not drawn into a controversy from

116

time to time is either stupid or irrelevant. Hans Küng is neither ... The mass media are interested in a theologian only in so far as he generates heat (and Dr Küng has generated a great deal of that). But scholars are interested in him only to the degree that he sheds light (and he has shed far more of that).' That the Roman Catholic archbishop felt he had to leave the hall shortly before my doctorate was bestowed did more harm to him than to me. My brief commentary was: 'I am happy that the first British Catholic to be made a Doctor of Divinity by Glasgow University was the Archbishop of Glasgow; I am happy to be in his company.'

In the evening there was a big party in Newark Castle with around 200 people present. All the Scots, women and men, danced exciting Scottish dances well into the night. However, this didn't prevent me from taking a trip the next day into the peaceful Scottish Highlands, though under grey clouds: a mostly bare hilly landscape with lochs and glens, and the impressive Blair Castle.

One couldn't have imagined such a feast in Tübingen (the winter festival in the New Aula and the summer festival in the castle for the teaching bodies – valuable because of the greater personal contacts, going beyond all the faculties – had just been cancelled for fear of student demonstrations), nor so relevant and friendly a question-and-answer session with 600 people as that of the Scottish Catholic Renewal Movement. It seems that nowhere have people so deliberately and thoroughly given up good academic traditions as in the Federal Republic of Germany, to which unfortunately I have to return the very next morning – to the Catholic Academy in Munich, to give a lecture on 'The Church's Ministry of Leadership – Variables and Constants').

Join in, flee or stand firm?

When it comes to discussing university reforms in detail it's often difficult to decide whether to join in the game or to refuse to play. I am not prepared for my sphere to be invaded by rebellious and intolerant Marxists. My whole Swiss character instinctively rebels against being intimidated, humiliated or pressurized. When at the climax of the conflicts over the emergency laws in the summer semester of 1968 a threatening group of perhaps 50 rebellious students (mostly non-theologians) invades my lecture, shouting and whistling, and demands a discussion on the emergency laws, I gently push aside the young woman activist who wants to seize the microphone, hold it firmly and ask, 'Have you read the wording of the draft law?' 'No,' she replies. I ask the invaders, 'Who has read it?' No one says anything. 'Then we must read the proposed paragraphs before our discussion.' I take the text from my brief case and give the microphone to the student. Sullenly, she begins to read out the text of the law, in a rather boring and laborious way, but breaks off after a couple of minutes: 'It doesn't make sense,' she remarks. 'Then it doesn't make sense to discuss it here,' I say, and stop the lecture, since the rebels don't want to leave the lecture room.

I am annoyed only because I get hardly any support from my own students. They just sit there on their benches like the old Romans in the arena, watching the outcome of the battle of the gladiators, but only half-interested. I am furious that in Tübingen the academic freedom to teach is being trampled under foot in this way, and that the anti-authoritarians are so authoritarian. I announce that I shall not be giving any more lectures this semester – we are still about two weeks from the end of the semester – since academic freedom isn't guaranteed. I'm going to Switzerland for the summer vacation and if democratic conditions aren't restored, I won't be returning to Tübingen in the autumn.

Joseph Ratzinger has had similar unpleasant experiences and is probably even more furious than I am. But while 'Hans Küng with the blood-lust of a toreador opposed the disruptions and sought substantive discussion,' writes Hermann Häring, whom we have already met, an eyewitness at the time who is later my assistant and finally professor of dogmatics at the University of Nijmegen, the unrest had quite a different effect on Joseph Ratzinger: 'The gentle and somewhat shy professor had a hard time in the unrest, and couldn't defend himself against it. The whistles with which his lectures were interrupted must have seemed to him to be arrows piercing his body and mind. Certainly we felt compassion for him, but sometimes there was also a touch of *Schadenfreude*; we didn't know what was going on in his mind. He withdrew into himself, probably discussed the problems only in his most intimate circle, and sought profound answers with a theological significance – as befitted a theologian. For him, what happened there had something to do with the "spirit of this world", with the end of the West and a faith which was collapsing. Presumably he never understood, for example, that in the matter of the "student revolution" Küng was fundamentally on his side.'[5]

An attempt to democratize the student community

By way of explanation, I must add that Joseph Ratzinger was one of those succeeding me in the extremely uncomfortable office of dean during those turbulent times. So he had to endure far more sessions and meetings, provocations, aggressions and disruptions than I did. As dean in the Catholic student community in the summer semester of 1968, with his assistants he took on a strong group of students who wanted to establish a fundamentally democratic regime – the general assembly of the community of all Catholic students as the supreme decision-making organ. The student pastor would have only an advisory function and a veto only on liturgical and pastoral questions.

Before the public meeting held by the community-structure working group on 25 June 1968 to provide information, I am presented with an unofficial agenda headed 'neither complete nor in every instance verbatim'.[6] I can no longer reconstruct clearly what was presented by the student gathering and what was presented by Professor Ratzinger and his assistants. What is certain, though, is that the students didn't rely on Marxist arguments for the new statutes of the university community but, among other things, on my book *The Church*, which many students found to be a liberation. It is also certain that in this book I didn't see the foundation of the community in merely sociological terms, but theologically in the light of the preaching of the gospel and the celebration of the eucharist. Unlike the Protestant exegete Ernst Käsemann, I not only allow the validity of the charismatic order (for example on the model of the community in Corinth) at the present time but also reflect at length on the role of those appointed to office and the 'apostolic succession'. I am concerned with the collaboration of ministers and laity, something like checks and balances in the church, including the right of the laity to have a say in the election of pastors and bishops.

Be this as it may, when asked right at the beginning of this meeting of around 100 people what his intentions are, Professor Ratzinger declares to the students: 'Your intentions deviate from what Küng has written. But they coincide with it formally.' I could certainly have agreed with Ratzinger's replies about the essence and functions of the church as described in the minutes. But he insists more on the authority of the ministry in the episcopal church, whereas in the light of the New Testament I also affirm democratic elements. Ratzinger and I could presumably also have agreed on these, but apparently the discussion, to which I had not been invited, went off the rails and at the end the Rottenburg chancery had its say. Ratzinger didn't talk to me about this, but one can still hear from students of the time that he hadn't been a 'liberal' even at that time.

It is understandable that all these events put a great strain on Joseph Ratzinger. When the Greater Senate is violently invaded he packs his things in his briefcase and leaves the room, which colleagues from other faculties regard as capitulation. But now his mentality is trapped in a different way. Only decades later do I learn from one of my doctoral students, at that time an active opponent of this radical line, that Ratzinger suspected me and my ecclesiology of being secretly behind these people.

A trauma that Ratzinger couldn't cope with

I ask myself whether the violent events in Tübingen were perhaps the same kind of shock for Joseph Ratzinger as the violent invasion of the Munich nunciature in November 1918 by revolutionaries of the Communist Soviet Republic were for the papal diplomat Eugenio Pacelli. This man, also as Pope Pius XII, obsessed with a fear of physical contact and Communism, had a deeply authoritarian and anti-democratic attitude ('Führer' Catholicism), predisposed to pragmatic anti-Communist alliances with authoritarian governments.

How deep the violation of the psyche of Joseph Ratzinger, who later is to become the enemy of all efforts to democratize the church and of liberation theology, goes is evident from his memoirs. Even now, after around three decades, they bear witness to an almost apocalyptic anxiety. Individual events are generalized: 'I myself have seen the rightful face of this atheistic piety unveiled, its psychological terror, the abandon with which every moral consideration could be thrown overboard as a bourgeois residue when the ideological goal was at stake. All of this is alarming enough in itself; but it becomes an unrelenting challenge to the theologian when the Church is used as its instrument.' I have cited these words at the head of this chapter. Ratzinger adds: 'The blasphemous manner in which the Cross now came to be despised as a sign of sado-masochism, the hypocrisy with which some still passed themselves off as believers when this was useful, in order not to jeopardize the instruments that were to serve their own private ends: all of this could and should not be made to look harmless or regarded as just another academic quarrel. Since, at the height of these debates, I was dean of my faculty, a member of the Greater and Lesser Academic Senate, and a member also in charge of designing a new constitution for the university, I experienced all these things at very close range indeed.'[7]

Now there was beyond question a basic terrorism from critics of society intent on improving the world, and I resisted it. And there was also an ominous pamphlet which raised the charge of 'sado-masochism' against Käsemann's and Moltmann's theology of the cross from an 'anti-authoritarian' perspective: the product of the offspring of a Bonn professor of theology and previously Moltmann's academic assistant, transformed from theologian to social worker instead of being active socially in a pastorate – a case which is truly not just of passing interest. Certainly there were also a few theologians who became atheistic Marxists. And the Evangelische Stift of the Protestant students of theology at that time turned into a place of left-wing political activists and was later even declared a 'nuclear-free zone'; things calmed down only when Eberhard Jüngel, appointed to Tübingen in the year of Ratzinger's departure, combining friendliness and acidity in his sovereign way, took over the office of 'ephor' (supervisor).

But even in 1969 one could also see the whole student movement in a less lurid light than Joseph Ratzinger in his pessimistic crisis of anxiety. This is certainly fed by the dualistic view of history held by his teacher Augustine, who after the culture shock of the capture and plunder of allegedly 'eternal' Rome in 410 by the barbarian Goths interpreted the whole of world history in his giant work *The City of God* as a fight between the 'state of God' and the 'world state', belief and unbelief, power and love.

Struggle for the truth

But who would have had more reason to complain about psychological terrorism and moral abandon than the Rector of the university during the turbulent summer semester of 1968, Ludwig Raiser, an active Protestant Christian? On 13 January 1969 he endured a three-hour occupation of the Rectorate by 150 students without negotiating or calling the police, and then made himself available for a public debate in the Festsaal. In a kind of interim summing-up after the summer vacation he had attested in a letter to the member of the teaching body: 'Almost overnight we have a neo-Marxist teaching structure, a political concept of scholarship and a syndicalistic plebicistic understanding of democracy.' He also speaks of 'shocking forms in which the theses and demands derived from this are presented'. But he immediately adds: even if we regard the student interpretation of what is happening as 'one-sided and distorted, their future expectations as utopian, we should seek to understand that in the world-wide unrest of young people an age is announcing itself for which the traditional forms of life and modes of behaviour will no longer be adequate'.

The difference between Joseph Ratzinger and me is probably that he has turned away from the whole student movement with horror and abhorrence and refuses to engage in the local intellectual controversy. To this degree I must agree with Ludwig Raiser: 'Our responsibility as scholars and teachers compels us to join in the thinking here. Though the ideologically fixated minorities may only seek the opportunity to propagate their prejudices when they call for discussions, the task remains of helping the great majority, which is critically doubtful but not fixated, to form a well-founded judgement.' Indeed, our 'struggle for the truth, carried on in intellectual freedom and mutual respect, will also win over the young generation, if we involve them in it, better than violence and angry repudiation, better also than merely holding firm to authority and tradition'. In this last phrase was Raiser also thinking of Ratzinger?

Here at any rate I am thinking of another academic assistant, the 'revolutionary' Karl-Josef Kuschel from Bochum, whom I have already mentioned. Subsequently I could put my trust in him in the 'struggle for truth' and help him 'to form a well-based judgement'. He does sterling work in our Institute, in 1972 has excellent results in the state examination in theology and German studies, is accepted by me and Walter Jens as a doctoral student, and alongside the academic adviser Dr Hermann Häring, who is also responsible for the administration of the Institute, will prove a skilful and loyal collaborator in working out my book *On Being a Christian*, which I shall be discussing later. All that is the basis of a friendship, unbroken since then, which has now lasted for more than 30 years and continues to the present day. At the end of 1975 he will write to me: 'As we said goodbye yesterday in front of the Wilhelmstift, you remarked to me, "That was a good year." That moved me greatly and I have special occasion to be grateful. It was indeed a good year, collaborating with you on something I was enthusiastic about. I wouldn't have wanted to miss it. I simply want to tell you once again that I feel very much at home with you, in work, in all that we do, read, hear and write together. I am very fond of you and all those who work with me, Frau Gentner, Frau Renemann and Frau Dinkel, and above all also Herr Häring. That is what I wanted to tell you – you know how much I also enjoy working on the new book ... ' (13 December 1975).

Evidently Joseph Ratzinger had no such positive experiences with 'revolutionaries' and with the 'great majority which is critically doubtful but not fixated'. As his memoirs attest, the trauma he suffered in Tübingen as a result of the student movement will burden him for decades, and time and again make him resort to 'authority and tradition' in all controversies. That must be sufficient explanation of why the time of departure had now come for him.

Ratzinger's departure in 1969

Ratzinger and I had close contact with each other even in the difficult year 1968. For example, on 25 May 1968 we went with Ratzinger's sister Maria to the Staatsoper in Stuttgart and enjoyed brilliant performances of Adolphe Adam's ballet *Giselle* and Mozart's *Concerto for Flute and Harp*. Indeed in the summer of 1968 we even considered two or three days holiday together in my house on the Sempachersee. On 29 November 1968 there was a sociable gathering of the professors in Ratzinger's house after the faculty meeting and on 12 December another in my house. There was certainly no lack of good personal relations.

But shaken by his negative experiences in the student revolts, Ratzinger decides to leave Tübingen. This is made easy for him since he has a call to Regensburg in Bavaria up his sleeve; his brother is a canon there and the brothers and sister can live together. I know the theological college, lodged in the old Dominican house; it was there on 29 January 1959 that I had the honour and joy, on the initiative of Professor Georg Engelhardt, of giving my very first lecture at a German college (on 'Justification'). Only in 1967 did the theological college become the University of Regensburg – not to be compared, of course, with the University of Tübingen, now 500 years old (in the US, Ratzinger's step was compared with a move from Harvard to Idaho State University). When I hear of his call there I tell Ratzinger how important it is to me that he should stay in Tübingen; we should get together and consider what the ministry in Stuttgart could do for him – perhaps a third assistant. Ratzinger promises that he will get back to me.

But it is characteristic of him that he avoids conversation and a couple of days later writes me a letter in which he asks me to be understanding about his imminent departure from Tübingen. Perhaps he's afraid that I would put him under pressure to remain in Tübingen for at least another semester. After the twofold burden of teaching in Tübingen and Basle to cover Ratzinger's free research seminar, it would really have been understandable for my colleague not to burden me once again with the whole teaching load in the next semester. However, he doesn't want to stay but to start work in Regensburg immediately. A pity, I think. 'Ratzinger changes his chairs like shirts,' people mock in the German faculties and want to award the 42-year-old dogmatic theologian the 'Itinerant Prize for German Dogmatic Theologians' on his fourth change of chair.

'Serves Küng right,' remark some of my Tübingen colleagues in the faculty. 'Why did he want to have Ratzinger in the faculty?' But I regret that least of all. I remain convinced that in these three dramatic years I had the best possible colleague.

However, I also don't regret that I stayed in Tübingen and so can assimilate the events of 1968 constructively, unlike my colleague, who retreats into his Bavarian idyll. I personally have suffered no damage, at any rate no trauma in my career. Nor did I ever enter, as Ratzinger did, into an 'active alliance' and a 'friendship' with a Protestant theologian such as Peter Beyerhaus. My friend in the Protestant faculty – alongside Eberhard Jüngel, called to Tübingen rather later – is the systematic theologian Jürgen Moltmann. He thinks that student generations change every two or three years. And soon the whole horrific episode will be over. But was it only a horrific episode?

The end of the red decade

There is yet further agitation by the Marxist students who dominate the student bodies and there are further 'strikes', with pamphlets, banners and megaphones: against economy measures, abolition of posts, regulated times of study and student dues. The revolutionary activities lead to a growing gulf between the students and the townspeople. Those who gain in the fight for jobs between professors, assistants and students are the state authorities, who now increasingly limit the autonomy of institutions of tertiary education.

But at a very early stage it is clear that the student revolts will ultimately fail in their megalomaniac programme (the overthrow of society as a whole!). At the end of 1968 important decisions are made in wider politics. On 30 May Charles de Gaulle announces parliamentary elections in a radio address aimed at redirecting the conflict from the street into institutionalized courses – after a general strike, the collapse of public life and big Gaullist counter-demonstrations. The parliamentary elections at the end of July produce a clear vote against the chaos of the days in May. However, de Gaulle resigns as state president on 28 April 1969 after the failure of a regional reform.

On 29 May 1968 – despite all the protests – the German Bundestag passes the emergency laws, and this ushers in the collapse of 'extra-parliamentary opposition'. The active alliance between students, intellectuals and workers has failed. The Socialist German Student Federation (SDS) hasn't succeeded in transforming the emergency opposition into a permanent opposition movement. In August 1968 the dispute between the old and new Left escalates – over their different assessments of the invasion of Czechoslovakia by Warsaw Pact troops and the violent suppression of the 'Prague spring'. On 21 March 1970 the German Student Federation is officially dissolved because of insuperable differences of opinion. The American SDS (Students for a Democratic Society) is also at an end; it can no longer agree on aims, forms and opponents in the struggle.

The terrorist actions of urban guerrilla groups (the Red Army Faction in Germany, the Red Brigade in Italy) are also unacceptable to most Marxist students; since these have abandoned the moral basis of the 1968 movement. But Andreas Baader, a man who never completed his studies, and the pastor's daughter and former Tübingen student Gudrun Ensslin, with Ulrike Meinhof, founder of the RAF, who, as I have already mentioned, had set fire to two department stores in Frankfurt in April 1968 as a protest against the Vietnam War and 'consumer terrorism', are arrested and sentenced to three years imprisonment for attempted arson that endangers human life. Even more radical on their release, with around two dozen fighters they declare a state of war. Various attacks on banks and assassinations follow, until the Baader-Meinhof group is arrested in May 1972.

But a second RAF generation has already grown up. The climax comes in 1977. The federal advocate Siegfried Buback and his escort and later the Dresden Bank chief Jürgen Ponto are murdered on the streets, and the employers' president Hanns-Martin Schleyer is kidnapped. There are also Tübingen students who sympathize with the terrorist scene. That is evident on 16 May 1977, when the council of Protestant theological students sends a bouquet of flowers and a declaration of sympathy to 'dear Günter Sonnenberg', who is in the Tübingen Surgical University Clinic, severely wounded in an exchange of shots with the police after the murder of Buback. The General Students' Committee of the university immediately endorses this as 'morally and politically right'. There is unrest and indignation in the university and among the population and a dismayed declaration by the professors of the Protestant Faculty in the face of such 'intellectual confusion'. The matter is discussed for three days in the council of Catholic theological students and there is a very long paper on the results.

After all the murders of representatives of the state and business some fear a state crisis and a civil war. But Chancellor Helmut Schmidt, a consummate statesman, doesn't declare 'war' on this terrorist network, doesn't call up troops, and provokes no hysteria about security as George W. Bush did after 11 September 2001. The RAF wants to obtain the release of Andreas Baader and his accomplices from prison by hijacking a Lufthansa plane. Helmut Schmidt reacts in a moderate and appropriate way but clearly recognizes the moral dilemma. The state should rescue the hostages but shouldn't allow itself to be put under pressure; either way there will be deaths, and guilt cannot be avoided. The highjacking of the plane ends in Mogadishu with the death of three terrorists and the liberation of 86 passengers by a German special unit. Only a few hours after the announcement of the liberation of the hostages Schleyer is murdered, and the main terrorists – Baader, Ensslin, Raspe and Möller – commit suicide in Stammheim prison, Stuttgart (18 October 1977). Ulrike Meinhof had already committed suicide in Stammheim in May 1976.

In this way the 'red decade (1967–77)', which Gerd Koenen, Tübingen president of the Humanist Student Union, calls the 'little German cultural revolution', having begun with violence (the death of the student Benno Ohnesorg), also ended with violence. The same year sees the death in Tübingen, on 4 August 1977, of the philosopher Ernst Bloch, founder of a 'creative Marxism', who had made a brilliant reconstruction of the philosophical traditions under the universal 'principle of hope' and raised the fist of revolution in the Festsaal of the university in support of the students. Jürgen Moltmann echoed him strongly in his *Theology of Hope*, but philosophers didn't respond in the same way. As is shown by the biographies and articles on the centenary of his birth on 11 September 2003, the heritage of Theodor W. Adorno, who died at too early an age, is contradictory and on the whole has little promise for the future. I am glad that I attempted to learn from Bloch (in stimulating conversations and colloquia) and from Adorno (from his and Horkheimer's books) but haven't used either the one ('Bloch music') or the other ('Frankfurt School') for my theology.

Subsequently some 1968ers and their sympathizers become middle class. Some of them simply disappear and one hears no more of them. Others embark on the 'march through the institutions' and attain important positions in the world of the media, in education, in the trade unions and in politics; some even become ministers. When asked about their revolutionary past and errors, most of them reply that they did everything right in the situation of the time but now the situation has changed. They themselves have remained the same. They hardly notice that they have set in motion similar mechanisms of repression and concealment to those of which they accuse the former Nazis. An unreadiness to repent can appear in brown, black or red garb.

Thus even three decades later, the 'red decade' still needs to be assimilated and the RAF myth needs to be demystified (there was yet a third generation which between 1984 and 1993 murdered and likewise obstructed justice by a conspiracy of silence). The discussion which flared up in 2007 about early release or even pardon for the last unrepentant RAF members in prison for multiple murder oscillates between demonization and trivialization. A balanced assimilation of the events, developments and results at that time doesn't seem so easy, even for theologians.

Though I share many unpleasant experiences of these years with Joseph Ratzinger, I have tried to make creative use of them for my theology, my view of the world and my knowledge of people. If we leave aside the mad revolutionary ideas which automatically lead to the absurd, the political projects of a chimaeric world revolution and the fantasies and eruptions of violence, the 'dawn of the young intelligentsia', to use Michael Schmidtke's phrase, and the deliberate cultural revolution bring about a 'change in mentality' which like many others I would not want to be without – and which many continue to miss in Joseph Ratzinger:

- towards a new relationship to authority, tradition and institutionalized power;

- towards an emphasis on self-determination, political participation and involvement;
- towards a self-critical treatment by Germany of its history;
- towards toleration of others and interests in the wider context ('Third World');
- towards the relationship to nature and other spheres of life;
- towards relations between the sexes.

To this degree we contemporaries have all been stamped – positively or negatively – by 1968. It was in fact a thrust towards modernization that brought major progress both for the women's movement and for the ecological and peace movements (the later 'Green' party) and the solidarity movement with the Third World. Didn't Joseph Ratzinger leave Tübingen for a good Catholic Bavarian tranquillity too early? But some observers of the theological scene raise another question.

Was I wrong about him?

In his memoirs written in 1998 Joseph Ratzinger still speaks of my 'winning openness and straightforwardness which I quite liked' and a 'good personal relationship' in our time in Tübingen: 'I must say that at that point I felt closer to Küng's work than to that of J. B. Metz, who on my recommendation had been invited to Münster to occupy the chair in fundamental theology.'[8]

Joseph Ratzinger's departure from Tübingen is still something of a riddle to me. On 26 October 1969, now already a professor in Regensburg, he gives a fine farewell meal in the Krone Hotel in Tübingen for his old faculty, in the best of atmospheres. He also thanks me personally for our good collaboration. Only many years later do I read a report by Dr Karel Floss, a Czech philosopher whom I prize highly, still intensely interested in theology and the church, a translator and (after the opening up of the Eastern bloc in 1989) a senator, who had remained in contact with me and other Western theologians during the Communist regime and to whom I had sent many books. At the end of July or beginning of August 1969 he visits Joseph Ratzinger in Tübingen. Ratzinger receives him courteously but soon hands him over to his assistant Martin Trimpe, who spends the evening with him. Shortly after midnight, on a tower with an enchanting view of Tübingen by night, according to Floss's report there is an enigmatic conversation in which Trimpe tells Floss that the collaboration between Ratzinger and Küng is over. It has to be broken up for the health of both parties, since continued collaboration with Küng is impossible if Ratzinger and his colleagues are not to go completely to seed. Küng, Trimpe says, will increasingly make a name as a skilful journalist about whom no one will hear anything in 20 or 30 years. When Floss asks what Trimpe is driving at, he replies that Ratzinger is going to Regensburg, where Bishop Graber is willing to guarantee him all he needs for peaceful, honest scholarly work. For Floss that was a second shock, since he knew that all those conservatives who in Czechoslovakia, too, were terrified of the consequences of the Council and especially the rejection of strict Thomism, had sought refuge with Graber. Thus Karel Floss's report,[9] which very recently he confirmed to me in a letter: 'Every word from that night in Tübingen is deeply imprinted on my soul' (31 May 2006).

Now I am certainly the last person to put the midnight remarks of an assistant about his professor on the scales. And I have never taken seriously the charge of being a 'journalist'; it usually comes from colleagues who would like to write better and be read more, but have neither the gift nor the style. Ratzinger agreed with me in including my big book *The Church*, published two years previously and universally welcomed as honest scholarly work, in our series Ökumenische Forschungen, published by Herder. I don't know what my detrimental influence on Ratzinger's closest colleagues is meant to be, and this was never the object of my curiosity. As for the impossibility of further collaboration between Ratzinger and me, the assistant may have overdrawn or even caricatured the personality of his master – I don't know. The one thing that is certain is that Ratzinger retreated from Tübingen, beyond doubt in the front line of scholarship, into theologically well-behaved Regensburg and the province of a reactionary German bishop, representative of Marianism and curialism.

I got to know of this conversation only years later. And now one must put the question asked by another contemporary witness, Hermann Häring, academic adviser in our Institute for Ecumenical Research, soon to get his doctorate in theology, who in 1980 is to become Professor of Dogmatics in the University of Nijmegen as successor to Edward Schillebeeckx. By perceptive publications he has proved to be the greatest expert on Ratzinger's theology and a critical interpreter of it.[10] Häring's view is that I was badly wrong about Ratzinger. Not only did Ratzinger fail to note that I was basically on his side over the student revolts, but he clearly already differed from me in his interpretation of Vatican II. Granted, in 1968 he had signed the Declaration for the Freedom of Theology which in the end 1322 theologians from all over the world joined in signing, and also in 1969 a Tübingen declaration on the election of bishops and the limitation of their time in office, worked out not by me but by the church lawyer Johannes Neumann and other colleagues. But hardly had Ratzinger left Tübingen than he withdrew his signature from this second declaration, allegedly under pressure from his colleagues. Did he already see himself as a future bishop? Certainly Ratzinger couldn't have guessed that at an age when all the other bishops of the Catholic Church would have had to offer their resignation, he would be appointed Bishop of Rome, a position which (so far) is the only one not to have an age limit.

From the beginning of our time together in Tübingen I was aware that he had the chair of dogmatics and the history of dogma and I the chair of dogmatic and ecumenical theology. We each engaged in dogmatic theology from different backgrounds: Ratzinger from the Latin Middle Ages (Augustine–Bonaventure), I from the Middle Ages (Thomas Aquinas) but also from the Reformation (Luther), from modernity (Hegel) and from postmodernity (Barth). My hope was that we should not only supplement each other well but also learn from each other; that just as I was also intensively concerned with the theology of the church fathers and the Middle Ages, he would also be intensively concerned with the theology of the Reformers and present-day historical–critical exegesis. After all, in the end of the day both of us wanted to bring the Christian message to men and women of today, most of whom, even in his view, do not live their spiritual and religious lives in the Middle Ages.

So I am convinced, and recall that conversation with a Swiss Jewish woman in Jerusalem in which it was clear that christology is not just to be developed 'from above', from the incarnation of the Son of God, but also 'from below', from the man Jesus of Nazareth. That is how Jesus' disciples first perceived him and that is how we can perceive him today, before asking more deeply, 'Who is he?' Indeed, I was happy when during a lengthy conversation in my car in 1968 or 1969 Joseph Ratzinger accepted the possibility of a christology 'from below'.

But there, Häring thinks, I was likewise deceived. Presumably Ratzinger had thought that the attempt would itself demonstrate the failure of the concept of a christology 'from below'. In fact I am horrified when I see in book form the lecture series 'Introduction to Christianity' which he had given to a packed and attentive audience in the Auditorium Maximum. I note how he not only sees some articles of faith in the framework of the early church and the Middle Ages, but also how he evidently does not accept modern research into Jesus, caricaturing it out of all recognition and therefore doing the deepest injustice to exegetes such as Bultmann and Käsemann, without mentioning them by name. Here someone who can think very precisely writes broad generalizations, evidently out of deep emotion. Contrary to my original plan, already in *The Church* I had had to describe the proclamation of the kingly rule of God by the Jesus of history and had presented the proclamation of Jesus in the light of Bultmann on the one hand and the (truly orthodox) Catholic exegete Rudolf Schnackenburg on the other, establishing an important distinction between the two (*My Struggle for Freedom*, VIII: How a book comes into being). How can Ratzinger, I asked myself even then, so stray into misinterpretations and insinuations in the interpretation of the New Testament? After the event, this has become clearer to me: we dealt with the Bible in very different ways.

Is the Bible to be understood in a modern and critical way or traditionally and dogmatically?

How differently Ratzinger and I dealt with Holy Scripture was already evident in our Tübingen lectures, but I became aware of it only later. It is finally confirmed by his 2007 Jesus book, which builds on his earlier studies. Whereas in exegetical questions I always seek the consensus of professional exegetes and am generally restrained in disputed questions, in his lectures as a systematic theologian Joseph Ratzinger dares to interpret individual biblical passages in a very independent way – and uses the findings of professional exegetes selectively and arbitrarily. Certainly he affirms the historical–critical method in principle, but he is more than hesitant in applying it. Fundamentally his exegesis is governed by dogmatics. Even as a student, Joseph Ratzinger has an ambigous relationship with his generally admired teacher in New Testament exegesis, as he reports in his memoirs (*Milestones*, p. 53). Because of his use of the historical–critical method, this Friedrich Wilhelm Maier became a victim of the 'Modernist' hunt under Pius X, lost his chair, spent many years as an army and prison chaplain, and was only readmitted as professor in 1924, under the moderate Pope Benedict XV. It amazes the student Ratzinger that this man and priest of deep faith can never completely overcome the trauma of his dismissal and harbours a 'certain bitterness' towards Rome, which has neither regretted its wrong decision nor has ever openly and honestly corrected its own erroneous views about the Bible (p. 51). Will Ratzinger, passing such a cold-hearted judgement half a century later, ever understand what such unjust disciplining means for someone whose whole professional and intellectual existence and credibility it puts at risk?[11]

As is already heralded in his 1968 *Introduction to Christianity*, later in his contribution to a volume which he edits on 'The Conflict over Scriptural Exegesis' (1989),[12] Ratzinger paints a gloomy picture of the historical–critical method: 'Faith is not an element of the method nor God a factor of the historical event with which it reckons.' Historical criticism attempts to 'construct' the human history behind the biblical history of divine action. This is then to serve as the criterion for exegesis: 'No one can be surprised that in this procedure the hypotheses increasingly bifurcate and finally become a jungle of contradictions. In the end one hardly knows what the text says but only what it should say, and from what elements one can derive it' (p. 16). Critical exegesis recognizes neither 'the *analogia fidei*, i.e. the understanding of the individual texts in the light of the whole', nor the role of the church tradition and church ministry, 'which has the decisive say in the exegesis of scripture'. It builds up a false opposition: 'In the light of this one could say that exegesis is done either critically or through authority, but not both at the same time. To interpret the Bible "critically" means to leave an authoritative exegesis behind ... In no case can "tradition" be a criterion for exegesis. All in all, traditional exegesis is regarded as pre-scientific and naïve; it is only the historical–critical interpretation that appears as the real disclosure of the text' (p. 10). Beyond question, Ratzinger has decided for an exegesis of scripture in which 'the tradition' and in concrete the church's ministry has 'the decisive say'.

He accuses critical exegesis of philosophical prejudice and calls for a criticism of criticism (pp. 24-34). He thinks that critical exegesis emphasizes false discontinuities according to 'the dictate of a so-called modern or "scientific" view of the world which establishes what may be and what may not be' (p. 36). By contrast, according to Ratzinger, an exegesis orientated on the church must open itself to the action of God in history.

It is illuminating that in the same volume probably the most important Catholic New Testament scholar in the US, Raymond Brown, paints a completely different picture of historical–critical exegesis in relationship to church tradition.[13] According to Brown's description, critical exegesis is by no means godless and destructive, in no way closed to the tradition. With numerous examples he shows how the critical perception of the historical plurality of Holy Scripture can contribute in ecumenical dialogue to breaking up old oppositions and redrawing the biblical lines which have led to their origin, for example in the question of Mariology and the veneration of Mary.

I take the middle way sketched out by Brown between Ratzinger's uncritical traditionalism and an uncritical Protestant biblicism. For this reason I attempt to construct my theology on the basis of the consensus of professional exegetes. Occasionally I have been accused of advocating the normative authority not of scripture but of exegetes, but that is wrong. I am well aware that the views of exegetes can change. Even professional exegetes aren't infallible; even their results must be examined critically. Nevertheless, in many questions of biblical understanding a consensus of the exegetes can be established which has a firm and convincing methodological foundation. Even if such a consensus isn't unshakable, it is to be accepted by systematic theologians. They may deviate from it only as far as historical criticism takes them and then only with the utmost restraint. That post-biblical tradition and the magisterium interpret a passage differently can stimulate critical reflection, but does not justify a divergence from the state of modern historical–critical research. So much on our different positions.

But now Joseph Ratzinger is already in Regensburg and in Tübingen we never had an open conversation about all this, just as Joseph Ratzinger has never sought intensive conversations with Jürgen Moltmann, Ernst Käsemann or Ernst Bloch. Instead he preferred to talk with the outsider in the Protestant faculty, Professor Beyerhaus, or the lecturer Ulrich Wickert, a failed patrologist. Wickert is active as a Catholic systematic theologian and even wants to inflict his highly unbiblical Mariology on me. However, he is unable to convince me.

I leave aside the question whether in his *Introduction to Christianity* Joseph Ratzinger was really referring to me with his tale of the stupid 'Hans in luck' who keeps exchanging his lump of gold for increasingly worthless things (horse, cow, pig, goose, whetstone which finally falls into the well), as some follow Hermann

Häring in believing. Ratzinger has energetically denied this on various occasions. At all events, since I didn't feel involved, at the time I saw no occasion to protest against his caricature of a theology which allegedly 'underinterprets in stages the claim of faith which it feels to be oppressive'.

But perhaps I should have taken more seriously the fact that here a colleague in the faculty for whom I felt nothing but friendship is working with a technique of insinuation and a polemic of defamation which hardly allows him to recognize the truth of another position. And the question has been raised time and again: has Joseph Ratzinger fundamentally changed?

Who has changed?

Joseph Ratzinger has always disputed that he has changed; he has defended himself vigorously against the charge of his critics that he is a turncoat, and in his autobiography he strongly emphasizes the continuity. I think that he is relatively right to do so. In some respects one can say that, just as Ratzinger the professor went from Tübingen to Regensburg in 1969, so as Pope in 2006 he returned to Regensburg to lecture.

From the beginning to the present day Joseph Ratzinger has seen himself 'really at home' in traditional Bavarian Catholicism – as Benedict XVI's trip to Bavaria in 2006 has demonstrated to the world – a Catholicism which is 'deeply woven into the living culture of that land and its history'.[14] He saw and sees himself as a theologian of tradition, who persists essentially in the theological framework marked out by Augustine and Bonaventure. For him the 'early church' or the 'church of the fathers' is the measure of all things.

This is the early church as he understands it. He doesn't see Jesus of Nazareth as his disciples and the first Christian community saw him but as he was defined dogmatically by the Hellenistic councils of the fourth/fifth centuries, which in fact split Christianity more than they united it. The Jesus of history and the undogmatic Jewish Christianity of the beginning hardly interest him, so he also has no deeper understanding of Islam, which is stamped by their environment. Nor does he show much understanding for the diverse charismatic structure of the Pauline communities and the different possibilities of a 'succession of apostles', and also of 'prophets' and 'teachers'. He isn't interested in the church of the New Testament but in the church of the fathers (of course without mothers).

For Ratzinger, the early church is the church of the church fathers, more precisely of the Latin church fathers rather than the Greek, and not of those before the Council of Nicaea in 325 who still clearly subordinate the Son to the one God and Father (deemed the heresy of 'subordinationism') and know no 'original sin' bound up with the sexual act. Ratzinger doesn't see the relationship of Father, Son and Spirit as the Greek church fathers do, starting from the One

God and Father (that is why the Orthodox churches still regard the introduction of '*filioque* = and from the Son' into the creed as heretical). Rather, he follows the Latin Augustine, of whom the Greeks thought little, who unbiblically starts from a 'nature' of God common to three 'persons'. Augustine is responsible for the Western doctrine of original sin and theologically lays the foundations for the Middle Ages of the Roman Catholic Church.

All this confirms that Joseph Ratzinger is from the beginning, and as Pope still remains, a theologian of the Latin Roman Catholic paradigm of Christianity which in many points is opposed to that of the Hellenistic early church but, as I have said, reaches its climax in the first centuries of the second millennium under the Roman Popes. However, Ratzinger in Tübingen still takes very seriously the main reason for the split which continues to persist between the Greek Eastern Church and the Latin Western Church in the eleventh century, namely the Roman claim to absoluteness made by the Popes of the Gregorian reform in the eleventh century. He is fond of citing Pope Gregory the Great, who vigorously rejects the 'blown-up title of universal Pope', which 'attributes the universal' to the Bishop of Rome at the expense of the other bishops. Ratzinger comments on this: 'Must not the dialogue with the Eastern church immediately reach quite a different stage if this text . . . is again taken completely seriously and the form of relationship is determined by it?'[15]

In his last series of lectures on ecclesiology in Tübingen he has even put forward the position that the Eastern churches can be committed only to those councils in which they took part; indeed that they would have to recognize the papal primacy only in its first-millennium form, without the Roman absolutism of the eleventh century, which led to the split between East and West. Thus he can still say after 1982: 'Rome must demand from the East no more than the doctrine of primacy that was formulated and lived out in the first millennium.'[16] If only he had said this to the Ecumenical Patriarch Bartholomew I on his visit to Istanbul in 2006! Instead, he again put forward courteously in a disguised way – of course without success – the medieval ideal of a papal church which rules the world at least spiritually by its monopoly of the truth, a church which after Vatican I called for the submission of Eastern Christianity, too, to the Pope's claim to primacy (which it had always rejected) and his infallible magisterium. He could have gone further, but didn't want to. Why?

Stand still – or move forward

What comes after the Middle Ages historically interests Joseph Ratzinger less as a fruitful further development than as a pernicious false development and phase in the decline of the West. For him the Protestant Reformation is the beginning of apostasy from the true 'Christianity of the fathers', characterized in predominantly negative terms in his 2006 Regensburg lecture as 'de-Hellenization', whereas in fact it represents a reform of the medieval church, which had become decadent, by a return to the gospel.

And his view of the world is especially shaped by his predominantly polemical grappling with modernity, with modern philosophy and a secular view of society and the state. Only one 'enlightenment' is really acceptable to him, the classical Greek enlightenment. He regards the clothing in Greek dress of a message which comes from the semitic sphere as a divine dispensation of such a kind that no other dress is either necessary or legitimate. The secular Enlightenment of the seventeenth/eighteenth centuries is unacceptable to him; in that Regensburg lecture which declares Hellenism to be the maxim of all that is authentically Christian he dismisses it all the more as 'de-Hellenization'. For him, even as Pope, modernity is essentially – after the alleged apostasy of the Reformation from the church – apostasy from Christ, then even from God and finally from humankind, as the catastrophes of modern times, which this theologian of the early church regards with horror, seem to him to prove.

And he must also regard with horror what happened to him – as a consequence of this development – in the student revolts in Tübingen in 1968 which confirms him in his pessimistic view of the world. Here, as he writes by hand in the Regensburg Faculty Book in February 1977 (it can be read in the authorized internet documentation of the Faculty of Catholic Theology), he experienced 'the upheaval in the life of church and state, the student revolts and their parallels within the church, so to speak at one remove'.

In this sense Joseph Ratzinger hasn't changed. It's quite fair to say that he has simply stood still. He wanted to stand still – with the Latin early and medieval church and theology which he had got to know and love in his studies through Augustine and Bonaventure and on his way up the hierarchy. The theologian Ratzinger has contributed little himself to theology even in his book on Jesus. Nor would he probably claim to have done so. In this respect he is of course right when he says that it is not he but I who have changed. In fact I didn't want to stand still, but to move forward.

In the logic of Vatican II

I don't dispute that I've changed. Not only have I thoroughly studied the councils of the early church, Augustine's doctrine of the Trinity and of grace and Thomas Aquinas, but in my student years I also tackled Reformation theology in the person of Karl Barth, the figure of the century. Moreover I was introduced by the Gregorian in Rome and the Sorbonne in Paris, presumably more con-structively than Ratzinger in Munich, to modern philosophy, especially Descartes, Kant, Hegel and Sartre, so that I ventured a brief work on Sartre's humanism and a major work on Hegel's christology. Thus at an early stage I got to know the positive side of modernity, which also cannot simply be from the

133

devil. There is an enlightenment which, like the early Greek one (by no means only pious), could likewise be a 'dispensation' and theologically at any rate needs to be taken as seriously as the Middle Ages and the Reformation. However, I also had to learn where the inhumane frontiers of modernity lie and how after the First and Second World Wars a new paradigm shift to postmodernity begins.

Hermann Häring, who as a student and assistant in Tübingen had both Ratzinger and me as teachers and later analysed both our theologies more precisely than any one else,[17] is right when he observes than the reformers at the Council, and I in particular, did not simply stand still at Vatican II but continued to move forward. We were led to that by the Council with its compromises, half-measures and ambiguities. In this respect I have in fact regarded my books *The Church, On Being a Christian, Does God Exist?* and *Eternal Life?* as taking the Council forward critically and constructively. In my later trilogy *Judaism, Christianity* and *Islam*[18] I have analysed precisely the paradigms of Christianity which I addressed briefly above in the context of the two other Abrahamic religions and here in particular I have given a comprehensive description of the original Jewish–Christian paradigm which Ratzinger hardly takes into account.

Of course all this was a tremendous labour of historical research and critical and self-critical reflection which took decades. In 1958 Joseph Ratzinger committed himself to writing a dogmatics. But he stopped at individual drafts in the hope of a synthesis. And when in spring 1977 he was nominated Archbishop of Munich, this dogmatics had not yet taken shape; only a brief treatise 'On the Last Things', originally Tübingen lectures, was prepared in Regensburg and published in 1977. In addition to that, Ratzinger can publish only brief elaborations, predominantly reviews and lectures, meditations and sermons. Later he will complain that – because he is 'in the service of the church' – he has no academic *oeuvre* to show after his doctorate and habilitation theses. And he is glad at the age of 80 to be able to present the first part of a more spiritual and meditative study of Jesus of Nazareth, which fundamentally he could already have written in Tübingen.

Yes, I concede that I've changed and feel it an honour when Hermann Häring applies to me Bert Brecht's famous story about seeing Herr Keuner again. A man whom Herr K. hasn't seen for a long time greets him with the words, 'You haven't changed.' 'Oh,' says Herr Keuner, and goes pale. Of course I haven't changed in the sense of an inner 'logic of development' of my consciousness and social learning as described in developmental or educational novels. Rather – if one wants a comparison at all – I've changed more as in political, historical or social novels, which react above all to external developments and upheavals. So initially I change – of course at the same time pursuing theological research – in response to the impulses of the Second Vatican Council, or, as Cardinal Suenens, one of the four Council moderators, used to say, '*dans la logique de Vatican II*'. But time and again I am also provoked by the contrary experiences that the Catholic church community has with the post-conciliar (or better pre-conciliar) Roman

Curia. And that applies above all to the great controversial question of infallibility, which has emerged in 1968 from the Pope's encyclical against contraception.

However, fortunately in the life of a professor of theology there are not only such big questions but, as with everyone, also the 'small' everyday questions. In this respect, too, in 1968 I had to make some by no means unimportant decisions which I must report before I go on to speak about the great enquiry, *Infallible?*.

Decisions for housekeeping and secretarial work

I feel increasingly ill at ease in my basically attractive house in Gartenstrasse, which is now being developed into a wide through road. There is more traffic, more noise, and above all, so near to the Neckar, always more mist than in the higher areas of Tübingen. And now the city tennis courts are being laid out directly below my house. I have a couple of weeks' coaching there but don't find it as easy to go straight back and sit at my desk, feeling fresh, as I do after swimming. Moreover the constant noise of the tennis balls disturbs me, since as often as possible I work outside on the small veranda. And, I think to myself, why should I spend tens of thousands of Deutschemarks over the years in rent instead of investing the money in a house of my own, even if at first I would be in debt?

One day an attractive 'rustic house in the best area of Tübingen' is advertised in the *Schwäbisches Tagblatt*. Well aware that dozens of people will be interested, I write immediately and on the front of the envelope containing my letter put, 'Away after Thursday, please let me know as soon as possible.' Things turn out as I expect. This envelope catches the attention of the owner, he sees who has sent it, and invites me to view the house on the Wednesday. It's a very attractive house and tailored to my needs. I have to travel to Switzerland on the Thursday; my parents make me an interest-free loan, and on my return I sign the contract, on 13 December 1967. In Easter Week, April 1968, I very happily move up to Waldhäuser Strasse, which is then still very narrow and bordered by bushes. It's a completely new feeling to have a garden, light rooms and a sun terrace to the south. Waldhaüser Strasse 23 is still my address.

A change has also become necessary in my domestic arrangements. It is proving increasingly impossible for one and the same person to cope with the house-keeping and the secretarial work. Because of my intensive academic and jour-nalistic activities far beyond Germany the correspondence has steadily grown and its linguistic demands have become more complex. Even so capable and obliging a woman as Odette Zurmühle can't cope. Having suffered from tuberculosis from her youth, she has again fallen ill and on 1 November 1967 returns to her native Switzerland, where she resumes her original activity as a teacher. I haven't for-gotten her great services during my first period in Tübingen.

At my request my old Dutch friends, with whom I keep in regular contact, now make a smooth transition possible. Inka Klinckhard and her mother bridge the weeks in Tübingen and also organize the move to Waldhäuser Strasse 23. There Dr Margret Gentner takes over my secretariat. My first housekeeper is a middle-aged Tübingen woman, but after a year she has become such a burden on me with her discontent at her own life and her constant sighing, lamenting and gloomy face that, despite her competent work in the house and garden, on 10 March 1969 I replace her with Charlotte Renemann. At that time 67 years old, Frau Renemann is an affirmative, open woman from Wilhelmshaven, the mother of three successful sons. She has a feeling for intellectual work, and for a decade (up to her death on 26 February 1979) with great dedication and an easy manner she helps me to make our house a happy and hospitable home.

From the beginning to the present day it has eased my work tremendously that my personal secretariat has always been in my home. In the Institute for Ecumenical Research in Nauklerstrasse, from 1965 onwards Annegret Dinkel serves as Institute secretary alongside the academic adviser, Dr Hermann Häring. She lives close by and so brings the Institute post every day on her journey there or back. All who have worked with us in the Institute over the years have the happiest memories of the cheerful parties that we had in my house or in the Institute and also the annual expeditions which I have mentioned. According to the Greek philosopher Democritus, a life without feasts is a long journey without an inn.

I can never be sufficiently grateful to all the women who have supported me over the decades in joy and sorrow and have actively been involved in my various tasks. Each of them in her own way has ensured friendly 'foreign relations', both with my assistants and academic aides and also with many visitors from Germany and abroad; even the postmen and craftsmen like coming to our friendly house. I have devoted a small 'memorial tablet' especially to my secretaries in my book *Women in Christianity*.

It also seems to me to be a stroke of providence that in 1968 I could move into an attractive rural house and reorganize my life and work. For I would never have guessed the dimensions that the dispute over the truth would assume in the next decade.

IV

Infallible?

'Jesus would not have understood any of it.'

The theologian Karl Rahner on the infallibility definition of Vatican I,
Der Spiegel, *28 February 1972*

It goes without saying that the dispute over the truth inevitably came to a head the moment a public authority in modern society claimed at least in certain instances to be able to formulate the truth *infallibly*, a priori free of error, i.e. in such a way that the statement cannot be false and consequently never needs to be corrected. The First Vatican Council did precisely this in 1870 in a solemn declaration, despite the opposition of many important bishops. The Bishop of Rome, if he makes a final decision on the basis of his highest apostolic authority as the supreme teacher of Christianity that a doctrine about faith or morals is to be maintained by the whole church, possesses infallibility on the basis of divine support, so that such decisions of the Bishop of Rome are intrinsically (*ex sese*) unchangeable and irreformable, and not based on the assent of the church.[1]

Infallible decisions by the Pope in 'the supreme exercise of his office'? No court in the world, not even the Supreme Court of the United States of America, attributes such *suprema auctoritas* to itself. This is a tremendous challenge for the modern world and also for many thoughtful Catholics. The Second Vatican Council extended the infallibility of the Pope to the College of Bishops without discussion. Famous test cases for the new infallibility are Pope Pius XII's 1950 definition of the bodily assumption of Mary into heaven and Paul VI's encyclical *Humanae vitae* against birth control. For me this is the occasion for my book *Infallible? An Enquiry*, published in 1970.

Not just theology

The year 1969 ends badly for me, but the year 1970 begins well. Exhausted by completing my book *The Incarnation of God*, on Hegel's christology, and much more, on 21 December I fly to America. The Catholic University of Chicago wants to award me an honorary doctorate in the humanities at the beginning of 1970. To go to Switzerland for Christmas ceremonies as usual would be too complicated, so I decide to go to America via the Caribbean, which has long fascinated me, in order to spend some peaceful sunny days in Jamaica. This Commonwealth country, which has been independent from Great Britain only since 1962, with a population 97 per cent of which are black or of mixed race, is of special interest to me.

But I find the long transatlantic flight to New York, the connecting flight of again almost five hours to Jamaica's capital Kingston, and finally the car journey across the island to the north coast, to peaceful Ocho Rios near Montego Bay, very trying. When I walk into the village the next day from my hotel, built in white British colonial style and run in the traditional English way, a strong feeling of nausea overwhelms me. I break into a fever. I return to the hotel immediately and am confined to bed for several days, providentially looked after by a couple from Zurich who have travelled with me, Dr Werner Bubb, a doctor who works for Lufthansa, and his wife. As I look time and again through my window at the same tall palm trees swaying gently in the wind, I recall the famous title of a book by the French ethnologist and founder of structuralist anthropology, Claude Lévi-Strauss, *Tristes tropiques*, 'sad tropics'.

But here I also get to know the more friendly side of the tropics. After four days I am back on my feet. At dinner every evening the three of us hear the marvellously monotonous and at the same time exciting sound of reggae, which combines the popular dance music of Jamaica (such as the calypso) with rhythm and blues; I am still fond of 'Banana Boat Song' by Harry Belafonte, the Jamaican born in New York in 1927 and later deeply involved in the peace movement.

During the day I can now continue my work, which is also my hobby, on the white sandy shore, together with regular swimming in the deep blue water; lengthy periods of idleness bore me. When I have to revise material that I've already worked out laboriously I regard it as a game, as this is. At the request of many Catholic and Protestant Christians I reshape the 600 large pages of my book *The Church* into an easily understandable short version of about 250 small pages with as many sub-headings as possible – without hermeneutical reflections and exegetical arguments, historical considerations and practical applications, without quotations from Vatican II and excursuses, footnotes and bibliography. What is decisive about the nature of the church is to be said under the title 'What is the Church?', to bring out programmatically what the church should be today: how far it is to remain what it is and how far it is to become what it isn't at present.

The book is to be published simultaneously by the Catholic Herder Bücherei and the Protestant Siebenstern Taschenbuch Verlag, 'perhaps a sign', as I write in the foreword, 'that the dawn has finally begun to break between the two theologies'. This short version – I have no illusions – aims at making 'a small contribution towards bringing the ecclesiastical–confessional systems entrenched on both sides and their representatives along with their theologies into the ecumenical movement more quickly and energetically than hitherto'.

The days of this working holiday fly past and I avoid becoming 'tropicalized', like our hotelier, much as I enjoy the Planter's Punch made out of Jamaica rum which is offered free of charge at noon on the shore. I just join a plantation tour to see the island. Well warmed and refreshed, on 6 January I fly via Miami to cold Chicago.

Interdisciplinary work in practice

On 7 January 1970 the celebration of the centenary of the Catholic University of Chicago, Loyola University, takes place in the Grand Ballroom of the Drake Hotel on Michigan Avenue by Lake Michigan, rich in tradition. It is only a few years since I spoke in Chicago for the first time on the topic of 'Church and Freedom', a topic which at that time was taboo. Now the theme of the whole centennial symposium is 'Freedom and the Humanities'.

The most important speech is given in the morning on 'The Scientific Profession and Degrees of Freedom' by one of my fellow candidates for an honorary doctorate, the physicist and novelist Lord Snow, who with his lecture on 'The Two Cultures and the Scientific Revolution', published in 1950, had sparked off a long discussion on the breakdown of communications between the sciences and the humanities. Now Snow is speaking on the freedom of intellectuals, who in principle can decide where, when and how they work and what they work on. The man speaks to me from the heart. Even if after 1968 the aura of the professor has disappeared, the university professor still is and in fact remains something of a dream profession. However, I must immediately add that this freedom calls for a great sense of responsibility, self-discipline and a desire to achieve. There are also colleagues who settle themselves comfortably into their positions, constantly repeat themselves in their lectures and don't produce any major works. But if one makes use of this academic freedom, one can seek the truth in research and teaching with a love of scholarship and no cares about existence, and share one's insights with others.

The academic convocation for bestowing honorary degrees takes place that afternoon on the campus of Loyola University on Lake Michigan. I am proud that this time I am being given a doctorate not in theology or law, but in humane letters. Of course I am highly delighted as a theologian to be singled out with such an illustrious group of colleagues of different disciplines: with the sociologists Peter Berger and Michael Polanyi, the psychotherapist Viktor Frankl, the philosopher Paul Feyerabend and the linguist Noam Chomsky. The most entertaining time is a conversation with the Austrian behavioural scientist and Nobel prize-winner Konrad Lorenz, focusing on the collaboration between innate and acquired elements in the behaviour of higher animals and the 'ethological shaping' that he has discovered. I know people who are more at ease with a well-trained dog than with other human beings; dogs are less complicated, more honest, reliable, obedient – one just has to find the right one. Hence also the effort to breed dogs with appropriate appearance and character. When I talk to Konrad Lorenz about his book *Man Meets Dog* (1950), he explains to me in some detail how he is attempting to breed the ideal dog from the two primeval strains of wolf and hyena – so far without success. I tell him that unfortunately I can't treat myself to a dog; the poor 'companion for life' at my side would have to spend far too much time alone.

Towards the evening of the day after the great celebration, after a ceremonial banquet, I fly to nearby Urbana, the state capital, where I give a lecture on 'Church and Truthfulness' to the giant University of Illinois. I am looked after – the world is a small place – by a professor from my home town of Sursee, the famous and knowledgeable Romance scholar François Jost, with whom I discuss God and the world well into the night. The next morning I return to Chicago. There in the afternoon I appear on the much-watched 'Kup's Show', which has a national audience. The presenter Kup (Irv Kupcinet) confronts each of the three partners in the conversation with their special interests: Norman Vincent Peale with the 'positive thinking' that he propagates ('Change your thoughts and you change your world!'), Charlton Heston with his portrayals of Ben Hur and Moses in the American blockbusters (he loses my sympathy later when as President of the National Rifle Association he serves the interests of the gun lobby). And of course the presenter asks me about the reform of the Catholic Church and prospects for ecumenism.

In my meetings with personalities from the most varied spheres of life, with clever and original contemporaries, I feel less inclined to talk about my own concerns than to listen and learn. My world doesn't just consist of 'religion' nor my scholarship just of 'theology'. The more time goes on, the less I am in danger of becoming a 'specialist idiot' instead of the master of a discipline, 'specialist idiot' being one of the great insults used by the 1968ers of professors who didn't in principle grapple with problems going beyond their specialist areas. Over the coming years much will be written and discussed about interdisciplinary studies. I have written little about them but practised them from an early stage. It would be impossible to list all the colleagues from other spheres of knowledge with whom I have collaborated actively, in seminars and doctoral colloquiums, symposiums and congresses. The guest speakers listed in the reports of the Institute for Ecumenical Research of the University of Tübingen under my direction (1964–96) alone number 170. And when later the Rector of the university invites me in a gathering of emeriti to give a report on my five decades at the University of Tübingen, I can describe my whole scholarly development through the names of colleagues from all the faculties from whom I have been able to learn over the years – not to mention the numerous colleagues in the wider world whom I had the pleasure of appreciating at guest lectures or guest semesters.

It strikes me all the more that in theology we have remarkable internal problems of a kind that are not to be found in the secular world. No one elsewhere would ever arrive at the idea of claiming infallibility. On the contrary, as my former Tübingen colleague Ralf Dahrendorf, now EC Commissioner, told me, even in the Supreme Court in Washington, which makes final judgements as the supreme legal authority, judges with different opinions often take some time to arrive at a verdict.

On 9 January in Chicago I give the final paper in the symposium on 'Freedom in the Church: Is the Church Infallible?' This is a problem which doesn't exist in other disciplines. Three hours later I return home via London and Amsterdam. And to theology.

The truth in truthfulness

One day a brief note circulated in the Council hall of Vatican II. It contained a single sentence, with no indication of where it came from, but it conjured up a knowing mischievous smile on the face of all the bishops who read it: '*Senatus non errat, et si errat, non corrigit, ne videatur errasse* – The senate does not err, and if it errs, it does not correct, so that it does not seem to have erred.'

Already in the lectures on moral theology at the Gregorian in Rome I had been struck by an excessive overvaluation of the sixth commandment and a strange undervaluation of the eighth. In the sixth commandment on sexuality there was no *parvitas materiae*; there were no slight sins but only intrinsically grave ones. The position with the eighth commandment on truthfulness was the opposite; there were only slight sins, unless the circumstances were grave. It then struck me even more at the Council how often in the discussions 'the truth' was put forward in an untruthful way. Thus basic attitudes such as freedom and truthfulness in the church itself seemed to me to be more important than any possible instructions to men and women 'in today's world', especially where sexuality and marriage are concerned. Therefore towards the end of the Council I give my first lecture on the church and truthfulness to bishops, theologians and journalists, and it is widely reported in the press.

To present the truth in truthfulness: any claim of the church to truth is repudiated if it is presented with lies or mendacity. Even decades later I cannot find fault with anything in my lecture on the church and truthfulness, though Fr Henri de Lubac rebuked me the next morning in St Peter's on the basis of a report in *Le Monde*: 'One doesn't speak like that about the church; after all, she's our mother – *c'est quand même nôtre mère*.' During those years truthfulness will remain an important theme, in scholarly work and in lectures. Here I am concerned to see the church less as 'mother' (in Rome at all events, it is not the church of Jerusalem but the *ecclesia Romana* that is propagated unhistorically as the 'mother of all churches'). I understand the church, as rediscovered by Vatican II, as the 'people of God' and '*communio*': as a great communion of believers whose servants are or should be the Pope, bishops, priests and theologians.

My basic Roman lecture with expansions appears in September of that same year, 1968, as a book under the title *Truthfulness. The Future of the Church*. The church's imprimatur from the chancery of my home diocese of Basle is given on 17 August 1968. I am able to react to the encyclical *Humanae vitae*, which bears the date of 25 July and appears in August, both in the preface and with a reprint of my 'Word on Sunday' on Swiss television to which I have already referred. But a fundamental question is at issue here.

Dealing honestly with errors

'*Errare humanum est* – to err is human.' That is a piece of old Roman wisdom, which hardly anyone will dispute in everyday life. And indeed one is regularly advised, not least in sermons, to concede as soon as possible errors that one has made. That also applies to serious historical errors of peoples which have resulted in great crimes. One thinks of National Socialism and its crimes against humanity, but also of Turkish nationalism or Japanese militarism. Other great European nations such as France find it difficult to assimilate their historical guilt. And the incomprehensible guilt which the Bush administration (together with Israel) has brought upon itself through its aggressive imperialistic policy in Afghanistan, in Iraq, in Palestine and in Lebanon has destroyed a great deal of the moral credibility of the United States and will burden US policy for years.

Of course one can also accuse Christianity of every possible mistake and error, of crimes and vices, false developments and signs of decadence. Even conservative defenders of the church's status quo today can no longer dispute serious errors of the church's magisterium all down the centuries. So to speak classical errors are now largely conceded, though their importance is often minimized or ignored, for fear of the authority of the magisterium. There are a wealth of examples: the excommunication of the Ecumenical Patriarch of Constantinople, Cerularius, and the Greek church, which formally marked the split with the Eastern church that has now lasted almost 1000 years. Or the prohibition of levying interest at the beginning of modern times, when the church's magisterium changed its view far too late, after manifold compromises. Then there are the condemnation of Galileo and corresponding measures which are essentially responsible for the alienation of the church from science which hasn't been overcome even now. There is also the condemnation of culturally adapted forms of worship and names of God in the Rites Dispute, which is a main reason for the widespread failure of the Catholic mission in modern times in India, China and Japan. Until the First Vatican Council and the capture of Rome by Italian troops (20 September 1870) there is the preservation of the medieval secular power of the Pope with every possible worldly and spiritual means of excommunication, which largely robbed the papacy of credibility as a spiritual service. And finally, at the beginning of the twentieth century, there are the numerous condemnations of the new historical–critical exegesis of the biblical authors, research into the sources of Old and New

142

Testaments, historicity and literary genres, the *comma Johanneum* (the trinitarian supplementation of 1 John 5.7 added only in the fourth century), the Vulgate. And there are also the condemnations in the dogmatic sphere, especially in connection with 'Modernism' (the theory of development and the understanding of the development of dogma) and some years later with Pius XII's encyclical *Humani generis* against the 'errors of the time' (1950), and the church disciplinary measures which accompany it. An infinite amount of human suffering is associated with these self-righteous actions of a church leadership which is often both ignorant and arrogant.

And it isn't just to err that is human, all too human. Another human, truly human capacity, which animals do not have, is to learn deliberately from mistakes. Anyone who doesn't want to learn from mistakes is condemned to deny or repress them, with all the negative consequences. When in 1971 the Marxist philosopher Ernst Bloch massively corrected articles from the 1930s about the Stalin show trials in which he identified Marxism with morality but did not draw attention to his corrections and concede his errors, it did him enormous damage. Nor did Martin Heidegger concede error when in 1953 he produced a new edition of his 1935 *Introduction to Metaphysics* without correcting his remarks about the inner truth and greatness of the National Socialist movement.

Finally, not only Popes have difficulty in openly and honestly conceding errors. In Rome errors are usually corrected only 'implicitly', in a concealed way, without candour. Of course the question becomes extremely explosive for Catholics in the case of a dogma defined as infallible according to the doctrine of Vatican I. I experienced this unique event personally in St Peter's Square in 1950.

Marian dogma – even against one's better judgement

I certainly hadn't argued with Joseph Ratzinger in the refectory of the German College over the Marian dogma proclaimed by Pope Pius XII on 1 November 1950 when he had come to us in Rome that year with other German theological students. At that time I was a convinced supporter of this dogma. Rather, he had argued with his own Munich faculty, in which 'the atmosphere was a few degrees cooler' (*Milestones*, p. 58): people there had great reservations about it.

The 'small episode' related at length by Ratzinger (pp. 58f.) is illuminating. It immediately makes clear the practical relevance of the question of the understanding of dogma which at first seems theoretical. In the 1940s, under Pius XII, the dogma of the 'bodily assumption of Mary into heaven' was propagated with all the means of propaganda and church politics – what Cardinal John Henry Newman called a 'luxury dogma', such as that of the 'immaculate conception of Mary' (1854). Like the bishops, the theological faculties all over the world are asked for their judgement – of course in the hope of a positive answer. But the answer from Ratzinger's Munich faculty is 'emphatically negative' (p. 58). And there are good reasons for this. For, as even Ratzinger recognizes, in a scrupulously documented article, the Würzburg professor of patristics, Berthold Altaner – author of the handbook *Patrology*, which is basic to knowledge of the 'teaching of the fathers' and has also been translated into other languages – 'proves in a scientifically persuasive manner that the doctrine of Mary's bodily assumption into heaven was unknown before the fifth century; this doctrine therefore, he argued, could not belong to the "apostolic tradition". And this was his conclusion, shared by the teachers in Munich'; hence the answer to the Roman enquiry about a new Marian dogma was 'emphatically negative'.

At the Gregorian we too read Altaner's article attentively. But our Roman teachers, who have been involved in the formulation of the new doctrinal document, immunize us against historical criticism with precisely the same argument that Ratzinger repeats in his *Milestones* (in fact it comes from the nineteenth-century Catholic Tübingen school and from John Henry Newman, as Walter Kasper has described precisely in his Tübingen dissertation). The criticism of the new dogma, so Ratzinger too now argues, is based on an approach which is not only historical but historicist. One may not identify tradition with what is attested in texts; because of this view of the 'overlap of revelation over scripture' Ratzinger had had his habilitation thesis rejected by the Munich faculty (cf. Prologue, note 4). The consequence is that even if there is nothing about a particular doctrine or history in the Bible and it is completely unknown for half a millennium, indeed even if like the legend of Mary's ascension it appears first only in an apocryphal fifth-century writing addicted to miracles, it can nevertheless be a truth of faith revealed by God.

In autumn 1950, in my third year of philosophy already under the influence of certain Roman dogmatic theologians, I too will have nothing to do with historical objections to the new dogma. And those German theological students who come to Rome and have lunch in the college to celebrate the promulgation of the dogma in 1950 seem to me to be being hindered by their 'rationalist' or 'historicist' professors from attaining true knowledge, namely that such a dogma has 'developed' over the centuries under the influence of the Holy Spirit slowly, slowly, quasi 'organically' from a 'kernel'. It is asserted that Mary's ascension to heaven is already 'implicitly', 'inclusively', contained in the address of the angel in the Gospel of Luke to 'Mary full of grace'. Ratzinger could also have said that.

Joseph Ratzinger maintains this standpoint, which is shared neither by the old Orthodox churches of the East nor by the churches of the Reformation nor by the critical theologians of the Latin church. However, for me the promulgation of this dogma in 1950 was not the end but the starting point of further reflection. For precisely the experiences of my seven years in Rome and the assent of faith required even to 'non-infallible' papal statements of doctrines, for example in encyclicals, make me ask: does one really have to assent to every dogma proclaimed by the church – in some circumstances against one's better judgement?

Ratzinger decisively affirms precisely this. In so doing he refers to his doctorate supervisor Gottlieb Söhngen, who while thinking in the light of the sources, always with great earnestness also put the question of the truth and thus also the present-day context of what is believed. As late as 1949, a year before the definition of the Marian dogma, Söhngen spoke passionately against the possibility of such a dogma in a top-flight ecumenical group. He was then asked by the Protestant Heidelberg systematic theologian Edmund Schlink (who later confirmed this to me in precisely the same words): 'But what will you do if the dogma is nevertheless defined? Won't you have to turn your back on the Catholic Church?' After reflecting for a moment, Söhngen replied: 'If the dogma comes, then I will remember that the church is wiser than I am and that I must trust her more than my own erudition.' Ratzinger thinks 'that this small scene says everything about the spirit in which theology was done here – both critically and with faith' (p. 59).

Critically and with faith? In the Catholic Church does 'with faith', I ask myself, mean that I dispense with 'criticism' as soon as 'the church' in its 'wisdom', or more precisely the Roman 'magisterium', prescribes a statement of faith? And are the Roman or Romanized theologians, who provide the basis for completely new dogmas, 'wiser' than the Germans, who cannot find them in the New Testament and the old Catholic tradition?

In the 1960s it is no longer the Marian dogma that stands at the centre of the discussion of the infallible magisterium but the question of contraception. Since the invention of the contraceptive pill the Roman magisterium has had colossal difficulties. It failed to see that it had already made a mistake in the 1930s, in reaction to a (correct) Anglican doctrinal decision in favour of contraception, when it ruled that any contraception is a grave sin. This is the problem of the 1968 encyclical *Humanae vitae*, which has time and again been blindly confirmed by Rome.

The prohibition of the pill – a second Galileo case

'That was brilliant, to combine the question of infallibility with the question of birth control and to build up your book *Infallible?* from that,' Cardinal Julius Döpfner once says to me, half in admiration and half in indignation. And my answer? 'It was Pope Paul VI himself who made this connection, not me.' At the First Vatican Council in 1869-70 the most-discussed case of error in papal history was that of Pope Honorius, who had been condemned as a heretic by an ecumenical council and several later Popes. But now, hundreds of years later, after the Second Vatican Council, the prime example of an error by the magisterium is the condemnation of birth control, which sparks off world-wide opposition and at times even subjects the Pope to ridicule. At the Trier Katholikentag Cardinal Döpfner is confronted with a protest poster: 'In an emergency the magisterium can stick it all together' (a reference to a UHU glue advertising campaign).

Evidently the Pope, protected in the Vatican, doesn't realize what dangerous ground he is moving on; he can hardly leave it as victor. For how is he as a celibate male to impose his authority on a question which is existential for countless people and on which every woman and every man feels more competent than the Holy Father? And this, as I warned time and again, is a 'Galileo question' that can only be answered with a yes or a no. 'The earth moves round the sun – or it doesn't.' 'Take the pill – or don't.' Here any apologetic theological dialectic, any attempt to veil it as a 'both – and' comes to grief. How could a Pope emerge from this situation with his teaching authority undamaged?

According to all opinion polls the encyclical *Humanae vitae* (emphatically endorsed also by Paul VI's successor but one, Pope Wojtyla) has not succeeded to the present day in gaining majority assent ('reception') even among Catholic believers or in preventing or even stemming the use of contraceptives in various countries. What was banned by the state under church pressure in individual Catholic countries is happening illegally, often endangering women. This is a Pyrrhic victory for the magisterium: with this encyclical the Catholic Church has lost power over the conscience of believers! People's mentality and practice can't be changed by such a doctrinal document. It doesn't result in a searching of the conscience over contraception but in a searching of the conscience over the limits of the church's magisterium. Because I call for that clearly and unambiguously, whether I want it or not, this criticism poses a question to me.

The question of truth – a public matter

Thirty years later the American journalist Garry Wills publishes a book under the title *Papal Sin: Structures of Deceit* (London 2000). By means of indisputable facts he shows that Popes Pius IX, Pius X, Pius XII, Paul VI and John Paul II made themselves guilty of grave intellectual dishonesty in so far as in what moral theologians call *ignorantia affectata*, cultivated ignorance, they did not want to maintain the truth. So not individual actions but structures of deceit are immanent in the system. Of course they include above all Paul VI's encyclical *Humanae vitae*, but also the 'conspiracy of silence' which under John Paul II, equally unteachable in sexual questions, surrounds the paedophile priests (and the Polish bishops and priests who collaborated with the state security service in Communist times).

More than any other papal doctrinal statements of the last decades, the encyclical *Humanae vitae* has made the question of truth a public concern in the church: the population explosion, birth control and church doctrine are questions not only for the church but for the world. And I attract more public interest than the many theologians who are very reluctant to adopt an unambiguous position over the question of the authority of the church's magisterium for fear of sanctions.

146

I have to meet many commitments abroad in addition to my lectures, seminars and sessions. But it is a myth that I am constantly travelling. For I also use weekends and semester holidays, normally travel very quickly there and back, and hardly ever go sightseeing (even if a city is completely new to me). As I am often told, I am easier to reach in Tübingen than most of my other colleagues; our secretariat functions admirably.

However, the invitations to give guest lectures don't always come in the order one would like and often I hesitate about saying yes because of my experience that soon another equally important invitation could arrive and dates could clash. Although I was in the US at the beginning of 1970, on Easter Eve I have to fly back to New York to give the first of my four lectures at Princeton Theological Seminary, a famous college of the American Presbyterian Church, on Easter Monday; the President, James McCord, had invited me during the Council in the very first television conversation spanning three continents (New York – London – Rome). All in all it's enjoyable, but often rather strenuous.

On the Friday of Easter week I take the Metroliner to Washington, DC. For the first time I am invited to lecture at the Catholic University, which is under the control of the bishops, and here in fact can speak freely about 'Infallible Church?' On the Saturday a top-level two-day symposium begins on 'Co-responsiblity', into which my lecture on infallibility fits very well. Then from 6 to 10 April there is a gospel festival at Pittsburgh Theological Seminary, where Karl Barth's son Markus teaches and his father's desk is venerated as a relic. This is a scholarly congress on the four Gospels, from which I can learn a great deal for the description of Jesus in my new book. After a lecture for the centenary of Wilson College in Chambersburgh, Pennsylvania, on 12 April I fly from New York, not to Stuttgart but to Scotland. In Glasgow and Edinburgh, then in Liverpool and London, as usual I have a full programme, so I am glad to be back in Tübingen on 17 April 1970. The next week I begin my lectures for the summer semester on christology and the seminar on 'What is the Christian Message?'

At the same time the American weekly *Esquire* (April 1970) publishes photographs of the '100 most important people in the world'. Only five women are included and the US dominates in this investigation, which has been produced over four years on the basis of hundreds of interviews with key figures in every sphere. The Catholic hierarchy is represented only by Pope Paul VI; Germany by Hermann Abs, Günther Grass, Axel Springer and Franz Josef Strauss; Switzerland by the psychologist Jean Piaget and me. Of course I'm delighted, but have no delusions about this honour, since any such selection is also governed by subjective interests. I see it as a political issue. For not least from my travels and an extremely varied public I have become aware that in my commitment to truth and truthfulness in the church I have a difficult position and need any support I can get. In a *'res publica* – public matter', publicity, communication through the mass media, plays a very important role. My way will soon be difficult enough.

Infallible? An unavoidable enquiry

I have often been misrepresented. All my life as a theologian I have by no means been concerned only for the freedom for which I had to struggle. At the same time I have been concerned with the truth, which I have sought with curiosity and incorruptibility. Wasn't it inevitable that in this quest I should come up against the problem of the church's infallibility? At the Gregorian in Rome in the 1950s I already learned that not only is the Pope infallible when he speaks *ex cathedra* as the supreme pastor and teacher of Christianity and in so doing exercises his 'extraordinary magisterium' as the councils do from of old. The College of Bishops is also infallible if together with the Pope it teaches that a particular doctrine of faith or morals is to be observed definitively (the ordinary magisterium), i.e. 'the teaching office which is exercised every day'. It is understandable that this ordinary magisterium of the bishops is increasingly claimed by the Vatican, in view of the unpopularity of the extraordinary magisterium of the Pope, in order to justify and spell out what the Pope says. In particular the 1950 dogma of the bodily assumption of Mary into heaven, about which the church knew nothing for 500 years, can most easily be grounded in an appeal to the faith of the Christian people, the liturgy and the everyday magisterium of the bishops, which can be confirmed by an (intimidating) opinion poll without an honest *status quaestionis*.

And now there is the tremendous challenge of this encyclical *Humanae vitae*, which wants to ban as a grave sin not only the pill and mechanical means of contraception but also the interruption of sexual intercourse to prevent conception. With it the Pope is going against the whole civilized world with reference to an infallible magisterium. At a very early stage I ask myself: formal protests and material objections are important, but mustn't this claim also be investigated thoroughly and professionally? There is a question to theology here; critical theological research into the foundations is needed.

This is a difficult scholarly venture. Who is to embark on it? It is clear to me that only a few theologians could write such a book and even fewer would want to. After all, to do so one must be as expert in Roman theology as in German exegesis and the history of dogma. One must have a degree of independence, say as a university professor, and at the same time a rare steadfastness. One must have an appropriate scholarly method and a precise and understandable style. And one must *want* to write the book. It had become clear to me before the Council in our personal 'dispute over dogmas' (*My Struggle for Freedom*, VI) that even Karl Rahner would never write such a book. And who wants to take on the serious conflict with the Roman authorities that would result?

In connection with the Inquisition proceedings against my book *The Church*, on 30 October 1969 Karl Rahner's assistant Dr Karl Lehmann had written to me from Munich: 'I hope that the battles that you have fought with Rome haven't taken too much out of you. But since as a Swiss Democrat from childhood you have had the right marrow in your bones, which we lack, in many respects you are the only one who can rightly fight through something like this. "Stand firm, Count" also applies here.' In the twelfth century the gentle Count Ludwig II of Thuringia was driven on by the cry of the smith of Ruhla to efforts against the nobility who were oppressing the people.

Gentle in heart and by no means predisposed to confrontation, I am certainly not a 'man of conscience' in the sense that on every occasion I appeal to my conscience instead of being concerned about my knowledge. Now this is a fundamental question for theology and the church and has remained so to the present day. I know that I must use my knowledge to the best of my abilities. So I decide on this book, for which I have already done important preparatory work in *The Church* (1967), with its long chapters on church ministries and the Petrine office. There I demonstrate with precise scholarship that the bishops became the successors of the apostles only on the basis of an extremely complex development; exegetically, historically and theologically the notion of a direct and exclusive apostolic succession of the bishops stands on feet of clay (*My Struggle for Freedom*, VI). I have also thoroughly studied the records of the Vatican I discussion of infallibility. It is unnecessary now to engage in major exegetical and historical research. Rather, it is important to analyse what I have already researched, supplement it, and make a comprehensive, topical and constructive synthesis.

I haven't been able to write any other book so quickly. I have all the themes in my head and have all the material perfectly under control: from the Gregorian (1948-55) the traditional Roman doctrine, from the historical studies in *Structures of the Church* and *The Church* the doctrine of Vatican I, from *Truthfulness* the discussion in the papal commission on the pill. Immediately after completing *The Incarnation of God*, which was to appear on the 200th anniversary of Hegel's birth in 1970, I begin writing *Infallible?*. It isn't difficult to orchestrate my themes. The manuscript is ready on 16 May 1970, just before Pentecost. It is published by the Catholic Benziger Verlag precisely on the 100th anniversary of the infallibility definition of the First Vatican Council on 18 July 1870 and immediately becomes a bestseller.

My title *Infallible?* speaks for itself. But the subtitle *An Enquiry*, i.e. an investigation, is also important. In parliamentary language the term denotes a request to the government for information. That is honestly meant. I don't want to present a fixed dogmatic thesis which is above discussion. But I do want to spark off a serious discussion in the church and society and openly challenge the leaders of the church to give an answer that is theologically convincing. The cover, an idea of my Swiss publisher Dr Oscar Bettschart, head of Benziger Verlag, a brave Catholic whose thinking is along the line of the Council, is striking. The word 'Infallible?' appears at the top in white against a shiny black background; at the bottom, in small print, is my name, and between the two, more than four times as big as 'Infallible?' is a giant trendy question mark in pink; the graphic artist had offered an even bigger one. That this question mark already states the issue abundantly clearly isn't due to me, but to the problems which are hanging in the air. Since I cannot and will not fob people off with the superficial traditional answers, I must investigate their foundation. The question of the foundation of the doctrine of infallibility is posing itself again today.

Are the foundations of this doctrine secure?

In order to evade the inconvenient question, some Catholic theologians want to ignore what simply cannot be denied: that Pope Paul VI can appeal to Vatican II for his condemnation of contraception. Article 25 of its Constitution on the Church has again accentuated what Vatican I says about the extraordinary infallibility of the Pope, but in addition has also reformulated the infallibility of the everyday magisterium of the bishops (in union with the Pope). 'Although the bishops, taken individually, do not enjoy the privilege of infallibility, they do, however, proclaim infallibly the doctrine of Christ on the following conditions: namely, when, even though dispersed throughout the world but preserving for all that among themselves and with Peter's successor the bond of communion, in their authoritative teaching concerning matters of faith and morals they are in agreement that a particular teaching is to be held definitively and absolutely.' And haven't the bishops, in consensus with the Pope, for half a century taught the immorality of any form of contraception? Ultimately Cardinal Alfredo Ottaviani had an easy task in convincing Paul VI of this consensus by means of a long list of official statements by bishops and whole conferences of bishops.

Subsequently people will accuse me time and again of having not reproduced Roman teaching exactly, but in an exaggerated, indeed 'distorted' way. But this is at best a weak attempt at justification particularly by German theologians (often they know better) who don't always want to accept the precise Roman texts since otherwise they would inevitably have to show their colours. No Roman authority or Roman theologian ever accused me, with seven years' study of philosophy and theology at the Pontifical Gregorian University, of not having reproduced the Roman doctrine exactly – how easy a denial would have been! On the contrary, numerous Roman confirmations of the infallibility of the condemnation of contraception by the ordinary magisterium can be found, which I have also cited in my book.

This is precisely the point: simply because I have reproduced the Roman teaching so exactly, the question of its basis now arises sharply. For of course these statements of Vatican II and Vatican I raise questions. Basically every Catholic theologian should raise them, though they are notoriously difficult to answer and so far haven't been answered clearly and unambiguously in Catholic theology.

Don't misunderstand me. Of course from the beginning I have supported in spoken and written words the basic intent of the Second Vatican Council to balance the (incomplete) First Vatican Council and its stress on papal prerogatives (confirmed in Article 18 of the Vatican II Constitution on the Church) by working out clearly the significance and function of the episcopate (Articles 19-27).

However, in this context unfortunately most bishops, theologically uninformed, thought it completely unproblematical, indeed desirable, for their own infallibility, the infallibility of the episcopate scattered over the earth, in questions of faith and morals, to be formulated alongside the infallibility of the Pope. And hardly any theologians had drawn attention to the dangerous nature of this teaching. It didn't occur to anyone that this very infallibility of the episcopate would be exploited by the ideologists of Roman primacy to support papal ambitions. But did no one really care about the lack of a foundation for such a momentous new Council statement on the infallibility of the episcopate?

It is amazing that in Article 25 of the Vatican II Constitution on the Church, on this question there is only a reference to the Vatican I statement about the *magisterium ordinarium* (Denzinger, 1712), and not a word about infallibility. In addition there is a reference to a Vatican I schema, but this doesn't have the slightest dogmatic authority because it was neither discussed nor approved. In that case, where does the view of the infallibility of the episcopate come from? As far as we know today, it was cooked up by the Counter-Reformation theology of the Jesuit cardinal Robert Bellarmine and the Roman scholastic theology which followed it. It is understandable that I had also to study this very 'thesis' at the Gregorian and painfully prepare it for the examination. However, it is now clear to me that this is no 'catholic' (= universal) doctrine but a new Roman special doctrine which does not occur in the theology of the Middle Ages, let alone the church fathers. And wasn't this to be talked about at the Second Vatican Council? Didn't it have to be?

It is almost unbelievable, but nevertheless a fact, that the new teaching about the infallibility of the episcopate was neither discussed nor examined at Vatican II but blindly taken over from Counter-Reformation Roman scholastic theology as prepared by the Curia. As I have already reported, 'the suppressed question of the infallibility of the church' (*My Struggle for Freedom*, VIII) caused me deep concern. Certainly I had succeeded in prompting and working out a speech against the infallibility ('inerrancy') of the Bible understood in fundamentalist terms; it was given by Cardinal Franz König of Vienna, but cancelled out by the Theological Commission. However, it seemed to me impossible to work out an address on the infallibility of the church limited to ten minutes, to be given in Latin and yet be generally understandable, let alone find another bishop prepared to deliver it.

Thus the highly problematical Article 25 on the infallibility of Pope and episcopate passes the Theological Commission and the plenary session of the Council without any objection or even hint of criticism. Granted, the bishops got heated about the collegiality of the Pope and bishops and the importance of episcopal consecration. But in the end they were robbed of their success in debates, compromise formulas and votes by a *nota praevia* prefaced to the chapter

151

on hierarchy in an authoritarian way by the Pope along the lines of Vatican I – still an important ideological presupposition for the Roman efforts at restoration in doctrine and practice. But there wasn't a single word about the problems of infallibility.

I often thought that it wasn't easy to be a Council theologian if one didn't want uncritically to assent to all its decisions. I often longed for Tübingen and its free air, in which I could research peacefully and teach without hindrance. I could only hope that Paul VI, a shrewd and foresighted man, would use proportionately the unlimited teaching authority newly confirmed for him. But in precisely that we were all deceived, as the encyclical *Humanae vitae* shows.

Making the church capable of correction: Walter Kasper

So often in what follows people will doubt my constructive intentions and denigrate me, as if I was concerned to cause the Pope and bishops – the anonymous bureaucratic word 'magisterium' is used frequently only with Vatican I – unnecessary difficulties and engage in opposition for the sake of opposition. Nothing could be further from the truth. Anyone who reads my book *Infallible?* will quickly note that I set out to offer a constructive solution to the leaders of the church who because of allegedly incorrigible dogmatic statements are in an aporia, incapable of correcting themselves and condemned to repeat errors. This solution could also be offered ecumenically. For it is clear to anyone that the two papal dogmas of Vatican I (the primacy and infallibility of the Pope) have deepened the schism with the Reformation and Orthodox churches.

Here the baby shouldn't be thrown out with the bath water. In a few paragraphs I make it clear that the church is dependent on true statements of faith: both on short summary confessions of faith (*symbola*) and if need be also on statements of faith which provide definitions against heresies (*dogmata*). But how am I to be able to explain that such true statements – spoken by a human person – are said to be infallible by divine guarantee, that they are thus a priori guaranteed to be free of error on the basis of special support from the Holy Spirit? There is no testimony to this in Holy Scripture and the great Catholic tradition. On the basis of the records I have to demonstrate that neither Vatican II nor Vatican I, to which it refers, cited scriptural proof or a universal ecumenical testimony of tradition for this thesis.

Anyone who reads without prejudice my book *Infallible?*, which is constantly being reprinted even a good 40 years after it appeared, can see with what careful consideration and evidence I argue step by step and finally propose a positive solution which still seems to me to be viable. If on the one hand we want to take seriously the promises given in the New Testament to the church as the community of faith, and on the other we cannot deny the many factual errors of this church, we can only say that the church is maintained in the truth of the gospel despite (not without) errors which are time and again possible. And as the records show, the statements of Vatican I and II could be corrected relatively easily because such a fundamental solution of the problem did not lie within the perspective of the fathers at that time.

Won't Rome and the episcopate see how much credibility the Roman Catholic Church would gain if it honestly recognized its errors and corrected them? And since the encyclical *Humanae vitae* is being largely rejected even within the Catholic Church and has shown irrefutably what difficulties are presented by an 'infallible' church which is therefore incapable of correction, one could expect them to be self-critical. After all, there are wise, understanding people in key positions in the church, people such as Cardinal Johannes Willebrands of the Secretariat for Unity, who on 12/13 September 1970 visits me in my lake house, or Cardinal Hermann Volk of Mainz, with whom on 18 October I discuss the state of the church with a *Spiegel* editor on the second German television channel, or the Primate of Belgium, Cardinal Léon Suenens, with whom I have long conversations in Brussels on 25/26 February 1971.

My former assistant Walter Kasper, now a professor in Münster, also campaigns for self-critical reflection. I had recommended him for Münster in my place and also proposed him for the editorial committee of *Concilium*. On 4 September 1969 I write to him: 'Should Ratzinger accept the call to Regensburg, which cannot be ruled out, I could think of no one better to propose here in Tübingen for his chair of dogmatics than you. I would firmly commit myself in this direction, although perhaps not everyone in the faculty will be of the same opinion.' I successfully propose him as Ratzinger's successor the following year: 'It is vitally important that in the sphere of Catholic theology the chair of dogmatics, which can show great names from Johann Adam Möhler and Johann Evangelist Kuhn to Karl Adam, Joseph Rupert Geiselmann and Joseph Ratzinger, should again have a first-class occupant.'

Without referring to me, on 12 December 1969 Walter Kasper writes a major article on the centenary of the Vatican definition on infallibility in the Catholic weekly *Publik* which perfectly reproduces my view: 'Thus the overcoming of church triumphalism by Vatican II also affects the church's understanding of the truth and calls for a new, deeper understanding of the concept of infallibility, which is so open to misunderstanding. More than any other, this concept is part of the past of Vatican I which has not yet been coped with. If we understand it rightly, it means the trust and faith that the church is fundamentally maintained in the truth of the gospel by the Spirit of God despite some errors in detail. Infallibility would then have to be understood dynamically and not statically; in and through the church the eschatological conflict with the powers of untruth, error and lies constantly takes place in the belief that here the truth will time and again prevail and never finally be lost. So on the basis of its faith, particularly in the conflict over the right knowledge of the truth, the church can be a sign of hope for human society. It must bear witness by its own example that to keep on seeking and moving forward in the certainty that the truth will prove itself is never meaningless but constantly necessary. The way that the church itself has taken from Vatican I to Vatican II is a testimony to this hope.'[2]

What a pity that Walter Kasper doesn't stand by this view boldly and faithfully when I (and on the periphery even he to some degree) come under fire from Roman-thinking traditionalists, instead of distancing himself from his (my) words in a pedantic and pettifogging letter that he sends to various authorities (and to me). I'm reminded of the saying, 'There's nothing like starting young!' But happily I have colleagues with the courage to take up this 'enquiry', which for others is truly a challenge.

A deadly threat to the Catholic faith?

'This book is a singular document in the history of theology,' writes the Tübingen theologian Herbert Haag in 1989, in the preface to the pocket-book edition of *Infallible?*, now with the subtitle *An unresolved enquiry*. 'Since it was first published in 1970, it has sparked off an international and interconfessional debate without precedent in more recent theology.'

And what a debate! I have great difficulty in following it, let alone assimilating it. It goes far beyond the theological publications and is therefore almost impossible to survey. In the next two years there will be several composite volumes, a monograph, numerous major articles, countless statements and reviews, even in the daily press. Important representatives of Catholic theology express their opinions, whereas some others, even 'progressive' or 'political' theologians, seem resolved on a wise silence.

However, I already have an invitation to give guest lectures in Australia and intend to distance myself somewhat from the infallibility debate during a well-earned research semester by a study and lecture trip round the world. But I am still in Tübingen, and no one can accuse me of evading the debate. I am grateful above all to the Jesuits in the philosophical and theological college of Sankt Georgen in Frankfurt; on 28/29 November 1970 the respected theologians Heinrich Bacht and Otto Semmelroth have invited me to a top-level symposium there. This is an extremely commendable enterprise. The dogmatic theologians Walter Kasper, Karl Lehmann, Karl Rahner and Hermann Volk, the fundamental theologian Heinrich Fries, the church historian Georg Denkler, the Old Testament scholar Norbert Lohfink and the New Testament scholars Rudolf Pesch and Rudolf Schnackenburg sit round a big rectangular table. I am delighted that all the contributions are objective and informative, and the discussion is fair and friendly. This is the way to reach agreement.

But one person stands apart and amazes everyone, Karl Rahner. He is late, and the only free place at the table is next to me. He soon speaks and addresses me quite directly with a weighty passionate voice, emphasizing every word: 'Herr

Küng, you may say that I am conservative traditionalist or petty bourgeois, but I have to tell you that I feel that your book is a deadly threat to my Catholic faith!' I answer him immediately, calmly but firmly: 'I understand your concern, Father Rahner, but if you look more closely it is not your Catholic faith that is threatened by my book but your dogmatic method, which constantly starts from particular dogmas and wants to return to them.' None of the other professors feels that his Catholic faith is under 'deadly threat', although of course all present their critical questions, along with endorsements.

Beyond doubt Karl Rahner clearly remembers our Munich 'dispute over dogmas' on the eve of the Council in 1962. I have already reported it (*My Struggle for Freedom*, VI). Even at that time I hadn't just opposed a 'positivistic' interpretation of dogmas which wants to take every dogma literally, of the kind practised in Roman theology. Presumably Rahner has read the paragraph in my book *Truthfulness* about the 'manipulation of the truth' where, without naming any names, I had criticized his 'speculative' interpretation of dogma which for reasons of a formal orthodoxy preserves each individual dogma word for word and literally, but at the same time reinterprets the whole wording in a modern sense, so that while his text is often violated, the interpreter always (still) appears to be Catholic. I opposed and still oppose that – inconvenient though this still is after the Council – in favour of a 'historical' interpretation of dogma which seeks to understand each dogma anew for the present from its historical situation. Of course this also applies to the Vatican dogma of infallibility, which, as is well known, came into being in the atmosphere of church restoration in 1870.

In the Frankfurt symposium it is evident that a clarification of the substantive issue would be possible and that most of the leading German theologians have kept calm. The following day, 30 November 1970, at 9.30a.m., I am invited by the Prime Minister of Rheinland-Pfalz, Dr Helmut Kohl, to a personal conversation in the Mainz chancery. Two years earlier I had thanked him for his generous reaction in a dispute within the church and at the same time sent him my book *Truthfulness*. Kohl had thanked me with a friendly letter on 18 October 1968 and invited me to visit him some time. Still quite fresh, two years younger than me and Prime Minister for only a year, Kohl is a convinced Catholic in the spirit of Vatican II, welcomely open to the renewal of the church and theology, with an extremely sober view of the church's situation and the abuses in it. It is a very illuminating conversation, interrupted only once by a telephone call from *Bild-Zeitung*, during which I also get to know Kohl's 'right hand', the intelligent and friendly Juliane Weber, and the Education Minister and later Prime Minister Bernard Vogel. As we part, Kohl tells me that one day he will invite me to his home in Oggersheim, where perhaps we will have the opportunity for a longer conversation.

So I go home with the feeling that I have withstood the first fiery trial over the question of infallibility well. Yet Rahner's direct attack on my Catholic orthodoxy doesn't bode well for the future.

Progressive theology united: the 1970 World Congress

In 1970 again events pile in on me and developments overlap. Often I have to be active in quite different arenas. The provocations of Rome on the one hand and my various publications on the other compel me to work at great speed. For as well as these 'extraordinary' tasks there are 'ordinary' tasks of which of course I shall say little: lectures and seminars and the correspondence which increases with every publication and controversy. All this is at the expense of sleep and entertainments such as concerts, the theatre and the cinema. It's just as well that I don't also have to look after a family and bring up children.

Before *Infallible?* my big book on the christology of the philosopher Hegel, *The Incarnation of God*, finally appears. I had begun it in Paris in 1957 and continued it in Madrid, London and Münster. I finally publish it in Tübingen in February 1970. For me it is a thorough preparation for my future christology and doctrine of God. The last part anticipates my paper at the World Congress of Theology that *Concilium* had decided on at its annual conference in Zurich in 1969, which concluded with a marvellous trip over Lake Zurich to the island of Ufenau. Five years after the end of the Council a great stocktaking is to be carried out on 'The Future of the Church'. I had proposed the individual topics within this overall theme in the Foundation: 'The Function of Theology', 'What is the Christian Message?', 'The Presence of the Church in Society'; 'The Structures'.

Thus from 12 to 17 September 1970 around 1000 theologians from 32 countries and four continents gather in the Palais des Congrès of the Belgian capital. Despite the counter-propaganda above all from the now arch-conservative cardinal Jean Daniélou (under Pius XII still an advocate of the '*nouvelle théologie*'; he is to die in 1974 in the company of a 24-year-old Paris *danseuse* of doubtful reputation), Cardinal Léon Suenens assumes the honorary presidency and gives the opening address on three problems left by the Council: the problem of the two different ecclesiologies within the Constitution on the Church; the problem of the two sources of revelation, scripture and tradition; and the problem of the hierarchy of truths.

Yves Congar, Karl Rahner, Edward Schillebeeckx and I are in charge of this congress, which is intended to inspire post-conciliar theology. That isn't easy, since the 1968 movement is now also having an impact on international Catholic theology and some younger theologians regard us as being a conciliar establishment. Latin American liberation theology also makes itself heard for the first time in the person of Gustavo Gutiérrez. On 14 September Rahner and I, together with the American exegete Raymond Brown of Baltimore, give our concise answers to the question 'What is the Christian Message?' Rahner's highly dogmatic statement is attacked in the discussion which follows as remote and abstract, so that he refers to my statement which had been formulated in an easily understandable form in the light of the Jesus of history. In his view this is a way in which one could sum up the Christian message for today.

156

Progressive theology appears united. In the decisions of our study congress on common theological guidelines, in the preparation and working out of which I played a major part, two resolutions are particularly important for being a Christian and the problem of infallibility:

- Resolution 4: 'The Christian message is Jesus Christ himself. He, the crucified, risen and living Lord, is the criterion for the proclamation and action of the church of Christ.'
- Resolution 6: 'The great christological confessions and definitions of the past also have abiding significance for the church of the present. However, they cannot be interpreted outside their historical context or merely repeated in a stereotypical way. In order to address people of different ages and cultures, the Christian message must time and again really be stated anew.' This is precisely my conviction.

Karl Rahner: the great disappointment

My attention is still centred on the discussion of *Infallible?* As expected, on 18 July 1970, the centenary of the Vatican infallibility definition, Pope Paul VI made a statement. I follow the radio news very attentively. But although the Italian edition of the book is on sale in Rome even before the German edition arrives – and on the Via della Conciliazione which leads to the Vatican – the Pope takes no notice of my 'Enquiry'. I am relieved – I think I have got over a dangerous hurdle.

But I have forebodings when on the eve of the Brussels Congress an article by Rahner's pupil Karl Lehmann appears in *Publik* (11 September 1970): 'Hans Küng on a Collision Course?' It is aimed, not at answering my 'Enquiry', but at questioning my orthodoxy. This is a wrong signal for the discussions which are now beginning. My reply, a precise analysis, is in the hands of the editors of *Publik* on 7 November 1970. They evidently like it. But then come ten weeks of to-ing and fro-ing between editors and authors: telephone calls, letters, conversations. Of course Karl Lehmann, chairman of the Theological Advisory Council and adviser to the Faith Commission of the German Conference of Bishops, hasn't the slightest interest that my article exposing him should be published. Only on 29 January 1971 may a castrated version appear in *Publik*. This isn't a good story, and certainly Karl Rahner is in the know.

Rahner doesn't say a single word to me about my infallibility book throughout the Brussels Congress in September 1970, when we sit together every day. In the meeting of the *Concilium* editorial committee in connection with the Congress the discussion turns more on liberation theology and the dispute between Latin American and North American theologians. My proposal to devote an issue of *Concilium* to the question of infallibility doesn't secure a majority, but there is no hurry. After the Congress Walter Kasper, now professor in Münster, tells me of a lunch with Rahner in a Brussels restaurant; gesticulating vigorously with knife and fork, Rahner had engaged in polemic against my book, about which he was now writing a long article.

In the difficult discussion over my dissertation on *Justification. The Teaching of Karl Barth and a Catholic Reflection*, in 1957 Rahner had given me very effective help by a major review in the *Tübinger Theologischer Quartalschrift*. And in 1962, after our vigorous argument in Munich, he had accepted my *Structures of the Church* for his series Quaestiones disputatae, although he didn't like its theses. Why shouldn't he now also support me in the tricky debate on infallibility?

On 22 October 1970 I had complained to him in a letter about Lehmann's article and way of working and asked him for an objective review: 'by no means simply assent, but a real help'. 'You should correct me where you think that I'm wrong ... But the truth shouldn't be repressed unfairly, as happens so often, or wiped off the theological agenda. So I wanted once again to ask for the weight of your standpoint in this question which is decisive for our church and for Christianity, for you to give me the same understanding criticism as you offered of my first book on justification: not for my sake, which is not so important, but so that "the cause" may be served.'

In fact Rahner's article appears on fourteen closely printed pages in November 1970 in the Jesuit journal *Stimmen der Zeit*. But for me it is a tremendous disappointment. Even the title has no objectivity: instead of 'Critique of the book *Infallible?*' it has a personal focus: 'Critique of Hans Küng'. But if this critique is directed against me personally, why didn't he speak directly with me, since I spent many days sitting beside him? Clearly he wanted to shoot me down as an individual and as a Catholic theologian.

With unusual animosity – after a few unsuccessful semesters in the Guardini chair of the philosophy of religion in Münster, since 1967 he has again been professor of dogmatics there – he launches a general attack on my person and theology. This culminates in an invective which is meant to deprive me of credibility throughout the Catholic world and which also goes promptly round the world through agency reports. He, Rahner, has 'first of all to say in all honesty' that with me he lacks a 'shared platform for a conversation within Catholicism' and that he can carry on a conversation with me 'only as with a liberal Protestant, indeed a sceptical philosopher'. And this after our joint appearance in Brussels? This after the platform we shared there about the Christian message? In saying this Rahner, not a petty informant but a leading Catholic theologian, is providing material for the intervention of that Roman Inquisition which only a few years previously had imposed a publication ban on him.

I am infuriated by this personal attack and ask myself what Rahner's reasons can have been. Our discussions about the interpretation of dogma and celibacy must have irritated him more deeply than I thought. Our discussion of celibacy must have gone home, not least against the background of his close friendship with the writer Luise Rinser, of which I have since been made aware.

A dogmatic theologian in need over arguments

It is thanks to the fairness of the chief editor of *Stimmen der Zeit*, my friend from the German College, Fr Wolfgang Seibel, SJ, that I am allowed to give an equally long answer to Rahner's article. When I re-read my article 'In the Interest of the Cause' I am amazed that I found the patience to respond to and criticize Rahner's extremely complex accusations – not without praising him for his earlier services. I criticize:

- the vagueness and inaccuracy of his remarks and the gaps in them;
- his misunderstandings, misinterpretations, insinuations and crude general-izations;
- his moral verdicts like 'arrogance', which had earlier also been applied to him;
- his tormented ambiguous attitude to the errors of the church;
- his evasion of the clear Roman statements about the infallibility of the epi-scopate (*magisterium ordinarium*);
- his pedantic theological wish list addressed to me ('Kung could have, should have, must ... ').

In Rahner's opinion, given rather high-handedly, I should above all have explained what I meant by error. To this I replied: 'Glad as I am to help my neighbour in need if he asks for it, I am unwilling to be summoned by him to his own bit of land to sweep the snow from his garden path, on the supposition that it is the only way in which I can reach the street. I have already cleared my own path with exegetical, historical, philosophical and systematic theological labours, though I am happy to be asked to scatter salt, and if necessary do more shovelling.'[3]

But things are very bad for Rahner. I am not the only one to say that his own 'transcendental deduction' (or is it really only an assertion) from a priori infallible statements is a 'failure'. It has convinced hardly anyone and will soon be for-gotten. And since Rahner has manifestly evaded an answer to the 'Enquiry' grounded in scripture and tradition, there is no overlooking the fact that no one so far has been able to provide a proof from scripture and tradition for an infallibility of particular church statements allegedly guaranteed by the Holy Spirit.

It has become clear that the penetrating enquiry *Infallible?* has hit the nerve of Rahner's theology and that is why the old master reacts in such a prickly way with attacks on the Catholic orthodoxy and Christian humility of his younger colleague – and shows himself up. So far it had hardly struck the Rahner enthusiasts that his theology is now utterly based on the dogmas of the church. But the church of Jesus Christ isn't grounded in dogmas; these are dams, not the foundation of the church. The church is founded – as the Brussels Resolution 4 affirms in consensus – on Jesus Christ himself as he encounters us in the Christian message which has its original record in the New Testament and to which (according to the view of the church fathers) the dogmas of the church are accountable. But wasn't and isn't the Christian message our common platform, the common ground on which we can and should discuss our differences?

It can no longer be overlooked that the pervasive weakness of Rahner's theology lies here. Most of all it lacks an exegetical foundation and support for its argument from the history of dogma. On various occasions Rahner himself has expressed his low estimation of exegesis and has used the history of dogma seriously only for his treatise on the sacrament of penance. The conclusion is that Rahner simply hasn't faced the decisive question of my book, namely how a propositional infallibility is to be grounded in the New Testament, the original Christian message. Speculating 'transcendentally', he hovers silently above any biblical and historical proofs with the flapping of dialectical wings. Unfortunately in his neglect of research into the New Testament and the history of dogma, despite his admirably bold advances, from a methodological point of view he has remained a Neo-scholastic theologian, 'the last great Neo-scholastic'. Faced with the argumentation of *Infallible?* on many levels and with good backing, with his dogmatic method he is in need and feels faced with a 'deadly threat'. In this distress he must now be glad to find helpers in his need. And he does so.

The 14 helpers in need: a new style?

It is understandable that Karl Rahner wants to write a reply to my response. In it he concedes, now at any rate without further personal denigrations, that he and I are possibly 'agreed on the real basic substance of Christianity' – 'that also seemed to be clear in Brussels'. No report which would have cancelled out the earlier defamation of me comes from the press agencies.

What is less understandable is that Rahner rejects my proposal of a 'personal conclusion' by me in the same issue of *Stimmen der Zeit*; he wants to have the last word, which is usually the basic right of the accused. For me this is a sign of weakness. At the same time he emphatically confesses that he is a 'system–immanent' theologian. However, this system–immanent theologian has beyond question failed to win the first battle over infallibility; indeed, in wanting to destroy my credibility as a Catholic theologian he has lost a great deal of credit among various theologians and non-theologians by his personal attack, so that the turn away from Rahner's theology in subsequent years began with his 'Critique of Hans Küng'.

Karl Rahner makes himself the servant of the Roman system as a system–immanent theologian in quite a different way from his letter to chaplains on celibacy. He takes on the editorship of a composite volume 'On the Problem of Infallibility'. He is supported by 14 helpers in need. Not of course 14 saints, like those holy men and women who were appealed to for help in every possible need in the fourteenth century. In Rahner's community of helpers, half of which consists of members of the partisan German Faith Commission, the traditional three holy women – St Margaret, St Barbara and St Catherine – who in any case aren't wanted in matters relating to the magisterium, are replaced by three theologians from abroad. At any rate the authors include three 'moderates' who are well disposed towards me: my Roman professor of dogmatics, Juan Alfaro; my predecessor in the Tübingen chair, Heinrich Fries; and my co-peritus at the Council, Otto Semmelroth. But there is not a single critical exegete or critical historian of dogma.

Karl Rahner's claim that this volume 'On the Problem of Infallibility. Answers to an Enquiry by Hans Küng' 'has been produced without an official commission from anywhere' is defensive and at best a half-truth. The book meets the wishes of the conference of bishops, and Rome is in the picture. Where the old Holy Office of the Inquisition has given itself the new pious name 'Congregation for the Doctrine of the Faith', this is called the 'new style' of the Inquisition. It lets others look after the business. And of course one must be grateful if as a theologian one is now no longer given short shrift and investigated, interned, censured, demoted, banished or, as in even earlier times, tortured and burned. Thank God for the Enlightenment!

It is a chief feature of the 'new style' of the Inquisition that it works in a more 'decentralized' way and leaves part of the inconvenient business to the national conference of bishops. On 9 January 1971 I find myself invited by the German Faith Commission to a conversation with several of its representatives in Stuttgart: Cardinal Hermann Volk, my boss during my years as assistant in Munich, and Bishop Friedrich Wetter, my fellow-student at the German College, supported by Joseph Ratzinger, professor of dogmatics, and the New Testament scholar Heinrich Schlier. Schlier in particular, himself a fine and clever scholar, attempts to teach me in an overbearing manner from the New Testament what in his view is 'Catholic', until I finally tell him that I have been a Catholic from my childhood and don't need to be taught by a convert.[4]

The abiding impression I take home from this conversation in Stuttgart is that none of the four gentlemen, not even Joseph Ratzinger, has an inner understanding of my ultimate motive, namely on the basis of the new exegetical insights to utilize the New Testament for the present situation of the church and especially for the ecumenical problem of church order which has been pending for so long. They are simply concerned to measure my theology by the doctrine of the church which has now been made dogma, but needs to be investigated. Of course the gentlemen sit in strict secrecy to judge someone who is absent. Only a few days later a statement by the German Conference of Bishops on *Infallible?* is published which, after all that has gone before, could hardly prove unpartisan.

So the dispute is 'only' over whether a priori statements, guaranteed by the Holy Spirit to be infallible, are possible. And in respect of this, a precise examination of the arguments shows that not a single one of the 14 Rahner helpers in need can provide a proof for the possibility of guaranteed infallible statements, if they attempt one at all. What is difficult about this debate is that now one plus 14 Catholic theologians are proceeding against one of their number without allowing him even to begin an answer – an unprecedented event in more recent Catholic theology. Karl Rahner above all is responsible for this. He is approached from various sides, but even refuses to accept my article entitled 'In the Interest of the Cause' in response to his personal critique, although he refers to it on various occasions in his own contribution; instead he prints the (manifestly contradictory) statements by the German, Italian and French conferences of bishops against my book. He seems to have little confidence in the 'infallibility' which he defends if he relies on such authoritarian methods for its defence and despite his 14 helpers in need fears even the briefest response from the one who has been attacked. Unfortunately, too, he cannot manage to distance himself publicly from his denigration of my Catholic orthodoxy and Christian attitude, with which I would be confronted even in Australia.

It is certain that Rahner found little sympathy for his action even among good friends: 'The discussion between you and Fr Rahner has disturbed me and even frightened me somewhat,' Walter Dirks, one of the most prominent Catholic laity and editor of the Frankfurter Hefte, writes to me on 21 January 1971: 'It is remarkable that our mutual friend Rahner occasionally lapses into reactionary positions in a way which is difficult to explain.' In fact the only explanation of this is Rahner's Roman 'system–immanence'. The discussion of Rahner's composite volume on Südwestfunk by Walter Dirks leaves nothing to be desired in terms of sharpness and clarity in its criticism. To what he calls the 'wicked words: no end to Küng' he opposes the words 'no end to Rahner'. He calls the right to drum up opponents of Küng's infallibility book a 'bad right'; he also finds bad form the reprinting of the statements of some conferences of bishops, the malicious feelings expressed in some statements, and above all the fact that Rahner didn't even accept my response to his first article. Immediately afterwards in the same radio programme (presented by the announcer under the slogan 'Today still no end to Küng') there was a brief, very affirmative discussion of my little book *Why Priests?*

But what is to be done? I do little myself, just to avoid breaking off the battered human relationships. I also invite Rahner to a session of my senior seminar on the infallibility discussion in the summer semester of 1972 at the University of Tübingen, and happily he comes. And when Rahner's orthodoxy is in turn attacked by Cardinal Höffner of Cologne, at the request of Westdeutscher Rundfunk I am glad to defend him publicly and without *Schadenfreude*. Since his time in Münster Höffner has been regarded as a friend of Professor Ratzinger.

First confrontation with Joseph Ratzinger

Only two years previously Joseph Ratzinger had bid a friendly farewell to us in Tübingen. But the way in which he now distances himself from former colleagues surprises us. As I have reported, on arrival in Regensburg he almost immediately withdraws his signature from the proposal for a 'limited period of office for residing bishops' (in fact eight years). The next year I get a friendly letter from him (6 July 1970) in which he tells me that because of a lack of suitable doctoral dissertations and work on his own publications, but also because of the distance, he wants to give up the editorship of the series Ökumenische Forschungen which we share, but will still be available for the next two volumes by Urs Baumann and Peter Lengsfeld.

'Naturally it would have given me pleasure had we been able to continue the series together,' I reply to him (18 July 1970), 'but of course I can understand the reasons why you are no longer able and willing to continue the joint editorship ... At all events I want to thank you most warmly for making it possible to start the series with me and for contributing to it. As a small token of thanks I am sending you my new little book on infallibility. In it I have sometimes been quite blunt, since both in theory and practice this problem has become very acute. It seems to me that we have to go through this somewhat difficult strait in order to gain more space. This book, too, has been written with the intention not of destroying the church but of building it up.'

I am also glad about his clear statement contradicting the most recent rumour that he assented to the habilitation of Gotthold Hasenhüttl only to avoid a row with me. That is utter nonsense. I now ask my Protestant colleague Professor Jürgen Moltmann to become co-editor of Ökumenische Forschungen and Kleine ökumenische Schriften along with Professor Eberhard Jüngel and Ratzinger's successor Walter Kasper, the Catholic dogmatic theologian, who has been called to Tübingen. They all gladly agree.

But now it pains me, just a year later, to see the volume 'On the Problem of Infallibility' (1971) written against my book *Infallible?* Joseph Ratzinger, whom I hadn't criticized any more than my other colleagues in my book, is among the attackers, and by no means among the gentle ones. In retrospect, after I have analysed the framework of his understanding more precisely, I can understand his reaction better. Like Rahner, he too sees his basic understanding of Catholic theology deeply put in question by *Infallible?*, although my *Structures of the Church*, *The Church* and *Truthfulness* (the two latter published in our joint series) would have prepared him better for it than others and given him a deeper perspective.

At any rate, unlike Rahner, Ratzinger doesn't denigrate me personally and finds words of recognition for the work of a colleague to whom he acknowledges 'years of untroubled collaboration in Tübingen'. He says that the author shows 'convincingly that in the light of the explicitly "Roman" type of theology (as represented above all by the Pontifical Universities of Rome and the theologians of the Curia) the statements of the encyclical (*Humanae vitae*) are to be regarded as objectively infallible and having the same status as a dogma. One must also agree with him when he continues that this is "the Roman, though perhaps not also necessarily wider Catholic doctrine" ... That this is the diagnosis of a crisis (thus *Infallible?*) is manifest: the indisputable seriousness of this book rests on that.'[5]

Very soon, on his way into the Roman hierarchy Joseph Ratzinger will maintain what was clear to me with my Roman education from the start. This doctrine of infallibility is by no means only the teaching of Roman universities but also of the Roman Popes and Congregations. Indeed, as we saw, it is the teaching of Vatican I and Vatican II. And Ratzinger himself, rising higher and higher on the Roman career ladder, will one day solemnly declare as Prefect of the Congregation for the Doctrine of the Faith that the prohibition by God himself of the ordination of women, although not solemnly defined, is still an 'infallible' doctrine – of the 'ordinary', everyday magisterium.

The Ratzinger of 1971 now thinks that after an eloquent complaint about my alleged use of the 'language of class struggle' (his 1968 trauma) he can accuse me of seven 'historical inaccuracies' and almost seven deadly sins. In my 'summing up of the debate' I scrupulously investigate every single one; there isn't much 'inaccuracy'. Rather, it proves that this accusation of 'historical inaccuracy' is a tactical defensive measure which robs me of credibility as the author of *Infallible?* and at the same time is meant to divert attention from my precisely presented 'Enquiry'.

An example? The discussion whether Pope Leo the Great in the fifth century used the title *Summus pontifex* or *Pontifex maximus* introduces a historical splinter which is meant to divert attention from the dogmatic beam in Ratzinger's theological eye. He too can know that at a time when bishops and theologians of both the Eastern and Western churches still did not read any privilege for the Bishop of Rome as Peter's successor out of the saying that Peter is the 'rock' of the church, Leo I, Bishop of Rome, wanted to demand the obedience of the other bishops and even the ecumenical council with an appeal to this biblical saying. But he was completely disregarded by the Ecumenical Council of Chalcedon in 451 and made aware of his limits, something that Ratzinger keeps quiet about. There is no trace of a recognition of papal infallibility.

But of course I take Joseph Ratzinger's main question very seriously. In my justified concern for an 'alternative' to Roman theology, don't I advocate a view of the ministry, the apostolic succession and the authority of the ecumenical councils which breaks not only with the typical Roman scholastic theology 'but with the whole Catholic tradition', in other words which is 'quite centrally opposed to the basic formulas of the early church, the significance of the term "Catholic" in the history of dogma'? Am I perhaps on the whole more Lutheran than Catholic? Here indeed Ratzinger raises the central question of the criterion of the Catholic, indeed of the Christian generally, though I want to pose it more precisely than he does.

Criterion for the Catholic: early church or New Testament?

I am somewhat amazed that Joseph Ratzinger doesn't take more seriously the New Testament view of the church which I have already described at length in *Structures of the Church* and *The Church*, and which is reflected in the broad consensus of present-day exegesis – questions of the twentieth century which could be treated on the basis of the state of knowledge at the time either by the Counter-Reformation Council of Trent (sixteenth century) or by the anti-modern Vatican I (nineteenth century). In Tübingen I had shared with Ratzinger the opinion that the tradition of the early church – because in many respects it was nearer to the New Testament – should be given greater weight than the typically Roman medieval tradition. But can I, like Ratzinger, regard the church and theology of the church fathers in the time after the New Testament (above all the fourth and fifth centuries) as the criterion for what is Catholic? The difference between this patristic theology and church and the New Testament is too great if one takes this really seriously!

But in the Prologue I have described how my clever colleague had always been bad at this, because even as a theological student he was willing to accept his-torical–critical exegesis only as far as it didn't disturb his patristic view of the church and theology, gained above all from Augustine (354-430) and his Bavarian Catholic form of Catholicism. He pays only limited attention to more recent Protestant and Catholic exegetical research into the primitive church. It would be highly inconvenient for his understanding of the church, orientated as it is on the later church fathers. This reminds me of the enigmatic comment by the pro-minent Protestant exegete Ernst Käsemann, who on leaving the hall after Rat-zinger's Tübingen lecture of 1967 'On the Importance of the Fathers for Present-day Theology'[6] remarked to me: 'Now I know once again why I can't be Catholic.'

I am no less Catholic than Ratzinger and want to remain so. But may I as a Catholic put the church, or more precisely the Hellenistic Roman tradition, above Holy Scripture? Must I orientate my Catholic understanding of the church primarily on the 'fathers', trained in Greek philosophy, on their dogmatic form-ulations which can be understood only in terms of Hellenistic thought, on an episcopal church with in part highly authoritarian church leaders, but still without a recognized Roman primacy of rule?

I orientate my understanding of the church primarily on the gospel, which is attested to me not by an 'overhang' of obscure Gnostic revelations old and new but exclusively by the New Testament, which of course must be reinterpreted for any new time. That is why Ernst Käsemann and Karl Barth accepted my book *The Church* as Protestant. My response to Ratzinger in 'Fallible? A Summing Up' starts from that. In Ignatius and Polycarp, in what is still almost the New Test-ament period – the 'apostolic fathers' – the original meaning of the word 'catholic', which at all events is supported by the New Testament, is that 'catholic church' means the 'whole', 'total' church as distinct from the individual local churches (including the church of Rome). What does that mean for our understanding today?

From Roman Catholicism to authentic Catholicity

I thoroughly agree with Ratzinger when he doesn't want to understand the term 'Catholic' as a 'completely random term' but as a 'historical entity'. Nevertheless, he makes it too simple when he uncritically identifies it with 'the reality of what is Catholic as it has come into being'. Hasn't he considered all that he has to swallow in this 'reality of the Catholic' which has 'come into being'. I know that in many respects he is as critical as I am about 'Catholicism as it really exists'.

But in that case what does 'Catholic', 'Catholic theologian', mean for me? In the light of the original term anyone can call himself a catholic theologian who feels indebted in his theology to the 'catholic', and that means the 'whole, universal, comprehensive, total', church. This is to be understood in two dimensions: being bound up with the church of all ages on the one hand and with the church of all nations and continents on the other. This is catholicity in time, interested in the continuity of the Christian faith, and catholicity in space, a universality of Christian faith embracing all the different groups.

I must emphasize that catholicity in time and space doesn't allow one to ignore the paradigm of Jewish Christianity (P I) or that of the early Greek fathers and Hellenism (P II), which is what Joseph Ratzinger did at a very early stage; he did it again as Pope in his 2006 Regensburg speech and also in his 2007 Jesus book. From the beginning this ends up in the Greek formula 'of the same substance (*homoousios*) with the Father' of the First Council of Nicaea (AD 325). Nor does catholicity in space and time allow one to dismiss the medieval Roman Catholic paradigm (P III) as in fact un-Christian, as Protestant theologians often do, nor, conversely, does it allow one from the lofty standpoint of Roman Catholicism to diagnose the Reformation (P IV) and the Enlightenment (P V) as 'de-Hellenization' and the progressive decay of the Christian West, responsible for the modern relativism of values and random pluralism. Such a constricted Hellenistic–Roman Catholicism is incapable of a real dialogue with modern philosophy, with science, with democracy as we understand it or indeed with modern theology generally. It is an obstacle to ecumenical understanding, goes against any authentic inculturation of Christianity, and prevents a formulation of the Christian message in the context of Indian, Chinese or African thinking.

I want to be a catholic theologian in such continuity and universality of Christian faith. But couldn't a theologian calling himself Protestant or evangelical also be catholic in this sense? Certainly, and I want to make Joseph Ratzinger reflect that authentic catholicity isn't a possession of Catholics which they inherit as a matter of course. Catholicity becomes Catholicism, an ideology, when the 'reality of the Catholic as it has come into being' – with all the accretions and distortions in piety, theology and church order – is simply accepted, instead of being subjected to a criterion. And for Ratzinger, too, this criterion cannot be other than the original Christian message, the gospel of Jesus Christ. That means that the theologian who is catholic in the authentic sense must have an evangelical disposition, just as conversely the theologian who is evangelical in the authentic sense must be open in a catholic direction. In this sense we can be ecumenical theologians, whether catholic or evangelical. In other words, authentic ecumenicity means an 'evangelical catholicism' centred on and ordered by the gospel of Jesus Christ.

Won't Ratzinger learn to make distinctions within the 'reality of the Catholic as it has come into being', a 'discerning of the spirits' in respect of church developments as recommended by Paul? Certainly any development 'in accordance with the gospel' is to be affirmed: for example the order of three ministries (bishops – priests – deacons). In some circumstances a development 'beyond the gospel' is to be tolerated, for example the adoption of some pious customs from ancient or Germanic religions. But any development 'against the gospel' is to be done away with: this includes certain abuses, particularly those perpetrated in the eleventh century in the church of the West, and the Roman centralism, absolutism and imperialism in doctrine, morality and church discipline often criticized at Vatican II, which is not backed by the fathers of the early church, let alone by the gospel itself. Rather, this claim to rule on the part of the medieval Roman system is the main reason for the schism first with the East and then also with the Reformation churches, and also for the present crisis in the Roman Catholic Church. That is also the significance of the infallibility debate for the whole of Christianity.

It doesn't surprise me that Joseph Ratzinger, who like other Catholic dogmatic theologians takes little trouble to assimilate the New Testament understanding of the church historically and critically, still shows little understanding of the concerns of the Reformers. But since he wants to take the early church of the fathers as a criterion, couldn't he show more understanding for the concern of the Eastern churches in the matter of infallibility?

A reconciliation with Eastern Orthodoxy is possible

Joseph Ratzinger should have been given cause for thought by the fact that the whole of Eastern Orthodoxy clearly rejected the 1870 infallibility definition as a Roman innovation, indeed as heresy. Resistance could be felt right up to Vatican I even in the Eastern churches united with Rome. At that council the Melkite Patriarch of Antioch, Gregory II Jussef, had protested against the dogmatic constitution on papal primacy and infallibility and voted on 13 July 1870 with a clear '*non placet*'. Even today, members of the Melkite church haven't forgotten that at that time the Patriarch had been humiliated by Pope Pius IX, who was psychopathically fixated on his own infallibility.

It was almost a century later that Gregory's successor Patriarch Maximos V, well known to Ratzinger and me, spoke out at Vatican II, as I have reported, in favour not only of reasonable birth control but also of a change of the papal primacy of rule into a primacy of service: 'If the primacy of the Roman bishop is freed in this way from its exaggerations in teaching and practice, it will not only cease to be the great stumbling block for the unity of Christians but will itself become the greatest force in promoting and preserving this unity.'[7]

In the infallibility debate, the same Patriarch Maximos speaks critically in a lecture in London on 13 November 1971 about the centralization of the church since the eleventh century, and supports my position: 'Can it (the Roman church) give theological and historical reasons for its claims over against the other churches? ... Its view of papal infallibility is too related to persons in respect of the infallibility of the church and in practice wipes this out. This is a theology which today has been abandoned by the serious theologians of the West but is nevertheless a theological view which in practice since Gregory VII (eleventh century) formed the basis for the life of the Roman Catholic Church. One cannot dogmatize the historical development of an individual church, a development which, however legitimate it may have been, is bound up with a given socio-political combination of circumstances.' Doesn't this accord precisely with the view which Professor Ratzinger put forward in his last year in Tübingen, as I have reported?

The schism with the Old Catholic Church could end

I find confirmation not only from Eastern Orthodoxy united with Rome but also from a colloquium in Berne on 24 January 1972, to which the dialogue commission of the Roman Catholic Church and Old Catholic Church in Switzerland has invited me. This Old Catholic Church came into being after 1870 from Catholic circles which rejected the two papal dogmas that contradicted old Catholic tradition.

After the publication of *My Struggle for Freedom*, I received a long letter (dated 7 November 2002) from a former Jesuit, Hubert Huppertz, who had married and finally with three sons had entered the ministry of the Old Catholic Church; his wife and daughter remained Roman Catholic. After re-reading the controversy with Rahner his conclusion was: 'You argued honestly and consistently, but in his thinking Rahner was trying to get round the allegedly unchangeable.' Then he said something about me that he didn't want to be understood as an accusation: 'I'm not surprised that the name "Döllinger" doesn't appear in the first 40 years of your memoirs – *damnatio memoriae*!'

Ignaz von Döllinger (1799-1890) was probably the most learned Catholic theologian and church historian in nineteenth-century Germany and at the same time the most acute opponent of the definition of papal infallibility and primacy of jurisdiction. He rejected these 1870 dogmas and insisted on the existing theological basis for the Old Catholic Church. He didn't regard his excommunication by Rome in 1871 as binding, but never joined the Old Catholic Church. Huppertz now thinks that I am 'Döllinger's "son" in at least five respects. 1. You have rejected a hierarchical career; 2. You have put obedience to your conscience in first place; 3. In faithfulness to Christ you have remained faithful to the church; 4. You can sleep peacefully; 5. You needn't destroy your unpublished works. However, in one respect you are incomparably superior to Döllinger: you get your manuscripts ready for publication and you write your memoirs.'

Hans Küng – a second Döllinger? My Neo-Catholic opponents would have applied such an Old Catholic label. My reply to my correspondent (11 November 2002) runs: 'As far as Döllinger is concerned, I have to concede that I have not occupied myself with his publications; in any case the reference to him would have been counter-productive and would have made it easy for my opponents to classify and denounce me. You know that I have always stood up for the concerns of the Old Catholics and with *Infallible?* have risked my own neck. I have returned to that time and again, not least in one of my most recent publications, *A Short History of the Catholic Church*. I still haven't completely given up hope that perhaps there might be a reconciliation under a new Pope – provided that there is a voluntary renunciation of power on the part of Rome, something that I have always called for.'

In a postscript I add: 'A Döllinger biography would be important. Are there also differences from HK?' To which the Old Catholic promptly replies: 'Differences: 1. Up to now age, just 75 as compared with 91. But the difference is getting less every day. 2. The role in institutional politics which Döllinger played during his life (he was a member of parliament) – HK's indirect political influence. 3. Döllinger's rejection of democracy under the traumatic experience of the French Revolution – HK Swiss direct democrat. 4. Döllinger's role in the hierarchy: as the court clergyman the provost of the St Kajetan Foundation was the second highest clergyman in Bavaria – HK avoided, in a truly primal Jesuitical way, any swing in the direction of official "acceptability". 5. Döllinger's step beyond confessional limits. His bridge-building into Judaism. The beginning of his controversy with Islam, within the limits of the mentality of the middle of the nineteenth century – HK's step beyond the limits of the world religions and his view of the common basis of all humanity: the global ethic. 6. Supporter of celibacy as the root of a morally credible priestly existence – HK's plea for freedom.'

My conversation partners in Berne at that time, professors from both churches, agree that the Old Catholic schism could be ended if a solution to the questions of primacy and infallibility along my lines were acceptable to Rome. What about the churches of the Reformation?

The Reformation protest could become immaterial

'When I read it, I increasingly had the feeling that I had an atomic bomb in my hands.' Thus already the General Secretary of the World Council of Churches, Dr Willem Visser 't Hooft, soon after the appearance of *Infallible?* 'For if these new ideas are accepted in Catholicism, a completely new situation will arise. Then Protestantism will no longer have any serious reason for protesting.'

Of course the infallibility debate is also followed with excitement in Protestant circles, though only a few Protestant theologians – honourable exceptions are my Tübingen colleague Eberhard Jüngel, the Swiss Lukas Vischer and the Dutchman G. C. Berkouwer, the latter a Protestant observer at the Council – support their Catholic colleague who is standing up for fundamental Protestant concerns. There is no question that the Reformation churches, too, could accept the doctrine understood in this sense: an indefectibility, indestructibility of the church as the overall community of faith, whose faith will never perish despite all the error of individuals holding office.

For me the clearest analysis is offered by the contribution of the Lutheran theologian Walther von Loewenich, which I also make the focal point of our composite volume 'Fallible. A Stocktaking'. He says that the book *Infallible?* reminds him of Martin Luther, who once remarked in connection with his 95 Theses on Indulgences that he had merely belled the cat; he had had the courage to say out loud what others were thinking quietly. Unlike Catholic theologians who want to see or construct a 'break' in my thinking and who complain about a tone and style which has been heightened because they are so sleepy, von Loewenich states that in substance *Infallible?* hardly goes beyond earlier publications by its author, but now after a century of taboos does what others have neglected to do, namely 'grab the bull by the horns', renouncing subtle theological arts of interpretation. Hence the whirlwind.

Joseph Ratzinger has taken particular exception to the fact that I have shown understanding for the way in which Martin Luther reacted in the Leipzig disputation when to avoid inconvenient issues his opponent Johannes Eck with tactical skill pinned him to the question whether ecumenical councils could err. Luther had to affirm this in respect of the ecumenical council which a few decades earlier in Constance had had the great Czech scholar and Reformer Johannes Hus burned at the stake, contrary to its solemn promise of 'free passage', and had condemned many of his statements, though they were backed by the gospel. In one chapter of my book *Infallible?* I also discussed with much historical material the question of the infallibility of councils, which was not asserted from the beginning.

Indeed, Loewenich says, for centuries the church 'lived without an "infallible" juristic principle': 'It is promised that it will remain maintained in the truth of God through all error. This view must also meet with ecumenical understanding.' So 'meaningfully' the decisive question in this discussion 'shouldn't be, "Is Küng still Catholic?", but rather, "Will Catholicism struggle through from doctrinal narrowness to authentic Catholicity?"'[8] Truly, Catholic theologians too should have no illusions at what is at stake here for the ecumenical world. My proposal over the problem of infallibility is an ecumenical solution: only if one puts oneself on the Catholic side of the discussion of the primacy and infallibility of the Pope as defined by Vatican I is an ecumenical understanding possible. Here beyond doubt questions also arise for the other churches, which likewise call for an answer and for which in *Infallibile?*, in agreement with competent theologians from the churches concerned, I have proposed ecumenical solutions. For the churches of Eastern Orthodoxy this is the question of the infallibility of ecumenical councils, but for the churches of the Protestant Reformation it is the question of the infallibility (inerrancy) of the Bible.

Of course the success of an ecumenical solution primarily depends on the efforts made on the Catholic side. And I have time and again taken stock of those justified Orthodox and Protestant concerns that the Catholic Church has already met since the Council and those that it has not. But it is certain – as a result of this debate – that now in Catholic theology, too, there is reflection on the fundamental difference between the Catholic Church and the Roman system. Thus Karl Lehmann states: 'There is virtually no doubt that in the ecclesiology above all – roughly speaking – of the second millennium there was a growing accumulation of this indefectibility of the whole church in the papal head and its curial organization. Here a magisterium of a distinctive kind was combined with a specific legal aim and each supported the other (cf. also the relationship between primacy of jurisdiction and infallibility).' New insights will be a great help towards an ecumenical understanding in the church's critical reflections on itself.

Who 'invented' the doctrine of infallibility?

My book appears in French on 5 March 1971 from the Catholic publishing house Desclée De Brouwer in Paris, *Infaillible? Une interpellation*, and I have abundant opportunity to refer to it there in the press and on radio and television. There is no attack on my Catholic orthodoxy at the symposium on infallibility in Paris on 12/13 May 1972 which I have already mentioned, arranged by the Centre Catholique des Intellectuels Français, but there are several very constructive contributions. The symposium is attended by as many prominent figures as the Frankfurt colloquium; here the Dominicans in particular have a brilliant representation, with my friends Yves Congar, Bernard Dupuy, Claude Geffré and Henri Legrand.

What is most interesting to me is a paper by the younger French historian Claude Langlois, who describes precisely how infallibility is 'a new idea of the nineteenth century': as a cultural counter-event to the French Revolution suddenly elevated by the ideologists of the counter-revolutionary restoration, above all by the French aristocrat Joseph de Maistre with his book *Du Pape* of 1819. Between 1840 and 1870 a broad wave of 'ultramontanism', which has its heart 'beyond the mountains (Alps)', is promoted above all by the popular Pope Pius IX, though in contrast to his initially democratic moods he soon proves completely reactionary. A new form of Roman Catholicism develops from this, governed by the triangular relationship between Marianism, doctrinalism and infallibilism: the dogma of the immaculate conception of Mary (1854), the Syllabus of Errors (1864) and finally the definition of infallibility (1870). This eventually gives the Pope a monopoly of truth in the church. Never in the 2000-year-old history of the Catholic Church has he in fact had the sole say, as he does now.

But if this is so much of an innovation, three questions above all are of burning interest. Here are really new insights which in part have surprised even me.

First question: Who 'invented' the doctrine of infallibility? What is sensational for me, too, is a discovery by the American historian Brian Tierney, whom I also get to know personally at Cornell University in Ithaca, New York. This first-class medievalist has discovered on the basis of many years of studies who 'invented' the doctrine of papal infallibility which became so popular in the nineteenth century but which is nowhere explicitly taught throughout the first millennium. For even in the Gregorian reform of the eleventh century, which introduced papal absolutism, the doctrine was strictly maintained that a Pope could err in faith. Thus the 'inventors' of papal infallibility are not, as has long been assumed, the papalistic theologians and canon lawyers of the high Middle Ages. Rather, the 'inventor' is the eccentric Franciscan Petrus Olivi (died 1298), often accused of heresy. With his doctrine of infallibility he wanted all subsequent Popes to subscribe to a decree of Nicholas III in favour of his trend among the Franciscans, which required rigorous poverty. Therefore in 1324 Pope John XXII condemned the doctrine of infallibility as the work of the devil, the father of lies. The consequence is that initially the infallibility of the Pope was a heresy that was condemned![9]

Second question: What about the infallibility of the ecumenical councils? One result of the researches by the Jesuit Hermann-Josef Sieben is that not even Athanasius, the great champion of the first Ecumenical Council of Nicaea (325), believed in it. Indeed the authority of the ecumenical councils had quite a different basis. A council doesn't have authority simply because according to certain presuppositions it is 'ecumenical', still less because it could produce infallible statements with the support of the Holy Spirit. Rather, it is authoritative in so far as it attests the apostolic faith, in so far as, to use a happy formulation by Athanasius about the Council of Nicaea, it 'breathes scripture', in short in so far as it is an authentic and credible expression of the gospel.[10]

Third question: What about papal or episcopal infallibility in the New Testament? It doesn't surprise me that not a single exegete speaks at any time in the debate in support of the question of the infallibility of the apostle Peter which is fundamental to Vatican I. On the contrary, the German Catholic exegetes Josef Blank, Rudolf Pesch and Wolfgang Trilling, not represented in any way on the Vatican II Theological Commission, but representative of present-day exegesis, agree that there is not the slightest support for an infallibility of Peter and *a fortiori* of the Bishop of Rome. For all three exegetes, in any case the saying about Peter as the rock, which occurs only in the Gospel of Matthew, is not a saying of the historical Jesus but a post-Easter formation of the Palestinian community, or that of Matthew.[11]

Jesus would not have understood any of this

Even Karl Rahner concedes in a *Spiegel* interview on 28 February 1972: 'If I hypothetically, unreally hypothetically, imagine that I had read out the 1870 definition of the First Vatican Council to Jesus in his lifetime, in his empirical human consciousness he would probably have been amazed and not understood any of it.' The only amazing thing is that we contemporaries with our 'empirical human consciousness' should understand something that Jesus the Christ, to whom the whole Christian tradition appeals, would not have 'understood anything of'.

Of course Jesus would also not have 'understood anything of' the Inquisition practised in his name, indeed (he himself was denigrated for his criticism of false legal and temple piety) he would perhaps have called militantly for a 'cleansing of the temple'. Karl Rahner and his colleagues have contributed to the fact that I am increasingly stamped as 'anti-Pope' and that all my future scholarly works on quite other topics will not overcome the cliché of 'papal critic and church rebel' used by some people.

'A Swiss defies the Pope' is the headline to an article in *Die Zeit* (35/1971): 'But whereas the theologians Congar, Rahner and Schillebeeckx had to submit to Vatican methods of investigation a few years ago, Hans Küng appears to be the first to force one authoritarian position after another out of the Roman censorship authorities.' Indeed, in February 1971 the Congregation for the Doctrine of the Faith has published the public rules of procedure – 'Procedure for the examination of doctrine' – which have long been called for. The 'Declaration on the Freedom of Theology' signed in 1968 by 1360 theologians, which I had drafted, has led to some improvements: the 'author' (no longer 'the accused') is now to be judged only by his own books, articles and speeches; he is to have a defender (*relator pro auctore*, though nominated by Rome); the relevant bishops are to be involved at an early stage. But still there is no possibility of inspecting the records and no serious chance of surviving the Inquisition proceedings without capitulating. Granted, it is said that these doctrinal proceedings aren't a 'criminal trial', but of course penalties are provided for. Should it prove in the course of the proceedings that the author of a book to which objection is made stands by his opinion and is unwilling to retract his 'error' by any 'saving means', he must expect sanctions. Archbishop Giuseppe Tomko of the Doctrinal Congregation, later deservedly made a Curia cardinal, who presents the new procedure at a press conference, avoids the question with a macabre joke: 'There is no provision for the electric chair or the gas chamber.' But he concedes that in the future, too, an unworthy servant of the church will suffer disciplinary measures. And truly the withdrawal of the church's permission to teach, banishment from a chair or suspension from priestly authority, can still cost a theologian his head or compel capitulation.

This is what had happened recently to the 44-year-old Croatian-born Ivan Illich, who as head of the CIDOC Institute which he founded in Cuernavaca, Mexico, had criticized the close link of the church with powerful figures in South America and the prohibition of the pill. He was called on to retire and indeed gave up his presidency – in the words of the Prefect of the Congregation for the Doctrine of the Faith, Cardinal Šeper, a 'spiritual sacrifice'. But six months later he nevertheless had to undergo a highly painful investigation in the Palazzo del Sant'Uffizio ranging from his 'errors' about the church and clergy and his support of the pill to his friendship with Che Guevara and his relationship with women. Illich refused to answer a single question and exclusively published the extensive questionnaire in the Mexican paper *Excelsior*. This was taken up in various other papers, some in Italian, so that for the first time the details of the proceedings of the Doctrinal Congregation in such a so-called colloquium were made known. The Congregation wants to avoid such embarrassment in future.

On 10 August 1971 *L'Osservatore Romano* confirms: 'Investigation into Küng Begun'. At a lower 'Catholic' level that means 'Blow against Modern Theologians Drives them out of the Universities'. That is the headline in the Catholic *Bildpost*, with photographs of Schillebeeckx and me, in close company with the president of the Humanist Union, the author of a book 'The Misery of Christianity or a Plea for a Humanity without God', who wants to ban theology from the university in favour of religious studies. However, these events remind other press organs of the Soviet Union, where for decades there have been proceedings against religion, and also against anyone intent on reform with 'scientific methods'. Thus one can also read in the papers 'What Sakharov is for the Kremlin, Küng is for the Vatican'. But I don't get involved in debates at this level. In response to the wave of rumours I can only remark laconically: 'At present I'm wondering whether to become a collector of Vatican postage stamps.'

In the meantime, for me, as for the great majority of Catholics at least in the northern hemisphere – in contrast to the church's magisterium – the problems over infallibility are basically settled. At any rate it no longer represents an intellectual challenge, though it is a challenge in church politics. So I will continue to engage in the discussion. But in my mind I have in any case long moved into other fields, and what can be experienced and assimilated there has fascinated me and moved me infinitely more.

V

Global Trip and Global Theology

'Goethe would have spoken about Christianity
better had he heard your lecture on the Christian message.'

The political scientist Theodor Eschenburg on 8 December 1970 to the
author of On Being a Christian

Since I am not writing the 'story of a soul', I don't want to spend time here on the heavy inner burdens put on me in getting through the whole controversy over infallibility, truth and truthfulness and all the attacks, insinuations and slanders that went with it. In the face of sustained church shortcomings, confronted with the immobility and high-handedness of hierarchical representatives, one can sometimes get extremely angry and indignant, becoming joyless and despondent when contemplating the log-jam of reforms that keeps piling up. And if I still see being a university professor as my dream profession, I must now pay a price for the association of my profession with 'profiteri', with 'confessing'. I get no sympathy in some circles for my abhorrence of the unctuous and dishonest way in which many churchmen talk, while I work hard to speak honestly and precisely. Be this as it may, fearlessness and intrepidity, stubbornness and resolution don't come cheaply. And if I stood alone in the great controversy which is steadily becoming more acute, I would go under.

Sympathetic support

How glad I am that I have fellow fighters all over the world, happily also among theologians and those of like mind; that above all in my closest surroundings I have people around me who support me in every way with their sensitivity and empathy, with their sympathy. That is true above all of my team in the house and in the Institute for Ecumenical Research, who read all my publications critically. Later I will sometimes be asked why I have had so many quite extraordinary colleagues – now more than ever. Doubtless one of the reasons is that I don't get any run-of-the-mill doctoral students (in any case their church superiors have warned them against this adventure). Instead people come, students and colleagues, who have made a deliberate choice, who don't want to take the comfortable way of assimilation to the church but the challenging way of an honest search for truth. They are more those with above-average, in some cases even exceptional, gifts. I have already spoken on several occasions of Hermann Häring, who gained his doctorate in theology in 1970 with a dissertation *summa cum laude* on the picture of the church in the Bultmann school and who later continues to be involved in many of my intellectual adventures. At the beginning of the 1970s Karl-Josef Kuschel, who has exceptional gifts, starts his career as an academic assistant and in 1977 crowns it with a dissertation on 'Jesus in Contemporary German Literature' and a doctorate, also *summa cum laude*. Third in the alliance is my Swiss compatriot Urs Baumann, who as early as 1969 introduced himself with a dissertation on 'original sin' and the crisis in its traditional understanding which has not yet been overcome. In the 1970s, like his two colleagues, he aims at habilitation and stands loyally at my side during all the decades in the Institute.

In this context my family, with whom I remain in the closest contact, even in Tübingen, is also important to me. It is more than understandable that my mother, rooted in the traditional Catholic faith but positive about the new orientation brought about by Vatican II, sometimes worries about her son who is always in the papers, attracting both positive and negative comments. So at this time I write to her (25 May 1971): 'I'm always glad to hear that you like what I'm doing. I'm particularly pleased that you read the discussion volume about my book *The Church*; you can see from that how everything has been received, that all is going well and you needn't worry. I'm also glad you like the record ('What is the Christian Message? Why I Remain in the Church', produced by Chris- tophorus Verlag, Freiburg im Breisgau).' It is also a great support that my five sisters and their husbands stand at my side. So I write to my 'dear little sister' (Hildegard) on 20 January 1972: 'It's very important to me to know that our family is on my side – apart from the understandable hesitations of our Mutti. It would be intolerable if even those nearest to me didn't understand my position. Conversely, it strengthens me greatly time and again, particularly when I'm in the lake house, to live in surroundings and a society which has no problems with these things. I'm particularly grateful to you for your involvement. Generally speaking I shall steer a firm course, though at present the waves are very high. The controversy over the infallibility of the church authorities was due, as these particular controversies show.' As for steering, during these stormy times I hardly use the sailing boat that we share. Raising and lowering sails takes considerably more time than swimming. But at precisely this time, in case I need it in the future, I renew my cantonal 'ship's driving licence'.

Support from theological friends

Of course now – after the conversation with the Faith Commission of the German Conference of Bishops, represented by Bishops Volk and Wetter and Professors Ratzinger and Schlier – the support of like-minded colleagues in theology is of great importance to me. That applies not only to my colleagues in Tübingen, where among the Catholic theologians Herbert Haag, Norbert Greinacher and Johannes Neumann are particularly supportive. If I wanted to mention by name all my theological friends in every church and on every continent I would never end.

Since I can no longer count on Karl Rahner and Hans Urs von Balthasar, I am particularly delighted with the 'peacemaking observations on a theological feud' by Otto Karrer, a highly educated and long-standing Catholic ecumenist:

When I read Karl Rahner's article in *Stimmen der Zeit* (December 1970) I was perplexed that Rahner allowed himself to make this attack. I speak as an old friend of his. It is difficult for me to fathom how the initiative for this attack could have come from him, of all people. After all, he was once under a cloud and today is now the recognized master of a theological conceptual system. Küng is quite different: a critical thinker and a prophetic theologian who refers directly to the gospel. Even after reading *Infallible?* and Rahner's critique I have no doubt about Küng's orthodoxy, but can understand that his intellectual nature, this time once again in unconcerned historical and theological criticism, may be provocative to one person or another with Roman inclinations. Of Arnold Ehrhard in the entry under his name in the *Lexikon für Theologie und Kirche* (ed. Karl Rahner) we read: 'His striking work *Der Katholizismus des 20. Jahrhunderts* brought him serious attacks, which he brilliantly repudiated. Suspicions of Catholicism reformism and Modernism did not shake his loyalty to the church. He was also a brilliant orator and preacher.' Küng's topic is similar: the identity of the church in historical change; everything living is in constant development. Today in the Catholic Church there is the hope that we have learned from the mistakes of that time. Is it to be a lack of Catholic faith to be convinced that the church will be maintained in truth despite all indisputable errors?[1]

Shortly after that, Otto Karrer's colleague, Dr Liselotte Höfer, writes to me from Lucerne: 'Meister Otto (which is what she calls him) is already making ironic comments that you are bombarding him with letters. And now here I am, too, with a very big request ...' In fact it is only a little request, which I am glad to accede to, as I have to others. On 8 December 1976 my fatherly friend Karrer, long under a cloud, who almost twenty years previously had surprisingly used the intimate second-person form of address to me, a young assistant priest in the Hofkirche in Lucerne, dies and is given an honourable resting place in this church. But I am subsequently surprised how after Karrer's death and the foundation of an Otto Karrer Society, which I support with a large sum of money, a biography many hundreds of pages long is written by the same Liselotte Höfer which says virtually nothing (probably prompted by the other side) about

177

Otto Karrer's relationship with me. This is just one of many signs that now for me the church climate has changed.

I have ties of friendship with the 30 prominent theologians from different countries and disciplines who form the editorial committee of *Concilium*, which gathers every year in Pentecost week – moving between Nijmegen, Paris, Zurich, Madrid and Tübingen. I have already said much about it in *My Struggle for Freedom*. Edward Schillebeeckx, a member of the Foundation with Rahner, Congar and me, is closest to me in his theology. My relationship with Karl Lehmann is warm, but not without tensions; until 1 October 1971 he is Professor of Dogmatics in Mainz, and then in Freiburg im Breisgau. He asks me for material for his seminar on the infallibility debate, which I quickly provide. He makes an understandable objection in connection with his former boss: 'You are very resolute and also very harsh in your verdict on Rahner as the "last great Neo-scholastic". For many years I myself have had many of the critical reservations about Rahner's theological method which you have expressed. But one must also give him his own place in the history of theology, and this is quite certainly not exhausted by his having been the last great Neo-scholastic.' I don't want to argue with him now about this (perhaps Rahner wasn't the last great Neo-scholastic), but it is soon to prove that Rahner's theology, which is extremely important for the theological breakthrough before the Second Vatican Council, loses importance amazingly quickly after the Council; his kind of speculative interpretation of dogma has no future.

Unfortunately I can't go along with Karl Lehmann's desire for me to take over as director of the pastoral theology section of *Concilium* in succession to Rahner, for whom he is deputizing. I would have liked to see him as the successor, but couldn't dismiss the argument that two pastoral theologians should be envisaged as directors of the pastoral theology section, one of whom if possible shouldn't be from the German-speaking world. In fact the editorial committee chooses Norbert Greinacher of Tübingen and Casiano Floristán of Madrid; unfortunately this leads to Lehmann's alienation from *Concilium* and his move to the conservative counter-product *Communio*.

Lehmann also writes to me about the new 'aid' from the German bishops for those in priestly office. I study it closely: 'It certainly won't surprise you that I have some reservations. Basically, it is still the case that today the New Testament evidence isn't taken completely seriously and so people aren't capable of really meeting the problems of the present.' At the same time a circular letter from the Bishop of Rottenburg, Carl-Joseph Leiprecht, has arrived with a 'working basis' for the Synod of Bishops being prepared for in Rome which is to meet there in September 1971. Here too I must offer clear criticism. I write to the bishop: 'I have the most serious reservations about this "working basis", which is quite unsuitable for helping in the present crisis of the church's ministry but will rather accentuate it ... Clear decisions on the most important practical reforms of the church's ministry, especially the abolition of the law of celibacy which, as is becoming more evident day by day, is having catastrophic effects on the whole church, would be more important than a comprehensive theory of the leadership of the church, which the next synod of bishops cannot achieve.' I enclose for the bishop my manuscript on the nature of the church's ministry which is soon to be printed in the context of a memorandum of the university's ecumenical institutes.

The reaction of the Federal President's office is also welcome. The personal adviser to the Federal President Gustav Heinemann informs me that Frau Heinemann read some of my book *Infallible?* to her husband on his sick-bed 'and both were equally refreshed'. Heinemann, co-organizer of the 'Confessing Church' in the Nazi period and an important representative of German Protestantism, sat next to me at table at Karl Barth's 70th birthday celebrations in Basle in 1956. He sent me the second volume of his speeches and writings, but it only reached me just after his death on 7 July 1976.

Concentration: being a Christian against a world background

Extremely pleasant prospects open up for me in July 1971. I have the freedom to leave behind me all that I have said, written, published, replied to and assessed since the publication of *Infallible?* in 1970, all that has occupied me and oppressed me, strained and often tormented me day and night. At last I can look forwards again, not constantly with an eye on Rome, to which by no means 'all roads lead', but going out into the big wide world, getting to know new ways, people, lands, cultures. This is no new journey to Rome but a second journey round the world, not as in 1964 in 25 short days, but lasting a whole six months, from July to December 1971.

I am anything but a backpacker or globetrotter. I am concerned deliberately to widen my horizons and at the same time to gain a new foundation for my theology. On my journey I also want to start on a book which the controversies so far have shown to be urgently needed: a new introduction to Christianity with a good scholarly basis. Why should one be a Christian? Why not simply a human being? What does it mean to be a Christian in today's world?

What is called for is a new foundation for Christian theology. After my fundamental criticism of infallibility I can no longer base theology simply on particular dogmas in a Neo-scholastic way. But after the results of historical criticism of the Bible I cannot base it on an uncritical understanding of the Bible in an old Protestant way either. Even the modern speculative attempts at mediation such as those by Karl Rahner or Karl Barth, which I have joined in in my own way, eventually lead nowhere and are hopeless. I have experienced them above all in my years of studying the christology of the philosopher Hegel and in serious study of exegetical research into Jesus. This is documented in the last chapter of my book on Hegel, *The Incarnation of God.* I see myself compelled to apply another theological method and to sketch out how the development of historical criticism itself compels us to rethink Christian theology in the light of the Jesus of history.

I begin my thinking from the centre and strive for a more solid foundation and concentration of Christian belief for a new time. As I have reported, I presented my summary of the Christian message with a foundation in historical criticism at the World *Concilium* Congress in Brussels in 1970; over long years in Rome, Paris, Münster and Tübingen I have worked at the exegetical problems. I keep testing my summary of the Christian message on the most varied occasions, for example at the Christmas celebrations of the two Rotary clubs of Reutlingen-Tübingen on 8 December 1970; I feel encouraged by the keen attention with which this very heterogeneous public follows my remarks on the elementary topic 'What is the Christian Message?' And Theodor Eschenburg, father of political science in the Federal Republic, delights me even more when on saying goodbye he remarks: 'Goethe would have spoken about Christianity better had he heard your lecture on the Christian message.' It will be a test of another kind that at the desire of Herder Verlag I record this lecture on the disc I have mentioned; this happens in Freiburg im Breisgau on 22 March 1971 – after two days cross-country skiing in the Black Forest with my Basle friends. But all that is just a prelude.

Broadening horizons: experience of the world

I take my Brussels paper and a few books with me on my big journey. I will travel more than 50 times in planes big and small, extremely modern and extremely decrepit. In between, everywhere I will have a great deal of time to reflect and to think about the foundations of the 'Introduction to Christianity' which I have to work out; in the end it will be entitled *On Being a Christian*. I first thought that it shouldn't be a big book but a short, compact one with relatively few notes, like *The Council and Reunion* and *Infallible?*

I owe the realization of this journey on the one hand to my alma mater, Tübingen, which has obtained a research semester without teaching duties for me from the Stuttgart Ministry of Education, and on the other to the University of Melbourne, which has invited me to Australia for a week to give lectures in my summer holidays; there are also invitations from New Zealand and the US. All this is covered by a 'round the world' ticket valid for six months. I plan at least the main stages of this trip as carefully as possible and choose quite a different route from that of seven years previously.

On 16 July 1971, the eve of my departure, I answer correspondence until 4.30 in the morning. Among others, I write to the philologist and professor of rhetoric Walter Jens, as I can't get to speak with him – since the revolutionary year of 1968 I have become more and more friendly with this man of letters and quasi neighbour and his wife Inge Jens, herself a German scholar and author. I send him a short word of thanks for the spontaneous offer of the use of his swimming pool: '. . . for the extraordinary generosity with which you gave me your house key – as a Catholic theologian I can sing a lengthy song about the power of the keys. Swimming has done me a great deal of good, particularly over the past energetic weeks, so I can start on my journey to Moscow and round the world early tomorrow without being completely exhausted. I shan't return to Tübingen until the end of November.' Homesickness will dog me round the world, even when it doesn't make me ill. I travel alone.

That same evening I also write to our honorary professor of scholastic philosophy, the prelate Alfons Hufnagel, in Rottenburg, who had invited me to a farewell meal in which I cannot take part: 'I don't want to neglect to thank you, not only for this invitation but also for all that you have done for us in Tübingen, and also for me personally. The *imprimatur* of some books which are not completely unknown is associated with your name, and it has always been a joy and an encouragement to see with what objectivity and fairness you treated these matters. I have been particularly impressed by the fact that you have always stood by your decisions, even if this has not always found praise beyond the Alps. If the Bishop of Rottenburg has held his protective hand over me, I have you to thank in a special way. So I would have liked once again to have expressed my warm thanks to you.' In five years he will no longer be with us; he dies in the night of 6/7 April 1976 – at the time I am in Rome for difficult negotiations.

I am concerned above all to expand my horizons as well as to achieve a more solid foundation and concentration on the present. My old mentor from the German College, Fr Wilhelm Klein, writes to me from Bonn about the ecumene which spans the world: 'When I travelled the world at your age, the narrowness of the biblical sphere began to dissolve through the incarnation of God in the immeasurable *amor che muove il cielo e le stelle*. How far we still are from the true ecumene, from the earth to creation and creator which we children of men have attempted to grasp in our narrow infallibilities! So write your Introduction to Christianity as a small way into biblical messianism.'

For a long time now I have seen Christianity in a twofold confrontation: with 'secular' humanism on the one hand and with the great world religions on the other. I want to investigate and answer the question of being a Christian as concretely and practically as possible against the horizon of our time: a critical survey of Christianity in the context of competing ideologies, tendencies, movements. Having got to know the United States and its intellectual and spiritual situation very well in the past decade, I now want to get to know the second superpower better – and especially the Russian Orthodox Church.

Holy Russia

My name is known in the foreign office of the Moscow Patriarchate, not least because of my activity as a peritus at the Second Vatican Council, which observers from Moscow attended earlier than any other Orthodox churches. I communicated with Archpriest Vitaly Borovoy from Leningrad, who made the contact with the head of the church's foreign office, Metropolitan Nikodim. I am also certainly known from the infallibility debate, which has also been followed in Moscow; in it I occasionally draw a parallel with the 'infallibility' of the General Secretary of the Communist Party of the Soviet Union. So I write to the official Moscow church authorities, who of course are still under the strict supervision of state organs and certainly also the Soviet secret service. It's difficult to get a firm answer from Moscow. At any rate I am promised the support of the Patriarch, and I also receive the necessary visa in good time.

On 17 July 1971 I fly from Stuttgart via Prague to Moscow, very apprehensive about how I will be received there. What a pleasant surprise! The Orthodox presbyter Nikolai Gundayev, his charming interpreter Irina Firsova and a car with chauffeur are waiting for me at the airport and I am driven to the Budapest Hotel in the centre of Moscow, where we have an evening meal together and still have time to visit Red Square by night. For all my days in Moscow I am constantly accompanied by this small team, which makes my stay in Moscow and on trips into the surrounding area extraordinarily pleasant and stimulating.

There is a special reason why I wanted to fly to Moscow on 17 July: the next day the feast of the most important Russian saint, Sergei, is being celebrated in the biggest Russian monastery, just over 40 miles from Moscow. So we go to Zagorsk very early in the morning. It was here that Sergei of Radonezh (1314–92), originally a hermit, founded the Monastery of the Trinity, some distance from Moscow and at that time in the Russian 'wilderness', in the solitude of the trackless forest. It is near to what was to be called Sergei Posad (in 1920 renamed Zagorsk and then given back its old name in the revolution of the 1990s). With its ascetic spirituality it became the model for around 180 further Russian monasteries. Sergei, who supported the reunion of the faith under the leadership of Moscow but rejected the dignity of metropolitan, remained simply a spiritual leader who embodies the ideals of Russian holiness in an exemplary way: simplicity, humility, compassion, and involvement in society and in the nation.

So here in the Church of the Trinity with its splendid decoration I can experience what has always been the grandeur and fascination of Russian Orthodoxy. There is the splendid liturgy shaped by Byzantium which with precious brocade vestments, richly decorated episcopal crowns and candles decked with flowers speaks to both mind and heart at the same time. There are the countless icons, images for pious remembrance, meant to strengthen prayer, but from an early stage already images for cultic veneration. They make Christ and the saints of the past present to believers today. There is the monasticism, largely embodied in the more senior clergy. And there is the attractive poly-phonic choral singing, which I got to know at the Russian College in Rome, and which today still speaks very deeply to both East and West because it combines homophonic Byzantine art singing with polyphonic church music, above all that of Venice. This found its way to Russia via the Mediterranean islands occupied by Italians or via Poland and the Ukraine.

Before the service, I have received through my escort permission from the metropolitan in charge to receive communion. When I take my place in the line, an excited supervisor approaches me and wants to drag me away by the arm, but my escort tells him that I have permission. As I struggle towards the exit at the end of the service, I meet a group of around 30 theological students from the Roman Congregation for the Evangelization of the Peoples (Propaganda Fide), who greet me enthusiastically. Had they known that I was going to receive communion, they say, they would also have done so; however, their Roman escort had forbidden them. Once again it is evident that 'the people' want an ecumenical world.

Afterwards I have the honour of being received by the Patriarch of Moscow and All Russia, Pimen I; he was only enthroned the previous year. It's a friendly but rather formal reception; I don't get the impression that the Patriarch wants a deep conversation. I am subsequently told how the Communist system has a hand in the game right from the choice of the Patriarch and in general keeps the Patriarchs on a short leash. The subordination of the church to the state has unfortunately always been one of the weaknesses of Russian Orthodoxy. More than formerly under Byzantine supranational authority, the church here was part of the state and always subject to political manipulations by the rulers. Thus since according to the later Orthodox view the First Rome had become heretical and the Second Rome (Byzantium) had fallen to the Turks (1453), the ideology of Moscow as the Third Rome developed: the last bulwark of orthodox Christ-ianity. However, Communist rule fundamentally destroyed this myth. Two decades later all my experiences in Russia will go into the second volume of my trilogy on the Religious Situation of Our Time: *Christianity* (II, 11-12 'Moscow: The Third Rome' and 'The Russian Revolution – and the Orthodox Church?').

I am delighted that in Communist Russia so many pilgrims have come to this feast. I am also allowed to take part in the meal in the refectory, since the Moscow Spiritual Academy and the priestly seminary are also in the monastery precinct. I can view the rooms – including the former rooms of the tsars – but find it hard to discover what kind of theology is being taught here. Certainly the church fathers play the main role; it is impossible for an independent theology to develop in the Soviet period. I had already got to know the most important Russian theologians abroad: George Florovsky, John Meyendorff and Alexander Schmemann, with whom I spent a whole evening theologizing in New York and with whom I got on excellently. It is sad that this particular theologian had to die so early.

Unholy Russia

I spend an incredibly rich day at the patronal festival of St Sergei. We return to Moscow in a good mood. However, the Soviet stars on the Kremlin towers shining red in the darkness remind me that we are no longer living in Holy Russia but in the atheistic Soviet Union. It is true that under Brezhnev's leadership the worst excesses of Stalinism have been overcome. But every time we drive past the Lubyanka, the headquarters of the still-powerful secret service Cheka–NKVD–KGB, in which countless people have been put on trial, tortured and executed, I must also think of what George Florovsky called the '"night" culture from old Slavonic paganism'; this is said to have maintained itself in Russia under the 'Christian "day culture"' of the spirit up to the Stalinist regime of terror.

Now of course there is both a day side and a night side to every culture. But Alexander Schmemann in particular made clear to me that the consequences of two centuries of Tatar enslavement of Russia are still tangible today: a 'Tatarism', a lack of ethical principles, and a repulsive combination of submission to the strong and suppression of all the weak. I also took a Dostoievsky novel, *The Demons* (1871), with me on this trip. Dostoievsky, the former St Petersburg revolutionary, warned by his own personal experiences and by his acquaintance with the anarchist Bakunin, and alarmed by terrorist murder, wanted to show the Russian people, especially the intellectuals and students, that nihilism and terrorism, direct violent action without any practicable constructive programme for the future, were the symptoms of a terminally ill society. To all this the monastery offered, and offers even in the Soviet period, a counter-reality of holy values with the possibility of conversion, purification and renewal. The youngest brother Alyosha lives this out in Dostoievsky's *The Brothers Karamazov*: in the midst of a dark world of the passions the hopeful vision of an alternative orthodoxy of mutual love.

The very next morning I have a taste of the complicated Soviet surveillance system; we have to drive round a lot to get me a visa for Tashkent. But there is still enough time for a first visit to the Kremlin, its main cathedral where tsars used to be crowned and patriarchs elected, but also where excommunications such as that of Leo Tolstoy (1901) were proclaimed. It is now a museum. Alongside the Kremlin churches is the imposing Congress Palace with its modern architecture. Then we have lunch directly opposite, in the roof restaurant of the Rossiya Hotel, the largest hotel in the world, with a splendid view of the Kremlin, Red Square and St Basil's Cathedral. In the afternoon I am shown the Soviet achievements: the Moscow television tower, the astronauts' memorial and the grounds of the 'Exhibition of Economic Achievements' of the Soviet Union (Sputnik). The next day we go to the Tretyakov Gallery with its great Russian works of art, many public buildings in Stalinist style and a few with modern architecture (e.g. the Comecon headquarters).

On the evening of the next day, 21 July, we are in the main Moscow railway station and leave on the dot of midnight to travel in a comfortable sleeper to Leningrad, formerly St Petersburg. In the Second World War it was besieged and destroyed by the Germans over almost 900 days, but now has largely been rebuilt. I am lodged in the pompous baroque Europa Hotel and am pleased to get to know this city on the Neva, generously planned by Peter the Great in classical baroque style and occupied in 1712; with its great harbour it has always been regarded as Russia's gateway to the West. Instead of a religious reformation, Peter the Great – a memorial of him on horseback dominates the Decembrists Square on the Neva – ordained a political secular enlightenment for the country. There was an internal Europeanization which for the first time confronted Russian Christianity with rising modernity. Not only state order but also church order was rationalized, centralized and disciplined by the police. With priestly seminaries and schools the church was to become an instrument of enlightened moral education.

But that made the Orthodox Church a guarantor and support of the tsarist regime. That is evident not least from the great churches, for example the mighty St Isaac's Cathedral or the Sts Peter and Paul Cathedral in the Peter and Paul Fortress, a prison in which among many others Dostoievsky languished. No wonder that Lenin, whose brother Alexander had been executed in connection with the murder of Tsar Alexander II (1881), had a deep hatred of everything religious. Consequently his Communist Party, which came to power here in St Petersburg – beginning with the 1917 October Revolution in front of the grandiose green Winter Palace of the Tsar – fought not only against feudalism but also against religion as the 'opium of the people' with all the means at its disposal. Thousands of churches were destroyed or closed, millions of people, believers and unbelievers, were sent to the Gulag archipelago. I was shaken when I read the works of prominent Russian critics of the regime which had only just become known, above all those of Andrei Sakharov, Dmitry Medvedev and of course Alexander Solzhenitsyn. Only in the 1980s, with the perestroika of Mikhail Gorbachev, with whom I later appeared in Lausanne as a speaker, would a change also come about for the Orthodox Church.

Abiding respect for the Orthodox Church

Since my visit to Russia I have felt a deep respect and admiration for the Orthodox Church, which has safeguarded its survival despite a variety of life-threatening crises, despite the Islamic conquest of most Orthodox Christian countries, despite the decades of Communist oppression. And for me the Orthodox Church, because it has not adopted Roman centralism and absolutism, is on the whole a form of Christianity which is considerably nearer to its origins: a proven *koinonia*, *communio*, fellowship of churches with equal rights.

Of course I could also note how the Orthodox Church is threatened with the danger of a liturgism which in fact reduces the life of the church to the liturgy and distorts contemporary proclamation without inspiring social and political reforms. For me the Russian 'saint' of our time remains the important preacher, writer and reformer Alexander Men who, initially an acclaimed biologist, had himself ordained an Orthodox priest at a time when Khrushchev declared that in twenty years humanity would have overcome all religions. I met him after the collapse of the Soviet bloc at a meeting of a Catholic Academy in Weingarten in Swabia, and got on as well with him as I had previously with Alexander Schmemann. I then sent my book *Eternal Life?* to him in Moscow. Soon afterwards came the shattering news that he had been murdered with an axe in the early morning on his way to church, presumably by agents of the secret service. That was one great hope less for a reform of the Orthodox Church of Russia, large parts of which seem to have embarked on a period of restoration.

In Leningrad we visit the Winter Palace and the Hermitage with its countless artistic treasures (including Scythian and Siberian gold work) and a unique jewellery cabinet, and finally also the 'Versaillesque' Summer Palace outside the city. We save a good deal of time by travelling back to Moscow in the sleeper, so that I can not only visit the museum in Dostoievsky's house but in the Patriarchate can also express my thanks to the deputy chairman of the church's foreign office, Metropolitan Dimitrov Juvenali, for the excellent way in which I have been looked after and discuss relations with Rome with him. My packed but highly informative stay ends with a cheerful meal in the attractive modern country restaurant of Archangelskoye. At the next table is the French film star Marina Vlady, lead character in a film about a scene from life by Chekhov. Will Communist Russia ever open up to the West, I wonder, here and at the airport when I say goodbye.

From Moscow I take a night flight to Tashkent. The almost five-hour flight of nearly 2000 miles seems to go on for ever. The seats are narrow. Next to me is a portly Russian woman who keeps flirting with her partner and leaning on me in the process. However, in the capital of Uzbekistan I receive a warm welcome from the likeable presbyter Viktor Trusevich and the monk Nikolai Chestov and his companion. They live in a simple one-storey priests' house by the bishop's church; I stay in a hotel.

In Moscow it is 18° Celsius, in Tashkent 35°. Here I find myself in a quite different and far more friendly atmosphere. Tashkent is a giant industrial city with one and a half million inhabitants and broad boulevards; the old city was destroyed by an earthquake in 1966 and has now been rebuilt in modern style. But it also has a market full of soft fruit, whereas in the hotel in Moscow one gets only dried grapes, because the Soviet Union can't manage to transport soft fruit in an edible form to Moscow. In the morning we go sightseeing in the city; there are some monumental buildings, the modern university and the old mosque, the seat of the mufti. Then two congenial Uzbeki guides take me round the Soviet museum, above all an economic exhibition of the predominantly Muslim Soviet republic of Uzbekistan. I am given a personal performance of Uzbeki dances in traditional dress, which I find very beautiful; then we visit churches and the cemetery. I can learn at close quarters how much the life of a presbyter of the Orthodox Church is bound up with simple people and how he enjoys a sympathy which is not always shown to the senior hierarchy.

There are still many believers in Russia and all over Eastern Europe, clergy even more than laity, whose spiritual and religious lives are lived, consciously or unconsciously, completely within the Hellenistic–Slavonic paradigm of the early church. Their liturgy has hardly changed, and their theology even less. This gives the Orthodox churches a strongly traditionalist and monastic character; on the other hand they are very religious and festive. In 1971, on my visit to the main cathedral of Russia, which had been turned into a museum, I would never have dreamed that two decades later I would be allowed to film the Easter service of the Patriarch of Moscow and All Russia in the old splendour. I summed up my feelings and impressions for the German TV project *Spurensuche* ('Tracing the Way') in a statement I made in front of this Cathedral of the Dormition of Mary. It still expresses my conviction of the hopes and dangers of Orthodoxy:

I cannot conceal my sympathy for the Orthodox Church. In many respects it is closest to earliest Christianity. It does not have the same centralistic government as my own church, and it allows at least its priests (but not its bishops) to marry. It also allows the eucharist to the faithful in both kinds, bread and wine. And it has survived under all kinds of political systems, even the last persecution for 70 years under the Communist regime, with thousands of martyrs. That is above all because of its grandiose liturgy, its hymns. All this is very gripping for someone from the West.

However, we cannot overlook the fact that the distance from earliest Christianity is enormous. The average believer has difficulty in recognizing Jesus' supper in the ceremonial liturgy. And the link with the state, too, is not at all characteristic of earliest Christianity.

But all that is a challenge for the Orthodox Church today to use the power of its liturgy to increase the element of proclamation: the message itself, preaching, and also the education of children in the schools ... And I also think of the bond, indeed the reconciliation, with the Latin church of the West, with which after all it was associated for 1000 years. A great task of the twenty-first century is to do away with this schism, which has lasted more than 900 years. However, here it is above all and primarily Rome that has to make a move (*Tracing the Way*, pp. 214f.)

But now to another world.

The world of Islam: Afghanistan

On 24 July 1971, two hours before my departure from the airport, all my papers are investigated by a frosty security official with dark glasses and some of them are photographed. Then in fine weather my unforgettable flight begins from Tashkent over Tajikistan, over the Pamirs, the 'roof of the world' covered with ice and snow, to the Hindu Kush (Persian *hindukuh* = 'Indian mountains'). There are endless bare mountain chains riddled with crevasses, but also snow–white peaks between 5000 and 7000 metres high. My destination is Kabul. So I have left what at least earlier was the Christian world. Indeed, I am now experiencing in a quite concrete way that the 'ecumene', the 'inhabited earth', is far greater than the Christian world. Here so to speak in the heart of Asia I am again experiencing the world of Islam, in an almost exclusively Muslim country.

Afghanistan: as I gaze out of the window, I think that it would be as difficult to wage war in this almost inaccessible country with its high mountain chains and deep-cut valleys like crevasses as it would be in the Swiss Alps, a factor which also helped my country to preserve freedom. After the conquests by Alexander, the Arabs, Genghis Khan and Timur Leng, Afghanistan became part of the Mughal empire – whose founder Babur came from Afghanistan and rests in its capital Kabul in a mausoleum in the Babur Garden – then part of the Persian empire until it achieved independence around the middle of the eighteenth century. In the nineteenth century Great Britain risked two extremely costly and unsuccessful wars (1838-42 and 1878-81) to integrate Afghanistan as a powerless buffer against Russia for its Indian colonial empire and prevent any modern developments (such as the railway). After yet another unsuccessful war in 1919 it finally had to grant the country independence, which was also assured by the young Soviet Union in 1921.

On my visit in 1971 the kingdom of Afghanistan is still a very isolated and socially backward country with an unstable domestic political situation; it has 15 million inhabitants, including many nomads, and is threatened by a drought and frequent sandstorms despite abundant water from the mountains. Genghis Khan's and Timur's troops had destroyed cities which flourished in the thirteenth and fourteenth century along with complicated irrigation systems. Various rival groups of people live in the land: 40 per cent Pashtuns, who are regarded as the authentic (Aryan) Afghans, 25 per cent Tajiks, 20 per cent Hazars and around 5 per cent Uzbeks. The majority of the population is built up of numerous tribes, sub-tribes and large families. King Zahir Shah has made a first freely-elected parliament possible, but that soon becomes the battleground of the tribal representatives against the reform policy of the government. I see from their wrestling bouts and cavalry fights in open spaces that the Afghans are a proud and militant people. The women (not the nomad women and those who have been emancipated) usually wear veils, often veils which conceal everything but their eyes.

But by comparison with the Soviet Union I feel more at home in Kabul, a relatively free and hospitable city which spreads over a large basin between the mountains at a height of 1890 metres. It is a capital which is growing fast, with around 400,000 inhabitants (in 2007 there are 3.5 million); at the same time it is the administrative, educational, commercial and industrial centre of the country. The country (in 2007 with around 30 million inhabitants) is 99 per cent Muslim; more than four-fifths are Sunnis. But there is religious freedom in this picturesque confusion of streets and houses whose pulse beats in the bazaar in the old city, where silversmiths and coppersmiths, cobblers and tailors have their open workshops.

Of course there are also Christians here. I am met by Archbishop Angelo Panigati, who is attached to the Italian embassy. On the Sunday I am allowed to preach in Kabul's over-full church. Archbishop Panigati, who is popular every-where, presides over the worship. The spirit of the Second Vatican Council makes its mark even in Afghanistan; several dozen confessions and denominations are present at the eucharist and the Archbishop tells me that all are invited to receive communion. Does he then have no problems with Rome? 'None,' he replies, 'the Afghanistan Conference of Bishops allows it, and that's me.' I quote the Russian proverb: 'The heaven is great and the tsar is broad!' It's an extremely cheerful, harmonious liturgical celebration with coffee to follow. How easy, I think to myself, it would be to produce the Christian ecumene if all church authorities and bureaucrats didn't cling to their status.

During the day I meet a group of the Peace Corps, America at its best. Sargent Shriver, who in 1961 at the request of his brother-in-law, President Kennedy, founded this American organization of voluntary development aid workers which became the model for development work in many countries, fully deserved his title story in *Time Magazine*. And the happy faces of these young people in my photograph album still remind me of the new peaceful paradigm of world politics which developed after the Second World War, promoted above all by the United States.

We have supper with a small international group in a little Muslim castle and an extremely lively discussion follows. No one can imagine that the Soviet Union, which had recently built the first daring all-the-year-round road with the help of a long tunnel over the 3000 metre high Salang Pass, could be so blind, after the experience of the British, as to march and fly into this country a couple of years later. Nevertheless, it did, and after ten years the occupation came to an end with the ignominious retreat of the Soviet army. Far less could my American friends have understood that the US would ever embark on the adventure of waging a massive war by land and from the air against radical Islamists in this Muslim land, instead of engaging in diplomatic, secret-service and financial operations ('In Afghanistan an ass with a sack of dollar notes gets further than a whole army,' as a tribal leader remarked). And least of all would I myself have thought that one day a government of the Federal Republic of Germany focused on humanitarian actions would think that Germany had 'to provide military defence in the Hindu Kush ... in unconditional solidarity with the US'. 'I don't know what German soldiers want over there,' a former Chancellor will tell me in a personal conversation, 'they'll have to stay there for years, possibly decades.' And that's what happened.

But on that peaceful summer evening in Kabul in 1971 I discuss above all with the distinguished and learned professor El Ham of the university the core theological question for Islam, for which the word of God has not become 'flesh' and assumed a human form but has become 'book', a book dictated word for word by God or his angel. Mustn't this word of the eternal God at the same time also be understood as the word of the Prophet and therefore also historically? The Islamic scholar assents to this view in the course of the discussion; indeed it has also been put forward by a famous Pakistani scholar, Fazlur Rahman, and justified at length. But when I go on to ask my Afghan colleague whether he may also put forward this view at the University of Kabul he replies seriously: 'No, if I did, I would have to emigrate.' And just as Fazlur Rahman emigrates and finally teaches at the University of Chicago, so too his Afghan colleague later emigrated. I don't know where he went.

The golden temple of the Sikhs

Of course, while in Kabul I buy beautiful lapis lazuli jewellery for my sisters and female colleagues. 'Haste is the work of the devil,' the Afghans say, but my programme is tight and on 25 July I have to fly on, with Afghan Airlines, two hours to the south-east over bare mountains into the Indus valley, into West Punjab, since 1947 Pakistani, and to Lahore. Here we have a stop of almost an hour – in a packed, sticky plane at noon in a temperature of over 40 degrees. All my clothes are damp with sweat, and unfortunately I see nothing of the beauty of Lahore.

However, I know that the tensions between Pakistan and India could lead to a war at any time, for in March 1971 Bengali East Pakistan (1500 kilometres from West Pakistan) had declared its independence as 'Bangladesh' with the help of India. Bloody oppression by the Pakistani central government and army led to a stream of ten million refugees pouring into India; only after the Pakistani defeat in the India–Pakistan war of 1971/72 did Pakistan recognize the independence of Bangladesh.

Finally we go on to Amritsar in India, the capital of Indian East Punjab, the other side of the border, which is very close. There our luggage is scrupulously searched. For this Punjab is also the restless land of the Sikhs (literally disciples), a religious community comprising around ten million members. The Sikh religion was founded at the end of the fifteenth century by Nanak, who attempted to unite Hindus and Muslims on the basis of an aniconic monotheism. Their holy scripture is the Adi Granth, which consists for the most part of poems and hymns

190

by Nanak and his nine successors, the gurus (teachers); here the doctrines of reincarnation and karma are combined with Indian bhakti piety, with the love of God. Only since the seventeenth century has Sikhism been given a strict military organization, rejecting the Hindu caste system. Since then all male Sikhs add 'Singh' ('lion') to their names, carry a dagger, and wear a turban over their hair, which they don't cut. The women add the word 'Kaur' ('princess') to their name. The light-skinned West Pakistanis, of Aryan origin, speak Urdu (a mixture of Hindi and Persian), the darker-skinned East Pakistanis (Bangladeshis), related to the Dravids of South India, speak Bengali.

Towards evening I am driven in a rickshaw to the main sanctuary of the Sikhs, the Golden Temple. One can hardly imagine a more colourful scene anywhere in the East: the Sikhs peacefully gathering round their main temple with their garments and turbans in so many different colours. The 'Golden Temple', gleaming in the middle of a small holy lake, founded by the fourth guru of the Sikhs in 1577, rebuilt after its destruction and clad in gilded copper plates, is open to all. I too have no problems crossing the great bridge to the temple and its central sanctuary among a crowd of Sikhs.

In the eighteenth century a strong Sikh kingdom had come into being, but after two Sikh wars, in 1849 the British made it a province of British India; after 1966 it then became the Indian federal state of Punjab. In 1971 I notice little of the existing tensions between Sikhs and Hindus. But even at this time demands are being made for an independent Sikh state ('Khalistan'), and in 1984 fundamentalist Sikhs with weapons entrench themselves in the Golden Temple, which will finally be stormed by Indian troops. The fatal consequence is several hundred dead Sikhs, and a short time later, in reaction, the murder of the Indian Prime Minister Indira Gandhi on 31 October 1984 by Sikhs in her own bodyguard.

The India of the Hindus

The next morning, 26 July, I once again visit the Golden Temple and am fascinated. But at noon I fly on with Indian Airlines to Delhi, which is an hour away by plane; there I am met by the Jesuit Frank Loesch. In the evening there are various discussions in the Jesuit College. But since I already know Delhi and its grandiose Mughal buildings well from a previous visit, early the next morning I go to the airport. I fly on over Hyderabad southwards, to Bangalore, the most important industrial city in South India, more than 900 metres up on the South Indian plateau, and therefore characterized by a better climate. European and American businesses are increasingly settling in this well-laid-out garden city, and ever bigger technology firms, which make use of the favourable location.

Here I make contact with one of the most important Indian Protestant theologians, M. M. Thomas of the United Theological College, who has written the widely-read book *The Acknowledged Christ of the Indian Renaissance*. Father

Amalorpavadas, head of the national liturgical and catechetical centre, is an outstanding conversation partner from the Catholic side. I speak in both centres on 'What is the Christian Message?' and 'The Church's Ministry – What Must Remain', always with discussions of every possible question. All the professors of the Catholic faculty are also invited to the lecture in the United Theological College.

Nowhere do I encounter difficulties, although in all the lectures I am starting from the current problems of the church and the need for reform. In Bangalore, too, people in both Christian churches have looked forward to my visit. However, in Bangalore the announcement of my appearance has stirred up the Indian hierarchy, above all the Archbishop of Bombay, Cardinal Valerian Gracias, whom I know from the Council, and the Archbishop of Bangalore, Simon Lourdusamy, who has just been called to Rome. They fear that there will be stormy discussions, but nothing of the kind happens. My lectures on the Christian message today go down well, and the discussion is pleasant and constructive.

In Bangalore I have the good fortune to be lodged among the people in the clergy house of Ignatius Anthappa, pastor of the St Theresa Community, who gained his doctorate at the Gregorian on Christian and Hindu mysticism and has friends in Switzerland. However, I am told that as a result he would forfeit the chance of becoming the next Archbishop of Bangalore. In the slum area around the clergy house I can see and hear a good deal; I get an insight into the church's programme of feeding children and also a little understanding of the wretched situation of the girls working in the textile industry in the basements – just one aspect of the poverty and need of the lower classes in India. The dance drama of a group of girls who also use classical Indian dance forms to depict a Christian content is in marked contrast to this. Here people are deeply rooted in tradition and at the same time open and ready for the new.

The Indian sub-continent between the Himalayas, the Arabian Sea and the Indian Ocean, with almost half a billion people, increasing by millions each year, is a highly diverse country with a highly diverse religion, which is involved in an economic and social upheaval. On my second visit to India I also get to know Hinduism better. I find it far more difficult to understand than the prophetic religions, because it does not appeal to any founder personality and cannot be ascribed to any particular god. It is an 'eternal', old indigenous religion, which hasn't been founded but has grown up. For anyone coming from one of the three sharply-defined prophetic religions, the mystical basic attitude, tending towards unity; the boundless openness and tolerance; the effortless recognition and assimilation of strange ideas; the striving for infinity and the capacity for development of Indian religion are impressive. Alongside polytheistic traits and orgiastic rituals there are also monotheistic convictions, the strictest asceticism and meditation (yoga), and highly spiritual philosophies such as the Shankaras. Of course I also see the negative side: authoritarian systems of family and society, less value attached to women and girls, no concept of 'personality'.

How can one understand such an open, growing, religious system which presents a living unity in an amazing diversity of views, forms and rites? Only decades later could I grasp the unbroken continuity of religions which have undergone very different epochs, constellations, 'paradigms'. The conceptual tools of paradigm analysis helped me later in the TV series *Spurensuche* at the end of the 1990s to grasp both the abiding religious substance of the Hindu religion and also the changing overall constellations of convictions, values and modes of procedure (paradigms) in the various eras. And to crown this work, in July 2006 my loyal companion and adviser on all the television trips, Dr Stephan Schlensog, now General Secretary of the Global Ethic Foundation, produced a comprehensive synthesis in a big book on 'Hinduism. Faith, History, Ethic', which competently takes further my trilogy on the three prophetic religions.

But in 1971 I am simply concerned to see and hear, observe and reflect on as much as possible. For me – as in Christianity – this also includes the limits and negative sides to Indian religion, which mustn't be concealed, Thus for example I ask myself whether the cyclical view of the world in Indian religion, according to which everything, the course of the world and the life of the individual, happens in a cycle of coming into being and passing away, is perhaps a reason for that individual fatalism and social determinism which form the main obstacle to reforms and the social improvement of the Indian masses. Or whether the caste order which, while abolished in the Indian constitution, is in practice apparently ineradicable because it has a religious foundation, is a tremendous burden on the new democratic India that is being built, and much else. Can't there also be a reformed Hinduism of the kind that neo-Hindu reformers programmatically called for as early as the nineteenth century?

In the evening of 28 July I fly from Bangalore to Madras on the Gulf of Bengal, a city of millions, the view of it shaped by colonial building. Its pride is the broad beach, extending over many kilometres and sometimes more than 200 metres wide, which is the second largest in the world. But as well as many beautiful buildings, here gigantic slum areas are growing up, and of course I'm interested in how these poor people can be given concrete help. It is interesting that here the churches have first put up quite simple 'sanitation units' instead of great prestigious buildings. These are simple structures for toilets with washing facilities, always under the supervision of slum-dwellers, who are responsible for order and cleanliness. Of course children's playgrounds and much else are provided.

I speak both in the Catholic Sacred Heart Seminary and to an ecumenical group in the residence of the famous bishop Dr Lesslie Newbigin, the chief architect of the model union of the Protestant churches of South India in the Church of South India. The Catholic church paper has several positive articles about me on the front page and a caricature with a limerick:

> There was a young man called Küng,
> whose praises anyone sung.

Though the things he said
Will sound better when he's dead,
For the moment he is a bit too young.

I take the opportunity to visit Tiruchirapalli, generally called Trichy, which is an hour's flight away; it's a well-known Hindu place of pilgrimage and a cultural centre of the region. I am welcomed by a German doctor, Frau Dr Aschoff, who for years has been working for countless poor patients. I also visit the South Indian temple site in Dravidian style, which is typical of those here: rectangular pyramidal towers without windows, but with countless cult figures in the niches. I also climb up Rock Fort Hill, the summit of which is crowned with a fortress.

But above all I am interested in the work of an English Benedictine, Bede Griffiths, who has built a Christian ashram here, a centre for religious studies and meditation. Highly respected by the Hindus, this Christian lives in a completely Indian style in his outer dress and inner attitude. Thus he goes much further than those Jesuits whom I got to know years before in Calcutta, who celebrated a liturgy adapted to Indian customs. Bede Griffiths, with whom I am quickly on the same wavelength, shows in exemplary fashion how far the inculturation of Christian belief in India can go: a truly Indian Christianity.

Sri Lanka and Buddhism

From Bangalore, on 1 August 1971 I fly to the biggest island in the Indian Ocean, on which the other great religion of India, which has practically vanished in India because of the decadence of its monasteries and the Muslim invasions, has found a new homeland. On Sri Lanka the older, strongly monastic form of Buddhism has rooted itself to such a degree that here the most important canon of the scriptures of this Theravada Buddhism have been written down in a central Indian language, Pali.

For almost three centuries the country was occupied by the Portuguese and Dutch and from 1802 to 1948 it was under British rule. The capital, Colombo, the economic centre of the country and one of the most important ports in Asia, has many poor districts, but displays a colourful medley of Hindu and Buddhist temples, and also mosques and Christian churches. The city centre with the government buildings and the Davatagaha Mosque, the oldest in the city, is impressive. The Tamil opposition – Hindus and Christians, whose home is above all in the north and east of the island – had developed into a powerful Marxist–Leninist popular liberation front which in April 1971 was able to wage a first revolt with attacks on police stations. The background is not so much religious differences between Buddhist Singhalese and Hindu Tamils as economic problems. The carefree years of the tropical island which Prime Minister Sirimawo Bandaranaike (wife of the murdered Prime Minister) had promised with her programme of low taxes, cheap accommodation, free education and transport, seems to have been beyond the financial resources of the island state. It has to live above all on the export of tea, rubber and coconuts, and now has an enormous budget deficit, high unemployment, growing foreign debt and inadequate support from the countries of the Eastern bloc. The left-wing course has to be revised, and restrictions are on the way.

But I am interested above all in Buddhism. I am driven about 75 miles in a car – unfortunately by a chauffeur who won't stop fiddling with the accelerator – through many palm groves into the central hill country, where there is a marvellous view of the tea terraces, which are admirably looked after. By a lake in the centre of these plantations lies Kandy, the former capital of the Singhalese kingdom and today the most important pilgrimage centre in the country. Here the holy tooth of the Buddha is venerated. The Buddha, the 'Enlightened One', has long fascinated me; in terms of content and spirituality the Buddhist religion embodies probably the strongest antithesis to Christianity.

Western people too are impressed by this 'middle way' between the extremes of the loss of the senses and self-torment – neither hedonism nor asceticism. The 'four noble truths' of Buddha Gautama – the core of his Benares sermon – seek to lead to insight into why one suffers, in order to grasp the cause of suffering and do away with it. The cause of suffering is none other than selfishness, greed, which leads from rebirth to rebirth. Only by recognizing this greed and rooting it out can suffering be overcome. To achieve that, human beings must take the eightfold path of the Buddha. It leads to redemption from selfishness, from the endless cycle of births in the seeming world (maya) of suffering, through extinction (nirvana) and liberation to the infinite.

However, this primal Buddhist message was as little talked of in Buddhist Kandy as Jesus' Sermon on the Mount is talked of in an Italian place of pilgrimage. Rather, here a monasticism which forms its own monastic hierarchy and has developed a function in supporting the state is massively present. Of course I also look at the temple elephants, which play a major role in the colourful processions here and are taken to a nearby river to drink and bathe. I keep asking myself how this development has come about. Over the course of the centuries the simple religion of Buddha, which regards everything external as maya, as unreal appearance, becomes a religion in which relics such as the Buddha's tooth, the many buildings and other external features seem tremendously important, as does that thinking in terms of merit which wants to achieve salvation through pious works. Numerous parallels with medieval Christianity occur to me here. There are also paradigm changes in Buddhism, which I shall investigate a decade later in connection with my Tübingen dialogue lectures with the Göttingen Buddhologist Heinz Bechert.

Indonesia: tolerant Islam

On 3 August I fly from Colombo to Singapore, former 'outpost of the British empire', and in this pulsating city state get a foretaste of the liveliness of the Chinese mainland. The population – two million at the time of my visit (76 per cent Chinese, 15 per cent Malay) – grows steadily to three million. Later I get to know this city on the southern tip of the Malay peninsula, soon to become the most important transportation, industrial, commercial, financial and services centre of Asia, better and introduce my television film on Chinese religion with pictures from the 'lion city' and a Chinese lion dance.

The very next day I have to fly on to Jakarta, since the Goethe Institute has invited me to give lectures there. This modern capital, with its national memorial, central museum and some broad boulevards, but no real city centre, already has three million inhabitants. Indonesia is a country with splendid exotic vegetation, beautiful women and handsome men; it has 3000 islands and the longest series of volcanoes on earth, which fortunately cause damage only rarely.

That evening in the tropical warmth I have a very deep discussion with the excellent student chaplain Franz Magnis-Suseno, a Jesuit, about what distinguishes Christianity from the other religions. It cannot be just general concepts such as justice, love, meaning in life, being and doing good, humanity. More precisely, the specific feature of Christianity is the person of Jesus Christ himself, of course with all his relations to God and human beings. Christian theology has to be constructed from this centre. That is the topic of my lecture on 4 August to a general audience invited by the Protestant theological faculty. The churches have a chance of unity only if they reflect again on that to which all churches appeal.

Indonesia, the country with the largest Muslim population in the world, is the land of a gentle Islam – by comparison with some countries in the Middle East. 90 per cent of the population are Muslims, who are in general very tolerant towards Christians and Hindus. The flight from Jakarta to Yogyakarta is marvellous. The volcanoes of Java with their cones more than 3000 metres high tower above the clouds, illuminated by the sun, peaceful and majestic. How could I have guessed at that time that in 2006 'Yogya' would not only be threatened by the nearby volcano of Merapi but also be visited by a fearful earthquake with more than 5700 dead and 36,000 wounded?. The Jesuits have their schools in Yogyakarta – the old capital, already with a population of a million in 1971, but little industrialized. It is a stronghold of the batik industry and of silversmiths; there on 6 August I give my lecture on 'What is the Christian Message?' in the Catholic faculty; it is translated into Indonesian and appears the next year in printed form. Here too there are numerous discussions, after the lectures, in the breaks, at meals.

The dean of the faculty, Fr Tom Jacobs, and the Buddhist specialist Fr Jan Bakker kindly escort me the next day to the most grandiose Buddhist building in

Indonesia, about 40 kilometres away. This is Borobodur (erected around 800), a seven-storey pyramidal monument on a square with sides about 125 metres long. Borobodur represents a three-dimensional mandala with gates and stairways towards the four points of the compass and 1500 bas-reliefs with scenes from the life and pre-life of the Buddha, a purification which leads from the region of sensuality, with voluptuous women's bodies, animals, plants and monsters, to the pure heights of religious symbols, all crowned by 72 stupas with sitting sculptures of the Buddha. From the top of Borobodur there is a glorious view over the fertile land to the volcanoes; there we talk about the religions and their impor-tance for modern men and women – notions which later I bring into lectures and which, I am told, also go down well with Indonesian non-theologians.

The next day we go to neighbouring Prambanan, to the largest Hindu temple site (ninth century) in central Java, destroyed in the sixteenth century by an earthquake and rebuilt only from 1937 on. The biggest temple, almost 50 metres high, dedicated to the god Shiva, shows scenes from the Ramayana epic on its stone reliefs. There is a raised stage for big dance and theatre festivals. In front of the main temple – I'm lucky and for me this is a tremendous experience – a performance of this oldest epic in Sanskrit literature is taking place: the story of the life and fate of King Rama from Ayodhya, the seventh incarnation of the god Vishnu. It's a remarkably colourful play with 450 actors in splendid garments, with lengthy songs and dances but also with demonic masks and an amusing scene featuring apes who, according to the epic, build a bridge from the Indian con-tinent to Sri Lanka to rescue Rama's wife Sita from the clutches of the demon king Ravana.

We talk a lot about '*Indonesianisasi*' ('Indonesianization'), which mustn't stop at externals but should grow out of new reflection on the Christian faith. Jesus' message of non-violence has something to say in a country of gentle and sensitive people who after a Communist rebellion in 1965 allowed themselves to be torn apart in mur-derous rage in a massacre of tens of thousands of Communists and Chinese (who were friendly to the Communists). 'Amok', too, is a Malayan word for 'rage': killing in blind rage, first observed among indigenous Malays. On my return, out of grati-tude I send the German-speaking theologians the standard six-volume lexicon *Religion in Geschichte und Gegenwart* and a three-volume Bible lexicon.

It gives me special pleasure that to end with, though needing some effort, I manage to fly east on 8 August to the little island paradise of Bali, to which, the Balinese say, the Hindu gods fled in the face of Islam and where everyday life, art and religion are still always interwoven. It's a delight to travel through the fertile land with many attractive people on the streets and thousands of temples. Almost every farmstead has a shrine where flowers, rice and fruit for the gods and spirits are placed every day. I particularly remember the temple site of Pura Besakih on the southern slope of Gunung Agun, with an enchanting view of the sea. But I was especially impressed by the evening dances in a village with few tourists, above all the Ketjak or ape dance, presented with hissing and shrieking from rough throats in a monotonous rhythm; this is a motif from the Ramayana, but danced by young men with wild passion, whereas the gentle Balinese women in precious costumes do variations on Indian motifs.

Of the many wood carvings that I am offered I choose a little black winged lion which still protects my lake house in Sursee. And in Tübingen I am reminded of Indonesia every day by a piece of Javanese batik – a coloured silk weave produced with the use of wax – given to me at that time by Indonesian friends, depicting an attractive girl fearlessly defending herself against a monster with two giant pairs of scissors. From Bali's insignificant capital Denpasar with its many traders I fly on to Australia via Yogyakarta and Jakarta. In this way I once again regain the Western, 'Christian' world from the worlds of Islam, Hinduism and Buddhism.

At the antipodes: Australia

After a twelve-hour journey I arrive in Perth around midnight on 12 August 1971. Perth is one of the most isolated cities in the world, separated from Sydney by a gigantic continental desert and more than 3200 kilometres from any other large city, but in a beautiful setting on Swan River, which is like a lake, and generously laid out with a giant park. I am now again among white people whose language I understand – and that's a great relief. They just have their distinctive accent, which is evident as soon as they pronounce the word 'Austrailian'. And of course they have their special history, which began 200 years ago with British penal colonies on the east coast. Learned treatises still argue whether this white colonization with its cruel decimation of the primal inhabitants ('Aborigines') who had immigrated millennia before should be understood as an imperialist invasion or 'patriotically', as an achievement in civilizing. Be this as it may, today not only Perth but also the other Australian cities make a very cultivated, more cosmopolitan impression. It's winter here, but the climate in Perth is a sunny Mediterranean one; the flowers are blooming and many people are swimming and surfing. Australia more than any country is a nation of sports.

Time and again I have to present myself to a totally unknown public in a country which is completely new to me, and for that I constantly need a new attitude to the people whom I want to convince of my cause, which is by no means taken for granted by many of them. Here I am helped by my openness to people of different origins, nations, skin colour and religion, an openness which has been given me by nature, shaped by education and encouraged by theology. Nowhere do I play the 'professor', so I am delighted when my host from Yogyakarta later writes to me: 'What impressed us most and drew us to you was the combination of theologian and friend ... the days for which we could have you with us remain a powerful memory, and perhaps there will be an occasion for us to meet again – wherever.'

I am given a very warm welcome in Australia, already in the mercantile city of Perth – gigantic cargoes of steel, aluminium and stone go from Western Australia to Japan and China. But before a public appearance I never forget to ask a higher authority to grant me the right tone for the right word and the understanding and good will of the public, particularly in a country which is fond of presenting itself as egalitarian. And my visit to the University of Western Australia, which is seldom visited by a European theologian, is enjoyable from beginning to end.

However, my real destination is Melbourne – a three-hour flight away – Australia's second largest city, still very English in its architecture, the capital of the state of Victoria and until 1926 the seat of the federal government. It is still a leader in culture, gastronomy and fashion. It was founded not as a penal colony but by settlers in the time of the gold rush. A punctual arrival there has dictated my so far packed timetable. There is a television interview as soon as I arrive. Trinty College has invited me and I stay in the fine residence of the Principal, Dr Robin Sharwood, on the campus of the University of Melbourne; the Catholic archbishop – the Roman system is functioning – has refused to share in the invitation. My short but intensive teaching begins the very next day, 15 August, with a Sunday sermon in the Anglican St Paul's Cathedral. Then from Monday to Friday (16 to 20 August 1971) there are major lectures every evening, which pack Wilson Hall with 1300 people. My general topic is 'Jesus – A Challenge for the Church'. On the first evening I speak on 'Is the Church Infallible?' and then give three lectures on Jesus: 'Jesus the Troublemaker'; 'Jesus' Destiny'; 'Jesus the Peacemaker'. My final lecture is on 'Is the Church Democratic?' All this is to great applause and at the end is received with a standing ovation. Later, around 120 tapes of these lectures circulate throughout Australia.

My hosts ensure that I also have a day out in the neighbouring hills. There I have the experience of seeing how tremendously wide the Australian cities spread, since there is an abundance of space and every family lives in its own house with a garden; soon Melbourne will extend for 100 kilometres along the coast, a sea of one-family houses on the plain. I have good memories of the conversations with my perfect host, the philosopher Max Charlesworth, whose advice I later ask about the Aborigines, and with the patrologist Eric Osborne, who is working hard for the United Faculty of Protestant and Catholic professors and students and often visits me in Tübingen. There are also the radio and television interviewer John Collins and Fr Gerald O'Connor SJ, on whose family estate a big reception is given in my honour with dozens of guests.

I spend the weekend visiting the federal capital Canberra in the north of the Australian Alps, and going far into the Australian interior. Because of the irre-solvable rivalry for the status of capital between Melbourne, often compared with Boston in temperament and atmosphere, and the lively port of Sydney, since 1913 Canberra has been stamped out on the ground half-way between the two according to the plans of an American architect. It has two centres, a government and a commercial centre, in concentric patterns, interrupted by rather sterile gigantic radial streets – all enormously spacious and very loosely laid out, especially in the residential areas. Since 1927 it has been the official seat of government; the Australian National University, where excellent specialists in religious and cultural studies work, is particularly important for me.

On Sunday 22 August 1971 I hold a service here for the German-speaking community. In the evening the Society for the Study of Religion and Theology gives a reception. In a long conversation which follows in the home of Professor Otto van der Sprenkel I meet the charming orientalist Tony Johns and for the first time Julia Ching from Shanghai, who is to become a very valuable adviser and friend in the future in connection with many questions about the world religions. I readily confess that from the beginning I was fascinated by her quite different, Chinese, facial expressions, gestures and thinking. Julia Ching's large and important family had been split up by the Chinese revolution. Some decided for Mao and others for Taiwan. She herself became a Christian in Taiwan and for some years was a member of a religious order, but she later married the American scholar Willard Oxtoby, who likewise became a good friend of mine. Both then became professors in the University of Toronto, where I once spent a guest semester. These contacts are important for my understanding of Chinese culture and religion and I shall be mentioning them again later.

On 23 August I fly from Canberra to Australia's oldest and biggest city, Sydney. It's not just its new Opera House built into the harbour, looking like a ship, an architectural jewel with its roof designed to look like three sails, that makes Sydney with its natural harbour and waterfront extending over dozens of kilometres one of the most beautiful cities in the world. It is shown to me with pride in an extensive boat trip after a drive over the wide spans of the eight-lane Harbour Bridge, a technical marvel of the early twentieth century, for lunch in the villa of a Swiss industrialist. However, one mustn't dangle one's feet in the water, since there are sharks lurking everywhere.

I didn't come to Sydney primarily for sightseeing, though, but at the invitation of the Australian and New Zealand Conference of Theology, for which I again have to speak to a large audience about infallibility and Christian ministry. As fate has it, Archbishop Charles Moeller, the Under-Secretary of the Vatican Congregation for the Doctrine of the Faith, has been invited by the Catholic Newman Association at almost the same time. This Louvain professor, whom I know well from the Council, is personally well disposed towards me. He sleeps in the same guest apartment, in the bed that I am to use the next day; 'the sleeping arrangement' seems to be Küng's 'only concession to obedience towards Rome' is the headline of an article in the *Sydney Morning Herald* of 21 August 1971. When we are alone together we have very friendly conversations. In them Moeller reveals to me that he has been to Pope Paul VI and managed to have the word 'infallible teaching' deleted from the encyclical *Humanae vitae* in connection with the condemnation of birth control. I explain to him that despite his good intentions, unfortunately he hasn't done us a service here. The change disguises the strict Roman view of the *magisterium ordinarium*, the everyday teaching office, namely that on the basis of the accord of the episcopate with the Pope the prohibition of contraception has to be regarded as 'infallible teaching'. It seems that scales fall from Archbishop Moeller's eyes when he recognizes that he has prevented a clear solution to the question of infallibility.

Before that, a two-day congress of theologians takes place at the University of Sydney; as well as presiding at the worship, on both days I have to give a paper, here too on the question of infallibility and then on the problem of ministry. And as in Melbourne there are a press conference, interviews, discussions and television.

With the lectures in Perth, Melbourne, Canberra and Sydney – as always combined with many side events – I have fulfilled all but one of my obligations in Australia. But now the University of Melbourne has offered me an honorarium of a kind I have never received before or since: fourteen days holiday in Australia at a place of my choosing, from 26 August to 10 September 1971. After studying the prospectus sent to me I choose a little island near the 1900-kilometre-long Great Barrier Reef with the beautiful name Daydream Island.

So I fly north from Sydney to tropical Queensland, to Mackay, where I view the coast and visit a sugar-cane field. Kangaroos are rarely to be seen in the wild, but there are eucalyptus bushes and gum trees *en masse*; from Australia more than 600 species have spread all over the warmer regions of the earth. From Mackay I continue by helicopter to Hayman Island, but this holiday resort seems to me to cater too much for the masses; from there I go by boat to Hook Island and the under-water observatory, where one can admire the fishes of the Great Barrier Reef. Finally I go by helicopter and boat to Daydream Island, where there is room only for a single hotel. There in an attractive large room I can enjoy a view on the one side of the mainland and on the other towards the Whitsunday group of islands and the Pacific; the legendary English seafarer James Cook sailed past them on Pentecost (Whitsunday) 1770 on his discovery of the east coast.

Free days at last: the daydream island

'Daydream'– at last I can get some rest: no commitments, what a blessing! At last I have a few free days after a strenuous Tübingen semester and a no less strenuous journey around half our globe – measured purely mathematically at the equator about 20,000 kilometres. At last I have time to assimilate some of the numerous impressions of the most varied landscapes and cities, cultures and languages, individuals and conversations.

The planned expansion of my horizon has indeed come about. The scope of my vision has widened tremendously. The line in the distance at which sky and earth, sky and sea, seem to touch becomes clearer when a ship appears on the horizon or the sun disappears over it. The geographical and even more the intellectual area which I can now survey to introduce my 'Introduction to Christianity' almost transcends my power of comprehension. Yet I must make the attempt and quietly consider how I can grasp and conceptualize the reality of this world.

Even in the holidays I enjoy structuring my day. I can't sleep into the day, I look forward too much to the sun, my elixir of life, physically and psychologically, as long as it isn't too burning. And I love to swim before breakfast, which in the holidays is a large English one, so my lunch can be mostly limited to fruit. Of course I read newspapers, which I get everywhere, but in Australia I find it difficult to obtain any news about home; so little of importance seems to be happening there. Basically I don't miss this news. But wherever I am, I want to follow closely what is happening in world politics and be able to assess it. World politics and the most important developments in the global economy are part of my horizon. In later years I have the good fortune through my activity in the InterAction Council of former heads of state and government to keep getting information about Australia at first hand from Prime Minister Malcolm Fraser (1975-83), who for me embodies the healthy Australian pioneer spirit.

And sport? I swim three times a day, morning, midday (with a siesta afterwards) and evening, in the swimming pool or in the sea. Occasionally I go water-skiing. But I am even fonder of snorkelling and diving. Here I use oxygen equipment for the first time and also have my first healthy underwater shock: suddenly my diving mask clings to my face when I breathe in – no oxygen, I can't breathe. I'm anxious to surface immediately. But I mustn't rise too quickly, quicker than my own water bubbles, because in the rapidly decreasing water pressure bubbles could form in my lungs – a frequent cause of fatal accidents to divers. Fortunately I was only a few metres deep; above the surface I tear the mask from my face. What's happened? The trainer forgot to fill the oxygen flask!

Of course this doesn't deter me from diving. The bright world of plants, corals, underwater creatures and fish is too fascinating. Little sharks swim around here, but I'm told that they aren't dangerous and in fact they do me no harm. That's not the case with other tiny living beings which are presumably responsible for an ear infection, so that inflammation (along with a chill) blocks both my ears and I can hear only as if through a wall. It's an unpleasant feeling to hear oneself speaking. I don't talk a lot on this 'daydream island'; the Australian holiday public isn't very interested, nor do I want to tell my life story to everyone. But unfortunately there is no doctor, nor do the aspirin which I am offered help. So on 8 September I go by boat to the mainland, where at any rate there is a new hospital in the little town of Proserpine; the doctor there gives me ear medication, but the wrong kind. There is no improvement up to the end of my stay on the island.

In Canberra I had seen in a bookshop the American author Henry Miller's novels *Tropic of Cancer* (1934) and *Tropic of Capricorn* (1939). I thought that although they were autobiographical retrospects on Miller's turbulent years in

Paris and New York they were perhaps the right reading on my way beyond the Tropic of Cancer. At all events, what I read was illuminating and certainly not without higher literary qualities. Miller is regarded as the eloquent, sometimes intoxicatingly prophetic 'father' of those writers who made a name for themselves around the middle of the twentieth century by deliberately breaking all taboos in the depiction of sexuality. But in his liberation from Puritan constraints Miller is far from reaching the level of Dostoievsky, whom he emphatically praises. Dostoievsky's *The Demons* already showed total laxity and lack of constraint, a world obsessed with sexuality, brutality and crime. However, in his amorality Miller, the eternal Bohemian, lacks the 'counter-world' of sacred values and criteria (as clearly represented in Dostoievsky's *The Brothers Karamazov* by the starets and Alyosha) which doesn't come even when in later years he settles in Big Sur on the Californian coast and gathers a host of admirers around him there. It is no help that finally, disgusted, he turns away from fashionable sex and com- mercialized gratification – this isn't what his attempt at liberation was meant to be about.

It is important to note for my future book that there is evidently something like an amoral 'night culture' not only in Russia but also in Paris and New York, in short, in the secularized West. It is grounded, not in a 'pagan past' or in 'Tatar oppression', but in a libertinistic pseudo-liberation of which one must be critical.

The new horizon: the great ideologies

So alongside the great religions, the great secular ideologies must also be taken seriously as the constantly-present horizon against which I have begun to write my 'Introduction to Christianity'. If I am interpreting my observations so far all over the world rightly, both technological evolutionary humanism and political social revolutionary humanism are in crisis.

If I think back to all my experiences in the Western world, the great ideology of a technological evolution which is automatically to lead to humanity is shat- tered. The progress of modern science, medicine, technology, commerce, communication and culture is certainly unprecedented; it surpasses the boldest fantasies of Jules Verne and other futurologists. Nevertheless, to a growing degree, precisely in the most progressive Western industrial nations, people are doubting that dogma in which they had long believed, that science and tech- nology are the key to universal human happiness and that progress comes about unavoidably and as it were automatically. What disturbs me most is no longer the danger of a nuclear destruction of civilization, which though still very real has been diminished by the political agreements between the superpowers. It is the great global and economic policy with its contradictions, the growing gulf between rich and poor peoples, and the growth of all the problems at a national level that are swamping governments. And it is even more the local problems that

203

are becoming evident in all the great metropolises of the world and threaten the future of all urban agglomerations: behind an often imposing skyline an urban landscape with increasingly polluted air, contaminated water, streets filled with refuse, clogged traffic, a lack of living space, excessively high rents, noise everywhere, damage to health, rising aggressiveness and crime, more and more ghettos and heightened tensions between races, classes and ethnic groups, expanding apparently without limits. At any rate this is not the grandiose 'secular city' which optimistic theologians such as the American Harvey Cox, my conversation partner during a week in Montreal, had dreamed of at the beginning of the 1960s.

Wherever I go, in Leningrad and Tashkent as in Melbourne and Sydney and even in the developing countries, in New Delhi or Jakarta, the same phenomena make themselves felt. They can't simply be set down and taken into account as the probably unavoidable dark side of great progress. Some things are beyond doubt the consequence of short cuts and abuses. But taken together, they all derive from this ambivalent progress which is so desired, planned and worked for, a progress which, if it goes on like this, develops and destroys authentic humanity at the same time.

But I don't want to paint things in black and white and say goodbye to hope along with ideology. What needs to be given up, it seems to me, is technological progress as an ideology which, governed by interests, generates pseudo-rational illusions of what can be done. We need to give up faith in science as a total explanation of reality ('world-view') and technocracy as a healing substitute religion. But what mustn't be given up is a concern for authentic human progress and the hope of a meta-technological society: a human way of working nearer to nature, a more balanced social structure and the satisfaction also of non-material needs, those human values which first make life worth living and cannot be quantified in money terms.

But if on the other hand I think back to my experiences in the Soviet Union, the great ideology of a political–social revolution which is meant automatically to lead to humanity is also shattered. From Leningrad via Moscow to Tashkent, nowhere in the heavens is there evidence of the advent of a classless free Communist society. Rather, in a quite different way from in the West there is the threat of the overwhelming power of the state: through the identification of state and party a socialist statism at the expense of the working population. Individuals are comforted with an appeal to the distant future happiness of humankind and are compelled to increase output in a merciless system with harsh quotas.

But here too I don't want to say goodbye to hope along with ideology. It seems to me that what needs to be given up is revolution as an ideology, which overthrows society by force and erects a new system of rule by human beings over human beings. What need to be given up are Marxism as a total explanation of reality ('world-view') and revolution as the panacea of a substitute religion, which is what some 1968ers are still dreaming of. But what mustn't be given up is the effort to make a fundamental change in society and the hope of a meta-revolutionary society beyond stagnation, revolution and an uncritical acceptance of the given, along with total criticism of the existing situation.

Won't it perhaps be possible in a more distant future to combine the two, the longing of a political–revolutionary humanism for a fundamental change in circumstances, for a better, more just, world, a truly good life, with the demands of a technological evolutionary humanism for the possibility of concrete realization, for an avoidance of terror, for a pluralistic order of freedom which is open to problems, a freedom which compels no one to a faith? And don't Christians in particular perhaps have a decisive contribution to make to that? The description of this horizon is to form the beginning of my book. These are my reflections. But I can't go on dreaming of the future on this beautiful little island. The present calls. I must set off again.

New Zealand: episcopal pastoral letter against a theologian

On 10 September I go first by boat to the mainland, then by helicopter to the small airport of Mackay, and on to the capital of the Australian state of Queensland, to Brisbane, the up-and-coming economic and tourist centre of the Gold Coast, which has had a university since 1909. In Brisbane I have to talk on the question of the essence of Christianity, which now constantly preoccupies me, under the title 'Jesus – The Challenge for the Church'. With my blocked ears, which echo, speaking isn't easy. The audience can't think themselves into the speaker's situation, one must simply act as if nothing were the matter. When will my ears open again? But I can be more than content with the weeks in Australia. Everywhere the media response has been wide and generally speaking very positive.

The very next day I leave Australia and fly about 2000 kilometres east, between the Tasman Sea and the Pacific Ocean, to New Zealand and its largest city, Auckland on North Island, which has expanded tremendously. Although I don't arrive until towards midnight, I get a warm welcome from the Anglican Principal of St John's College, Dr Raymond Forster, and am taken to the college. I learn from him – and here I am suddenly back in the reality of the old world – that the Roman Catholic Archbishop of Auckland, Reginald Delargey, felt the need to have a pastoral letter read out in all Catholic churches warning against the theologian from Tübingen. One could be proud of such a unique distinction if it weren't so sad. What is worrying this churchman? But in Europe such negative propaganda brings me positive points.

For I have media at my disposal which reach further than episcopal pastoral letters. On 12 September 1971 I give the *New Zealand Herald* an extensive interview which, however, avoids unnecessary polemic against the bishop. I also have a full programme in Auckland. I preach on 12 September and give my two lectures on 13/14 September to full houses. Unfortunately there is time only for a drive around Auckland before my planned sailing.

When at the end of my visit Raymond Forster asks me whether I would like to visit Reginald Delargey, I immediately say yes. As others couldn't have expected, but I did on the basis of my knowledge of such gentlemen, the bishop welcomes me privately with marked warmth, as if nothing had happened – having shown himself to be a good Roman Catholic in public by his pastoral letter. We talk about some things in the church and see much in the same way. At the end of our discussion he gives me a bronze medallion of Paul VI's visit to the South Pacific and remarks (thereby betraying himself), 'Let's say goodbye in friendship. Who knows, next time you come back here, perhaps you'll be a cardinal.' As I go out I say with a smile: 'There's little hope of that, and I'm not aspiring to it.' Things in fact turn out as expected, namely the other way round. Five years later Archbishop Delargey, with his conformity to Rome, becomes a cardinal – by this he certainly achieves the greatest happiness on earth for himself, which I don't envy him. I congratulate him cheerfully. 'I see your Grace got there first. And for me there is absolutely no hope. Nevertheless, congratulations and all blessings.'

The second most beautiful country in the world

'New Zealand is the second most beautiful country in the world,' I am told before my departure by Placidus Jordan, the experienced journalist and later Benedictine father, with whom I have made friends. Had he not been Swiss, he would certainly have put New Zealand in first place: a land with about the same surface area as the Federal Republic of Germany, but with a population not even the size of Switzerland. However, whereas Switzerland is surrounded by powerful neighbours, New Zealand's nearest neighbour, Australia, is 1600 kilometres away. Whereas the Confederacy dates its foundation from the federal letter of the three original cantons, dated 1291, which still exists, New Zealand was 'discovered' only in 1642 by the Dutchman A. J. Tasman, but taken over politically by the British government in 1838-40 and declared independent in 1907 as a dominion in the British Commonwealth.

Here, however, people tend to forget the Maoris who, coming from central and east Polynesia, settled New Zealand as early as 900. They were then cruelly decimated by immigrants in a number of wars; today they make up only around 10 per cent of the population. Whereas little Switzerland embraces four linguistic cultures, in New Zealand one often feels more English than the English, and people are sometimes annoyed at the increasing immigration from Asian countries. In 1987 a legal judgement conceded to the Maoris that the Treaty of Waitangi, concluded with their ancestors in 1840, had precedence above all other laws, especially in questions of land law; the original inhabitants are thus still getting some of their rights.

The country, consisting of two large islands, which is more than 1700 kilometres from north to south, is of extraordinary beauty and diversity, with its endless wide national parks and countless untouched areas. On North Island, towards the equator, there are volcanoes, thermal springs and geysers; on South Island, to which I now fly from Auckland, are the great New Zealand Alps (Mount Cook is 3763 metres) with glaciers, fiords and lakes; as a Swiss one can indeed feel at home here. I fly direct to the city at the south end of South Island, Dunedin, on fiord-like Otago Bay. Antarctic expeditions start from this settlement founded by Scottish Presbyterians in 1848, planned as an octagon. I stay in the college named after John Knox, the Scottish Reformer, and feel very much more at home at dinner with the professors, mostly Scottish Presbyterians, who know about my Scottish John Knox cap, than with the ambiguously friendly Roman Catholic Archbishop of Auckland.

In Dunedin on 16/17 September I give four public lectures and discuss vigorously with professors and students – now again with open ears. For at the other end of the world I have come across a pupil of the internationally renowned Tübingen ear, nose and throat specialist Professor Dietrich Plester, whose medication works quickly. There is also of course sightseeing. But this time it is not so much the port that is interesting as the wonderful landscape of Otago province around Dunedin. In the evening of the second day of lectures I can drive with a New Zealand theologian, Professor Ian Breward, who is both knowledgeable and friendly, to Central Otago, which in the summer is the hottest and in the winter the coldest region of South Island, to the famous Lake Wanaka. It's a unique experience to drive through a landscape with so little traffic, so few roads and uncultivated nature. By the sea in our log cabin we are very much alone. However, it's got very cold and I'm grateful for two pullovers lent to me which I wear one on top of the other.

By comparison with Switzerland and other densely populated European countries New Zealand is a very peaceful land: today it has a population of 4 million with 40 million sheep and 10 million cattle. For the next two days I enjoy the peaceful beauty of the country and also a gold mine (closed down). On 19 September we go from Lake Wanaka to the no less attractive Lake Wakatipu, to Queenstown and then by boat to the gloriously situated Peak Farm with dinner in the Presbyterian manse. Looking at this lonely farm on a green hill, I catch myself romantically dreaming how beautiful it would be if one could escape all the hustle and bustle of this hectic life and retire here to such a farm where in the evening the sheep are cheerfully and peacefully gathered in by a dog. But instead of realizing such fantasies of dropping out, I later have to content myself with conversations about New Zealand, albeit with the highly competent Jim Bolger, to be Prime Minister from 1990 to 1997, who is also a member of the InterAction Council.

The next day we travel south, via Cromwell – named after the famous Scottish Reformer, revolutionary and 'Lord Protector' Oliver Cromwell – back to

Dunedin where until 1 a.m. I deal with the correspondence which has arrived from Tübingen. On 21 September I return north by plane for a very strenuous lecture trip. To describe it in rather more detail: in the early morning I fly from Dunedin to Christchurch, the largest city on the east coast of South Island, on the edge of the Canterbury plain, 'the most English city outside England', built like a chessboard with numerous parks and gardens by the River Avon. There is a press conference as soon as I arrive. Around 10.30 I give my first lecture at the university on the Christian message, there is a short snack at lunchtime, and at 1 p.m. I give a second lecture on the Christian ministry, with a discussion. I then fly on to Wellington, the capital of New Zealand, on the south end of North Island, built on the steep slopes of a bay in Cook Strait. I remember it for the storm wind which blows through the strait between the two islands; some manuscripts are snatched from my hand as I get out of the plane and I have to pick them up quickly on the runway. In Wellington too – first settled in 1840, a former church of St Paul still bears witness to the neo-Gothic wooden architecture of the nineteenth century – I give my lecture on the Christian message, followed by a discussion,

22 September is another big travelling day. I fly from Wellington via Auckland out of New Zealand north to Nouméa in sub-tropical New Caledonia, which is part of French Polynesia. One can already see from the plane the gigantic nickel mining area there; the island is one of the world's greatest producers of nickel. James Cook gave it this Roman name of Scotland (Caledonia); later the French annexed it. There on the first morning I deal with the post, plan my further journey and do some shopping. 'When do the shops open?' I ask. 'At nine, but the Chinese open at eight.' This is part of the answer to the question why the Chinese are so successful everywhere.

Then finally there is a short twenty-minute flight to the coral Île des Pins, which because of its volcanic core doesn't in fact have any palms but pines (*Araucaria cooki*). What originally seems to be an exaggeration by my Zurich travel agency in fact proves to be true. The only really quiet hotel to my taste between Australia and California, where I can read and work quietly, is not the Château Royal in Nouméa but the Relais de Kanuméra on this island. I want to spend my well-deserved summer holidays here at the end of September and write my book.

The island, surrounded by coral reefs, is a reserve of the Melanesians who inhabit the Western Pacific north-west of Australia and are distinguished by their loose curly hair, broad noses and thick lips from the Polynesians who inhabit the islands of the central Pacific. Theirs was a culture without metal until the arrival of the Europeans, and this is still evident in the only larger building of our hotel, the restaurant, which is built in South Sea style out of marvellous tropical wood with no nails. I don't really live in the hotel but in a South Sea hut covered with straw, though it is made modestly comfortable with a ventilator and a shower. Because of a specially constructed central pillar, the roof of this hut doesn't rest directly on the side walls, but has space for air to circulate. I soon notice two rats running around up on the walls. To the daughter of my host in Auckland, a biology student, I owe a 'relaxed' relationship with these long-legged creatures. She let me stroke a cute young rat which she was observing for her university studies. So I give these rats a few days. But when they become increasingly dependent, and by night even run over my bedclothes and wake me up, I point them out to the management. Poison in the shower drains quickly finishes them off.

My life here has little in common with the exotic and erotic character of Paul Gauguin's or Max Pechstein's paintings of the South Seas. But the simplicity, calm and extraordinary beauty of this solitary life on the beach of the big bay now really puts my thoughts to rest. 'There is nothing more beautiful under the sun than to be under the sun,' remarked Ingeborg Bachmann. Music is all I miss, so after supper I like to listen for a long time to the soft harmonious sounds of the South Seas. A small table is enough for me to work on during the day. I usually put it out on the white sand by the clear blue water, where hardly anyone passes; this is a glorious spot of earth just for me. Evidently it isn't high season, and my conversations are usually limited to a little small talk. The Melanesian chambermaids chatter a lot, but speak hardly any French or English. I always take my notepad with me to meals, look over what I've written and write some more. When I'm asked what I'm writing, I reply, '*Mes impressions.*'

I eagerly await the post, which comes across to us from the mainland only twice. I'm always particularly excited about the reports which my deputy in the Institute, Dr Hermann Häring, regularly sends to my staging posts; he calls them 'a little peephole into Tübingen'. Apart from all the personal and administrative details, these tell me for example about the list of professors who support me in Rome compiled by Dr Bernd Jaspert of Marburg; or about the election of our church lawyer Johannes Neumann as Rector, a ceremony which has to be transferred to the Senate Hall in the Botanical Institute under police protection because of the student disruptions; or about Karl Rahner's intrigues over the call of my former assistant Alexandre Ganoczy to a chair of dogmatics in the University of Münster; or about the visit of an editor of Herder Verlag, who (in vain) seeks to have Josef Nolte's book against dogmatism toned down a bit.

But with no other diversions, without radio and television, when I am not swimming or walking along the shore I work happily without interruption on my 'Introduction to Christianity'. I slowly realize that if I am to do it thoroughly, such an introduction will require more research and reflection and therefore also more pages than I had originally planned. The basic plan and basic intention slowly emerge. Beyond question the centre of my theology lies here, and it's worth taking the trouble to work it out.

My central project

For whom am I writing this introduction? I've been able to think a great deal about that before and during this long journey and begin the preface with the following clear sentences:

> This book is written for all those who, for any reason at all, honestly and sincerely want to know what Christianity, what being a Christian, really means.
> It is written also for those
> who do not believe, but nevertheless sincerely enquire;
> who did believe, but are not satisfied with their unbelief;
> who do believe, but feel insecure in their faith;
> who are at a loss, between belief and unbelief;
> who are sceptical, both about their convictions and about their doubts.
> It is written then for Christians and atheists, Gnostics and agnostics, pietists and positivists, lukewarm and zealous Catholics, Protestants and Orthodox (p.19).

Joseph Ratzinger certainly wouldn't have prefaced his 1968 Tübingen *Introduction to Christianity* with such statements; after all, fundamentally he only wanted to address Catholic Christians who were to be reintroduced to the traditional creed. On the basis of all my reflections on Christian and non-Christian readers and the contemporary horizon I can now also define precisely what my introduction sets out to be. 'It is an attempt, in the midst of an epoch-making upheaval of the church's doctrine, morality and discipline, to discover what is permanent: what is different from other world religions and modern humanisms; and at the same time what is common to the separated Christian churches.' It was clear to me from the start that my book *Infallible?* with its uncomfortable enquiry could be felt by the leaders of the church to be a challenge, indeed a provocation. But I tell myself that this book about being a Christian must be accepted even by the government of my church as a welcome aid in the difficult situation of the church and society. I was to be deceived in this. However, my expectation that this book would be extremely helpful to the many people throughout the world addressed in the opening sentences was not to be disappointed. It aimed to discover – and this aim again distinguishes my introduction from that of Ratzinger, which relies on 'the tradition'–

> what this Christian programme originally meant, before it was covered with the dust and debris of two thousand years, and what this programme, brought to light again, can offer today by way of a meaningful, fulfilled life to each and every one.
> This is not another gospel,
> but the same ancient gospel
> rediscovered for today.

210

The original Christian message for today

To avoid any misunderstanding, in the preface I want to indicate that as the author of this book I don't want to present myself as a good Christian but do think that being a Christian is a particularly good thing. However, at the same time I also want to point out that it is my theological task to work out the decisive and distinguishing features of the Christian programme for the contemporary reader from its origins in a way which is historically precise yet up-to-date, based on the most recent research, yet understandable. That will require the utmost effort from me, in both the presentation of the content and the form of the book.

As far as content is concerned, I don't want just to tackle individual questions and areas of theology but to describe the whole of the Christian message against the background of today's great ideologies and world religions. In that case, as an individual I must attempt to overcome the specialization of the discipline of theology – which a team cannot do – and offer a coherent systematic synthesis unified down to the last detail.

As for the form of the book, I want to avoid all biblical archaisms and scholastic dogmatisms along with all fashionable theological jargon and speak in the language of today's men and women. That means that I must take the greatest possible trouble over the language that I use, to make it simple and understandable to contemporaries without any theological training, while being at the same time precise, differentiated and exciting.

All these are truly no small demands on an author who doesn't disguise his basic attitude. Since I have experienced so much untruthfulness in the church and theology, I am quite clear that I must speak the truth incorruptibly – without traditionalist prejudices and church–political qualifications and unconcerned with the formation of theological fronts or fashionable trends. Specifically that means intellectually honest arguments and undiminished theological criticism, which I don't avoid because I have an unshakable trust in the Christian cause.

I deliberately don't want to start from theological questions and traditional dogmas, although I know the classical Christian tradition better than most of my critics from my training in Rome and my personal research. I have treated the dogmas of christology thoroughly in my book *An Introduction to Hegel's Theological Thought as The Incarnation of God. Prolegomena to a Future Christology*. I don't need to repeat all this in my 'introduction'. Rather, I want to start from the broad and complex questions of present-day men and women and with a wealth of information advance in ever greater concentration to the centre of the Christian faith.

So all in all I am providing not only information but orientation. I want to take more seriously than is customary in theology the foundations in being human, in universal religions, in what lies outside the church, yet at the same time crystallize the distinguishing Christian features more sharply than elsewhere, so that the reader learns to distinguish essentials from inessentials. What I mean by broadening the horizon and concentration is a Christian theology which is at the same time a world theology.

The magic of the South Seas

The days on the Île des Pins, uniformly happy under the sun, are also fruitful for my work, so I postpone my departure for some days at the expense of other stops. I know and have experienced that there are also the 'sad tropics'. But on this solitary coral island, a reserve for the original inhabitants, the dream of the simple life is a reality for me, at least over these weeks: a life in harmony with an untouched nature, in freedom, relaxation, being natural – and at the same time the opportunity for mental concentration.

Visitors with whom I want to make closer contact appear only rarely. One of these is an Australian, a brilliant diver. One day I swim with him right across the bay to the reef. Suddenly a giant fish several metres long swims past us. Remarkably I feel no fear, but am eager to take a closer look at him. We have no bloody fish on our hooks which could attract sharks from a considerable distance. But the big fish doesn't return. I am more terrified by a ray perhaps three metres long, a cartilaginous fish which lies invisible on the sea bed like a flattened disc and, terrified by us, suddenly rises with its broad pectoral fins like wings. It is less dangerous to hold on to the shell of a giant tortoise which can also swim well.

It's a special experience for me to go out to sea with the Australian in a sailing boat; giant shoals of flying fish pass it. Finally we arrive at a big somewhat rounded rock in the water. My companion knows it and jumps into the water; I follow, and around three or four metres down, under the shadow of the rock, we find half a dozen bright red giant lobsters with big claws and thin antennae which are directed at us in a warning. We shoot two with our harpoons and surface. But I don't enjoy that very much; I'm not the hunter type. Later, what I find worse is the slow slaughter of an apparently ancient giant turtle; it robs me of the appetite for turtle soup.

One day a young Italian couple strays on to our island. After I've listened to their free and easy conversation for a while, to their surprise I speak to them in Italian. I get to know them better: Principessa Vittoria Odescalchi, from the family of Pope Innocent XI (1761-89), who had an antipathy to all splendour and nepotism, with her husband, Marquis Sanfelice di Monteforte. They're on their honeymoon. We get on well and talk about God, the world and Rome. The next day I travel with them far out to another reef in their motor boat. There, despite the higher waves, I can dive deeper than ever before and swim through whole underwater abysses with caves, surrounded by hard and soft coral and bizarre, multicoloured fish – an unforgettable, fascinating underwater landscape in an unreal blue-green light with an infinite number of mossy, cup-shaped, mush-room-like, spiky flowery forms, many of them moving gently in the water without a sound. I will see my two Italian friends again in Rome, but without souvenirs of the dive; if one takes coral out of the water and exposes it to air, it dies and its colours fade. I deny myself a comparison with the old dogmas.

But now I cannot postpone my departure from this unique island any longer. On 17 October 1971 I fly back to the capital, Nouméa, where happily people haven't heard earlier of my quiet presence on the solitary island. After my departure the New Caledonian journal *La Voix de Cagou*, dominated by integralists in the orbit of the nickel industry, publishes a poisonous article with the banner headline: '*L'anti-pape est venu à Nouméa prêcher l'évangile selon Mao* – The antipope has come to Nouméa to preach the gospel according to Mao.' Complete nonsense: here too I have spoken about Jesus' challenge for the church today in a lecture to the clergy and gone on to speak in a priests' seminary. How far the Roman propaganda against the 'antipope' has got! Months later the 'Authorities of the Archdiocese of Nouméa' are attacked in the same journal (22 February 1972) because they have displayed my book *Why Priests?* – written by 'someone who has been excommunicated, who denies the Pope and fights against the Roman Church'. Should I level a libel charge through a lawyer there? It wouldn't have got anywhere.

On the evening of 18 October I fly on to the Fiji islands, cleft by volcanoes and surrounded by coral reefs, and land safely at Nandi airport on the main island of Viti Levu, one of the 360 larger islands, hardly a third of which are inhabited. Since 1971 they have been an independent member of the Commonwealth and a member of the United Nations. Ethnically and linguistically the roughly 215,000 Fijians are Melanesians, with curly hair and negroid features, but culturally they are Polynesians. When I ask about the influence of the different ethnic groups, it is explained to me with a smile that the few Chinese have the highest posts in the banks and businesses. But today the Indians, brought to the country by the British towards the end of the nineteenth and beginning of the twentieth centuries originally as sugar-cane workers, and now around half the population, are independent farmers on rented land and have all urban trade in their hands. That also strikes me as I walk down the business street of the neighbouring city of Lautoka. And what about the indigenous Fijians? By far the greatest part of the land belongs to them; they are responsible for the 'art', and thus for crafts, wood carvings and folklore, welcomed by the growing number of tourists. This is an exaggeration, but it explains the ethnic tension between the English-speaking Indians with their large families and the Fijians, who don't speak English.

The next day I fly from Nandi over the wooded and sparsely settled hills to the small capital, Suva. As so often in these islands, the south-east side exposed to the trade winds gets a great deal of rain while the leeward side is relatively dry and covered with savannah, suitable for rearing cattle. In Suva, a typical colonial city, I am welcomed by Dr George Knight, president of the Pacific Theological College, who kindly starts by showing me Suva and its surroundings by car. In the evening I give my ministry lecture and have dinner with the Anglican bishop

213

and the Methodist president; as I have by now come to expect, the Roman Catholic bishop once again sends his apologies, though presumably he would have liked to have taken part. The next morning I lecture on the Christian message, as always followed by a lengthy discussion with professors and students.

In the afternoon we drive to a typical Fijian village where people still live quite traditionally, as in the interior, as landowners among village and island chieftains. One can understand why George Knight emphasizes not only the good colonial order and infrastructure on a British pattern but also the successes of the Christian mission – we also visit one of the mission stations. These Fijians who are so friendly today were still notorious cannibals a century ago, so that sailors circumnavigating the world avoided the islands. No one wanted to have them, and it wasn't until 1874 that Great Britain took possession of them. With the British there then came Indians and Chinese, at first only to work in the sugar-cane fields.

From Suva on 21 October I fly to Samoa, which is still idyllic, or more precisely to West Samoa, and the capital and largest harbour of Apia. I am invited to lunch in the Congregationalist College, but stay in perhaps the most famous hotel in the South Seas, the Aggie Grey. It was praised by the distinguished Scottish writer Robert Louis Stevenson, who is buried in Apia, and plays a major role in his exciting and entertaining South Seas stories (*On the South Seas*, 1896). The main rooms of the hotel are still furnished entirely in the South Sea style, but an increasing number of new tourist apartments are being built in the large park. The owner, Aggie Grey, with beautifully styled silver hair, wearing a pearl necklace with several strands, proudly tells me how she had a liaison with a German officer in the time when West Samoa was a German colony.

Since 1962 West Samoa has been constitutionally independent. During the evening, in the church not far from the hotel, one can hear the pious melodious singing of ordinary believers, just one of the signs of how these hilly islands have largely been Christianized, though they have retained their traditional social structures, which are based on close ties of kinship among chosen heads. The stories about free love among the Samoans (*Sex and Temper*), later shown to be imaginary, come to mind. The American ethnologist Margaret Mead told them about Samoan girls between the two world wars; her claims about the anti-authoritarian education on Samoa proved to be projections and the thesis of the peaceful character or 'nature peoples' to be a legend. In any case it is better not to speak of 'nature peoples'.

What an honour it is that in 2006 the long-serving Prime Minister of Samoa, Atua Tupua Tamasese, with his wife Filifilia, both admirers of my books, visit me in Tübingen and as a present bring me a large tapa, an artistically painted wall decoration made of raffia, and in addition a beautifully framed photograph of his grandmother Vaaiga from 1905, together with carved wooden combs; the tapa now adorns my South Sea casita (the roofed part of my terrace). In June 2007 I am able to congratulate him on his election as supreme head of state.

The world of tribal religions

Already in South India, but especially in Australia (the aborigines), in New Zealand (the Maoris) and now in the South Pacific (the original Melanesian and Polynesian inhabitants), I have become increasingly aware that everywhere the ethnic religions formed, and in part today still form, the background to the 'high cultures' which presuppose writing. However, these original inhabitants aren't simply 'nature peoples', but in their way people with a culture. They shouldn't be romantically transfigured and idealized as they were by Margaret Mead, far less slandered, outlawed and oppressed as 'uncivilized', as they were by the first Europeans after their 'discovery'. As if these peoples had no culture and religion! Even today – and I will be able to observe this yet more closely at a later date in Central Australia, New Guinea and Africa – many ways in which these people behave are fundamentally different from ours. But does that make them worse? May we regard these people as uneducated and lazy because even today they prefer hunting, gathering, dancing and celebrating to agriculture, breeding cattle and building houses?

Of course it is evident, particularly in the South Pacific, that a 'return to nature' is impossible; history can't be turned back. But I now know that I still have much to learn. At all events we shouldn't oppose 'nature peoples' to 'civilized peoples'. The original inhabitants also have a culture, even if they have developed no writing, no science and no technology. Their thought is completely logical, completely plausible. Many years later I proposed the tribal religions as a topic for the first film in the German TV series *Spurensuche* and therefore travelled to see the Aborigines in Australia and tribal groups in Africa.

Unfortunately in West Samoa I have to make up for the time I spent on the Île des Pins, so I fly on to Pango-Pango on American Samoa; however, apart from the very beautiful bay and an Intercontinental Hotel, there isn't much to see there. I fly on the next day to Tahiti, the largest of the Society Islands in French Polynesia, which are colonies administered from distant Paris. Around two-thirds of the population live in the capital Papeete, a typically French colonial city with government and business buildings. I go out into the country, but my real destination is another island north-west of Papeete, Bora Bora, which is reached in a small plane. In my opinion it is rightly called 'the most beautiful island in the world'.

Bora Bora is a volcanic island whose sole surviving cratered hill, Mount Temanu, is almost 800 metres high. My Bora Bora Hotel is at its foot, with a view over the blue-green lagoon to the edge of the crater, which consists of a ring of small palm islands; our plane landed on one of them. It's an indescribably beautiful view, which I enjoy by day up on a small terrace of the hotel, whose bungalows are surrounded by trees. Here I go on working contentedly on my book in a fresh breeze and beautiful weather. But time and again I love to go snorkelling, which right next to the shore offers such a wealth of corals and fishes that one can completely forget oneself. It seems to me that the different species of fish can be compared with different types of human beings: thick, thin, shy, lazy, sleek and also bluffers who, beautifully clad in yellow stripes, try to swim straight into my face with an impressive gesture but at the last movement turn off sharply and seek the wider sea.

Back in the Western, 'Christian' world

I am fortunate with the weather, since even on Bora Bora it often rains heavily and for days. After six sunny days, on 1 November 1971 I fly back to Papeete and from there north-east to Los Angeles. That this flight lasts seven hours shows the distances which one must still reckon with even in the age of jets. On 3 November I have to lecture in a large hall in Hollywood on 'Jesus – Challenge for the Church'. This topic hits the jackpot because a few weeks previously *Time Magazine* had devoted its title story to Jesus: 'Jesus has finally "made it",' Professor Andrew Greeley writes to me from Chicago. He has prompted the lecture service of the Thomas More Association to co-ordinate what invitations I can accept and organize the whole lecture trip, which in America is backed by clear agreements with the individual organizations so that I am not taken over completely. People in Chicago also want to know precisely where I have an after-dinner speech, a conversation with professors or a meeting with students; usually the whole day is filled with engagements from early morning until late evening – apart from the siesta which I always request.

Of course I don't give any pious revivalist sermon even in the Baptist Temple in Philadelphia, where I get a standing ovation from an audience of 2000. Rather, I note quite soberly the changes in the American churches since my first appearance at the time of the Council in 1963. The considerable loss of priests and ordinands particularly in the Catholic Church leads to the well-known concerns for reform which I tirelessly repeat. But then comes the decisive change: the important thing is not so much individual reforms as a new turn towards Jesus who, if one takes him seriously as a historical figure in the challenges of his time, is also a great challenge for us in the church today. So now I have a whirlwind tour right across the United States, lasting almost three weeks, usually in places in which I haven't spoken before.[2]

It is very strenuous. But I have the satisfaction of seeing more of the American continent after my various lecture tours since 1963 than most Americans, some of whom haven't even been from the east coast to the west coast or vice versa.

On 24 November I finally fly back to Europe, overnight to Amsterdam, where with my friends I can dictate in peace the chapters of my 'Introduction to Christianity' that I have written so far. At the same time I have the opportunity to visit the Dutch Cardinal Bernard Alfrink in Utrecht to discuss the church situation and also Cardinal Léon Suenens in Brussels. On 3 December 1971 I fly to Hamburg to watch my TV portrait and to plan a further four-part television series on 'Why I Can Still Be a Christian Today'. Then I go straight on to Frankfurt, where I have to take part in the working group of the ecumenical institutes. The important topic is the reform and recognition of church ministries. On 5 December 1971 I am finally back in my beloved Tübingen.

One of my assistants expresses amazement that I have come back unchanged from this six-month trip. I am as I always am, and hopefully always will be. Shouldn't I have adopted some specific globe-trotter features or at least grown a beard? But what has changed in me can't be seen from the outside. After all my various experiences I am still a Christian, Catholic theologian – perhaps more consciously than ever. And with the effort at broadening my horizons, which I have achieved, I can now think more globally than before. In future I want to practise even more strongly a Christian theology which at the same time is 'ecumenical' in the broadest sense of the word, orientated on the whole 'ecumene', the whole 'inhabited' earth, and in this sense a 'world theology'.

I am glad that this second trip round the world has taken place with so many positive experiences and without greater complications, and also without any accidents. But one needn't travel round the world to have an accident. I cause one myself a month later, when on 14 January 1972 I'm driving back to Tübingen from an exhausting graduate conference of the Catholic Academy of Hohenheim, Stuttgart. I'm not driving very fast, which is my reputation, but relatively slowly, because I'm tired and am listening to classical music. On a quiet forest road I don't observe the priority at a crossroads. And that's where it happens. The other car suffers little damage, but mine is a write-off. I'm in one piece, but a new car is called for and I'm grateful that the Catholic Academy with the help of its insurance makes a not inconsiderable contribution to the cost.

Business as usual

When one describes a life in which so many extraordinary things have happened, it's easy to overlook the ordinary, the normal: that during the semester a professor has to give his lectures punctually. The lectures have to be prepared, but whenever possible I co-ordinate them with my publications. As well as the lectures, the weekly seminars are to help to clarify my own thoughts through discussion and to discover talented students in the process. Faculty meetings take place several times a semester, though for me they are at the lower end of the scale of popularity, because they are all-too-often about disputed points such as the distribution of resources or the often controversial assessment of doctoral or habilitation students.

When I look back over the rotating lectures on dogmatics in the 1960s and 1970s, I note that – alternating first with Joseph Ratzinger and then with Walter Kasper – I have lectured on almost the whole spectrum of dogmatic topics: from the doctrine of God and christology, through the doctrines of grace and justification, to the doctrines of the church and the sacraments. Moreover I have given special lectures on Hegel's christology, on infallibility in the church, on the proclamation of the word, on discipleship of Christ and on prayer, meditation and worship. Then there are the seminars. As well as the themes surrounding *On Being a Christian* – what for various theologians is the Christian message, the new books on Jesus, the Christian element in ethics and the infallibility discussion – I am keenly interested in semester topics such as Ernst Bloch's understanding of God, the Neo-Marxist and Neo-positivist critique of religion, the problem of natural theology in Karl Barth (together with Eberhard Jüngel), theology and science (with Ludger Oeing-Hanhoff), and finally 'How Do We Talk about Justification Today?'

My regular duties also include membership of the Senate commission for the future of scholarship. Happily I was a member of the university building committee for only a short time and of the faculty study commission for rather longer. For a while I have edited the *Tübinger Theologischer Quartalschrift* with Johannes Neumann. As well as the working group of the university ecumenical institutes, which sometimes causes a great deal of work because of the memorandum on the church's ministries and then also the question of an ecumenical papacy, activity for *Concilium* is a constant burden, since as one of the four theologians I am a member of the Foundation and as director of the section on ecumenism also a member of the editorial committee. With Walter Kasper, I have edited issues on a whole series of highly interesting topics: *Do we Know the Others?*, *Apostolic by Succession?*, *Post-Ecumenical Christianity*, *Polarization in the Church?*, *Christians and Jews, Luther Then and Now.*

However, on 7 May 1974 Walter Kasper unexpectedly resigns from *Concilium*, allegedly because the Tübingen faculty won't grant him enough money for assistants (as director of my own Institute I haven't been directly involved in the decisions). This reason doesn't convince me; rather, I ask whether this isn't a resignation with an eye to Rome, for church–political motives. But as so often I make a virtue of necessity. I find a quite excellent new fellow–director in the person of the theologian Jürgen Moltmann, well known throughout the Protestant world, with whom collaboration is as smooth as it was previously with Walter Kasper. The topics we now deal with are *Why did God make me?* and *An Ecumenical Confession of Faith?* What Jürgen Moltmann writes about the annual *Concilium* meetings in his autobiography is confirmation of my conviction that 'catholic' needn't be understood in the sense of demarcating a confession. Just as I, constantly orientated on the gospel, can describe myself as 'evangelical', so Moltmann can write, 'I could identify well with this independent catholicity. In this sense *Concilium* made me "catholic". I became, so to speak, a Protestant Catholic, even if not a Roman one.'[3]

Because of problems relating to publication, finance and sometimes individuals, the *Concilium* Foundation requires quite a lot of time. On different occasions there are meetings at short notice in Amsterdam, Düsseldorf or Paris. Every year in Pentecost week there is first the Foundation meeting and then that of the editorial committee. Happily I am given the necessary mental and physical strength to cope with extraordinary situations.[4] When I go to bed in the evening I sometimes hardly remember from what bed I got up that morning.

Sleep, laughter and hope

But normally I am far more in Tübingen than one might think, given my numerous trips abroad. Despite my mobile life I remain healthy. Two things help me. First, sleep. I can sleep anywhere even during the day, in the train, in a car, on a plane, in an office. I go to sleep quickly and usually wake up refreshed after half an hour at most. At night, though, a good five hours sleep is normally sufficient – I don't need an alarm clock – with an additional half-hour siesta during the day. This is one of the good Roman habits I have kept all my life.

The second thing is if at all possible to sleep in my own bed at home. At night one travels more quickly with less traffic and can begin the next morning as usual. So often I drive home around midnight. However, on the way home, twice when I've been over-tired I've gone to sleep for a second and both times this almost cost me my life. On the good advice of my friend Walter Jens, in later years I never drive home alone, but have myself driven. At least the organizer saves the cost of an overnight stay.

'As a counterbalance to the wearisome things of life heaven has given human beings three things,' one can read in Immanuel Kant, 'hope, sleep and laughter.' Despite all the difficulties in the church, I've never given up hope. And one often hears laughter in our house on all sides; all in all we have a strenuous but usually also a happy life. We laugh a lot, real laughter which comes from inside, from the heart. Modern biology shows that healthy laughter is the best medicine; instead of 'stress hormones', adrenalin and cortisol, 'happiness hormones', endorphins, are distributed which bring relaxation. For me only music, which has been called the sweetest medicine, can compete with laughter.

And the Lord gives me much in sleep. When my eyes close late at night, when I can't see my way through a complex question or formulate the answer, I often say to myself Psalm 127.2, 'The Lord provides for his beloved in sleep.' Of course I too know what psychoanalysis and brain physiologists have discovered by detailed research, that the human brain indefatigably assimilates the impressions of the day during the night. But I also know what neither psychoanalysts nor brain researchers can tell me: that I am in God's hand and therefore needn't worry unnecessarily about tomorrow.

But what does 'unnecessarily' mean here? Will laughter soon disappear for me? Won't the extremely unpleasant controversies and wearing battles which are pending deprive me of sleep and even of hope? However, to begin with these are only evil forebodings, and I have by no means given up hope.

VI

Battle for the Truth – or a Struggle for Power?

> 'It is truly a drama of a special kind: a powerful institution – the
> Catholic Church, which insists that it is in possession of the "whole
> saving truth revealed by God" – against an individual. From Rome to
> Bonn a powerful apparatus is endeavouring to make the church
> magisterium insist on ancestral rights as it sees itself threatened by
> meditations which a Tübingen professor develops in his study ...'

> The literary scholar Walter Jens on the documentation Um nichts als
> die Wahrheit. Deutsche Bischofskonferenz contra Hans Küng
> *(1978)*

There may be, sometimes must be, conflict. There is nothing intrinsically bad
about conflict. Conflict is often necessary: in politics, in business, in scholarship,
in society, even in the church, conflict also about the truth. But the means by
which a conflict is carried on are the all-important thing, whether a conflict over
the truth is carried on in truthfulness and fairness. A conflict over the truth
mustn't degenerate, especially in the church, into a battle for power carried on
with violent worldly or 'spiritual' means.

Problems for the Doctrinal Congregation

After the Roman Congregation for the Doctrine of the Faith has published the
order of procedure called for since the Council it is ready to go on the offensive.
On 22 June 1971 the 24-member plenary assembly of the Congregation, to
which all the important personalities in the Curia belong, resolves after strictly
secret discussions, endorsed by Pope Paul VI on 25 June 1971, that disciplinary
proceedings should also be opened against my book *Infallible?* According to the
investigations by the Congregation it contains statements which seem to be
incompatible with Catholic teaching.

Neither a copy of the decree nor the document of papal approval nor information on my right to appeal are sent to me. What I do receive are subtly devised
'*quaestiones*', formulated in Latin, questions about 1. The authentic magisterium in
the church, 2. The infallibility of the College of Bishops and the Roman Pontiff,
3. Indefectibility (the church abiding in the truth) instead of infallibility, 4.

Infallible statements. And the notice is short: within 30 days I am to declare in writing whether and how I can reconcile my theses and assertions with Catholic doctrine.[1] I am suddenly in a great hurry.

The express letter from the Prefect of the Congregation for the Doctrine of the Faith, Cardinal Franjo Šeper, dated 12 July 1971, arrives only a few hours before I leave for my lecture and study trip round the world. In a letter from Moscow I reply to the cardinal that it is quite impossible for me during such a trip to go into the complex questions in an appropriate way. I therefore ask for patience until my return. He needn't know when that will be.

On 6 December 1971, on my return to Tübingen after almost six months, I set to work to draft an extensive reply. As four years earlier in connection with my book *The Church*, I now receive from the Doctrinal Congregation a kind of Christmas present: an admonition dated 17 December 1971 relating to questions on *Infallible?*

In August, *L'Osservatore Romano* had formally confirmed the rumours that there was an investigation into me. At that time I was already in Australia. On his own initiative the young Protestant theologian Bernd Jaspert (later a church historian at the University of Marburg), with the Americans Paul Knitter SVD (of Marburg, later professor in Cincinnati and New York) and Leonard Swidler (professor at Temple University, Philadelphia), both Catholics, initiated an ecumenical declaration of solidarity in a very short time. Only two weeks later they sent this with more than 325 signatures (of many prominent professors of theology from the German-speaking world and the United States) to the Doctrinal Congregation.[2] The signatories expressed deep concern about the way in which the investigation by the Congregation into the two books *The Church* and *Infallible?* was being carried out: 'The method of this investigation radically contradicts the spirit of Christ; it dishonours a man who has always understood himself as a loyal son of his church, and who afterwards as before holds himself to be obligated to the message of Jesus Christ.' They declared their solidarity with the author and 'demand that unconditional and unrestricted access to the pertinent dossier of the Sacred Congregation for the Doctrine of the Faith be granted him so that he may respond in every appropriate manner out of a full knowledge of the objections brought against his books'.

My own lengthy answer to the Congregation which I work out on my return and scrupulously allow to be checked by others – in order to avoid any appearance of anxiety or panic – takes the same line, but I don't send it until 24 January 1972.[3] After apologies for the delayed reply, in the first part I make a fundamental objection to the proceedings of the Congregation, for four reasons:

1. No access to the records: I continue to be denied a sight of the Inquisition dossier 399/57/i which was begun in 1957 after my dissertation on justification appeared.

2. No defender: I am free to choose only an advocate nominated by the congregation (*relator 'pro auctore'*).

3. No definition of competence and court of appeal: are the previous proceedings before conferences of bishops and their organs closed as a result of the Roman proceedings?

4. No duration or time limit for either side: after four-year proceedings against *The Church* I am to respond to questions within 30 days.

I conclude the first part of my letter by saying that 'certain curial prescriptions and practices in no way correspond to a modern sense of the law'. The second part contains 'preliminary observations on the questions of the Congregation'. Of the four lengthy arguments the first is the most important: 'If any official department of the Catholic Church ought to know a well-founded answer to this question, then that should be the Roman Congregation for the Doctrine of the Faith. But here again to appeal only to those documents of the magisterium which are the object of my questions is a vicious circle in which what must be demonstrated is presupposed. I am willing to be convinced by arguments at any time. I therefore ask the Congregation to give me in at least brief form a reasoned argument for the possibility of infallible statements, one which does not ignore the difficulties over certain texts of the magisterium which I have pointed out, but takes them into consideration.'

In point 2 I explain that so far 'not a single author has offered a convincing argument for the possibility of infallible statements'. As I shall be holding a senior seminar on infallibility with prominent opponents of my book in the summer semester of 1972, I request the participation of a representative of the Congregation (expenses paid). In the fourth section I declare myself ready for further study and dialogue and finally attempt to convince Cardinal Šeper quite personally of the honesty of my motivation and my constructive intentions in the present crisis of the church.

It is necessary to have read the precise wording of this letter, which covers many pages and aspects, to recognize the weight of my questions to the Congregation and the many difficult problems that the letter contains. It isn't surprising that the Congregation initially veils itself in silence. But of course it hasn't given up.

The news magazine *Der Spiegel* of 13 March 1972 reports on these events and comments: 'For the first time the Küng case now confirms what critical Catholic theologians have long feared, namely that the methods of the Congregation for the Doctrine of the Faith have changed little, although since January of last year it is working according to a new regulation. In no constitutional state in the world are there proceedings of the kind that the Pope still thinks appropriate for the Catholic Church.'[4] The result is a flood of newspaper headlines such as: 'Professor Küng a Heretic?', 'Küng Turns Down a Trip to Canossa', 'In Conflict with the Curia on the Church's Side', 'A New Luther?', 'God Save the Küng'. And in a series on 'uncomfortable contemporaries', 'The Reformer who is True to the Church'.

Quiet work

I note the whole media rumpus, but it doesn't keep me from my studies. After New Year 1972 – I celebrate it skiing with my school-leaving friends in Eigenthal at the foot of Mount Pilatus – I can finally resume work on my 'Introduction to Christianity'. My research seminar still lasts until the middle of April. I work every day in my lake house from early morning until deep into the night. Music is for me what black coffee is for others – from the Renaissance to Stravinsky, depending on my mood; it's an elixir of life that keeps me awake. But unlike up in the Alps under a blue sky, in Sursee, as everywhere else in the foothills to the Alps, lake and landscape are shrouded with grey mist. Every morning I swim in the cold lake, the temperature of which is little above zero – my only exercise during the day, 'extraordinarily refreshing for hot theologians' heads'. Every evening I celebrate the eucharist with a consecutive scripture reading in the district hospital – last year the Gospel of Mark, now the Sermon on the Mount. On Saturday evening or Sunday I celebrate the eucharist in my parish church of Sursee.

On 27 November 1973 I will write to my colleague Johannes Neumann: 'This morning I swam for the first time in my lake in a snow-covered landscape. It's tremendous fun, though the water can't be much colder without freezing.' In winter the holiday houses of my parents and sisters are uninhabited, and it's very quiet by the lake. Only once was there an intruder in my absence: a labourer who had broken out of prison sought lodging and left some things in disorder. But when I'm living in the house – Frau Renemann is responsible for the house, Dr Margret Gentner for manuscripts and correspondence – one needn't have the slightest fear.

Rest is also important to me in Tübingen. And when nearby an enormous white dog is left alone regularly on Sundays and holidays, reacts badly to church bells and yowls and barks for hours, I finally have to report him to the police. I keep the weekend in particular as free as possible of visitors and am nowhere so happy as on my terrace, occupied with my book. In the meantime I have prepared a first rough draft of the little book 'Introduction to Christianity', which ultimately will be entitled *On Being a Christian*. But there are many questions of method.

Where to begin: from 'above' or from 'below'?

Neo-scholastic christology takes it for granted that the beginning should be dogmatic and 'from above', with the 'divinity of Christ'. At the Gregorian in Rome the first christological thesis I had to study was: 'That Jesus Christ is the natural Son of God and true God is demonstrated with certainty from Christ's own words and the testimony of his first disciples.' However, there is no

223

historical–critical exegesis of any of the scriptural proofs quoted, and if for example Mark 10.18, 'Why do you call me good? No one is good but God alone', is quoted as a difficulty for this thesis of Jesus' divinity, the answer in the textbook (by Charles Boyer) is simple: 'Christ, asked of as man, wills to teach that the source of all good is to be found in the Godhead, without affirming or denying his divine nature.'

Of course Joseph Ratzinger doesn't make it as simple in his 1968 *Introduction to Christianity*. After rejecting an enquiry into the Jesus of history, because he claims that this is impossible, he wants 'simply to try to understand what is stated by the Christian faith, which is not a reconstruction but a present reality' (p. 201). So Ratzinger wants to begin firmly from 'above', from the traditional statement of the creed today: I believe 'in Jesus Christ, the only begotten Son of God'.

The sharpest criticism of Ratzinger's christology comes initially from Walter Kasper, now professor of dogmatics in Münster, who doesn't want to start from the 'Platonic dialectic of visible–invisible on which Ratzinger's scheme is based', but 'from the concrete interweaving of the human being into nature, society, culture and history': 'Against the horizon of a historical way of thinking the unique and irreducible significance of the earthly Jesus and his fate can be given a clearer basis ... The historical question of the earthly (historical) Jesus thus becomes an immanent element of theology, and it becomes impossible to shove it aside in a caricature.'[5] In fact Ratzinger's depiction of the positions of Adolf von Harnack and Rudolf Bultmann is a caricature.

It already became clear to me during my work on Hegel's christology at the end of the 1960s that today I cannot begin from above in either a contemporary or a scriptural way – either Neo-scholastically or following Hegel. Jesus Christ, not a human being in whom God reveals himself but 'a (divine) person in two natures (one divine and one human)'? Such words and ideas shaped by Hellenistic language and thought are incomprehensible today. This doctrine of two natures didn't solve the fundamental christological difficulty in the fifth century, but led to a further split in the church. Indeed, according to present-day exegesis it is in no way identical with the original message about Christ in the New Testament. As I make clear in a section on 'The Christ of dogma?', it would be more appropriate to the facts and the historical thinking of men and women today to show how the first disciples begin from the real human being Jesus, from his historical appearance and message, his life and fate, his historical reality and influence. Whereas both in his *Introduction* and in his 2007 book on Jesus Joseph Ratzinger begins with this unity and understands it a priori in trinitarian terms according to the dogma of the fourth/fifth centuries, I attempt in accordance with the Synoptic Gospels to begin from the Jesus of history and like his disciples ask, 'Who can this be ...?' (Mark 4.41) and go on to investigate his relationship to God, whom he calls his Father. So this is an approach 'from below', but one which presses forward 'above'.

Of course my method doesn't give free play to a 'Christ of the enthusiasts', who aren't very bothered about scriptural testimony and history and construct their own Christ. By contrast I take more seriously the 'Christ of literature'; for this chapter the work of Karl-Josef Kuschel and his dissertation on 'Jesus in German-language literature of the present day' (which was published in 1978) provides a good deal of extremely valuable information. Walter Jens's reading of this chapter – he supervised Kuschel's dissertation with me – is the beginning of an intensive scholarly exchange between us which leads to a deep personal friendship.

I am particularly grateful to the perceptive and consistent Tübingen scholar Ernst Käsemann, a Bultmann pupil, for the conviction that one can know far more about the Jesus of history than Karl Barth and Rudolf Bultmann thought possible and necessary. Jesus isn't a phantom, but a historical person with human features. And if one can learn about him only from the foundation documents of the faith, and in the end it is often impossible to decide what is historical and what isn't, the great contours of the message, the conduct and the fate of Jesus of Nazareth and his relationship with God, come out so clearly and so unmistakably that it is evident that the Christian faith has a support in history and that therefore discipleship of Jesus is possible and meaningful.

But already since my return from my long world trip I am confronted with a development which causes me to revise my manuscript thoroughly.

Was Jesus a revolutionary?

In Germany in 1972 there is a tremendous discussion of a question which is sparked off by the revolutionary student movement and the South American liberation movement. Wasn't Jesus of Nazareth a political revolutionary? In Tübingen the question introduces me to prominent theologians who help me to discover and develop my own standpoint.

On the left wing there is the Protestant theologian Jürgen Moltmann, who on the basis of his leanings towards socialism and his friendship with the Neo-Marxist Ernst Bloch, resident in Tübingen since 1961, puts forward theses on a 'theology of revolution' (though a non-violent one). At a discussion in the theological study group on 8 January 1969 I had had to object that for all the justification of social criticism one cannot so easily reinterpret Jesus' message of the kingdom of God as a message of a kingdom of human beings to be brought in by political and social revolution. There was much that I just could not agree with. To follow Moltmann in finding 'God in the revolution' seemed to me to be all too simple, as if 'the human future can only be a revolutionary one' and 'the problem of the use of violence and non-violence is a pseudo-problem', thus Moltmann in *Evangelische Kommentare* in 1968![6] Much as I treasured his extremely stimulating *Theology of Hope*, I sometimes missed a critical exegetical basis. He didn't think that he had laboriously to catch up on the historical–critical exegesis which he conceded that he had also neglected in his student years. And instead of subjecting the unfulfilled apocalyptic expectation of the return of Christ to an eliminating but interpretative demythologization, he exploited it as a utopia for a socialist society to be brought in by revolution. 'The "theology of revolution" had its day, and I also made my contribution to it,' he writes in his memoirs (2006), but without correcting the false hopes and actions of 1968.

On the right there is the Protestant New Testament scholar Martin Hengel, a recognized specialist on Hellenistic Judaism and in this connection also on the revolutionary Zealot movement against the Roman powers of occupation. In 1970 a book of his was published with the title *Was Jesus a Revolutionist?* Unlike many Christian 'revolutionaries' (to use the more accepted term), he had thoroughly worked through the sources and has an excellent knowledge of their social context. Even if I don't share his somewhat conservative political views, I have to agree with his exegetical conclusions about Jesus.

Now I can provide a precise foundation from the texts of the New Testament. According to the Gospels Jesus of Nazareth was a very clear-sighted, resolute and, if need be, militant and at all events fearless young man of about 30 years of age. He was certainly not a representative of the political and religious establishment; he was not a conformist, an apologist for the status quo, a defender of law and order. He called for a decision. In this sense he 'brought the sword', not peace but conflict, in some circumstances extending into the family. There is no doubt that he fundamentally questioned the religious and social system, the existing order of the Jewish law and temple, and to this degree his message had political consequences. But at the same time for Jesus the alternative wasn't political and social revolution. Mahatma Gandhi and Martin Luther King in their practice of consistent non-violence could more consistently appeal to Jesus rather than Che Guevara, who romantically glorified violence as the midwife of the new society, and following him the Catholic priest Camilo Torres or even Ernst Bloch,

In this sense I think I may say that Jesus was more revolutionary than the revolutionaries. In my book I describe in detail what this means: unconditional forgiveness instead of hitting back, readiness to suffer instead of using violence, praising the peacemakers instead of songs of hatred and revenge. The revolution set in motion by Jesus was decidedly a non-violent revolution, a revolution in the most inward and hidden parts, from the centre of the person, from the human heart, but aimed at society. It involves not taking the same line as before but radical rethinking and conversion, away from egotism towards God and fellow human beings.

The chapter on 'Jesus – a revolutionary?' has finally become a quite fundamental chapter, with many footnotes. And this now has serious consequences for the whole book. The next chapter on 'Jesus – an ascetic or a religious?' must be treated just as thoroughly and the whole literature about the Qumran writings found in caves by the Dead Sea must be assimilated. And so it goes on, chapter by chapter. In this way the book changes its character: my little book 'Introduction to Christianity' finally becomes my big book *On Being a Christian*, for which I must go on to revise all the introductory chapters. But this means that completing it is postponed month after month. However, that is the only way in which I can systematically incorporate the results of New Testament exegesis and thus lay a solid foundation for my theology. At the same time I have a criterion for answering difficult topical problems, such as the one which is being discussed a great deal now.

The pros and cons of a 'political theology'

Johann Baptist Metz, Professor of Fundamental Theology in Münster, born in the same year as me and a fighter with me for the reform of the church, has recently become a member of the *Concilium* Foundation together with the French Dominican Claude Geffré. As a pupil of Rahner with originally an anthropocentric orientation of his theology, after 1968 in a variety of short articles he sketched out the programme of a 'political theology'. He has me completely on his side when he rejects the internalization, spiritualization and individualization of the Christian message and against it emphasizes its power for social ethics and its social relevance.

I want to share in advocating such a theology which is critical of society, but would prefer not to call it 'political theology'. Why? Because this term seems to me to be hopelessly compromised. It was compromised right at the beginning by Emperor Constantine's court bishop, Eusebius of Caesarea, who was the first to develop under this label a religious and political imperial theology according to the programme 'one God, one Logos, one emperor, one empire'. It was compromised in our time by the Catholic constitutional lawyer who unintentionally prepared for the National Socialist Führer state, Carl Schmitt; under this term Schmitt developed the contours of a totalitarian state.

Moreover, in our days the concept of 'political theology' is time and again understood as 'politicizing theology', not least because there are some who give it a different function, so that it becomes a critical revolutionary concept with postulates such as the nationalization of key industries or the possibility of voting out the representatives of the people at any time. The earlier anti-modernism and anti-socialism with a direct 'Christian' foundation is now followed by a criticism of capitalism and a socialist theory of society with an immediate 'Christian foundation'. Of course Johann Baptist Metz has never provided a comprehensive synthesis, and even in the issue of *Concilium* on *Christianity and Socialism* (5/1977) which he edited he doesn't speak out clearly on socialism.

I do, though, think that I can join him in his justified theological concern and make this clear to him in a long conversation at a *Concilium* meeting in Nijmegen. I also later confirm this to him explicitly in writing: 'I want to emphasize once again how very important it seems to me – personally and for theology in

Germany – for us to work together as well as possible, to get to know each other's theology better and take up each other's concerns. Everything that I said to you in that late hour in Nijmegen was meant seriously. So I am also delighted that through the *Concilium* Foundation we shall presumably see rather more of each other than once a year' (10 May 1971).

Johann Baptist Metz presses for me to be accepted as an adviser to the Synod of German Bishops in Commission I: 'Not because I would simply share his theological and ecclesiological position,' he writes to Prelate Karl Forster of the Secretariat of the German Conference of Bishops (25 June 1971), 'but because I am of the opinion that a broad and representative spectrum of theological views must be guaranteed for the work of this commission and therefore a position like his cannot be excluded a priori.' Metz along with Rahner also supports the Catholic German Students Union (CGSU) which, by a decision of the German Conference of Bishops in spring 1973, is 'no longer recognized as representative of Catholic students' and is therefore denied further financial grants.

All the appeals of theologians, theological students and student pastors cannot prevent the liquidation of the work of Catholic student communities extending beyond particular regions – this is comparable to the death sentence on the journal *Publik* in autumn 1971. And even more than on German 'political theology', the aims of which remain vague, controversy focuses on Latin American liberation theology, which I shall be discussing in detail in connection with my trip to Latin America. All this raises for me the fundamental question: what may be given up in this great conflict in the church and what must remain?

Has the church lost its soul?

On 20 March 1972 I speak in the Great Hall of the Lucerne Kunsthaus, where the symphony concerts take place during the weeks of the International Music Festival. Of course I am delighted that in this city by Lake Lucerne, where I went to school and worked for almost two years as an assistant priest, more than 2000 people come to hear me, many of them even sitting behind me on the steps of the orchestra podium. But they have also come because of the topic: 'What Must Remain in the Church'. Seven years after the Council this has become an urgent issue, since as a consequence of the log-jam in reforms after the Council and the Roman provocations (see Chapter II above), the church is visibly in crisis. The American weekly *Newsweek* publishes a major investigation under the title 'Has the Church Lost its Soul?', a question which I take seriously and which I want to pose as one of the 'architects' of the Second Vatican Council.

I begin with a brief analysis of the changes in the situation since the Second Vatican Council (1962–65). First, the numerous positive points – what has changed for the better: an understandable liturgy which is close to the people and improved sermons which are close both to scripture and to our time, and thus a popular piety which is more concentrated on the essentials; a more open training of theologians and a greater participation of the laity in decision-making processes at parish and diocesan levels; new awareness of the urgent needs of the world, a new freedom of thought, discussion and action in the church; mutual recognition and ecumenical understanding between the Christian churches; a relaxation of and essential improvement in relations with Judaism and the other world religions; an affirmation of freedom of religion and of the conscience.

But then unfortunately there are the equally numerous negative points – what has changed for the worse: unsatisfactory answers to the deeper restructuring in contemporary society; disorientation in Christianity; a crisis in the Catholic Church because of the postponement of reforms; birth control and the morality of marriage, the question of celibacy; mixed marriages; eucharistic fellowship; a reordering of the election of bishops and the Pope. As a result, tens of thousands of priests have left the service of the church and there is a catastrophic lack of men to follow them. At the same time attendance at Sunday worship is declining and there is a crisis of Catholic schools, journals, publishing houses, associations, a general lack of inspiration and imagination for the constructive solution of present problems. And behind all this there is a fundamental lack of constructive spiritual leadership in Rome and among the bishops.

The result is a disturbing loss of credibility. However, I would never have claimed what the German Press Agency reported on 8 March 1972 from Washington on the basis of an interview with me in the American monthly *Intellectual Digest*, that under Paul VI the credibility of the Catholic Church has reached its lowest level for 500 years. This is a report that goes through the German press and brings me much blame and malicious letters. What I did say, repeat on 13 March and now confirm precisely in Lucerne, was: 'The present Pope began with perhaps the greatest credibility of the Catholic Church in the last 500 years. Now that we are coming to the end of this pontificate, I think that credibility has once again sunk so low that we cannot explain how this could have come about. This is no criticism of the person of Paul VI, for whom as a human being and a Christian I have every understanding, but a criticism of the state of the church and the reactionary course of the present church leadership in Rome and elsewhere.'

What must remain in the church

To offer orientation in this critical situation, in my lecture I concentrate on the essentials and rule out two problem areas: social problems generally and specific problems of church reform. So I relegate to the periphery, as not being central, disputed questions such as infallibility, birth control and the pill. Consequently curiosity grows about what is really central in Christianity, what is the 'soul' of the church. At all events the pious devotions which have disappeared, the rules

for fasting which have been abolished, special dress for clergy and women religious, or even confession which used to be necessary are not central – these are
sheer left-overs from the ecclesiastical Middle Ages which aren't requisites.

But in that case what is central, what is the 'soul' of the church, what must
remain? My answer is that what must remain, the distinguishing mark of the
Christian, is not an idea, a principle, a basic attitude but quite simply, in a word, a
person: this Jesus Christ himself and his spirit – with all the practical consequences. I paint a lively and exciting picture of this Christ which I have worked
out for myself in the past months, of his life and teaching, his struggles, suffering
and death and belief in his new life in God's eternity.

With him as criterion I sketch out some political and social consequences with
reference to war and peace, economic power, consumption and the crisis in
meaning. And also stimuli for the church: against the polarization between
conservatives and progressives, for faith without narrowness, morality without
legalism and church discipline with an ecumenical breadth. I conclude my lecture
by saying:

> The church must change even more in order to remain itself. And it will
> remain what it should be if it remains with the one who is its origin: if in all
> its progress and change it remains faithful to this Jesus Christ. It will then be
> a church which is closer to God and at the same time closer to men and
> women. Then the Catholics with their emphasis on tradition will become
> more evangelical and at the same time the Protestants with their emphasis
> on the gospel will become more catholic, and in this way – and this is
> decisive – both will become more Christian.[7]

'He spoke for a full two hours to an audience which listened in silence,' reports
the *Luzerner Neueste Nachrichten* (22 March 1972), followed by 'sustained applause
without a break'. I have been understood in my homeland and in the next weeks
I speak on the same topic in various cities of Switzerland (Schaffhausen, St Gallen,
Basle, Zurich) and Germany (Berlin, Frankfurt, Worms).

'His Holiness's loyal opposition'

All that is 35 years ago. As I sadly re-read this programmatic lecture in 2007, I ask
myself whether it couldn't have been something like a comprehensive and at the
same time concrete programme of government after the Council for an open
church leadership. Instead of this, with such a programme I increasingly find
myself in the opposition as a result of the resistance of the Pope, the Curia and the
episcopate.

Long after this lecture, at a dinner party in Hamburg in the house of a friend,
Dr Karl Klasen, President of the Federal Bank, the then Chancellor Helmut

Schmidt, sitting on my right, puts a critical question to me in a friendly way: 'Aren't you and your friends for the Pope something like what the Jusos (the radical young socialists) are for me?' I reply to him with a smile: 'It would be easier for you, Chancellor, if your Jusos were as intelligent and moderate an opposition as we are for the Pope.' To which Helmut Schmidt retorts: 'Of course you're right.' He gets on considerably better with the American Ambassador Arthur Burns (formerly, from 1970 to 1978, Chairman of the Federal Reserve) than with his boss, President Jimmy Carter.

Thomas Mann once said that he was born to be a representative and not a martyr. No more am I. But it is also my experience to be forced into opposition. I recall my private audience with Paul VI at the end of the Council (*My Struggle for Freedom*, IX: Audience with Paul VI), considerably less devout than that of Thomas Mann with Pius XII, when the Pope had the idea that he could persuade me to enter the church's service by his verdict that he wished I had written nothing, '*niente*'. It dawned on me then that in the future I must work even harder on a theology for my fellow men and women, even if the Pope and his people didn't like this. 'I have compassion (not on the high priest, but) on the people', someone else said. And more and more complaints about a church system which has become rigid are now coming to my ears in a variety of forms: conversations, telephone calls, letters, news from the church and the world. If one notes the results of surveys in the various countries one knows that in most controversial questions the opposition has by far the largest majority behind it. But others have the (legitimate) power to achieve something.

In Rome people are now speaking openly of a 'Paolinian restoration', i.e. a return of Paul VI to Pius XII's conservative course — against John XXIII — not least to support the 'right-wing course' of the new Italian government. But I think that it is of the utmost importance that my friends and I should form a loyal opposition, taking up the term used in the United Kingdom, where people are convinced of the need for a strong opposition in quite a different way from that in the Roman Catholic Church: 'His Holiness's loyal opposition!' Unfortunately such an opposition can't be elected in the church, since in the process of centralization which has been going on in the Roman Catholic Church for centuries all the originally 'democratic' elements — above all the election of Pope and bishops by people and clergy and the limitation of their power — have been eliminated. It is well known that since the eleventh century the Roman Catholic Church has been made an absolutist organization by that 'revolution from above' (Gregory VII) in which over time — and reinforced since Vatican I (1870) — Pope and Curia have also forced the formerly powerful episcopate into complete dependence.

Opposition needs publicity

So if opposition to the Roman Curia, which is gaining force all over the world, is to be effective, it needs the media, just as the opposition in absolutist France before the French Revolution was prepared for by writers such as Montesquieu, Voltaire and Rousseau. In the controversy over church and infallibility – not a revolution but a radical reform – I would have been lost from the start without the support of the public.

I have never sought publicity or to be a publicist, but rival colleagues have sometimes enviously accused me of being a master of the 'journalist's craft' and of exerting 'influence on the public' in this way. That's a convenient excuse for these defenders of the traditional bastions. Can't they concede that in public controversies my concern is with the truth, which must be done in truthfulness; that my main arguments come from Holy Scripture and the great Catholic tradition; that my public reputation is founded on my scholarly publications from my dissertation onwards; that it isn't journalistic cleverness but clear theological argument and language that have gained me credibility in public?

However, when I appear on the media I must all too often show myself in a particular role and content myself with short statements, which leave me unsatisfied, since they don't give appropriate expression to my real concerns. So after some reflection I have readily accepted an offer from Norddeutscher Rundfunk, Hamburg to produce a television portrait of my life so far. After various preliminary discussions in June 1971 – before my second world trip – there were several days of filming with the author and producer Peter Rosinski and the theological adviser, my friend from student days, the Jesuit Dr Wolfgang Seibel, first in Sursee, in the parish church, in the lake house and on the lake, and then in Tübingen, in the city and at my home. This is an interesting and fruitful collaboration which takes time, but is pleasant. There are many shots which are both informative and aesthetic: cutting and shortening cause the producer and the editor Wolfgang Lüning some difficulties. Then on 3 December 1971 – the penultimate stop on my journey round the world – as I reported, I see the finished film in the Hamburg studio.

I am enthusiastic, since what I had hoped for has been achieved. It is possible to see my theological and pastoral concerns behind all the public controversies and polemic; it is possible to know the person Hans Küng behind the theologian, scholar and publicist. I am still deeply grateful to Peter Rosinski and Wolfgang Seibel: the more precise view into the workshop of a mass medium which is so often vilified remains very important for me. This 'Attempt at a Portrait' is broadcast on 14 March 1972 and often repeated. And now I have the offer to do another three studio broadcasts in Hamburg as discussions with the public on the topic 'Why I am a Christian Today'; they are broadcast in November. But what a stroke of ill fate: in the middle of August of that year Peter Rosinski loses his only daughter – seemingly because of an unsuccessful operation; she is only eleven.

We theologians have as a publicity organ of the loyal opposition which goes all round the world our international theological journal *Concilium*, which had originally been planned as the voice of the Council and not as an opposition journal. However, it has taken on this role as a result of the reactionary Roman policy. For example, only through *Concilium* was it possible in 1968 to prepare an impressive Declaration for the Freedom of Theology and gather 1360 signatures of theologians all over the world for it. But could the same thing still be achieved in 1972? Anxiety about reprisals is going the rounds again. Such a figure certainly couldn't be achieved, and even in the *Concilium* Foundation, while Edward Schillebeeckx would go along with a declaration, after the infallibility debate Karl Rahner and possibly also Yves Congar certainly wouldn't. So another course has to be adopted.

After the disappointing Synod of Bishops in Rome in October 1971 I think that action has to be taken against the present stagnation and frustration and that a Declaration against Resignation has to be worked out and disseminated. Before Christmas 1971 I compose a first draft, which is subsequently read critically by my team, corrected and supplemented. The judgement of our excellent church lawyer Professor Johannes Neumann is particularly important to me. But without our outstanding secretariat I would have had difficulty in drumming up an internationally representative group of theologians. This time my selection has to be pragmatic. I mustn't aim at a large number or equal representation of the different nations, but must rely more on personal relations, accepting an over-representation of Tübingen theologians, and at all events get a group which has the necessary weight to attract international attention. In the short space of time available I don't succeed in getting theologians even from France, Belgium and Italy.

Finally the Declaration is signed by 33 prominent theologians, whom I shall list here so to speak on a roll of honour, because they represent a reforming élite in the time after the Council. In this way I can express my gratitude to some, whether they are still in contact with me or have taken quite different ways: Jean-Paul Audet (Montreal), Alfons Auer (Tübingen), Gregory Baum (Toronto), Franz Böckle (Bonn), Günther Biemer (Freiburg), Viktor Conzemius (Lucerne), Leslie Dewart (Toronto), Casiano Floristán (Madrid), Norbert Greinacher (Tübingen), Winfried Gruber (Graz), Herbert Haag (Tübingen), Frans Haarsma (Nijmegen), Bas Van Iersel (Nijmegen), Otto Karrer (Lucerne), Walter Kasper (Tübingen), Ferdinand Klostermann (Vienna), Hans Küng (Tübingen), Peter Lengsfeld (Münster), Juan Llopis (Barcelona), Norbert Lohfink (Frankfurt am Main), Richard McBrien (Boston), John L. McKenzie (Chicago), Johann Baptist Metz (Münster), Johannes Neumann (Tübingen), Franz Nikolasch (Salzburg), Stephan Pfürtner (Fribourg), Edward Schillebeeckx (Nijmegen), Piet Schoon-enberg (Nijmegen), Gerard S. Sloyan (Philadelphia), Leonard Swidler (Phila-delphia), Evangelista Villanova (Montserrat), Herrmann Josef Vogt (Tübingen), Bonifac Willems (Nijmegen).

Against resignation: points of orientation

Thanks to good relations with the media it is possible to have the Declaration 'Against Resignation'[8] published in Tübingen before Easter, on 25 March 1972, simultaneously published in the *Corriere della Sera* (Italy) and in the most important Catholic media: in *Publik-Forum* and *Herder-Korrespondenz* (Germany), in *The Tablet* (United Kingdom), the *National Catholic Reporter* (US), *Vida Nueva* (Spain), *De Bazuin* (the Netherlands) and other papers. The Dutch documentation centre idoc, since the Council operating internationally from Rome under the efficient direction of Leo Alting van Gesau, distributes the text to the international press. Paradoxically, two whole-page insertions appear in the same Vol. 8 of idoc (15 April 1942), one from *Concilium*, which announces the issue on the reciprocal recognition of church ministries edited by Walter Kasper and me, and the other from *Communio* (Vol. 1), the new conservative counterpart of *Concilium* founded by Hans Urs von Balthasar with the support of Henri de Lubac and Joseph Ratzinger.

The Declaration begins like this: 'The Catholic Church finds itself in a crisis of leadership and trust on many levels. Six years after the Second Vatican Council the third Roman Synod of Bishops has come to an end without tangible results. In the conciliar period the church's leadership tackled both old and new questions and to an astonishing extent led the way towards solutions. But now in the post-conciliar period it seems incapable of achieving constructive results on such urgent issues as justice and peace in the world and the crisis of the church's ministry. The intrinsically peripheral law of celibacy has undeservedly become a test question for church renewal.' There follows a very realistic analysis of the present difficult situation. The reasons for the present crisis in leadership and trust do not simply lie with particular persons, but in the development of the church system since the Middle Ages. The crisis can be overcome only if the whole church 'again considers its centre and foundation: the gospel of Jesus Christ, from which it took its start and which it has to understand and live anew in every new situation'. So this is by no means just a social and political starting point, but a theological one.

But of course I also raise the political–strategic question. Is a serious reform possible at all in view of the 'superior power and closed nature of the church's system'? We should also address bishops and pastors. My five points of orientation, to overcome stagnation and resignation, rest on many experiences, conversations and actions. Here I shall sum up briefly what is spelt out at more length in the Declaration.

1. *No silence*. Everyone in the church, whether ordained or not, whether man or woman, has the right and often the duty to say what they think and what they believe should be done about the church and its leaders: 'Those bishops – and with the national conferences of bishops they often make up a strong minority or even the majority – who consider certain laws, ordinance and measures a disaster, should come out and say this publicly and call straightforwardly for change.'

2. *Personal action*. Don't just complain about Rome, but do something about it oneself: 'Whether one is a pastor, chaplain or lay person, all members of the church have to do something themselves to help the renewal of the church in their sphere of life, large or small. And particularly in modern society the individual has possibilities of positively influencing the church's life. In various ways one can press for better forms of worship, more intelligible preaching and more relevant pastoral care, for ecumenical integration of communities and Christian commitment in society.'

3. *Acting together*. The officially established parish councils, priests' councils and pastoral councils could become a powerful instrument of renewal in parishes, dioceses and nations, but the free groupings of priests and lay people could also help particular causes in the church to achieve a breakthrough: 'One parishioner who goes to the pastor doesn't count, five can become a burden, fifty can change the situation. A pastor in a diocese doesn't count, five get noticed, fifty are unbeatable.'

4. *Searching for interim solutions*. Many reforms have been achieved only by pressure from below; pressure on the church authorities in the spirit of Christian brotherliness is legitimate: 'Wherever a measure taken by a superior church authority openly contradicts the gospel, resistance can be permitted and even required. Wherever an urgent measure on the part of church authorities is unacceptably delayed, provisional solutions may be set in motion in a prudent and balanced fashion, as long as church unity is maintained.'

5. *Not giving up*. The temptation to leave the church either outwardly or inwardly should be resisted: 'Particularly in this phase of stagnation the crucial point is to hold out serenely in trusting faith and to maintain staying power. Resistance was only be expected. But there can be no renewal without struggle. Thus it remains crucial not to lose sight of the goal, to act quietly and decisively and to maintain hope in a church that is more obligated to the Christian message and hence more open, more humane, more credible, in short more Christian.'

Concealing the use and the misuse of power

The 'Manifesto of the 33 Theologians' proves to be a publicity bombshell. The daily papers report it on both sides of the Atlantic. In the Vatican there is a great stir, the ghost of revolution is going the rounds. Offence is taken above all at the point made that pressure on the church authorities in the spirit of Christian brotherliness is legitimate.

Whereas elsewhere in the Vatican the voices of the opposition are silenced as far as possible, barely four days after our publication there appears on the front page of *L'Osservatore Romano* (29 March 1972), not in journalistic fairness a reprint or at least a summary of our declaration but rather a big article against it by a curial heavyweight, namely the Prefect of the Vatican Congregation for

Catholic Education, the French Cardinal Gabriel Garrone, the former Arch-bishop of Toulouse. I know him from the Council as one of the exponents of conciliar renewal. But now fully Romanized as a Curia cardinal, he denounces our 'points of orientation' as 'a project of contestation', indeed 'demagogic pressure' directed 'against the spirit of faith and the tradition of the church'. As if issues in church law such as celibacy and the reception of married priests back into the ministry were Catholic 'basic values and basic truths'!

The conflict over the truth is now increasingly becoming a power struggle. But as has been customary in Rome since the Council, the exercising of power by the Curia is disguised as 'service': 'The plan of action which the "Manifesto" envi-sages in fact completely rejects the view that power in the church is not a force which must be kept in equilibrium by other forces or can even can be rejected but a "service" of the authorities which is guaranteed divine support.'[9]

Or − a second way of disguising power − it is claimed that anyone who exercises authority in the church today has no power; on the contrary he stands against the dominant power, the force of public opinion. In this way it is thought possible to justify means of power such as the removal of the church's permission to teach, declarations of repudiation, a refusal to allow any inspection of the records, any statement by the person under investigation or any possibility of appeal.

Or − a third way of disguising power − there is the assertion that one isn't exercising rule over the faithful but 'protecting the faith of simple people', who don't write books or articles, and this is 'a democratic task, to give voice to those who have none'. At the same time there is a complaint that 'simple people' everywhere are constantly putting the same peripheral questions (birth control, celibacy, mixed marriages, the ordination of women) instead of being concerned to disseminate the gospel. In this way Pope and bishops are 'lording it over our faith', instead of − to use a saying of Paul (cf. 2 Corinthians 1.24) − 'working with you for your joy'.

These 'first reflections' by Garrone are followed by further articles in the *L'Osservatore* against the 'disobedience' which is allegedly expressed in this 'Declaration', against 'rebellion' and 'anarchy'. For example, it is said that no theologian 'has the task of giving the Christian people guidelines for its behav-iour'.[10] A valid overall judgement on the present church requires 'complete information, pastoral competence, a feeling for practical life and objective realism; these elements are to be found in the College of Bishops, and not in groups of the faithful, however qualified they may be'. The German and Italian Conferences of Bishops second this declaration by the College of Bishops. So too does the Archbishop of Westminster, John Heenan, who shares the responsibility for Charles Davis' departure from the church; by contrast Davis sees the Declaration of the 33 theologians as not radical enough, because they nevertheless want to remain in the church.

As far as I can see, Cardinal Franz König of Vienna takes a moderate position against both resignation and escalation:[11] a public statement cannot damage the church but only benefit it. The theologians too should be treated by the bishops with goodwill. In the US the *National Catholic Reporter* of 31 March empathically defends the Declaration as a '"pastoral letter" from theologians to all the Catholic people': 'That is in itself a refreshing breakthrough, as well as a sign that the theologians who have for so long been advising hierarchs are clearly impatient with the magisterium's failure to implement as church policy the progressive actions of Vatican II.' Moreover, while the Declaration endorses the resistance in the church, it doesn't extend it in revolutionary fashion to the political sphere, as the Catholic left wing in America does. It also takes up the question of celibacy, but not the wrong attitude of the church to women.

Of course my name is mentioned time and again in this connection. I am something like a *bête noire* for those inclined towards Rome. However, to the present day I can stand by these points of orientation and, as far as I can estimate, I have observed them myself. What this Declaration has achieved, however, is quite another matter — in view of the 'power of circumstances', specifically the church power structures dominated by Rome. For all my admiration of Friedrich Schiller's *William Tell*, I could never make my own his statement 'the strong one is most powerful alone'. The success of such initiatives, in the church in particular, depends at every level — parish, diocese, nation — on the behaviour of countless agents: whether they are governed by fear or courage, cowardice or boldness, folly or wisdom.

A power struggle in the church

Of course the renewal of the church depends above all on those with power in the church: the Pope, the bishops and the priests. Whether there is more collegiality in the church between Pope and bishops, and also bishops and clergy, whether there is more democracy, freedom, equality and brotherliness along the lines of the earliest church depends on whether those holding power in the church — since the methods of the French Revolution cannot be applied to them — are themselves prepared to make reforms possible, thus voluntarily or perhaps under pressure granting participation, shared responsibility; in short giving up power and sharing power.

However, 'No farewell to the world is more difficult than a farewell to power,' remarked the French statesman Talleyrand, unsurpassed master of adaptation to changing regimes (*ancien régime* — revolution — Napoleon — restoration), and he should have known. Importantly, similarly compliant behaviour can also be observed among churchmen and theologians before, during and after the Second Vatican Council. How difficult is even the limited renunciation of power in the church!

At the same time it is my experience that everyone who possesses power tends to misuse it unless limits are set. This conviction led Montesquieu, the most important state philosopher of the French Enlightenment, as early as 1748 in his *magnum opus* entitled *De l'esprit des lois* (The Spirit of the Laws) to call for the abolition of absolutism (in favour of a constitutional monarchy according to the English model) and a division of powers. This doctrine certainly had a great influence on the French Revolution and the US Constitution, but not the slightest on the Vatican and the Roman Catholic Church.[12]

Much though the freedom of the papacy has helped the church over the course of history in the face of state absolutism and totalitarianism, papal absolutism has damaged the church itself. In an atmosphere of restoration and reaction, at the First Vatican Council absolute papal power was cemented with the solemn definition of the papal primacy of jurisdiction over all churches and each individual Christian and with the definition of papal infallibility – this despite warnings such as the wise words of the Anglo-German politician and historian Lord Acton, 'Power tends to corrupt, absolute power corrupts absolutely.'

Even the Second Vatican Council, despite infinite troubles and debates over collegiality, didn't succeed in limiting the absolute papal power over the Roman Catholic Church. The internationalization was only external, the collegialization only apparent and the decentralization only cosmetic. Contrary to the intentions of the Council there was no fundamental reform, but only a modernization of the Roman Curia – in the spirit of the old absolutism, in which right at the beginning of his pontificate Paul VI in his address on the reform of the Curia had called for 'absolute obedience' (cf. *My Struggle for Freedom*, IX). The church community pays the price of this papal sole rule in things great and small – one thinks only of this Pope's encyclicals on celibacy (1967) and the pill (1968). That is why I felt obliged (cf. Chapter II above) to publish my book *Infallible?* as 'an enquiry' in 1970.

These controversies play at most a secondary role in a conflict over the truth. Primarily there is a struggle for power in the church. Here I see myself disappointed in one hope: that this 'successor to Peter' will reflect on the Sermon on the Mount. Jesus of Nazareth calls in some instances for a renunciation of rights in favour of the other, to go two miles with the one who has forced me to go one with him (Matthew 5.41), and renunciation of power at my own expense, to give my cloak to the one who has taken my tunic (Matthew 5.40).

I have never called simply for an abolition of power, and even in the church that is illusory. But I have called for a relativization of power with a Christian conscience and the use of power to serve rather than to dominate. When John XXIII summoned the Council, to the horror of the Curia and contrary to its thinking in terms of power and power politics, he used his power for service and shared it with the bishops. In this way he proved to be '*Servus servorum Dei* – servant of the servants of God' (Pope Gregory the Great), not just in fine words. Unfortunately no one has so far followed him on this course, so since then, again contrary to the will of the Council, a triumphalist and powerful church has celebrated itself in colossal demonstrations of power and pomp, while at the local level millions of people are running away from it because in many controversial dogmatic, moral and disciplinary questions the rulers threaten to oppress the ruled, the institutions the persons; order threatens freedom and power threatens law.

Who knows, perhaps we who have committed ourselves to fundamental reforms in the Catholic Church have lost the battle for power in the church. But does that mean we have also lost the battle over the truth? By no means!

Battle for the truth

For me there is no doubt that scholars too have power. 'Knowledge is power,' said the English philosopher Francis Bacon in the seventeenth century. In my grammar school in Lucerne we often mocked the way in which our (very competent) geography teacher added, 'and geographical knowledge is world power', which no longer sounds so pretentious in an age of global geopolitical reflections and operations. But should I perhaps now as a theologian produce a parallel formulation: 'And theological knowledge is God's power'? No, such a remark would be not only pretentious but almost blasphemous.

At a very early stage I became aware that even a theologian with his knowledge has power and can misuse this power — as a court theologian or enthusiast. Even during the Council, in 1964, in a 'Theological Meditation' entitled *The Theologian and the Church* — dedicated to 'Karl Rahner, at sixty, in gratitude for his theological work' — I clearly supported a theology for which critical examination and attachment to the church aren't a contradiction. I have never understood 'criticism' in purely negative terms, but always as a presupposition for something new. Nor have I understood belonging to the church as theological conformism and dogmatism but always as service to the church, the community of the faithful, whose holy scriptures, creeds, definitions and great theologians deserve respect.

In my book *The Church* I included a long section on the succession of teachers in the church, which is to be respected not above, but with, the succession of the apostles and prophets. And in *Infallible?*, in the concluding chapter on the 'relatively recent and unclarified concept of the teaching office (magisterium)' I argued for a clarification of competences: that according to Paul 'pastors and teachers in the church, leaders and theologians, each have their own charism, their own vocation, their own function'. Bishops and pastors have the task of leadership, theologians that of scholarship. Of course the two cannot be completely separated, and for that reason I resolutely pleaded for 'collaboration in trust', since both sides 'have every reason to listen to one another, to inform, to criticize, to inspire'.

This collaboration had borne much fruit in the Council. But after the Council it was increasingly replaced by a renewed monopoly of the bishops, who thought that they should decide even on complex doctrinal questions and that they had to examine their own theological teachers. Not only in Rome but also in many countries, once again pliant court theologians again came to be consulted instead of critically constructive theological specialists.

It was also in the 1970s that the philosopher Jürgen Habermas, increasingly liberating himself from the Marxist presuppositions of the Frankfurt School, began to work out a critical theory of action and society which he finally summed up in his *Theory of Communicative Action* (1981). Here Habermas attempts in the light of the human community of communication and argumentation to develop norms which are also to apply unconditionally in a democracy. He defends reason as the principle of non-violent communication against communication in authoritarian and totalitarian systems, distorted by violence. Against any 'oppressive dialogue' he pleads for conversation, for insight without compulsion, for rational decision: discourse free of domination. A communicative reason orientated on understanding can and should create a unitive social consensus by way of argument. All this is fundamental to safeguarding democratic social life.

Isn't such non-violent, rational communication also important for the functioning of a faith community if one wants to resolve conflicts in the church without compulsion and achieve a consensus by rational arguments? For Habermas, religion, which has no social relevance for the Frankfurt school, takes on increasing importance during these years. It is important for enlightening ourselves about the conditions that make our lives humane and not comfortless. But conversely, in questions of the truth of faith is religion and especially the Roman Catholic Church open to Habermas' call for inter-personal conversation carried on rationally, for discussion free of domination? Unfortunately Habermas didn't put this central question in his public dialogue with Cardinal Ratzinger, head of the Congregation for the Doctrine of the Faith (held at the Catholic Academy in Munich on 19 January 2004), and virtually no observer noted this (or wanted to note it).

In the last resort I am concerned with the truth of faith and not just the question of power, of who has the say in the church. However, I am concerned with the truth not understood primarily as a system of ecclesiastical statements of faith which (according to an old catechetical formula) 'the church prescribes for belief', but in quite concrete terms with the Christian truth, the gospel, the Christian message, with Jesus Christ himself. Time and again this Jesus has to be reinterpreted and followed in discipleship with all that means for God and human beings. Shouldn't Christian truth also be discussed in an atmosphere free of compulsion – without the Damoclean sword of disciplinary sanctions which always threatens? Shouldn't the better arguments decide, particularly in the battle for the truth? This battle hasn't yet been decided.

Attempts at a conversation free of domination

On 9 January 1971, as I reported in Chapter IV of this book, I had made myself available for a conversation with Cardinal Volk, Bishop Wetter and Professors Ratzinger and Schlier. There was little 'conversation free of domination' to be detected here. Rather, at least outwardly (what I believe in my heart is of no importance) and possibly even against my better judgement (the church has a monopoly of the truth) I was to submit obediently to authority. Of course such an understanding had to fail. Can't it be achieved in another way?

In 1971 I responded in long articles to two friendly but now suddenly notably apologetic Catholic critics – Avery Dulles (US), a dogmatic theologian, and Gregory Baum (Canada), a political theologian, on the infallibility question. But what was more important for me was a basic article in the *New York Times* under the title 'Why Infallibility?' in which on 3 June 1971 I summed up the main arguments for the publication of my book. In the summer semester of 1972 I again enter the scholarly discussion on infallibility. I invite the most important opponents to Tübingen to my senior seminar to discuss their contributions to Rahner's composite volume 'On the Problem of Infallibility. Answers to Hans Küng's Enquiry'. So no one should accuse me of not being ready for conversation.

To my delight, almost all of them come: on 3 May Heinrich Fries, on 10 May Joseph Ratzinger, on 7 June Karl Rahner and on 14 June Karl Lehmann. Only the Freiburg theologian Adolf Kolping, author of a pamphlet 'Infallible? An Answer', pleads a dental operation and refuses. All the sessions are harmonious and each concludes with a good private dinner. In all these discussions, each lasting three hours, Karl Lehmann is the only one who, driven by us further into a corner than his predecessors, to the annoyance of his two assistants concedes that in some circumstances an 'infallible' definition could also in fact be wrong. I write to Edward Schillebeeckx on 28 June 1972: 'The infallibility seminar here, at which Rahner, Ratzinger, Lehmann and Fries appeared in person, went very well. The guests were treated in a very fair and friendly way. But not once were I and my cause put on the defensive. Rather, it is again evident that no one can give a reason for the infallibility of particular statements. So a whole series of objections have been shown up to be worthless.'

This was in fact a 'discussion free of domination' and I want to add further arguments. But what will the next act of the drama be? Already while reading Rahner's composite volume I had considered whether it would be useful likewise to bring together the happily numerous assents to my book and organize my own volume. But I didn't even get round to the task of surveying the potential material closely. A personal stocktaking in the face of the many misunderstandings and insinuations of my opponents didn't appeal. However, on 29 June 1972 I nevertheless begin this highly unattractive task. Despite a great deal of preliminary work and considerable assistance from Dr Hermann Häring I don't manage to complete it by the beginning of the holidays, to be precise by 5 a.m. on 2 August.

And now I must have a holiday, so I drive to Switzerland. There on 18 August I resume work in the lake house; by 31 August I have completed a first draft. It has become a long treatise, which I revise thoroughly after my return to Tübingen, while the other contributions are being edited.

'Fallible?': the results of the infallibility debate

In January 1973 the imposing work finally appears, again published by the brave Benziger Verlag, under the title 'Fallible? A Stocktaking'. It is 525 pages long and contains 16 contributions from highly qualified specialists on biblical, historical, social and theological problems. About 190 pages of it is my personal stocktaking, which goes in great detail into all the important and some less important questions of the controversy. It is amazing how many titles the multi-language 'Bibliography on the Infallibility Debate' which concludes the volume comprises in ten pages of small print: composite volumes, longer articles and statements, reviews, reports in newspapers and magazines – and all this in three short years. With this bibliography Karl-Josef Kuschel has laid the foundations for the infallibility archive in our Institute for Ecumenical Research; it is his first published scholarly work. His co-author is the American Bernadette Brooten, from Idaho, who for the moment is working as an academic assistant in our Institute; later she specializes in research into women and brings the insights of American feminism into the debate about a contemporary theology.

The welcome result is that I can establish a fundamental agreement in three respects between the important parties in the dispute. First, even my opponents recognize that in principle the church's magisterium can err (even if it hardly ever openly and honestly corrects its errors). Secondly, all share my scepticism about the concept and practice of infallibility and attempt to reinterpret or even rename it by way of qualification. And thirdly, they all endorse my basic thesis: despite all indisputable errors, the church abides in the truth.

So where isn't there agreement? Only over the possibility of infallibly true statements guaranteed by the Holy Spirit. None of the doctrinal statements of the Pope or the whole episcopate in matters of faith (for example the 'bodily assumption of Mary into heaven', 1950) or morality (for example the 'sinfulness of contraception', 1968) can be false because of the support of the Holy Spirit and consequently all Catholics must obey them unconditionally.

And what is the status of such infallible doctrinal statements? It cannot be disputed or overlooked that not a single one of the prominent disputants has proved their possibility or even attempted to do so. On the contrary, the debate has brought new insights, once again summarized briefly here:

1. The inventor of papal infallibility is not orthodox scholasticism (for example Thomas Aquinas) but a thirteenth-century Franciscan, Petrus Olivi, who was often accused of heresy.

2. The teaching authority of the ecumenical councils does not rest on their production of infallible statements but on their roots in the gospel.

3. There is no support for an infallibility of the Bishop of Rome either in the New Testament or in the tradition of the first three centuries.

Anyone who has read 'Fallible? A Stocktaking' will agree with me that I haven't contented myself with answering the objections of my critics in every detail but have sought to work out a fundamental agreement among those involved in the dispute. At the same time I have also made clear the impossibility of proving so-called divinely guaranteed infallible statements and taken seriously the new insights that have emerged in the discussion. In addition I have constructively demonstrated and spelt out a possible consensus for the future: 1. What it means in concrete terms for the church to be maintained in truth; 2. How one can live with errors in the church; 3. What are the criteria of Christian truth; 4. How to proceed in the case of conflict. I can't describe all that here. But what happens to the results of the debate?

'Infallibility' reinterpreted — counter-arguments ignored

The greatest expert on the rise of the idea of infallibility, the American historian Brian Tierney of Cornell University, writes to me after receiving 'Fallible? A Stocktaking' (3 April 1973):

As I read your discussion of the whole controversy I began to feel optimistic. Really I think that we shall win this fight over infallibility, though it will take a long time. The striking fact is that, so far as I can see, no sophisticated theologian is really defending the doctrine that the council of 1870 actually defined and intended to define. In the end surely this will become plain to everyone. Theologians criticize you because you attacked an 'old-fashioned' doctrine of infallibility instead of discussing their nuanced modern theories. But they never notice that their nuanced theories are really incompatible with the dogma of 1870 that they pretend to defend. This seems to me especially true of Karl Rahner. For many years his teaching has been alien in spirit and content to the definition of 1870. It is sad that he cannot admit this — even to himself.

According to Tierney the consequences of this position are serious:

The attempt to preserve the doctrine of infallibility at all costs is corrupting the whole language of Catholic ecclesiology. Theologians who don't really believe in what was defined in 1870 insist on defending the definition. Naturally their work becomes evasive and paradoxical — to me nonsensical — until it is hard to believe in their intellectual honesty. (Of course I do not think they wilfully lie but they will not candidly face unpleasant truths.) It is also important of course that papal infallibility is the greatest obstacle to the growth of the ecumenical movement.

These are remarkably clear words. After my efforts perhaps after all an outsider can think himself a little into my situation. Time and again the hierarchy requests me to examine my views. After the great stocktaking 'Fallible?' I can honestly claim that I have thoroughly examined my views and worked over all the objections.

But conversely there is total negativity: not a single representative of this 'magisterium' in Rome or Germany has grappled with the arguments presented in the stocktaking volume. One notes among these representatives of the 'true faith' what Jean-Paul Sartre analysed as '*mauvaise foi*', which is better translated 'confused awareness' than 'bad or false faith'. With this crooked basic attitude these gentlemen of the magisterium, most of whom wouldn't be capable of explaining to our contemporaries what being a Christian is in accordance with the Bible and our time, content themselves with detecting possible 'heresies' and attempting to confirm their own, allegedly orthodox, views. It oppresses me that evidently no exegetical, historical or systematic thought makes any progress against lazy thinking grounded in dogma or the deliberate disregard of uncomfortable truths. Be this as it may, I don't receive the slightest reaction to this stocktaking book either from the German bishops or from Rome. Even a decade after Vatican II, Neo-scholastic Roman court theology prevails in the Roman Curia and especially in the Congregation for the Doctrine of the Faith – and is hardly attacked.

In this situation, I tell myself, I will surely receive help in the controversy from Geneva, from the World Council of Churches, which represents non-Roman Catholic Christianity. After all, in the end I stand for quite decisive Protestant and Eastern Orthodox concerns.

Ambiguous experiences with the World Council of Churches

Since it was founded in Amsterdam in 1948, the World Council of Churches (WCC) has performed tremendous services for the unity of the Christian churches. It has had my complete support since my years of study in Rome (1948-55) and even more since Vatican II (1962-65). But my personal experiences with the WCC are ambiguous.

I was envisaged as a speaker at the plenary session of the General Assembly of the World Council of Churches in Uppsala in 1968. But because there were objections from Rome I was replaced by the chief editor of the Roman Jesuit journal *Civiltà Cattolica*, Fr Roberto Tucci. In 1970 the ecumenical institutes were invited to a conference in the Château de Bossy above Lake Geneva, home of the Ecumenical Institute of the WCC. However, it wasn't so much the General Secretary, Eugene Carson Blake, and the executive committee who were behind this invitation as the director of the WCC library, Dr Hans van der Bent, who had visited me in Tübingen. This Dutchman, a sterling ecumenist, was unhappy about the direction of the social policy of the World Council, which recently had become all too one-sided: a 'World Conference on Church and Society' had taken place in Geneva in 1966 which, utterly motivated by the *Zeitgeist*, presented a 'theology of revolution' for discussion. However, at the WCC General Assembly in Uppsala in 1968 the talk was more cautiously of 'renewal' rather than 'revolution', though this nevertheless sparked off a vigorous dispute between the different trends of political theology and above all a lasting conflict with the evangelicals, who sensed here a betrayal of the gospel. Be this as it may, now, from 27 to 30 June 1970 at the beautiful Bossey Institute, more than 30 directors of ecumenical institutes from all over Europe, America and even Australia meet; however, they have extremely different orientations and some have only a peripheral interest in theology. There are illuminating exchanges of information and we get on well.

For me it is fundamentally more important to inform myself personally about the orientation of the ecumenical movement and I have lengthy conversations with the real founder, first General Secretary and long-time head of the WCC, Dr Willem Visser 't Hooft, a charismatic with a talent for organization, a Reformed theologian with firm convictions yet ecumenical breadth, who has never primarily been concerned with his own person but with the shared Christian cause. Although by now he is retired, he has taken the trouble to come to Bossey. In personal conversation I note that he is unhappy with the new 'revolutionary' orientation of the WCC but naturally doesn't want to comment publicly on the policy of his successor and the present leadership. What a pity, I also think, that the Catholic Church doesn't have a Pope of the stature of Visser 't Hooft. But would this independent man, rooted in the gospel, ever have risen to bishop and cardinal in the Roman system?

The new General Secretary, Eugene Carson Blake, is a pragmatic and liberal American Protestant, formerly a brave fighter for the civil rights movement, but without theological ambitions. He doesn't think it necessary for himself or one of the leading members of the WCC staff to make the short journey from Geneva to Bossey to welcome personally over the three days the professors, some of whom are important, and possibly to talk with them. Instead, at the end of the conference (30 June 1970) we are invited to the headquarters in Geneva. And since I have spoken critically about the new orientation of the WCC, I am now nominated spokesman for the group.

We are received in a large room where the General Secretary is enthroned on a platform with members of his staff. He jovially bids us welcome. As spokesman, speaking up to him from below, I can't stop myself remarking that I feel as if I were at a papal audience. I say that we would like the undoubtedly important

245

questions of social development, such as the problems of the Third World, racism and poverty, peace and disarmament, to be discussed further. But at the same time we would like theological dialogue towards a resolution of the questions bound up with the split in the churches to be pursued more vigorously. In the name of my colleagues I then make three requests: 1. In future all significant theological currents should be represented in the joint commissions of the WCC and the Vatican Secretariat for Unity; 2. The criterion for selection should be professional scholarly competence; 3. Competent scholars and institutes should be involved in the preparatory stage and not just at the end.

Carson Blake receives my statement graciously and seeks to pacify us. The WCC has no monopoly of the truth and we should cultivate above all links between us. These are fine words which get nowhere. Still, there is no conflict and we go on to have a friendly conversation. In this situation I don't want anyone to burden me with the problems of infallibility, an ecumenical question *par excellence*. My *Infallible?* appears a few days later, on 18 July 1970, the centenary of the definition of infallibility, and in any case I have spoken a good deal about this problem on the radio, in lectures and interviews. The Geneva conference doesn't produce a concrete result.

Strange alliances

I have invited Peter Beyerhaus, Director of the Institute for Missiology in the Protestant Faculty, to join me on the drive back from Geneva to Tübingen. Very interested in the views also of conservative Protestants, I had held a joint seminar with him on ecumenism and with him had resisted a red demolition squad at our seminar. At that time I still thought that one could convince any scholar with rational arguments. And now I, who am no Bultmann disciple, have five hours in the car to give a detailed account to my colleague of historical–critical exegesis of the Bible and the concerns of the Protestant exegete Rudolf Bultmann, whom he finds totally uncongenial. But every time he seems finally convinced under the pressure of quotations and arguments, he begins all over again. I take all conceivable trouble, and do so three or four times, until finally, while not despairing of communicative reason, I doubt the capacity of reason to make any progress in the face of sentiments and resentments, traditional prejudices and emotional positions.

Beyerhaus, who produces virtually no scholarly publications but constantly agitates, will develop into an opponent of the World Council of Churches and an ideologist of the evangelical movement 'No Other Gospel'. And he is the fundamentalist theologian with whom Professor Ratzinger, as his memoirs of 1998 first betray to me, tried to 'plan a common course of action ... one of the most precious gifts given me by my years in Tübingen'.[13]

To be fair: relatively liberal ecumenists, too, can reveal remarkable limitations.

When on a later occasion our Ecumenical Institute wants to engage in a serious conversation with the World Council of Churches, I agree a date in February 1976 with my highly esteemed colleague Dr Lukas Vischer, Secretary of the Faith and Order section and well known to me from the Council. We have met occasionally at my guest semester in Basle and on ecumenical occasions. He is a member of the editorial committee of the ecumenism section of *Concilium*. Together with the Catholic dogmatic theologian Johannes Feiner, who is also Swiss, he wrote an excellent 'New Book of Faith' in an ecumenical spirit and sent it to me in July 1973. But immediately before the meeting in Geneva I receive the surprising news that the meeting of our Institute with Dr Vischer must be moved from WCC headquarters to the Calvin Auditorium next to Geneva Cathedral. Whoever or whatever stood behind this decision, no one can give me a convincing reason for the move. Has the Vatican intervened through its local 'observer'?

In fact, I hear on good authority that the leaders of the World Council of Churches have for some time allowed themselves to be intimidated by Rome into not inviting me to any commission or assembly. 'Don't spoil things with Rome' seemed to be the slogan in Geneva after the Council. And shrewdly leave the reform concerns of the Reformers to the reform Catholics? This has advantages for me, as the great guru of American management counselling, Peter Drucker of Claremont, California, once explained to me: 'You can either go to meetings or you can work, but you cannot do both.' Because of this unecumenical alliance between the Vatican and Geneva at my expense, I have a good deal more time for research.

I never discovered precisely what went on behind the scenes in the newest case in Geneva, but it is clear that I must firmly reject the 'shifting' of the meeting: either I go through the main entrance of the World Council of Churches or I don't go at all. On 15 February 1976 on the spur of the moment I send a telegram saying that we are turning down the meeting.

This makes clear what fundamentally I already know: my theological positions, which seem dangerous for Rome and its power structure, are uncomfortable for Geneva and its church diplomacy. I will receive some signs of sympathy from the World Council of Churches but little practical support in my battle for an ecumenical openness on the part of the Roman Catholic Church. It often oppresses me to see how little support officials of the Protestant churches give to those Catholic theologians who stand up for Protestant concerns. Later I put it like this: such Protestants prefer being photographed with the Pope to protesting.

Two years later, however, I appear in a fine photograph with the WCC General Secretary Philip Potter, Carson Blake's successor. It recalls a happy ecumenical occasion in Berne on 9 May 1978. Potter and I speak at the 450th anniversary of the Reformation in Berne in the Holy Spirit Church, packed with 1800 people; another 800 follow the transmission in the Catholic Trinity Church. I close my 'Questions to the Reformation' with seven 'imperatives of ecumenical hope': 1. Ecumenical conversations must not remain without results. 2. The church leaders are challenged to take concrete ecumenical steps. 3. Ecumenical impulses from the grass roots (hospitality in worship and the eucharist, interconfessional religious instruction, etc.) are to be taken up by church leaders instead of being banished into no man's land ('for the Holy Spirit does not just sit in the Holy See'). 4. Free churches are to be included in ecumenical agreements. 5. Step-by-step plans for union are to be worked out and implemented between confessions. 6. Ecumenical efforts must be set against the background of the world and its problems. 7. In the present ecumenical stagnation, what is ecumenically possible must be noted. The most essential element in all ecumenical efforts is a concentration on the centre: on God and on Jesus Christ. Philip Potter, too, argues for a 'conciliar fellowship of the churches'. We get on well together.

The June 1970 Bossey conference also had a welcome result, at least incidentally.

Reciprocal recognition of ministries

As soon as I realize at the Bossey conference that no concrete results are to be expected, I first speak with the Protestant theologian in whom I had most confidence at the conference. He is Professor Edmund Schlink, the director of the ecumenical institute of Heidelberg University, an ecumenically inclined Lutheran with profound knowledge and critical perception. He had invited me to Heidelberg for a seminar on justification soon after I was called to Tübingen. We often saw each other at the Second Vatican Council, at which he was present as an observer for the Evangelical Church in Germany.

I now propose that we bring to life a working group of the university institutes to tackle the trickiest question of Catholic–Protestant dialogue, the reform and reciprocal recognition of church ministries. Schlink immediately agrees and we also win over the other four institute directors from Germany present at the conference: from the Protestant side Wolfhart Pannenberg of Munich and Hans-Heinrich Wolf of Bonn, and from the Catholic side my highly-esteemed predecessor in the Tübingen chair, Heinrich Fries of Munich, and my friend from the German college, Peter Lengsfeld of Münster.

This working group of university ecumenical institutes with their teams meets in Frankfurt on 7 November 1970. We agree on the distribution of tasks relatively quickly. From a sociological perspective Lengsfeld and his team will take on the crisis of the ministry in the Catholic Church and Wolf, or on behalf of him Yorick Spiegel, the crisis in the ministry from a Protestant perspective. Schlink will deal with the apostolic succession and the fellowship of ministries from a systematic perspective, I and my Tübingen team will cover the nature and form of the church's ministry, and finally Pannenberg and Fries will deal with ordination and its sacramental character.

There are few detailed questions to which so far I have devoted so much attention as the question of ministry; for me − after settling the problems of justification − this is the real issue that separates the churches. I devoted almost 300 pages to it in *Structures of the Church* (Chapter VI) and investigated more deeply than most Catholic theologians how Martin Luther, because of the resistance of a totally secularized and blinded episcopate which was unwilling to reform, was forced into the desperate situation of either having to ordain pastors himself or having them ordained as 'emergency bishops' (but soon unfortunately they are Summepiscopi) by the local princes − a system which only came to an end with the German Reich in 1918.

Not least a treatment by Schlink of the apostolic succession had helped me in the early 1960s to clarify systematically the exegetical findings which I had learned above all through my Tübingen colleagues Ernst Käsemann (Protestant) and Karl Hermann Schelkle (Catholic). The importance for the apostolic succession of the laying on of hands by ministers as it developed in the early church can be seen more clearly than elsewhere in Lutheranism. But at the same time − and this is important for the Reformation churches − according to the New Testament two further ways into the church's ministry can be recognized and acknowledged for today. There is the call of ministers by those who have themselves received no mission (in the Acts of the Apostles the laying on of hands by prophets and teachers). And according to the authentic letters of the apostle Paul there is the free charisma of those who feel themselves called to the ministry of leadership (1 Corinthians 13.38; 16.15) or presiding (Romans 12.18) in a community of believers.

On 26 June 1971 I discuss the question of the church's ministry of leadership, its variables and constants, before an audience of 500–600 priests of various ages in the Catholic Academy in Munich, and receive a good deal of assent. But it would have been surprising with such a difficult ecumenical problem if collaboration in our ecumenical working group had continued without difficulties. These emerged at our meeting in Königstein near Frankfurt on 2/3 July 1971.

On Sunday 4 July I begin by revising our text, for which my assistants Dr Hermann Häring, Dr Friedhelm Krüger and Dr Joseph Nolte were also responsible and which we had discussed in several sessions of the doctoral colloquium. My draft begins from the church as a community in freedom, equality and brotherhood; the slogan of the French Revolution has support not in the clerical absolutist constitution of the medieval church but in the church of the New Testament. In the light of the New Testament evidence I look at the development of the traditional understanding of the ministry and only then turn to the systematic question of the form and essence of the church's ministry, concluding with thoughts on the image of the church leader today. Revision of the text is completed in a week, on 9 July.

Since this draft is now three times as long as the original study and overlaps a good deal with the drafts by the other institutions, the working group agrees that because of the urgency of the problems we face, my manuscript may be published separately in the middle of July 1971. It is appears under the title *Why Priests?*, dedicated to 'my brothers in the church's ministry as a help between the times'.

The book also appears in French and Italian translations the same year, in 1972 in Dutch, English, American, Spanish editions, and in 1973 in Portuguese. This theology of ministry with an utterly biblical foundation not only evokes much assent but also brings out defenders of an image of the priesthood reserved for celibate males. To my regret the aged retired Archbishop of Strasbourg, Jean Weber, whom I regard highly, produces an article which is widely disseminated especially in the US, with malicious attacks on my Catholic orthodoxy. Unfortunately *Time Magazine* (7 August 1972) presents *Why Priests?* as a fundamentally Protestant work, but then publishes letters from readers in my favour, above all one from the well-known Catholic theologian Gregory Baum (2 September 1972): 'Even if other theologians attach greater importance than Küng to the church's historical experience, they realize that the biblical witness never simply confirms the church. The Bible continues to embarrass the church, disapprove of its collective behaviour and undermine the authority of the merely human. Hans Küng is not marginal, but central in the Roman Catholic Church's quest for a new future.' Where one cannot defend oneself, one is dependent on friends, and how good it is when in this case they are there.

Now the denunciations pile up. When the editorial committee of *Concilium*, invited to Brescia by our Italian publisher Queriniana and its shrewd and clever representative and theologian Rosino Gibellini, meets on Lake Garda in the Gardone Riviera from 24 to 28 May 1972, the Vatican correspondent of the *Corriere della Sera*, Fabrizio de Santis (whom I know from the Council), starting from a caricature of me in the traditionalist paper *Chiesa viva* (No. 8, 1972), writes an article on us which, though amusing, is open to misunderstanding, with the headline 'The Fathers of "Pop-Revolutionary" Theology'. A protest letter from our committee follows with well-known signatories: E. Schillebeeckx, Y. Congar, J.-P. Jossua, M.-D. Chenu, A. M. Greeley, G. Baum, H. Küng, J. B. Metz, G. Gutiérrez, C. Floristán, J. Pohier, C. Duquoc, D. Power, C. Geffré and R. Laurentin. However, the editors choose as a title 'The Revolutionary Theologians'. De Santis apologizes to me: neither the first nor the second title is his. He then writes a second, better-informed article (7 June 1972) about our meeting, which for him is a 'summit of Catholic intelligence'.

At the same time I receive the news, with warm greetings from Fr Roberto Tucci, SJ, chief editor of *Civiltà cattolica*, later a cardinal, that with 42 per cent *Concilium* is the most-read theological journal at the Gregorian, whereas the house journal *Gregorianum* has a readership of only 2 per cent. The rising controversies again confirm that all these doctrinal and structural questions are not just about theological theory but about political practice; they aren't concerned just with a conflict over the truth but with a power struggle.

Apostolic succession − primarily a question about power

Our original manuscript is abbreviated, revised and adjusted to the results of the other institutes for the memorandum of the working group. There is still a vigorous discussion of the so-called 'sacramental character', that spiritual mark which is allegedly stamped by ordination on the soul of each man who is ordained. Lengsfeld affirms this mark on purely social grounds, but Pannenberg does so on highly theological grounds. I reject it because it is an invention, unknown in the Eastern churches, of the Latin church father Augustine, who used 'character' simply to make it clear that one may not repeat baptism, and it was then transferred by later theologians to ordination to the priesthood. In the end we find a mediating formula for this dispute which doesn't trouble anyone.

In 1973 the memorandum is finally ready for printing under the title 'Reform and Recognition of Church Ministries'. It consists of 23 theses which are explained by six contributions from our institutes.[14] For me the most important is thesis 8, about which there has been consensus among us from the start. 'The ministry of founding and leading the community has been exercised in different ways depending on tradition and situation, not exclusively on the basis of a laying on of hands by the apostles or by appointment through those commissioned by them. It also took place on the basis of a mission through communities and charismatics, and in the free missionary exercise of a corresponding charism.'[15]

This thesis is highly uncomfortable for Rome. Objections were already made to it in the proceedings against my books *Structures of the Church* and *The Church*, in which I had given a thorough and comprehensive description of the ordering of ministries in the light of the New Testament. But in Rome people aren't accustomed to grappling with the evidence of exegesis. Paul VI himself has no inkling of the problems posed by the New Testament. And in the Doctrinal Congregation the Bible is used as a quarry from which to dig out material to support the church system as needed, regardless of the fact that the Pontifical Biblical Commission, the majority of whom are professional exegetes, often puts forward opposite positions.

However, one should be clear that for Rome the question of the apostolic succession is primarily a question of power. For the traditional Roman doctrine creates the possibility of disqualifying a priori all Protestant and Anglican pastors as not validly ordained and therefore refusing eucharistic fellowship with these churches. Excommunication of individuals and churches and a refusal of communion to them has been the instrument of power used since the Middle Ages and the Reformation to maintain the absolutist Roman system and the Roman Catholic claim to monopoly, to be alone the 'church of Jesus Christ' − and this despite all the corrections made by Vatican II.

My well-founded conviction is that 450 years after the Reformation it is time to understand better this doctrine which divides Christianity and which over the centuries has in practice been of little use to the Roman Catholic Church, and to correct it in the light of the New Testament. Our memorandum is to provide the theological basis for that. However, it would make little sense to send it to Rome or to the bishops. Serious note will be taken of it only as a public document. Therefore it must be published immediately.

To give it more weight and urgency, we want to enclose with it a simple response card on which readers can indicate their assent to the theses. People accustomed to democracy take this for granted. The head of Grünewald Verlag, Dr Jakob Laubach, who is also the publisher of the German edition of *Concilium*, agrees to my request by telephone. However, this leads to a 'serious row' between him and Bishop Hermann Volk, which is settled only after a year of silence. And what the publisher forgets to say in his memoirs is that despite my urgent insistence the response card that we wanted isn't inserted.[16]

Our memorandum gets a positive discussion in the papers. Even Karl Rahner comments on it at length and on the whole positively (*Frankfurter Allgemeine Zeitung* of 14 February 1973). Soon afterwards, however, the notoriously one-sided 'Faith Commission' of the German Conference of Bishops, which could easily have supported our memorandum, publishes a declaration the main author of which is presumed to be Professor Joseph Ratzinger. In fact it clarifies nothing, but smoothly and without convincing reasons rejects our solution to the old disputed question with its biblical basis. However, an existential question for our communities, many active Christians and especially married couples of different confessions can't be settled so easily with such doctrinal dictates.

Demand for eucharistic fellowship

This unecumenical attitude of the hierarchy and its Faith Commission is disowned by both Catholics and Protestants. Opinion polls show that among the people a steadily increasing majority of both wants eucharistic fellowship. That becomes dramatically clear at the ecumenical meeting at Pentecost 1971 in Augsburg. It opens with 32 acts of worship, in several of which the eucharist is celebrated together or open communion is practised. The Roman Catholic Bishop of Augsburg, my basically good-hearted but theological unenlightened prefect at the German College, Josef Stimpfle, is alarmed, and thinks that he needs to take action against all this. But in the big working party on worship a clear majority accepts the resolution that joint celebrations of the eucharist are to be accepted for ecumenical groups and married couples of different confessions, and that every Christian, regardless of confession, may be allowed to receive communion in any Christian church. In this way the one Christian church would be visible in the different confessions.

But how does the Roman Catholic Church react to this new 'Pentecost miracle'? It simply ignores the wish of its faithful, indeed for decades it prevents any further ecumenical meeting. Of course this is out of a well-founded fear that the same demands would be made and a shared eucharist would simply be practised. Only 32 years later, in 2003, an 'ecumenical Kirchentag' is again allowed to take place, in Berlin. Previously, Roman pressure had forced out of Protestant church governments agreements that in no case might open communion be practised for members of other confessions. Pliant representatives of German Protestantism also object to justified ecumenical demands by Catholic and Protestant reform groups with excuses such as 'it's too early'. Once again there is an unholy alliance of church governments to prevent ecumenical actions.

My pupil Gottfried Hasenhüttl, now Professor of Dogmatics in Saarbrücken, who also invited other Christians to his Catholic service at the Berlin 'ecumenical Kirchentag', is punished not only with a withdrawal of his permission to teach but even with suspension from priestly duties, though countless Catholic priests would have done, and do, the same thing in their parishes. No means of maintaining the existing power structures can be too bad.

These events show once again how unteachable this 'magisterium' is: incapable of conversation, it refuses any substantive discussion and requires blind submission in controversies. This is not primarily divinely revealed 'truth' but an unrestrained use of church power. This authoritarian way of going on confirms me in my conviction that I should never submit blindly to such a magisterium – contrary to the biblical and rational arguments. But of course I also know that people will not stop at any means of deterring me from my conviction.

In the middle of February 1972, although I am on my research semester, I must return from Sursee to Tübingen. However, this is for a happy event, the awarding of a doctorate to my excellent American pupil Ronald Modras of Detroit, with his dissertation on Paul Tillich's view of the church. To my delight, immediately before my world trip two other pupils had gained doctorates in theology: the New York Jesuit John Dwyer with a dissertation on Paul Tillich's theology of the cross and my former assistant Christa Hempel with a work on the discussion of the doctrine of justification. Some semesters previously I had prepared the way for her by a motion in the faculty that by a change in the regulations women too should be admitted to doctorates in Catholic theology.

Now and again my highly intensive work on my 'Introduction to Christianity' is interrupted by festivals. On 22 February I am back in Sursee to take part at last in the famous Basle Fasnacht with my friends the next day. I go into the centre of the city with thousands of others in the pitch-black night, where on the dot of 4 a.m. the various 'cliques' begin their 'morning walk' in old country fashion with drums and pipes, but also with giant illuminated masks of an extremely original kind. Arm-in-arm we walk with them through the streets and alleyways of the old city, crowning it by eating the traditional flour and onion broth in a restaurant early in the morning.

However, pipes and drums cannot drive away my anxieties about the church. The most recent events obscure rather than illuminate the horizon.

VII

öööö

The Demand for Capitulation

'Humiliter se subiecit – *he has humbly submitted.*'

Traditional submission formula of someone censured by the Vatican
(*in* L'Osservatore Romano)

'Concern for the church': I truly have no less concern for the church than my
opponents. However, I always understand 'church' in the sense of the Bible and
Vatican II (Chapters I and II of the Constitution on the Church) as the fellowship
of believers, as the people of God, and not as 'hier-archy', the 'holy rule' of the
few who have power over the many. I am all for 'offices in the church'; without
them the church doesn't function. However, those ordained to them shouldn't
exercise power over the community and lord it over them, but be at their
'service'. In theory that would also be conceded by Pope and bishops. But what
does it look like in practice?

The change in the reform cardinal Suenens

It is above all the fate of Cardinal Léon Suenens, Archbishop of Mechelen-
Brussels, that worries me. At the end of March 1969 there has been a vigorous but
quite private conflict – reciprocal accusations in letters – between him and Pope
Paul VI, who isn't used to such resistance. On 23 June 1969, the eve of his name
day, in an address to the College of Cardinals the Pope publicly intervenes in the
debate sparked off by Suenens' interview in April 1969 (cf. Chapter II above) but
without mentioning any names. The Pope makes known his wish for reform of
the Curia, but generally speaking defends the Roman system against the allegedly
'unjust', indeed 'disrespectful', criticism that has been made.

Though the reaction of the public and especially of active Catholics to Suenens' interview has been very positive, and so many bishops secretly agree with
him, hardly one speaks out publicly, and at the 'Extraordinary' Synod of Bishops
in October 1969 Suenens sees himself isolated. This is a very awkward situation:
not only do the Curia cardinals spurn him, but most of the presidents of the
bishops' conferences – only those bishops most intent on falling into line have
been invited – turn their backs on the 'cardinal of contestation'. This is what

every bishop fears in this authoritarian Roman system: standing in isolation with demands for reform. It is almost unbearable for Suenens, who in the Council was a highly respected and popular cardinal and also enjoyed communicating on other issues.

By the personal intervention of – if I am rightly informed – Chiara Lubich, the founder of the Focolare movement, after a silence there is finally a meeting in the Vatican in 1972 between the Pope and the cardinal. Paul VI, shrewd and calculating as ever, begins by embracing Suenens warmly. Then a conversation takes place, the main point of which is passed over in Suenens' published memoirs.[1] There isn't a word about the Pope's reaction to Suenens' criticism of the way in which he carries out his office. According to the memoirs the conversation turns above all on the promotion of a 'Marian' ecumenism, even if both are convinced that this would hardly fall on open ears with Cardinal Willebrands and the Secretariat for Unity. Suenens tells the Pope of various ecumenical conversations and the two main obstacles to an ecumenical agreement: 'Mary (for the Protestants) and the papal primacy (for everyone)' (p. 204).

The private 'letter of thanks on the day after the audience' which Suenens sends to the Pope brings more enlightenment and signals a change in their relations: 'This letter marks a change in our relations in the sense that the problems thrown up by the Council would increasingly give place to new tasks, namely preparing for the acceptance of the charismatic renewal which has come about in the Catholic milieu in the United States' (p. 205). The letter itself says that Suenens has chosen the topic for his lectures in the United States. 'In the decade between 1960 and 1970 the church concentrated especially on examining its "institutional" aspect; the new decade 1970-80 requires us to emphasize the spiritual, "pneumatic" aspect of the church. And that allows me to let the problems of the structures rest ("*laisser en repos*") in order to take up a concern that I have encountered all over the United States: a thirst for prayer, for the discovery of Jesus as a person, and for the Holy Spirit' (p. 205).

There is indeed a change in relations between the cardinal and the Pope – however it does not begin with the letter to the Pope but before or during the audience. At any rate, later in Brussels the cardinal reveals to me the real motive for this change: the urgent request of the Pope that while he may continue to formulate his criticism in the future he should not proclaim it to the whole world and the church but rather communicate it quite personally to the Pope. I'm shocked when Suenens says that he has agreed. That is what the Romans time and again attempt to achieve, *silentium obsequiosum*, 'obedient silence', in public; what one believes in private doesn't bother them much, but it mustn't be spoken of and above all mustn't appear in the media. I am convinced that criticism of Paul VI made personally will achieve little unless at the same time it is supported by the public. Suenens, I'm afraid, will thus be more and more domesticated by Rome and personally immobilized.

The cardinal tells me that he will now commit himself to the charismatic movement. I think to myself that this is certainly less dangerous, but what will it finally achieve? In this way one easily sacrifices church reform to enthusiastic 'piety' in an otherwise unchanged Roman system. In fact the great cardinal of reform, whom I cannot see in any other light, has capitulated to Rome.

Jan Grootaers, whom I know from the Council as a journalist and observer and who later becomes a professor in Louvain, rightly mentions two contradictory basic lines in his nuanced assessment of the life of Cardinal Suenens. There is his commitment on the one hand to liturgical renewal, the ecumenical movement and new orientations in ecclesiology, and on the other to a Marian apostolate and the charismatic movement: 'The contrast between these two basic lines is abundantly clear in the considerable distance between the efforts towards a fundamental reform of the liturgy in the spirit of the early church, ecumenical openness and an ecclesiology of the people of God on the one hand and a Marian piety, tending towards Mariolatry, of Irish origin and with a very disciplined and clerical organization on the other, i.e. the Legion of Mary and then the charismatic movement. In both cases we have a way of thinking which *de facto* ignores the renewal of the Second Vatican Council even if there are declarations of intent which go in another direction.'[2]

I fully agree with the conclusion of this man who knows the cardinal well: 'So the change of direction was radical. *De facto* it meant that Suenens finally renounced any involvement in the direction of the post-conciliar reform movement, say, in the inner structure of the church or the anti-collegial way in which Pope and Curia exercised authority.'[3] Thus the reform cardinal, who saw himself as a representative and champion of the Council, has become a 'charismatic cardinal'.

Of course this doesn't lead me to break off relations with Cardinal Suenens; we maintain our friendly relationship. In October 1973 we see each other again in Rome, and I shall be reporting that in due course. Later, on 2 February 1978, I have a long conversation with him in his palace the night after a lecture at the Dutch university of Tilburg on 'The New Question of God' by the distinguished Belgian reform theologian and sociologist of religion Jan Kerkhofs, who had gone to Brussels. The next morning, after a celebration of the eucharist, we continue the discussion until my flight after lunch. The conversations turn above all on the probably imminent papal election and the precarious situation of the church. I hope that Cardinal Suenens will perhaps take up his 'resting' plans for reform on the election of a reforming Pope.

Charismatic movements in the Catholic Church

Beyond doubt Suenens has succeeded in breaking up the monopoly of apostolate that Catholic Action, directed by the hierarchy, had in some countries, especially Italy, in favour of the Legion of Mary and other Catholic lay movements.

256

Catholic Action derives from Pius XI's 1922 encyclical *Ubi arcano* and is propagated in the face of growing secularization as 'the collaboration and participation of the laity in the hierarchical apostolate of the church'. It developed in different ways in different countries: by gender and age (men, women, young men, girls) in Italy or specialized according to social milieux (workers, rural population, freelance professionals) in Belgium, France and the Netherlands. But recognition and leadership by the hierarchy was always decisive. In Germany, where there are parish youth groups, Catholic committees, women's federations, popular associations and some other associations, the concept of Catholic Action was never popular. But in Italy Catholic Action, with the help of '*comitati civici*', was also very much involved in politics, especially in the electoral campaigns against the Communists.

The relatively independent Legion of Mary was fought against for decades by Catholic Action. At the World Congress of the Lay Apostolate in Rome in 1967 Catholic Action formed the overwhelming majority and occupied all the positions of leadership. Giovanni Battista Montini, now Paul VI, comes from this milieu. So Cardinal Suenens can chalk up as a success the fact that the Pope finally accepts the Legion of Mary and the charismatic movements which came into being in the USA and at Pentecost 1975 conditionally gives them his blessing.

As the author of Suenens' Council speech on the charisms (*My Struggle for Freedom*, VIII: The laity and their charisms), which was the basis for Article 12 of the Constitution on the Church, I can welcome this development. I have sympathies for many aspects of the charismatic renewal, but only if at the same time, in the spirit of the Council, it is commited to the reform of the church and society. For decades the Irishwoman Veronica O'Brien, a close friend of Cardinal Suenens, has been a central figure among Catholic charismatics; as a delegate of Frank Duff, the Irish founder of the Legion of Mary, she works in several European countries. She too visited me in Sursee, with the Frenchwoman Yvette Dubois, and we got on well. But of course my main interest remains the reform of the church, for which Cardinal Suenens was a great hope, and to this degree I am very disappointed by his most recent development.

After the election of Karol Wojtyla on 16 October 1978 all reform hopes for Suenens definitively have to rest. For with John Paul II a Pope appears on the stage for whom Catholic Action plays no role and who from the beginning sets his hope completely on the 'new' charismatic movements which are faithfully submissive to him, conservative in their basic attitude, with no interest in internal reform, but rather orientated on the 'evangelization', or better 'Catholicization', of a world that has become godless. Vatican II mightn't exist as far as they are concerned; they are content with the spiritual leader whom they cheer on, even if they no longer know his dogmas and by no means follow his moral teachings. As early as 1981 a great international congress of these *movimenti* is held in Rome to which Catholic Action isn't even invited. In future the *movimenti*, native above all to the lands of the Counter-Reformation, in Italy, Spain, Ireland and Poland, will

257

flock *en masse* to the great papal demonstrations and bring with them many sightseers, seekers after meaning and sympathizers. At the Youth Day in Berne in June 2004 (John Paul II's last visit to Switzerland), with their banners they form easily recognizable cohorts who in an utterly un-Swiss way greet every statement by this pontiff with frenetic applause. They are also the elect at the World Youth Meeting in Cologne in August 2005, who welcome Wojtyla's successor Joseph Ratzinger at the airport with chants of 'Benedetto' and everywhere spread the impression that 'the youth' are again submissive to the Pope.

But with Karol Wojtyla, from the beginning the powerful Opus Dei is behind everything. Whereas the Legion of Mary turns to everyone, including the marginalized and neglected, such as streetwalkers, Opus Dei deliberately turns to the powerful in politics and the banks, the media and the universities. The efficient co-ordinator of papal power and media and financial power for the expensive papal events is the director of the Vatican press agency and Opus Dei man Joaquín Navarro-Valls.

None of this disturbs Cardinal Suenens in any way. In the surprising development sparked off by the new Pope, he becomes the '*cardinal charismatique par excellence*'. Almost 90 at the time, he appears as the most important protector of a new generation of 30-year-olds who have no knowledge of the Council and John XXIII. Even Suenens hardly cites the Council any more. Instead, he has the honour of presenting the publication of the official reports of the international charismatic congresses of 1981 and 1987 to the media. But I am anticipating developments. We are still in 1973 and I feel that my decision not to climb the hierarchical ladder was the right one.

Unfair conditions for a 'colloquium'

The Inquisition proceedings against *The Church* have now been going on for six years and those against *Infallible? An Enquiry* for three. The Vatican has combined the two proceedings. So many conversations and colloquiums, so many articles and composite volumes, so many letters to and fro.

My last letter to the Congregation for the Doctrine of the Faith is dated 24 January 1972. So far it hasn't been possible to agree with Rome on either the date or the topic for a discussion. That isn't my fault. Fair conditions for a colloquium are refused time and again: I am not allowed to inspect the records, there is no possibility of an appropriate defence, no name is given of the defender assigned to me by the Congregation, and there are no realistic deadlines for either side. My letter is still unanswered. I attach importance to my statement that contrary to all the rumours which are time and again spread by my opponents I was and am ready for any authentic conversation, but have rejected and still reject any inquisition. The issue is to be the truth and not 'absolute obedience'!

I used to be surprised that Joseph Ratzinger, at the time a Council theologian, wrote sharp statements into the speech which Cardinal Josef Frings gave at the Council against the practices of the Holy Office that contradicted all modern sense of the law, but later himself argued for such practices and as head of the Congregation for the Doctrine of the Faith often ordered them. However, the new publications of the records of Cardinal Frings by Norbert Trippen show that the decisive statements were not in Ratzinger's handwritten draft of the speech but were formulated personally by Cardinal Frings and delivered unscripted. As Frings remarked: 'I am well aware of how heavy, how difficult and thorny the task is of those who work in the Holy Office for many years to protect the revealed truth. However, it seems to me appropriate to require that in the dicastery too no one should be accused, judged or condemned (*damnetur*) for his correct or incorrect faith without first knowing the arguments put forward against him or the book written by him, before he has had the opportunity to correct himself or the book which seems to be his undoing.'[4]

In the correspondence with Rome, why do I concentrate so much on the formal questions? Because on the conditions laid down so far I can only be the loser in a discussion of theological doctrinal questions. This is not even a fair scholarly procedure. I am dealing with that investigative authority founded in the Counter-Reformation (*Suprema Congregatio Sancti Officii Inquisitionis*) which, while it has changed the name 'Inquisition' (most recently *Congregatio pro doctrina fidei*), has changed its methods little. Made famous and notorious by its burning of Giordano Bruno and condemnation of Galileo, together with the Congregation of the Index which it later took over, it has banned on pain of excommunication more than 4000 books of often highly-respected intellectual figures and tortured countless theologians even in the twentieth century, if no longer physically, at least psychologically. I have reported on the devastating diary entries of the French theologian Yves Congar, who ended up totally exhausted (*My Struggle for Freedom*, III: Purging theologians); the lives of some theologians were in fact obliterated, not least that of Pierre Teilhard de Chardin, who wasn't allowed to publish any theological writings even when he had been banished to the US.

To be brought before this court of the faith in present conditions, even after Vatican II, means having as much chance as Alexander Dubček, who in the 1968 'Prague spring' wanted to bring about a 'socialism with a human face', thus doubting the dogmas of the Communist system; he is now invited to a 'colloquium' in the Politburo in Moscow. His cause is lost from the start. And what will a theologian achieve in the church's highest court of faith when confronted with eminences and excellences clothed in scarlet and purple, all of whom believe that they possess the truth and don't intend to study seriously and discuss the theological problems set before them? They only want to persuade, pressurize, compel the accused to concede that he is in the wrong and that 'the church' – which is what they are – is in the right. For the Party song can be revised for this mentality: 'The church, the church, is always right!'

Nor should it be forgotten that during these years I have derived a good deal of strength from the fate and resistance of the Soviet writer Alexander Solzhenitsyn, though of course I can't compare myself with him. I have devoured his first novel, *A Day in the Life of Ivan Denisovich*, along with his first two highly auto-biographical novels on the Stalinist system, *Cancer Ward* and *The First Circle of Hell* (1968). Under vigorous attack for years, excluded from the Soviet writers' association in 1969 but awarded the Nobel prize for literature in 1970, Solzhe-nitsyn isn't allowed to travel to Stockholm to receive the prize, but bravely fights on.

In the same issue of a Protestant Sunday paper which publishes an article about me with the title 'A Christian with the Utmost Ecumenical Openness', I am deeply moved to read Alexander Solzhenitsyn's pre-Easter 'Lent Letter' to Pimen, Patriarch of Moscow, in which he utters a shattering lament about the desperate state of the Russian church dominated by the Communist regime. In it he also commemorates the 'two completely honest priests Yakunin and Eshliman', who seven years previously had written a famous letter to Pimen's predecessor about 'the voluntary enslavement of the Russian church' and as a result were removed from office.[5]

In 1974 Solzhenitsyn is finally expelled and deprived of citizenship; he is welcomed by Heinrich Böll and then finds a second home initially in Zurich. I have followed his fight for the truth in the Soviet system with passionate interest and unqualified admiration. My mother gives the first volume of the docu-mentary report *The Gulag Archipelago* which appears in 1974 to her 'dear son on his birthday, 1974'. Solzhenitsyn's later problematical support of traditional values, first in the USA and then under a sometimes reactionary and nationalistic aegis in Russia, hasn't diminished my admiration for this writer, who always wanted to support 'the laws of humanity in an inhuman system', but it has warned me about the follies of a conformist old age.

In later years the literary scholar, historian and writer Lev Kopelev, a fellow-prisoner with Solzhenitsyn, who has given him a memorial in the *First Circle of Hell*, makes a similarly strong impression on me. Freed from the gulag in the course of the 1954 de-Stalinization, even after the end of the thaw he supports dissidents, the last one being Andrei Sakharov, and steadfastly refuses to obey a summons to KGB headquarters. He isn't arrested, but is ultimately deprived of his citizenship. In view of his fate and our personal acquaintance and like-mindedness it is a special delight for me in 2006 to receive the Lev Kopelev Prize for Peace and Human Rights in Cologne, Kopelev's new home until his death in 1997.

In 1972 it is certain that for the sake of my cause, and also that of many others whom Rome is overwhelming with unfair procedures and who cannot defend themselves well, I must maintain my resistance in the Roman system: I will not enter the headquarters of the Inquisition without legal guarantees of a fair con-versation. But I am still interested in theological dialogue and now take a step towards reconciliation which surprises many people.

'Operative agreement' with Karl Rahner

I am concerned to draw a line of reconciliation under the debate on infallibility with my most important theological opponent, Karl Rahner. Now that I have published my stocktaking in 'Fallible?', it seems to me time to write a lengthy open letter to him (*Publik-Forum*, 1 June 1973). I note 'an abiding small difference' between him and me in our understanding of infallibility:

> A decision on this question could not at present be forced out of either you or me (even by the Roman Congregation for the Doctrine of the Faith), though we wrote yet more articles and made yet more composite volumes. So I would like to ask you: isn't it time to drop this question between us and simply leave the verdict on the answer to posterity? I am not very concerned to be right ... At all events, if possible I would like to make peace with you in this matter. That doesn't mean that you should accept my view, but that you should allow that my view is Catholic. Hence a wish that is very close to my heart: that you stop calling me a 'liberal Protestant' – to the delight of our common opponents – and explicitly accept me as the Catholic theologian which I want to be, despite all my evangelical concentration.

Rahner responds in the same issue:

> You have written me a conciliatory letter, the tone of which did me good ... It makes no sense to want to enumerate each other's real or (seen from the other side) supposed sins of polemic. Nor am I concerned to talk about a 'liberal Protestant'. That quite apart from the fact that I have not called you a 'liberal Protestant', but only said that in this one question I cannot carry on the dispute otherwise than with a liberal Protestant, for whom a council and scripture are not absolutely binding.

There follows quite a complicated description of the state of scholarly discussion in which it becomes clear that Rahner sees the 'small' differences as being rather 'greater' than I do. But then he writes: 'Dear Herr Küng, let me return once again to the matter which in our controversy I once called an "operative union". ...' And here I must now foist on the reader a bit of Rahnerian verbal and theological dialectic:

> I say that if you make sure that an anti-Roman irritability does not run riot among your friends, if you concede to Roman statements a – relatively – binding character which is all that they claim for themselves, since no definitions are to be expected, if you make even clearer that there are (as you yourself say) true binding statements of faith which also maintain

themselves through time and (as you write) can require an unconditional life-or-death confession in a particular situation (however, who in the church combines such statements with such a demand?), if we all (you and I and all those who want to be Catholic theologians) serve the cause of Jesus in our time without qualification, with all the strength of our hearts and minds, and do not do otherwise (varied though this task may be), then I too would be ready for us to drop our conflict for a few years, and wait.

Here in a rather complicated way Rahner has said that our discussion isn't about a decision that divides faith or the church, but about a further theological task that needs time and 'cannot and need not be decided' by a statement from Rome 'in the immediate future'. Finally, Rahner expresses the hope that his interpretation of the First Vatican Council can be made to agree with my 'opinion, though this can be expressed in a better, more Catholic, way'. The letter ends: 'I very much look forward to a friendly meeting. Yours, Karl Rahner SJ.'

The commentary by the editor, Manfred Plate, in the always constructive Catholic journal *Christ in der Gegenwart* dated 24 June 1973, runs:

We may regard this fine document by two leading Catholic theologians of our century as a very important sign of the times. It should be a model for the way in which difficult questions of theology and ecclesiology are discussed or, better, for the spirit in which such discussions take place. Only in this way can the church become credible. The two letters also differ from some superficial talk which regards itself as progressive, or from the barren complaints of those who only look back at the past. The questions remain, the burden of history remains, but the forward perspective, into the future, brings liberation. The solution to our problems lies in the end-time.

The friendly meeting does take place, in Tübingen. At the instigation of my colleague and friend Norbert Greinacher, I invite Karl Rahner to lunch in my home on a visit that he makes to Tübingen. The meal with the three of us is very friendly. After the dessert the conversation happens to touch on Joseph Ratzinger. 'Ratzinger is so intelligent,' Rahner observes ironically, 'that he can defend even the most stupid cause with intelligent arguments.' I chuckle and look at him, whereupon he quickly adds, 'And of course so can I.' He is right in both respects. I quietly think to myself that I would never want to have to defend a 'stupid cause' in theology.

However, in Rome people remain unimpressed by my conciliatory dialogue with Rahner. The Doctrinal Congregation thinks nothing of an objective theological dialogue and of Christian reconciliation. There they are pursuing quite a different plan.

A concerted action: Vatican and episcopate

In a secret meeting on 26 April 1972 the Doctrinal Congregation had already decided to work out an official 'Declaration on the Catholic Doctrine of the Church', which is to be defended against 'some errors of today'. I cannot expect that it will take note of the international scholarly discussion of my books and our memorandum on the reciprocal recognition of church ministries. Rather, instead of the biblical evidence, the doctrinal document will contain only statements by the more recent Popes, the Council of Trent and Vaticans I and II. In the end the document will have 60 footnotes, none of which refers to a single scholarly theological publication. So this is a magisterium which hardly refers to the foundation document of the church, Holy Scripture, as the foundation for its truths but above all to its own documents, i.e. to itself.

Now a concerted action by the Roman organs, the German bishops and the church media is prepared in top secret and at top level against one of its theologians. On 5 July 1973 it is finally ready. The plan is to take me by surprise, so that I have no time for prompt, even simultaneous reaction. The action takes the following course. A letter from the apostolic nuncio dated 4 July[6] tells me that the Declaration will be published, 'tomorrow, 5 July, at 11 a.m. Central European Time'. In fact it is only brought to me a day later, on 5 July, by a courier from the Bonn nunciature to my Tübingen home. Half an hour after that the same letter, with which the Declaration is enclosed in Latin and German, is delivered by express post as a 'duplicate'.

An hour later, also on 5 July, in Rome there is a special Vatican press conference which has hastily been called. The letter along with the Declaration is presented to the public by spokesmen for the Doctrinal Congregation and commented on – flanked by two articles in *L'Osservatore Romano* and a further press release. In Germany the Roman action is supported by two declarations of the Conference of Bishops and by personal interventions from several bishops, likewise going back to Roman initiatives.

The Declaration by the Doctrinal Congregation bears the title *Mysterium Ecclesiae* (The Mystery of the Church), thus the opening words of the original Latin text.[7] It is published without naming any names, but the press conference in the Vatican makes it clear that it is directed against Professor Küng in Tübingen, as the simultaneous letter from the Congregation indicates.[8] Sections 1 and 6 relate to my book *The Church*, and sections 2 to 5 to *Infallible? An Enquiry*. The report of the Roman intervention goes round the world; as is customary in authoritarian regimes, the church media reproduce only the 'official' view of things. How shall I defend myself?

At the same time I receive the covering letter of the Doctrinal Congregation dated 4 July 1973. I hear later that originally I was simply to have been confronted with an ultimatum through the public Roman action: either sign this declaration immediately or have church sanctions imposed. Through last–minute negotiations with the Secretary of the Congregation for the Doctrine of the Faith, Archbishop Jérôme Hamer, who personally brings the Declaration by plane to Frankfurt, the German cardinals Döpfner and Volk and Bishop Leiprecht of Rottenburg succeed in establishing the possibility of a colloquium with the Congregation as an alternative. But the accompanying Declaration by the German Conference of Bishops, likewise dated 5 July 1973,[9] is completely in solidarity with *Mysterium Ecclesiae* from the start.

Of course the public waits to see how I react. The same day I defend myself in a press statement.[10] I protest at the procedure of the Doctrinal Congregation. This evidently did not see itself in a position in all the long years to carry out and conclude the proceedings against my two books in accordance with the procedural order decreed by Pope Paul for the Congregation for the Doctrine of the Faith of 1971. Instead, contrary to law and fairness it now intervened in the pending proceedings with a general public declaration on the questions arising from the two books.

Should I spell out the situation quite clearly? I think yes: 'This procedure and the declaration with simple assertions which have no substantive foundations make it clear that the Congregation for the Doctrine of the Faith is incapable of making a contribution that takes us further in the questions of church, ministry and infallibility which today are being discussed throughout the world in Catholic theology and in ecumenical circles. As a result, this same Roman authority again appears as both prosecutor and judge and through the whole proceedings – now also in full public view – shows that it is trapped in what it has started.'

It's almost unbearable: countless telephone calls, letters, conversations, press reports, radio and television broadcasts follow. All rather a lot for just one man who faces a gigantic apparatus with considerable legal, political, financial and media power. That is why I put a relevant quotation from Walter Jens at the head of the previous chapter. This is beyond doubt a trial of strength, which I can lose. But what is decisive for me is the test of truth, and who gives way.

An 'enquiry' about the possibility of error unanswered

It isn't difficult to demonstrate this oneself on the basis of the Roman document. I immediately set to work to compose a newspaper article on the Declaration on the basis of the abundant material available. It goes to the press next day under the title 'Incapable of Learning? *Roma locuta, causa aperta*'.[11] I begin by pointing out that in the period after the Council Rome has published a whole series of important documents, none of which has resolved pending questions but which have made them even more open and acute. Rome has again missed the opportunity to offer a guide to the undeniable questions that have arisen, in the style of the encyclicals of John XXIII. Instead of this, it has lapsed into the former methods of the Inquisition authority, which has already acted against so many famous Catholic theologians who are still alive.

However, I also acknowledge important Roman concessions that are made: for the first time in a Roman document, in the Declaration, under pressure from my 'Enquiry', the 'historical conditioning' of formulations of faith regarded as timeless is not just touched on or rejected, but positively made a topic of discussion. The incompleteness of dogmatic statements and the possibility of improving them is emphasized. The meaning of statements of faith is at least partly dependent on the terminology of a particular time and situation and in some circumstances has to be reconstructed by theologians. Statements of the magisterium also often bear the traces of a time-conditioned way of thinking. Not all dogmatic formulas are equally or eternally appropriate for the communication of the truth of revelation. Sometimes new declarations and statements have to be added, and sometimes old formulas have to be replaced with new ones. Thus despite everything my 'Enquiry' has had some success: I remark that 'It is worth emphasizing that all this can be read in a Declaration by the Congregation for the Doctrine of the Faith.'

But – and this is my decisive question about truth and falsehood – doesn't 'historical conditioning' also include the possibility of error? 'Shouldn't one have been able to expect, on the basis of this relatively intensified awareness of the problem, that the "Enquiry" into infallibility would be honestly and seriously addressed? Could these doctrinal formulations, historically conditioned in so many ways, dependent on the situation, incomplete, capable of being improved and expanded, also perhaps be *false*? Doesn't granting "historical conditioning" also entail the "possibility of error", which indeed the history of theology and dogmas appears to substantiate? Or why should the Holy Spirit, whom those in office are so fond of seeing busily at work, necessarily prevent errors in individual cases?' I ask for evidence.

At this central point I cannot hide my deep disappointment and say clearly: 'The "Enquiry" into an infallibility of specific statements or authorities guaranteed by the Holy Spirit was not responded to, but rather evaded. Where one expects reasons one hears affirmations, where one expects explanations one hears admonitions, and finally it is conceded that the dogma of infallibility should not be "demonstrated by an investigation of the foundations of our faith", but that the Roman doctrine should "be called to mind".' Thus, I note soberly, there is only 'recollection' where one expects a reason. 'Whether this Roman doctrine can still be explained for today was the very question that was asked.'

Here I must now remind the '*beati possidentes*', the 'happy possessors' of the truth, at least briefly of the errors of the past: 'How much in dogmatics, exegesis, morals, church discipline and politics has been "called to mind" for believers by the same Roman faith authority since the time of the Reformers, and nevertheless has ultimately had to be given up *de facto* by Rome! Nevertheless,' and again I point to the positive solution of the fundamental question, 'despite all errors the church has not simply fallen away from the truth of the gospel; time and again it has been maintained and renewed in it. What reasons can be given against such an interpretation? The arguments put forward in *Infallible?* and later reinforced in many ways have in any case not been refuted. Thus the "Enquiry" remains: *causa aperta.*'

But in conclusion I refer to something 'pleasant': 'In the document not only were no names mentioned, but likewise no formulas of excommunication and condemnation were used. This too seems to have been learned in Rome from the development so far: questions like those that are pending cannot be answered by condemnations; a cause such as this cannot be settled with disciplinary measures: the creation of martyrs does not pay.'

So I end on a positive note, with a confession of critical solidarity with Rome, fully in keeping with my line so far: 'Catholic theologians – and the author has always unhesitatingly described himself as a Catholic theologian – will certainly pay attention to Rome. And they will even do so gladly whenever constructive, helpful and reasoned answers are given to the needs and hopes of this time. In the course of the centuries Rome has shown that it is capable of learning. So the hope is not unfounded that the Roman faith authority will learn, and that out of an organ of the inquisition of faith one day an organ of the proclamation of faith will nevertheless come, in line with the task of the Congregation as Paul VI described it in the decree on the reform and change of name of the Holy Office of 7 December 1965. The protection of the faith is better served today not through the exclusive persecution of errors but through the positive promotion of Christian doctrine.'

A question of style instead of a question of truth or law?

Cardinal Julius Döpfner had only my press statement of 7 July in his hands. But he felt pressed (or was he pressed?) to respond immediately with an accusatory letter and a public press release.[12] It's remarkable: the whole machinery of the Roman system is let loose on a single theologian in order to discredit his Catholic faith before the world public. And for that he must be duly grateful.

But if this theologian ventures to defend himself, his accusers don't openly face the question of truth, 'Is what he says true?', or even the legal question, 'Are the proceedings against him lawful?' Rather, it is made a question of style. The President of the Conference of Bishops complains in his letter about my 'tone and style', but doesn't say a word about questions of truth or law. This isn't a new experience for me. Time and again church officials complain about the 'tone and style' of their critics instead of going into the substantive question, whereas their critics are meant to accept as quasi God-given their official tone, which is often hierarchical and heartless, and their arrogant style of exercising office.

To tell the truth, even on re-reading my press statement several times, with the best will in the world I can't discover a single statement in it that isn't pertinent and argumentative, and at the same time plain and clear. The hierarchs aren't accustomed to this from their theologians. Evidently they don't know 'boldness' – a New Testament virtue. Thus Döpfner's press statement says that I have 'made statements' about the Congregation for the Doctrine of the Faith some of which have a 'defamatory character'. Of course none is specifed. I am not the only one who asks myself what could have been 'defaming', 'denigrating', in the press statement quoted above. At any rate 'the most important Catholic theologians of this century – from Karl Adam to Chenu, Congar, de Lubac, Teilhard de Chardin, Karrer, Rahner, Schoonenberg and Schillebeeckx – all had serious difficulties with this authority', which appears as 'prosecutor and judge' at the same time, and which 'still under Pius XII' acted with 'regular purges, with dismissals, bans, and prohibitions on teaching and publication'. Is it to be 'defamatory' if in the face of such actions which defame one all over the world one defends oneself against the same Inquisition authority? That is truly more than a question of style, it is a question of law and above all a substantive question.

Of course I know very well what 'tone and style' people in Rome expect of theologians who are criticized by the Curia: 'humility' and 'obedience'. My fellow-student from the German College, Julius Döpfner, has been able as often as I to read in *L'Osservatore Romano* the triumphant news about this or that author who, defamed and harassed for long enough, has finally 'humbly submitted': '*humiliter se subiecit*'. A triumph for the magisterium – even if history is later to prove right the one who has been humbled. Today such discriminatory and defamatory formulas of submission aren't used – usually in fact all the power of the state is no longer available to implement the verdict. But in effect the public capitulation of the 'deviant' is still required. That is still the issue – with milder forms and gentler methods. An exercise of power instead of a discovery of the truth! At any rate, the apologists for this system say, the 'style' of the Inquisition authorities has changed. What does this 'new style' mean for me? If I am now being offered a 'colloquium' in Rome, this is only in order to achieve in the end what had originally been worked for directly: my subscription and capitulation, the '*humiliter se subiecit*'.

This was the precise intention of the declaration *Mysterium Ecclesiae*. Happily the demand for submission was stopped by the German bishops at the last moment, but (less happily) in fact it had been only postponed. Am I to accept such a 'mystery' of the church, which has little to do with the Jesus Christ of the Bible? After a good Roman training in the German College I have learned that one must also be able to resist (cf. *My Struggle for Freedom*, III: A silent duel), not only for one's own sake but also and not least for the truth and the good of the many people who are affected. However, that won't be easy.

For me a question of conscience

In the two weeks after the Roman Declaration of 5 July 1973 I have hardly time to catch breath. In addition to all the telephone calls, letters and conversations there are countless interviews. The international press has registered the event as a 'Warning from Rome' (*Time Magazine*). An excellent article by Kenneth Woodward appears in *Newsweek*. Even the French Catholic daily *La Croix* comments with welcome understanding. I am grateful to my friend Andrew Greeley for a column syndicated all over the US which is clearer than Yves Congar's article in *Le Monde* or Giuseppe Alberigo's article in *Il giorno*. 'I have two hard weeks behind me. It was clearly a planned action on various levels at the same time. I needed all the hours of the day and also most of the hours of the night to defend myself,' I write to Greeley on 21 July 1973, 'but I think that the first phase is now over and I have survived in good shape. The second phase will probably be another exchange of letters. It isn't certain whether we shall have a third public phase.'

In fact every lever is now being pulled by the German bishops to get me to the 'colloquium' called for by the Doctrinal Congregation. From their perspective this is understandable. They have imposed the colloquium so to speak as a reprieve from my immediate 'execution' by the Congregation. But from my perspective it must be equally understandable that I will in no way submit to an inquisitional procedure disguised as a 'colloquium' in which in the end there is no other possibility for me of safeguarding my rights (something that is granted even criminals in civilized states) than ultimately to subscribe to the Roman dictate if I don't want to fall victim to Roman sanctions. After all, Rome isn't Moscow nor Tübingen Prague.

Cardinal Hermann Volk, in my year as assistant in Münster my boss and now Bishop of Mainz, attempts to convince me in a very personal letter dated 10 July 1973 to 'talk with Rome'.[13] That sounds harmless, but it isn't. He too says not a word about the 'just and fair conditions for such a conversation' that I have kept demanding since 1969 and that I also repeat to him.[14] What bishops who constantly have one eye on Rome find so difficult to understand is that for me the 'Infallible Enquiry' is a matter of conscience. So I attempt to make it unmistakably clear to the cardinal 'that I intend with all legitimate means to defend myself in this case, which truly is not only mine': 'I may neither act against my conscience, which in all fallibility I attempt to orientate on the gospel, nor disappoint the numberless men and women throughout the world who place their hopes for the future on this path and expect that I personally – as in recent days has been said in countless letters and conversations – will remain in the church with an unpretentious steadfastness.' At the same time I think that I must make an important point to the cardinal, who is responsible for questions of faith in the conference of bishops (and since 1968 has even been a member of the Roman Congregation for the Doctrine of the Faith), in view of the threatening scenarios with which I am confronted as a consequence of the Roman intervention:

'Having now for about ten years dealt with the Roman Inquisition authorities, I will perhaps be believed when I say that, if I must, *Deo bene volente* I will likewise endure yet another ten. In any case – and this should be said very clearly – any disciplinary measure would not be the end, but rather the beginning of the real debate, the end of which would not be foreseeable. I would not want to elaborate for you or for me the effects on pastoral work within the church, in the world of politics, the university and the state, and finally also in the ecumenical sphere.'[15]

At the end of my long reply I remind Cardinal Volk of our 'deep agreement over fundamentals and aims': 'I promise you ... that without concern for protocol or personal prestige I will gladly contribute in a Christian spirit to any honourable, honest and just solution. At the same time I request you and your fellow bishops to ensure that an honourable, honest and just solution is also striven for in Rome. I expect in principle no more and no less than to be able to research and teach in peace, in keeping with my calling as a teacher of theology in the Catholic Church. I will always stand by the church in full loyalty and clear fidelity.'[16]

My back is covered by Tübingen colleagues

With this letter I also enclose a reply to Cardinal Döpfner[17] and Bishop Leiprecht of Rottenburg.[18] I am greatly encouraged in this difficult controversy by the sustained support from my colleagues in the faculty of Catholic theology in the University of Tübingen, who on 27 July 1973 send a lengthy statement to Cardinal Döpfner and to the German archbishops.[19]

Professors Alfons Auer, Gisbert Greshake, Herbert Haag, Walter Kasper, Wilhelm Korff, Johannes Neumann, Rudolph Reinhardt, Max Seckler and Hermann Josef Vogt – who deserve to be gratefully singled out by me – think that 'proceedings of the kind that the Congregation for the Doctrine of the Faith is carrying out on this occasion are inappropriate'.[20] Professor Norbert Greinacher couldn't be contacted. Unfortunately the proceedings are 'the resumption of a practice which has damaged the reputation of theology as a science and the church as a whole': 'The undersigned hold that it is necessary that whenever the Congregation for the Doctrine of the Faith or the bishops believe it necessary to object to a specific opinion that is being taught, this must happen in proceedings that are not only orderly and correct but also appropriate to the matter in hand and built on a clear theological foundation ... Today in the constitutional and civil practice of civilized states governed by law it is taken for granted that anyone charged has the right of access to their file and an appropriate defence – and this not only in criminal proceedings.'[21]

The Tübingen professors – supported by some Munich colleagues under the former Tübingen church historian Peter Stockmeier, who intervene with Döpfner – finally put themselves behind the Declaration of the more than 1300 theologians dated 17 December 1968 for the freedom of theology, which they enclose, and ask the bishops to reflect on the negative pastoral consequences which would follow a procedure which contradicted present-day legal principles and the essence of theology. And at the same time they warn against a view which is rightly or wrongly attributed to their former colleague Joseph Ratzinger, though without mentioning his name: 'The German bishops will also have to test whether the counsel of those who, under the watchword "little flock", demand severe restrictions accords with the church's universal task of proclamation and its tradition.'

Doctoral students and bishops also involved: Bishop Kempf

Of course I am also denounced on many sides, especially by papers 'loyal to the Pope', in Switzerland especially by *Neues Volk*. My very doubt about the dogma of infallibility is said to be 'heresy' and the 'radical reforms' that I propose are 'nothing short of a radical destruction of the Catholic Church'. Thus my old 'arch-enemy' from Lucerne, a notorious sympathizer with Rome and an informer, Professor Alois Schenker (28 November 1973). My objection about this to the Bishop of St Gallen leads to the editors of this paper being warned in a conversation to show moderation and fairness. A Swiss religious whose merits lie elsewhere even attempts on various occasions to turn his sister, my mother, against me, so that I finally break off all contact with this monastic uncle. My mother understands.

A few weeks before the statement by my faculty colleagues, Heinrich Böll, who had been awarded the Nobel Prize for literature the previous year, had cast a 'look back in bitterness' on theology which unfortunately was in many respects only too justified. I thank him for his words, even if they are uncomfortable: ' . . . you shouldn't wholly give up your hope for theology and the theologians yet. Our business, too, isn't easy today: between superstition and rationalism, between false progressisms and a reactionary hierarchy, where we should be pulling up and planting in the same field at the same time. We do it as badly or as well as any of us can manage.'

In these words to Heinrich Böll, who is fighting for the 'Catholic part of humankind which is suffering and groaning' under precepts and infallibilities, I think that I can also speak for my colleagues in the faculty. The issue of *Der Spiegel* of 16 July 1973, which reports the Roman declaration *Mysterium Ecclesiae* against me and the disciplining of the church historian Professor Georg Denkler, who opposes celibacy, contains an interview with Heinrich Böll in which he laments the contradiction between the policy of *détente* in foreign affairs and the hardening of domestic policy and the persecution of writers in the Soviet Union: 'It is time to be energetic publicly.'

The 'Catholic part of humankind which is suffering and groaning' also includes the next generation of Catholic theologians. Unfortunately here it is becoming evident that in future only conformist theologians are wanted for doctorates and habilitations and consequently also for professorial chairs. Sooner or later theology will go into decline unless there is a correction of course. Granted, lay theologians cannot simply be controlled and manipulated by the bishops; at worst they can be blocked. But the diocesan clergy can have a direct influence on the academic course of the members of their dioceses.

When the Institute for Ecumenical Research was founded, I had accepted a member of the Rottenburg diocese as a doctoral student and wanted to make him an assistant. He accepted my offer with delight and then went to the chancery in Rottenburg – and was never seen again. Later he did his doctorate with Professor Kasper – and married; at least I couldn't be blamed for this 'priest's marriage'. Another habilitation student who was to complete his doctorate with me in 1976 and held an assistant's post in the Institute with a view to habilitation unexpectedly left to do his habilitation at another university. Not much later he then received a chair, having clearly dissociated himself from my christology in a newspaper article.

However, the most illuminating case is that of a doctor of theology from the diocese of Limburg with the very best qualifications, who wants to do his habilitation with me in 1974. After various conversations and exchanges of letters, also with the open and respected Bishop Dr Wilhelm Kempf, a former member of the German College, and his Vicar General, in the end this young scholar is allowed to do his habilitation despite 'the extremely oppressive personal distress of the diocese' (thus Bishop Kempf). However, the condition is that he does it not with Küng in Tübingen but with Professor Heinrich Fries in Munich! The habilitation student reveals the bishop's fears to me in a letter of 18 May 1974: 'It would be more favourable for the present situation of bishop and diocese to avoid anything that could arouse animosities. (To spell it out in my own words: "Bishop Kempf is concentrating his 'scholars' in Tübingen and is even sending one to Küng").'

When I tell the habilitation student that I fail to understand why he has given way he writes back: 'If you had experienced how the screws were put on me in the last stage of the conversations with Limburg, perhaps you would understand better why I didn't want to take any more risks. I feel that my resolution is modest and after months, indeed years, of "struggle" my will to win through 100 per cent is waning' (31 May 1974).

Yes, of course I understand. For Bishop Kempf of Limburg was himself denounced the previous year and the screws have been put on him – by Rome. Because he allegedly acted so generously towards his diocesan councils and in view of the collapse of the previous forms of pastoral care sought new solutions to the question of celibacy, on 26 August 1973 the Bonn nuncio Corrado Bafile – when we ate together during the first session of the Council still a relatively open

271

Vatican diplomat but now an apparatchik with leanings towards the Curia – writes a report to the Cardinal Secretary of State Jean Villot, in which he recommends that Bishop Kempf should be replaced as head of the diocese (with a suffragan). As the result of an indiscretion this letter is made public. The consequence is a storm of protest in the media far beyond the diocese of Limburg, which also includes Frankfurt. The 'de-nuncio' – after a conversation with Döpfner – withdraws his proposal as 'outdated'. Many people in the Vatican also think Bafile's proposal clumsy and feel that as a diplomat he is a '*uomo morto*', who will soon be replaced. In this case, for once the people have won a victory. Indeed, in this system even the bishops don't have an easy time. They too, indeed they in particular, must constantly reckon with denunciations – and are afraid.

A system of denunciation and supervision

In the Roman system, in every country the 'apostolic nuncio', in his person (since the beginning of modern times) a representative of the Pope to the state, but increasingly also the overseer of bishops, the recipient of denunciations and informers for the Curia, occupies a central place (above all in the nomination of bishops). The Vatican expert Hanspeter Oschwald rightly raises the question, 'But who first informs the nuncio, who informs the Curia? A prelate compared the system of information in the Catholic Church with that of the Kremlin. The selection or registration is restricted. This system could embrace everything, but doesn't, because not everything fits into the plan. Who gathers material in Germany about Kempf or about Küng, who knows what the Curia would like to see, and whose line and interests coincide with these supposed wishes of the Curia?'[22]

In this connection some victims of the church's Inquisition should be reported. Only a few attract considerable mention in the media: in the German-speaking world the Viennese theologian Adolf Holl, author of the book 'Jesus in Bad Company', or the Innsbruck dogmatic theologian Franz Schupp SJ, who attempts to introduce results from more recent linguistic philosophy into theology (he loses his chair and leaves the Jesuit Order), or Sigmund Kripp SJ, head of the Innsbruck Youth Centre Kennedy House (he emigrates to Germany and is expelled from the Jesuit Order).

But if one looks beyond the German-speaking world one can read the dramatic stories which the Australian theologian and historian Paul Collins has published under the title *From Inquisition to Freedom* (2001). As well as his own story and mine he deals with that of the American moral theologian Charles Curran whom we have already met (Chapter II above: Repression in the US and England), the cases of the theologian Tissa Balasuriya from Sri Lanka, who is committed socially and in interfaith dialogue, the British radio and television personality Lavinia Byrne (committed to the ordination of women), and Jeannine Gramick and

Robert Nugent from the US, who for decades have been concerned with homosexuals and AIDS victims.

Disciplinary proceedings against two works by my Tübingen colleague and Swiss fellow-countryman Professor Herbert Haag, 'The Biblical Doctrine of Creation and the Church's Doctrine of Original Sin' (1966) and 'Farewell to the Devil' (1969), have also been going on for a long time. He too has been presented by the Congregation for the Doctrine of the Faith with individual statements, torn out of context and translated into Latin, for his comments. Haag gives an answer to the objections to the first book but requires these proceedings to be concluded before he comments on the second book. However, his proposal is rejected by Cardinal Šeper in July 1973, who again requires comments on both books. Haag, inspired by a similar ethic of freedom, to whom any fearful thought in terms of authority is abhorrent, declares once and for all that for him the case is closed and that he attaches no value to further correspondence.

When Haag constantly refuses again to respond to Roman accusations that he has answered long ago, on 12 August 1977 Bishop Georg Moser visits him in his home and uses all his skills of persuasion to get him to send an answer to Rome. In vain. Herbert Haag, renowned in the faculty for his sovereign smile, still refuses. 'What shall I do then?,' the bishop finally asks, perplexed. Haag laughs, 'Lord Bishop, do what you want.' The bishop is in despair, 'But I must do something.' Haag once again, 'You can do whatever you want.' The bishop has no alternative but to say goodbye. And wonder of wonders, Haag is not troubled further. The excitement over the declaration *Mysterium Ecclesiae* had been far too great.

But I can't sort out my problems so easily. Rome would rather say 'goodbye' to the 'devil' and 'original sin' than to its own infallibility, the dogma of dogmas.

Fundamental objections to the proceedings

I also worked indefatigably on my 'Introduction to Christianity' in my summer holidays in 1973 in the lake house by the Sempachersee. Work on it had fallen behind not least because of the controversies with Rome and the bishops. I allow myself just a brief trip into Chur in the Grisons to dive with a classmate up in the hills in the cold beforested Lake Cresta – by comparison with the colourful life of the fish and corals above a South Sea reef, here there are almost uncanny dark green depths where only individual dark fishes can be sighted. Of course I have to put on a diving suit, which lets water in but as a warmer intermediate layer protects the body from the cold; a close-fitting suit would crush the skin in the depths. This is an experience which I don't want to repeat. I could now also do with protective clothing against the cold in my theological controversies. But it isn't so easy to make a warmer intermediate layer for oneself.

At the same time in Rome, in the Vatican Congregation for the Doctrine of the Faith, people seem to have been working even in 'Ferragosto', the traditional August holidays around the feast of the Assumption of Mary (15 August). I receive a formal admonition dated 16 August 1973 from the head of the Doctrinal Congregation, Cardinal Franjo Šeper, an ultimatum which invites me by 20 September at the latest to reply to the letter from the Congregation dated 4 July of the same year, which had been sent to me with the declaration *Mysterium Ecclesiae*.

In fact I don't hurry to respond, for what can I gain from this endless correspondence with the Inquisition authorities? But I had already prepared a meticulous answer in Tübingen, the first part of which deals with the legal and the second part the theological questions. Everything was discussed in our team and with friends. In the lake house I have thought about it a lot and added a third part. This answer, which is dated 22 September 1973,[23] I send to the Congregation in Rome precisely a month after the arrival of the admonitory letter. By way of introduction I object to the 30-day ultimatum from the Congregation, which took eighteen months to confirm the receipt of my earlier answer about the book *Infallible?* and two years to respond to my communication about *The Church*.

I spend several pages in Part I making fundamental objections to the legitimacy of the proceedings of the Doctrinal Congregation which had already been presented in my letter of 30 May 1968. They don't say a word even in their most recent letter of 16 August about the question of just and fair conditions for a colloquium which has now already been under discussion for five years. Above all I stress the points relating to inspecting the records, the choice of a defender and the possibility of an appeal. Hitherto, I say, I would have taken part in any authentic and fair colloquium on infallibility – in Frankfurt, Paris, Berne or Tübingen. I would gladly also take part in a genuine con-loquium, an authentic talking together in which each side could learn from the other, even in Rome: 'But a dictate in which one side demands the capitulation of the other or a colloquium which is only the disguised beginning of disciplinary measures is of no help either to the common cause or to me personally. Rather, it blocks a genuine solution of the question still pending and is prejudicial to the credibility of the Catholic Church.'[24] Hence the precise question: 'Can the Congregation guarantee me a genuine colloquium, or am I to expect a dictate in which what is not being "immediately" subscribed to is supposed to be endorsed? In other words, is the purpose of the colloquium to ascertain the truth, or is it submission and the initiation of disciplinary measures? Is the Congregation prepared to implement the theologians' "Declaration on the Freedom of Theology?".'[25]

In Part II of my response I have to state on the substantive theological questions that the Roman Declaration only tries to 'call to mind' the well-known statements of Vatican I and II without saying 'how they are to be answered and explained theologically'. Therefore I ask the Congregation once again 'to produce, at least in abbreviated form, an argument that would prove the possibility of infallible statements. In this argument the difficulties I have raised concerning some texts of the magisterium should be addressed, not ignored.' Is the silence in the most recent Declaration as opposed to former public silence about infallible statements to be taken to mean 'that there are no such "infallible statements"'?

Unfortunately the Congregation hasn't sent any experts to the Tübingen senior seminar on the infallibility debate at which numerous experts from other universities – including Professors Heinrich Fries, Karl Lehmann, Karl Rahner and Joseph Ratzinger – took part. As a further instance of my concern to make myself available for serious theological discussion and to answer all the arguments against my book I would send Cardinal Šeper my composite volume 'Fallible? A Stocktaking', with its dedication 'non in destructionem sed in aedificationem Ecclesiae'.

Part III of my letter, first worked out in the lake house, attempts to convince Cardinal Šeper in a 'personal word' that both sides have now said what had to be said. It is time to conclude 'this affair, which is unpleasant on both sides and holds out no great promise for the future' and 'let Catholic theologians debate these difficult questions freely on the basis of the declarations issued to date'. After the long letter there is a brief conclusion: 'In short, the unpretentious proposal which I ask the Congregation to consider with benevolence is this: Without further colloquiums or other consequences, stop the proceedings against me which have been going on for years and out of which nothing good can come for either side.'

Precisely 30 days later, on 22 October 1973, Cardinal Šeper confirms receipt of my lengthy reply of 22 September: 'Your letter raises numerous difficult questions which need to be examined with care and attention.'[26] But meanwhile I haven't been inactive.

The fate of someone 'ready for conversation': Professor Pfürtner

Likewise on 22 September 1973 I had written to Cardinal Döpfner and asked for his support to ensure that there was no injustice in my case as there was in the case of the moral theologian Professor Stephan Pfürtner, a Dominican, since 1966 at the University of Fribourg, Switzerland.[27] After fifteen years of work in the field of empirical sexual anthropology, sociology and ethics and pastoral work with young people, on 3 November 1971 he had given a lecture in Berne on topics of family and sexual morality with some unconventional theses (especially on sexual intercourse before marriage). On the basis of a denunciation by the local bishop secret 'extraordinary proceedings' of the Doctrinal Congregation were carried on, resulting in a call to recant publicly or be dismissed from his chair. Professor Pfürtner had no knowledge of these secret proceedings, and of course had no legal hearing with a right to see his file or have his own advocate. 'Extraordinary proceedings' in which no 'ordinary' norms apply are the old Inquisition back with a vengeance.

Without denying his views, Pfürtner engages in various conversations with religious superiors and bishops and finally accepts the offer of a 'colloquium' made to him bona fide by the Swiss Conference of Bishops. On 11 April 1972 he attends the 'colloquium' with the Prefect of the Congregation for the Doctrine of the Faith, Cardinal Franjo Šeper, in a remarkably quiet Palazzo del Sant'Uffizio, where he sees no one but the porter; the cardinal had forbidden all his colleagues to make any contact with him that morning.

A humane and pastoral bishop, Franjo Šeper, the Archbishop of Zagreb, had been appointed by Paul VI to replace the former doctrinal Grand Inquisitor Ottaviani. Although modest in appearance, he is already completely bound up in the system of the Inquisition: he doesn't listen to arguments, go into the question of human rights in the church or have any knowledge of most recent research in sexual anthropology and sociology. He simply repeats the theses of the textbooks on moral theology – no wonder that there is no consensus. What will happen? Pfürtner is simply to 'obey', says the cardinal, obey the 'church' and his superiors in his Order. Pfürtner leaves the eerie Palazzo of the Inquisition beaten, without anyone else having seen him. That is what happens to someone who engages in a 'colloquium' with the Doctrinal Congregation without any legal guarantees.

What are the consequences? They are serious. Under pressure, the General of the Order threatens to withdraw the Dominican's permission to teach if he doesn't resign. Attached to this is the condition that he mustn't publish anything or make any public verbal statement on questions of social ethics which hasn't been presented to the curia of the Order in Rome. Faced with this alternative, Pfürtner makes his own choice. He resigns from his chair and his priestly office and leaves the Dominican Order, but not the Catholic Church.

Ten years earlier, in the debate over Hochhuth's *The Representative* (1963), the whole Catholic milieu – press, organization, clergy and politicians – felt that they had to protect Pius XII. But after the post-conciliar Roman provocations (see Chapter II above) and especially Paul VI's 1968 encyclical *Humanae vitae*, the mood had changed and there had been a change in mentality – from an uncritical veneration of the Pope to critical loyalty or even repudiation. So there is a great stir among Swiss church people about the scandalous treatment of this distinguished scholar. But all actions in favour of him are useless. At the beginning of the semester, on 22 October 1973, Pfürtner doesn't appear for his lectures. The only official communication is that 'Lectures in German will be announced later.' There is great disappointment among the students. In this way Pfürtner's lecturing activity at the university is unobtrusively ended.

Pfürtner will soon discover that the Inquisition has a long arm: he will not get a theological chair approved by the Catholic Church anywhere in the world. It is to the credit of the Protestant faculty of the University of Marburg that it finally offers him a chair, with exemplary tolerance; he needn't give up his membership of the Catholic Church. One can understand Stephan Pfürtner's 'conclusion' from today's perspective: 'The hope that dawned at the Council that the Congregation for the Doctrine of the Faith would abandon its baneful history as the medieval Inquisition authority and with its new name would take on a new face was deceptive. This authority is evidently not really reformable; rather, it must be abolished.'[28]

Where it has a direct grip, as at the Pontifical Gregorian University, the proceedings are even more rapid and any 'colloquium' is dispensed with. Professor Fr Pedro Brugnoli SJ, almost the same age as I am, has a connection with a Catholic reform group '7 November', founded after Vatican II, and is the author of a very moderate, balanced book, 'The Courage for a Free Church' (1971). I hear from Rome that on the instructions of the Doctrinal Congregation he receives a terse, harsh letter from the Jesuit General Fr Pedro Arrupe, in which without further reasons he is told that his links with this reform group are unacceptable: 'I am sorry to have to tell you that you must leave the Gregorian and return to the province.' Without any statement from Brugnoli the order is carried out in the holiday month of August 1972. And am I willingly to submit to such a procedure – with or without a 'colloquium'? I hope it won't be thought ill of me if in all this I quietly ponder the remark of Wilhelm Busch, Germany's most popular humorist: 'Only the greatest calves choose their butchers.'

Against this background it becomes even clearer why I write to Cardinal Döpfner in my letter of 22 September 1973: 'The way in which the well-intentioned "colloquium" of the Swiss bishops was used to provide a "legal" basis for disciplinary measures has made me doubly cautious about occasions of this kind.' But time and again Rome and the German bishops accuse me of a 'lack of readiness for conversation'. Now there are certainly people who avoid direct confrontation as far as possible and show little readiness for conversation. I am not one of them. On the contrary, already at the Gregorian and in Paris I personally sought out my professors, and if I had a serious problem, asked for a conversation. And now as a professor in the University of Tübingen I like making contact with colleagues inside and outside our faculty. So why should I be afraid of conversations with those holding power in the church? Already accustomed to red and violet before my years of study in Rome, I have less fear of contact than others. I also cultivate contacts on all sides elsewhere. In short: conversations, yes, Inquisition, no.

The coming Chancellor: Helmut Kohl

I have already reported an early contact with the then Prime Minister of Rhineland-Pfalz, Dr Helmut Kohl. He had invited me to Mainz and promised me a telephone call before Christmas, but because of other engagements that didn't happen. I wrote to him on 10 January 1972 and praised him for having adopted his own standpoint over both the ratification of the treaties with the East and the Industrial Constitutional Act.

At the same time I mentioned that I could come for a day to Mainz from

Sursee if I took the plane from Basle at 3.40 p.m. and could fly back to Basle from there at 8.50 p.m. Helmut Kohl gladly accepted this suggestion, so we met in the state chancery in Mainz on 25 January. He had me picked up at Frankfurt airport and generously paid for my flight. We talked about the present rifts in church politics and also my oppressed personal situation. He offered to get a chair for me in Mainz if there were serious difficulties in Tübingen. We agreed on a further meeting.

At the beginning of 1973 I get a letter from Dr Kohl: 'I read your last book over Christmas and thought of you. It's a pity that we didn't meet again in 1972. Perhaps we can soon remedy this' (3 January 1973). I reply on 25 January 1973 and enclose my book *What Must Remain in the Church*, which has just been published. 'What I said in my last conversation with you, you will find without any reference to party politics in my little book under the heading "stimuli for society". It should really be possible for the Christian Democrats to show themselves more Christian than the Social Democrats and the Free Democrats, who so far have been much better at winning over committed Christians. An implicit C would sometimes be better than an explicit one.' Kohl thanks me, but says that a meeting I propose for 10 February is impossible because of his commitments abroad.

I am still in my lake house when a letter reaches me from Kohl dated 21 August, in which he thanks me for my information: 'I hope to see you soon in Mainz, cheerful and with courage unshaken.' On 11 September a telephone call comes from the Prime Minister inviting me for a conversation and an evening snack on 18 September at his home in Oggesheim. He has reserved a good suite for me in a hotel nearby and will pick me up from there in his car and take me back. Since June 1973 Dr Kohl has also been Federal President of the Christian Democrats; he is a rising star and doubtless extremely busy with his commitments in Mainz, Bonn and throughout the Republic. Even during our rustic snack with the best Pfalz wine he is called away from the table for a long telephone conversation.

We discuss every possible problem of church and politics and spend a particularly long time on celibacy, which sometimes also commends itself to politicians. Hannelore Kohl, a charming and intelligent woman – unlike her husband also at home in French and English – agrees with me vigorously when I comment that living alongside a very busy politician surely can't be easy: she doesn't like the constant public appearances and prefers to see to the upbringing of her children. I see no reason to worry about her. I couldn't have imagined that one day she would commit suicide in loneliness because of a serious illness, an allergy to light. The only thing that comforted me then was that church people, who are otherwise strictly against active help in euthanasia, didn't dare to condemn this woman, who enjoyed the sympathy of the nation, and that my fellow-student from the German College, Bishop Anton Schlembach, made Speyer Cathedral available for her funeral.

I have splendid conversations with Dr Kohl, two years younger than me, dynamic, lively and often laughing mischievously. He has a gift for these intense personal conversations and cultivates personal relations, which at that time didn't serve to maintain power in a 'Kohl system', as they did later. Was his invitation to me a political calculation? He has an understandable interest in getting as much authentic information as possible about the Catholic Church in Germany, in the world, and especially in Rome. And it is particularly important for him as a politician that with my concern for reform I speak for large parts of the Catholic and Protestant population; such a contact can be as important for him as one with a bishop.

Of course the curiosity is mutual. With a burning interest in domestic and foreign politics from my youth in Switzerland onwards, though as a theologian I am restrained in my political comments, I am anxious to learn as much as possible from the world of politics for my own assessment of the situation. How does such a skilled politician assess problems and persons, for example his opponent Willy Brandt, but also individual friends in the Party? When I object that he is too tolerant of Franz Josef Strauss, the devious President of the Christian Social Union, who is both ambitious and critical, but with whom he has a friendship, he says that he has to have a good deal of stamina. At any rate he feels best as Prime Minister of Rhineland-Pfalz; only the role of a Renaissance Pope, this seasoned Catholic comments with a smile, would have been even better. At that time he was already saying quite clearly that he was a candidate for Chancellor following Rainer Barzel: 'I'll be next.' This is a quite justified political effort to gain the democratic mandate of the people. He stands just three years later, but in 1980 loses out to Strauss, finally becoming Federal Chancellor in 1982.

Kohl also proves to be well informed in matters of church politics. He has a sober view of the state of the hierarchy without any illusions. He had also invited the bishops of Rhineland-Pfalz; he remarks with a laugh that Cardinal Volk of Mainz is something 'beyond good and evil'. He wants to hear from me above all about Paul VI and his intentions. He has no allusions about the Vatican; he is one of those Catholics who is less impressed by Roman pomp than some Social Democrats and liberals who with a show of reverence not evident on other occasions walk through the rooms of the Vatican alongside a *cameriere di spada* in Spanish court dress for a special or even a private audience. I had sent him the letter I had composed in reply to the Doctrinal Congregation and he had read it through sentence by sentence; he advised me to delete the reference to the parallel with the Soviet system so as not to cause unnecessary offence. I didn't want to take his advice to write personally to the Pope at the same time, as this could have resulted in new complications. At any rate I can reach him, Kohl tells me, if things really become urgent; otherwise he will talk about the matter with Cardinals Döpfner and Volk soon.

Our conversation lasts until towards midnight. When it ends he takes me into his well-stocked wine cellar and chooses more than a dozen excellent Pfalz wines as a present for me; these are stowed first in his car and then in mine. Friends for life? At all events this is privileged treatment, for which I am grateful. Not everyone would be admitted to Kohl's wine cellar; I hear that Rainer Barzel, for example, never had that satisfaction. The next morning at 7.30 a.m. I drive back to Sursee in three hours.

A further brief correspondence leads to a second meeting with Kohl in Oggersheim on the eve of Corpus Christi, 29 May 1975. As well as the current political situation and my problems with the hierarchy we talk above all about the Christian element in the Christian Democrat Union. I make it clear how the classic concepts of democracy, 'freedom, equality, justice and brotherhood (solidarity)', can also be interpreted, criticized and integrated in the light of their Christian roots. I express my hope that he may succeed in steering a clear and resolute Christian course in a very difficult situation. On 11 June Helmut Kohl thanks me for my letter of 6 June: 'I hope that we can continue this kind of conversation and that I may again ask for your support.'

Anyone who thinks that as a result of these conversations and this correspondence with the coming German Federal Chancellor I have become a supporter of his Christian Democrat party is wrong. Willy Brandt, the representative of the President of the Social Democrats, invites me to become a trustee of the Heinemann Civic Foundation, the board of which is primarily made up of prominent SPD members. What I write to him also applies to the Christian Democrats: 'Given my public commitments in so many directions, I must not only avoid over-commitment generally but also renounce active collaboration with a political party' (10 August 1976).

Where I can make a concrete contribution with my experiences I do so gladly. I will have no inhibitions later about taking part in a weekend conference of the SPD Basic Values Commission, nor about accepting an invitation to a lecture in the Hofburg in Vienna from the socialist Federal Chancellor of Austria, Dr Bruno Kreisky, which I will describe later. I have already spoken of my dinner with the serving Social Democrat German Federal Chancellor Helmut Schmidt; relations with him will outlast all others. On 8 May 2007 the 88-year-old will give the eighth Global Ethic Lecture at the University of Tübingen. For me he is a model of the clear-sightedness and steadfastness that I all too often miss in the church sphere.

Roman festivals – informative encounters

I know that even in the Roman Curia there are those who regard some of my concerns as justified. On Saturday 22 September 1973, the day on which I send off my long letter to the Congregation for the Doctrine of the Faith (in the house we refer to it as the 'Letter to the Romans'), Archbishop Simon Lourdusamy, who has moved from Bangalore to Rome as Secretary of the Congregation for Evangelization Propaganda Fide, visits me in the lake house; he is on his way to a mission congress in Munich. There is plenty to discuss. In the evening, as usual I celebrate the eucharist in the local parish church and then pack my bag. The next day I am going on a long-planned trip to Greece – and on for a less enjoyable visit to Rome.

From Zurich on 23 September I fly to Athens with a small group of friends from my class to celebrate the 25th anniversary of our leaving school; there we first relax in the sea in Lagonissi, between Athens and Cape Sunion, and swim and snorkel until we suddenly encounter a swarm of jellyfish which bring us out in a heavy rash. Then we go across Greece by car and visit the great classical sites on the mainland and the Peloponnese, only some of which I know. One sees everything differently if one has learned Greek for years and can make the trip with a Greek teacher, an old friend, who has written novels such as *Socrates Dreams* and *Beautiful Damaris*. These two untroubled weeks in Greece strengthen me for the following week, when much will be required of me.

On 7 October we fly from Athens to Rome, where I show our little group the 'holy city' from my own quite personal perspective. We mostly go on foot through the many lively alleyways along which I have walked countless times in my seven student years in Rome, wearing my scarlet gown. We follow my route to the Gregorian University, past the Quirinal and the Fontana di Trevi, or from Santa Maria Maggiore to Michelangelo's Moses in San Pietro in Vincoli and from there to the Colosseum, the Roman Forum and up on to the quiet Palatine hill, my favourite place in ancient Rome, and of course also to St Peter's, where we go up the dome. We look at the eerie Palazzo del Sant'Uffizio to the left of St Peter's from outside and from above. It gives me great pleasure once again to see so much of the art and culture of ancient, medieval and baroque Rome which I have continued to love, and then to celebrate cheerfully at supper in Trastevere or the Piazza Navona.

But that brings a happy art and cultural trip to an end. Twenty-five years previously I had not only left school in Lucerne but gone on to begin my studies in Rome in the Pontifical German College. This became my destiny and now in October 1973 it is celebrating a jubilee. I haven't been in Rome for eight years, but I want to take part in the 400th anniversary of the re-foundation of our Pontificium Collegium Germanicum Hungaricum, at which many senior clergy from Rome and Germany are expected. Won't it seem provocative if I refuse to take part in a 'colloquium' in the Congregation for the Doctrine of the Faith but come to Rome for the celebrations? But this is the kind of occasion when I will be able to have informative conversations without becoming entangled in Inquisition proceedings.

On 9 October my companions make their way home to Switzerland, but I visit my lodgings in my old college on the Via San Nicolò da Tolentino 13, near the Piazza Barberini. The Rector, Fr Claudius Mayer-Lauingen, gives me a warm welcome: he tells me that he has been asked whether I am coming to the college jubilee more often than whether the Pope is coming. And at breakfast I happen to sit next to a fellow-student from Poland who tells me with great joy, 'When in Poland I say that I met Cardinal Döpfner in Rome, they'll say "Good". And Cardinal Šeper, "Very good!" And the Pope, "Excellent!" But when I say "Hans Kung", they'll say "Really?"' So he asks me for written confirmation on a bit of paper with the date and a signature that he can show to anyone in Poland. I write above it: '*Veritas in veracitate* – the truth in truthfulness.'

As planned, I use the occasion for important meetings. The previous day, Monday 8 October, I was invited by Cardinal Léon Suenens for a conversation and lunch in his residence on the Via Aurelia. I ask him to intervene for me with the most powerful man under Montini, the sostituto ('deputy') in the Secretariat of State, Archbishop Giovanni Benelli, and also with Pope Paul VI. 'You make life difficult for your friends,' the Cardinal remarks with a smile. But he completely understands that I don't want to get entangled in Inquisition proceedings. Cardinal Suenens will report to me immediately after his two audiences in the Vatican on the Thursday.

I meet Cardinal Julius Döpfner on Tuesday 9 October in the evening in the German College – after supper in the refectory, at the so-called 'patres recreation' which is held in a separate room, apart from the students' recreation, with a glass of liqueur. 'May I still venture into your presence?' I ask him with a mischievous smile. To which he replies in a friendly way, 'That's all I needed!' Can I have a personal word with him? Yes, but the only possible time is tomorrow at 5 p.m., an hour before the Pope's visit to the college; he is leaving the next day.

On Wednesday 10 October 1973 I join in celebrating the great college festival, at which those in the senior year are ordained priest in Sant'Ignazio by Cardinal Julius Döpfner, and the 'first-years' are officially admitted to the community. It's a moving celebration – I think back to my own ordination in the same place on the same day nineteen years previously and all that I have experienced since then as a presbyter of this church. But in 1954 there were sixteen candidates and now, in 1973, there are only four – a sign of the times. I am one of the first after all the bishops to lay hands on my brethren.

After this, as ever, I go on foot through the small alleys back to the German College. I had been well received by members of the college, young and old. Of course there were discussions: 'In this climate and in the presence of numerous heads of the hierarchy it was unavoidable that the "three great figures" of the week – Küng, Kempf and Curia – made feelings run high' (*Frankfurter Rundschau*, 12 October 1973). However, in the circumstances Bishop Kempf hasn't ventured to travel to Rome.

The Prefect of the Congregation for the Doctrine of the Faith, Cardinal Franjo Šeper, also appears at the great banquet – a real Roman *pranzo* with many courses. Of course he sits with Cardinal Döpfner and other bishops at the table of honour. All those honoured are greeted with the *Litaniae Hincmari*, attributed to the powerful Archbishop Hincmar of Reims from the ninth century, solemnly sung by choir and community. There is lively conversation at all the tables.

After the closing prayer I deliberately don't go forward for the greetings, but keep near the exit and there first greet the Vatican ambassador Dr Alexander Böker, who is well up with my case through his counsellor, another former German College student, Archbishop Heinrich Josef Krahé. We speak openly about the negative effects a further escalation of the actions against me would have on relations between state and church in the Federal Republic. Then I talk with Archbishop Josef Schröffer, formerly Bishop of Eichstätt, but now Secretary of the Roman Congregation of Studies. I also make him aware of the consequence of further actions against me. He excuses himself by saying that he isn't a member of the Holy Office.

At the same time I watch Cardinal Šeper slowly preparing to leave, greeting many people; of course he's noticed me a long time ago. Will he pass me by or greet me? He approaches Archbishop Schröffer and then remarks, seemingly in complete surprise, 'There he is, the great Küng!' I reply, 'What does great mean?' We shake hands in a friendly way: 'I hope that you haven't taken what I've written to the Congregation personally.' He comments on the coverage of me in the media: I may not have a powerful apparatus at my disposal, as he does in the Vatican, but I have an equally powerful publicity apparatus. Be this as it may, the ice has been broken: a human contact without censure, demands and threats and a friendly farewell. However, the cardinal is glad that no photograph had been taken of us; that would have put him in a bad light with his colleagues in the Vatican. I then hear that the well-known Munich prelate Michael Höck and another former member of the German College who went there in 1924 had admonished their contemporary Šeper: 'If you don't talk to Küng ...'

Paul VI in the German College

An hour before the Pope's visit, at 5 p.m., I have my conversation with Cardinal Julius Döpfner. He has come through an operation well; this time he is less tired and seems very jovial. His main objection is that my reaction to the Roman action has been impossibly sharp. With a mixture of pleasure and displeasure he remarks, 'And the way in which your sentences are constructed ...' Yes, they've clearly been thought out precisely and aren't easy to contradict. I want to know what was wrong with my letter. He doesn't give me an answer; he is again concerned with tone and style. I remark that in general the letter has been well received, even by the bishops present here such as Friedrich Wetter, Bishop of Speyer, with whom I have a long conversation on the roof terrace of the college with its marvellous view over the city to St Peter's. I emphasize to Cardinal Döpfner that in my letter I had wanted to indicate that I was by no means disposed towards confrontation, but I wouldn't avoid it if it was forced on me. The result is that Cardinal Döpfner promises me that he will talk about further procedure with the action man in the Holy Office, Archbishop Hamer.

The visit of a Pope to Roman colleges is extremely rare. It is more than 200 years since the last papal visit even to the German College. There must be no slip-ups; around 30 papal bodyguards are expected round the college. Two weeks previously in the presence of journalists the Rector had criticized a Catholic news agency report 'Pope and Küng in the Germanicum'; there had been no thought of a direct encounter. The evening before, a letter from Paul VI to all Jesuits had been published in which he called for reflection on the Ignatian principles, and especially for obedience to the Apostolic See. His Paternity Pedro Arrupe, the Jesuit General, known as 'the black Pope', used the occasion to welcome the white Pope personally to the German College and assure him on this occasion of the loyalty of the College and the Jesuit Order. Evidently this wasn't taken for granted in the present situation.

In fact the Swiss in the German College had been against the papal visit: one couldn't constantly carry on about the Pope round the table and then invite him to the college. But punctually at 6 p.m. the Pope is there. The spokesman for the students is an Austrian. In the college church he bravely campaigns for 'mutual trust'. Formerly centralization and the Counter-Reformation had dominated, he says; now there is co-operation and ecumenism. The time requires priests to 'integrate themselves more and more deeply into the world'. Old students think that this greeting to the Pope is too bold. But Paul VI isn't a man who reacts spontaneously. His long address in Italian is conventional; he sees the college as 'a hothouse for apostles'; the priest is to be 'in the world, but not of the world', and above all loyal to the Pope. He embraces the student spokesman with a stiff liturgical gesture; the enthusiasm of the students is muted.

I had sat at the back of the church on the left-hand side to spare Paul VI a direct encounter which could have been painful for both sides here, in public and under the eye of the media. Next to me I see the head of the German College, Brother Wilhelm Dankl SJ, revered by all, pious but critical. He has fallen asleep. He will be able to celebrate 40 years at the college, and later he is presented personally to the Pope, who gives him a friendly greeting. As a papal gift the college receives an artistically framed altar picture, four metres high, by a Flemish master. Later, two coats of arms are discovered on the other side of the canvas, one of Bavaria and the other of Pius XI. This is evidently a gift from German lands which is gathering dust in the Vatican warehouses and for which a place must now be found somewhere in the German College, not without difficulties.

Conversations with Roman professors

The next day, Thursday 11 October 1973, is the day on which the new priests celebrate their first mass. I am in Sant'Ignazio early in the morning with Otto Wüst, my friend from Sursee and now the Bishop of Basle. At 10 a.m. Cardinal Léon Suenens is in the Vatican. An hour later he calls me. The sostituto in the

Secretariat of State, Archbishop Giovanni Benelli, doesn't seem to be particularly interested in any action against me; this is more a concern of the Doctrinal Congregation. However, Küng must do '*quelque chose*'. But what? Benelli too doesn't quite know. The best thing would be for me to state that I agreed with the Declaration by the Congregation. '*Impensable* – unthinkable!,' Suenens replies, whereupon Benelli, more a diplomat than a theologian, says, '*Laissons cela aux temps meilleurs* – let's leave it to better times.'

But in the private audience in which the cardinal explicitly brings up my case, Pope Paul VI makes the amazing remark, '*Non viviamo più nel tempo della inqui-sizione* – we're no longer living in the time of the Inquisition.' However, the Pope too thinks that Küng must do something – which he too doesn't specify more closely. He certainly means some gesture of submission, but at the expense of the truth?

At 8.30 on the evening of 11 October I am invited to my old alma mater, the Gregorian, for a conversation with professors. I had already suggested this myself in a letter to my Spanish former professor of dogmatics, Professor Juan Alfaro, who had always stood up for me. There is a good number of German-speaking professors, several of whom I know well from my student days: as well as Alfaro the church historian Friedrich Kempf (brother of the bishop), the moral theologian Josef Fuchs, the philosopher Peter Henrici (a nephew of Balthasar), the specialist in Soviet philosophy Gustav Wetter, and others.

I express my thanks for the invitation and begin by saying how proud I am to have studied at the Gregorian. I've learned a great deal, though I've made use of my knowledge in my own way. There is benevolent laughter, and even more when I mock myself over the report, presented in all seriousness by Karl Josef Becker, the professor of dogmatics, that the Frankfurt historian of dogma Her-mann-Josef Sieben SJ (see above Chapter IV: Who 'invented' the doctrine of infallibility?) is 'desperately unhappy' about what I have done with his historical research into the infallibility or fallibility of the first ecumenical councils. Becker can't really explain what the poor dogmatic historian is so 'desperately unhappy' about in my use of his results and what is wrong with it (of course Sieben fears for his good Roman Catholic reputation). I remark with amusement that I am desperately unhappy if historians of dogma are desperately unhappy simply because a dogmatic theologian happily makes use of their research. Of course, if a historian of dogma says that he is 'desperately unhappy' he can avoid any uncomfortable substantive discussion. When I relate this anecdote to my Tübingen friends we jokingly invent the term 'Fr Sieben syndrome' for this kind of unhappy reaction.

It's a successful evening and I'm glad that now important Gregorian professors understand my positive concerns better. That's even true of the former Rector Fr Edouard Dhanis, who puts various questions to me. He is the man who drafted the declaration *Mysterium Ecclesiae* directed against me, so I had been asked beforehand whether I had any objections to his presence at this conversation. Of course not. Later it is betrayed to me that Dhanis is isolated at the Gregorian because he is acting in this way as a minion of the Curia.

The sharp criticism of the present papal regime expressed in private at the Pontifical Gregorian University is amazingly broad and sustained. Fr Maurizio Flick, who supervised my licentiate work on Karl Barth's doctrine of justification, even refused to be consultor to the Congregation for the Doctrine of the Faith. Unprecedented! In my student days it was the highest honour for a Gregorian professor to be called to this most secret of all bodies in the Roman administration. The three or four gentlemen concerned were collected from the Gregorian every Monday in a black Vatican limousine and driven to the Palazzo del Sant'Uffizio. We students were aware of this, and it made an impression on us. With their suggestions and verdicts, draft texts of encyclicals and other documents, these 'experts' could write church history behind the scenes. I am indebted to Frs Hürth and Tromp that in 1957 no proceedings were opened against my dissertation on justification. However, in the past two years the ex-Holy Office has changed little and the Gregorian fundamentally: the whole order of studies has been adapted to the times, the lectures are now in Italian instead of Latin, and there are also seminars in various other languages. We even continue our lively discussion for a moment on the Piazza della Pilotta, and two of the professors escort me back to the German College.

In the service of the ecumenical world: Cardinal Willebrands

On Friday 12 October 1973 I am invited to lunch by Cardinal Johannes Willebrands in his residence in the new block of the Vatican opposite the barracks of the Swiss Guard. He has heard about my arrival at the German College through our mutual friend the Dutch Germanist Frans Thijssen, a passionate ecumenist, who had put me in touch with Willebrands for the first time in the 1950s, and indicates that he would like to see me soon. Of course the conversation with the head of the Vatican Secretariat for the Unity of Christians is very important to me.

He embraces me warmly: 'So, a heretic!' As always we get on very well. He tells me that some of the younger generation in his own family have great problems with the Catholic faith. Of course I know that since he is more of an outsider among the Curia cardinals, his hands are often tied. We talk in depth about the situation of the church and especially about the Soviet Union, which he has visited. It goes without saying that for the two of us papal primacy and infallibility are a main obstacle to ecumenical relations. But it is now clear that as a Dutchman and as President of the Secretariat for Unity, which comes under the doctrinal supervision of the Congregation for the Doctrine of the Faith, he doesn't want to expose himself in the infallibility debate: 'Rome needs you: people who hold out here,' I tell him. Sometimes he can do good. Our opinions differ only over the question of eucharistic fellowship, on which he has already had an argument with Jürgen Moltmann. Following the line of the Curia completely, he wants to continue to wait – for how long?

Finally he tells me that Cardinal Šeper has let him know that he is prepared for a personal conversation if I want to see him. I do. Willebrands picks up the telephone: Šeper is sick, but nevertheless invites me to tea in his apartment at 4 p.m. It's in the same Vatican block, round the corner, where Cardinals Ratzinger and Kasper will also live later. There is still a good half-hour before then, and Willebrands, knowing my Roman custom, invites me to have a little siesta on his sofa. Then he insists on accompanying me. He brushes aside my objection that it could compromise him to be seen with me.

I don't envy a Curia cardinal his apartment in the shadow of St Peter's, dignified and spacious though it is, and furnished with heavy furniture and pious pictures. Can the view of Bernini's grandiose colonnades in St Peter's Square replace the Swabian Alb or the Swiss Alps? Or big windows a terrace with a view of green countryside? I can understand that people sometimes feel homesick.

The head of the Doctrinal Congregation in private: who capitulates to whom?

The Prefect of the Congregation for the Doctrine of the Faith, Cardinal Franjo Šeper, like all Roman cardinals at home simply dressed in a black gown with no decorations apart from his ring, and in slippers, receives me in a 'brotherly' way but without the familiar second person usual between those who have been at the German College. Would I like a cup of tea? Slivovitz? The Croatian's eyes light up. That makes some things easier to discuss, he remarks. The conversation is lively and not unfriendly. But the cardinal's manifest effort from the beginning is to dissuade me from my 'enquiry' into matters of infallibility and to persuade me to fall into line and engage in an official colloquium in the Palazzo del Sant'Uffizio or make an act of assent. However, without the legal guarantees that I keep asking for I must decline.

'You want us to capitulate,' he finally exclaims. 'By no means,' I reply, ' I don't expect you to concede that I've been done an injustice or to confirm that I'm in the right. I only want a cease-fire once everything has been said by both sides.' And a cease-fire is rather different from a capitulation. But he finds it difficult to drop the whole matter (which has already been my proposal, put in writing). 'A pity,' he remarks, half seriously and half in jest, 'a pity that you aren't a priest in my diocese of Zagreb. Do you know what I would have done with you there as your bishop? I would have ...' The cardinal visibly enjoys the idea: 'I would have sent you to the remotest corner of my land, to a Croatian farming community. There you could have learned what the faith of the Catholic people is.' Of course this is sheer wishful thinking. 'What a good thing it is,' I say to him with a smile, 'that I'm a free Swiss citizen and live in the diocese of Basle and not in the diocese of Zagreb.' I tell him that I also think I know a little about the Catholic faith.

But then he puts a question to me which perplexes me: 'The Holy Father didn't know that you were coming to Rome. But a while ago he asked me, "What do your think, eminence, I have to do to win over Hans Küng?" What should I now say to the Pope?' I am brought up short. Had I known that, I could have asked Paul VI for a private audience as I had done eight years previously at the end of the Council. I reflect and then say modestly, 'I'd like the Pope to let me carry on with my research and teaching in peace,' an answer which understandably cannot satisfy the cardinal. But what else am I to say? Joseph Ratzinger had long been won over by Paul VI. But I cannot be won over with Roman honours and posts, and I hope that I will also be able to continue to resist Roman pressures. My problem is that I cannot renounce the truth recognized over long years in scripture and tradition simply to become *persona grata* again to the Summus Pontifex.

In fact I have no greater wish than for this Roman (and episcopal) 'teaching office' to leave me in peace at last after all the personal and public admonitions and condemnations. That's a small wish for me but a bigger wish for Rome; the unqualified Roman monopoly of opinion, truth and power in the church seems to be threatened by such tolerance, threatened by a single theologian. People seem to fear my pen as the king of France once feared Voltaire, and I am no mocker and freethinker – at most a free thinker.

The 'hammer' of the Doctrinal Congregation: Archbishop Hamer

Cardinal Šeper, too, is ultimately perplexed and after an hour and a half proposes that I should 'have another talk with Hamer'. He is referring to Jérôme Hamer OP, the Secretary of the Congregation for the Doctrine of the Faith – for me an old acquaintance, whom I had visited as a young professor at the Angelicum, the Dominican university in Rome, and asked critically about Barth's theology; I had seen him again in Paris. But meanwhile the Belgian has made a career in the Curia; he has already become archbishop and is on his way to a cardinal's hat – at some cost! The Flemish and Dutch are annoyed that their Fr 'Hamer', in German simply 'Hammer', pretends to be French and allows himself to be addressed as Monseigneur Amère. However, this cannot disguise the fact that as the strong man of the Doctrinal Congregation, the tall, thick-set Dominican constructs the arguments, plans major actions and negotiates with the German bishops.

I prefer to talk with real Romans rather than with all these senior clerics. So I am glad to have an invitation for that evening from my diving friends from the Île des Pins, Giorgio and Vittoria Sanfelice di Monteforte, whose first child I sadly couldn't make time to baptize. We meet in the splendid penthouse of their Palazzo Odescalchi, then eat in a restaurant on the Piazza Navone, basking in memories of our days together and discussing my Roman 'experiences' and future prospects. This is Rome as I like it.

The next day, 12 October, the day of my departure, I have lunch around 2 p.m. in the fine secondary residence of the Secretary of the Doctrinal Congregation on Monte Mario. Monseigneur Jérôme Hamer, *plus français que les Français*, loves the cut and thrust of conversation. He thinks clearly and talks fast. I enjoy the elegant to-ing and fro-ing in French, which also allows irony and humour: not an interrogation but a real dialogue at a high level.

We quickly get to the point. First of all we talk about theological questions. Hamer doesn't attempt to prove to me that the 1870 infallibility definition is solidly grounded in scripture and the great Catholic tradition; he just bases himself on the First Vatican Council, whose decree as a Catholic one has to accept. I repeat the view for which there is a broad foundation in my publications that in 1870 Vatican I was blind to the deeper problems – that despite all errors the church can be maintained in the truth of the gospel – and that the whole question cries out to be developed from there. So it isn't a matter of completely denying this council definition. With my Roman training I don't find it difficult to distinguish all his traditional objections; the discussion keeps coming back to the question how the church's magisterium could function without infallibility and what would have to happen particularly in a case of conflict. These are all complex questions which I have answered both in *Infallible?* and in the stock-taking 'Fallible', but which he clearly hasn't studied sufficiently.

However, the political implications seem to him to be much more important and he speaks about them with amazing openness. My extraordinarily rapid and clear public statement (whose 'sharpness' Cardinal Döpfner had criticized) has 'fouled up' (I no longer remember which French word he used) the whole Roman Declaration. For instead of the true Catholic doctrine being at the centre of public interest, everything now centres on my person. The Congregation, he remarks, deliberately didn't mention my name in the Declaration: 'But in the covering letter you said quite clearly,' I interrupt with a smile, 'that everything has been "declared" solely for my sake.' 'If on the one hand you want the Declaration to apply to me but on the other don't have the courage to mention my name in it, you mustn't be surprised if your ambiguous position meets with a very critical response from the international public.' And I add maliciously: 'Had I been in your place I wouldn't have written the letter,' whereupon, stifling a laugh, he stares down at the ground for a long time.

But what the Secretary of the Doctrinal Congregation is most curious about is media politics. He tells me that my statement has appeared simultaneously in a Flemish and a Dutch paper, in German, French and Italian publications and in the *New York Times*. I explain to him that the *New York Times* thinks the questions being discussed here important enough to fly its Roman correspondent to Stuttgart and Tübingen to get authentic information. Hamer is amazed that I was capable of reacting to all the Roman moves in the media so quickly and precisely, almost the same day: '*Vôtre secretariat est phantastique*,' a compliment which I am happy to pass on. Our small but highly qualified and efficient team works in my house and this makes it possible for me to react quickly and intelligently without friction. We also know the important addresses. The archbishop thinks that my reaction will spur on '*l'orgeuil de l'Épiscopat allemande* – the pride of the German episcopate'. That wasn't quite my impression; the German episcopate seems to be treading carefully, to say the least, over many things – at any rate where Rome is concerned.

My conclusions about this discussion with Hamer are that: 1. People in the Vatican have the impression that this whole concerted action against me has gone wrong from the start; at any rate my first clear statement has struck home. They didn't reckon with such critical international reaction. 2. However, I cannot convince the strong man of the Doctrinal Congregation to let the discussion on infallibility mature. I probably can't count on a 'cease-fire'.

The archbishop doesn't in any way indicate what the next step by the Congregation will be. However, it soon becomes clear to me that Hamer is pursuing a double strategy: on the one hand to win over public opinion in Germany by what was meant to be a clever Declaration and on the other to compel me to fall into line by direct pressure. It has also become clear to me that the great strategist of the Doctrinal Congregation isn't necessarily a great politician as Max Weber understands the concept. He certainly has 'passion' and 'responsibility' for 'boring through thick planks', but hardly the necessary 'proportion'. Be this as it may, sharply though the arguments are exchanged, our discussion is carried out in serenity, without personal wounds. I have a friendly cup of coffee with the Monseigneur and leave his residence at 5.30 p.m. I am driven to Fiumicino and at 8.15 p.m. get on the plane for Zurich.

Before that I had said goodbye to the porter of the German College, Silvano (he has now also become a book binder). He has never forgotten that his former 'servants' chaplain' had fought on his behalf to make it possible for him to marry and have a family (*My Struggle for Freedom*, III: An uncomfortable memorandum). '*Arrividerci!* Come back soon, Signor King,' he cheerfully calls after me. It's going to be a long time before I return. I am very pleased to be picked up in Zurich about 9.40 p.m. by my mother, my sister Rita and brother-in-law Bruno, to be back in my homeland and to celebrate the 'feast of thanksgiving' (eucharist) the next day – it's Sunday – with the community.

The headline over my interview in *Die Zeit* (19 October 1973) is 'No incense or scent of heresy'; my visit to Rome is said to have taken place with proceedings pending. My comment is: 'We're not in an association where the truth can simply be dictated.' Or can it?

The proposal for a cease-fire rejected

I send a short report on the conversations to Dr Helmut Kohl on 29 October 1973, ending: 'In my opinion it is essential that those in positions of responsibility in Germany – primarily Cardinals Döpfner and Volk – do not set in motion further unwise initiatives from Rome. A decisive no by the German authorities would also be heeded in Rome. If this happened I would keep quiet, so long as I wasn't challenged again.'

Of course, despite all the Roman 'gentilezza' I'm not deceived. These gentlemen – one hardly has to do with ladies in the Vatican milieu – who can be very friendly, jovial or charming in informal conversation would prove extremely stiff and formal in an official 'colloquium', dressed in judges' robes. They would know no mercy but only 'the truth' and 'the law', as these are understood in Rome. So I know what is at stake. And I have to assume that my proposal that the matter should be dropped by both sides will not be accepted. Rome always wants to be right. A single unpunished dissident who shows that one can also think otherwise endangers the whole system.

At the end of November 1973 I ask Cardinal Julius Döpfner once again for a date for a conversation, but if it is to include Cardinal Volk it can't take place until 19 February 1974.[29] At 3.30 p.m I am at the archbishop's palace in Munich, Kardinal Faulhaber Strasse 7, for a conversation which is to last for two and a half hours. It's a stalemate: the Congregation won't halt the proceedings and I can't expose myself to an Inquisition hearing ('colloquium') in which from the start I am fighting a losing battle without legal guarantees.

Cardinal Döpfner tells me about a letter from Rome, which evidently has his approval, but he doesn't want to show it to me – in the end isn't he on the other side? A double game? Finally I ask him bluntly, 'Which side would you take if there were a ("legitimate") condemnation by Rome?' He thinks for a moment and then says, 'Of course that would be hard, but it would have to be endured.' In other words, he would be on Rome's side, though he concedes that the question of theological truth doesn't seem by any means clear to him either. 'My country – right or wrong.' And similarly 'My church – right or wrong'? I would love one day to see a bishop who for the sake of the truth of the gospel, like Paul, resists Peter face to face (Galatians 2). Since the conversation in Munich, of course my scepticism has increased. If there were renewed reaction on the part of Rome I feel that I might expect only qualified help from the German bishops.

What I fear then happens. Finally, on 30 March 1974, in reply to my letter of 22 September 1973, I receive from the Doctrinal Congregation the detailed answer that is already known to Cardinal Döpfner.[30] The decisive point is that the Congregation doesn't accept my proposal for a cease fire: it wants my capitulation – as soon as possible. If I accept the declaration *Mysterium Ecclesiae* immediately, I am told, the current proceedings will be ended. If not, the Congregation has offered me the possibility of a 'colloquium'. But according to the guidelines such a colloquium amounts to a hearing which is used to conclude secret proceedings without the person concerned and with no possibility of appeal.

At this point it wouldn't make sense to repeat arguments and counter-arguments once again. For me what remain essential are:

1. My repeated request for just proceedings, for inspection of the records and for fair conditions is met with excuses by the Congregation.

2. To provide a foundation for the infallibility of church dogmas, as Vatican I defines them with an appeal to the Holy Spirit, a reference is made in a circular argument to Vatican I, which in a completely different situation has provided no convincing basis for them. That is why – after the encyclical *Humanae vitae* – I thought that I had to write my book *Infallible?* as an 'enquiry'. Or is the church perhaps right simply because it has solemnly defined that it is right? The Doctrinal Congregation argues like a cat biting its own tail.

At the same time, Archbishop Jérôme Hamer now thinks that he has to go on the offensive in public. He seeks to justify the inquisitorial proceedings of the Doctrinal Congregation in an interview covering many pages in *Herder-Korrespondenz* of May 1974. He doesn't have much success, as is shown by an unflattering article about him in *Der Spiegel* of 27 May. On the contrary, Hamer is fanning even further the displeasure among the population over Roman practice. He is answered in the June issue of *Herder-Korrespondenz* by the Tübingen church lawyer Johannes Neumann, who gives me brilliant advice on all legal questions, under the title 'Things Could Be Done Better', and in *Publik-Forum* by the Saarbrücken New Testament scholar Josef Blank, who goes deeper theologically: 'A Tricky Question for the Congregation for the Doctrine of the Faith. The Problem for the Roman Congregation as an Authority which Administers the Truth.'[31] No one could have demolished Hamer's arguments in a more convincing and more brilliant way than these two. I finally respond in the *Frankfurter Allgemeine Zeitung* and several Swiss papers on 25 July 1974: 'On Roman Proceedings over the Faith.'[32]

Will the bishop stand firm?

And what about the Bishop of Rottenburg, Dr Carl Joseph Leiprecht, who is responsible for Tübingen? He continues to be left out of all these negotiations. I had numerous conversations with him, dating from my time as a young deacon. However, they were mostly at his invitation, because some complaint or admonition from Rome had arrived (evidently I never deserved praise) as on 5 July and on 24 October 1973. The conversations were serious, but always open and friendly. Despite all the difficulties, Bishop Leiprecht, who had bidden farewell to me as personal peritus at the Council after the first session for reasons of church politics, remains well-disposed towards me. He avoids public disputes and prefers conversations in small groups. He expresses reservations, but attempts to mediate and smooth the way, with an understanding of the lively to-ing and fro-ing of a church which studies and proclaims. He hadn't been informed even about the letter from the Doctrinal Congregation dated 30 May 1974. When Cardinal Döpfner tells him about it, he asks me for a photocopy. In a letter of 30 May he confesses to me that he is 'very anxious about the further course of the controversies', which has been intensified by that *Spiegel* article of 27 May (about Hamer): 'If things go on like this, I fear that they will not turn out well. You should try to do everything possible from your side to ease the tensions.'

Five days later, on 4 June 1974, I receive the surprising news that Bishop Leiprecht is resigning. The same day, before the news appears in the papers, I write to him: 'I can understand that this excessive burden has become too heavy for you. But you can be certain that your resignation will be extraordinarily regretted not only among the people generally but also in our discipline – and that is less to be expected. I personally have special reasons for being grateful to you for all your understanding and tolerance and all your interventions on my behalf in Rome and in the diocese.'

When he leaves office Bishop Leiprecht takes the whole Küng dossier with him and later destroys it; no one knows why and what for. But I hear later from a well-informed source that the bishop retired because in his state of health he wouldn't have survived this controversy. Truly it isn't easy to be a bishop in this system. My friend from Sursee, Otto Wüst, first a suffragan bishop and then Bishop of Basle, once tells me when we are talking about supporting certain reforms: 'Yes, you could do it, but I couldn't; I couldn't take it.' After Leiprecht's resignation Cardinal Döpfner said in the Vatican that it was enough to lose one Bishop of Rottenburg; that must be enough and his successor mustn't also be burdened with this affair. But on the Piazza del Sant'Uffizo they don't want to drop the matter.

From the beginning I have had an open and cordial relationship with Leiprecht's successor Georg Moser, former student chaplain and director of the Stuttgart Academy, whom I had examined for a doctorate on 19 July 1962. I invite Dr Moser, suffragan bishop since 1970, to dinner in my house on 29 March 1976, after his appointment as Bishop of Rottenburg (12 April 1975). We also talk about the devastating lack of priests in his diocese and in other dioceses in Germany. He tells me quite frankly: 'I just don't know how things are going to go on.' I reflect for a moment; should I tell him that he has a duty to say this publicly? But the thought suddenly flashes through my mind: could this intelligent, affable Swabian withstand the storm in public, the sensational reports in the gutter press, the protests of the 'papal loyalists' and finally the massive pressure from Rome? No, he would have to decide on such bold action himself and not at my insistence.

What I say to Bishop Moser as we part must have gone on ringing in his ears. I urgently ask him to get in touch with me immediately in strict confidence if any action from Rome against me should come his way; we would then consider together how best to react. After all, as a former student in Rome and an expert at the Council I already had many years of intimate experience of Rome behind me. It is clear to me that should the worst happen in my controversy with Rome I will not spare him the public statement that I wouldn't dare to ask him to make over the shortage of priests and celibacy. And, I think to myself, will this bishop then stand firm? With united forces, yes, but hardly by himself.

The Roman proceedings contrary to human rights

It is understandable that excitement should become most tangible in my Swiss homeland, with its democratic leanings, where in the case of the professor of moral theology Stephan Pfürtner, who had been compelled to resign, the Catholics and their bishops saw themselves outplayed by Rome. In February 1974 the Swiss bishops accepted the following recommendation of the Synod of all Switzerland on the magisterium and theological research: 'In every case the person concerned in proceedings over doctrine shall have the right to determine his own defender and to inspect the records.'

With reference to this, on 16 June 1974 the diocesan synod of Basle passes an almost unanimous resolution with reference to the United Nations Charter: 'Proceedings which do not accord with these conditions and thus with human rights (UN Charter, articles 10 and 11) and even more so any condemnation which may follow from it, contribute to a heightened polarization in our church, endanger the credibility of the church authorities and burden pastoral care and ecumenical collaboration. The questions thrown up by Professor Küng are not problems which had been created by him; rather, they concern a broad public. He has merely taken them up and presented them for discussion. The problems which such questions provoke can be resolved only in an open dialogue and not through mere words of power.'[33]

Thus alongside many individual voices the synod of the largest Swiss diocese, Berne, calls for the Roman proceedings to be stopped. Of course these various activities have my full consent, but I refrain from any agitation and don't appear in public gatherings relating to my own cause, although I often want to. I could certainly become a tribune of the people (since 1973 there has been the first TV talk show in Germany), but I want to remain a professor. At the beginning of June 1974, in a short time a small committee in Lucerne collects around 20,000 signatures – my sisters Marlis, Rita, Margret, Hildegard and Irene are involved – and presents them to the Swiss bishops at their assembly.

That makes an impression on the Swiss bishops, who are not 'prince bishops' with the authority to raise taxes like the German bishops, and at the beginning of July 1974 leads the President and Vice-President of the Swiss Conference of Bishops, Bishop Nestor Adam of Sitten and Bishop Anton Hänggi of Basle, to travel to Rome. Their intentions are good, but their plan is a bad one. Instead of first briefing himself through me, my own bishop Hänggi prefers to make an intermediate stop in Munich to see Cardinal Döpfner. Does this help him?

In the Vatican the two bishops have conversations with the Roman Doctrinal Congregation and, as I feared, are outmanoeuvred. They are told that 'all the acts on which the Congregation bases its actions' are already in my hands. Our bishops don't see the subtle qualification ('on which the Congregation bases its actions'): not a word about inspection of my dossier 399/57/i!

The press release which the two bishops issue in Zurich after their return had been subtly prepared by the Doctrinal Congregation and resulted in a counter-declaration from me the same day.[34] Indeed 'mon secrétariat est phantastique'! Cartoons show the two bishops coming back from Rome like small boys, in cut-off trousers. There is a great stir on all sides: telephone conversations with Cardinal Döpfner, with Bishops Adam and Hänggi, Professors Kasper, Lehmann and Neumann – newspaper, radio and television interviews follow. The ball is back in the Congregation's court. I say that if the Secretary of the Congregation for the Doctrine of the Faith, Jérôme Hamer, wants to come to Switzerland, as has been announced, I am ready to hold a public colloquium with him over the proceedings. Of course the eloquent member of the Curia doesn't want to accept this offer.

Only on 4 September 1974 do I finally have a clarificatory conversation in Solothurn with Bishops Adam and Hänggi, who are very well disposed towards me. Nothing concrete comes of it; the Swiss bishops are powerless. I face the Swiss public on 16 September in Zurich in the much-watched television series 'At First Hand', in cross fire from the television presenter Alphons Matt and the political theorist Professor Arnold Künzli of Basle. I don't a priori reject the designation 'loyal rebel' if the emphasis is put on 'loyal'. In fact I oppose the anti-conciliar restoration and renewal of the absolutist power structure. The current controversies are also a battle for public opinion and I'm glad that the television broadcast has a broad and positive response and that the Neue Zürcher Zeitung doesn't write superficially about me as a 'rebel' but as 'the unmistakable personality who combines in himself the theologian, pastor and fighter in the spirit of the Council' (18 September 1974).

On 21 September 1974 I am back in Switzerland, in Lucerne for the marriage of my cousin Walter Gut with the widowed Gert Zust. With this marriage the plan for a lay order for men inspired by Hans Urs von Balthasar, in which my cousin was to have played an important role, is finally laid to rest. On 24 September I am invited to dinner by Professor Karl Lehmann at his house in Freiburg im Breisgau. After the open friendly conversation in my report to the Institute on 31 October 1974 I take back my reservations about Lehmann's inclusion in the working group of university ecumenical institutes in Heidelberg expressed on 4/5 May 1974. I had been afraid that the capacity of our group to function freely could be damaged by a new member who advocated rigid and barren hierarchical positions on the recognition of ministries, eucharistic fellowship and even the papacy. I still haven't given up hope that this quick-thinking theologian, who had already worked on the not very helpful episcopal 'aid' for the clergy but could also do other things, will not develop into a pliant court theologian. Finally, on 2 and 3 October, I have conversations in Zurich with Dr Hanno Helbling, literary editor of the *Neue Zürcher Zeitung*, and in Sursee with Konrad Lienert of the *Zürcher Tagesanzeiger*. All these conversations time and again centre on Rome, the bishops and all that goes with that.

But I have long been concerned with a book which is infinitely more important to me than *Infallible? An Enquiry*, now four years in the past, namely *On Being a Christian*. Won't this book perhaps finally convince my opponents in the German episcopate and in Rome of my constructive intentions?

VIII
𝕭𝕺𝕮𝕭𝕺𝕮𝕭𝕺𝕮

The Adventure of a Book

'Hans Küng's On Being a Christian *is one of the most amazing theological books not only of the 1970s but of the whole period after the Second World War. It broke through the current standards of Catholic systematic theology and to the present day provokes vigorous resistance from professional colleagues in this discipline, a resistance which exhausts itself in sweeping criticism or sovereign silence.'*

Hermann Häring, Professor of Theology and the Philosophy of Science at the University of Nijmegen, 1 March 2006

'*Habent sua fata libelli*,' says an old Latin phrase, 'books have their destinies'. How long have I been working on my 'Introduction to Christianity', which I wanted to finish so quickly? It certainly takes patience and yet more patience to write such a comprehensive book which has been worked out down to the smallest detail: sitting down time and again and working far into the night – and that in the midst of all the controversies and struggles. Happily I can switch from one thing to another very quickly. And I am strengthened by the saying of the apostle Paul, who knows from experience 'that hardship develops experience, and perseverance develops a tested character, something that give us hope, and a hope that will not let us down' (Romans 5.3f.).

A change of publisher with consequences

Since the statement on 'What is the Christian Message?' which I worked out laboriously for the 1970 *Concilium* World Congress in Brussels I have held several seminars connected with it: on 'The Essence of Christianity' according to the great theologians of the twentieth century, on 'New Jesus Books', and on 'The Distinctive Christian Element in Contemporary Ethics'. The first draft of my book was written during my trip round the world in 1971. But the infallibility debate, the constant correspondence with Rome, bishops and theologians, and the stocktaking volume 'Fallible?', which took so much time, cost me weeks and months.

The repressive policy of the Roman and German magisterium has also had unforeseen effects on Catholic publishing. Hitherto it had been taken for granted that a Catholic theologian had his books published by a Catholic publishing house; mine were published by Johannes Verlag, Benziger Verlag and Herder Verlag, and all sold large numbers of copies. But it is this that annoys our hierarchs, and Cardinal Hermann Volk, whose theological writings haven't sold more than a couple of thousand copies at most, says this openly in Stuttgart. Above all the hierarchy wants to ensure that a book such as *The Church*, which has already gone through several editions with Herder, appears with the corrections called for by the magisterium. But since Rome and some bishops cannot persuade the author to make these corrections (Rome did succeed in having corrections made to the Dutch Catechism), pressure is put on the publishing house. And pressure can be put on Herder Verlag, probably the biggest Catholic publisher in the world (founded in 1807), in so far as in addition to missals it publishes many official church texts which it cannot afford to lose. Even my good personal relations with Dr Hermann Herder-Dorneich can't help here. The publishers simply can't resist and it is explained to me that they can't go on publishing *The Church* without the corrections called for by the church authorities. That is how the official post-censorship functions after the abolition of prior censorship.

Contrary to its own fundamental interests, Herder Verlag gives me an occasion to leave. For a long time Dr Klaus Piper, an independent publisher with a broad intellectual range and literary sensitivity, whose basic interest is in the humanities and who is always on the lookout for young talent, has had his eye on me. He is the son of the Reinhard Piper who founded the publishing house in 1904. On 6 March 1973 he had sent his editor, Dr Hans Rössner (whose dark Nazi past became notorious only decades later), to see me in Tübingen. So I had a good introduction to a general publisher which couldn't be pressurized by the church and which offered quite different possibilities of distribution. The dissemination of my ideas is the one thing that is important to me – royalties, though welcome, are incidental. Piper promises to publish the new book with a first impression of 50,000 copies.

So I leave the Catholic publisher for a secular publisher, definitively for all my future works – and because this could be seen as a precedent for other authors, some speak of a 'historic' decision. It's a pity for Herder, especially because now all my previous books, which have appeared with Catholic publishers, are re-issued in the Piper series as pocket books. In this format, for example, by 1992 *The Church* had already sold 20,000 copies. Even my 1957 dissertation *Justification* has been reprinted time and again by Piper Verlag. It is understandable that Catholic publishers feel left in the lurch by their own church leaders,

But my 'Introduction to Christianity', which is to bear the title *On Being a Christian*, is still far from finished. In a research semester in 1973/74 – my third in what are now already 28 semesters in Tübingen – I make good progress, mostly in the quiet of my Swiss lake house. Even in the Christmas period, which I spend first with my sister Rita and my brother-in-law Bruno (Frei) in Wengen, then on the Kleiner Scheidegg by myself in an old wooden hotel at the foot of the north face of the Eiger, I work on my book as if possessed, interrupted only by brief ski trips. On Christmas Eve, though, there is a Föhn, a strong mountain wind sounding as if an express train was thundering up above through the Eiger, Mönch and Jungfrau. The hotelier moves dinner to the cellar bar and forbids us to light candles in our rooms. As a precaution, in the evening I put my book manuscript, of which there is no duplicate, in my very resistant 'world-trip bag', which I could throw out of the window into the snow if there were a fire. But we survive the night; in the morning, in front of my bed there is a thin layer of snow which has come in through the cracks, and outside, in front of the hotel, there is a wall of snow four metres high.

After New Year I am pleased to have a visit from my cousin Walter Gut, who in the meantime has become Minister of Education for the canton of Lucerne. For him I write a cheerful 'Open Letter to a Community Mayor' to try to activate the population of central Switzerland to found a university in Lucerne – but in vain. The outcome of the plebiscite a few weeks later is negative, above all because the university is expected to be enormously expensive. I have more success with another public appeal.

For the Jesuits in Switzerland

At the height of the Kulturkampf, after the First Vatican Council and its defi-nition of papal primacy and infallibility, in the revised 1872 constitution of the Helvetic Federation the Protestant cantons had enacted confessional articles directed against the Catholic cantons. The founding of new religious houses and the public activity of Jesuits – deeply committed to papal infallibility – were prohibited. After long efforts the abolition of these articles is put to the Swiss people in a referendum to be held on 20 May 1973. My name is quoted three times on a pamphlet of the action committee in favour of preserving the articles: as a representative of the opposition to Roman centralism and absolutism and thus indirectly against the abolition of the ban on Jesuits and new religious houses. Once again I can't avoid making a public statement.

Of course I stand by my criticism of the Roman system. But I see myself compelled also to take a public stand in favour of the abolition of the articles against Jesuits and new religious houses. For what was understandable a century ago is incomprehensible, unjust and impracticable today. These two articles in the constitution have lost their significance, the assertion that the Jesuits pose a danger to the state has become ridiculous. Despite all the difficulties, after Vatican II members of religious orders in particular – and especially the Jesuits – are working for a reform of the Catholic Church in the spirit of the gospel and for an understanding with the other Christian churches. Hence my clear recommen-dation to vote *against* a no: 'Those who on 20 May vote *against* the abolition of the confessional articles are contributing to a new deterioration in the confessional climate; are confirming the prejudice of reactionary Catholics that Protestants are unwilling to learn; and are disowning the Catholic forces of renewal and understanding at work in the Swiss Catholic Synod and the Swiss Conference of Bishops, as they are in Catholic parishes large and small and in their pastors.'

For the Yes: 'Those who on 20 May vote *for* the abolition of the confessional articles are voting for equal rights and unlimited freedom of belief, conscience and culture; are voting against discrimination not only against Swiss Jesuits and members of religious orders but against all Swiss Catholics; are contributing to tolerance and peaceful co-existence in our country; and are helping to remove a stain from our free, democratic and legal constitution.'

In broad circles extending beyond the Protestant population, more credibility is attached to my statement, which appears in many Swiss papers, than to those of the bishops, who are likewise appealing to the people. At any rate the result shows that intervention here was both necessary and successful: in the vote on 20 May 55 per cent are for the abolition of the articles and 45 per cent against. Happily my positive expectations are not disappointed.

However, such political interventions occupy only the periphery of my life as a theologian. I devote every free moment to my central project of the 'Introduction to Christianity', which is now well-advanced.

Not a Jesus domesticated by the church but a real Jesus

The approach 'from below' which I have chosen is considerably more laborious than an approach 'from above'. I have had to study many books on Jesus and consult biblical commentaries. Indeed I have even given consecutive sermons ('homilies') at the daily worship in the district hospital of my home town of Sursee on the whole of the Gospel of Mark – learning from the excellent new commentary by the Zurich exegete Eduard Schweizer – and later also on the Sermon on the Mount. In this way I come to know Jesus of Nazareth better and better as a historically well-documented and clearly identifiable historical figure despite all the uncertainties in detail, a figure who has to be understood in the light of the historical situation of Israel at that time.

But precisely in this way it also becomes increasingly clear to me that for the church this Jesus becomes not simply the confirmation of the 'reality of the Catholic that has come into being' (thus Ratzinger) but once again an invitation and a challenge: 'Jesus has often seemed to be "domesticated" in the churches, turned almost into the representative of the religio-political system, justifying everything in its dogma, worship and canon law: the invisible head of a very clearly visible ecclesiastical machinery, the guarantor of whatever has come into existence by way of belief, morals and discipline. What an enormous amount he has been made responsible for in church and society in the course of Christianity's

2000 years! How Christian rulers and princes of the church, Christian parties, classes, races have invoked him! For what odd ideas, laws, traditions, customs, measures he has had to take the blame!' So one has to remember him, the real human being Jesus, who existed before any church, to become certain of the true foundation of Christianity for our whole lives as Christians.

That is what I want to do: to tell once again from the beginning the unique history of Jesus of Nazareth, what he proclaimed, did, fought for and suffered, and reflect systematically on it for our time. At the beginning of the 1970s the great importance of remembrance and narrative for human and religious identity is in the air, but this is not what prompts me. Long before any demands for a narrative theology, which often all too much remains a theory, I am keenly interested in the increasingly dramatic story of the man from Nazareth.

It is extremely exciting for me to work out very precisely, with the help of modern exegesis, how with his message and his conduct the young man from Nazareth broke through all the schemes which religion had developed then, as it has now, in other words to establish in the midst of the controversy with student revolts and liberation theology that Jesus wasn't a political revolutionary opposing the occupation forces but preached non-violence and precisely in this way became more revolutionary than the revolutionaries (cf. Chapter VI above). Then in the midst of the discussions about religious orders at the same time I could work out that he was not an ascetic or a religious but someone who liked to go to parties, whose attitude towards the world was more free than that of the ascetics. Finally, I could work out how he was not a politician or social reformer, and therefore not a priest or theologian in whose controversies with the religious and political hierarchy of the time there are all too many parallels with today's Catholic hierarchy. Conversely, it emerged that some traditional Catholic moral positions can be recognized in the casuistry and compromise of the Pharisaism of the time which show Jesus to be more moral than the moralists.

To this degree my scholarly research never takes place in an ivory tower, but is embedded in all the experiences, feelings, annoyances of the time. But everywhere I take the utmost trouble not to introduce any 'pre-understanding' into the New Testament texts. Rather, these are to proclaim their own message and precisely in this way to bring Jesus to light: his winning love of his fellow men and women, which is open to those who particularly need him (the 'neighbour') and which excludes no one, not even the opponent or the heretic. It is a pragmatic, creative love which in a particular situation is even ready to serve without thought of rank, to renounce without receiving anything back, to forgive without limit.

Good news which leads to conflict

I want to make clear for today's situation that this Jesus does not proclaim a new theological theory and a new law, nor does he proclaim himself. He proclaims the kingdom of God, which for today means God's cause; the will of God is the human cause, human well-being. For the well-being of men and women Jesus performs charismatic healings and at the same time *de facto* relativizes hallowed institutions and traditions, cult and law.

So one can understand the charges against him: isn't he – thus the priests and scribes – a false teacher, a pseudo-prophet, one who leads the people astray, a blasphemer? Indeed the dispute is ultimately about God, in whose name he acts and as whose ambassador he appears. However, Jesus doesn't appeal to a new God but to the God of Israel – albeit understood in a new way, not simply as God of pious observers of the law, the 'righteous', but as father of the lost, weak, poor, oppressed, 'sinners'. He addresses this God in a quite unusual way as his and our 'Father' and proclaims his forgiveness to men and women, who are in turn to pass it on to their fellow human beings. All this is summed up in the prayer 'Our Father'.

Thus I attempt to make it clear that the conflict with the powerful in state and religion was unavoidable. Jesus' arrest, condemnation and violent end were a consequence of his attitude to God and human beings. There was a violent reaction to his non-violent action from the guardians of law, justice and morality: his historically indubitable death on the cross. The extreme torment he suffered there appears to be the curse of the law; the one who for his disciples is God's envoy and messiah appears to those faithful to the law to be the representative of the lawbreakers, the sinners. And so he dies abandoned by his fellow men and women and by God.

But – and Judaism offers many stimuli for this faith – everything was not over with his death. I have investigated carefully the Easter experiences which have been handed down in various contradictory traditions and legendary elaborations and can only be amazed that in 2007 a film about 'The Tomb of Jesus' can still be shown which the Israeli-American archaeologist Joe Zias and other renowned experts have rightly called deceit and soap opera. According to the authentic witnesses the decisive element of the faith of the community is completely unambiguous: the crucified Jesus lives for ever with God – as hope for us. I make clear what 'resurrection' means: not a return to life in time and space, nor even its continuation, but rather acceptance into that incomprehensible all-embracing first and last reality which we call God. And for the world of religions and ideologies this means that this Jesus Christ differs unmistakably from the many exalted gods and divinized founders of religions, from Caesars, geniuses, heroes of world history in appearing, not as the risen, exalted divine figure but as the humiliated, crucified one. The cross is rightly the basic symbol of Christianity.

The essence of Christianity

In the light of this history of Christ Jesus I can thus give a precise answer to the fundamental questions of Christianity which I have put to myself, and hope that my answers will find a broad consensus.

What is the distinctive feature of Christianity? Concentrated as much as possible, it can be said to be Jesus Christ himself. He is the living, normative embodiment of his cause: the embodiment of a new attitude to life and a new lifestyle. For men and women today he offers the basic model of a view of life and a way of living – though these can be realized in many ways. In his person he is an invitation, a call, a challenge. And he makes a new life possible in concrete terms both for the individual and for society through a new basic orientation and attitude, through new motivations, dispositions, actions, indeed a new horizon of meaning and a new goal.

So who is a Christian? A Christian isn't simply someone who attempts to live a humane, a socially concerned or even a religious life. Christian concentration and openness to the world need to be combined: non-Christians, too, can be humane, socially concerned, even authentically religious. However, the only true Christians are those who attempt to live out their humanity, social concerns and religion in the light of Christ, in his spirit, according to his standards: attempt – no more and no less.

The discrepancy between Jewish–Christian and Hellenistic understanding

Throughout I strive for a scholarly responsible expression of the Christian message of the kind that Joseph Ratzinger would also demand. However, historical accuracy and a critical interpretation of history are presuppositions for this. Unlike Ratzinger, I accept the challenge of historical–critical exegesis; Edward Schillebeeckx is the only other dogmatic theologian who does this. Exegesis grounded in historical criticism calls for a dogmatics with a responsible attitude to historical criticism. Thus I can basically agree with my friend the Flemish-speaking Belgian theologian: 'Towards a New Consensus in Catholic Theology?' is the title of my article in the *Tübinger Theologischer Quartalschrift* (Vol. 4, 1979). I couldn't have suspected that it would be my last contribution to our journal and that only a few months later I would be excluded from the editorial group without an explanation or a word of thanks from those who all owed their involvement with it not least to my vote.

In my theological works I have increasingly taken the trouble to write everything in a language in keeping with that of the intellectual discussion of our time which is also good German. My English translator Edward Quinn once complimented me: 'You're a dangerous author; you make me feel that I can read German easily and then I attempt it with your colleagues ...' (4 April 1979).

I could now have concluded my 'Introduction to Christianity', which is really too long. I've worked through the reports of Jesus' death and resurrection interpreted by Paul and John. But what will my opponents say if I don't say anything about the later dogmatic developments of christology, for example about the interpretations of the death of Jesus: died 'for us', his death as an atoning sacrifice, the doctrine of satisfaction? Or about the interpretations of his origin: the incarnation of the Son of God, the virgin birth, Mary as Mother of God, the christological dogmas of the fourth and fifth centuries?

I have an excellent knowledge of this material, which I already studied in Rome for my examinations and have taught in Tübingen for my students. And I succeed in describing these difficult developments precisely yet comprehensibly in around 50 pages. Then – well prepared by my book *The Church* – I write about the same number of pages on the inspiration of the Bible, the Holy Spirit, the many forms of the church with its different constitutions, charisms and ministries, and finally the service rendered by the Petrine office.

Something that Joseph Ratzinger simply doesn't want to take account of both in Tübingen and later in his Jesus book is that everywhere, whether one likes it or not, one comes up against the tremendous discrepancy between the original Jewish–Christian understanding and the Hellenistic understanding which developed after that. One might think of the title 'son/child of God' – just one of the many dozens of titles given to Jesus in the New Testament. In the Hebrew Bible the title 'son of God' is given to the people of God, the pious, the prophets and above all the King of Israel at his enthronement (Psalm 2.7); in the New Testament, above all in Luke's Acts of the Apostles, also to Jesus exalted from death to God: 'begotten' as son on Easter Day (not at Christmas) (Acts 13.33).

All this is expressed in Jewish Christianity in categories of action and relationship. But when 'son of God' is transferred to Hellenistic cultures, at an early stage it is moulded in the categories of a static Greek ontology ('two natures/wills', 'one hypostasis/person', 'one being with the Father'). These are all concepts which were almost incomprehensible at that time to the Jewish Christians and are today for the majority of Christians, who haven't studied Greek philosophy. To put it plainly: I by no means reject the classical Hellenistic christology and doctrine of the Trinity from the fourth and fifth centuries, but interpret them in the light of the biblical origins and attempt to take up their intentions in the language of our time.

So I produce a critical–constructive dogmatics on the basis of critical–constructive exegesis. I do the same with the eleventh-century doctrine of satisfaction worked out by the father of scholasticism, Anselm of Canterbury. Later, as I have already indicated, I shall speak of three successive paradigms of Christianity which continue simultaneously: the original Jewish–Christian paradigm (I), the paradigm of the early church and Hellenism (II) and the medieval Roman Catholic paradigm (III). These will then undergo further epoch-making revolutions: the Protestant Reformation paradigm (IV) and the paradigm of modernity and the Enlightenment (V). So in our time, too, in the transition from modernity to postmodernity (VI), aren't new processes of inculturation and therefore also new interpretations of the Christian message possible, indeed necessary? At any rate I take a great deal of trouble to work out formulations for a christology which is responsible to scripture, meaningful and pastorally helpful.

A basis for dialogue with the Jews

I have long been convinced that the serious theological dialogue with Judaism which began after Vatican II can be carried on meaningfully only on the basis of a christology 'up from below'. Anyone who wants to carry on a conversation with Jews or Muslims on the basis of the traditional Hellenistic doctrine of the Trinity and incarnation will begin a pseudo-dialogue that will very soon come to an end. But one can go a relatively long way with a Jew in the light of the Jew Jesus of Nazareth. Questions such as that of the validity of the law, which also have parallels in controversies within present-day Judaism, then become urgent.

My first main partner in the dialogue was Dr Pinchas Lapide, born in Vienna. He emigrated to Palestine in 1938, fleeing from the Nazis; in the war he was an English officer, then a diplomat in the state of Israel and finally professor at Bar Ilan University. From the middle of the 1970s he lived as a writer in Frankfurt am Main. I had a dialogue with him which was broadcast on Südwestfunk on 25 August 1975 about the decisive point of dispute: the Jew Jesus of Nazareth who stands between Jews and Christians. Lapide shows an unusual understanding of all that is Christian yet remains a convinced Jew. Therefore he is particularly congenial discussion partner for us Christians, though one who makes extraordinary demands. He teaches us to understand better what is both Jewish and Christian.

However, Lapide underestimates the conflicts which Jesus, whom he wants to make a liberal Pharisee, has with the Jewish law. I must contradict that. Jesus' arrest, condemnation and execution cannot simply be explained as a judicial murder by the Romans. In 1976 I give Lapide the opportunity to be the first non-Christian to have a book on 'Jews and Christians', an 'Encouragement to Dialogue', published in my 'Theological Meditations'. I write to him that 'It is an ardent and informative testimony to Judaism, combined with an extraordinary ecumenical breadth in relationship to Christianity' (25 February 1976).

So no one needs to teach me about 'truthfulness' in the dialogue with Jews and Muslims. At a very early stage I also grapple with other interpretations of Judaism: with that of the knowledgeable and congenial writer Shalom Ben-Chorin, who visits us in Tübingen (21 June 1975), and also that of the Marxist philosopher Ernst Bloch, with whom I hold a colloquium in the company of the Protestant theologian Jürgen Moltmann and the philosopher Helmut Fahrenbach (30 June 1975). I will work all these experiences and insights into the first volume of my trilogy on the Abrahamic religions, *Judaism* (Part Two B: The Dispute between Jews and Christians).

And Christian practice?

Finally comes the hard work. As always, I write out every page twice by hand, dictate it into a machine, have the typescript checked and corrected, and also read and improved by my closest colleagues, Hermann Häring and Karl-Josef Kuschel. Then I read it, improve it and give it the best literary polish I can. The completed chapters are read critically by my friend and colleague Walter Jens, and I also have the difficult chapters checked by experts: the sections on the world religions by Julia Ching (Canberra) and Professor Heinrich Dumoulin (Tokyo), the New Testament chapters by my Tübingen colleague Gerhard Lohfink, and the new sections on theological ethics by my colleagues Alfons Auer and Wilhelm Korff.

Parts A ('The Horizon'), B ('The Distinction') and C ('The Programme') of my 'Introduction to Christianity' are definitively completed on 6 June 1974 at 1 a.m. At 2.08 I take the night train to Holland to be in Westerhellig near Nijmegen punctually at 8.30 for the meeting of the *Concilium* Foundation. Isn't it understandable that after Parts A–C I'm exhausted and decide simply to omit the planned Part D ('Practice')?

But when I disclose this decision to my faithful literary adviser Walter Jens, he protests vigorously. This Part, for which I've already gathered a great deal of material (on political theology, liberation theology, autonomous ethics), must certainly be in. And Hermann Häring and Karl-Josef Kuschel are ready, with exemplary commitment, to read, reflect on, discuss and improve the versions of the manuscript which are constantly rewritten, often worked on till late at night. This means that my secretary has to type some pages up to twelve times – when there are as yet no computers.

So I get back to work. First comes the section on the practice of the church. Why remain in the church? Then again in summary the concrete demands for reform and the call against resignation in the church (which is spreading wider and wider); finally brief descriptions of the nature and functions of the church. A second large section discusses the practice of the individual: first the affirmation of autonomous norms of the human (here already we have the later 'global ethic'!), then the foundation of a theonomous ethic for those who believe in God, and finally the characteristic of a specifically Christian ethic, which lies in 'discipleship of Jesus Christ'. This shouldn't consist either in imitation or in veneration. Rather, everyone should become involved in Jesus' way and take his or her own way – and everyone has their own way – following Jesus' directions. These are all also questions of social relevance that I had already reported in connection with liberation theology, which is broadly discussed here. Finally there is the central

Christian message of the cross, all sides of which are reflected on critically: the misused cross, the misunderstood cross and the understood cross. The practical conclusion is that one shouldn't seek suffering but endure it, shouldn't just endure it but fight it, and finally shouldn't just fight it but assimilate it.

I am delighted to conclude the book with the topic of my youth, the central theme of the Reformation, the justification of human beings before God (or social justice?), 'What is ultimately important and what is not'. The final chapter culminates in suggestions for a practice of freedom: in the legal order, in the struggle for power, from the pressure of consumption, to serve. I finally sum up in one page of the epilogue what it is to be human. This is taken up and surpassed in being a Christian, which is understood as radical humanism that can integrate and overcome even suffering, guilt, death and meaninglessness. At the end I summarize the whole book in a single sentence, which will remain my motto for life:

> By following Jesus Christ
> man in the world of today
> can truly humanly live, act, suffer and die:
> in happiness and unhappiness, life and death,
> sustained by God and helpful to men.[1]

Meanwhile the title of the book has also been determined. I had decided for 'On Being a Christian? An Introduction' – I like titles with critical question marks. But my publisher Klaus Piper, with his sure instinct for titles, suggests *On Being a Christian* – and nothing else. It's a quite unusual title, which doesn't even make it clear whether one is to think of adding a full stop, an exclamation mark or a question mark, in other words whether *On Being a Christian* is an 'is' or a 'should'. But that's what makes it interesting, and in fact it will so quickly become established that it will soon be popular to speak of 'being a Christian'.

It is Saturday 27 July 1974, between 1 and 2 a.m., when I can write the final sentence. With Hermann Häring and Karl-Josef Kuschel, who have supported me to the last minute, I can now say 'The book's finished.' I play the Hallelujah Chorus from Handel's *Messiah*, but then I'm overcome and have to turn away; I don't want the two of them to see my tears. We remain together until dawn and celebrate the completion of the tremendous work. The three of us will never forget these precious hours all our lives, and are still true friends.

To Hans Urs von Balthasar, who had just sent me the first volume of his impressive *Theodramatics*, seeking the way from the theatre to the Christian faith, with the understatement 'a bit of gipsy theology', I had written in gratitude: 'It's a real adventure to come from the Jesus of history to the proclaimed Christ and not evade any uncomfortable questions in the process. As I've already said to you, I have only one concern, to make clear the foundation on which men and women today can stand in faith, and here I want not least to address people outside the

307

church. At the moment I've no idea whether all this will bring me yet more difficulties with Rome. But I mustn't pay too much attention to that, and think of my potential readers, who expect the truth in truthfulness.' I add: 'It would delight me enormously if I had got past the complications of a church politics which helps no one. Unfortunately the infallibility story isn't yet finished.' This last statement proves correct.

The disciplinary proceedings on doctrine are 'stopped'

Again there are to-ings and fro-ings between Cardinal Julius Döpfner and me.[2] Again I reply on 4 September 1974 to a letter from the Doctrinal Congregation. Again I report a series of weighty difficulties over the legality of the proceedings and at the same time spell out some theological statements on the criterion of faith and the magisterium. I say that since I am working every day and am constantly ready for any corrections which with good reason may be required of me, I would like to claim 'the "time for reflection" that has generously been offered me by the Congregation to "examine my doctrinal views", which is the duty and task of any serious scholar and especially a serious theologian'.[3]

Meanwhile *On Being a Christian* has been printed. To my great delight I hold the first copy in my hands on 3 October 1974 while I am still in Sursee, and on 10 October – the twentieth anniversary of my ordination – I can launch it at a press conference at the Frankfurt Book Fair.[4] Will the bishops now understand my constructive intentions better? I send *On Being a Christian* simultaneously to Cardinal Julius Döpfner and Professor Karl Lehmann in Rome at the beginning of October, during the synod of bishops – I intend this as a *captatio benevolentiae* ('courting goodwill'). Karl Lehmann immediately reads 400–500 pages and wants to 'get back to the immense achievement' (24 October 1974); he is also concerned to reach an agreement in the future (2 December 1974). Cardinal Döpfner dryly thanks me after his return from Rome on 4 December. He has read 'some select passages'; he says that I have 'devoted much strength and work, and the pastoral concern with which the book is motivated' is 'detectable'. But he has also 'found a series of statements which I am convinced are not useful for this aim, indeed make it more difficult. They will not exactly promote a reasonable conclusion to the doctrinal proceedings in Rome.'[5]

It's depressing. *On Being a Christian* doesn't much interest the President of the German Conference of Bishops, but the 'doctrinal proceedings in Rome' do. During this stay in Rome he had 'opportunity to discuss the question of the doctrinal proceedings several times': 'I hope that in the end a reasonable solution will result, despite all the difficulties. However, it has also become clear to me that such a conclusion cannot be reached without your collaboration. At the moment I cannot say more than that.'[6] But what does 'your collaboration' mean? On 11 December I thank Cardinal Döpfner for his intervention in Rome and his efforts towards 'a reasonable solution': 'This still seems to me to consist in a standstill on both sides.'[7]

However, the Doctrinal Congregation won't stand still. And all this has been set up in advance with Cardinal Döpfner. On 14 February 1975, at his suggestion there is a conversation with him in Munich, attended also by the church lawyer Professor Johannes Neumann from Tübingen and Dr Josef Homeyer, the Secretary of the German Conference of Bishops and future Bishop of Hildesheim, who has previously been active in Rome behind the scenes. In it I am verbally informed of the content of two new declarations, one by the Doctrinal Congregation and the other by the Conference of Bishops. But I may not see the declarations, although they are already lying finished on Döpfner's desk! Again the same dishonest game; the plan is to overwhelm me. As I write to a Dutch colleague this week: 'A new storm will descend on me, directed from Rome and Germany at the same time; it will be on the radio.' As a son of the Alps one must indeed be very weatherproof to want to go on enduring all this after the adventure of the book.

In fact I am now virtually swamped with documents from the magisterium, most carefully prepared in Rome and by helpers in Germany. Three days after the conversation in Munich, on 17 February 1975, the Doctrinal Congregation publishes in Rome a declaration which at first sight is amazing: for the moment it will formally 'stop' both proceedings against the books *The Church* and *Infallible?*[8] This is a major operation to silence me – on Roman conditions – the significance of which isn't immediately clear. For it is apparently happening in the hope (this will be discussed soon) that I will stand still, which I certainly can't promise. As with the 1973 declaration *Mysterium Ecclesiae*, the Congregation is acting like a general staff opposing a whole army of 'enemies of the church': the German Conference of Bishops unreservedly supports the Roman declaration with a declaration of 17 February which is more than twice as long.[9] Both documents, which could easily have been handed to me in Munich, are now sent to me at home by a courier at deliberately short notice, with a long covering letter from Cardinal Döpfner.[10] On 20 February he comments on all this yet again in a press conference after the spring meeting of the bishops in Bad Honnef with a written declaration which is much longer yet again, but he combines it with a personal statement of respect for me.[11]

In all these declarations, unsupported by any serious theological arguments, it is judged that my views 1. of the 'dogma of infallibility', 2. of the magisterium of the church and 3. of the eucharist, which 'in an emergency could be validly celebrated by the baptized without priestly ordination', do not correspond to the 'teaching of the church'. On 19 February there is a telephone conversation with me, wanted by Cardinal Döpfner before the press conference (for what?), but nothing new transpires.

Should I perhaps express my thanks for this 'stop' to the proceedings? On 20 February I make my own press statement,[12] accompanied by interviews and a half-hour broadcast on First German Television, in which I make it clear:

1. That the two 'declarations' do not refute anything that I have brought forward with detailed theological arguments;

2. That the stop to the proceedings is a public admission by the Doctrinal Congregation that the secret proceedings against me have proved impossible to carry through, especially because no one has wanted me to see the record. I rejected Inquisition proceedings but not a real colloquium;

3. That the Doctrinal Congregation was unfortunately unwilling to accept my proposal for a standstill and has renewed its attack on my orthodoxy. But I welcome the fact that at least the German declaration in principle recognizes 'room for attempts at clarification in the church'.

It is important that for the future I don't promise any 'penitential silence', which is apparently what Rome and the bishops had expected. Rather, at the end of my press statement I emphasize:

Therefore I will not allow myself to be deterred from continuing to fulfil my theological ministry to my fellow men and women in critical solidarity with the Catholic Church and in an ecumenical spirit, and to teach what can be presented as Catholic teaching in the light of the New Testament and the great Christian tradition. I will certainly time and again reflect as a responsible theologian on the method and content of my theology, just as I hope that the Roman Curia will adopt the theological principles of the German Conference of Bishops, even if this must have major consequences for the method and content of Roman theology.[13]

Professor Karl Lehmann, amazingly well up on the course of things, writes to me on 16 February 1975 that he is 'very glad and happy that it has proved possible to prevent the imposition of any disciplinary measures ... No one but you could have achieved this solution. Perhaps you are nevertheless not completely content with the outcome. That too is perhaps understandable. But as far as I know the proceedings, I can assure you that an attempt has been made by all those involved really to achieve the best.' There are numerous commentaries in the international press which describe the ambiguous situation: 'Conflict Removed?', 'Renunciation of Serious Disciplinary Measures', 'A Breath of Wisdom', 'Küng's Questions Remain', 'Muzzle from Rome', 'Stranglehold with Velvet Gloves'.

Nevertheless, perhaps I now have a breathing space. How wonderful it would be to stop the dispute! In a personal letter to Cardinal Döpfner dated 26 February 1975,[14] despite all my reservations I offer him an 'honest, heartfelt word of thanks' for his efforts at mediation which have avoided the threatened general confrontation. I express particular gratitude to him for the declaration of respect that he made at the press conference, recognizing 'my deep commitment and pastoral concern' and also that I 'speak a simple and understandable language'. 'At no point was there any question of condemning all Professor Küng's theology; it was a matter of correcting some – albeit very important – points. This criticism has nothing to do with Küng's integrity as a priest and a Christian.'

That is my hope, as I express it to Döpfner. 'Now that a period which has been unpleasant for all concerned has come to an end, as you have made clear in public ... it would delight me greatly if in future we worked together for what is probably more important for both of us: the common Christian cause.' But this hope is to be disappointed. For – something that I don't go into in my press statement – the conference of bishops surprisingly combines with its statement on the proceedings against *The Church* and *Infallible?* sharp criticism of my book *On Being a Christian* and thus opens up a new theatre of war. To whom do I owe these new attacks? And what use are all the proceedings on doctrinal questions if those who start them don't think of stopping them? In the present situation it seems to me advisable to pass over this unexpected attack on *On Being a Christian* in silence. But how am I to keep silent in the long term when I am constantly being attacked by the other side in articles and addresses? Thus a large poster in Bonn announces Professor Dr Adolf Kolping on 'The Küng Case. A Stocktaking of the Pros and Cons'. And in July 1975 Pope Paul VI uses the occasion of the beatification of Carlo Steeb, the founder of a German religious order, to criticize sharply the 'damaging and liberal tendencies' at the University of Tübingen.

At this moment, however, an enquiry from the Stuttgart delegate to the Bundestag, Peter Conradi, addressed to the German Federal Government, about the restriction of my freedom to teach by 'instructions from abroad', doesn't seem to me to be necessary.[15]

I couldn't have suspected that despite everything, the (understandable) dispute over infallibility would be followed by a much more dangerous dispute over *On Being a Christian* (which even today I understand far less).

An unexpected bestseller

I had never really expected it. I was convinced that one can't plan a bestseller; a good book and the *Kairos*, the right time in history, must coincide. A book of 200 pages, which the 'Introduction to Christianity' had originally been planned to be, could perhaps have made it, but not On *Being a Christian* with 676 pages in relatively small print. Even the outstanding promotion and a well-attended press conference put on by Piper Verlag in the Bayerischer Hof in Munich could hardly achieve that. Yet soon after it appears, the book climbs the bestseller list of *Der Spiegel* and soon reaches the top. For months it remains at number two between Solzhenitsyn's *Gulag Archipelago I* and *Gulag Archipelago II* – 100,000 copies had already been printed by January 1976 and 160,000 by April. What an opportunity for the church, I think to myself, at a time when pastoral letters and pious literature hardly receive any attention. There are numerous grateful letters from readers and complimentary remarks. Editions of the book are prepared in English, Dutch, Italian, French, Portuguese, and later also Russian and Korean. The later '20 Theses on Being a Christian' which attempt to sum up the essentials then appear in Finnish, Danish, Czech and Hungarian in addition to the languages mentioned.

Disapproving colleagues think it is above all Rome and its actions against me that have achieved this global success. However, to avoid this deliberately distorted view I may point out that the dissertation on *Justification* by a then completely unknown young man became a theological bestseller and even now sells on and on. *The Council and Reunion*, the work which presented the programme for Vatican II, became an international church bestseller, followed by *The Church* and *Infallible? An Enquiry*. But *On Being a Christian* was the first to become a general bestseller – like its predecessors, also in other European languages.

The recipe for media success, 'the more controversial the better', applies only to a limited degree in the religious and theological book sector. The Swiss Jesuit Ludwig Kaufmann (of the Zurich journal *Orientierung*), who is well disposed towards me, asked whether the conference of bishops didn't function as Küng's advertising agency. But my book *On Being a Christian* is really a scholarly work by no means intent on controversy. On the other hand, the publicity for markedly controversial books such as Horst Hermann's 'The Seven Deadly Sins of the Church' and 'Heretics in Germany', or Hubert Mynarek's 'Eros and the Clergy. The Misery of Celibacy' is limited. Conversely, my book is immediately given multi-page reviews in foreign papers such as the Dutch *De Tijd* and the Spanish *Vida nueva*. And so much attention is paid to it in Russian and Estonian even in the Soviet samizdat (underground literature) because of its careful grappling with atheism that the Moscow atheistic journal *Nauka i religiya* (Science and Religion), of which a large edition is printed, publishes a polemical article by one B. J. Kryvelyov in which the 'Freethinking Pater Küng' (the title of the article) is presented as a 'heretic' and even the Vatican is over-trumped.

That a book on being a Christian can have such success confirms me in the conviction that a new approach to the old gospel in a new time would meet with interest and sympathy. By contrast the conventional christology which my colleague Walter Kasper offers at almost the same time under the title *Jesus the Christ* would be limited to the traditional Roman Catholic public, despite its use of exegetical material, because of its method, language and content. It was also to be foreseen that Paul VI's 1975 encyclical on 1650 years of the Nicene Creed, which left traditional dogmatic christology once again unexamined, would hardly be noted. Only a dozen ultra-conservative theologians, Protestants (Beyerhaus, Wickert) and Roman traditionalists (around Bishop Graber) – all friends of Ratzinger – gathered in Regensburg in January 1975 and discussed the 'heresies' which were allegedly spreading right across the confessions. Hadn't one expected all the more that the Catholic hierarchy would have welcomed such a successful book as *On Being a Christian* with great delight, even if perhaps it could have wanted more traditional dogmatics? But everything turns out quite differently. However, the first attack comes from an unexpected side.

My image in Der Spiegel

On the whole, the influential political journal *Der Spiegel* had supported my concern for reform. So there was no reason to refuse to allow it to look at the proofs. But in the issue of 16 September 1974, as a result of his own resentment or on higher instructions, the churches' editor Manfred Müller, a former chaplain, caricatures my book even before it appears. As my Catholic colleague Otto Hermann Pesch writes to me on 18 September 1974, such a preliminary report, which no one can check, has a 'devastating effect'; some readers would get the impression that I was wanting to develop my attacks on Rome in a new, more comprehensive, way.

I had already drafted an answer, well thought out and highly polished, 'My *Spiegel* Image' (for what follows, English readers should know that *Spiegel* is the German for mirror). The editors of *Der Spiegel* see it but refuse to print it – too big a blunder? Now I ask the *Frankfurter Allgemeine Zeitung*, which so far has pursued the strategy of either ignoring *Der Spiegel* or just quoting it indirectly. But the editorial conference decides to publish my response on 21 September, 'as its importance extends far beyond the occasion and is of general interest regardless of its polemical approach'.

I can quote only my introduction here:

> Is this to be my *Spiegel* image? A radical church critic and destroyer of dogmas, who with a smile, as the accompanying photograph shows, 'dethrones' the most sacred truths of faith, deprives his church of its foundation and in so doing lacks only one thing: the courage once and for all to part company with it? That is what people would like me to do: in the shady papers of traditionalist groups and, one hears with amazement, now also in the enlightened *Spiegel* (dated 16 September 1974). But that by way of anticipation: I cannot recognize myself in this *Spiegel* image. And why is there such a difference between looking out of a mirror and looking into it? The mirror distorts. In the showcases of publicity, caricature can sometimes be amusing. And here the author of the article, for all the bestial seriousness that is put on show, displays stylistic delight: from the 'aggrieved' Vatican to the dogma which 'gets into difficulties' whereas Küng 'moves back'.

In this style it also goes on to the difficult theological statements, and attacks the distortions of my account, from the virgin birth to the resurrection. Then comes the general conclusion:

Haven't people at *Der Spiegel*, which has given an instructive and precise account of my cause in many articles, noticed the fatal coalition of interests into which they are being drawn with Catholic traditionalist groups and the Vatican inquisition of the faith? Is *Der Spiegel* now to be as interested in my departure from the church as Catholic extremists in Rome and elsewhere? Is the old game again to be played out here between the extreme right and the extreme left, to liquidate the critical centre? Are the 'church high-ups' here to be called on in all seriousness to 'stop tolerating' this theologian and 'if possible' 'help' him to leave the church by 'removing his licence to teach'? Without any irony, given the way in which this *Spiegel* article has been written it can stand unabbreviated and unchanged in any traditional-istic inquisitorial pamphlet. However, for me any left-wing Inquisition would be no better than a right-wing one, just a bit more hypocritical.

I end with a request: 'It would be good if *Der Spiegel* went on pursuing its declared aim of providing information and enlightenment to the public in matters of religion and theology as well.' My whole response is now a bold direct confrontation with *Der Spiegel*, which is also taken up by the *Basler Nachrichten* and the *Neue Luzerner Nachrichten*. How will it turn out? Wisely none of those theologians who envy me my publicity says a word. This is too dangerous ground.

Dialogue with Der Spiegel's founder, Rudolf Augstein

Happily, however, after this unusual confrontation *Der Spiegel* doesn't wage a minor war against my book and my theology. Granted, the churches' editor is defended in a *Spiegel* 'house bulletin', but that was the least that the editorial board had to do for a colleague who had been censured for his effective publicity. *Der Spiegel* opens a new Vatican series with a quotation from *On Being a Christian*, and on 22 October 1974 this leads me to write a personal letter to its editor, Rudolf Augstein: 'For all the differences in position, it is important to me that no false fronts are formed and that *Der Spiegel* does not lose credibility in church and theological matters, which, as for example this first article of the Vatican series shows, it thoroughly deserves. At any rate that should not be my concern.'

Rudolf Augstein had become a public figure in 1972 with a 500-page theo-logical book on 'Jesus Son of Man',[16] for which he had evidently been badly advised by his ghost writer. The specialists had torn it apart because of its ten-dentious selection and interpretation of scriptural texts and the arbitrary use of specialist literature. I had been more restrained than others towards this book, because I saw behind it the real concern and the deep disappointment of the former Catholic at the blocking of reform at Vatican II and wanted to respect that. At any rate Augstein's last chapter, to which the whole book leads, seems to me worth serious consideration: 'What will happen without him?' Yes, what will happen without Jesus Christ?

Augstein's clear alternative to the Christian faith is: 'There is no God whom we know or about whom we can speak' (p. 408). We must 'live without religion' (p. 422). We are not spared 'being suspended over nothingness' (p. 423). However, we must 'survive' (p. 423). But how? By 'coping with life in a rational, utterly banal way' (p. 425). We must attempt 'to make ourselves, our life and society the best we can in meaningful work, meaningful joy and meaningful hatred' (p. 425). 'If we improve nothing and fail, at least we are no worse off than before' (p. 426).

So that is the alternative to Christian belief in God. I respect it and don't want to belittle it. Often atheists live more credible lives than Christians. Nevertheless I have questions for Augstein. Are we to bring up our children and the younger generation without faith to such a rational and banal way of coping with life: without a final orientation, without deeper meaning, without higher ideals, without a great and living hope? Are they to have no other support than themselves and their reason, which can so easily deceive, confuse, lead astray, given over to all the addictions, compulsions, ideologies of our time? Aren't we to be able to give them answers to the questions of human life which aren't repressed by any ban on questions?

I begin with these words in my 'Word on Sunday' broadcast on First German Television on 3 December 1974, the First Sunday in Advent (although this and my two following 'Words on Sunday' were well received by the public, I was later always kept off this television broadcast, which was controlled by the hierarchy). I didn't think it worth mentioning Augstein's insinuation that 'the undeterred Swiss and Council adviser Hans Küng, born in 1928', would probably, like Rahner, 'if it came to an oath in Rome, insist that there are inerrantly defined doctrines of the Popes and councils' (pp. 126f.). I'm no Rahner. In my letter to Augstein I dryly remark: 'I haven't answered the groundless insinuation in your Jesus book that if it came to an oath in Rome I too would give in, but I think that I've refuted it in recent years by word and deed.'

Finally I remind Augstein that I once thought 'a personal conversation with you (and no publicity afterwards) would be useful to clarify positions on both sides. It might become clearer through such a conversation than through publications how serious is the controversy in which I am engaged with Rome. I don't know whether such a conversation in a private context would appeal to you.'

Rudolf Augstein's reply on 4 November 1974 is friendly: 'It would be good for us to meet.' He says on his coming article: 'My review, which is not meant to be a "review", will, I hope, be as little unfair as your behaviour towards me has been so far. Of course it can't be "restrained". And surely it shouldn't be? Restraint in this case would mean that I adopted a position only on the periphery or not at all. Look forward to seeing you as soon as possible, Yours, Rudolf Augstein.'

On 8 November 1974 I send Rudolf Augstein my statement at the press conference on *On Being a Christian* and observe: 'Whether my post-infallibilistic theology – which is more than the resumption of a controversy (that for me is already settled) – deserves censure from the Vatican, I would answer with a no and a yes. My book certainly doesn't stabilize the system; that much can be said about it now. And there can be no question of the "conversion of a rebel" (thus the *Deutsche Zeitung*); it's more a matter of going on calmly and consistently. Be that as it may, I look forward eagerly to your "review" and hope that it takes us further. And I'm delighted that you're interested in a meeting.'

Augstein's article on *On Being a Christian* proves gracious. He has confirmed what he indicated in his last letter, so I can reply: 'Your article certainly isn't restrained, nor is it unfair. Only the triple charge of "untruthfulness" – regardless of the individual arguments – seems to me to be unfair and misguided: why must I be untruthful if I argue for another well-founded position which *you* think untrue?' Like other ex-Catholics, Augstein seems unable to get over the fact that someone who is subjecting his Catholic Church to radical criticism nevertheless wants to remain in this church.

I say that despite all the differences in basic positions we can sort that out in a conversation. 'For today let me content myself with thanking you for dealing so thoroughly with my book and correcting the false impression given by the Müller article. I'm also honestly grateful that this time no immediate journalistic reaction is being forced on me. But very soon, contrary to your expectations, a renewed controversy could be forced on me by Rome. Though what do they have there against so constructive a book as *On Being a Christian*?'

An unwelcome programme of reform

We may recall that without the least discussion (even Cardinal Döpfner says nothing to me), without any serious theological investigation, certainly without formal proceedings, in its declaration of 17 February 1975 on the conclusion of the doctrinal proceedings against *The Church* and *Infallible?* the German Conference of Bishops added a third part, about *On Being a Christian*. In it the conference made the sober official statement that while 'its theological efforts and pastoral aim can be recognized', it is possible to note 'a series of statements which, it seems, cannot be made to accord with the above-mentioned principles'. And then 'for example' more or less the whole list of traditional dogmatics is cited: 'christology, the doctrine of the Trinity, the theology of the church and the sacraments, the position of Mary in salvation history'.

So my book, which is a help to countless men and women, is to be publicly disparaged by the conference of bishops and its theological and journalistic helpers. This is an own goal: it could have considerably improved the largely unsatisfactory state of proclamation, preaching, religious instruction and adult education by giving a solid basis to what it is to be a Christian at the level of present-day research and spelling it out. I receive approval for *On Being a Christian* almost every day from both Catholic and Protestant Christians. Over three evenings from 12 to 14 June 1975 before an audience of 5000 at the Evangelical Kirchentag in Frankfurt I discuss with the Protestant theologian and journalist Heinz Zahrnt, who has done much for the contemporary under-standing of the question of God through his book *The Question of God. Protestant Theology in the Twentieth Century* (1966), the basic questions of being a Christian: 'Who is a Christian? Who is Christ? And who is God?' My introduction is given tremendous applause: 'Here I stand as a Catholic Christian. I can do no other!' After this truly ecumenical dialogue many people ask themselves what still divides the confessions.

But what evidently stirs up the Catholic bishops even more than any dogmatic statements is the repetition of my 'demands for reform' (which are also those of countless other Catholics). They even give page numbers (English pp. 491f., 525-27) in their censure. Evidently in the view of these 'lords of our faith' one may not even mention such concerns any more. They are too uncomfortable, too blasphemous, too popular. So I shall briefly sum them up for the present-day reader to assess. Ecumenically, there must be genuine, increasing integration of the different churches: through reform and reciprocal recognition of church ministries; through a common liturgy of the word, open communion and increasingly frequent common celebrations of the eucharist; through common construction and common use of churches and other buildings; through a common fulfilment of service to society; through increasing integration of theological faculties and of religious instruction; through concrete plans for union worked out by the leaders of the churches at national and universal levels.

For the Catholic Church in particular, what remained unresolved at Vatican II must be demanded with increasing urgency, fought for and finally inplemented by both congregations and their leaders: election of bishops by representative bodies of the clergy and laity; the election, too, of the Pope by a body consisting of bishops and laity; a personal decision by priests and bishops whether they want to marry or remain unmarried, depending on their personal vocation; the right of the laity to share in decision-making with their pastors and bishops in a system of checks and balances; equal rights for women in church law, in the decision-making bodies of the church and theology, and also the possibility of ordination; a constructive attitude to sexuality; birth control also by 'artificial' means in accordance with the conscientious decision of the partners.

These are the reform concerns of countless Catholics all over the world. Of course what is wrong with these reforms isn't discussed. Meanwhile the Vatican has made tremendous progress in the restoration of the Roman system, as is shown by a five-part *Spiegel* series beginning on 24 October 1974 entitled 'Inside the Vatican'. It gives a very accurate description of personnel and management methods in the Vatican City State. That each of the five articles is prefaced by a quotation from *On Being a Christian* can't have made my book any more popular at headquarters in Rome.

At the same time the commission for 'reform' of the Code of Canon Law is quietly working away under the presidency of the reactionary cardinal Pericle Felice; it is merely making a few formal improvements to church law as it was before the Council in order to prevent any reforms. Here the already finished text on the sacrament of marriage appears 'very unsatisfactorily under various perspectives (biblical, theological, ecclesiological, anthropological, psychological and canonical)', as the well-informed Council theologian Giuseppe Alberigo, seeking allies outside Italy, had written to me (18 February 1974). On 21 January 1977 it becomes evident that even in Italy the norms of church law on sexual morality can no longer be established easily. The law to legalize the termination of pregnancy resolved on by parliament comes into force despite the most vigorous opposition from the Vatican and the Conference of Bishops. But a more fundamental reform concern lies in the background.

Towards a revaluation of women

The discussion of *On Being a Christian* and my theses on the position of women in the church and society overlap. The issue is far more than the sacrament of marriage. For the new version of church law prepared in the Vatican by celibate clergy is utterly male-centred in the pre-conciliar spirit. At the end of 1975 the Tübingen Catholic faculty is united in feeling that it must react to these conservative developments.

Within the group of editors of the *Theologische Quartalschrift* – the oldest theological journal in the world still in existence, founded in 1819 – it is decided to produce a thematic issue on 'Women in Church and Society' to be edited by the Old Testament scholar Herbert Haag and the dogmatic theologian Walter Kasper (2/1976). On 15 January 1976, on top of everything the Roman Congregation for the Doctrine of the Faith publishes a 'Declaration on Certain Questions Concerning Sexual Ethics'. It is disappointing all along the line, and the editors of the *Theologische Quartalschrift* now believe that they owe it even more to their task as teachers of theology 'to make a contribution to the clarification of questions of content and method by a balanced statement'.

The issue is introduced by two professors of sociology, Rosemarie Nave-Herz and Hilde Kaufmann, who offer a survey of the changed role of women in our society and the change in women's self-understanding. At the centre of the issue are an article by our church lawyer Johannes Neumann on 'The Position of Women in the Catholic Church Today' and right next to it – agreed with Neumann – my 16 theses on 'The Position of Women in Church and Society'. How explosive these theses are is evident from the headline chosen by the editors of the *New York Times Magazine* of 23 May 1976, 'Feminism: A New

Reformation', with a subtitle 'A Dissident Catholic Theologian Nails his Theses for the Liberation of Women to the Church Door'. I'm not very keen on the parallel with Martin Luther. In any case it isn't historically certain that Luther in fact 'nailed' his theses to the door of the castle church in Wittenberg; he may simply have proclaimed them and sent them out. At all events my theses are now disseminated by the most varied media all over the world, hardly to the delight of the Roman Curia.

In fact in these 16 theses, in line with *On Being a Christian*, I develop a comprehensive reform programme on the position of women in church and society. The most controversial is thesis 15, which I shall therefore quote verbatim:

> There are no serious theological reasons against a presbyterate of women. The exclusively male constitution of the college of the Twelve must be understood in terms of the social and cultural situation of the time. The reasons given in the tradition for the exclusion of women (through the woman sin came into the world, woman was created second, women are not created in the image of God, a woman is not a full member of the church, the taboo of menstruation) cannot appeal to Jesus, and bear witness to a fundamental theological defamation of women. In view of the functions performed by women as leaders in the earliest church (Phoebe, Prisca) and the completely changed status of women in business, scholarship, culture, state and society today, the admission of women to the presbyterate should not be delayed any longer. Jesus and the early church were ahead of their time in the revaluation of women; today's Catholic Church is lagging far behind its time and also behind other Christian churches.

Thesis 16 forms the conclusion:

> It would be a misunderstanding of ecumenism to delay long overdue reforms such as the ordination of women in the Catholic Church with an appeal to the greater restraint in more conservative 'sister churches'. Instead of being used as an excuse, such churches should be invited to reform; here some Protestant churches can serve as a model for the Catholic Church.

I am horrified when I read all this again today. Not at the content, but at the fact that even after 25 years, in essential points these 16 theses still await fulfilment and can be printed virtually unchanged in 2001/2 in my short book *Women in Christianity*. They were also backed by my colleagues in the faculty and a majority of leading theologians, and supported by broad areas of the Catholic population. The Vatican surely noted them. Be this as it may, on 27 January 1977 a long 'Declaration on the Admission of Women to the Ministerial Priesthood' was published by the Vatican Congregation for the Doctrine of the Faith – likewise exclusively made up of celibate males! – on the orders of Pope Paul VI, which was surprising in its terseness. The central statement is that the Catholic Church 'in fidelity to the example of the Lord, does not consider herself authorized to admit women to priestly ordination'. As if Jesus himself, who was no priest, had ordained men to the priesthood! Is that in the Bible? Later Cardinal Ratzinger, on behalf of John Paul II, declares the view that the ordination of women is against the will of God to be 'infallible doctrine', referring to the ordinary magisterium of the whole episcopate. Infallible?

But I hear from members of the Pontifical Biblical Commission involved in the preparation of the Declaration that it passed by a majority of 12 to 5 the thesis that the church can indeed entrust the ministries of the eucharist and of reconciliation to women without offending against the intention of Jesus Christ; the Doctrinal Congregation constructed its own biblical arguments which have nothing to do with what the Biblical Commission presented to them.

In these events, too, it once again becomes clear that in principle historical–critical exegesis does not find its way into official Roman teaching as represented by the Doctrinal Congregation, so even reforms justified by the Bible can be blocked. If reforms were implemented there would have to be change, but if dogmas are repeated, the old balance of power can be maintained and with it an outdated picture of women. Instead of the *aggiornamento* of the Council there is now a post-conciliar immobility in all areas.

Against a split in the church

As we saw, many Council documents were the results of compromises forced on the progressive majority at the Council by the conservative Curia, which dominated the Council apparatus. But compromises mean that both sides refer to them in different ways, and this contributes to confusion and polarization in the post-conciliar church. Here very soon at the extreme right of the spectrum a group comes into prominence which initially enjoys the sympathy of the Roman Curia but is finally called to order, not least at the wish of Pope Paul VI himself. For once the practices of the Inquisition are used against the 'right wing'; in public this immediately provokes comparisons with my own 'case' and requires me to make a statement.

While I resolutely support reforms, I am equally resolutely against any split in the church. We must above all avoid the mistakes of modern Protestantism – sectarian encapsulation, mutual excommunication and the constant splitting off of churches. We must never become the church only of a particular party, mentality, age group. Even conservative people, whether individuals or groups, must have a home in the Catholic Church. Being Christians together is more important than being traditional or progressive.

Convinced of this, I now put in a good word for the traditionalist followers of the former Archbishop of Dakar, Marcel Lefebvre, the 'Priestly Society of St Pius X'. On 6 May 1975 in Fribourg, Switzerland, episcopal approval is withdrawn from this 'priestly fellowship' and so its priestly seminary in Ecône in the Valais has no foundation in church law. Thereupon traditionalist Catholics bitterly complain that Rome is treating progressive theologians far more leniently – me in particular.

In an article in the London *Times* of 28 August 1975 with the headline 'Rome Must Find a Way to Cope With the Growing Conflict within the Church' and a long interview with Hanno Helbling, the features editor of the *Neue Zürcher Zeitung*, on 3 October 1975 I take a stand on Ecône. I call for justice for the traditionalists too and plead for an overcoming of the polarization in the Catholic Church and for mutual tolerance. I regret this conflict for the sake of those concerned. I have personal experience of the psychological burden of lasting harsh treatment by the church authorities.

However, contrary to the widespread parallels which are drawn I must emphatically point to the differences between me and Ecône and Mgr Lefebvre: I have never disputed the Catholic orthodoxy of the Roman authorities nor discredited the Second Vatican Council as heretical. Nor have I ever founded my own ('progressive') association or attempted to implement my view in an exclusivist doctrinaire way by the training of priests or even having my own priestly seminary. Any tendencies towards splits are alien to me. I really cannot understand why a separate association and a separate priestly seminary have to be founded for the concerns of Archbishop Lefebvre; there are truly more than enough conservative priestly seminaries and bishops in our church.

On the other hand – and I address these words to Rome – I also do not see why in some circumstances one cannot celebrate a eucharist in Latin; we have done that at the annual meeting of *Concilium* with theologians from different language groups, all of whom of course understand Latin. Nor do I see why Catholics who still want to practise the old communion by mouth instead of communion in the hand (which is still older!) should be prevented from doing so. Not everything among us needs to be regulated in a uniform way, even when it comes to renewal. There should be as much freedom as possible, as much compulsion as necessary and – according to Augustine – in all things love. Or at least justice.

Justice for the traditionalists too

In one respect Archbishop Lefebvre and his followers can and should be given their due: it cannot be disputed that in some cases the development after the Council has gone further than the Council decreed, not only *de facto*, but also *de iure*, i.e. with the assent of the church government. For example, according to the Council's Constitution on the Liturgy, in principle Latin as the language of the church of the so-called Latin rite should have been preserved; the vernacular was allowed as an exception only for individual parts. This is a lazy compromise which calls for a clear solution. After only a few years Pope Paul VI allows all the Catholic liturgy – including the eucharistic prayer (the 'canon' of the 'mass') – in the vernacular.

This is right. By no means all the church's problems over the following years and decades can be solved in accordance with the letter of the Council documents. Now in particular, ten years after the conclusion of the Council, well-considered progress beyond the Council documents is necessary on many questions. Indeed the present stagnation and polarization can be overcome only if Rome and the bishops consistently – and by no means ultra-progressively – seek and establish a solution to the questions left open by the Council in the light of the New Testament and the great Catholic tradition, explain it sufficiently to the people – which does not always happen – and finally resolutely implement it.

The *Neue Zürcher Zeitung* reports details of the Roman dealings with Archbishop Lefebvre, which according to the paper represent the clumsy use of an old instrument, the Inquisition, in a modern situation. In fact the Curia doesn't deny what Lefebvre attests: three Curia cardinals entrusted with his case had asked him to attend a 'conversation' ('*entretien*') about 'some points' in the visitation report on Ecône. But this conversation – on 13 February 1975, continued on 3 March – had proved to be an interrogation about the content of a statement on Vatican II made earlier by Lefebvre. Lefebvre, alone, had been confronted with three cardinal prefects of Roman congregations and a secretary. The session had been taped. A copy of this tape had been first promised, but then refused him; at first he was also to get a transcript, but later was only allowed to look at it. Once again, the Inquisition fears the light of publicity.

All this confirms to me that a similar torture would have been inflicted on me had I agreed to such a 'conversation' ('colloquium'), with no opportunity of winning the 'trial' which in any case wouldn't have been an orderly one. This is the quite normal style of the arbitrary Roman administration. In Rome there is still a tremendous lack of modern legal order and practice. Therefore my commentary on these occurrences must also make it plain that: 'As I have called for justice for myself, so I call for justice for our traditionalists, though that does not mean that I approve of their views. It is wrong that they are being subjected to "conversations" which are in fact interrogations; that promises are given which later are not kept; that the arrogance of office is practised against them in Roman self-glorification. In short, no Inquisition against Ecône' (*Neue Zürcher Zeitung*, 3 October 1975).

Rome should have thought of other ways of coping with conflicts. It seems to me that this unhappy heightening of the conflict could have been avoided with rather more understanding for the persons concerned, open and self-critical conversations and better theology, orientated on the New Testament instead of on medieval church law. Be this as it may, on 10 May 1976 I get a letter from the group centred on Ecône expressing their delight that I have also acknowledged the authentic zeal and idealism of their priestly brotherhood. They invite me to visit Ecône one day so that I can see what it is like; if necessary this could be done incognito. I reply (24 May 1976) that I'm delighted to hear that this priestly brotherhood doesn't reject the Second Vatican Council as such and that I would have no objections to visiting Ecône at some point.

In July 1976 the Pope suspends Archbishop Lefebvre from his priestly and episcopal office, but Lefebvre continues to celebrate his masses according to the old Latin rite and thousands attend. When he had been elected Superior General of the missionary order of the Spiritans in 1962 he had also made inaugural visits to the houses of the order in Germany. He travelled quite modestly in a Citroen 2 CV. He was jovial and on his departure was surrounded by many admirers. Unfortunately, an eyewitness tells me later, the 2 CV wouldn't start. Lefebvre spent some time tinkering with the engine, and lo and behold the car started. There was general jubilation: 'Our great Superior General can even repair cars!' However, this jubilation subsided later when it became known that Lefebvre staged the same repair act on other visits in precisely the same way.

On 7 July 2007 Benedict XVI again allows the medieval Tridentine Latin mass in the face of the resistance of many bishops, for in his memoirs Joseph Ratzinger had spoken out more extensively and bitterly against the liturgical reforms of Vatican II than about any development after the Council (apart from the Tübingen student unrest). However, this could result in a new split in the church – into congregations with a medieval Latin mass and congregations with the Vatican II eucharistic celebration orientated more on earliest Christianity. Thus there is an incomprehensible revaluation of the medieval mass, which is remote from Christian origins, and at the same time a dangerous failure to understand the pastorally destructive effects of such a new split.

I never visited Ecône, since the controversy over *On Being a Christian* increasingly came to a head, in a highly unpleasant way.

A dirty game

I want to be fair: in all these controversies I could hardly imagine a better negotiating partner among the German bishops than Cardinal Julius Döpfner. And I concede that with my theological position and consistent demands for reform I am an extremely uncomfortable person to have around. Doubtless in my case Döpfner took a great deal of trouble – always also in the interests of the hierarchy – to arrive at a *détente* and if possible a constructive solution.

On the other hand I cannot conceal the fact that the cardinal didn't ultimately prove to be an honest broker in the conflict. To be so he should have constantly and honestly kept me completely in the picture. But he maintains regular contact with the Curia, exchanges information, makes agreements. When it comes to the

Roman authorities he is, as Karl Rahner once maliciously said to me during the Council, 'a rubber lion'. He has again left me uncertain about the latest Roman declaration against me, although it is already on his desk. Nor has he indicated to me that even before the 'stop' to the proceedings on *The Church* and *Infallible?*, a troop of theologians has been summoned up behind my back, as with *Infallible?*, to write a book – not to give *On Being a Christian* a scholarly evaluation but to put it under concentrated new fire. The German Faith Commission has prompted the new book, entitled 'Discussion of Hans Küng's *On Being a Christian*' and presents it in Rome as a counter-action against me, the theologian who is so fearfully dangerous for the church.

This time the organizer of the book isn't Karl Rahner but – and I am surprised at this – my fellow-countryman and former mentor Hans Urs von Balthasar.

I have few theologians more to thank than him, and I acknowledge that in *My Struggle for Freedom*. He wrote the best introduction to Karl Barth's theology and advised me on the choice of my dissertation topic. He read my manuscript, suggested various improvements and finally published *Justification* in his own Johannes Verlag. Until most recently he remained my always stimulating conversation partner and found even my book *Infallible?* as he told me, 'a very powerful book'.

But at a very early stage Karl Barth told me that Balthasar thought that in my case 'the chicken had become fully-fledged rather too early'. I was never interested in joining the lay order of unmarried men which Balthasar planned but never really realized. Theologically, from Rome onwards I had stood on my own feet and three years after my dissertation received my chair in fundamental theology in Tübingen. Balthasar would very much have liked the chair, but Rome blocked him. Again, two years later I was an official Council theologian, whereas Balthasar, whom the Bishop of Basle, like many pastors, thought an arrogant intellectual, had remained in Basle and regarded the Council with increasingly sceptical, indeed hostile, eyes. And this man who once complained to me that his much-praised books, such as the one on Bernanos, hardly sold above 800 copies, was soon able to see copies of *On Being a Christian* moving beyond the 100,000 mark. This must have been difficult for him.

Hans Urs von Balthasar is the man who, having disparaged the first volume of his own *Theodramatics* as 'gipsy theology', attacks his former 'protégé'. As soon as I hear of the book I write to him in a friendly way to ask him whether my information is correct, and if so, whether I may be allowed to write a response, as is usual in discussion volumes: 'I really cannot think that you would do something of this kind without telling me about it' (10 October 1975). A hand-written reply comes as always on a postcard, this time frosty: 'Since you always know such things before they happen, it seemed to me superfluous to tell you about it' (14 October 1975). To my second letter, which says that he hasn't answered my second question whether he would accept a reply from me to the criticism (16 October 1975), he replies with the excuse, 'One hears better when everyone isn't talking at once' (7 November 1975). I suspect what is coming my way. But in the end Balthasar doesn't have the courage, like Karl Rahner before him, to name himself as editor of the volume. Instead, he commends himself in a private circular letter to certain Swiss clergy as a 'guide in a foggy landscape'. The obscurantist himself as a guide: what a pity, I think.

No final say for the accused

Grünewald Verlag of Mainz also refuses to publish an answer from me in the composite volume, even though it would be useful in clarifying the substantive question. They don't hesitate to use my name and the title of my book – 'Discussion of Hans Küng's *On Being a Christian*' – in large letters in the title and in publicity, to propagate 'being an anti-Christian' – still without an answer from Hans Küng.

The publisher Jakob Laubach trivializes and excuses this denigration in his memoirs, which I have already cited: although I would have been content with a brief answer to all the criticism, possibly even just one page, he allows himself the excuse, 'Perhaps the book would have become too big ...' At any rate his comment added from the perspective of 1997 reconciles me: 'I thought the later "measures" against Hans Küng utterly inappropriate. And it is high time, particularly on the part of those in office in the church, to recognize his merits for a contemporary and generally understandable account of the Christian faith' (p. 109). But that is twenty years later: too late, after all the machinations against my book from the official Catholic side, which also made a negative impression on some Protestants. In 2007 a Protestant woman pastor wrote to me: 'If I had read your book 50 or 40 years ago, It would have improved my preaching, teaching and pastoral care.'

To Karl Lehmann I express my surprise and displeasure that he is 'taking part in this enterprise which is doubtful from the start'. 'Of course I cannot have anything against several authors discussing my book. But it should be an authentic discussion and not one without the author. Individual contributions may be more or less objective, but the context is wrong from the start. And since I already know the standpoints of some of the authors, I expect nothing good to come of it. At any rate, with this composite volume I am again being forced into a confrontation which I do not want in this form but nevertheless have to endure ... I simply do not understand how something like this is still possible in the Catholic Church in 1976, above all with colleagues all of whom are known personally to me' (13 January 1976).

The question for me now is, 'What shall I do?' Publish yet another composite volume like the one against the theologians who attacked *Infallible*? That seems to me too involved and too difficult – who would contribute to it in this exacerbated situation? So should I simply keep quiet? The opponents who have been gathered are too important and their attacks too vigorous. They so to speak throw me to the wolves of the Doctrinal Congregation. They are backed by a theological pamphlet by my former Tübingen colleague, Professor Leo Scheffczyk of Munich, under the title 'Faith Breaking Out or Breaking Up?' and an article by the equally ultra-conservative Gregorian dogmatic theologian Jean Galot SJ, both of whom take me to task for various heresies. The Swiss church newspaper for the clergy and other church magazines also have as an insert a leaflet about 'Discussion of Hans Küng's *On Being a Christian*' which is so defamatory that I have to protest to the editors. Finally the cases of the dismissed professors Stephan Pfürtner, Franz Schupp, Horst Hermann and also Uta Ranke-Heinemann (daughter of the German Federal President), and those of the numerous pastors, chaplains, teachers of religion and lay theologians who have been silenced, are a warning to me to be 'sober and vigilant' in accordance with the biblical saying.

So I decide on resistance. I mustn't yield to the superior power of these dogmatic theologians. I now hold the seminar for the summer semester of 1976 on my opponents' composite volume instead of on the Apostles' Creed. And to fight back I decide to produce a long article in my defence. On 1 April 1976 I write to the features editor of the *Frankfurter Allgemeine Zeitung*, Marcel Reich-Ranicki, who with Walter and Inge Jens has already been a guest in my house. 'I have made great efforts to reduce the controversy with my eleven opponents along with a description of the situation of present-day Catholic theology to this number of pages. You will see for yourself that this is probably the decisive controversy at present over the course of Catholic theology.'

Agreement from exegetes

In fact on 22 May 1976 the *Frankfurter Allgemeine Zeitung*, at that time liberal and well-disposed towards me, prints uncut my 'Answer to My Critics – Theology for Today's Men and Women?'[17] It was clear to me from the start that I mustn't give an answer on extremely difficult theological problems in the features section of a daily newspaper in dogmatic and scholastic terms, but in language understandable by everyone and in a polished style – without cynicism and unfairness, but not without wit and irony. Here are the introductory sentences:

> The doves are now also cooing it from the rooftops of the *palazzi* of Rome: the dispute – apparently put aside a year ago – is going on, unfortunately. One bit of progress is that the Pope and bishops seem initially to have convinced themselves of the inadvisability of authoritarian disciplinary measures. But now it is the professors of theology who are continuing the dispute. There were still fifteen of them in the infallibility debate. This time – after refusals – they have arrived in the strength of a football team: eleven, once more against one. However, they have vigorous support in the stands

from a handsome number of theological banner-wavers and the trumpets of arch-conservative Catholic postillions. Isn't the individual's cause lost from the start? What is one individual to do when many are camped in front of his goal? How is he to catch all the balls when each player has brought his own? He would need at least eleven arms and at the same time to be able to guard against tackles, shoves and fouls. So what is to be done?

In truth this 'Discussion of Hans Küng's *On Being a Christian*' is less a discussion volume than a partisan work by carefully chosen professors, the majority of whom are members of the episcopal or papal faith commission, which is likewise one-sided in its composition, 'all honourable men'. The contributions of Walter Kasper, my Tübingen colleague, and Karl Lehmann are objective and fair. The Mainz dogmatic theologian Theodor Schneider is constructive; he concedes the notorious difficulties of the classical doctrine of the Trinity, endorses criticism of it in the light of the New Testament and recognizes my concern for continuity with the great tradition: 'Küng consciously stands on the ground of the church's doctrine of the Trinity and correctly reproduces its content in all brevity. In the light of this it would be a mistake to impute "heretical" thoughts to him or to want to insinuate such an impression.'

The exegetes in particular recognize my position: orthodoxy isn't their problem nor suspicion of heresy their concern. The Freiburg Old Testament scholar Alfons Deissler remarks: 'Here the essentials of the Old Testament message of God come out as they rarely do in non-exegetical literature.' The Vienna New Testament scholar Jacob Kremer comments: 'The book offers a "by no means uncritical" , largely "excellent evaluation of the wealth of exegetical investigations which even professional exegetes can hardly keep up with"; this may be reckoned "among the best accounts of Jesus of Nazareth in recent times".'

Even later, there is no serious criticism on the basis of historical–critical research, which is so strongly present in my book. The article 'Responsible Faith' by the Protestant Zurich exegete Eduard Schweizer (*Neue Zürcher Zeitung*, 30 November/1 December 1974), which is not in the composite volume and which agrees with me all down the line, can be taken as representative of most German-language exegetes.

But unfortunately some colleagues from Catholic dogmatics are not as objective as this Protestant exegete. One significant example must be mentioned here, which sheds especially clear light on the basic questions under debate.

'No understanding without initial goodwill'

What is most disappointing in the whole volume – and I cannot conceal that here – is the article by Joseph Ratzinger, who evidently was deeply shaken in his Catholic faith, or rather his theology, by my book. How, I ask myself, can someone who was once such a kind and skilled colleague fail to show his former Tübingen partner any of the objectivity and fairness which are the presuppositions for a scholarly discussion?

My answer is brief and keeps to Ratzinger's statements, which speak for themselves: 'Should I perhaps go into the countless misinterpretations, insinuations, condemnations from the dogmatic theologian Joseph Ratzinger?' His verdict on me is grotesque: 'being a Christian' is a 'label which in reality remains an empty formula'; what is Christian is demoted 'from its life-and-death seriousness to something of questionable literary interest'; Christian faith is 'made rotten from its foundations'; the fellowship of the church disappears 'literally into meaninglessness'; such teaching becomes an 'unconcealed presumption'; a theology 'without a location and ultimately not binding'; 'so to speak going its own way, alone with itself and modern rationality' into a 'lack of seriousness'; a 'school certainty, a party certainty but not a certainty for which one can live and die, a certainty for comfortable times in which the ultimate is not demanded'; such a theology 'ultimately lands up in the abstruse', 'doesn't go anywhere'. Faced with such falsifications and slanders, I can only say 'No, I don't want to discuss at that level.'

'I would only ask my readers for that initial goodwill without which there can be no understanding,' writes Joseph Ratzinger, now Pope Benedict XVI, in 2007 in the Foreword to his book *Jesus of Nazareth*. He never showed this 'initial goodwill' to my *On Being a Christian* at that time. Now, after 30 years, in 2007, I understand Joseph Ratzinger's theological position and motivation better, and why he evidently met my book with initial antipathy, with which there can be no understanding.

Jesus of Nazareth 'has had a long gestation', Joseph Ratzinger writes in the first sentence of his Foreword, and refers to the completely uncritical Jesus books of our youth. In fact initial antipathy is a factor in this long gestation:

- When the student Ratzinger flees from the historical–critical exegesis of his New Testament teacher Friedrich Wilhelm Maier into dogma and rebukes his Munich theological faculty for showing scepticism about Rome and the 1950 Marian dogma;
- When the Tübingen Professor Ratzinger in his 1968 *Introduction to Christianity* offers a complete caricature of research into Jesus and shows no understanding whatsoever of exegetes such as Rudolf Bultmann and Ernst Käsemann;
- When as Prefect of the Congregation for the Doctrine of the Faith Ratzinger brutally launches proceedings over 24 years against other Jesus books (by Schillebeeckx, Boff, Sobrino), against liberation theology and against an authentic Asian and African theology;
- When Ratzinger as Pope Benedict XVI in his 2006 Regensburg speech, imprisoned in the Hellenistic theology of the fourth and fifth centuries, throws

out both the Enlightenment and the historical research of Adolf von Harnack as 'de-Hellenization';

- When finally Ratzinger works into his 2007 Jesus book, with its 'long gestation' texts, lectures and sermons which were obviously written earlier, and time and again, while calling the historical method 'indispensable', robs it of its force wherever traditional view or dogmas are touched on.

This book is 'in no way an exercise of the magisterium ... Everyone is free, then, to contradict me,' Ratzinger writes in the Foreword, and massive objections from specialists have followed – after the extravagant praise of his naive admirers.[18] First of all it is striking that in his Jesus book the author postpones historically precarious questions from the virgin birth to the 'empty tomb' to a planned second volume, and interprets Jesus' walking on the lake, the transformation of water into wine and Peter's abundant catch of fish in symbolic theological terms without saying anything about the historicity of these narratives. Contrary to the broad consensus of exegesis, he doesn't begin from Mark as the earliest Gospel but makes the Gospel of John as a whole, written around AD 90 (which of course also contains earlier material), the historical source of an eye-witness, instead of following the example of the conservative Tübingen exegete Martin Hengel, whom he elsewhere quotes with approval, and understanding it as a 'wide-ranging but by no means completely free "Jesus poem"'.

The method is unhistorical because the dogmatic theologian Joseph Ratzinger goes about things the wrong way round. He reads the Synoptic Gospels in the light of the Gospel of John, and understands Johannine christology completely in terms of the dogmas of the councils of Nicaea (fourth century) and Chalcedon (fifth century), so that according to him the Jesus of history already confesses himself to be 'of one substance' with the Father. Basically, Ratzinger hasn't written a historical book but a learned spiritual interpretation of scripture – leaping over all historical problems – which already finds a hidden christology in the notion of the kingdom of God, and also in the Sermon on the Mount and the Lord's Prayer, a christology of which according to other Synoptic witnesses Jesus evidently wasn't aware.

Joseph Ratzinger could have already written such a Jesus book in Tübingen. It confirms the insight I already had on his departure from Tübingen (cf. Chapter III above): Joseph Ratzinger has stood still because as a Bavarian Catholic in the Hellenistic tradition, interpreted in Roman terms, he wanted to stand still. To this degree he represented and represents a different basic model of theology and church, as different from mine as in astronomy Ptolemy's geocentric picture of the world is different from Copernicus' heliocentric picture – which for the astronomers and theologians of his time, thinking in Ptolemaic terms, likewise 'gives no certainty for which one can live and die', 'ultimately lands in abstruseness', 'doesn't go anywhere'. Hence Ratzinger's verdict on my book *On Being a Christian*, driven by antipathy and incomprehension, is understandable. But as a scholar thinking historically, in *On Being a Christian* I couldn't bring myself to sacrifice myself to an unhistorical spirituality, to read the later tradition of faith everywhere into the words and actions of Jesus, and thus to clothe the Jesus of history with the Christ of dogma. We must deepen this insight further.

A comparison between Ratzinger's Introduction and On Being a Christian

On 1 March 2006, at the invitation of the Karl Rahner Academy in Cologne, Professor Hermann Häring compared Ratzinger's *Introduction* and my *On Being a Christian*, both of which he had originally heard as lectures when a student. Häring's knowledgeable comparison, which shows him to be a master of hermeneutic, demonstrates even to non-theologians various perspectives which still form fluid front lines of this theological dispute. Here are just some of Häring's questions.

What is the audience? Ratzinger's potential readers are Catholics orientated on the church, whom he wants to introduce to the truth of their world of faith. *On Being a Christian* explicitly breaks open this circle of readers and is addressed to contemporaries who are not a priori orientated on Christianity.

What is the basis of the arguments? For Ratzinger without any qualification it is the creed of the Catholic Church formulated for all times, and he wants to reintroduce Catholic Christians to its language and thought-world. However, for *On Being a Christian* the foundation is the Jesus of history attested in the New Testament accounts, who precedes the later dogmatic creeds and formulas and from whom the faith can be understood anew in a new era.

What then are the form and intention? In a confusing age which lacks orientation Ratzinger's *Introduction* aims at regaining a living Catholic spirituality, drawing on the tradition of faith. *On Being a Christian* aims beyond that at a new practice of faith, which calls for renewal and self-criticism and thus for a new Christian spirituality and a new overall understanding of Christianity.

So what is the decisive direction of understanding (leading hermeneutic)? For Ratzinger's *Introduction* this is the consensus of the first five Christian centuries (*consensus quinquesecularis*) in which dogmatic theology received its classical form, and the church (with few exceptions) was not yet split. For *On Being a Christian*, while the early church consensus remains important, it has to be seen in a broader context and ultimately to be measured against the original, biblical message of Jesus as God's messiah, which is to be given new answers in times of upheaval.

What are the open or concealed interests (assessment in terms of a critique of ideology)? Ratzinger's *Introduction* remains completely within the system: the well-being and confirmation of the institutional church are to be guaranteed unconditionally, Christian faith is always obedience to the church. *On Being a Christian* is critical of the system as far as the church is concerned; it also exposes errors and failures in the church and calls for fundamental reforms by the criterion of the message of Jesus himself, and thus represents a consistently evangelical position in the context of the Catholic Church.

And what is the actual effect? Ratzinger's work stabilizes the official structures and faith systems of the Catholic Church. Fundamental criticism and relativization are avoided and are not justified or legitimate even in the name of Jesus. *On Being a Christian* crosses these limits set by Ratzinger in that if need be church structures can be assessed and in any case relativized by the message, action, destiny and person of Jesus.

What is the pre-existing framework of thought (epistemic system)? For Ratzinger this is undoubtedly Hellenistic philosophy and theology, represented in Platonism or the work of Augustine: hence the theology of the early church still has a normative significance which cannot be superseded. For *On Being a Christian* the framework is initially the broad treasury of academically responsible nineteenth- and twentieth-century scholarship, but against the wider background of religions and ideologies it is a hermeneutic critical of ideology which presents itself as an all-embracing scholarly system here reintroduced into Christian theology.

Finally, what are the weaknesses and strengths of the two 'Introductions'? The weakness of Ratzinger's *Introduction to Christianity* is that it doesn't expose itself to any critical dialogue internally or externally; at a critical point in time it attempts to give answers which the church has known for centuries. These are not subjected to any criticism; the changed situation is predominantly interpreted as a false way. The strength of this approach is that it creates a strong symbolic church identity which in the long term can create an expression of itself in a newly aroused need for religion and the presentation of religion on the media. The disadvantage of *On Being a Christian* is that with its new systematic approaches the book presupposes a comprehensive argument with culture that makes enormous demands for which the Catholic hierarchy is evidently not prepared. The strength of *On Being a Christian* is that it takes account of the needs of contemporary society. Here the Christian message is formulated for secular spheres of culture without damage to its heart in the gospel and thus the foundations are laid for an institutionalized reform of the Catholic Church.

How one can come to terms theologically

But what about the other dogmatic theologians in the 'Discussion of Hans Küng's *On Being a Christian*'? Some are certainly against me, but that doesn't mean that they are a priori in agreement with Joseph Ratzinger. In the face of what this time is a dogmatic position, presented in an ice-cold and demagogic way, they certainly don't appear as mediators but as skilful arrangers of the theology of the magisterium which is avoiding a conflict. In my answer in the *Frankfurter*

Allgemeine Zeitung, to which I now return, I shed critical light on these different strategies.

From the perspective of the Roman Curia, my other dogmatic opponents are in fact by no means all orthodox Catholic theologians; at least the first two similarly had dealings with the 'Holy Office', the doctrinal Inquisition. Each has his way, one loud, the other soft, of coming to terms with official doctrine at critical points. In my answer I refer to three typical possibilities of coming to terms – which are also perceived by other theologians: here I only indicate them, since non-theologians aren't very interested in how one can come to terms in a more or less elegant way with what is questionable in the church.

Accommodation 1: One reinterprets church teaching. An example is Karl Rahner on the question 'Did the historical Jesus found a church?' As a master of theological dialectics he transforms his historical no into a dogmatic yes.

Accommodation 2: One flees into aestheticism and mysticism. An example is Hans Urs von Balthasar on the question of 'demythologizing', which for him simply means spiritualizing. This man who in his younger years had written a much-noted reform work under the revolutionary title 'Razing the Bastions' (1952) now opposes reforms: why should one 'advance against institutions like Don Quixote against the windmills'? In an 'emergency' all the countless people who suffer under institutions (on matters of birth control, divorce, celibacy, the most various kinds of arrogance among clergy) can hardly gain any help from his 'spiritualized' theology.

Accommodation 3: One harmonizes the history of dogma. An example is the dogmatic historian Alois Grillmeier on Jesus as son of God. He calls for a 'new sketch of the Christian, which can be understood, surveyed and followed'; with my book *On Being a Christian* he has it in his hands, but he doesn't want to pay attention to it. He drops it. His own contribution culminates in a sterile appeal for a stereotyped repetition of the Hellenistic formulas and notions of Trinity and incarnation of 1500 years ago, as if the doctrine of two natures were absolutely biblical, hadn't split the early church, and could still be 'understood, surveyed and followed' by those who aren't historians.

Scandalous silence about key christological statements

I keep to the theses which Karl Rahner and I recently worked out together at the *Concilium* World Congress in Brussels in 1970: 'The great christological confessions and definitions of the past also have abiding significance for the church of the present. But they cannot be interpreted outside their historical context or even repeated as stereotypes. The Christian message must time and again be expressed anew to people of different times and cultures.'

But my opponents don't see what an opportunity the overall sketch in *On Being a Christian* represents. These dogmatic theologians are responsible for every possible sweeping charge being levelled against me (liberalism, disloyalty to the church, a loss of faith) so the whole discussion goes off track and misses the basic intentions of the book; they argue about the 'divinity of Christ' and his pre-existence before all time. Above all, there is a concern to block off this kind of theology and the consequences which follow from it. The success of the book is assuming dangerous proportions.

After reading the anti-*On Being a Christian* volume I understand why people didn't want to allow me even one page to reply. I could simply have had the relevant page of *On Being a Christian* reprinted, behind which stands the historical, philosophical and theological work that I did in my Hegel book on *The Incarnation of God*.

However, Grillmeier, like all the other authors of the volume, simply suppresses my central statements on the christological problems. He ignores my explicit endorsement not only of the great intentions and classical formulas of the Council of Nicaea in 325 but also of Jesus' divine sonship (the *vere Deus* of the Council of Chalcedon in 451, interpreted in keeping with scripture and the time): 'The whole point of what happened in and with Jesus of Nazareth depends on the fact that, for believers, God himself as man's friend was present, at work, speaking, acting and definitively revealing himself in this Jesus who came among men as God's advocate and deputy, representative and delegate, and was confirmed by God as the Crucified raised to life' (*On Being a Christian*, p. 449). Isn't such a statement sufficient for one to be acknowledged a Catholic?

I never heard anything more from Hans Urs von Balthasar after the composite volume, which he followed up with another poisonous letter to the *Frankfurter Allgemeine Zeitung*, to which I wasn't allowed to reply. After his massive breach of friendship I had no occasion to seek contact with him again. But I did visit his grave, to the left of the Hofkirche in Lucerne, the church where I had begun as an assistant priest in the 1950s and to which I had invited him for a series of sermons. How sad that what had begun so well ended so lamentably.

Thus the leading Catholic dogmatic theologians of Germany (the Protestants stand aside and above all stick to Karl Barth) reject the view of *On Being a Christian* governed by new exegesis, philosophy and history – above all Balthasar, Rahner and Ratzinger. The moderates among them – Kasper and Lehmann – write more articles and are happy soon to exchange an increasingly uncomfortable professorial chair for a more comfortable bishop's throne. Ultra-conservatives such as Grillmeier and Scheffczyk are rewarded with the red hat at an age when they no longer qualify for electing a Pope; it can't be bestowed on Balthasar because his fate, interpreted in different ways, is to die the day before the ceremony. Most of my opponents now rest in peace and I hold nothing against them. But the dogmatic self-blockade of those days has unfortunate consequences: many important theological issues are made taboo, and German Catholic dogmatics, previously highly respected on the international scene, stagnates.

Subsequent Catholic theologians need to look out. The most recent warning example is that of the Franciscan theologian Joseph Imbach, a Swiss at the Franciscan College in Rome. Earlier I had accepted his text 'Living in Fear?' in my series 'Theological Meditations'. But some months later a passage in his report of my press conference in Rome in the Lucerne *Vaterland* ensures that a denunciation goes to the Vatican Secretariat of State and from there to the Congregation for Christian Education. Its president, Cardinal Schröffer, a former student of the German College without theological ambition, calls for a statement from the General of the Franciscan Conventuals. This requires Imbach at least to recant the conclusion of his report and declare the whole thing an '*incidente di lavoro*' ('a little mishap'). He refuses. Now two other of his other articles, published in Italian specialist journals, cause offence. He fights on with humour and without bitterness for an unblinkered Catholicism. But in 2003 the Doctrinal Congregation finally withdraws his permission to teach, first for a year and then for an indefinite period, because of a publication on miracles. In 2005 the Herbert Haag Foundation for Freedom in the Church, of which I am president, awards Imbach its prize 'For Freedom in the Church' and as a result of a successful campaign for donations a teaching post in the Protestant Theological Faculty in Basle is financed for him.

The criticism by German dogmatic theologians of *On Being a Christian* contrasts sharply with the high praise which this book gets from the media all over the world. Here are a couple of sentences from the *Church of England Newspaper*, in which Richard Holloway writes: 'No other Catholic thinker has so much talent as Küng, of combining a coherent Christian vision with precise scholarly detail and translating his ideas into such simple and powerful language. This book is ... a high-flying vision of Christian life and faith, which addresses both intuition and intellect.'

On Being a Christian *launched in Rome*

On 21 March 1976 I had been at the launch of the Spanish edition of *On Being a Christian* at a press conference in Madrid, with an excellent introduction by the respected Jesuit José Gómez Caffarena, Director of the Fe y Secularidad Institute, where the next day there was also a seminar for 25 theologians. The day after that I gave a lecture at the university. *Ser cristiano* quickly became a bestseller in Spain. But press conferences can have their tricky moments, for example when a journalist or a press agency doesn't report the essentials but only the answer to a particular question: thus there was excitement at a report in the German and Swiss press that in Madrid I again called for 'far-reaching reforms' – from the abolition of the prohibition of contraception to the election of the Pope and the bishops by representative bodies of the clergy and laity, There was no indication that my real topic was *On Being a Christian*. Of course the Vatican also reads such reports.

On 4 April I fly to Rome for the launch of the Italian edition of *On Being a Christian*. Of course I have no illusions. I'm again approaching the lions' den. But if the highly-respected publisher Mondadori asks me, why shouldn't I do it? In any case I love the open game. Once again I stay in my old German College and in the afternoon – after various press interviews in the morning – visit my 'special friends' of the Doctrinal Congregation to talk about the state of the proceedings: at 5 p.m. Cardinal Franjo Šeper in his private apartment at Piazza della Città Leonina no. 1, and at 6.30 p.m. Archbishop Jérôme Hamer, the Secretary of the Congregation for the Doctrine of the Faith, in his residence on Monte Mario. Right at the start the latter can't conceal his amusement and secret admiration, that I can dare to hold a press conference the next afternoon *'sous le nez de Sa Sainteté* – under His Holiness's nose'. I say that it is quite normal for me to present my Italian book personally to the Italian public.

But I don't seem to have convinced the Prefect and the Secretary of the Congregation for the Doctrine of the Faith to let me continue my theological work in peace. I also make great efforts in the conversations to discover their plans, but they aren't showing their cards. I remember the fox from Aesop's fable who doesn't allow himself to be lured into the cave of the old, apparently sick, weak lion because so many tracks lead in but none lead out. I will never allow myself to be lured into the Palazzo of the Holy Office and the traps of the proceedings there.

The press conference is very friendly and normal – despite a spanner in the works from Vatican Radio. Right at the beginning I observe that I have come 'to present my book here in Rome to the Italian public for what it is: a truly Catholic but also a truly ecumenical book. Almost 30 years ago I studied theology here at the Pontifical Gregorian University and the Pontifical German–Hungarian College. I have never regretted my seven years in Rome – to which were later added four years during the Council. I am proud of them and have been able to make use of them. Almost 30 years of Catholic and ecumenical theology have gone into this book. It isn't a look back in anger but a realistic exploratory look forward. It isn't a reckoning with the 30 years in which it has slowly become clearer to me what being human and being a Christian can mean: for men and women of the present in the light of the gospel.'[19]

On the last evening I am invited to dinner by my friends from the Île des Pins, Principessa Vittoria Sanfelice di Monteforte and her husband. The next day I fly back to Stuttgart/Tübingen, report to my team on events in Rome and in the evening happily celebrate the birthday of my colleague and friend Jürgen Moltmann with him and his wife Elisabeth.

But the question remains: how will the hierarchy react? What will the future be? Read once again the words by Walter Jens at the head of Chapter VI and you can recapture a little of my feelings. Where people can hinder or prevent the publication of my works they do, in an authoritarian way and quite unconcerned for the legal situation. From Brazil Leonardo Boff reports that despite the contract

335

which has been signed and a translation which is almost complete, the publishing firm Vozes, which belongs to the Franciscan Order, may not publish my book *On Being a Christian* because of the intervention of the Doctrinal Congregation (the Brazilian Superior General of the Franciscans has been entrusted with carrying out the order) (10 August 1976). I agree that the book shall now be published by the respectable publisher Imago, which also publishes Freud's collected works. I gladly dispense with any royalties because of the economic crisis in Brazil.

The campaign of the hierarchy against me is effective even at a local level. Since I had my house by the lake, people in the nearby district hospital of Sursee had been glad for me to come to celebrate the eucharist every working day. But moving the eucharist in March 1973 from morning to evening, which has often been customary since the Council, didn't suit all the sisters. And when my pastor and friend Franz Xaver Kaufmann retired for reasons of old age in December 1973 and was replaced by an arch-conservative successor who was at the same time head of the Marian Schönstatt Movement in Switzerland, with a marked Roman orientation, this pastor gathered some of the faithful around him and at the same time alienated the majority of the by no means traditionalist Catholic population of my home town. Fewer and fewer sisters came to my eucharist in the hospital, and finally only two or three. Evidently my evening eucharist was no longer wanted.

So on 8 September 1976 I write a farewell letter to the sisters saying that I won't be involved in this service in future: 'I think back with joy and gratitude to the twelve years of my preaching and pastoral care which have perhaps given most to me personally. I was concerned only to preach the gospel of Jesus Christ and to celebrate the eucharist in his memory, and one shouldn't impose oneself. And if I am sad to say goodbye in these unexpected circumstances, I do so without bitterness and resentment against certain persons.' I don't receive an answer to this letter either from the sisters in the hospital or from the Superior General, but a few months later I have one from a former superior with whom I had always had good relations. Her encouraging lines do me good.

Experiences in northern Europe

I receive encouragement not least from visitors from all over the world; of course my readers grow with the increasing number of translations. Three Finnish Lutheran theological students who are thinking of doing doctorates on my theology at the theological faculty of Helsinki are particularly important and dear to me: Eero Huovinen, Risto Cantell and Simo Salo. They visit Tübingen on various occasions and are able to see whatever they want. But they are above all interested in my coming to Finland one day. However, I have to postpone this trip because of constant other claims.

336

Normally I scrupulously fulfil commitments and hardly ever excuse myself for sickness, indisposition or overwork. But I did have to make one exception that is still painful to recall, for the Gifford Lectures, which are held in rotation at the universities of Glasgow, Edinburgh, St Andrews and Aberdeen. According to the foundation document the lecturers may be believing, agnostic or freethinking scholars, provided that they are 'able, reverent men, true thinkers, sincere lovers of and earnest inquirers after truth'. The Gifford Lectures have been given not only by famous scholars of religion such as F. Max Müller, Andrew Lang, William James and J. G. Frazer but also by Nathan Söderblom, Reinhold Niebuhr, Karl Barth, Emil Brunner and Rudolf Bultmann. What an honour it is then for me, still relatively young, to be invited by the University of St Andrews to give the 1974 Gifford Lectures.

On the other hand, how could I have foreseen when I accepted the invitation that the preparation of the Gifford Lectures would fall during my confrontation with Rome and the German bishops and the concluding phase of *On Being a Christian* and all the activities connected with the launching of the book at the Frankfurt Book Fair? I simply didn't have the strength to prepare a series of lectures lasting over several days in English, which would then be published as yet another book. So on 4 October 1974 I withdrew and of course I wasn't at all surprised that I never heard anything from St Andrews from that day to this. Perhaps people there will forgive me when they read these memoirs. Please accept my apologies.

After Easter 1975, when things have calmed down again, I accept the invitation to Finland. At any rate I don't need to prepare different lectures in a foreign language for each day. I want to gain a first impression of Scandinavia, so on Easter Monday 1975 I make a stop in Copenhagen and on Easter Tuesday a second stop in Stockholm. I arrive in Helsinki on Easter Wednesday, 9 April. From my youth I've had a soft spot for Finland, since this very large country with a small population, a bit like Switzerland, was attacked during the Second World War by the Soviet Union and therefore enjoyed our complete solidarity. I have dinner with the professor of ecumenical theology, Kalevi Toiviainen (born in 1929 and almost my exact contemporary), whose three pupils have worked out a grand but also intensive programme of travel for me. It helps that my '20 Theses on Being a Christian' have now been published in Finnish.

At 7 a.m. the train leaves for Seinäjoki, where I give a lecture to the pastors in the evening on 'Is the Office of Pastor Still Necessary?' Then it's off to Bishop Yrjö Sariola in Lapua. At 11.55 p.m. we take the night train to Rovaniemi, the capital of Lapland, where we arrive at 7.55 a.m. After breakfast, a sauna and a bath at 9.15 we fly to Ivalo, north of the Arctic Circle, where we arrive just over half an hour later and are lodged by friends in a comfortable Finnish wooden house with a view of the frozen snow-white lake. There is marvellous sunshine until towards midnight, which invites cross-country skiing to Kanispää across a marvellous peaceful boundless white snowy landscape with gentle hills and treeless slopes almost devoid of human beings.

On 12 April we go with the frontier-zone pastor Tapio Leinonen at great speed by snowmobile over the apparently endless Lake Inari to Murmansk, finally visiting a Lapp family, though conversation with them is difficult. On Sunday 13 April there is worship in Ivalo. And in all the free hours of what are already very long days, hardly followed by proper nights, I answer on tape every possible and impossible question from my three young Finnish friends. We discuss the whole panorama of theology. These are great days with a lot of sun, and a sauna in the evening. I'm proud to be the only one of the four of us who dares to run naked through the snow-covered forest. Training in the Sempachersee has paid off. But no one is willing to cut a hole in the ice for me, though I could have stood it.

On 14 April we fly from Ivalo to Helsinki and on to Turku (Swedish Åbo), the see of a Lutheran archbishop with a Swedish-speaking university, until 1812 the Finnish capital. Here I give a lecture on 'The Distinctively Christian'. The next day I go to Helsinki for a licentiate seminar in the theological faculty and lunch with the assistants. In the evening I give a lecture in the great auditorium of the University of Helsinki with a discussion presided over by the highly-respected Chancellor of the University and President of the Lutheran World Federation, Mikko Juva (later an archbishop). These are all extraordinarily rich days, quite unforgettable, from which I have to return to Tübingen on 17 April after various further meetings, among others with the Roman Catholic bishop Paul Verschuren. In my lake house an Arabia coffee set in cobalt blue – with attractive gold-speckled mocha cups – which is as beautiful as it is sturdy still reminds me in my lake house of my fine Finnish experiences. However, I find the later dissertations of the three friends of that time – in so far as they were finished at all – very disappointing.

Two years later I have the opportunity also to get to know other Scandinavian countries. I gladly accept an invitation from Professor Peder Højen to go to Copenhagen, where on 28 March 1977 I give my standard lecture on 'What Must Remain in the Church', together with a seminar on my '20 Theses on Being a Christian', which also appear in Danish the next year.

The next day I fly on to Oslo and there at the invitation of Professor Inge Lønning, also a bold Lutheran and dean of the faculty, who later often visits us in Tübingen, give a double lecture on 'Ludwig Feuerbach and his Atheism'. On 30 March I add a seminar on the '20 Theses on Being a Christian', but still have time for an expedition to the big television tower on a mountain near Oslo from which I enjoy the broad view over the hilly landscape. I'm accompanied by the Catholic theologian Dr Kari Børresen, who also studied at the Gregorian in Rome, an enthusiastic feminist who has written a critical dissertation on the nature and role of women in Augustine and Thomas Aquinas under the title *Subordination et équivalence* (1968). The same day I travel back to Tübingen. These are beautiful, intensive, stimulating days. All the press reports are positive. 'Your visit was an inspiration for our theological milieu which will quite certainly continue to have an effect,' Dean Lønning writes to me. 'We hope that next time you have more time at your disposal' (15 February 1977).

Experiences in East Germany

How different were my experiences in the eastern part of Germany, which was occupied by Soviet troops after the Second World War. I don't for a moment believe in a permanent division of Germany – so convinced am I on the basis of my Swiss origin of the unity of the nation despite different languages and cultures. Even if my first trip to the German Democratic Republic in October 1972 is rather easier because of my Swiss passport, the border checks and border controllers are repulsive. The often dilapidated buildings, bad streets, shabbily clothed people and the omnipresent Communist propaganda slogans form a somewhat gloomy background to the oppressed mood in the population.

The churches and their institutions are islands of freedom (though a freedom at that time still wholly limited to the religious sphere) in this evil totalitarian regime. Thus for example it was possible for the Caritas association of Cologne, headed by a former student of the German College, to avoid the import ban and smuggle a copy of *On Being a Christian* into the GDR. And when I ask a Catholic theological student why he is studying theology, he says that in the church one still has most freedom from the totalitarian Communist system.

On 27 October 1972 I give a lecture in the Berlin Pastors' Training Centre, neutrally called the 'Language School', again on 'What Must Remain in the Church'. The next day I go by train to Leipzig. Here I stay with the Oratorians, where I get much inside information about what life is actually like in the GDR. I make very good contact above all with the excellent New Testament scholar Wolfgang Trilling; he is my key Catholic witness for an unideological historical–critical interpretation of the classic New Testament passages on Peter.

In the afternoon I visit the brave Catholic pastor Karl Herbst, who for many years has distributed contemporary explanations of sayings of Jesus to various places all over the GDR; three years later the police confiscate his copying apparatus because he doesn't have written permission. Herbst moves to West Germany. In the afternoon of 29 October I have a conversation on ecumenical matters with Protestant theologians in the home of the Protestant lecturer Ulrich Kuhn. Then in the evening I give my standard lecture on 'What Must Remain in the Church', of course to only a small audience. This lecture has so many facets that very different discussions can follow depending on the place and the audience. The next morning I speak in the Protestant seminar of the university about the infallibility debate. Despite the different political systems, many problems of both churches aren't fundamentally different from those in West Germany.

But I can't feel right in a system under totalitarian government. I find it oppressive that people – shut off from the rest of the world – should simply go on working all their lives. On the afternoon of 30 October I return to West Berlin to give a lecture on the same topic in the great Congress Hall. On 31 October I go to Frankfurt for the Reformation festival and the day after to Worms. How glad I am to be back home, even if mountains of post await me!

Concerns for fellow men and women

The correspondence has steadily increased: not just the official correspondence with faculty and university or with colleagues and friends for opinions and recommendations; not just business correspondence about my books in different languages or with the Foundation and editorial committee of *Concilium*. To begin with I needed one or two filing cabinets to keep the correspondence in, after throwing out all the less important items. Now it's four or five. More and more people from all walks of life approach me – in writing or by word of mouth – with their private concerns and needs. A theological student wants to do practical work in a particular French Dominican house. A German theologian who has a doctorate from a (church) university in (secular) France wants state recognition for it from the Federal Republic of Germany. A reader wants to gain a papal audience through me for his Indian yogi. Often people pose difficult questions. May and should a married and therefore laicized Catholic priest assume a pastorate in the Old Catholic Church? May a Catholic theologian who has converted to the Protestant church convert back to the Catholic Church? Can I find a pen friend for a homosexual in a penal institution? Won't a religious who has married continue to have all too many psychological problems? Can a Greek Orthodox professor who speaks German well get a guest chair in our faculty? An American fellow student from the Gregorian, who has worked as a professor for several years, had to be laicized because he married and now despite literally hundreds of applications to universities and colleges hasn't found a job. Can he do anything other than sell insurance? There are problems of celibacy for clergy, sexual problems for married people, bureaucratic problems for church officials ... And I am often asked why, with all my difficulties and tribulations, I haven't left the Catholic Church.

There are so many more questions and complaints. I take the trouble to answer as many as possible, by letter, standard letter, offprint, bibliographical reference. Sometimes I can help as a pastor, sometimes I can't; sometimes I write to a bishop or another authority, and often the correspondence goes to and fro several times. Sometimes I'm just perplexed. For example, what advice shall I give to one of my Catholic diploma theologians who, after getting all the necessary dispensations from both authorities, has married a Protestant assistant minister and now has an eighteen-month-old daughter? Conversations with the church authorities of the two churches lead to a squaring of the circle: unless the Catholic theologian gives his child a Catholic baptism, he won't get a Catholic post. But conversely, if the

Protestant pastor has the child baptized a Catholic, she won't get a Protestant post. And this a decade after Vatican II! I often think of Karl Barth, who said that he would like to be Pope just for a day, to set many ecumenical matters right.

But there are countless questions on which I simply am not competent (so far, I haven't been able to study the problem of assisted euthanasia); or questions over which the enquirer should seek pastoral help locally and not from me (to make a Catholic son-in-law acceptable to Protestant parents); or for which I would have to study a whole sheaf of legal documents or other writings. Here I sometimes refer to the saying of Jesus that he has not been appointed a 'judge or arbiter' (Luke 12.14).

I'm often saddened by the great worries of my friends, most of which have to do with the deterioration in the church. Art Yzermans writes to me about the 'bad times' in his formerly so hopeful home diocese of St Cloud. Giancarlo Zizola, one of the most competent commentators on the Roman scene, writes of his departure from the daily paper *Il giorno* where his critical religious column has finally become dangerous for 'church and lay strategists of restoration'. Erwin Kleine in the Netherlands writes about the collapse of his health. The Canadian theologian Gregory Baum, born in Berlin, writes of his resignation from the priesthood for love of a woman. A younger theologian in a British university city has had his sex changed surgically and can't find a job as a woman. I slowly begin to understand what the Apostle Paul means in his 'tearful letter' (the last three chapters of 2 Corinthians) by 'the pressure on me of my anxiety for the churches' (11.28).

I can agree to the numerous requests for a personal conversation only if I am told what it is about and I am really competent for it. For example, I am not competent to deal with the many people who claim to have received a private revelation and want to convince me that it is important for the salvation of my soul or the salvation of the world, or with those who are educated or half-educated in science or philosophy and want my judgement on their personal global system for the definitive solution of the great questions of humanity. Whenever possible, I reply with a friendly comment, especially to those who are completely disturbed psychologically: they always arouse my compassion. But if more letters keep coming, sometimes one or two dozen, I can no longer deal with them.

Now and then I also have pleasant surprises: a bunch of flowers when it isn't my birthday; Basler Leckerli, a sweetmeat from my homeland; one or more bottles of wine after I have read a book or an attractive gift from a distant land; or often from a manager of General Foods International a big packet with sachets of Maxwell House coffee, enough for the regular morning and afternoon coffee for our team for a long time. Nothing is forgotten: thank you, James Griffin!

From Korea, where many of my books are translated and I have never received any royalties, I am provided with Ginseng tea for life. A Korean who made me guess his age, which I deliberately underestimated but not enough, three times

341

gave me the explanation for his youthfulness: Ginseng!

However, I also have other means of keeping healthy: moderate eating and drinking, fresh air and sun, swimming and music, a siesta and human contact. As well as the many 'problem letters' I also receive quite a number of supportive letters. I am really touched when a fellow member of my course in Rome, Franz-Joseph Kötter of Münster, writes to me in a long letter when the crisis is again coming to a head: 'You are so close to me and I know that we are bound together as if the past 22 years since Rome had hardly been ... I wish you strength so that, guided in the Spirit, you can say the right thing to all these people. You have a very great gift for doing that' (20 December 1977).

A prize for civil courage

That same year the city of Munich gives me an experience and an encouragement of a special kind. On 11 July it awards me the medal for civil courage. In the morning I take part in a faculty conference in Tübingen at which Gerhard Lohfink is elected to the New Testament chair. I drive off in the afternoon; Karl-Josef Kuschel accompanies me. We talk intensely about the structure of my next book on the question of God. Discussion with my proven collaborator in *On Being a Christian*, who can weigh up arguments and think in terms of concepts, has become indispensable.

The celebrations are held on the Tegernsee in the house of the most famous Bavarian popular writer Ludwig Thoma (1867-1921), who had opposed hypocrisy, bourgeois narrow-mindedness, Wilhelmine Prussianism and clerical Bavarian politics, but later went into the national conservative camp. This award 'for civil courage' is important to me. It is bestowed on me by the Lord Mayor of the City of Munich, Georg Kronawitter, at a fine supper in Thoma's house, to the accompaniment of Bavarian zither music. Next to me at the table are the founder of the prize, Hans Hellmut Kirst (who wrote the trilogy of novels *08/15*), and the great actors Kurt Meisel and Ursula Lingen. The company, which numbers perhaps three dozen guests who evidently expected a serious theological speech of thanks, reacts with increasing enthusiasm to my light-hearted words. Karl-Josef Kuschel proves capable of driving me back to Tübingen that same evening in two and a half hours.

But now I need some relaxation. On 19 July 1975 we go to the lake house and celebrate 1 August, the Swiss national day, with the family. On 12 August, after a short lecture in Innsbruck, I go with Marianne Saur (more of her later) to Salzburg, where the festival offers us four great experiences. Leonard Bernstein conducts Mozart's Piano Concerto K 453 from the keyboard, and there are works by Shostakovich and Sibelius. The next day we see Mozart's *Marriage of Figaro* conducted by Herbert von Karajan, peerlessly staged by Jean-Pierre Ponnelle, and not spoiled by any whimsical theatrical direction. In the morning of the Feast of the Assumption we hear Haydn's *Nelson Mass*, with which I am very familiar from a gramophone record, and in the evening see *Everyman*, the play about the death of a rich man, in Hugo von Hofmannstahl's version with the ideal cast of Curd Jürgens and Senta Berger.

The very next day, 19 August 1975, I begin the manuscript of *Does God Exist?*, which I shall be writing about in the next chapter. And I look forward to the appearance of the '20 Theses on Being a Christian' on 26 August. For me personally that closes the discussion of *On Being a Christian* for the moment. I don't want to stand still or stiffen up, but resolutely to continue on my way. But what will the way of my church be: further forward, or back into the time before the Council?

IX

Problems of the Hierarchy and Problems of the World

> *'How does it happen that when a man rises on the ladder of church dignities, his theological openness, mobility and responsibility tend to fall (Goethe, "Had St Paul a bishop been ...").'*
>
> Karl Barth (at a conference on baptism and vocation), 16 March 1966

After the Council the Catholic hierarchy again seems to many Catholics to be increasingly remote from reality, in some of its positions even unworldly. But doesn't this development also become evident in other churches? So where possible I should accept these events with rather more humour and reflect on what the Reformed theologian Karl Barth describes as 'an occasional problem to be given special treatment (perhaps for an hour in the evening)': 'How does it happen that ... ?' Barth refers to Johann Wolfgang von Goethe's poem 'The Wandering Jew' (1774):

> The priests who lived in yesteryear
> were priests just as they always were
> and also as they are today
> when lofty office comes their way.
> Though once as busy as a bee,
> or like a serpent roaming free,
> now cloaked, becollared, far from care
> the bishop rests in his armchair.
> And by my life it can be seen
> that had St Paul a bishop been
> he would have had an ampler girth –
> of that in clergy there's no dearth.

The end of the conciliar era

On 21 January 1971 the Joint Synod of the German Dioceses met; as I reported (Chapter III above), the bishops had rejected me as an adviser despite the wish of many members of the synod. In several meetings over five years up to 22 November 1975 more than 300 excellently motivated and informed members of the Synod discussed forward-looking documents idealistically and realistically with the bishops: on worship and collaboration with the laity, religious instruction, youth work and relationship to the working class, church service and pastoral care of foreigners.

But the practical implementation of these documents didn't receive the necessary support from the bishops, far less from Rome, on the critical points (divorce, contraception, sexual relations before marriage). There was no unqualified affirmation of birth control and distancing from the encyclical *Humanae vitae*, no participation of remarried divorced persons in the eucharist, no relaxation of the law of celibacy, no say of diocesan bodies in the election of bishops. Indeed, to the present day the Vatican hasn't thought important demands worth answering. Lay preaching, allowed for a trial period by the Synod and then practised successfully, is later forbidden by the Vatican and the bishops: better no sermon than one from a lay person? At any rate the collaboration of the laity in parish and diocesan councils was revalued in Germany by the Synod, something quite unique in the Catholic Church. Synod 72 of the Swiss dioceses also had a similarly unhappy fate: excellent discussions, proposals and documents got lukewarm support from the bishops and were ignored by Rome. Unfortunately the whole vast expenditure of intellect, time and money didn't produce any practical results.

Now the hierarchy again has the leisure to turn its attention to me. After the controversy over *On Being a Christian* in the *Frankfurter Allgemeine Zeitung*, Cardinal Julius Döpfner reports that he is not asking my colleagues, who have been thoroughly investigated, for a 'serious examination' of my method and the substantive statements to which objection has been made, but me. That is on 24 June 1976. On 28 June I reply to him that I have seriously examined all the literature that has appeared in connection with my views on the question of infallibility and the church and published the composite volume 'Fallible? A Stocktaking', but this hasn't met with any theological response. As for the discussion of *On Being a Christian*, I have taken the trouble since the publication of the book to clarify, examine and deepen the disputed dogmatic questions. This can be demonstrated by a three-day doctoral colloquium on a comparison between Walter Kasper's *Jesus the Christ* and *On Being a Christian*; a further three-day doctoral colloquium on the composite volume 'Discussion of Hans Küng's *On Being a Christian*'; several colloquiums lasting several hours with well-known exegetes such as Professors Joachim Jeremias and Gerhard Lohfink on the substantive questions under debate, especially christological questions; and a seminar towards the end of the summer semester on the discussion volume which ended with a disputation between Walter Kasper and me. I have had conversations or exchanged letters with the majority of the authors of the composite volume. And so on. What else should I do to 'examine' myself? And is such an examination a one-way street?

345

But not a single bishop with whom I have to do, directly or indirectly, is interested in a real theological discussion of controversial questions, in real solutions to problems. They imagine that by virtue of their office they are in possession of the truth, so they don't recognize the legitimacy of the questions. They won't see that there are problems which call for new solutions, new formulations. For them the only truth is the unqualified confession of the traditional formulae repeated word for word, not critical investigation, reinterpretation and implementation in accordance with the results of modern scholarship. They don't expect thought but obedience – in accordance with the truth that they possess.

Sudden death of a mediator: Cardinal Döpfner

Just a month after his letter, on 24 July 1976, Cardinal Julius Döpfner dies suddenly of a heart attack at the age of 62. The day before, he had drafted a letter to me which was to have been typed and sent on 24 July. In it he thanks me for my letter of 28 June. Meanwhile the Faith Commission of the German Conference of Bishops has concerned itself with the new situation and on the basis of suggestions made to it proposes 'a conversation intended to clarify some central theological questions raised by *On Being a Christian*'. 'I hope that this conversation will lead to a clear agreement in the common cause of our faith and remove some confusions which have arisen in connection with your book.' It is agreed that I may invite a colleague to the conversation. Döpfner wants to bring Cardinal Volk, Bishop Moser of Rottenburg and Professors Lehmann and Ratzinger. The conversation is to be held at the Catholic Academy of the diocese of Rottenburg in Hohenheim, Stuttgart, in the second half of September or October.

But now Cardinal Julius Döpfner is dead. Time and again he has been my conversation-partner in the years since my book *The Council and Reunion*, though at that time, unlike Cardinal König later, he didn't dare write a foreword to it. The death of this moderate, human and congenial President of the Conference of Bishops and indefatigable mediator is widely regretted, and particularly by me. Already as a student at the German College I had admired the vigorous temperamental young Bishop of Würzburg – a passionate climber, particularly friendly with the Swiss students at the College. For all his theological limitations, his constant excessive concern for the Roman Curia and corresponding tactics, before, at and after the Council there was no better in the German episcopate.

Döpfner's abiding merits are threefold. He resisted the constant pressure of Rome to revise the 'Königsberg Declaration' issued by the German Conference of Bishops which after the encyclical *Humanae vitae* (1968) allowed partners freedom of conscience in the question of birth control (that was still being called for in July 2006 at a 'Forum of German Catholics'). He made the Würzburg synod possible. He promoted the institution of married pastoral workers in the face of resistance from Rome, with the secret (but vain) hope that they could one day be ordained priests. And he attempted to defend me within what he thought was the realm of possibility.

In his heart Döpfner was convinced that I was right in many things. Thus at a service in the sacristy (not the church) of St Johann in Tübingen he made benevolent remarks about me: 'He's right, but he's too soon!' On the contrary, I was convinced that I was too late with some ecumenical concerns (450 years after the Reformation!) and that my proposals for being a Christian today came at just the right time. I don't expect the Catholic hierarchy to adopt my theology. But I do expect it to tolerate my theology as Catholic theology. With the sudden death of Julius Döpfner eight months after the end of the German Synod, under permanent stress as President of the Conference of Bishops, it seems to me that the conciliar era has finally died.

A dangerous constellation

The letter from Cardinal Döpfner of 23/24 July 1976 is sent to me on 31 August by the now acting President of the German Conference of Bishops, Cardinal Joseph Höffner. This former Bishop of Münster, by now 70, a former student of the German College who is completely fixed in dogmatic terms, a specialist in the social sciences, has been Archbishop of Cologne since 1969 as successor to Cardinal Frings.[1] He accepts Döpfner's proposal for a conversation, but this can't take place until October. I receive the letter in my lake house in Sursee and answer it on 4 September: 'I gladly declare myself in principle ready for a conversation to clarify some central theological questions relating to *On Being a Christian*.'[2] I very much want Cardinal Volk and Bishop Moser to take part. I don't say anything about Professors Lehmann and Ratzinger.

On 12 October 1976 the Secretary of the Conference of Bishops, Dr Homeyer, announces that the conversation can't take place until the second half of November.[3] He now wants to agree a date with me and then also with Cardinals Höffner, now President, and Volk, Bishop Moser and Professors Lehmann and Ratzinger, who have already told Cardinal Döpfner that they are ready to take part in the conversation.

Now the time has come to clarify certain features of the conversation. In a letter to Cardinal Höffner dated 19 October 1976 I write that I would have no objection to Professor Lehmann, who has proved to be an objective conversation partner on the disputed points, but I don't see 'any help in clarifying existing substantive questions in a conversation with Herr Prelate Joseph Ratzinger' – in Regensburg he had adopted this Roman title, taboo for professors in Tübingen – 'who in his contributions to the discussion so far has not shown himself to be an unprejudiced partner in a discussion. On the contrary, I fear that his participation could result in an emotional atmosphere which would not serve the conversations.'[4]

None of this is an indication of a fundamental antipathy to the person of Joseph Ratzinger, of whom I thought highly in our three years together in Tübingen; after the first conversation with the Faith Commission in Stuttgart, on 23 January 1971 he had written me a friendly letter about an academic matter and added: 'I hope that you will return happy to Tübingen after our conversation in Stuttgart.' Later, I was very unhappy, indeed dismayed, at the theological level of his two contributions on *Infallible?* and *On Being a Christian*. In them he showed himself amazingly incapable or unwilling even to reproduce my views correctly, far less pass objective judgement on them. I found some of his remarks not only wrong and unfair, but even insulting.

At the time I was far from clear why someone who knew me so well could react in such an unobjective and emotional way. It seemed as if lightning had struck the unenlightened pious corner of his pious Bavarian heart. Or was it simply that his failure to grapple seriously with the historical–critical exegesis of the New Testament was having its effect here? Or was the shock of the Tübingen student revolts so deep that he had transferred some of his traumas and resentments to my person and theology? Or did he sense, like Karl Rahner at one time, 'a deadly threat' to his own dogmatics? Be this as it may, my objection after his two articles is more than justified and moreover is accepted by Cardinal Höffner. Six weeks later Dr Homeyer writes to me in a letter of 9 December[5] that in the meantime 'Professor Ratzinger has asked to be released from his participation in the conversation'; Ratzinger's place will be taken by Professor Otto Semmelroth, a Jesuit from Sankt Georgen, Frankfurt – this is certainly welcome to me.

I deliberately don't propose a colleague from systematic or exegetical theology but a specialist in procedural questions in the person of our highly-respected church lawyer Johannes Neumann. So as not to be entangled in Inquisition proceedings in which I would be fighting a losing battle from the start, in a conversation with Bishop Moser I had already urged what in my letter to Cardinal Höffner of 19 October I now stated as a 'precondition for my participation', 'that this is not a conversation in the sense of §5 of the procedure for doctrinal complaints in the German Conference of Bishops'.[6] My starting point is that obscurities should be clarified and misunderstandings removed in an open and honest conversation. This includes the condition that the minutes of such an open conversation would not be used against me in any way: 'All I ask you, dear Herr Cardinal, is to guarantee this to me explicitly.' The explicit guarantee is then given by Dr Homeyer in the name of Cardinal Höffner.[7] I am told that to obviate any difficulties over the minutes, Cardinal Höffner is prepared 'at the beginning of the conversation to ensure that the tape recorder, i.e. the record, will not be used by either side'.

But despite all the assurances, it will soon prove that precisely this is what is done. It is clear that the death of Cardinal Döpfner has ushered in a situation which is disturbing for the church in Germany and highly dangerous for me personally. Georg Moser is envisaged as Döpfner's successor, but the Bavarian state government opposes the 'liberal' non-Bavarian. So Joseph Ratzinger becomes Archbishop of Munich. That means that the place of the mediator Döpfner is taken by two resolute opponents of mine: Höffner, who will presumably be the new President of the German Conference of Bishops, and Ratzinger, the Archbishop of Munich – both against me on the side of the Curia. And what will happen if the ailing Paul VI, who despite all his objections has held his protective hand over me, is replaced by a new Pope who perhaps isn't well disposed? Be this as it may, I have to fulfil my obligations, in Tübingen and shortly in England and the US.

A good reception in America

Happily I don't encounter either in Great Britain or in the US the resistance I encounter in Germany. On 31 October 1976 I begin this journey, on which Karl-Josef Kuschel again accompanies me. In London we visit my former Tübingen colleague Professor Rolf Dahrendorf, now Director of the London School of Economics, a skilled analyst with world-wide experience, with whom I enjoy discussing the church and the world, religion and politics. Then comes a meeting with Antoine van den Boogaard, President of the *Concilium* Foundation, and the publishers' representative Paul Brand. To arouse interest in *Concilium* we go to Cardinal Basil Hume, Archbishop of Westminster, who gives us a friendly welcome and shows great openness to our concerns. Dinner with our English publisher Tom Burns in a typical English club ends an energetic day.

From London one can reach the media of half the world. And of course I take every opportunity to present my book *On Being a Christian*. The next day, 1 November 1976, there is a press conference, an interview for Australian television, then interviews for BBC radio and television and finally also for *The Times* and *The Tablet*. In the evening we are invited to the residence of the Apostolic Delegate Bruno Heim, a Swiss, formerly secretary to the Paris nuncio Angelo Roncalli, later John XXIII. He loves to cook and we have a friendly Swiss conversation. He is a specialist in heraldry and will also sketch out the coat of arms of the next (but one) Pope (John Paul II), at whose request the cross is moved from the centre – in favour of a giant M (= Mary)!

On 2 November 1976 we fly to Boston. Before the flight I am pressed into a lengthy conversation for television at Heathrow Airport. It is the day of the election of Jimmy Carter as US President: for me too this is a sign of hope after the Nixon–Ford era. From 3 to 5 November on three evenings I give the W. B. Noble Lectures on *On Being a Christian* in Harvard Memorial Church.[8] For my discussion with three colleagues from Harvard Divinity School, who keep changing, I use the '20 Theses on Being a Christian' which I have already formulated; during the day – often even at breakfast – I discuss them with various groups of students and professors.

On 6 November we fly to Chicago and here enjoy the hospitality of my friend Andrew Greeley and of the Thomas More Association, for which I give a lecture on 'Why Sunday Worship?' On 8 November I return to New York where the book launch takes place in the Overseas Press Club. In the US *On Being a Christian* is welcomed with far less prejudice and in a far more friendly way by the leading Catholic theologians than it has been by the German dogmatic theologians. The reviews of both the prominent exegete Raymond Brown and the conservative dogmatic theologian Avery Dulles (later also David Tracy and Andrew Greeley) are, as I write to the editor of the Catholic journal *America*, 'well-informed, thorough and fair'; if only 'some of my German critics of the book had studied it carefully and criticized it' (26 November 1976).

The year 1976 had also been a very energetic year for me, and I am glad that after my return as well as skiing in Lech I can devote every free hour in the Christmas season to *Does God Exist?* After the big chapters on the atheism of Feuerbach, Marx and Freud and the nihilism of Nietzsche I have progressed to the fine positive chapters on fundamental trust (as the basis also of a fundamental human ethic) and belief in God (as the basis for fundamental trust). But at the beginning of January 1977 I must descend from the clear bright heights of the Alps to the valleys below the cloud layer, where again I have business with the German Conference of Bishops.

Different spiritual worlds

The 'conversation' with representatives of the Conference of Bishops takes place in the Catholic Academy in Hohenheim, Stuttgart, on 22 January 1977. I am speaking and answering questions for four hours, from 10 till 2; the minutes produced afterwards number almost 100 printed pages.[9]

To be brief, in my introductory defence I make several points clear: 1. that I am moved by pastoral intentions; 2. that the selection of critical questions addressed to me relates to only a tenth of my book; 3. that my method 'from below', starting from the questions of men and women today, in no way excludes the reality of God; 4. that my readiness to learn and correct myself is clear in my publications and my university activities; 5. that my article in the *Frankfurter Allgemeine Zeitung* was a justified defence against the improper attacks on my Catholic orthodoxy; 6. that fundamentally only dogmatic theologians, and not exegetes, ethicists and practical theologians have difficulties with my book; 7. that neither in Italy nor in the US nor in Ireland, where I have presented my book, is there such excitement and controversy as there is in Germany; 8. that even in Germany the reaction of the wider public to *On Being a Christian* has generally been highly positive and particularly in conversation with Jews about Jesus it opens up hopeful perspectives. I haven't mentioned the remarkable contrast between the way in which I am treated by the German Conference of Bishops and my rating in the world, now numbered by the editors of six American church journals with Jürgen Moltmann as the only Europeans among the 50 most influential thinkers (representatives) of the Christian church in today's world – together with Billy Graham, Archbishop Helder Camara, Andrew Greeley and many others.

But my eight points make little impression on my conversation partners. However much I emphasize that I would not deny the traditional dogmas but want to interpret them for men and women of today, they want to bind me in the fetters of scholastic dogmatics and compel me to adopt a method 'from above'. Basically, as Ratzinger notes, this is a discussion between Ptolemaeans, for whom the sun goes round the earth, and a Copernican, for whom the earth goes round the sun: an understanding is difficult, if not utterly impossible. For both sides sun, moon and stars may be the same, but each sees them in a completely different framework of understanding, in a completely different overall constellation or paradigm. In the meantime I have studied Thomas S. Kuhn's classic *The Structure of Scientific Revolutions* (1962) and begun to apply his theory of paradigm shift to the history of theology. The symposium of our Institute from 22 to 24 April 1977 at Ising on the Chiemsee is wholly devoted to the question how far the theologies of Augustine, Thomas, Luther and the Council of Trent represent different paradigms.

This paradigm theory now explains to me something that at times it is almost impossible to comprehend: why an understanding between the representatives of the old theological paradigm and me seems as difficult to achieve as did one between the representatives of the old and new astronomical paradigms in the time of Galileo. The representatives of the old and new constellations live in different worlds of thought and language; they can therefore hardly communicate with one another. The same is true of us; we live in the same church, and more than once I have protested to Lutheran colleagues who want to suggest to me that these hierarchs and I aren't in the same church. We are indeed in the same church, but we see God, Jesus Christ, the Holy Spirit and above all the church in as different perspectives as Ptolemy and Copernicus once saw the sun, moon and stars. The remarkable thing is how little those holding office in the church have learned from previous paradigm shifts.

Whereas Cardinal Hermann Volk is at least concerned for an understanding and argues in terms of theology and Neo-scholasticism, Cardinal Joseph Höffner has examined my book only in accordance with certain dogmatic formulas, which he confesses he has found only on page 444, where they don't seem to him to be adequate. If he has really read the whole book as he asserts, and not just thumbed through it, he hasn't understood it. When Höffner, at that time professor of Christian social doctrine in Münster, had been in Rome in the 1950s, we students of the German College had spotted how, while he had an excellent knowledge of questions of social policy, he was completely backward in theology. At the time I said that Höffner seemed to me to be like a craftsman zealously at work in a constantly changing world, but carrying his Gregorian theology in his rucksack as emergency rations, in the naive and self-confident conviction that not the slightest thing had to be changed ('*theologia perennis*'). Society and social doctrine may develop, but theology and fundamentally also the church always remain the same. This is very much in line with the motto on the coat of arms of the Grand Inquisitor Cardinal Ottaviani: '*semper idem* – always the same'.

Meanwhile Höffner's theological emergency rations are going stale. Without noticing it, he has got stuck theologically at the level of the Gregorian theology of the 1930s. Using Karl Rahner's terminology, one could call him a Denziger theologian. He has in his head only the dogmatic formulas listed in Denzinger's *Enchiridion,* uses them unhistorically and thinks that even after Vatican II he can still solve the theological problems of men and women today with the old conciliar definitions and the Roman school books of his student days. So in an open letter he accuses even Karl Rahner of no longer standing on the ground of the teaching of the church because Rahner has spoken critically in the German Synod about the divinity of Christ and the indissolubility of marriage. On Christmas Eve, 24 December 1977, on Westdeutscher Rundfunk of Cologne, in a half-hour broadcast, anticipating the results of my book *Does God Exist?*, I had answered the question 'Do We Believe in a Son of God?' and ended with the clear confession: '*Credo in Jesum Christum, filium Dei unigenitum* – I believe in Jesus Christ, God's only Son.' Did Höffner hear it?

But what is to be the outcome of such a discussion? Towards the end of the Stuttgart conversation the guardians of the faith are somewhat at a loss over what to say to the public – in the end they can hardly avoid a press conference. Moreover, everyone's stomach is rumbling and Cardinal Höffner is muttering that '40 to 60 bishops' are waiting to celebrate his 70th birthday – for him now evidently more important than the true faith. It is hastily agreed that the main topic of the conversation has been 'the statements of the author of *On Being a Christian* about the person and saving work of Jesus Christ'. However, there is agreement that some of Professor Küng's christological statements are in need of expansion. The German Conference of Bishops thinks this urgently necessary to avoid misunderstanding. Küng declares himself ready to make an appropriate contribution to the clarification of the questions discussed. The restrained press release generally receives positive comments in the media, as though people graciously want to give me time.

Making old creeds understandable

However, after the event the bishops obviously aren't content with the result of the Stuttgart conversation. Four days later, on 28 January 1977, Bishop Georg Moser, who is clearly himself under pressure, writes a letter to me. He urges me to write a further letter to the President of the German Conference of Bishops at the latest by its spring general assembly (28 February to 3 March). He thinks that there are quite specific areas which in his view are 'in need of expansion' (the doctrine of two natures, Johannine christology, the form of unity between Jesus and the Father).

I take the trouble and on 21 February send the desired letter to Cardinal Höffner. In it I maintain some points that I already made in my introduction to the Stuttgart conversation. At the same time I cite at length the declaration on the dogmas of Nicaea and Chalcedon which I have already formulated in *On Being a Christian*. In the end my letter is more than ten pages long. I also send it to Bishop Moser with a brief personal note: 'The only reason that I have taken so much trouble over a detailed answer was your personal intervention in this matter, which convinced me. This is meant to be a small token of thanks on my part.'[10]

But none of this is any use: these efforts, too, aren't taken seriously. Again, after its spring meeting on 3 March 1977 the German Conference of Bishops feels that it has to issue a press statement: 'Despite the efforts to come to an agreement the German Conference of Bishops thinks the inadequate statements by Professor Küng, which are open to misinterpretation, so serious that he must be required once again to put them right and supplement them.'[11]

I have no alternative but to reply the same day with my own press statement:

Men and women of today are not helped in their difficulties over belief with the mere repetition of old creeds. I have never denied the creeds, but rather have attempted to make them understandable to present-day men and women. People also expect this from the bishops. The clarification of theological difficulties which I have not invented myself cannot just be foisted on to individual theologians. Unfortunately the bishops have not said a word in response to my constructive proposals: 1. Study projects on important disputed questions; 2. Study conferences with the best possible experts; 3. An unpartisan composition of the German Faith Commission.

And I add:

Of course I am prepared to make further clarifications to my theological position. Important fundamental questions will soon be clarified in my book on the problem of God. But precisely for that reason, as I said in my last long letter of clarification to the Conference of Bishops, I would be grateful if the German bishops left me to do my own theological work in peace.[12]

Couldn't they accept at least one of my proposals instead of constantly oppressing me and publicly disowning me? Elsewhere at any rate I am more appreciated. Shouldn't I move to America, as has been suggested to me more than once?

Three days with the Kennedys

After the end of the winter semester, on 22 February 1977, I again fly via London to Washington. I couldn't refuse an invitation from Eunice and Sargent Shriver-Kennedy to give three evening lectures on *On Being a Christian* at Georgetown University. Since I must go and come back in a rush I am allowed – for once in my life – to fly on Concorde: at twice the speed of sound, 18,000 metres up, far above the weather and its clouds and storms. It's a fantastic feeling. We take off from London Heathrow at 1 p.m., I feel a slight jerk when we break through the sound barrier, and then there is just a gentle rushing noise. We land in Washington, DC at 12.10 p.m. after not even four hours, whereas a propeller plane takes twelve hours and a jumbo jet seven. There I am picked up by Shriver's son Timmy, who wanted to see a Concorde land (it's been in service a year) with its nose lowered so that the pilot has sufficient view. Timmy, who later will become President of the Special Olympics for the mentally handicapped founded by his mother, takes me to the great family estate of Timberlawn with its spacious park in Rockville, Maryland. That evening there is a dinner with about 30 people including President Carter's security adviser, Zbigniew Brzezinski, the leading Congressman John Brademas, Senator John Danforth, later UN ambassador, and the columnist Mary McGrory.

For Eunice and Sarge I am the theologian who as few others in the US has his hand on the pulse of the time and yet answers philosophical, theological and political questions from the depth of the Christian tradition. For example, there is the question whether children in their first years at school should have just a general ethical education or should be given a specifically Christian education. At the same time, for them I am a theologian who talks even on difficult questions without abstruse theological jargon and is therefore capable of explaining his concerns to very varied audiences, whether to students of philosophy and theology at Georgetown University, to politicians on Capitol Hill, on the TV broadcast 'Good Morning America' or to the College of Preachers of Washington Cathedral. Most important, though, are the Rose Fitzgerald Kennedy Lectures, given over three evenings to an audience of 1000 on the overall theme 'What Must Remain in Christianity?'

It's fascinating for me, as well as engaging in all these activities, to share in the life of the Kennedys, the most famous family in America, discussing every possible question in the living room or even in the kitchen. I talk with Sarge about the German origins of the Shriver family, originally Schreiber, and his experiences with the Peace Corps. I talk with Eunice about the still unclarified questions of birth control and infallibility, discussed in the Center for Population Policy of the Kennedy Institute, or the Vietnam War. Eunice thinks that her brother would certainly not have sent more ground troops to Vietnam but would have got out more quickly. And it gives me great pleasure to watch her youngest brother, Senator Edward Kennedy, driving his sports car in a way which terrifies his oldest sister. Eunice later writes to me that the three lectures were a 'terrific success'. She has already read half of *On Being a Christian* and told their mother Rose Kennedy in Boston that she won't have much time when she comes to see her because she has to go on reading the book.

The basis for my getting to know Eunice and Sarge Shriver-Kennedy more closely was certainly my admiration for President John F. Kennedy, whom I met personally in 1963 in the White House at the end of my first lecture trip right across America. I am proud that he introduced me to his Vice-President Lyndon B. Johnson as 'a new frontiersman of the Catholic Church'. For me Kennedy was the 'idealist without illusions', as he described himself. Now, though, the period of idealizing heroic historiography has been replaced by disclosure literature, especially reports of John F. Kennedy's sexual adventures which have reached the public. Understandably, I have inhibitions about addressing this delicate topic directly and giving the impression of indiscreet curiosity. But on the journey to the airport in the car alone with Sarge I do finally touch on it. He plays it down. 'During President Kennedy's lifetime no one would have dared to spread such rumours,' but now 'this woman' (he meant Judith Campbell Exner) has spread unverifiable stories in public. Quite possibly I offended Sarge in putting the question before my departure, but not to have done so would have seemed to me dishonest. Meanwhile too many stories of Kennedy's sexual escapades, even in the White House, have been spread for it to be possible to dismiss them as 'rumours'. And for me they are not just forgivable 'peccadilloes', venial sins.

But of course my verdict on the charismatic statesman Kennedy, who had only a thousand days in office and whom I portrayed in *My Struggle for Freedom* (VII: A free man with a free mind) hasn't changed. Since with George W. Bush we have experienced the precise opposite of a Kennedy, the desire for a new Kennedy has again been kindled in the US and the Kennedy myth has taken on new radiance. At the instigation of neo-conservative ideologists and with the support of a fundamentalist Protestant following, George W. Bush staged the invasion of Iraq using Orwellian lies and under the cloak of the establishment of democracy, with devastating consequences for the Near East and the US. By contrast, in October 1962 John F. Kennedy coped with the most dangerous confrontation between the US and the USSR over the secret stationing of Soviet missiles and long-range rockets on Cuba not by an invasion of Cuba, which had been argued for by the generals, but by a sea blockade and shrewd negotiations with Khrushchev. This introduced a policy of *détente* with an agreement to stop nuclear tests, and peaceful competition to reach the moon (the Apollo programme).

Behind Kennedy's radiant life was hidden a lifelong history of illness which he bore with Stoic bravery. We were first made to realize its extent by the most recent biography, researched in the utmost detail, by Robert Dallek, Professor of History at Boston University.[13] Kennedy's illnesses had aroused in him an unquenchable hunger for life and driven him to his ambition. But all this in no way affected his political judgement as US President. Even according to the most recent biography, despite the aggressive desire of his generals for war he remained a model of wise statesmanship in a difficult situation. What I missed in so many church leaders at the Council I found in Kennedy the statesman: intelligence, historical knowledge, honesty and resolution.

From the White House now, in 1977, I receive friendly thanks from President Jimmy Carter, for me likewise a hopeful president, for my book *On Being a Christian* which I inscribed for him; his letter has the handwritten postscript 'He may come by to see me'. Unfortunately there isn't enough time, since I am already bound for the airport, to fly back to Europe via Boston. But inevitably, because it has been planned long since, in three months I shall return to America, this time though not to the East Coast but direct to the Midwest.

Ecumenical problems and opportunities: a Vatican III?

In the *Concilium* Foundation we had agreed that 1977, the twelfth year of our journal, should be celebrated with a congress in the US, where our journal has its difficulties. The President of the University of Notre Dame, Indiana, Theodore M. Hesburgh, a representative of American Catholicism known throughout the land and a member of several presidential commissions, was ready to act as host, together with our real partner, Archbishop John J. Egan, the Director of the Center for Pastoral and Social Services, as pleasant as he is efficient.

This link has been suggested by Andrew Greeley, a member of our board of directors, together with our friend David Tracy, likewise of the University of Chicago, and at the time President of the Catholic Theological Society of America. With me Johann Baptist Metz, whose turn it is to be president of the congress, represents the European side and devotes himself intensely to the preparations in the face of the many difficulties. There are good auspices for collaboration here. However, hundreds of theologians aren't to be invited to Notre Dame, as they were to Brussels in 1970, but only the members of *Concilium* and the Catholic Theological Society and – this is very important to us – a group of social scientists. In the last week of May 1977 finally 71 participants meet in a pleasantly democratic atmosphere and in addition there is a large guest audience.

In view of the standstill of the Catholic Church and the critical stage of ecumenical understanding the general theme is 'Toward Vatican III. The Work That Needs to be Done'. The enormous amount of material is divided according to the structure of *Concilium*. First comes 'Christian Faith': church and life, church and ecumenism. Then 'Christian Ethics': church and individual, church and society. Finally 'Church Praxis': church and reform, church and worship. There are two or three speakers from different nations and continents on each topic. Along with the Italian Council historian Giuseppe Alberigo and the American dogmatic theologian Avery Dulles I am given the topic 'church and ecumenism'. I use the opportunity for a stocktaking of the state of the Catholic

Church and the ecumenical world twelve years after Vatican II which is both comprehensive and deep.

In the next session, the Dutch church lawyer Peter Huizing SJ (formerly at the Gregorian, now in Holland) supports many of my reform concerns. In his concluding remarks he points to the great frustration in the church and theology. The problem is not to convince other theologians of the need for these reforms; rather, it is to find the secret of influencing the church authorities who have the power to bring about changes. When in 2007 after 30 years I re-read the 27 carefully-worked-out pages of my comprehensive and detailed reform programme I am deeply saddened: what opportunities we missed in past years in our church! How many people have left the ship, and how many have a spiritual thirst! Of course tensions are also to be expected in our congress because of its composition: between Europeans and Americans, North and South Americans, theologians and social scientists.

Dispute among theologians: politicizing theology

Despite the gloomy prospects for the future, the Notre Dame congress is a great success. My account, like those of Giuseppe Alberigo and Avery Dulles, is welcomed with much approval. However, things are different in the 'church and society' unit. Here Johann Baptist Metz, completely failing to recognize the situation in the US, presents four sharp theses in a 1968 mentality. Beyond doubt much of their substance is right, but they haven't been sufficiently thought through and above all haven't been prepared for by any publications. Metz argues for a church with a stronger emphasis on the North–South axis and the transformation of a church of the middle class into a church of the class struggle (Thesis 1). At the same time he radicalizes church life in a mystical–political way through discipleship and apocalyptic or the expectation of an imminent end (Theses 2–4).

He is followed immediately afterwards by the most important American moral theologian, Charles Curran. Systematically, point by point, Curran takes up Metz's theses and criticizes them well and truly in a balanced way, above all the apocalyptic expectation as a constant criticism of structures of oppression. Instead of playing off the 'rich churches of the North' and the 'poor churches of the South' against each other and generally promoting the class struggle, Curran calls on both to apply Catholic social teaching in church and society. He does all this very objectively and without any personal jibes, because beyond question he doesn't want to hurt Metz. But Metz feels mortally wounded and will not recover from this criticism for the rest of the congress. The situation is made even worse when the German Canadian Gregory Baum, likewise politically left-wing, with the best will in the world comes to Metz's help with a vigorous critique of the sociological school present at the congress. He says that they are all too uncritical of the political order and don't take account of the results of other sociologists,

357

above all from Europe. Of course this provokes Andrew Greeley, who has long since been wary of the 'political theologians' and the Latin American liberation theologians; he uses the opportunity to let fly with sharp polemic.

I keep out of this public debate; exposed as I am in my position in the church, I am concerned to keep a low profile among the leaders of the congress, where Metz is functioning as president. I was heavily burdened with planning it and preparing the organization, sometimes had to mediate between topics and authors, and finally had to bring together all the papers of the *Concilium* participants. Now I am faced with the shattered remains and attempt to knit together what possibly can't be knit together. Charles Curran behaves in a reasonable and conciliatory way. However, Metz is defeated and furious and will accuse me bitterly two days later in New York, when we are going down Broadway after a discussion with our publisher, of having taken Greeley's side. But I had only been attempting to mediate and in doing so drew Andrew Greeley aside and advised him to be moderate.

Greeley and I remain friends. But Greeley won't be reconciled with Metz and Baum and even tenders his resignation from the editorial committee of *Concilium*; he won't change his mind despite a friendly letter from me. After the congress Metz denounces reform theologians as 'highly conservative both politically and in terms of society' and in a press interview (4 September 1977) says that the concern for reforms within the church shown by me and many participants had 'not been a theme at this congress'. This announces a fundamental change in this 'political theologian' which culminates in his being invited by the head of the Roman Congregation for the Doctrine of the Faith, Cardinal Ratzinger, to his 70th birthday party in 1997.

Afterwards Archbishop Egan thanks me 'for all that you did to make things easier' (16 June 1977). He says that despite everything the congress has been a tremendous success and that the press response in *America*, *Commonweal* and the *National Catholic Reporter* and in the secular press has been 'extremely positive' – apart of course from ultra-conservative papers such as *The Wanderer* in the US or *Neue Bildpost* in Germany, which present me as the heretical leader of a church revolution. Anyone who wants an objective view can obtain it: all the papers are published – though some are heavily revised and the Curran–Metz criticism is not included.[14]

Endless quarrels: Cardinal Höffner

However, the Catholic hierarchy doesn't leave me in peace. On 22 April 1977 I have received a long letter from Cardinal Joseph Höffner.[15] Reliable sources indicate that this letter has been written by a well-known professor of dogmatics and a member of the Faith Commission. Is it Höffner's friend Ratzinger? I can only guess at his name. On 13 June I reply to Cardinal Höffner. I tell him that I have been in the US at a theological congress, I am surprised that they are still not content with all my verbal answers in the Stuttgart conversation and with my most recent written remarks. I must ask the cardinal to excuse me for being unable to send an appropriate answer to his letter 'until I have finished my book on the question of God and given the ceremonial lecture to celebrate the quincentenary of the University of Tübingen in October of this year'.[16] In the end of the day I am a professor of Tübingen University and not an employee of this Conference of Bishops and under its instructions. The lack of time isn't just an excuse; I am in fact under great pressure.

On 8 July I receive another letter from Cardinal Höffner in which he delivers an ultimatum: I must give him an answer to his letter of 22 April by 10 September at the latest;[17] the plenary assembly of the Conference of Bishops begins on 19 September. On 12 September I reply to him once again[18] that I am in the final phase of my book on the question of God and that the ceremonial lecture on the quincentenary of the University of Tübingen has absolute priority.

I add that nevertheless I have worked as hard as I could to spell out the substance and make specific the very complex questions he has raised, especially the christological ones, which in my view could not be answered in the form of a catechism: 'After spending several hours in Stuttgart giving you detailed answers and in addition addressing a long letter of clarification to the German Conference of Bishops; also after several thorough conversations with the Bishop of Rottenburg, I have once again carefully thought through the whole set of problems in connection with the question of God and the fundamental question of faith and knowledge and set it down in a book of almost 900 pages.' The clarification of the situation will be better served by thus putting the cardinal's questions in a broader theological context. *Does God Exist?* is to be published soon and I will immediately send him a copy in the hope that the German Conference of Bishops will be able to assess not only its pastoral intentions but also the weight of the substantive theological statements which will be presented broadly in this my 'answer to the question of God in modern times'.

But on 21 September I receive another impatient letter from Cardinal Höffner: he regrets that I have omitted to answer the basic questions of Catholic faith.[19] In my reply of 7 November I firmly reject the charge that I have again refused to answer questions in connection with my book *On Being a Christian*. I say that I have made clear confession of the divine sonship of Jesus and that I will be answering further questions in my *Does God Exist?*. I have 'never intended to deny the indispensable confessions of our faith and I see no fundamental contradiction between the statements in my book *On Being a Christian* and the statements of the first ecumenical councils. However, I think it necessary to interpret them for men and women of today. I would like to ask you emphatically in future to start from the fact that we both stand on the ground of a shared Catholic faith.'[20] The reference to the Tübingen ceremonial lecture had been anything but an excuse. This was a quite extraordinary occasion.

Quincentenary of the University of Tübingen: jubilee address on the question of God

Couldn't Cardinals Höffner and Volk, who had also once been university professors, appreciate the ecumenically important fact that a Catholic theologian was to give a ceremonial lecture at the great quincentenary celebrations of the University of Tübingen founded in 1477, in the Stiftskirche of Tübingen, a centre of the Reformation?

Professor Johannes Neumann, himself an influential member of the jubilee committee, reports in the Stuttgart colloquium to the cardinals, Georg Moser, Bishop of Rottenburg, and their professorial entourage how he proposed every possible candidate for the speech, but not his faculty colleague Küng. However, for this jubilee the professors 'did not want to hear anything about any epistemological questions or even about the history of the university, but about the central question of our human existence, about God'. 'It was then said that the only one we trust to do this in a language that we non-theologians understand is not this person or that, but Hans Küng. Some of these were extremely distinguished members of our teaching body. And if I may tell you that Hans Küng's On Being a Christian can be found among many secular works in this place where we have met, the university guest house, you will see that here Küng in particular has in fact found a vacuum in the bishops' preaching, which is why his book is so popular.'[21]

What is the reaction of the episcopal side at this colloquium? Not a word of satisfaction or even recognition, but confused silence. Cardinal Höffner finally says tersely, 'We want to come to an agreement.' Cardinal Volk adds that 'agreement' doesn't mean just any 'supplementation' but, as Höffner makes clear, the verbatim acknowledgement of church doctrine, say 'with reference to the pre-existence of Jesus Christ, the fruit of salvation and the binding nature of the councils', as the bishops understand them.

I have already long since explained this and much more, as it could be explained in the light of Holy Scripture and the great Catholic tradition. However, these gentlemen have nothing more to learn. Such a 'magisterium' in principle has nothing to learn, only to teach. After all, Höffner boasts, we are not a 'study group' which has never studied seriously either modern exegesis or the history of dogma or contemporary Catholic and Protestant theology: 'This is the college of bishops throughout the world' – as if he had asked all of them! And was a theologian just to nod his head sagely? But at this stage of the conversation, as I've said, everyone wanted to eat. With relief I think that even 'princes of the church' with no appetite for theology sometimes feel quite human pangs of hunger. But the question of God doesn't interest these men of God a jot. They live in another world, the world of the church.

From the beginning my great concern was for the question of God once again to be raised clearly, even in the framework of our secular university. And the theological week on 'The Question of God Today' which both theological faculties hold jointly in the jubilee year shows how much the ecumenical world has progressed at the academic level despite the unecumenical attitude of Rome and the bishops. I had suggested the week and invited my colleagues Jüngel, Kasper and Moltmann, together with the two deans Greinacher and Scholder, to my house on 27 October 1975 to plan it. It was held in the Festsaal of the University with a full and lively audience from 19 to 21 April, combined with major evening lectures by the General Secretary of the World Council of Churches, Dr Philip Potter, and the physicist and philosopher Carl Friedrich von Weizsäcker.

The central ceremonial act for the quincentenary of the university takes place in the Tübingen Stiftskirche on 8 October 1977. There, preceded and followed by a Handel organ concerto, I give my ceremonial lecture – after all the greetings, the last of them which is by the then German Federal President Walter Scheel. Without any prior warning, instead of giving a greeting he can't resist the politicians' temptation and delivers a ceremonial speech almost as long as mine. It is on 'Courage for Critical Sympathy', a topic being canvassed by the students, and is understandable against the current background: the student bodies dominated by the Marxists are obstructing all jubilee celebrations and prefer to organize strikes; the great mass of students remains passive. On the other hand, the employers' president Hanns-Martin Schleyer, who had been kidnapped by the Red Army Faction (RAF), is now to be exchanged for eleven Baader-Meinhof prisoners: Federal Chancellor Helmut Schmidt has to refuse – this after similar negative experiences – despite a request from Frau Schleyer, so as to show that the state isn't open to pressure.

For me it isn't easy after Scheel's all-too-long speech to give the ceremonial lecture announced in the programme on the difficult topic 'Can We Still Believe in God Today?' The terrible heat under the bright lights of the live television transmission makes sweat run down my forehead, which is an added complication. With many allusions to the history of Tübingen University, my first part is on 'Why people were against God'. It is because for centuries 'God's representatives' fought against science and democracy. I also attempt to give a balanced answer to political atheism. My second part is on 'Why yes to God?' A no to God is possible, but so too is a yes; today at any rate the classical arguments for atheism – the argument from psychology that God is a pure projection of our wishes and the argument from the philosophy of history that the end of religion has come – have been seen through. My basic answer is solidly grounded in my forthcoming book. A yes to God isn't possible on the basis of a compelling proof (like that, for example, for Pythagoras' theorem), nor is it possible on the basis of a vague feeling (feelings are all too often deceptive). Rather, it is possible only on the basis of a reasonable trust, for which there are no proofs but many reasons. So finally in the third part I come to my answer to the question 'How we can think of God today?' My conclusion is that 'today we are again faced with a decision on the basic question against the background of modern science'.

I present in very concrete terms what sounds abstract in summary. The applause in the large church is unusually sustained and I receive many compliments. But at the banquet which follows in the Museum Restaurant, attended by prominent political and university figures, the Prime Minister of Baden-Württemberg, Hans Filbinger, thanks everyone but the speaker. The church authorities probably wouldn't have agreed with everything said in the Stiftskirche today, remarks the conservative politician from Freiburg in a pert tone with a smug laugh. In his greeting he had quoted Cardinal Ratzinger on the 'baneful role' of left-wing politicians. The next year this pious Catholic is toppled as head of the state because shortly before the end of the war, as a marine judge, he had condemned deserters to death and had attempted all down the years stupidly to hush this up and later even to defend his death sentences as 'just'. 'The world's history is the world's court,' the Swabian philosopher Hegel had remarked.

My speech is widely reported in the media and later it is also broadcast by Swiss and Austrian television; the *Frankfurter Allgemeine Zeitung* devotes almost three pages to it. Probably none of my speeches has generated so many letters of assent and requests for a copy. Soon afterwards it and President Scheel's speech are published with great speed by Piper Verlag. The university Attempto Verlag immediately has my speech pressed as a gramophone record, 'The New Question of God'; the graphics on the sleeve are of a seeker by the most famous German woodcut artist HAP Grieshaber from neighbouring Reutlingen: the original still hangs in my home. I thank the artist for the depiction of the figure against a white background: 'Crawling and laden and horizontal to the earth, but at the same time – at least as I see it – held hovering by a hand, a fire, a force from the vertical ...' (12 December 1977). But I don't hear from a single bishop – apart from my own Bishop of Basle, Anton Hänggi. I have a sense of foreboding.

One of my plans for the quincentenary came to nothing. Despite a long letter I couldn't persuade the Polish composer Krzystof Penderecki to set to music for our ecumenical worship the eight Beatitudes of the Sermon on the Mount, each of which 'shows a tremendous contrast and a span, and presents a unique challenge both theologically and musically' (18 November 1976). In fact the Beatitudes have hardly ever been set to music since Wilhelm Kienzl's folk opera *Der Evangelimann* (1895). When I got hold of Penderecki, who was living in Germany, on the telephone he explained to me that it was impossible for him to compose anything completely new by 9 October 1977. I have my success with another proposal which likewise has to do with Eastern Europe.

Honorary doctorate for a Soviet dissident: Evgeni V. Barabanov

In 1977, as part of the quincentenary celebrations of the University of Tübingen, the faculty of Catholic theology honours with doctorates four figures who in different contexts, whether in Starnberg, Jerusalem, Rio de Janeiro or Moscow, attempt to gain a hearing for the Christian spirit in our world and to do justice to a Christian ethic. The best known is the physicist and philosopher Carl Friedrich von Weizsäcker, who has penetrated the fundamental problems of physics to the philosophical question of the essence of the truth. The Benedictine abbot Laurentius Klein is also well known; he has founded a study centre for Christian biblical theology, Judaistics and Islam in the Abbey of the Dormition in Jerusalem. The Bishop of Novo Iguaçu in Brazil, Adriano Hypolito, is honoured as a champion of human rights and social justice who has made well-based theological contributions.

Least known, but not least interesting, is a dissident from the Soviet Union, Evgeni V. Barabanov, who is doing theology in Moscow in extraordinary conditions. I had made contact with the intellectual underground in the Soviet Union at an early stage. It is intellectually a very lively group, all its members in their middle thirties, and my link with them is Senta Grünbeck of Munich, a trained teacher of religion with qualifications in Russian, who is in constant touch with them. So there are exchanges in both directions.

People in Moscow were keenly interested in *On Being a Christian*. I immediately had twenty copies sent to Moscow by a roundabout route. With a substantial financial contribution I ensured that the translator had something to live on, that paper was bought and the book could be printed abroad. When the book was finally distributed in samizdat, underground and unauthorized, there was a very heated discussion. Of course those who had grown up in traditional Orthodox theology were initially surprised at a historical christology developed 'from below'.

On 5 February 1976 I had received from Evgeni Barabanov the translation of his fine article on 'The Destiny of Christian Culture', which I published in my series of 'Theological Meditations'. Born in Leningrad in 1943, Barabanov has first been brought up a Communist (his father was in a high position in an armaments factory). At the age of 15 he discovered the New Testament for himself, and when he was 17 there was the first great conflict: the KGB secret police came to his father and showed him evidence against his son, photographs of his son taking part in worship, the young man kneeling in front of an icon. Thereupon Barabanov was sent to a psychiatric clinic for observation but was released after some months. However, as the 'case' wasn't over, he could be 'disposed of' any time the KGB wanted. At the Lomonossov University in Moscow Barabanov studied history and art history, and on the completion of his studies worked on the journal *Decorative Art* and with the publishing house 'Art'. In 1973 he was dismissed for sending a manuscript to the West. Since then Barabanov has lived with his wife Natasha and two children of four and five in Moscow, constantly under political pressure, afraid of raids on his house, arrest, interrogation, consignment to a clinic.

Another original article by Barabanov on 'The Aesthetics of Early Christianity' was also assessed very positively by our ancient historian Professor Hermann Josef

Vogt and was accepted for *Theologische Quartalschrift* (4, 1976). My proposal that an honorary doctorate should be bestowed on Barabanov is unanimously accepted in the faculty. I give the laudation for this Russian, who is attempting to make his way between church conservatism and modernism in the unshakable hope of a religious rebirth of his country. The Soviet embassy in Bonn sends an angry protest note, but we aren't impressed by it and award the doctorate nevertheless. Since then a large portrait photograph of Barabanov, who is absent from the ceremony, has adorned the Theological School.

Problems of the world and problems of the hierarchy; what a strange contrast! On the one hand there are my efforts to promote the Christian cause wherever I am, even in the USSR, and on the other there are the efforts of the German hierarchy to discredit me all over the world. Even Cardinal Julius Döpfner had used his New Year's Eve 1975 sermon to launch polemic against me by name from the pulpit of the Liebfrauenkirche in Munich. I hear of that only later. Paradoxically it is Senta Grünbeck, present at the time, who writes a letter to this cardinal; ten years previously he had blessed her in religious instruction (letter of 17 April 1976):

> Ten years ago I came to you, stirred by Küng's sermon in which he calls for loyalty to the official church. Hardly any of the few of my colleagues who reject Küng can give reasons for their rejection. Why do leading persecuted Christians of the East, who don't have the leisure to cling to formulations because faith is a matter of life or death, turn to Küng in particular? Don't our youth need to trust a man who can be said quite certainly not to be on the side of the hangers-on in real times of crisis?

And Senta Grünbeck ends her Easter letter as follows:

> These thoughts came to me during the 1975 New Year's Eve sermon and returned once more when at this time I brought greetings from Moscow to Küng from people who because of their belief in the resurrection have prison behind or ahead of them. Küng's spontaneous readiness to help brothers in need has strengthened my Easter faith. I want to communicate to you for tomorrow's Easter festival a 'Russian' Christ is risen, i.e. one loaded with feelings, in the hope that your fatherly goodness will again be strong enough also to be able to embrace people like Küng.

This letter doesn't seem to have had any effect on Döpfner. At any rate the conference of bishops now prepares a further major action against me in secret with all the means at its disposal. Here in particular I need the counsel of my church lawyer. But a few weeks after the Stuttgart conversation he had dealt me a bitter personal blow.

The loss of a legal adviser: Professor Neumann

The professor of church law, Johannes Neumann, returns his *missio canonica*, his permission from the church to teach, resigns his priestly office, leaves the Catholic Church and gives up his chair of church law. These are confusing and turbulent days after Easter 1977. It is an event widely reported in the press, behind which there is a deep human tragedy.

In a long statement Neumann explains that he has taken this step because of the inhumanity of the church system. I can easily follow his arguments; we both had an increasingly critical view of the Catholic Church after the Council. With his writing 'Human Rights – Also in the Catholic Church?', his alternative draft of a new marriage law (written with the Dutch Peter Huizing) and many other proposals, Neumann has been brushed off by the hierarchy. He says that the church 'system' has proved unreliable and 'irreformable'. He protests in particular against 'the order for the laicizing of priests which mocks any sense of law' and the 'blackmail' connected with it. In these circumstances, how is he as professor of church law to continue to explain the church's ordination law to candidates for the priesthood? 'The clergy ... are largely without rights and protection in the conflict with the church leadership.' In short, Neumann says that in the light of the self-understanding which has developed under the influence of many external historical and political factors, the Roman Catholic Church is fundamentally no longer capable of being reformed. He goes. But I stay, and since then our attitudes to the Catholic Church and the Christian faith have divided us.

Regardless of any personal factors which may have played a part in Neumann's decision, our faculty has lost an excellent specialist and a shrewd and pleasant colleague, the university an eminent member of the Senate and its last Rector before the introduction of a presidential constitution. And I lose a loyal friend. From the beginning he has been a congenial and a highly competent legal adviser and I have valued him above all other colleagues in the faculty apart from my Swiss friend Herbert Haag. He has more trouble than he expected in moving to another faculty (even that of legal science, which had co-opted him in an honorary capacity the previous year). He ends up in the sociology of religion department. Since then I have missed his voice, not only in the faculty and university but also in public inside and outside the church. I need his friendship and his professional knowledge more than ever in the increasingly difficult years which face me.

In February 1978, I send him the documentation 'For Nothing but the Truth', in which he plays such an important role, soon after it is published, with a short letter: 'Dear Johannes, You can imagine that much was going through my head – and my heart – as I looked out and collected this documentation. Your name has an indelible place here and I wish that so much in recent times hadn't happened. If I can help you in any way, you know that I will. All good wishes, Your Hans' (15 February 1978). His answer consists of a few friendly lines. Now he goes his own way, marries and moves far from Tübingen to a village in Baden; his life focuses increasingly on his family. At the climax of the controversy with Rome two years later, when I urgently need advice on church law, I will ask him once again for help – for a fee.

Tons of paper

Even the powerful and generally positive response from the media to my quincentenary speech on the question of God cannot make an impact on the agitators in the German Conference of Bishops. They won't even wait for *Does God Exist?* with its christological explanations, which they have been told about. Now the uncomfortable theologian is to be put under massive pressure and finally got out of the way. Only a month after the university speech, on 17 November 1977, the German Conference of Bishops distributes with all the means at its disposal a multi-page, long-drawn-out and dogmatic third declaration on *On Being a Christian*, announced as 'Word of the German Bishops to those involved in the Proclamation of the Faith'.[22] There are long sections (which are certainly boring even for many good Christians) on: 1. Jesus Christ, true man and true God; 2. God's giving of himself to us in Jesus Christ; 3. Curtailment of the reality of redemption.

To the annoyance of the bishops, the pastors and teachers of religion involved in the proclamation of the faith and the many interested people find *On Being a Christian* helpful. They are impressed, if not oppressed, by the list (with references) added to the declaration, of roughly twelve pastoral letters from the German bishops, three statements by the Apostolic See, a word on Europe, four statements by Cardinal Döpfner and four further documents. Of course there is hardly any mention of my book in these documents. But a multi-page documentation of the written proceedings between me and the German Conference of Bishops concerning *On Being a Christian* and finally an index and chronological table with another 25 entries follows. All this 'incriminating material' is also sent to me in Tübingen on the eve of publication with a covering letter by courier from Cardinal Höffner – as always at short notice.

One can only wonder: at a time which surely has other concerns, in a manoeuvre planned by a general staff, tons of paper are addressed 'to those involved in the proclamation of the faith' – all against just one theologian! How many people have worked for how many hours on this action and how many thousands of Deutschemarks have been spent on it? And what is the point of this unprecedented journalistic, personal and financial expenditure by the German hierarchy, doubtless in agreement with the Vatican, if they know 'the truth' on a sure basis?

I have no illusions. In this way they want at least to render harmless a serious, influential theologian, whose behaviour isn't conformist on every point, whom they cannot, as in former times, burn, ban or otherwise silence – of course for the well-being of the faithful. A hierarchy with a thirst for power now increasingly uses the sanctimonious argument that 'the faithful' have a 'right to be protected in their Catholic faith'. It should be noted that since 1970, following the long and proven practice of the US Supreme Court, a 'dissenting opinion' is also allowed to be published in the Constitutional Court of the Federal Republic of Germany. But in the Catholic Church of this Republic – despite the freedom of religion, conscience and opinion solemnly affirmed in 1965 by Vatican II – my 'dissenting opinion' is to be suppressed as far as possible and the one who presents it is to be discredited all over the world.

And all this although, as my own press release, likewise published on 17 November 1977, says, my book *On Being a Christian* 'is a real help to many Christians, pastors and lay people, both Catholic and Protestant, in their Christian faith and life'.[23] For many weeks it has been right at the top of the *Spiegel* bestseller list and is now certainly being read not just by potential 'heretics'. I regret that the bishops haven't waited for my remarks in *Does God Exist?* and object strongly to the publication of my personal letters to the President of the German Conference of Bishops in a tendentious context without my permission and the refusal to include a statement by me in the documentation on the same matter. Doctrinaire self-justification by the bishops without self-criticism has the wrong effect: 'In the present difficult situation of church and society, people expect from the bishops not condemnations but constructive answers to questions which are also theirs.'

The theologian Heinz-Joachim Fischer, who so far has always commented fairly on the proceedings, notes a lack of proof from the bishops: 'Küng is not known clearly and decisively to have rejected an essential statement of the church's faith, nor has this charge ever been levelled by the bishops. However, with their statement and the documentation of the correspondence the bishops are displaying their lack of evidence. Where they explain what theologians must do they become incomprehensible' (*Frankfurter Allgemeine Zeitung*, 22 September 1977).

But the bishops' wide-ranging journalistic campaign, which has been carried out over a long period, has of course borne fruit among many uninformed believers. I receive malicious and negative letters and also hate letters – not from readers of my books, but from readers of newspapers. There is one, for example, from Switzerland addressed to 'Dear Küng family' in Sursee (4 February 1977), to be forwarded to me: 'He should know that that's enough and we are still capable of beating in the enemy's skull in accordance with old ancestral custom ... We will find him *anywhere* in Europe. European Sanction Committee for Purging the Church. H. Ott.' But of course there is also approval from European neighbours. For example, a former pupil writes to me ironically from Luxembourg: 'The Bishop of Luxembourg is incurring some expense over the correct doctrine: he is sending the declaration by the German bishops on *On Being a Christian* by express post to all pastors, teachers of religion and so on. In that way Luxembourg is saved!' Indeed every bishop does it his way. Here is another example.

A bishop and his teacher of religion

The major episcopal action against me proves devastating for many 'sisters and brothers involved in the proclamation of faith'. Every German bishop also sends a letter of his own to the 'ladies and gentlemen involved in the proclamation of the faith', as for example does Bishop Heinrich Maria Janssen of Hildesheim, who at first contentedly notes 'that the theological controversy of past years has calmed down'. But 'the annoying controversy with Professor Dr Hans Küng continues'. 'With much restraint and some patience which has been wrongly interpreted we bishops have attempted to persuade Professor Küng to make additions, corrections or clarifications to his book *On Being a Christian*. Professor Kung has not been prepared to do this.'

Because Professor Küng has 'canvassed public support' against the criticism and reprimand of him by the bishops, Bishop Janssen goes on to say that the bishops felt compelled to prepare documentation on the controversy and thus make it clear 'that clarification and correction of the passages objected to in his book have been hindered by the recalcitrance of Professor Küng'. So the bishop encloses the declaration by the German bishops: 'I do this with an expression of my deep regret that a theologian who is undoubtedly so highly gifted can persist so blindly and obstinately in making remarks in his book which need correction, or even abbreviation and omission, which cannot stand in their present form if the faith is to be kept pure. This burdens so much that is valuable in Küng's books and makes it impossible for us to allow them without correction and repudiation.' Of course the bishop knows that 'Professor Küng is a mentor today for many of you and that his books are read by many people. I must ask you all the more urgently to consider carefully what the bishops have presented here and accordingly be critical when using Küng's books.'

That's how it all looks from the perspective of the bishop 'from above'. The perspective of the pastors and teachers of religion 'from below', as indicated by letters, looks quite different. Among all of them this action provokes inability to understand (the declaration is 'a great misunderstanding'), frustration ('an own goal') and anger (accusations that the authorities are 'weak and disgraceful', 'shameful'). For example, Jos Schnurer, a teacher of religion from Hildesheim, writes to me: 'I think that your optimistic statement that in future the official church will react in the controversy with you in a less hierarchical and dogmatic way no longer applies today – if it ever has. In my estimation and my observations as a Catholic Christian who is increasingly drawing a distinction between "being a Christian" and "being a member of an official church which is closed to change", we are in a time of almost unprecedented conservatism. The attempts again to bind the faithful seamlessly to the official church and to forbid criticism cannot be overlooked.'

The teacher of religion sends me his bishop's letter with the comment: 'In Lower Saxony – and probably not only there – at the moment a development is taking place which can only be described as the official church battening down the hatches against any effort to open it up to questions of our time. Thus for example in the sphere of education masses of private schools are being established and maintained by the bishops, lavishly equipped from church tax and with the teachers there bound to the "right line" in rigid instruments of school supervision. The "German scandal", which is what I call the uncritical and almost absolute tie of the official church to the "Christian" parties, is a further indication of my thesis that the official church is not in a position to adapt to the demands of the time.'

And on my statement that the most important controversial questions between Catholics and Protestants have been settled, he remarks critically: 'Do you know that for example in Hildesheim and in the diocese of Hildesheim the private schools under episcopal supervision accept very few Protestant pupils? Do you know that the teachers of religion in Lower Saxony aren't allowed to give integrated instruction, i.e. religious instruction common to Catholics and Protestants? And for years I have never heard of joint celebrations of the mass and meetings of Catholic and Protestant communities!'

The final conclusion of this teacher of religion on the basis of the bishop's actions is: '"Being a Christian?" For the official church "being a Catholic" is the maxim. Who speaks of Christianity if by that they understand more than an absolute confessional tie to Catholicism? Who can achieve it? Küng perhaps, but not a teacher of religion in Lower Saxony! That is why although I have permission to teach I have refused to give Catholic religious instruction. For me, despite *On Being a Christian* and *Does God Exist?* and "For Nothing but the Truth", it's no longer worth standing up for the official church, it's no longer worth criticizing. That doesn't mean that your books and your efforts remain fruitless.'

Of course for me such letters are depressing. I reply to the teacher of religion that I can sense his feelings all too well and could easily contribute further material. 'One can in fact doubt whether the official church will get any better in the near future. That I nevertheless involve myself in this particular church is for the simple reason that I am not concerned with the official church but with the church, and that is the fellowship of all believers. Would I do all these people, the many little and unknown ones, a service if I were to resign? I would like you to think about that.' So I present him with my remarks on 'Why I Remain in the Church'. Many people confirm my view: 'If Küng is disciplined or forbidden to teach – or if Küng recants – there is no longer a place for me in the church.' There is also comforting news such as: 'In the Cologne Carmel Mary of Peace, *On Being a Christian* is being read at meals.' I receive many expressions of thanks by word of mouth and in writing ('I haven't been shaken in faith but fortified') and calls to remain steadfast and not to let myself be led astray.

Dogmas instead of reforms?

One thing had immediately struck me: my demands for reform which were even emphasized with page numbers in the first episcopal declaration on *On Being a Christian* (English pp. 491, 525-27) of 17 February 1975 and at the same time rejected – I enumerated them in the previous chapter – are absent from the subsequent episcopal documentation and correspondence and totally disappear in the third declaration by the bishops. The reason is easy to see: these demands are too popular in the church and the wider public for it to be possible to use them against me. A referendum (of the kind that is possible in my Swiss homeland on all important political questions in the community, canton and Federation) would result in almost solid majorities for the reforms everywhere and overwhelming majorities on some questions.

Instead of reforms, which the people expect, bishops prefer to talk about dogmas. John XXIII had said in his opening speech at the Second Vatican Council that the 'salient point' was 'not a discussion of one article or another of the fundamental doctrine of the Church which has repeatedly been taught by the Fathers and by ancient and modern theologians, and which is presumed to be well known and familiar to all'. More important is the contemporary proclamation of the faith: 'a leap forward towards a doctrinal penetration and a formation of consciousness in faithful and perfect conformity to the authentic doctrine, which, however, should be studied and expounded through the methods of research and through the literary forms of modern thought'. Our post-conciliar bishops are far removed from this conviction of the great Pope of the Council, the conviction in which my book *On Being a Christian* was also written. As previously at the Counter-Reformation Council of Trent and at the anti-modern First Vatican Council, the Curia is doing all it can to shift the dispute as far as possible from reforms to dogmas. Here – with a reference to 'tradition' – they know that they have the whip hand and can ward off uncomfortable demands for reform from the start.

In fact I am concerned not only with theological questions but with religious practice. At a time when the churches are becoming increasingly empty, in Tübingen I am arguing vigorously for a new regular Saturday evening worship shaped by the teachers of the faculty of Catholic theology at which the celebrant also preaches. In fact this service comes about and proves popular. I preside over the worship on three Saturdays in 1977.

My pastoral activity isn't recognized by the bishop and the conference of bishops either and it hasn't deterred them from their major action against me. The incomplete and tendentious documentation by the conference, which comprises only about a third of the existing documents, leads me in my defence to make public all the documents and (since personal letters from me have also been published) a copy of the Stuttgart conversation. They will appear at the beginning of the following year, 1978.

Walter Jens, President of the PEN Centre of the Federal Republic, known as an author of books critical of theology, declares himself ready to edit this 394-page documentation volume for Piper Verlag and provide an introduction. He chooses the title 'For Nothing but the Truth. German Conference of Bishops against Hans Küng'. In keeping with the circumstances, his introduction accentuates what bishops, who are fond of unctuously 'reprimanding' people but aren't accustomed to forthright contradiction in their pulpits, take very much amiss. He writes: 'Church magisterium against Hans Küng: in this dispute on the one hand are the keepers of the holy grail of formulas, the apologists for dogmas who, it seems, would rather allow the exegetes in their own ranks to say that Jesus was mistaken than to say that the magisterium is mistaken ... the advocates of "pure doctrine", and on the other is a man who is unwilling to see why Luther's statement "I do not set myself up above the doctors and councils, I set up Christ over all teachers and councils" could not also be formulated as an authentic ecumenical statement by a Catholic Christian.'[24] For people outside the Roman Catholic milieu the behaviour of the German bishops is quite incomprehensible.

Church authorities against church teacher: an appeal for understanding

I have to stand up for myself theologically. At the end of our documentation I reply to the German bishops with an extended 'Appeal for Understanding'. In it I stress that conflicts are unavoidable even in the church; they are a sign of life and are in any case to be preferred to the graveyard peace of totalitarian systems. But conflicts must be endured, indeed used fruitfully. In them no group may outplay another – neither the 'pastors' the 'teachers', nor the 'teachers' the 'pastors'. Already in *Infallible?*, in a concluding chapter on the magisterium in which I take up Yves Congar's historical research, I have pointed out that the term 'teaching office' ('magisterium') is based neither on the Bible nor on old Catholic tradition. It has come into use in the present sense only since the end of the seventeenth century, and only from the nineteenth century does the distinction between 'teaching' and 'learning' church occur more frequently. Only with Vatican I (1870) does the expression 'magisterium', as 'teaching office', a term a bit like 'foreign office', enter church terminology in a technical sense.

If understood in a doctrinaire and totalitarian sense, the term 'teaching office' all too easily absorbs all other ministries, not least that of the 'teachers', which stands in third place in the table of charisms given by the apostle Paul in 1 Corinthians. For the community of faith today this means (and I argued for this at length in *The Church*) that both the service of leadership by the bishops and pastors and the service of scholarship by teachers and theologians each has its own task, function, competence and calling. Therefore Paul puts to the power-hungry who want to embody all church functions in themselves the rhetorical questions: 'Are all apostles? Are all prophets? Are all teachers?'[25]

In my 'Appeal for Understanding', in which I also hope to be speaking for many colleagues, I therefore emphasize the difference, but also what we have in common:

> The well-being of the whole community of faith and that of the individual is not helped by the establishment of one group at the expense of another. It is not helped by either a hierarchical church or a professorial church; it is helped only by joint involvement in the service of the common Christian cause, with the tensions which that brings. Don't we start from the same gospel of Christ, the proclamation of which we have to serve, each in a special way, whether through leadership (which predominantly includes preaching and the administration of the sacraments) or through research and teaching? And aren't we there for the same people, who today once again are beginning to take note of the ethical and religious dimension in the life of the individual and the community and who now expect from us not opposition but collaboration?[26]

That is how I finally end our documentation, with a plea addressed to the bishops:

> Let us finally stop this superfluous dispute over orthodoxy and the 'curtailment' of Christian truth. Let us stop the secret negotiations, endless correspondence, inquisitorial questioning, authoritarian interrogations, public condemnations. Let us break down the mistrust, overcome the polarizations and balance the oppositions fairly. Let us collaborate again on the true front on which we stand together, in order to meet the challenges of the time and to be a real help to people in their individual and social problems; in order to advance the unity of the still-divided churches and to give to the people in our country once again an 'account of the hope that is in us'[27].

Couldn't, shouldn't, mustn't the bishops have open ears for this call for reconciliation?

Around my fiftieth birthday: Chancellor Kreisky

I had never expected to reach 50. My life is too demanding, I work too much at night, I travel too much, take too many risks ... I think of my Lucerne classmate Heinrich Peyer, the missionary to Africa. He died just one day after his fiftieth birthday, on 4 December 1977, trying to save a black child from the river, and drowned: he in particular had deserved to live longer.

And now my own fiftieth birthday is upon me. The preceding week is filled with important events. On 3 March 1978 my book *Does God Exist?* is released to the bookshops. But my real birthday present is delivered on 8 March: the extremely helpful little book *Hans Küng. His Work and His Way*, edited by Hermann Häring and Karl-Josef Kuschel. It contains a chronicle of the events from 1928 to 1978 with essays on my big books so far. There follows a conversation between the two editors and me on every possible question relating to the church and finally a complete bibliography of my publications from 1957 to 1978 by my secretary Dr Margret Gentner, along with an appendix about the Institute for Ecumenical Research.

The book with its attractive photographs gives me much pleasure. It is meant to paint a portrait, sketch out the outlines of my work and my person and demonstrate continuities and discontinuities in the development:

> For many people in the church and throughout the world, Hans Küng may be a contradictory figure – too critical for some, not critical enough for others; too Catholic still for some, by others long since regarded as no longer Catholic; for some too religious, for others too crudely outspoken. Yet he is at one and the same time a theologian and a scholar, a pastoral worker and a writer, a preacher and a professor, a priest and a controversialist, a Catholic and an ecumenist. How does all this fit together? How does he see himself? By whom has he been influenced? What people has he met? What has left its lasting stamp on him?'[28]

Thus the editors. A brief answer to all these questions is given in the book.

Some time previously the chief editor of the Austrian Catholic press agency had asked me unofficially whether I would accept an invitation from Dr Bruno Kreisky, Chancellor of Austria, to come to Vienna; he had heard my speech at the quincentenary of the University of Tübingen and had been extremely enthusiastic about it. Of course I accept the invitation from this highly-respected socialist chancellor since I am to speak on the question of God and my speech is to take place in a historic setting.

Early in the morning of 9 March 1978 I fly from Stuttgart to Vienna for two days. There I am first received by Dr Kreisky at the Chancellery in Ballhausplatz, which for me is associated with a childhood memory reported in *My Struggle for Freedom*: at the age of six I heard in Switzerland at lunchtime on 25 July 1934 the first radio report which sank deep into my memory: the shock news of the murder of the Austrian Chancellor Engelbert Dollfuss in the Chancellery by the Nazis. Kreisky shows me the place where it happened and the portrait of Dollfuss, still decked with flowers. Then among other things I talk for a long time, almost too long, with this Chancellor of Jewish origin about the Chazars, who evidently fascinate him a great deal. They are that Turkic people of disputed origin whose realm lay between the Lower Volga and the Don, whose upper class accepted the Jewish faith and took over political leadership there in the ninth century, in terms of cultural politics playing an important role as mediators between cultural groups precisely because of their religious diversity; however, they then mysteriously went under and are last mentioned in the thirteenth century.

In the evening I go with him by car to the nearby Hofburg, once the imperial castle of the Habsburgs. An audience of 1700 including the Austrian President Dr Rudolf Kirchschläger, a convinced Catholic, have gathered in the congress centre there; for lack of space even the Minister of Education, Fred Sinowatz (later Kreisky's successor), has to sit on the platform steps. Only Cardinal Franz König has sent his excuses at the last moment for diplomatic reasons; he has invited me for coffee in his residence the next morning, where we have a friendly conversation.

The Chancellor introduces me in person. He mentions my speech at the University of Tübingen and says that such a theologian should also have a hearing in Austria. As in Tübingen I speak on the question of God and science; here too the theme is very topical. There is enthusiastic applause at the end. Aware of how many of his friends from the Socialist party have turned to historical materialism – I had studied the history of 'Austromarxism' previously – Bruno Kreisky ends by saying: 'This evening a door has been opened and now everyone must see for themselves what to do as a result.' Afterwards he thanks me very warmly by telephone: it had 'been a very big affair', and all were impressed by the 'intellectual power of the presentation'.

On New Year's Eve 1978 Kreisky, also a skier, invites me to drink a glass of wine with him at the famous Gasthaus Post on the Arlberg. We talk above all about the situation in the Middle East, which is always explosive. He explains to me at length that I am looking at things all too one-sidedly from the Israeli perspective. I also have to learn to understand the Arabs. Certainly all my life I have been critical about the Catholic Church's stance on the Jewish question. For me this terrible history of the anti-Judaism of the Christian churches remains a main reason for the racist antisemitism of the National Socialists. But I have also found that the occupation of Palestinian land by the Israelis since the Six Day War of 1967 is becoming more problematical for me the longer it goes on and the less people are willing to grant the Palestinians a state of their own. I have long regarded the dream of a Greater Israel as an illusion and by 2007 will think it irresponsible. I analyse this development in a long chapter in the first volume of my trilogy on the religious situation of our time, *Judaism*, and repeat it later in *Islam*.

Answer to the modern question about God

Already during my study of Hegel it became increasingly clear to me that the biblical message of a God who is in no way separate from the world but is active immanently in it can be grasped better in the light of a post-Copernican worldliness of God understood in modern terms than in the light of classical

Greek or medieval meta-physics. This is to be made clear in my new book on the question of God in the modern world, on which, well prepared for by my book on Hegel, I have been working from 1975 to 1978.

Originally I wanted to construct something for *Does God Exist?* out of the few dozen pages cut from *On Being a Christian* on the question of God. But rash superficiality isn't my virtue. And over the next years again and again I have to set myself a new deadline for this book because I lose so much time in the controversy with Rome, the German bishops, the eleven theologians and sometimes also with attacks on my Catholic orthodoxy and Christian integrity in the press, not to mention the steadily rising demands of correspondence and the media. Moreover I am fascinated by the great atheists influenced by Hegel: Feuerbach and Marx, then of course Nietzsche, and finally Freud, including their personalities as human beings. So I want to investigate not only their arguments and their systems but also their lives, what irritates them and their quite personal motives: how and why they came to deny God.

I had begun the book on 19 August 1975 in Sursee and at first made good progress. By my return to Tübingen on 4 October 1975 I had already to some degree sketched out large chapters on Descartes and Pascal and the history leading up to them and beyond them. After the big monograph which I had already written on Hegel the next chapter of the new book, on Hegel, needed to be an understandable summary of this notoriously difficult philosopher. As well as skiing I used the Christmas holiday in Lech to work out the chapters on Feuerbach and Marx (already dealt with in the early 1960s in my semester of lectures on philosophy, standing in for the philosopher Joseph Möller) and read the most recent extensive literature. So I was very well prepared for a trip to Budapest, where a symposium involving our discipline and the Roman Catholic Theological Academy took place from 23 to 25 April 1976. Thus I had occasion to present my 'Theses on Atheism' for discussion in this Communist country, a discussion which of course was allowed only in the narrow framework of academic theology without a wider public. We then visited the starting point of the Christianizing of Hungary, the famous Benedictine monastery of Pannonhalma (St Martin's Mount); there too we had an interesting theological conversation led by the excellent Archabbot Dr Andreas Szennay.

My lectures for the next two semesters of 1975/76 were devoted to the doctrine of God, the seminars to the Neo-Marxist and Neo-positivistic critique of religion and the Apostles' Creed. As always, I spent the summer holidays at Sursee. On 6 August 1976 my publisher Klaus Piper visited me and we agreed that *Does God Exist?* would be published in September 1978. Incidentally, the Polish philosopher Leszek Kolakowski wrote to his editor that he admired 'Küng's courage in publishing a book with such a simple, dense title as *Does God Exist?* when others would take a vague title such as "The Present Significance of Religion" and the like' (15 March 1978).

In 1976 I combined a visit to the Salzburg Festival (a grandiose performance of

Verdi's *Don Carlos* under Karajan) with a further trip through the beautiful countryside of Austria, a country so similar to our Switzerland: this time from Salzburg to Vienna and from there with our family quartet (my sister Rita, my brother-in-law Bruno and Marianne Saur) into Burgenland, to the Neusiedler See and Eisenstadt, where there was a folk festival in Esterhazy Castle, the place where Joseph Haydn worked. Then back from Vienna via Krems and the Wachau to Innsbruck and finally over the Arlberg to Sursee. Following that I could revise my chapter on Frederick Nietzsche's nihilism with Karl-Josef Kuschel in the lake house. Thus the larger and more difficult critical half of *Does God Exist?* was essentially finished.

My book isn't shy of confessions where appropriate. But there is no praising or preaching! Readers have the right first to inform themselves about the present state of the question and be given answers: clear but not finished answers. I don't want to 'prove' God but to provoke a free decision, for or against, a responsible decision, and perhaps also the revision of a previously held opinion. So these aren't proofs of God but good reasons which invite readers to put their trust in a primal ground, a primal content, a primal goal of human beings and the world, in God.

In this perspective, in the end, laboriously worked out over the course of three years, there are seven large consecutive chapters. First of all I descend to the depths: A. Reason or Faith, B. The New Understanding of God, C. The Challenge of Atheism, D. Nihilism – Consequence of Atheism. Then I slowly ascend again: E. Yes to Reality – Alternative to Nihilism, F. Yes to God – Alternative to Theism. Then as a conclusion and link to *On Being a Christian*: G. Yes to the Christian God.

Christological clarification is ignored

The documentation 'For Nothing but the Truth. Conference of Bishops against Hans Küng', edited by Walter Jens, was published on 13 January 1978. On 10 February I sent it with covering letters to Bishop Moser[29] and Cardinal Höffner.[30] Cardinal Josef Höffner replied on 16 February with a completely negative press release in which he defended the one-sided episcopal documentation and attacked our book.[31] At the same time he wrote to me that an understanding can 'hardly be arrived at by public appeals but only by your positive answer to the repeated questions and admonitions from the German Conference of Bishops'.[32] Unfortunately I have to infer from the press release and letter that Höffner is hardly showing understanding but wants to order me about in the same authoritarian style.

I send *Does God Exist? An Answer for Today* to Bishop Georg Moser and Cardinal Joseph Höffner inscribed with the date of 19 March 1978 – my fiftieth birthday. My handwritten dedication is: 'For Bishop Georg Moser (or Cardinal

Joseph Höffner), in the hope that my appeal to the bishops will be heard.' The book contains my clarification of central christological questions which has been asked for on various occasions by the bishops. In the section on 'Son of God', over a dozen pages I again make an effort, as promised in the joint press release after the Stuttgart conversation in January 1977, 'to contribute in an appropriate way to the clarification of the questions discussed'.

The chapter also explicitly takes up the christological formulas of the Councils of Nicaea in 325 and Chalcedon in 451 which are desired by the bishops, as they can be understood in the light of the New Testament: 'For believers, the true man Jesus of Nazareth is the real revelation of the one true God, and in this sense, his Word, his Son ... God himself encounters us in a unique and definitive way in the activity and the person of Jesus.'[33] What more is wanted of a Catholic theologian? In a long note I defend myself against the falsification of my theology in the declarations by bishops and theologians.

But none of this does me any good. In his letter of 3 April 1978 Bishop Moser doesn't see himself in a position to agree to my desire to disseminate the 'Appeal for Understanding'. He thanks me for *Does God Exist?* with a single dry sentence, without even mentioning the christological clarification; presumably he hasn't read it. But Cardinal Höffner in his letter of 24 April 1989 expresses the hope that he will 'find time to read the book'. Once more he emphasizes, as if I hadn't written anything, that I should 'examine the methodological approach and the substantive statements of theological thinking which are objected to in the declaration in the light of the principles laid out there'.[34] In other words, none of the bishops who are constantly oppressing me has, as far as we know, taken time to read this book. They were interested only in the repetition of specific dogmatic formulae and not in the figure of Jesus Christ himself.

Teacher about God in the great tradition

These completely barren disputes, which are basically an episcopal test of strength and cost me an infinite amount of time and energy, will not and cannot keep me from intensive scholarly work. I am passionately a theologian, literally 'one who speaks of God', a 'teacher of God', who may occupy himself as a scholar with 'God and the world'. For me there is nothing greater, more beautiful, more captivating. I am proud not only, like Joseph Ratzinger, to stand pre-eminently in the 'tradition of the church fathers' but also to stand quite consciously in a scholarly tradition of 2500 years in which it has not been possible to separate theology and philosophy: since the Ionic thinkers before Socrates sought the primal ground of all things; since Plato reflected on the idea of the good, Aristotle on the unmoved mover and goal of all things and Plotinus on the great One.

There has been theology in the strict sense since Origen, the most important Greek Christian thinker, the great exegete and systematic theologian who laid the foundation for scholarly Christian theology. And among the Latins it was the brilliant North African Augustine of Hippo, the first to write an autobiography, who left behind a tremendous theological *oeuvre* in a brilliant style, with logical acuteness and human warmth, which proved fruitful for the whole of the Middle Ages in the West. However, for me, in catholic breadth and evangelical concentration, this tradition also includes the Reformers and the great thinkers of the Enlightenment and modernity.

According to Paul there is not just an 'apostolic succession'. There is also a 'succession of teachers (scholars)'. Since my student days in Rome I have felt particularly close to Thomas Aquinas. At a time when the Arabs, who for centuries had been intellectual leaders, tragically gave up their great philosophy, in the face of the inquisitors of his church he created a powerful intellectual system of reason and faith, nature and grace, philosophy and theology; it only established itself long after his death, but it is still influential today. And since I had studied the tremendous Reformer Martin Luther in connection with justification, church and ministries, he was no less close to me, not to mention John Calvin, the most important systematic theologian of the Reformation. And there were so many others – to mention only the greatest – up to Friedrich Schleiermacher and Karl Barth, on whom I did my doctorate and who opened the door to me for a contemporary biblical theology, as I described in *My Struggle for Freedom*. One day I would later offer portraits of the *Great Christian Thinkers* in a small introduction to theology and in 1994 dedicate it 'to Eberhard Jüngel and Jürgen Moltmann, my theological companions in Tübingen, in gratitude for many intimate ecumenical discussions, always inspiring, sometimes passionate'.[35]

Originally there was a long chapter on the question of God in *On Being a Christian*. But Walter Jens had convinced me that the transition to the question of being a Christian was too long, so I had cut it out. However, immediately after *On Being a Christian*, on 19 August 1974, while still in my lake house, I began the book on the question of God. 'You're like Thomas Mann,' my friend observes, 'who in March 1943, the day after finishing his giant Joseph novel, embarked on his next massive work, *Dr Faustus*.' But one doesn't know how long and difficult such a work will be. I didn't want just to relax, but to go out again into the depths. After all, it's important to grasp the problems existentially, pose elementary questions and advance towards the fundamental question of a last certainty, all concentrated on the eternally new question 'Believe in God?' This is an extremely complex set of problems, perhaps not for a self-certain hierarchy, but certainly for men and women seeking in today's world.

Seeing a book of almost 900 pages, people often ask me how long I worked on it. It's hard to say, for the book which finally bears the title *Does God Exist?* had been preceded by another book which proved to be an extremely useful preparation for thinking through the question of God.

God's living nature and historicity: Hegel

In fact the way was a long one. The problem of fundamental philosophical certainty occupied me for three decades, since my three years studying philosophy in Rome (1948/51). I coped with it existentially by a reasonable fundamental trust in reality, for which there are many good reasons but no compelling proofs (*My Struggle for Freedom*, III: Venturing fundamental trust). For my further reflection I was helped by lectures at the Sorbonne on the great initiator of modern philosophy, René Descartes, and other seventeenth-century thinkers. So I was well prepared to begin my first Tübingen lectures on fundamental theology in 1960 in an unusual way with Descartes and Blaise Pascal: knowledge or faith? *Cogito ergo sum* or *Credo ergo sum*? In Rome I had studied Hegel's philosophy and Marx's theory of society and history thoroughly and therefore had no inhibitions about taking over the lectures on philosophy in our faculty in the summer semester of 1961 and dealing with the great atheists Feuerbach, Marx and Nietzsche; Freud and grappling with psychoanalysis in a balanced way followed later.

Feuerbach and Marx had learned important lessons from that philosopher with whom I too had occupied myself for fifteen years, G. W. F. Hegel. My book *The Incarnation of God. An Introduction to Hegel's Theological Thought as a Prolegomena to a Future Christology* (700pp.) had arisen out of it; it was to appear in 1970 on the 200th anniversary of Hegel's birth. In the same years as *Infallible?*, I thought, here was a clear sign that my philosophy and theology serve, as Paul puts it, 'to build up and not destroy' the church (cf. 2 Corinthians 13.10). Its long history is worth commenting on briefly.[36]

I describe Hegel's whole development with great intensity from original texts. In each chapter, beginning with his biography, I describe the development of his philosophical and theological thought generally, then the development of his christology, and end every chapter with a discussion of philosophy and theology. Thus five interwoven strata run through each chapter – usually spiralling inwards: an invitation to and discussion with Hegel, equally important to theologians and philosophers, which draws as much out as it penetrates inwards. This is a new genre of critical historical and systematic grappling with an author of his stature and at the same time an introduction to the world of German idealism which is important for discussion of Marx and Kierkegaard, for both Catholic and Protestant theology. It is probably my most difficult book, but one which despite all the problems of Hegelian terminology and syntax remains understandable; it also appears in Italian, French, Spanish and English editions and to my great joy finally seals the 1951 licentiate in philosophy with an honorary doctorate in philosophy from the University of Genoa in 2004.

I have learned an enormous amount from Hegel: the overall view of science, law, art, religion and philosophy, a thought which is dynamic and historical, with a systematic network, that investigates the opposites thoroughly; a dialectic which doesn't consist in the mechanical clatter of thesis – antithesis – synthesis but in reflection on the opposites in an ongoing dynamic which time and again can also lead to reconciliation.

But beyond the purely philosophical discussion of Hegel, my book takes the present discussion on the questions of God and Christ further and in so doing leaves behind the Neo-scholastic level of the objections made by Cardinal Höffner and others. From beginning to end, in all its strata it circles round two great questions of present-day theological thought: the historicity of God and the historicity of Jesus. Without prejudice I have attempted in extensive excursuses to subject the axioms of traditional theology such as the unchangeability of God and God's incapacity to suffer, the christological formulas of the Council of Nicaea in 325 and the doctrine of two natures of the Council of Chalcedon in 451, to a critical constructive examination. Certainly the living nature and historicity of God and at the same time the historicity and significance of Jesus can be presented better on the basis of modern philosophy than with static Hellenistic categories. That was also my great concern in *Does God Exist?*

Complications and implications

For a long time *Does God Exist?*, which is by no means a simple book, remains no.1 on the *Spiegel* bestseller list, and this despite an only moderately friendly review by Professor Karl Lehmann with some unnecessary sideswipes. Of course the theologian Lehmann is increasingly becoming a man of the hierarchy. As he explains later, he had drafted Cardinal Döpfner's last letter to me in July 1976. And it emerges from his failure to contradict my accusation in a letter (6 February 1978) that he formulated the three inquisitorial questions for Cardinal Höffner in connection with the Stuttgart conversation. So he is all the more infuriated that Rome passes over him as Bishop of Freiburg; piqued, he tells the nuncio and others that he is no longer available for becoming a bishop, as if he had a right to that. He allows himself to be comforted with the title of a 'Papal Prelate of Honour'.

A malicious article which Lehmann also had a hand in inspiring appears in the same issue of *Der Spiegel* as his review; in part it is a tit-for-tat response by the church editors there to my reply 'My *Spiegel* image' in the *Frankfurter Allgemeine Zeitung* and in part an annoyed reaction to the unnecessary mystification created by a new publicity representative at Piper Verlag. *Der Spiegel* refuses to publish the correction which I sent to the editors on 16 February 1978 with a threadbare objection from the editor responsible (22 February 1978); it isn't worth writing another *Spiegel* image.

I send a copy of *Does God Exist?* to the Freiburg dogmatic theologian Helmut Riedlinger, who was with me at the German College; he had described the good points of *On Being a Christian* without envy but had also criticized its alleged 'radical rationality'. Another copy goes to Cardinal Joseph Ratzinger, because he had agreed that an invitation should be sent to me by the Catholic Academy to a conference in Munich on the question of God (I couldn't accept it for reasons of time). I send him my book 'remembering that for all your criticism of *On Being a Christian* at that time you praised the passages on the question of God which already contained the theme of this new book. Perhaps more mutual understanding may be possible in the light of it.'

The intensively revised chapter on Sigmund Freud takes on a life of its own. On 3/4 April 1978 I have to give the Terry Lectures in New Haven, which had been given before me by philosophers such as John Dewey, theologians such as Paul Tillich and Reinhold Niebuhr and psychotherapists such as Carl Gustav Jung and Erich Fromm. My four lectures on 'Freud and the Problem of God' fit perfectly into this context. They are so enthusiastically received by the large audience that Yale University Press wants to publish them before the big book *Does God Exist?* appears in the US. My New York publisher Doubleday agrees, so they appear in 1979. In May 1986, to my great joy, I am then awarded the Oscar Pfister Prize in Washington by the American Psychiatric Association; the Protestant pastor Oscar Pfister from Zurich is the only theologian to have remained in regular contact with Freud. The book is reissued in 1990, now including my Washington ceremonial lecture 'Religion – the Final Taboo', about the repression of religion (as opposed to sexuality) in psychology, psychiatry and psychotherapy. I gave it in German also in connection with the centenary of the Psychiatric University Clinic in Basle.

The chapter on God and creation also has implications. In writing it I took into account the most recent results of astrophysics relating to the Big Bang and the development of the cosmos: evolution as an illustration of creation. Thus prepared, I had no qualms about accepting an invitation for a major television broadcast in Hamburg, 'To New Destinations', on the occasion of the 20th anniversary of Sputnik on 4 October 1977. There I heard about and saw the weather satellites which would soon be circling the earth and yet more pointers to the future, though at the same time the limits of space research became increasingly clear to me.

I had been invited as so to speak a 'heavenly expert', together with Jesco von Puttkamer of NASA, who kindly took me through the space museum in Washington, and the Nobel prize-winner for chemistry, Manfred Eigen, with whom I could discuss developments in microbiology and belief in creation. Puttkamer in particular was enlightened a great deal by my contributions showing how the advances into the universe and the new picture of the world which arises from it could be harmonized with the traditional statements of faith. As well as the demythologizing of the biblical picture of the world (for example the 'ascension'), what is of fundamental importance to me is that space travel shouldn't be speeded up, as it is in the Soviet Union, and the problems of the earth suppressed, but that the problems of our earth shouldn't be isolated, as they are by some in the West, overlooking the cosmic perspectives. However, to my regret I couldn't accept Puttkamer's kind offer to me of a grant from Georgetown University to study the philosophical and theological implications of this new development of space travel.

Later, in 1994, on the basis of the foundations worked out in *Does God Exist?*, together with Professor Amand Fässler and my colleagues from the Tübingen Institute of Physics I can hold a semester colloquium on 'Our Cosmos'. Then for 2005 I again work thoroughly through the whole set of problems and extend them with respect to the origin of life and human beings – all this is published in my book *The Beginning of All Things*. Finally, in July 2006, on the basis of this there is an interdisciplinary colloquium on the relationship between science and religion in Tübingen Castle with high-ranking specialists from Germany and Switzerland and in 2007 another on brain research, sponsored by the Templeton Foundation in Yosemite National Park, California.

The struggle over language

On Being a Christian and *Does God Exist?* supplement each other and, I hope, join together seamlessly. Where repetitions seem appropriate, of course especially in the last part, I don't avoid them. Each book is meant to be read on its own and be completely comprehensible. It is important to me to express the whole of belief in God as consistently and transparently as possible, even if on some individual questions patterns of thought rather than solutions are demonstrated. This whole opens up so many possibilities of entry, all of which lead to the centre, that readers are encouraged to do what they in any case often do with such books: begin where it gives them pleasure.

A further distinction comes to me at the beginning of 1979 which confirms me in my efforts to write books which are not only correct in substance but also have a literary polish. Together with the world-famous Swiss author and dramatist Friedrich Dürrenmatt I am accepted into the PEN Centre of the Federal Republic of Germany (for poets, essayists and novelists). The impertinent accusations by envious colleagues that my style is 'journalistic' have long since fallen silent, but German theology can use an invitation to work for good German in theology (and how difficult that often is!).

Previously – and I owe this to my excellent translators – I have been accepted into the American section of the international writers' association PEN. The distinguished American weekly *Christian Century* asked 89 of its scholarly reviewers to single out from 15,000 books on theology and religion published in the 1970s which 'most deserved to endure'. First place was given to *A Religious History of the American People* by the church historian Sidney E. Ahlstrom, and second place to *On Being a Christian*. In addition to my books, three more works by European authors appeared: Jürgen Moltmann's *The Crucified God* in fourth place, Eberhard Busch's biography of Karl Barth in ninth and Edward Schille-beeckx's *Jesus. An Experiment in Christology* in twelfth, while the South American liberation theologian Gustavo Gutiérrez came in sixth place with his *Theology of Liberation.*

Happily the significance of my books goes far beyond the Catholic Church and the German language area. In an interview the then Archbishop of Canterbury, Dr Donald Coggan, is asked whether present-day theology in Germany makes any significant contribution to the education of the Anglican clergy. His reply is: 'The books of authors such as Karl Rahner and Hans Küng are read in any respectable college and many have, for example, read Hans Küng's big book *On Being a Christian*. Yes, I think that's an important contribution.'[37]

If I am concerned always to write in a lively style, it isn't in order to shine but in order to have an effect. It isn't the style but the subject-matter that should shine. I don't write without art but without artifice; as a writer I don't want to be admired but understood. My concern isn't with literary effect but with the message that I have to present.

As a writer I feel a bond with colleagues in other countries. Even if I rarely put my signature to the many declarations presented to me, this solidarity calls on me to intervene urgently for persecuted colleagues, for example in Czechoslovakia: criminal proceedings are being instigated against leading members of Charter 77 such as Václav Havel, Jiri Dienstbier and Václav Maly, with whom I later have dealings, because of their commitment to human rights. With Norbert Grein-acher and Johann Baptist Metz I sign the statement of solidarity which goes out from Tübingen.

But my last phase of work on *Does God Exist?* is abruptly interrupted. A tragic death occurs in my house. For me it begins a completely new phase of my life.

X

ഇൻൽഇൻൽ

1978: The Year of Three Popes

*'Holy Father, excuse my language which, though frank, is governed by
my love for the Christian cause and our church. I am ready at any time
also to present these concerns to you personally should you so wish, and
should you have sufficient time at your disposal for a conversation about
these complex problems. God bless you in your primacy of service to the
Catholic Church and to the whole of Christianity.'*

The conclusion of my letter to the new Pope John Paul II,
30 March 1979

As I said at the beginning of this book, the course of the world and the course of
one's life come together. In 1978 – the year of three Popes – I am 50. For a long
time I had thought that I wouldn't reach a half century, given my gruelling life in
Tübingen and many trips across the world; the laws of probability indicated that
sometime, somewhere, something would go wrong. Yet I do attain this year of
which the Chinese sage Confucius, whose tomb I will soon visit, says:

> At fifteen, I had my mind bent on learning.
> At thirty, I stood firm.
> At forty, I had no doubts.
> At fifty, I knew the decrees of Heaven (*Analects* 2.4).

Indeed, at 50 I know the 'decrees of Heaven', the task that has been given to me.
But I couldn't have guessed the ill that would befall me in the next decade, before
I could say with Confucius:

> At sixty, my ear was an obedient organ for the reception of truth.

Dramatic changes to my life

In the midst of all the scholarly work and all the controversies with the church
hierarchy during 1978, my housekeeper Charlotte Renemann dies. Since 1969
this tall and silver-haired woman from Oldenburg, proud mother of three sons
who are successful in their professions, has run my household with great dedication. She took on the task of housekeeper at the age of 67 and performed it to

my complete satisfaction. It was amazing how she made Vatican emissaries wait at the door in a friendly yet masterful way. She is perpetuated in my television portrait by Nordwestdeutscher Rundfunk. We had a happy celebration of her 75th birthday on 27 January 1977.

But a good year later, on a quiet weekend – I am abroad and she is alone in the house – in her roof apartment (with a balcony and the most beautiful view over Tübingen to the Swabian Alb) she has a stroke by the wash basin. She lies on the floor for more than 24 hours while the water flows uninterruptedly through all the ceilings down to the ground floor. Finally, one of her sons gives the alarm to her neighbour when no one answers the telephone. Annegret Dinkel, our Institute secretary, is called and finds Charlotte Renemann lying unconscious on the floor and with hypothermia. She is rushed to the university clinic. I come back to Tübingen early and find her still alive, but two days later, on 26 February 1978, my loyal, cheerful and trustworthy housekeeper is dead. A small group of us go to her burial in the Bergfriedhof. With an address on this 'extraordinary woman' I give her a last memorial. A few months later in the Netherlands, also at a good age, Elisabeth Klinckhard dies; along with her daughter Inka she had so often offered me her friendly help (in Mexico, in Sursee and on our move to the house on the hill).

I am now confronted with two basic questions: who will run my household and what is to happen to my water-logged house? Frau Renemann had in fact been the only person to reply to my advertisement for a housekeeper at the time. I was lucky then, but it would be wrong to tempt providence. Some years previously I had got to know the sister of my Rotarian friend Dr Dieter Kemmler, Marianne Saur-Kemmler, an attractive, intelligent, warm-hearted and at the same time self-confident widow of about my age. She impressed me because for fourteen years she had devotedly cared for her incurably ill husband, a dentist, and run his practice, but at the same time with much skill and creativity had successfully taught German to the children of immigrant workers in her home town, the neighbouring town of Reutlingen.

I suggest to her one day that for the long term she might perhaps engage in a more demanding activity. And as the daughter of a Protestant businessman who has other priorities, she in fact begins to be interested in theology, finally becomes deeply involved in the last phase of *On Being a Christian*, and takes on the by no means simple task of making the index for my new book *Does God Exist?* (more than 1600 names from all the countries of the world). She has long had a competent housekeeper for her beautiful home in Reutlingen. When after the death of Frau Renemann I ask her whether she might like to take over the running of my house she makes her answer dependent on the assent of this housekeeper, Martha Walz, and above all her brother Dieter and her two sons, of whom one, Hans, is head of an agricultural machinery factory and the other, Uli, is following his father in being an excellent dentist.

In fact everyone agrees – on the one condition that the two households must be clearly separate (also in legal status) and that if the arrangement didn't work out, could be independent of each other. For me this isn't a very easy decision, since previously I have been sole master in the house. And now is it to be divided? But the planned model of two dwellings which shared a housekeeper and cleaning help seems to me a very good one and in the long run it would remove all worries about my household. So I accept the condition. In the judgement of the professionals, it would in any case be better to pull down my attractive but very narrow rustic house, built in the 1930s with light material, with a creaking wooden floor and rubble underneath it, than to spend a lot of money restoring it and extending it. Despite an intensive search it is impossible to find a more beautiful site in the best area of Tübingen, immediately above the university with a marvellous view of the Swabian Alb. So we decide to demolish the old house, which is done in a single day, and rebuild a functional two-family house with offices on the ground floor, my personal rooms on the first floor and Marianne Saur's rooms on the second floor.

The planning begins immediately. As with my lake house, I very much enjoy indicating the layout and dimensions of the rooms on graph paper; our Reutlingen architect, not insisting on his own originality, takes my design over almost unchanged. According to the building regulations of the city of Tübingen, the house may not be longer than the previous one, but it can be four metres wider, now with a bigger terrace than before, of the kind that I was accustomed to as a child. The most important innovation is a little swimming pool on the ground floor. Having grown up by a lake, swimming was what I had most missed in Tübingen until Walter and Inge Jens had generously offered me the use of their swimming pool. My own pool is to be an unrivalled source of health for me, a hard worker chained to his desk until late into the night. So I no longer need to nip down two streets to Sonnenstrasse 5 in the early morning in rain, snow and ice and be afraid of catching a chill.

We begin the building work as soon as possible. My friend Dieter Kemmler relieves me of the complicated negotiations with the city and the various firms. But Marianne Saur and I, following advice, concern ourselves with every individual functional and aesthetic detail of the new house, not least the reinstallation of my big library – it weighs 7.5 tonnes in the van when I move it out on 3 July 1978. A large filing room must also be planned.

During my 'homeless' period I have numerous commitments abroad. On 9 May I give a lecture in the Swiss federal capital, Berne, on the 450th anniversary of the Reformation, entitled 'Questions to the Reformation', which is followed by a dialogue with the General Secretary of the World Council of Churches, Philip Potter, and Professor Andreas Lindt. Broadcast on the radio, it has a wide audience. I am in Switzerland for the summer holidays. I have no lectures for the winter semester 1978/79 and in the last week of September and the first week of October I am with the faculty in Israel, in the second half of October and in November in the US and Latin America. I shall be giving a detailed account of this trip.

For the rest of the time while my house is being rebuilt I live in Marianne's house on the Achalm mountain in Reutlingen; she has recently suffered a fifth big burglary – another reason for moving to Tübingen. So I commute almost daily between Reutlingen and Tübingen, but give numerous lectures all over Germany on the topic 'What One Can Hold On To'.[1]

An ecumenical round table

On 8 December – all the guests still remember how the streets suddenly froze and were covered with sheets of ice – we have the topping-out ceremony in the attic storey of the new house, Waldhäuser Strasse 23. There is emergency heating. My faculty colleagues are invited to a festive dinner party in Marianne's house at New Year 1979, all in the best of moods. Just one accident disrupts the course of the building and literally could have broken my neck. One weekend in February 1979 three of us go to look at the building, which still has no lights, and I trip over a trapdoor which contrary to all the regulations has been left uncovered, and fall headlong into the empty swimming pool. My right arm spontaneously goes up to my head, but I have to pay for that with a fracture. I can only guess how this news immediately found its way into the papers – to the *Schadenfreude* of quite a few people.

At the beginning of July 1979 the house is ready for us to move in, and on 6 July the sorting of my library begins; according to my plans it will take two knowledgeable academic assistants almost two weeks to complete. The two apartments are finally occupied after the summer holidays. From now on Marianne presides with masterful grace over my house and takes care of invitations, shopping and a thousand other things, supported by her housekeeper, so I can concentrate wholly on my scholarly work. Time and again Marianne also reads my manuscripts from first version to the last; she checks how understandable and dramatic they are, and whether the pace is right.

Soon Marianne becomes a welcome member of our theological round table. This meets several times a semester, usually rotating between our homes. Professor Eberhard Jüngel, Professor Jürgen Moltmann and his wife Dr Elisabeth Moltmann-Wendel belong to it, and to begin with also Professor Walter Kasper, until he opposes me in the growing confrontation with Rome in the faculty. Jürgen Moltmann summed things up in a little speech on Marianne's birthday: 'Marianne Saur is a stroke of luck for Hans Küng and all of us here in Tübingen.'

And that is how we remain to the present day – in witty conversation with much laughter and if need be also in theological dispute – a unique friendly circle who also go on trips together: to Champagne, to Burgundy, to Sicily and to Bari to Frederick II's Castel del Monte. And it is precisely as Jürgen Moltmann writes in his own memoirs:

387

We remained pugnacious and clung to our mutual self-distinctions, but respect for the achievement of the others, and personal sympathetic participation in whatever happened to them, increased. And in any event, what we all had at heart was the truth of the Christian faith. Here we spared each other nothing out of politeness, as when Jüngel once called the Qur'an a 'frightful book' and I agreed with him or when Elisabeth disputed the doctrine of original sin, or when I was forced to defend Calvin and Calvinism or when Küng attacked the weaknesses of Protestantism. After 20 years we then reached the point of addressing each other as 'Du', the familiar form of address used for family and close friends.[2]

But back to summer 1978. While I was in my lake house in Switzerland, on 6 August Pope Paul VI died in his summer residence of Castel Gandolfo. A question which had occupied me for so long arose with sudden urgency.

What Pope do we need? Six criteria

I have already painted what I think is a fair portrait of Pope Paul VI in various sections of *My Struggle for Freedom*, which as a whole proves positive, despite all the ambiguity of his policy. I personally feel grateful to this man. I also say that publicly, now that I am asked for comments on his death from all sides:

> I personally am grateful to Pope Paul for holding his hand over me protectively all these years. I got to know him personally when he was a cardinal and then spoke to him again later. No one could have prevented him from imposing harsher penalties in the vigorous debate over infallibility, which could have gone as far as excommunication. I knew that in my case, too, his guideline was to proceed *con carità*, i.e. not with juridical, disciplinary means, but to attempt to find a solution, at any rate to avoid an open break. There were and are people in the church who didn't understand this attitude and wanted, probably still want, tough proceedings, and I am very well aware that it needed only a nod from the Pope for these forces to be brought into play.[3]

I couldn't suspect that we would soon have a Pope who would give this nod.

Of course I had reflected for a long time on a successor, concentrating less on a particular person than on the criteria which should be applied for the next papal election. In this connection I had already long been in contact with the likeminded American theologian, sociologist and well-known columnist Andrew Greeley of Chicago, who in an article in the *New York Times Magazine* had taken up the question of the election of the Pope very much along my lines. I was in tune with what he wrote. On 20 May 1976 I sent him a clearly organized draft, thoroughly discussed with my team, and then in Pentecost week, on 9 June 1976 I presented it, corrected and approved by Greeley, to the *Concilium* Foundation in Paris. Before that I had won support for the text from the President, Antoine van den Boogaard, and above all from Edward Schillebeeckx. The other two members, Claude Geffré (for Yves Congar) and Johann Baptist Metz (for Karl Rahner), agreed. The declaration, subsequently revised and approved by all of them, was to appear in the world press immediately after the death of the Pope with the title 'The Pope We Need'.

So the text is ready, but who is to sign it? I am in charge of the action, because I have the necessary contacts with the media and particular personalities. My initial plan is that this time the declaration shouldn't be signed primarily by theologians, but by as many important lay people in the Catholic Church as possible. Here I think first of the Kennedys, who have already been mentioned several times, especially the President's oldest sister Eunice and her husband Sargent Shriver-Kennedy, who in a letter of 28 May 1978 has invited me to give a guest lecture on 'Science and the Question of God' at Georgetown University on 19 October. I keep in contact with Eunice by letter. She likes to listen to tape cassettes of my lectures and keeps wanting more; she is also very interested in my writings. 'Send me your writings, I find more inspiration and refreshing new suggestions in your work than in that of others' (4 September 1979).

However, the month of August, when I am in my holiday home, is the worst possible time to persuade important people to sign such an important declaration at a few hours' notice. As yet there are no such things as faxes or emails. On 7 August 1978, the day after the Pope's death, from early to late I telephone from Switzerland all over the world, but my calls to Washington and Cape Cod, Massachusetts, to The Hague and Brussels, don't have any positive result. Dr Helmut Kohl, now Christian Democrat opposition leader in Bonn, had written to me recently after I had sent him a book, 'We should have a quiet conversation soon. Would that suit you?' (17 April 1978), but at the time I was too busy to make this visit immediately. Helmut Kohl, now on holiday in Austria, doesn't seem to me to be very hopeful for what to a politician is a 'bold undertaking'. The long-serving Dutch parliamentarian and minister Dr Marga Klompé, a bold exponent of conciliar and synodical renewal with many contacts, whom I once visited in The Hague, can be reached in the Vorarlberg in Austria only in a roundabout way: she is injured and can't be active. Nor can anything be done in other cases. So what next?

There is no other way, time is pressing. I must rapidly change the strategy and again turn to leading theologians. When it comes to 'the cause', I've never hesitated over expenses. Unconcerned about the telephone bill, which in such international actions rapidly reaches dizzying heights, I now first telephone Yves Congar, whose answer I await with some trepidation. '*Vous serez surpris, mais je suis d'accord.*' He agrees. With his support it's easy for me also to win over the other famous French Dominican M.-D. Chenu, together with Claude Geffré in

Paris, who is already in agreement, along with the church and council historian Giuseppe Alberigo in Bologna and the Belgian journalist and lecturer Jan Grootaers in Louvain, whom I know from the Council. My friend Andrew Greeley in Chicago has been in agreement from the start, as of course is Edward Schillebeeckx in Nijmegen, who was also involved in organizing the declaration.

I have a long telephone conversation with Gustavo Gutiérrez in Lima, Peru, the founder of Latin American liberation theology. I shall be mentioning him at length later. I read him the long text in English over the telephone and understand his response; he would have put even more emphasis on the poor in Latin America and all over the world, but he sees that it is impossible to draft another declaration now and he is in agreement. So finally, with my Tübingen friend Norbert Greinacher and me, we have at any rate ten internationally known theologians as signatories.

The only big disappointment in this action, which I have to carry out by myself from my lake house without the secretariat, is Johann Baptist Metz. I had counted on his signature, since he had already approved the text earlier at the *Concilium* meeting. I ask him also to attempt to get Karl Rahner, who is still cross with me over the infallibility debate, to sign. It would have been better if I hadn't done this, since instead of getting Rahner's signature, on 8 August Metz, after hours on the telephone, withdraws his own. He makes all kinds of excuses which culminate in the grotesque statement that it 'takes courage *not* to sign this document'.

To this day I still do not know who – for whatever reasons – has alienated whom. Above all it is quite incomprehensible to me that Rahner and Metz think that they have to go one stage further in a letter to the *Süddeutsche Zeitung* and make a short statement which in practice pleads exclusively for a 'socially concerned' Pope and is silent over the reforms within the church which are necessary. Later – after the election of Wojtyla – Metz flies off the handle when I tell him that he has got precisely the kind of Pope he had wanted: infallible and socially concerned. Moreover Metz himself soon has to suffer under the new/old Inquisition regime. In July 1979, to the general consternation of the critical Catholic public, his call to Munich as successor to Professor Heinrich Fries is prevented by collaboration between the Minister of Education, Hans Maier, and Cardinal Joseph Ratzinger. The result is that, unlike Ratzinger, Metz has to spend the rest of his life in Münster in Westphalia, which he doesn't like, and can't return to the Bavaria about which he was always so enthusiastic.

But even without Metz I have now collected sufficient important signatories and can send the text to *Süddeutsche Zeitung* and for the English-language world to *Time Magazine*. I then travel, since months before I had promised the Austrian television station ORF to go to Iceland, where at a meeting with scientists between 11 and 14 August 1978 I am to make a statement about God and creation against the background of the primeval Icelandic landscape. I mustn't disappoint the very committed initiator and instigator Dr Jos Rosenthal.

Hardly have I set foot in Reykjavik than I am summoned to the telephone at the airport: an editor from *Time Magazine* in New York tells me that they can't agree to my condition that my name and my photograph mustn't have a prominent place in the article. *Time* won't publish our joint declaration without my photograph. I have no alternative than to accept – in any case, now and then one must expect some misunderstandings. So the document appears with the photograph of the one who in fact is responsible for the whole thing.

The declaration 'The Pope We Need'[4] begins with the background of world politics and then says: 'The Pope has a decisive role in the Catholic Church. Who occupies such an office at this time is not a matter of indifference for the Catholic Church, Christianity and the world. So out of concern for the church and its service of men and women, as Catholics we want to make ourselves spokesmen for the many inside and outside the Catholic Church who want a good Pope for this church: above all a Pope who also helps to overcome the oppositions and conflicts which have broken out within the post-conciliar church, a Pope of reconciliation. Only the best is good enough for that, The Pope of this time must be ... ' and now follows the real statement under six headings, which are all elaborated very precisely; to quote them in full would go beyond the bounds of these memoirs. Here are the headings:

1. Someone open to the world
2. A spiritual leader
3. A true pastor
4. A collegial fellow bishop
5. An ecumenical mediator
6. A real Christian

Because of the later effects of this document, which quite a few colleagues had corrected and supplemented, it is important for the reader to have a concrete idea of its constructive argument and elegant tone. So I shall quote verbatim the last particularly tricky section on 'A real Christian':

The Pope need not be a saint or a genius, he may have limitations, mistakes and defects, but he must be a Christian in the true sense of the word: in thought, word and action orientated on the gospel of Christ as the decisive norm.

He should be a convincing preacher of the good news, grounded in a strong and well-tried faith and with unshakable hope.

He should preside in a relaxed, patient and confident way over this church, which is not a bureaucratic apparatus, a business enterprise, a political party, but the great fellowship of believers.

As a moral authority he should stand up with objectivity, passion and perspective not only for the interests of the institution but for the realization of the Christian message among men and women; here he should regard his commitment to the oppressed and disadvantaged all over the world as his special obligation.

It can be recognized that what is wanted is a 'socially concerned' Pope, who stands up for the poor but also for the 'poor devils' in the Catholic Church: the divorced and remarried; spouses who practise contraception; priests who have married; couples of different confessions who want to receive communion together, and so on. In other words, what is wanted is a reforming Pope with social concerns.

Our text ends with an appeal to the cardinals to discuss together the above-mentioned criteria before nominating candidates, make them the basis of their decision, and then choose the best possible candidate, from whatever nation. And now comes the great question: who will finally be chosen?

The 33-day Pope: John Paul I

After the death of Paul VI who despite his constant compromises was never really accepted by the 'hawks' in the Curia and the College of Cardinals, the conclave is deeply split. There are the 'Montiniani' who take Paul VI's line; their candidate is Giovanni Benelli, made Archbishop of Florence and cardinal only a few months previously, but before that for ten years the Pope's head of staff ('sostituto') in the Secretariat of State. This mediating party is opposed by the 'hawks': their candidate is Cardinal Giuseppe Siri of Genoa, who was already unpopular at the Council. The two groups block each other in the first round of votes. Finally, an Italian compromise candidate is found, who is acceptable to both parties: the Patriarch of Venice, Cardinal Albino Luciani, a kind, modest man, at whose election on 26 August 1978, which he certainly didn't aspire to, I am truly happy. He will certainly be a Pope of reconciliation and therefore – an innovation – he adopts as his name those of two very different predecessors: John Paul.

The day after the election I give Swiss television a positive interview. For not long beforehand, our University Music Director Alexander Sumski had been in Venice with the Tübingen Collegium Musicum and had given a big concert in St Mark's in the presence of the Patriarch. I learn that the Patriarch has my *On Being a Christian* on his desk, he had asked after me and sent friendly greetings. Soon afterwards I respond with a letter and send my *On Being a Christian* in Italian, *Essere cristiani*, with a personal inscription. He thanks me kindly; he says that Bishop Gargitter of Brixen, formerly at the German College, had given him the book soon after it came out in German. The Patriarch writes to me: 'I have read parts of it (my knowledge of German is imperfect) and have found some very fine passages. You have the gift of writing and you could do much good. I confess that

I remain doubtful about some points (I am no specialist), and on others in the end I have a different opinion.'

The letter impresses me. It expresses modesty, judgement and serenity. It ends: 'The only response I can think of is to send you my unpretentious publication *Illustrissimi*, with expressions of my high esteem. Albino Cardinal Luciani, Patriarch.' With his letter he send his 'Letters to Distinguished Personalities', which alongside saints and church teachers also includes men of the Enlightenment such as Voltaire. At all events these letters show me a friendly mediator with an open horizon, who evidently will not just ply me with dogmatic formulas.

I reply to the Patriarch in Italian: 'I am amazed at your book: here is a theologian and Patriarch who can write not only pastoral letters and pious sermons but letters (quasi-encyclicals) to the great figures of the past in an elegant and very humane style. I read this collection of letters from the Patriarch which you sent to me in Tübingen with pleasure and satisfaction. I have heard that you too are an alumnus of the Gregorian and gained your doctorate with a thesis on the "heretical" church reformer Rosmini, under the supervision of Fr Flick, who also accepted my licentiate thesis devoted to a non-heretical Protestant (Karl Barth).' On 15 April 1977 the Patriarch warmly thanks the *'caro professore'* in his own hand for the Easter greetings and observes on my compliment, '"*Quasi encichliche*"? *Ohimé!* These are just light-hearted scribbles (*scarabocchi scherzosi*), though with a pastoral intent.'

It will be understood from this brief prehistory that I am optimistic about Luciani's election as Pope. It's a good sign that he doesn't take the name Pius but the names of the two Council Popes. Immediately after the election I send him *Does God Exist?* with the dedication 'Caro Papa Giovanni Paolo I, I am delighted at your election and hope that your pontificate can respond to the urgent expectations of millions of people who thirst for God.'

Soon afterwards the report goes through the press that John Paul I has made the 'monstrous' statement that God is not only father but also 'mother'! *'Dio madre.'* One doesn't have to be much of an expert on the Roman Curia to suspect that to many of its members, some of whom are fanatically celibate, this must seem an almost blasphemous statement. But those who know the Roman Curia also know that powerful Curia cardinals have little inhibitions about saying very clearly to the Pope, their former colleague, that this or that offends against 'the tradition' or 'Catholic doctrine' (or their personal view of it) and that in future he must guard against such statements or actions.

At all events this Pope, who is depicted soon after the election as the 'smiling Pope', is amazingly serious at his solemn institution on 3 September 1978, completely without his usual smile. His address is also very conventional, evidently at least read, if not composed, by the Holy Office, where people still have the arrogant view that they must guard 'the truth' of the faith even of Popes and councils. The new Pope is not to enumerate further heresies, a suspicion held

393

about his predecessor but one, Angelo Roncalli, John XXIII, who is suspected by some members of the Curia of 'modernism'. I have my first doubts: will Papa Luciani be able to withstand the Curia? It is still too early for a verdict, since he has been in office for only a few days.

Enigmatic death of the Pope

A study trip of the Catholic Faculty had long been organized for the period from 23 September to 7 October 1978 to the 'Holy Land'. Here finally an important step towards peace has been taken. The previous year the Egyptian President Anwar as-Sadat had undertaken a bold visit to Jerusalem and ushered in a first relaxation of the climate with his speech to the Knesset (19/20 November 1977). By skilful and indefatigable negotiation on the part of the convinced Christian US President Jimmy Carter on his Camp David presidential estate, on 17 September 1978 the Camp David Agreement is finally concluded between Sadat and Menachem Begin, the former terrorist, now leader of the Likud Party and Israeli Prime Minister. Through the personal involvement of Jimmy Carter it leads to the Egyptian–Israeli peace treaty (26 March 1979), which, because it was fair, has lasted to the present day. Later I get to know President Jimmy Carter better within the framework of the InterAction Council.

Our study trip is led by our great Old Testament scholar Professor Haag, who has an excellent knowledge of Palestine. It's a trip which with its combination of information, devotion and recreation delights us all greatly. First we have three days in the south (Beersheba, the Negev, the Dead Sea and Qumran), then a week in Jerusalem, and finally four days in Galilee. Relevant passages from the Old or New Testament are read at every place we go to and we learn from our exegetes about the central message and deeper sense of the narrative, what is historical in it and what is possibly legendary; we also constantly see interesting features of the archaeological investigations which are often being carried on.

On Sunday 1 October 1978 I have the honour of taking part in and preaching at solemn worship in the Benedictine Abbey of the Dormition in Jerusalem, among the monks and many pilgrims. People are a little horrified when I entitle my sermon 'He is not here!' However, this was a remark made by a young man at the tomb from the short Easter account of the earliest Gospel according to Mark, which as yet has no legendary elaborations and is immediately followed by 'He is risen.' For our day, that of course means that he is not here, not even here in Jerusalem. So one may not attach decisive significance for Christian faith even to the biblical sites, the authenticity of some of which is in any case disputed. Christian faith, unlike Jewish faith, isn't tied to a land, and unlike Islam isn't centred on a place of pilgrimage. It isn't a Christian obligation to make a pilgrimage to Jerusalem, far less to Rome. Rather, the important thing is Jesus

Christ, his message, his conduct, his fate, his spirit and hence unpretentious discipleship in the everyday world.

Just before that, our harmonious journey has suddenly taken a dramatic turn: the shattering news reaches us in Jerusalem that Pope John Paul I died on 28 September 1978. He was only 65 and he had been in office only 33 days. After my return I receive a report from his secretary Don Lorenzi, who thanks me for sending *Does God Exist?* Unfortunately my book didn't arrive until after the Pope's death. A number of urgent questions arise.

Unexplained deaths and scandals in Rome

The surprising death of the relatively young 33-day Pope – he was found dead in bed one morning – isn't investigated either by an autopsy or by the police. It isn't surprising that to the present day the craziest rumours abound. I get so many enquiries from all over the world about what I think of this sudden death that finally I compose a text which I circulate. It culminates in the remark that I believe the members of the Curia, some of whom are personally known to me, capable of some things, but not of the murder of a Pope.

Others, such as David A.Yallop, the author of the 1984 bestseller *In God's Name*, think differently. He quotes me half a dozen times as a witness, unfortunately not always correctly. But of course he is right in his broad account of the way in which the Vatican is entangled in the world of finance and even the Mafia. That is certainly true of its excellent relations with Giulio Andreotti, several times minister and seven times Prime Minister, whose influence is as great as the cloud of scandal surrounding him. Moreover Andreotti is author of a book 'My Seven Popes'.[5] He is also thought to be privy to the murder of the investigative journalist Mino Peccorelli in Rome on 20 March 1979 or even to have instigated it; but since none of the key testimonies of Mafia bosses is thought credible, he can wriggle his way out of legal proceedings time and again. At the end of 2002 he is sentenced to 24 years imprisonment in the Court of Second Appeal for ordering the murder. However, the verdict is quashed by the Italian Supreme Court in October 2003 for lack of evidence.

The Vatican, which likes to preach law and justice all over the world, hasn't contributed anything to the explanation of manifest crimes, even though after the unexpected death of John Paul I, further amazing deaths occur which have still not been explained even today. There is the suicide (or poisoning?) in a Roman prison of Paul VI's former big banker and financial expert Michele Sindona, possibly recommended to the Pope by his patron Andreotti; the Sicilian, previously sentenced for fraud in America, had evidently also been a Mafia banker.

Then there is the grim death of 'God's banker', Roberto Calvi, head of the Banco Ambrosiano, Italy's biggest private bank, which went bankrupt with the disappearance of $1.3 billion. Bearing the name of Milan's most important bishop and church teacher Ambrose (fourth century), whose successors also include Archbishop Giovanni Battista Montini, later Paul VI, this bank enjoyed the special trust of the church, both the hierarchy and believers. In June 1982 Calvi, like Sindona a member of the dark secret lodge P2, which has revolutionary aims, was found hanged under Blackfriars Bridge in London, his pockets filled with stones – suicide or, as more than Calvi's family in Milan are convinced, a Mafia murder? And what did the Vatican contribute towards enlightenment here?

Banker Paul Marcinkus: covered by the Vatican

The Vatican Bank Istituto per le Opere di Religione (IOR) is the active partner in Calvi's venturesome financial operations. Moreover in 1982, without conceding any debt, it spends the sum of $240 million to buy off the Vatican from legal action as the chief shareholder in the Banco Ambrosiano, which has held and wasted the money of countless Catholic creditors. The moral damage to the Vatican is enormous.

Calvi's direct Vatican business partner was a large American clergyman, Archbishop Marcinkus from Chicago, of Lithuanian origin, more than 1.9 metres tall, and initially in the Secretariat of State. As a multilingual travel marshal and bodyguard ('gorilla') he had protected Pope Paul VI from being stabbed in Manila. In 1968 he was nominated a titular bishop and finally, without any banking experience, appointed secretary and in 1971 head of the Vatican Bank. He rose to become the most powerful American in the Curia.

I remember him very well. He served as deacon at the first mass of my friend Robert F. Trisco, also from the Archdiocese of Chicago, in my last year of studies in Rome, in the church of S. Agnese; I was subdeacon. I saw him again during the Council. One evening he came to our residence for a drink with the American bishops and periti. From what his friends say I gather that this Marcinkus, an enthusiastic golfer and tennis player, must face the music for Paul VI, who had unwisely invested large sums of money in the bank of his former archdiocese of Milan; Marcinkus had written letters of comfort for the Banco Ambrosiano when its bankruptcy could already be foreseen.

So the Milan state advocate issues a warrant for Marcinkus' arrest. He lives in a clergy house in Rome, but evades arrest by fleeing to the Vatican, where he lives a completely secluded life. The Vatican refuses to hand him over. After a long tug-of-war with the Italian judiciary the immunity of the Vatican official – even for a crime committed on Italian territory! – is finally established by a highly controversial decision from the Italian court of appeal with reference to the Lateran treaties. Who in Italy can withstand the power of the church? Not even the courts. At the beginning of the 1990s Marcinkus can return to America unnoticed. When I was giving a lecture in Phoenix, Arizona, in November 2005 I was told that he lived there in the retirement complex of Sun City, next to the golf course. After years of investigations the Roman public prosecutor's office produced a report in 2003 and the Calvi murder trial was to begin at the latest in 2005. However, on the evening of 20 February 2006 Marcinkus, a possible witness but now 84 years old, was found dead in his home.

Although prosecutors in various countries had called for it, Marcinkus was never put on trial for money laundering, setting up shell companies, the collapse of the Banco Ambrosiano or the death of Calvi. The award-winning British journalist John Cornwell, one of the few journalists who was able to have long conversations with Marcinkus and had also interviewed many of his friends and enemies, finds 'no evidence that Marcinkus was a murderer of either John Paul I or Roberto Calvi': 'What I did discover, however, was a remarkably jaundiced view of the "secular" estate, coupled with a subtle and "casuistic", as opposed to consequentialist, standard of business ethics.'[6]

Marcinkus openly confessed to Cornwell that he had plundered the Vatican pension fund to buy off involvement in the Banco Ambrosiano. I am reminded of similar financial behaviour by the British–Czech financial tycoon (and alleged agent of the Israeli Secret Service, Mossad) Robert Maxwell. Theo Sommer, the editor of *Die Zeit*, had drawn my attention to him at the World Economic Forum in Davos: 'If you want to see a man with a billion dollars of debt, look, he's sitting at the next table.' Not long afterwards, in May 1991, Maxwell fell mysteriously from his luxury yacht in the Mediterranean (or was he pushed overboard by Mossad, which feared that he would betray secrets?) and strikingly wasn't rescued by anyone.

It's a never-ending story. On 5 July the influential big financier Gianmario Roverado, who is regarded as the 'broker of Opus Dei', is kidnapped on his way to an Opus meeting in Milan and two weeks later is found murdered in Parma. At the same time, the Calvi murder trial continues before a Roman court; at it, among other things, the honorary chairman of the *L'Espresso* media group says that Calvi sensed a conspiracy against him and even had the windows of his Roman apartment fitted with armoured glass against a possible helicopter attack. The person thought responsible is Flavio Carboni, the former Calvi bag carrier, and with him his ex-girlfriend Manuela Kleinszig from Carinthia, Mafia banker Pippo Calò and further mafiosi.

Will the mysterious darkness which surrounds the relationships between the Vatican, Opus Dei and the Mafia ever be illuminated? For me the failure of the Vatican to act in this unprecedented history of scandal stands in strange contrast to the zeal with which it pursues my own case. The death of Calvi and so many other incidents (for example the equally unexplained murder of the commandant of the Swiss Guard and his wife by a member of the guard who immediately commits suicide) also makes me wonder whether there was something suspect about the death of John Paul I. At any rate, immediately after his death a pious lie goes the rounds that the Pope died with Thomas à Kempis's medieval book of devotions *The Imitation of Christ* on his bedspread. I hear directly from those around the present Archbishop of Milan, Cardinal Giovanni Colombo, Luciani's best friend in the College of Cardinals, that the evening before his death John Paul I had telephoned him and said to him: '*Mi prendono in giro* – they're leading me by the nose.' In fact the Pope died with a list of high-ranking names for nominations on which he possibly hadn't agreed on his bedspread. Perhaps the personal decisions expected of him had been the burden which had oppressed this evidently very sensitive Pope (allegedly he was also thinking of dismissing Marcinkus) – who knows? Some people also connect the heart attack of Cardinal Döpfner at almost the same age with excessive psychological burdens.

Be this as it may, many people saw John Paul I as a bearer of hope for a church with a concern for men and women in the spirit of the Second Vatican Council. And I am convinced that no ill would have befallen me under this Pope. But now a new Pope has to be elected. And after all the difficulties with the election of Albino Luciani that will be considerably more complicated.

A Pope from Poland: Karol Wojtyla

The second conclave in a very short time faces a completely new situation. The Italian cardinals, again divided, can no longer agree on an Italian compromise candidate. So the historic opportunity opens up of bringing a non-Italian into play. It is above all Cardinal König of Vienna, an expert on Eastern Europe, who, having rightly wanted a non-Italian in the previous conclave, now together with the German cardinals introduces the name of the Archbishop of Krakow, Cardinal Karol Wojtyla, into the discussion. Wojtyla is finally elected after the eighth round of voting and assumes the name John Paul II.

As I had long planned, on 13 October 1978 I fly to New York. From Monday to Thursday (16-19 October 1978), announced as 'the leading theologian who is controversial throughout the Christian world', I give four lectures in Riverside Church to an invited audience within the framework of the Fosdick Ecumenical Convocation 'Sermons in America' on the question 'How Can We Speak About God Today?'. After every lecture I receive whole packets of notes with questions and always respond to those which seem to me to be important. I do so from the pulpit from which ten years previously I had had to announce the murder of Martin Luther King.

On 17 October 1978, on the steps of Riverside Church, immediately before my lecture I hear of Karol Wojtyla's election as Pope. I immediately proclaim from the pulpit that we now have a Pope of Polish descent. I am by no means pessimistic about this. The Italian monopoly of the papacy which has lasted for more than four centuries must cease if there is finally going to be true reform. And as a Swiss I am a friend of Poland, since in the Second World War this country was divided up between Germany and the USSR. One of my best doctoral students, the American Ronald Modras, is a Pole. He gained his doctorate in 1972 with a dissertation on Paul Tillich's ecclesiology and is already professor at the University of St Louis, where I received my first honorary doctorate in 1965. I had welcomed Polish visitors to my home on various occasions and received friendly letters from Poland; I had sent some books to Poland and have contacts with the journal *Ancora*, highly respected by intellectuals and clergy, or reform groups such as 'The Common Way'. From 18 to 20 May 1979 our faculty even holds 'Warsaw days' (with lectures by our Polish colleagues Juros, Sobanski, Zuberbier and Charitanski).

However, often critical articles about me, usually written by conservatives, appear in the Polish daily press and in the papers. I also hear much that is doubtful about the still 'pre-conciliar' situation in which the church of the new Pope finds itself. As early as 1976 a very well-informed source in Warsaw tells me: 'Unfortunately we must note with sadness that your activity is little known in Poland because of the internal situation, which recalls the time before the Council. For fear of our episcopate none of the Catholic publishers here has the courage to bring out one of your valuable books. No one even thinks of publishing *On Being a Christian* ... Our church is largely isolated from the progressive theological theses which are developing in the West.' Later, at the height of the crisis, after my church permission to teach has been withdrawn, a personal friend of Wojtyla will emphatically explain on Swiss television by way of an 'excuse' that he can assure the Swiss people that the Polish Pope 'has not read a single book by Hans Küng ...' But as later becomes clear, he has long since made up his mind about me.

Still, despite all the reservations, at that time in New York I honestly welcome Wojtyla's election. It's a good idea to elect a man from the East in view of the still existing division of the world into West and East. There is still an 'iron curtain'. I am also assured from various quarters that Wojtyla is more open than the Archbishop of Warsaw and Primate of Poland, Stefan Wyszynski, who had sharply censured the publication of my first lecture in America on church and freedom in the Krakow weekly *Tygodnik Powszechny* (*My Struggle for Freedom*, IX: The church and freedom in Poland). However, Cardinal König, who had supported Wojtyla's election so strongly, is also deceived over him.

A long-planned trip by the *Concilium* Foundation to Krakow − our journal, which had once appeared in Polish, is to be revived in Poland − had been continually postponed because of problems with dates. Possibly Archbishop Wojtyla would have refused to see us, as he refused to see the German Chancellor Helmut Schmidt on the occasion of his visit to Krakow Cathedral. The Chancellor is annoyed, not least at the threadbare excuse that Wojtyla is away doing the 'Exercises', and doubly annoyed when the dean fobs him off with a cheap gift. Later, in a private audience, the German Chancellor attempts to convince the Polish Pope with great seriousness of the urgent need for a fight against the population explosion and in favour of birth control − with no success. Nevertheless, Helmut Schmidt concedes to me in one of our conversations: 'If I wanted to make my confession, I would do so to this Pope.' To which I retort with a smile: 'You can talk! You're a Protestant. You would never dream of making your confession.' But photographs of the new Pope which I see only after my return from North and South America are an early warning to me.

Deceitful photographs: an Opus Dei Pope

First photographs, which *L'Osservatore Romano* publishes in its German-language weekly edition (20 October 1978) immediately after the election, show Cardinal Karol Wojtyla in cardinal's dress with Cardinal Joseph Höffner and Franz Hengsbach, Bishop of Essen. They have been taken during lectures and discussion between 1972 and 1975 in the Centro Romano per Incontri Sacerdotali (CRIS) of the ominous Opus Dei in Rome which from an early stage has Wojtyla's whole sympathy – at the expense of the Jesuits, who have been dominant hitherto. Karol Wojtyla had been rejected as a doctoral candidate by the Jesuit Gregorian University shortly before I studied there because of his narrow-minded theology – I shall be speaking of this later. We know that he has already published a book in the Opus Dei series and, it is said in the Roman Curia, travelled through Latin America at Opus Dei's expense.[7]

As Pope, by every possible means he will promote this 'Work of God', this Fascist-type Catholic secret organization with the features of a sect which grew up in Franco's Spain and had the majority of ministers in Franco's last cabinet as members. It consists of laity (some of whom are committed to celibacy) and priests and is spreading especially among the powerful in politics, the banks and business, journalists and universities, initially in Spain and Latin America, and also in the Roman Curia. It wants to obliterate memories of the Second Vatican Council, and all down the line supports Roman Catholic conservatism. Its members, often recruited with doubtful methods, despise sex, chastise themselves and disparage women. Wojtyla withdraws this tightly-organized Opus, which aspires to power in the church and in time has several hundred thousand friends, supporters and sympathizers everywhere, from the control of the bishops and make it a *prelatura nullius*, so to speak an independent world diocese, in the face of much resistance also in the Curia. Some bishops and cardinals who reject Opus Dei finally speak well of it. Wojtyla beatifies and even canonizes its ambitious founder Josemaría Escrivá de Balaguer (he died in 1975), who wants to purge the church, allegedly polluted after the Council, and lead it back to the 'tradition'. He does so in record time, scorning all critical evidence and violating church regulations – for many Catholics who reject blind obedience and sectarianism this is a mockery. He nominates the sacked Vatican banker Marcinkus a titular bishop – Marcinkus is also said to have diverted millions to the Polish Solidarity movement. But he does nothing to explain the deaths and scandals all over the world which cry out for justice. At a very early stage Karol Wojtyla shows himself to be an Opus Dei Pope, firmly rooted in the conservative charismatic 'movements' and inadequately educated in contemporary theology. Joseph Ratzinger, who originally had his reservations about Opus Dei, allows himself to be given an honorary doctorate by the Spanish Opus Dei University and makes use of its services in power politics.

A second photograph makes me think: a full page in colour in the magazine *Quick*, otherwise known above all for nude photography, shows the face and hands of the Pope, deeply sunk in prayer, and this depiction is subsequently to be seen often in the media. The photographer relates at length how the photograph came about. After various shots he finally persuaded Pope Wojtyla to pray in front of the camera. Wojtyla said that he couldn't do this, but 'for the sake of the people' he finally knelt down and mimicked praying. A click of the camera and it was done. The beautiful picture travels round the world and is reproduced on countless postcards.

We now have a media Pope *par excellence*, who misses no opportunity to present himself in a pious way, in many respects like Ronald Reagan, who is soon afterwards elected US President. Reagan, too, is a trained and passionate actor and thus a 'great communicator' whose human aura makes people forget his reactionary politics and its victims. 'What does the United States need?', I am asked by Fritz Stern, an important German–American historian of Jewish origin, professor at Columbia University, whom I know from New York and who visits me in Tübingen. When I reply, 'The United States needs an actor,' someone who like Wojtyla can sell a reactionary doctrine and politics to the public with the charism of the great communicator, he is immediately prepared to accept an article by me for the journal *Foreign Affirms*. John Paul II himself reports in his *Rise, Let Us Be on Our Way* that someone had said to him, 'You would have been a great actor if you had remained in the theatre.'[8] Thus Wojtyla will far surpass Pius XII, whom the Tübingen church historian Karl August Fink used to call the greatest state actor of all time, with an image which is less detached and hierocratic and more pastoral and popular, no longer within national limits but beamed all over the world by the power of the mass media. The public appearances of Pope Wojtyla, like those of President Reagan, are prepared for in the media perfectly, down to the last detail, as if for Hollywood. Usually other people write the speeches. In the Vatican the wily press chief Dr Joaquín Navarro-Valls is responsible for everything; an Opus Dei man whom journalists call the Vatican spin doctor, he can 'sell' his boss in the best possible way.

What many television viewers still aren't aware of is that all the Vatican ceremonies, from the papal election to the funeral, are filmed by Televisione Italiana, which sells them to all the television companies in the world but at the same time produces only what has previously been agreed with the Vatican – sheer court reporting. But with these remarks on the election I am anticipating the developments in this pontificate which were to have devastating effects not least for Latin America.

Liberation theology: Gustavo Gutiérrez

Besides being a year of turbulence in Europe, 1968 was a year of new beginnings for the Catholic Church of Latin America. The assembly of Latin American bishops in Medellín, Colombia, has an importance for this continent comparable to the Second Vatican Council. Here the Latin American church and theology became aware in a new way of the social, political, cultural and religious situation which is marked by the tragic sign of underdevelopment. '*Liberación*' now became the great programmatic word for all those wanting to support the poor and marginalized of this continent, whose poverty is not a necessity of nature but the product of a cruel political and social system, those who want to make a stand for people exploited in an open or concealed way, for despised cultures and peoples (Indios) discriminated against. This marked a commitment to liberation, so that an underdeveloped people could receive basic food and basic culture and the disadvantaged could achieve full equality before the law.

In 1970, as I have described, European and North American theology is confronted for the first time with Latin American theology at the *Concilium* World Congress. Happily the 'father' of this theology, the Peruvian Gustavo Gutiérrez (like Greeley, Metz and me born in 1928), was accepted on to the editorial committee of our journal. Most of those on the committee were positive about liberation theology and I felt it an important enrichment for me and my theology from then on to maintain regular contact with Gutiérrez, who the next year publishes his basic work *Teología de la liberacíon. Perspectivas* (English *Theology of Liberation*). From the beginning we get on excellently. Later Gustavo will say to me on a visit to Tübingen: 'It's remarkable that you and I come from backgrounds which are different in every respect, but we always meet in the middle.' The secret is that we are both concerned, not with the person, but with the (Christian) 'cause'.

Over the next years I take great trouble to understand the concerns of liberation theology and adopt it as far as is possible and meaningful outside Latin America. In the editorial committee of *Concilium* we soon decide to publish a whole double issue, exclusively written by Latin American liberation theologians, with the title *The Mystical and Political Dimension of the Christian Faith*. It appears in 1974 in six languages with contributions from Leonardo Boff, José Miguez Bonino, Enrique Dussel, Segundo Galilea, Ronaldo Muñoz, Juan Luis Segundo and of course Gustavo Gutiérrez. I soon make myself knowledgeable enough to write a soundly-based chapter on the social relevance of the Christian message and on commitment to liberation for Part D of *On Being a Christian*. I can still stand wholly by it today.

From the beginning I try not only to read books and articles about Latin American theology and the church, but when opportunity arises also to get to know the countries and people of this gigantic continent (I visited Mexico as early as 1963). As I have already reported, there is an opportunity during my research semester of 1978/79 while our house is being rebuilt. In any case I am in the US for lectures from 13 to 22 October 1978; after Riverside Church in New York, at the invitation of the Kennedy Institute in Georgetown University, Washington, and finally in the University of Chicago, in both places on 'Science and Belief in God'. The next day I fly from Chicago to Miami and from there to Caracas in Venezuela.

Experiences of Latin America

In the Venezuelan capital Caracas – like all Spanish colonial cities, as we shall see, originally built on a grid pattern but with extremely modern buildings – on 24 October 1978 I meet up with my sister Rita and her husband Bruno, and Marianne Saur, who had her own programme in the US. With them in Bogotá, Lima and Cusco I get a lively impression of Colombia and Peru. From Cusco we spend eleven hours in the train, around 400 kilometres through the Altiplano, the high plateau of the Andes – Indios everywhere at the stations and in the fields – to the small port of Puno. From there we go in a speedboat across over Lake Titicaca, the 'Sea of the Andes', 190 kilometres long at a height of 3800 metres, to the island of the sun god and the Marian pilgrimage place of Copacabana. Finally we go on to Bolivia's *de facto* capital La Paz, where for the first time we get to know a population the majority of which are Indios. Then we fly further south to Santiago de Chile and Valparaiso and from there to the eastern regions: Buenos Aires, Rio de Janeiro, Brasilia, ending up in Salvador de Bahia.

It is impossible here to relate even the most striking impressions of this journey which is so full of experiences. What diverse landscapes! There are the high mountains of the Andes with snow-capped summits more than 6000 metres high, the alluvial lands of the plains and the giant cities on the Pacific and Atlantic coasts. And what differences in the population! There are the descendants of the Spanish or Portuguese immigrants, the Indios in the city markets or on the high plateau of the Andes and the many mestizos, people of mixed race. What gold and wealth in churches and palaces, what a culture of folklore, songs and dances and at the same time what indescribable poverty and what misery! And what grandiose ruined cities of pre-Columbian Inca cultures, for example on the slopes of Machu Picchu or in Tiahuanaco on the shores of Lake Titicaca – and what ugly industrial and poor districts on the periphery of the modern big cities, with shacks constructed from planks, sheet metal, palm fronds and other material. The divide between poor and rich manifestly widens with the population growth and urbanization.

403

The gold museum in Bogotá, the great wine cellars in Valparaiso, Rio's Sugar Loaf Mountain and the architecture of the brilliant Oscar Niemeyer in the new capital of Brasilia are sights that one doesn't forget. Above all, there are specific encounters which remain indelibly in the memory: for example, unusually in a military dictatorship, I speak directly to a policeman guarding the La Moneda residential palace in Santiago de Chile (he replies in a very ill-natured way), where on 11 September 1973 President Salvador Allende, the first freely-elected Marxist head of state in the world, was murdered at the instigation of the CIA. Or there is the procession of the 'Lord of Miracles' in the Peruvian capital Lima with the monstrous pushing and shoving of the tens of thousands of people who accompany an enormous statue and want to touch it. Or the conversation with very friendly young people in the *favelas* above the Sheraton Hotel in Rio, whom we were warned against. Or the Indio women wearing elaborate hats and colourful clothing in the market of the city of Cusco or in the village of Pisaq in Peru, some of whom have one child on their stomach, a second on their back and a third crawling behind them, an illustration of the gigantic population explosion in Latin America. Or in the thin air of La Paz (around 3700 metres above sea level in front of snow-covered Mount Illimani, 6640 metres high) a wide basin, hundreds of metres deep, covered with houses from its broad rim right down to its narrow floor; or the market of the Indios who, although the majority population, are bitterly poor. Only in 2006 is Evo Morales elected as the first Indio state president in Latin America. Or the children on the stations of the gigantic Altiplano, at a height of 4000 metres, who offer to sell us the three classic species of South American camel (llama, alpaca and vicuna) attractively cast in brass (today they stand peacefully on one of my bookcases with African wooden elephants, ivory elephants from India and an alabaster polar bear from Perm in the Urals). Children here on the broad plains in healthy air with agriculture and the tending of flocks are more fortunate than the children in the slums of the big cities.

All over Latin America there is problem upon problem, depending on the country: corruption, horrendous rates of inflation, ruined state budgets, immense foreign debt, economic and political dependence on the US and above all a lack of justice everywhere. There is a tremendous range of tasks.

The dangers of liberation theology

After this trip I am far from being a specialist on Latin America (later I will learn a great deal at our university in a working group of experts on Latin America and yet more from further trips there). But now I can talk in quite a different way from my own experience of Latin America, the *iglesia popular* (ecclesial base communities) and liberation theology, which is often denigrated even in Germany. I have already shown my positive attitude to the main concerns of liberation theology in *On Being a Christian*. So from the beginning I share the commitment of my friends Gustavo Gutiérrez and Leonardo Boff (from 1977 happily on the editorial committee of *Concilium*) and others. However, from the beginning I have also expressed criticism and have had two important reservations.

My criticism is that while I endorse a selective application of Marxist instruments of analysis to grasp and criticize the mechanisms of the capitalist economic system, I learned in the Roman study circles of the 1950s that Marxist solutions don't convince economists. So at the beginning of the 1970s, for the sake of the common cause, I warn that there should be no uncritical identification of the commitment of liberation theology with the political option for socialism and the socialization of the means of production.

After the annual *Concilium* meeting in 1973 I wrote to Gustavo Gutiérrez (26 June): 'There were vigorous efforts from Rome to put *Concilium* on the right track, which we have resisted for years. It seems to me important that we don't fix ourselves one-sidedly to a left-wing political course either; what other journals can do anyway would mean a slow death for *Concilium*. This certainly shouldn't prevent us from also taking firm theological positions on social questions. It was with this in mind that I very firmly supported the South American issue at that time.' But I have to note that my Latin American friends don't like such criticism and their own criticism of economics often doesn't seem to me to be competent. They don't take seriously the chapters devoted to this question in my forthcoming *On Being a Christian* and so offer an exposed flank to attacks which allege that liberation theology has been infiltrated by Marxism. It is only the collapse of the Soviet empire in 1989 that teaches some of them better.

There is another criticism that they don't like: liberation in society without liberation in the church isn't credible and will quickly meet with institutional reprisals. But my friends tell me with a superior smile that, now deeply involved in society, they have put 'behind them' my struggle in the church for structural reforms against Roman centralism and papalism. The demonization of the well-to-do and dismissal of other theologies as 'liberal' and 'bourgeois' is going the rounds among the 'political theologians', although most of them live good bourgeois lives. They needn't trouble with the Pope and his infallibility; they will leave such rearguard actions to me. In fact the liberation theologians left me a solitary figure in the great infallibility dispute. They brushed aside my early warning that they too would come under fire later if there wasn't a change in Rome.

Under the new Pope John Paul II and his German guardian of the faith, Joseph Ratzinger, who take a united front against liberation theology, they soon have to pay dearly for their attitude. On his first trip to Latin America in January 1979 the Polish Pope, stamped negatively by Soviet Marxism, vigorously criticizes liberation theology and 'disowns a whole group of theologians, pastors and bishops'. I write this on 30 January in similar letters to Gustavo Gutiérrez and Leonardo

Boff. 'But I hope you won't be discouraged. You can rely on my solidarity. Write to me if any statement from here would help you.'

There is a warning sign: the next year, on 23 March 1980 a heroic pioneer of liberation in Latin America, Oscar Romero, the Archbishop of San Salvador, is shot at the altar, directly from a car. He had grown up in the church establishment but the tremendous distress of men and women and the murder of a priest friend had changed his life and made him a committed defender of the rights of his oppressed people. He received no support whatsoever from the Vatican – any more than his socially committed and like-minded counterpart in Brazil, Helder Camara, Archbishop of Recife, defamed as a 'Communist bishop'. On the contrary, everything is done to ensure that no martyr cult arises at Romero's tomb in San Salvador Cathedral, and this true martyr remains unnoticed in the mass beatifications and canonizations by Pope Wojtyla. That is why later in my television series *Spurensuche* I began the sixth film on Christianity with a sequence about a poor district of San Salvador and a statement at the place where Archbishop Romero was murdered.

The liberation theologian Jon Sobrino, whom I respect greatly, and who had escaped the bloodbath in the Jesuit residence in San Salvador because he was on a trip abroad, had reservations about appearing in my film. His fears were justified. In 2007 the Vatican Inquisition will condemn him with a public 'Declaration' – in part on unjust charges similar to those against my christology. Here again it becomes evident how people in Rome see the reality of Latin America with European eyes and don't have the slightest sense of a 'contextual theology', the context of which is not the Greco–Hellenistic culture of the fourth and fifth centuries but experiences of injustice and oppression on the Latin American continent of the twentieth and twenty-first centuries. At the same time the violent Christianization of Latin America is transfigured and too few conclusions are drawn from the fact that at the time masses of the original inhabitants were massacred and rich cultures were largely destroyed. On his visit to Brazil in 2007 Pope Benedict XVI still thinks that Christianization was 'silently longed for' by the original inhabitants. Rome attempts to discipline Latin American theology and the Latin American church, like the Dutch before it, with reactionary doctrinal documents on the one hand and nominations of conservative bishops on the other, with equally destructive results.

John Paul II: not a Pope who engages in dialogue

After my return from the trip to North and South America, which lasted several weeks, at Christmas 1978 I send the new Pope John Paul II a book – not *Infallible? An Enquiry*, but *Does God Exist?* I hope that the Pope from Communist Poland can easily recognize in this book the fundamentals that we have in common, not least in the long critically balanced chapter on Karl Marx and what follows from him. In my inscription I express my 'hope' that the Pope may succeed in 'bringing GOD closer to the people of today'. Receipt of the book is confirmed by the Pope's Polish private secretary, Stanislaw Dziwisz, with a Christmas card, but there is no word from the Pope himself. And that will be the case, despite all my efforts at dialogue, for 27 years, until his death.

At the beginning of 1979 it is already known that the Pope wants to confirm the law of celibacy for the Catholic clergy of the Latin rite in a lengthy document published on Maundy Thursday. In view of the declining number of new priests this is a serious decision by the new pontificate. So after thorough reflection and discussion, on 30 March 1979 I send an urgent personal letter to John Paul II in which I ask him to have the problems clarified objectively and fairly by a commission representative of the whole Catholic Church. I make the same request over the issue of infallibility and therefore enclose my 'Theological Meditation' *The Church – Maintained in Truth?*, which has just been published. I shall be writing about that in the next chapter. At the same time I declare my readiness to come to Rome at any time to present the urgent concern personally to the Pope. There has never been any lack of readiness for conversation on my part.

My letter begins with an honest *captatio benevolentiae*:

I am impressed by the sympathetic humanity, the resolute action and the pastoral commitment with which you have taken up your service of the church and today's world, which is so infinitely important. I am grateful for the way in which from the beginning and now also in your first encyclical you have put Jesus Christ at the centre, so that from this centre of Christ-ianity can come a new concern for human beings, their hopes and needs. I am delighted that you have spoken out clearly for the progress of ecumen-ical understanding among the churches, and above all that you have intervened so powerfully for human rights in West and East, North and South. This is truly a new Christian humanism.[9]

I will never retract this recognition.

But then after a transition I openly come to critical questions which aren't mine alone. For 'many people are asking':

Can we credibly accuse present-day society, both capitalist Western society and socialist Eastern society, of mistakes unless at the same time we honestly and concretely concede and correct in practice the indisputable mistakes of the church?

Can we credibly fight against the poverty, illiteracy, unemployment, malnutrition and sickness in Latin America and the Third World which are connected with high birth-rates unless at the same time we resolutely support a kind of family planning which can be reasonably asked of people, and which includes conscientious contraception on the part of one of the partners?

Can we in today's society credibly stand up for the rights of women if we still regard women in the church as subjects with fewer rights and refuse them ordination with arguments which are not theologically convincing?

Can we work credibly for an active ecumenism if almost 500 years after the Reformation we still dispute the validity of Anglican and Protestant ministries and eucharists?

Can we credibly call for better Christian proclamation and practical pastoral work if our legislation is robbing more and more communities all over the world of their pastors and – just as seriously – of the regular celebration of their eucharists?[10]

This last point fills me with particular concern, as the celibacy encyclical of John Paul's predecessor but one, Paul VI, the first part of which discusses with amazing openness the difficulties faced by a law on celibacy, hasn't ended the discussion but intensified it. There is now a devastating lack of priests. I am convinced that further admonitions to obedience, loyalty and prayer won't solve this serious problem. And then I briefly cite the evidence from Bible and church tradition: while affirming the call of individuals to the unmarried state in the service of their fellow men and women, this does not justify a universal law for priests and bishops.

As in the opening words of my letter, in the closing sentences – put at the head of this chapter – I also attempt to win the Pope's heart. In vain. It will soon emerge that this man tolerates no criticism and doesn't want honest dialogue. From the beginning he surrounds himself with yes men – in the innermost circle Polish. I don't receive a reply from the Pope to my letter any more than I do from the sending of *Does God Exist?*, far less an invitation to the conversation I asked for. But did he get the letter and has he read it? The answer is certainly yes to both questions. However, this Pope, unlike his predecessor, doesn't want to talk with me but only about me. He does so first with the Bishop of Rottenburg, Georg Moser. In an audience he speaks with Moser of my letter and in so doing apostrophizes me as a 'world prophet', who is evidently unwelcome to him and disturbs him. The bishop can't explain this expression and I can only guess at its meaning.

At all events none of this bodes well for the future, as soon becomes evident. On 22/23 March 1979 I had launched *On Being a Christian* in Paris – a great success for Editions du Seuil, without any scandal. But at the beginning of April I read with consternation that the Congregation for the Doctrine of the Faith has condemned the book *Quand je dis Dieu* by the French theologian Jacques Pohier, a member of the editorial committee of *Concilium*. I write to him (4 April 1979): 'I don't know how you yourself are taking this. One can have very different views on it. But it's a defamation of your theological work, and in addition this first case of a condemnation after the Council is of fundamental importance. One needn't agree with what you write in your book to be against such methods. In fact this represents a return to the Index and thus also to the Inquisition. Can we do anything for you?' However, Jacques Pohier replies (13 April 1979) that first of all proceedings are taking place within the Order and that all his Dominican friends, who are also mine – Jossua, Geffré, Congar, Chenu – are of the view that it would be utterly inopportune to make a public intervention. For me, though, these Inquisition proceedings are of course a warning sign and are intended as such by the Inquisition.

A risky introduction – a strategic mistake?

I am sometimes asked – with different undertones and intentions – whether I didn't also make mistakes in the whole controversy with the Roman hierarchy. And countless times over the years I have been told a charming joke which came to my ears at a very early stage and which I've happily passed on, especially after I heard that Pope Paul VI had got to hear of it and, since he wasn't blessed with a sense of humour, wrongly understood it to be directed against himself rather than against me. It goes like this. The Pope has died, and in the conclave which follows the cardinals note that in many respects the previous pontificate hasn't been very successful: a change of course is needed. But since none of them had argued for this, they finally agree on the name of a certain Tübingen theologian who has long supported it. However, first they want to ask whether he would come to Rome for an election and accept high office. The theologian replies, 'No, I want to *remain* infallible!'

But those who know me know that I've never regarded myself as infallible, quite the contrary. Precisely because I've studied and written a great deal, I know what I don't know. And I also know how easily a mistake can slip in. So I keep checking all my manuscripts and have them re-checked. But perhaps I have sometimes appeared all too self-confident for uncertain souls, though only after I have formed a sure opinion with a great deal of effort. Of course I make tactical mistakes, like everyone else, and one can always discuss vocabulary and questions of style, as I do with the team and my friends. But strategic mistakes?

A prime example of a strategic decision in 1978 is whether to write an introduction for *How the Pope Became Infallible. Pius IX and the Politics of Persuasion*. The book has been written by an insider, the Catholic theologian, historian and long-time collaborator with the Vatican Secretariat for Unity Dr August Bern-hard Hasler. In his book he relates and analyses the way in which the infallibility definition of Vatican I was arrived at in 1870 and thus sharpens and popularizes my 'Enquiry' into the basis of the definition of infallibility. Was Vatican I a truly free council, was it a truly ecumenical council, and were the sacrifices worth while? And should the infallibility Pope Pius IX, who indisputably has the traits of a psychopath, be beatified, as is being planned in the Vatican?

Should I write an introduction to this book? That is an extremely tricky question. It is clear that Rome would take it amiss. So should I refuse support to the author, a fellow Swiss, who worked for a couple of months in Tübingen in 1965 to complete his dissertation? It should be said that as early as 1976 Dr Hasler had asked me to write a review of his dissertation, by now a two-volume monograph on 'Pius IX (1846-1878), Papal Infallibility and the First Vatican Council' (Stuttgart 1977) for the *Frankfurter Allgemeine Zeitung*. To begin with I had agreed in principle, but in 1978, the year of three Popes, the church–political situation changed. In January the documentation 'For Nothing but the Truth. German Conference of Bishops against Hans Küng' appears, edited by Walter Jens and with an explosive introduction. I have written an 'Appeal for Understanding' at the end. Moreover in the autumn my big book *Does God Exist?* is to be published. I write to Hasler (11 January 1978) that I can't take on this review at this particular moment. He keeps pestering me, as if I, who have risked more than anyone else in the matter of infallibility, were the only person on God's earth who could review his book (1 February 1978). Once again I make clear to him: 'It isn't a matter of my not being able to state my opinion freely and I will do so in due course.' I had already defended his book publicly. But it was also a matter of time: 'Sooner or later I will express myself again on this matter. But first I must see how I survive the next period' (6 February 1978). So I refuse to write the review.

Of course I have long since also asked myself the opposite question. Should I now keep silent on the question of infallibility for all time? Doubtless that would be extremely welcome to Rome and is probably what people in Rome expect after the 1973 declaration *Mysterium ecclesiae*. But – and Cardinal Döpfner is also aware of this – neither then nor later have I promised silence, but rather maintained my reservations about the whole proceedings. I know since my studies at the Gregorian that in Rome people like to emphasize to a potential dissident that what he personally believes is of little interest to the church authorities but that at least he should keep silent: *silentium obsequiosum* – obedient silence, especially towards the Summus Pontifex. In his lectures on moral theology Fr Franz Hürth SJ explained to us that 'decency' required this and he confirmed it to me personally when as a student in the early 1950s I asked him in his room about the limits of infallibility (*My Struggle for Freedom*, III: Critical questions).

Moreover most theologians were wise and obediently kept silent. The most famous case in the context of Vatican I is the learned Tübingen council historian and then Bishop of Rottenburg, Karl Josef Hefele. In protest against the infallibility definition, with several dozen other important German and French bishops he left the Council. But several months later he did publish the Vatican I infallibility definition (1870) in his diocese, the last German bishop to do so – and kept silent about it for time and eternity. No one learned from him what pressure from above, from below or from the side had moved him to capitulate. Thus at the end of the nineteenth century the infallibility debate ran into the sand in the Catholic Church, in which in any case a major campaign against the 'Modernists' was taking shape. So should something similar now happen again? Had *Infallible?* been written in vain, and was the 'Enquiry' to remain without an official answer? At the same time, should Catholic women continue to be forbidden the pill by the magisterium and ordination be refused them? Was this and much else 'infallible' teaching? All the theologians censured under Pius XII (de Lubac, Bouillard, Rondet, Chenu, Congar, Rahner) had maintained an obedient silence.

The question of strategy now arises for me again with Hasler's second book, *How the Pope Became Infallible*, which sums up his two volumes in a popular form and sharpens them. It is to be published by Piper Verlag in 1979. In a long telephone conversation from Switzerland Hasler beseeches me to write the introduction he wants. Of course I sympathize with my younger colleague and recall only too well how in 1970 after the publication of *Infallible?* I had hoped for the support of my older colleague Karl Rahner, in vain. And who would be the appropriate man to write an introduction for him if not the author of this 'Enquiry'?

But I never decide such strategic questions without much discussion. My team is in favour of an introduction, as are the Tübingen colleagues whose advice I seek, but two Rotarian friends with whom I discuss the question at length one evening on skiing holidays in Lech are against it. Rome could use this introduction against me. In the end I have to decide for myself. And I decide in favour of the introduction, but safeguarded by a second publication. It seems to me meaningful and helpful to sum up the 'state of the infallibility debate' for a wider public and in this way do August Hasler the service he desires.

Conscious of the risk, at the same time, based on my stocktaking of the infallibility debate in 'Fallible?' (1973), I write an easily understandable explanatory 'Theological Meditation' with the title *The Church – Maintained in Truth?* I answer this question clearly in the affirmative, even in the face of numerous serious errors in the church. In the light of the biblical message I explain abiding in the truth despite all errors as specifically as possible. I also think through the practical consequences consistently. A church guided by the Spirit? Living with errors? Criteria of Christian truth? The opportunities of a fallible 'magisterium'? What is to be done in case of conflict?

I understood all this as a stimulus to become aware again of the power of the truth by which the church has lived and – I trust – will live in the future. At the end of the meditation I refer to the ecumenical consensus with non-Catholic Christians which is possible only on such a basis and as in the introduction ask, following the French theologian Yves Congar, one of the great figures who paved the way for Vatican II, for the question of infallibility – in the new pontificate – to be investigated anew with objectivity and scholarly honestly and if possible for an ecumenical commission to be appointed to do this. Both the

411

introduction to Hasler's book and my own meditation are completed in 1979 and immediately go to the printers.

Or should I as a loyal Catholic theologian perhaps not be allowed to address such a petition to the supreme Catholic pastor, who likes to call himself *Servus servorum Dei* – Servant of the Servants of God? John Paul II has just come back from Latin America with new experiences. Am I hoping too much if I expect of the man who there has spoken out clearly against poverty, underdevelopment and child misery and who also wants to work for ecumenical understanding, particularly in respect of birth control (pill and condom), a decisive step towards the honest clarification of the oppressive question of infallibility – in an atmosphere of mutual trust, free research and fair discussion? I don't want to provoke a new dispute over infallibility by my introduction to Hasler's book and this 'Theological Meditation'. Rather, through the 're-reception' or interpretation of the papal dogmas of Vatican I called for by Yves Congar, the infallibility debate should be settled as soon as possible.

So was it a strategic mistake to write the introduction and meditation (I enclose only the latter with my letter to the Pope)? It was easy to say this later, since Rome took the two publications as an occasion, not to establish an ecumenical commission but to remove the church's permission to teach from me without legal proceedings. So was it a mistake? I acted conscientiously, with the best will in the world, after long reflection and much discussion with other competent people, and in full awareness of the risk. Indeed I saw it as my duty in the face of the silence of most theologians not to keep silent. One could also put the question the other way round: did Rome perhaps make a strategic mistake and underestimate the risk to itself? Many theologians and members of the hierarchy – not to mention the clergy and people – were and still are of this opinion. But I can have no inkling of the conflict that the two works on 'infallibility' will bring me at the end of 1979. First, the year takes its course dramatically in another way.

In the centres of the world

This much is clear: I am not a theologian of the Roman Catholic 'headquarters'; I have none of the characteristics of the 'court theologian'. And in time I have got used to not finding a hearing at the centre of the Catholic Church for my theology which, granted, is in some points uncomfortable. Instead I am welcome in many centres of the world, often in places to which theologians aren't normally invited, not to speak on some peripheral topics, but on the theme of theology, God-talk, in rational responsibility. I have mentioned my speaking engagements in the US.

It was particularly bold of me to speak at the World Economic Forum in Davos on 28 February 1979 on 'Should Managers Believe in God?' To this day I am grateful to the founder and president of the Forum, Professor Klaus Schwab, for coming with two gentlemen from Geneva to Tübingen specifically to convince me that despite my many commitments in 1978/79 I should include in my plans the considerable time needed to work out the lecture and take part in the Forum. I hold Klaus Schwab in extraordinarily high esteem because he has built up a unique institution and commands a horizon which extends far beyond economics. And I am well prepared for such an intellectual adventure: by years of studying for *Does God Exist?*, by my speech on the quincentenary of the University of Tübingen and by a succinct summary of the big book in '24 Theses on the Question of God'. These are completed on 20 April 1979 and serve as the basis for my Tübingen lectures on the Trinity in the next summer semester. The lecture in Davos is a great success, earns me respect in the world of business and politics, and encourages me to take part in the World Economic Forum more often in the future. At it I have valuable experiences and get to know leading figures from the world of politics and business.

An invitation to Israel from the Swiss–Israel Society under the aegis of the charming Dr Yakov Bach represents a challenge for me of a quite different kind. Bach meets me at Tel Aviv airport on 5 May 1979. Since there are not only believing Orthodox Jews in Israel but a majority of secular agnostics and atheists – which is understandable after the experiences of the 'chosen people' in the time of the Nazis and in the Holocaust – the topic 'Science and the Question of God' seems to me to be the right approach to the question of God. I speak on this first at the University of Haifa (6 May). I meet numerous Israeli personalities in the evening, at a reception by the Swiss Ambassador in Tel Aviv.

The next day (7 May 1979) I am in Jerusalem, first for tea with the famous Jewish historian of religion Gershom Scholem, who is already 83 years old. However, it isn't until a decade later, for my book *Judaism*, that I can move on to his special area of Jewish mysticism and the Kabbala. It is a special honour for me to speak in the evening on 'Science and the Problem of God' at a large public meeting of the Israeli Academy of Sciences. There are no serious objections.

I obtain information on the precarious political situation the next day (8 May 1979) from a diplomat in the Israeli Academy of Sciences. The Palestine problem is far from being solved; unfortunately the opportunity of a fair peace wasn't taken up after the Six Day War. Then I have lunch with colleagues in the Hebrew University, also well known to critical political theorists all over the world. In the evening there is discussion far into the night in the Rainbow Club, which meets in the Ecumenical Institute of Tantur on the road between Jerusalem and Bethlehem, about the tricky theological and political questions between Jews and Christians, Israelis and Palestinians. Everywhere I am given an extremely friendly reception by the Israelis, so only the best of memories have remained with me.

I get up the next morning at 3.15 a.m. I take the flight back from Tel Aviv to hold a press conference for the Italian edition of my book (*Dio esiste?*) in Rome punctually at 11.00 a.m. (9 May 1979) and the next day – with a slight detour – for the Spanish edition (*Existe Dios?*) in Madrid (10 May 1979). My very committed Spanish publisher Manuel Sanmiguel takes me himself in a small car for a three-hour drive over winding roads (there is as yet no motorway) to the Spanish university city of Salamanca, with the richest of traditions and glorious historical buildings. There I speak in the Aula Magna on 'Sciencia y el problema de Dió'. I return to Madrid overnight. The next morning I revisit the Prado museum for El Greco, Velasquez and Goya and at noon give the same lecture to the Madrid student community. Finally I fly home to Stuttgart via Zurich. I get back in the evening, glad to have these energetic weeks behind me and grateful to Dr Karl-Josef Kuschel for taking over lectures (Theses on the Question of God) for me.

But how sad it is that despite my efforts on all fronts of the world, rather than support from the headquarters of the Catholic Church and the German episcopate, all I get is a rap on the knuckles, so that some discussion in Davos and in Jerusalem unfortunately concentrates more on these church–political questions than on the question of God. Most of these 'successors of the apostles' wouldn't be capable of talking about the question of God before such different audiences. Here I could understand myself almost in line with Peter and Paul as 'apostle to the Jews and Gentiles'. I have always attached importance to seeing myself in the succession of the 'teachers'; I never come forward as a missionary revivalist preacher or as a theological specialist who may well have forgotten God, but as a professor of theology who adopts a standpoint on the central questions of God and the world. In this respect, too, I think that I've remained true to my original calling, though I have to fulfil it in quite a different way from the one I imagined. But I do everything with the basic attitude that I expressed 25 years previously on the prayer card for my first mass: 'Pray for me also, that God may open to me a door for the word, to declare the mystery of Christ' (Colossians 4.3).

Now I am to speak of this mystery of God in quite different centres of the world. Leaving aside appearances in German-speaking countries[11] (including the Communist GDR)[12] there are above all three occasions which require of me the utmost preparation: on 28/29 August 1979 in Peking at the Chinese Academy of Social Sciences, 'Nine Theses on Religion and Society'; on 5 September in Hamburg at the European Congress of Radiologists, 'Towards a Humanity in Medicine'; and on 29 September in Stuttgart to the German Federation of Artists, 'Modern Art and the Question of Meaning'. Here are some brief reports.

China after Mao

I had long wanted to get to know not only Hong Kong but also China itself, that land with a culture thousands of years old and with constantly changing political significance. On 8 September 1976 the Chinese state and party head Mao Zedong (Mao Tse-tung) had died. Ten years earlier, in May 1966, in order to eliminate his rivals, the alleged 'representatives of the bourgeoisie' who had infiltrated the Party, government, army and culture, Mao had declared war on them and in August 1966 had sent the students and pupils with the 'Mao Bible' on campaigns against 'old ideas, old customs and old habits': the Cultural Revolution, a 'great leap forward', in which, however, millions of Chinese were sent into the country for re-education or tormented in other ways.

My Chinese colleague and friend Julia Ching, whose aunt is a senior state official, soon to become a minister, but whose uncle is still in a labour camp, has helped me to make a detached and balanced assessment of the person and work of the 'red emperor'. Mao's Cultural Revolution did immense damage, cost hundreds of thousands of lives, devastated China's economy, and plunged the land into chaos and anarchy. After his death at the age of 82 the 'Band of Four' around his wife Jiang Qing, mainly responsible for the Cultural Revolution, were arrested; after the 11th Party Conference the left-wing party was removed from office and the Cultural Revolution was ended. The era of Deng Xiaoping began; the only woman in his cabinet is my friend Julia's aunt, as minister for water and energy.

However, in 1979 there is as yet no Western tourism, and an individual traveller without a Chinese escort is unthinkable. Julia is prepared to accompany me. But how are a Chinese woman from Shanghai with a Canadian passport and a Swiss citizen living in Germany to be able to travel together? So Julia asks Sargent Shriver-Kennedy whether his brother-in-law, Senator Edward Kennedy, who has good contacts with the Chinese, can help us. This request has unexpected consequences: Sargent replies that he would very much like to come with us himself, and later yet others are added, so that in the end our party numbers about twenty. We are now a delegation of the Kennedy Institute for Ethics, Washington DC, with a whole series of stimulating, mostly young scholars. For me the most exciting of these is the brilliant American ethicist Richard McCormack SJ, who replaced the Dutch gynaecologist André Helleger as acting President of the Kennedy Institute when Helleger died of a heart attack a few months before the China trip. Our status as a delegation gets us special treatment in many respects and an extremely interesting travel programme.

On 12 August I fly via Moscow to Tokyo, where I arrive at noon the next day and meet Julia, Sargent and the other Americans. That evening the small group of us has dinner at the Catholic Sophia University at the invitation of the Rector of the university, the distinguished Jesuit Giuseppe Pittau, who is later to succeed the Jesuit General Pedro Arrupe as the commissar 'Vicar of the Order', appointed in an authoritarian way by Pope John Paul II after Arrupe had resigned under papal pressure. The next day there are lectures for us at the Sophia about education in Japan, curricula in Japanese universities, bioethical problems and finally law and ethics in Japan. We have dinner in the Ginza, an entertainment district of Tokyo. The next morning there are lectures on the Japanese constitution and on law and ethics, and in the afternoon I give a paper on religion and science. Finally there is a conference with the president of Japan's Medical Association on the new responsibilities of doctors to the public.

On 17 August, after a visit to the imperial district, we fly to Hong Kong. Here the next day we visit a camp of refugees ('boat people'), above all from Communist Vietnam, and the day after that a reconstructed Chinese village from the Sung period. On 20 August we are at the Chinese University of Hong Kong. Here in a free academic atmosphere I have to discuss 'Religion and Science' in a seminar – good practice for my task in Communist Peking. At the same time I hear an excellent lecture by Professor Liu Shu-Hsien on Chinese philosophy which later prompts me to propose him for the first UNESCO Colloquium with representatives of the world religions on 'World Peace through Religious Peace' in Paris in February 1989. Liu explains that whereas Greek philosophy begins from cosmological questions about the origin of all things, Chinese philosophy begins from practical questions about the right way of life (Dao): human beings, seen in the cosmos as a whole. And whereas Roman law wants to protect the rights of the people, Chinese law wants to protect the rights of the ruler, who stands above the law. So in Chinese philosophy there is a far-reaching antipathy to laws and an insistence on ethics.

On 22 August 1979 we go by train to Guanghzou (Canton). China's first contact with Europeans (Portuguese) took place in the city at the mouth of the Pearl River in 1514, but it received its decisive stimuli from the Chinese reform movement of 1898 and the 1911 revolution. The monument to Sun Yat Sen, the first president of the Republic of China, whose 'Three Principles of the People' (nationalism, democracy and social reform) indicated the goals of the Revolution, bears witness to this. In this industrial and commercial centre of South China we have an elementary introduction to Chinese Communism and 30 kilometres north of Guangzhou visit a model commune, a production unit (village) and, again in the city, a hospital.

On 23 August we fly to Peking. The next day we have a great experience: in the middle of the 'Middle Kingdom' we visit the square of 'Heavenly Peace' and the extensive imperial Forbidden City. To enter it we have to go through a gate over which a gigantic portrait of Mao Zedong is still displayed. One may criticize the 'Band of Four' but not Mao. All through China the *bon mot* circulates that the thumb (Mao) is always hidden behind four outstretched fingers. But of course for its own self-preservation the party doesn't want to make any accusations against Mao. The icons are to remain not only at the entrance to the Imperial City but in the Chinese capital generally. Meanwhile it has become widely known that Mao, who is also glorified by many people in the West, is responsible for the death of tens of thousands of Chinese during his various campaigns against the 'class enemy', above all during the 'great leap forward' between 1958 and 1960, in order to implement industrialization and the agricultural revolution with the famine that followed. The Party officials now say that for 70 per cent of his time Mao was a force for good, but some put it the other way round: 30 per cent good and 70 per cent bad.

In the afternoon we are at the famous Peking University (originally the

416

Protestant American University), in the philosophy department of which the Cultural Revolution had begun. The Rector was led on to the campus with a dunce's cap and placard; professors were beaten and maltreated, students denounced and arrested. People want to forget that time. It strikes me how uncertain Chinese professors are when one asks them about their great sage Confucius. They don't want to censure him, although his static patriarchalism which had led to social conformity is certainly no longer contemporary. But they don't want to praise him either, although he is one of the first humanists and ethicists in human history and in Communist China one largely misses the respect for the other that he called for. The anti-Confucius campaign during the Cultural Revolution still has its effect in Peking; this applies above all to the prime minister and foreign minister Zhou Enlai, brought up as a Confucian, who in his moderate behaviour recalls a Confucian mandarin, always a kind of opposite to the brutal peasant leader Mao.

The whole of China seems to be wearing uniform, white shirt and white trousers. Men and women do the same hard work; doctors and taxi drivers get the same wages; people normally travel on bicycles (there are three million of them in Peking); there are only a few buses and cars. There is no Sunday but at least in theory a free day in the week and two weeks' holiday. There is no sport and there are no boutiques, and bound up with all this is a personality cult of the great leader similar to that in Moscow, extending beyond death. Happily we have priority over the hundreds of Chinese waiting to enter the mausoleum of the embalmed Mao.

We are also taken into the lonely Catholic Cathedral of Peking, where we meet a 'patriotic' priest, strangely clothed in a Roman gown, who still celebrates the Latin Mass facing the wall. Apparently he has heard nothing of the Second Vatican Council and gives unhelpful information in response to our very direct questions about the difficult state of the Catholic Church in the People's Republic: nothing about the number of bishops, priests, faithful, open churches. However, I hear from Julia Ching that many Catholic priests have also been accused by bands of Maoist fanatics and have been driven through the streets like cattle, but have earned much respect for Christianity through their refusal to yield.

For me, though, the supreme monument in Peking isn't the structure of the great imperial palaces but the incomparable Temple of Heaven, which is in a gigantic park. The temple proper rests on a rectangular terrace symbolizing the earth, nature, the human world, supported by richly painted pillars which stand for the seasons, months and days, with a three-storey roof, blue tiles and a golden pearl crowning it all. The Temple of Heaven is a symbol of the Chinese notion of the cosmic harmony of heaven and earth which outlasts all the stormy times. It fascinates me so much that two decades later I want to end my film on Chinese Religion in the TV series *Spurensuche* with a statement in front of it.

On 26 August 1979 we go by train to the Great Wall, begun by China's first emperor Qin 2200 years ago, but today without any protecting function: it could be a warning to those who build walls in the GDR and in Israel. On the way back we visit the famous Ming tombs of the imperial dynasty of the fourteenth to seventeenth centuries. In the evening there is a reception at the American Embassy with the US Vice-President Walter Mondale, Jimmy Carter's representative, who in 1984 was to lose as Democrat presidential candidate to Ronald Reagan. Happily I see him again at the InterAction Council in Vienna in May 2007. Things become serious for me on the fourth day in Peking, 27 August 1979.

In the Chinese Academy of Social Sciences

The two-day symposium takes place in the Peking Hotel, as many state buildings haven't been properly renovated. I am aware of my responsibility: I am the first Western philosopher and theologian to be allowed to speak about religion and the question of God in the heart of China, in Peking, at the Chinese Academy of Social Sciences, without any prior censorship. I limit myself to nine theses (9, because it is 3 x 3, for Chinese the perfect number!) about religion and science. I don't want to speak from a specifically Christian standpoint but from a universally human position, which can be shared by many people all over the world, and specifically also by the Chinese who come from a Confucian, Daoist or Islamic tradition.[13] My translator is Julia Ching, with whom I have discussed my nine theses, formulated in English.

Of course I present everything in a friendly tone without academic affectations. But it isn't my way to beat about the bush. Rather, I am resolved to use my freedom, and right at the beginning I advance to the centre of the Marxist critique of religion, which tends to identify religion simply with superstition. My first thesis is meant to provoke thought: 'We have to distinguish between religion and superstition.' How? Religion doesn't recognize anything relative, conditioned, human as an absolute authority but only the Absolute itself, which from time immemorial in our tradition we have called God. By this I mean that hidden, first of all and last of all reality which not only Jews and Christians but also Muslims worship and which the Hindus seek in Brahma, the Buddhists in the Absolute and, of course, traditional Chinese in Heaven or the Dao. Religion is certainly one of the most important factors in the history of their great country; it is and remains a social and political factor not only in Tibet but also elsewhere.

However, superstition recognizes as an absolute authority (and requires blind obedience to) something that is relative and not absolute. Superstition divinizes either material things or a human person or a human organization. In this respect, for example, any cult of the person proves to be a kind of superstition. A bit much for Maoists, I think to myself, looking at the many young faces – but there is no protest. The consequences are that not all superstition is religion; there are also un-

418

religious, very modern forms of superstition. Conversely, not all religion is superstition; there is true religion. But any religion can become superstition wherever it makes a non-essential essential, a relative absolute.

In theses 2–5 I come to speak directly on the question of God. I say that the question of the God of the old picture of the world is obsolete, but not the question of the God (the Absolute) of the new picture of the world; that God has been rejected in modern times because church and theology rejected modern natural science and also democracy, and that it is regrettable how many false gulfs have been opened up in modern times between belief in God and science. As in my Tübingen speech on the quincentenary of the university, in theses 6-8 I then describe how the strengths and weaknesses of the psychological argument against religion as a projection may be said to have been exposed, as have the strengths and weaknesses of the philosophical argument about the end of religion. However, the reality of God cannot be accepted on the basis of either a rational proof or an irrational feeling, but only on the basis of a reasonable trust.

Then I conclude with the challenging thesis 9. No one may be compelled physically or morally to accept a particular religion or a particular ideology. There wasn't always freedom for atheists; atheists must also be given freedom of thought, speech and propaganda in Christian countries. But there wasn't always freedom for believers in God either; believers in God must also be given freedom of thought, speech and propaganda in Socialist countries. This full freedom would help many believers (Christians, Muslims, Jews, Buddhists, Confucians, Daoists) to overcome their well-founded unease there.

Of course the answer to the question of God is in no way a recipe for all the urgent economic, political and social questions of the day. However, the question of God can have a deep positive influence on these questions, as it were 'from below', from the ground, by bringing into play basic convictions, basic attitudes, basic values. Not only are ideas dependent on an economic basis (thus Karl Marx) but economic development is dependent on ideas (thus Max Weber). Granted, religion can exercise a negative influence – we heard of the effect of Confucianism on the high birth rate. But it can also have a thoroughly positive influence, as has been shown in practice by the numerous believers in West and East who fight for social justice, the liberation of peoples and peace. On this religious basis believers have a well-founded answer to difficult questions of principle: why for example love is better than hate, peace better than law, freedom better than oppression, non-violence better than violence.

I ask whether in our most recent history we haven't experienced so many forms of superstition, so much blind faith in so-called supreme values such as nation, people, race, class, science, progress. Human beings have always believed in some 'God': if not in the true God, then in some idol. But after so many crises, an amazing amount has been clarified and many difficulties with belief in God have been settled. I repeat here in Peking that today one need no longer be against God because one is for heliocentricity and evolution, for democracy and

419

science, for liberality or socialism. On the contrary, one can be for true freedom, equality and brotherhood, for humanity, liberality and social justice, for humane democracy and controlled scientific progress, precisely because one believes in God and therefore in a true humanity. This, it seems to me, is a new situation, which is very different from that of Feuerbach, Marx and Engels.

Since here in the Academy of Social Sciences every sentence has to be translated consecutively from English into Chinese I have abundant occasion to observe my audience. But it is difficult to read these mostly unmoved faces; a few years later I speak to hundreds of students in Peking and find lively, often radiant, faces. However, in 1979 Mao's shadow still lies heavily over the country. And for a young Chinese generation which in the Cultural Revolution had been sworn to the fight against the 'Four Olds' – old ideas, old culture, old moralities, old customs – and for a classless society my nine theses strike a completely new note. Just one older scholar who verbosely and with deadly seriousness puts forward the orthodox Marxist standpoint speaks in the discussion, but without finding approval from the audience. The rest is silence. It is still too dangerous, in this ambivalent post-Mao period, even in the Institute for World Religions, to stand up for religion. Certainly the official ideology, a barely rational mixture of Marxist idealism and Maoist extremism, has largely lost its credibility for the younger generation. But the Communist Party still determines the daily course of things in China, and the future is uncertain.

At Confucius' birthplace

After my lecture my hosts treat me with marked friendliness, and at the dinner which follows in the Peking Hotel with the beautifully decorated round tables there is a very relaxed mood. Those sitting next to me put dish after dish on my plate in a friendly Chinese way; I enjoy them all, and the rice wine which people drink with the toast 'Kampé'. I seem to have won the respect of the Chinese with my critical self-critical theses. The 'Discussion about God in Peking' which has become possible after Mao is attentively noted in the German media. The comment in Die Zeit when the theses are published is correct: 'The theses show that in present-day China discussion is possible of a kind that would have been ruled out a few years previously.'[14]

At the end of the evening I have a nightcap in the German Embassy with ambassador Erwin Wickert, a writer and expert on East Asia who is highly regarded in Peking. In a famous novel, The Heavenly Mandate, he has depicted the history of the Taiping Revolt against the Manchu dynasty and now inscribes it for me as a memento (27 August 1979); his son Ulrich Wickert, later the popular presenter of 'Topic of the Day' on German television, returns that same evening from Tibet and tells of the unhappy situation there, increasingly dominated by the Chinese. There is no hope for the Dalai Lama.

The next day there are papers from the American side: ethics and population, ethics and medicine, ethics and scientific research, ethics and diplomacy, ethics and laws, ethics and economics, ethics and social sciences. But during the day I find time to get rice-paper rubbings of important Chinese reliefs, which still hang in my hall. In the evening we are invited to a farewell banquet in a marvellous traditional restaurant in the middle of a park with an enchanting lake. One could forget one was still in a Communist state if one didn't know that recently the 'Band of Four' around Mao's wife Jiang Qing had recently stayed there. In 1976 she had once again succeeded in overthrowing Deng Xiaoping, who had been removed from all high offices in the 1967 Cultural Revolution but in 1973 had been rehabilitated. He was then restored to all these offices the year after Mao's death (likewise 1976). Deng's politically pragmatic course of reforms is aimed at economic and technical achievements and a raising of the standard of living – but without democratization, without concern for environmental interests, without a more efficient use of resources and without preventing the growing trend towards wealth which is endangering the cohesion of China, though of course this is to be conceded openly only under Deng's successor Jiang Zemin.

On 29 September we fly to Jinan, where we also see a large commune, but in the afternoon we go by train to Qufu, the birthplace of Confucius around 500 years before Christ. We are the first foreign group to visit this historic place, known throughout China, and are even allowed to stay in the spacious residence of the Kung family, which time and again has been restored in the traditional style. The last traces of the destruction wrought by the Cultural Revolution are being removed from the big Confucian temple nearby; otherwise there is marvellous tranquillity here, and in this mood we can also visit the Kung cemetery and the tomb of Confucius, which all play a major role in the 1990s in our filming trip for *Spurensuche*. However, it will be some years before a Chinese state president – Hu Jintao in February 2005 – quotes Confucius and his emphasis on 'harmony', shortly afterwards admonishing the Party cadre to build up a 'harmonious society' and bring people, government and the different groups closer together through Confucian virtues such as honesty and unanimity. And only in 2007 will environmental problems and an economic policy which is both ecologically and socially responsible stand at the centre of the National People's Congress.

Next morning we travel back to Jinan, make contact with the medical faculty, and also admire the beautiful landscape by the lake. Then we fly from Jinan to Shanghai. There we visit another hospital which displays considerable technical, hygienic and organizational backwardness; but it is interesting to witness a throat operation by means of acupuncture. We visit the industrial exhibition and then a famous Buddhist temple which has been renovated, and finally meet the President of the Shanghai Court of Justice, whose stereotyped information about religion and law doesn't satisfy us at all. From there we return to Peking. The time to part company with the American delegation has come; I express warmest thanks to Sargent Shriver and Julia Ching, without whom our China expedition, extraordinary in every respect, wouldn't have been possible. Over the night of 3/4 September I take the plane from Peking with stops in Bombay and Athens to Geneva, where I immediately have to change for Hamburg.

Towards humanity in medicine

I have a terribly long flight of 35 hours in all, but I must appear on 5 September at a big medical gathering on quite a different topic. I give the ceremonial lecture for the European Congress of Radiologists in Hamburg, which I am still intensively revising in the plane with an eye to my audience. 1979 is an utterly hectic year. Some readers will ask themselves why I burden myself with such different and difficult tasks. When I think about it, extraordinary commitments usually have two characteristics. The big topics involved are prepared for somewhere in my life story and academic research, otherwise I wouldn't attempt them. And it takes the right time (*Kairos*), the decisive external stimulus, to make me decide to work on a special topic alongside lectures and major publications which requires much reading, thought and expressiveness. My early meeting and friendship with Julia Ching were the preparation in my life for the theses on religion and superstition, but the decisive stimulus was provided by the invitation from the Institute for World Religions of the Chinese Academy of Social Sciences.

There is a key experience behind my preoccupation with the question of humanity in medicine: the painful suffering and death, protracted over a year, of my 22-year-old brother Georg from an incurable brain tumour which had manifested itself for the first time on the day of my first mass in the crypt of St Peter's on 11 October 1954 (*My Struggle for Freedom*, III: In the grottos of St Peter's). But in this hectic year 1979 I would never have investigated this complex theme of a 'humanity in medicine' without the challenge of my Tübingen colleague Professor Walter Frommhold, the distinguished Director of the Institute of Radiology. He used all his arts of persuasion (his last trump is the amazing cure from cancer of the uncle of my closest collaborator Dr Hermann Häring) to press me to give the opening speech at the European Society for Radiology in Hamburg, whose President he is.

So I said yes, and at the same time – faithful to my principle of beginning wherever possible 'from below' with people's questions – arranged a day visit for myself and my three closest colleagues to the Radiography Institute. Here, in clinical gowns, we could see the instruments that had been perfected for diagnosing and treating cancer, and also the gentle approach of the head of the clinic in visiting the sick. We went on to have a long conversation in which some problems were clarified, and these were followed by further conversations.

My concern in the Hamburg radiologists' congress is to argue resolutely for an end to the hostility between medicine and belief in God, for which I had done the essential basic work in *Does God Exist?* This hostility had flared up acutely at the 31st Assembly of the German Naturalists and Doctors in Göttingen in 1854 – paradoxically the very year in which in Rome the Pope proclaimed as a dogma the 'immaculate conception of the Virgin Mary', for which there is no evidence in the Bible and ancient tradition. In the battle for the wider public the materialists won. They claimed that convictions of faith had no place in questions of science and medicine. The mechanistic context of the laws of nature had to be investigated to the end without philosophical or theological reservations. There is no active consciousness without brain activity, no soul standing independently over against the body. Medicine, too, had to start from quantitative measurements and experiments which could be checked and repeated. So religion had nothing to do with science; if it was anything at all, it was a private matter. Ludwig Feuerbach, father of the Marxist critique of religion, praises Martin Luther because he allowed his son to study medicine, since for him the medical man was by nature a materialist.

In 1979, however, far more than a century later, the situation looks quite different: to the crisis in belief in God has now been added the crisis of belief in science, particularly in medicine. After the experiences on the one hand of the criminal experiments by doctors on human beings in National Socialism and on the other of the breathtaking successes of medicine after the Second World War, some people are afraid of the unlimited possibilities of medicine. Even psychoanalytically trained doctors such as Alexander Mitscherlich warn against technological medicine and care of the sick which treats human beings like items on a conveyor belt; against a medicine of apparatuses which largely dispense with the use of human language for reasons of time and replace it by a wealth of symbols and measurements understandable only by specialists. In short, they warn against a dehumanized medicine which keeps the relationship of trust between doctor and patient emotionally sterile and reduces human contacts, friendly concern and personal support to the unavoidable minimum.

I grant that I, too, had once asked the director of our University Clinic for Internal Medicine how one could avoid being a complete prisoner of this medical apparatus on entering one of our clinics. Excusing himself with a smile, he said that the emergency doctors would often do too much for the safety of patients and stick a tube in every human orifice. As with preachers, I distinguish between those who soberly and objectively discuss a topic or even reprimand their audience and those who want to help people sensitively with their words in a scriptural and contemporary way, so with doctors I distinguish between those who quickly provide their treatment in a technically perfect way and those who look after their patients with gentle care.

I needn't report here all the points I made in my lecture in a balanced way to stimulate a sense of the ethical and religious dimension (the Hippocratic oath) and campaign for a healthy religious sense. With an enlightened understanding of faith it is possible to explain some things that certainly can be argued for without God but can hardly be given an indubitable unconditional, universally-binding foundation: five imperatives of humanity. These imperatives are for a new humanity and a new meaningfulness in medicine and above all for a new relationship to sickness, to therapy and to dying.

I can't spell all this out here; it will later find its way into my book *Eternal Life?* The fifth imperative, a new understanding of dying and help in dying, will occupy me more intensively than the others in future. At the end of the lecture the sustained applause from the radiologists and the enthusiasm of the congress president Professor Frommhold make me forget the extraordinary efforts involved both in preparing the lecture and in the long flight from Peking to Hamburg. And the printing of the lecture on two pages of the *Frankfurter Allgemeine Zeitung* of 7 December 1979 will, I hope, show the service I perform for the Christian cause.

That same 5 September, in a good mood I fly back to Stuttgart from Hamburg. Happy to be back in Tübingen, over the next few days I have to concentrate all my efforts not only on dealing with a mountain of correspondence but before the winter semester begins in the middle of October on completing another no less important lecture on again a quite different topic. However, it has likewise been prepared for in my life story, and has received special impetus from outside. This is a lecture for the German Federation of Artists on 29 September of the same hectic year 1979.

Modern art and the question of meaning

Perhaps one of the reasons for the growing alienation between Joseph Ratzinger and me, which a couple of weeks later is to lead to public confrontation, is our extremely different attitudes to the modern secular world, of which modern art is a part. For Joseph Ratzinger modern art, like so much that is 'modern' in a time of anti-Western National Socialism hostile to art, remains a largely closed realm during and after the war. By contrast, at school in Lucerne I was introduced so well to classical modernity – architecture, sculpture, painting – by my outstanding teacher of the history of art, Adolf Hüppi, that at the beginning of my studies in Rome, where everywhere I miss modern works of art, I can venture to guide my fellow students at the German College through a big special exhibition in the Palazzo Barberini, directly opposite our college, of Henri Matisse, whom I admire.

Time and again I occupy myself with modern art, especially, as I have reported, with modern church architecture. One may justifiably add to this the pilgrimage church of the Swiss Le Corbusier in nearby Ronchamp which I have visited often, brilliantly shaped by plastic ideas instead of geometrical patterns. I can by no means accept the conservative criticism of the Austrian art historian Hans

Sedlmayer, a former Party member and after the war a confessing Christian, who under a title which has become proverbial, *Art in Crisis: The Lost Centre* (1948), makes a passionate plea against the pressure towards autonomy, towards the purity of the arts, against the modern principles of pure architecture, pure painting, pure drawing, against the demands for truth in construction and authentic materials; against abstraction, objectivity, sobriety. According to Sedlmayr, all these are extremely pernicious absolutizings and polarizations which – in a rational constructivist or irrational surrealistic way – inevitably lead to the alienation of the arts from one another and the dissolution of art generally. This dissolution manifests itself especially in the turn to the lower spheres, to the primitive, barbaric, archaic and often even to the pathological, morbid, chaotic – all to the neglect of the higher spiritual, humane, metaphysical. I reject this purely negative view of modern art.

However, I cannot overlook the fundamentally pessimistic, often nihilistic basic mood of some artists. In my time as an assistant priest in Lucerne this was made evident to me by my congenial Lucerne art professor Max van Moos, whom I invited to my 'Dragonfly Club' for girls in the parish, although he was unpopular in church circles. He died a few years ago and in around 1000 pictures and 20,000 drawings in surrealist style presented a comprehensive *oeuvre* of grim pictures and messages full of remarkable dream ideas and visions of terror. As his obituary in a major German newspaper put it, in this way this painter made clear not only his own situation but that of modern men and women generally: the human being, having fallen victim to blind and evil greed, is now visited by nightmares without finding hope and grace. These are the 'sorry truths' of an artist plagued by great anxieties with which his unconscious has presented him all his life: the artistic confessions of a nihilist who after reading Nietzsche lost his belief in the church but not his belief in hell.

All this and some art exhibitions and art trips, especially in France, form the starting point of my lecture at the opening of the 27th annual exhibition of the German Federation of Artists in Stuttgart. The President of the German Federation of Artists, the brilliant constructivist sculptor Otto Herbert Hajek, has taken the initiative in persuading me to give this address. He won international fame first through his abstract sculptures ('space knots'), then through the 'colour ways' running through façades and streets by means of steel sculptures ('signposts'), and finally above all through the colourful paintwork of the Southern Plaza of the Adelaide Festival Centre in Australia. On such an important occasion, to which not only Federal President Carstens and Chancellor Schmidt but also Pope John Paul II would be sending greetings, I didn't want to content myself with a couple of more or less witty observations. Rather, I wanted to give a basic answer to a question that has concerned me for a long time, namely that of meaning in art – in the face of so many people who look at the works of classical modernity without comprehension. I wanted to do so as a contrast to many artists who with Theodor W. Adorno in his aesthetic theory think that in a time of meaninglessness a work of art can only depict meaninglessness in an aesthetically meaningful, i.e. intrinsically coherent way.

For me such an understanding of art – and here I can refer back to categories in *Does God Exist?* – is the expression of a fundamental lack of trust in reality. Of course no one can prevent artists from regarding everything, their own lives, art, the whole world as ultimately meaningless, absurd, chaotic, illusory, empty – in revolt, resignation or simply cynicism. And artists can express this lack of trust in reality in their art – in aesthetically coherent, even completed images.

They can. But – and in my lecture this is the alternative which I exaggerate to clarify it and which Adorno doesn't investigate – they mustn't! Artists, of course always supported by others, can say a fundamental Yes to reality despite its questionable nature, in the face of all the temptations of negation; in other words a fundamental trust instead of a fundamental mistrust – without any cheap optimism or any affirmative lies. They can express this fundamental trust in their art – even in deliberately ugly, critical, provocative and negative images – and this has largely happened in modern art (and not just in religious art).

But that also means respect for the artist. No human being and no institution, no state or church, but also no philosopher or theologian, has the right to arrogate to themselves a moral judgement on an artist's fundamental attitude on the basis of an artistic depiction, to be a judge of personal nihilism, decadence, amorality or even lies.

On the other hand, I now also want to invite artists to attempt to overcome the artistic crisis of confidence – confidence in art – which is often the consequence of a general crisis of confidence, confidence in reality, by a renewed Yes to a basic sense of this reality which is the hidden foundation of our life and our world, which permeates it and supports it. It is a Yes to a foundation of meaning to which thousands of artists have borne witness over thousands of years in thousands of images. One can ask what art would be like without religion, from which it has emerged since the Altamira cave paintings, the pyramids in the Egyptian desert and the great temples in Mesopotamia, India and Greece. In the final part of my lecture I attempt to illustrate this basic position in three stages: about art as heritage, anticipation and elucidation of meaning. To this degree graphic art has a value for orientation and living particularly in the age of the mass media. At a time when meaninglessness threatens, art contributes (even through the apparently meaningless) towards keeping the question of meaning present, towards provoking the question of meaning and facing the question of meaning.

Unsuspecting

The photographs in *Kunsstreport* of 1979 show me speaking to a packed room; many people are sitting on the floor or standing. There is lively approval, not least from the guests of honour in the front row: the Lord Mayor of the City of

Stuttgart, Manfred Rommel, son of the Field Marshal; the Bishop of Rottenburg-Stuttgart, Georg Moser; and the Minister of Science and Art of the state of Baden-Wurttemberg, Professor Helmut Engler. Who could have guessed that the last two would very soon become my opponents in a looming controversy over nothing less than my scholarly existence in the University of Tübingen and the Catholic Church? What seems to me to be an ominous reorientation has taken place relatively quickly in the Catholic church government, which the new Pope from Poland has demonstrated very sharply above all on his trip to America.

I am reminded every day of the memorable art festival in Stuttgart whenever a steel sculpture – ingeniously made of two opposed triangles inserted into each other – is illuminated in my garden. It looks different every time it's illuminated. My friend and contemporary Otto Herbert Hajek, in the presence of his wife Katya, a gifted poet, allowed me to choose it from the works in his workshop as an honorarium. He died on 29 April 2005. I gratefully remember him for his paintings, which similarly prefer geometric forms and the bright colours of red, blue, yellow and finally also gold. They form unique patterns for the graphics of the covers of several of my Piper paperbacks.

In the still distant year 2006 that lecture on art and the question of meaning will form the finale to my little book on 'Music and Religion. Mozart – Wagner – Bruckner'. But long before I can celebrate such small literary 'triumphs', I have to follow an unsuspectedly bitter path. I had written to a retired Protestant theological colleague with a sigh, 'Often I long for your current status; with retirement life can begin anew. But I've still almost twenty years before that. What else will happen?' (18 August 1976). I couldn't have suspected that after all my extraordinary efforts the hardest part of 1979 was still awaiting me and that in around ten weeks something like a 'forced retirement' would threaten me.

XI

೩)೧೩೩)೧೩

The Great Confrontation

'The publication of this declaration will certainly provoke stormy reactions from the public. These will by no means be limited to the diocese of Rottenburg-Stuttgart, nor even to the German Conference of Bishops; they will go beyond the German-language area and assume a world-wide character. On the basis of previous experiences we may expect that the press, radio and television will be involved internationally. Given this situation, it seems to me appropriate for the sake of the whole church that the planned proceedings of the Congregation for the Doctrine of the Faith against Professor Dr Küng should avoid any appearance of unjust or illegitimate harshness which could cause offence both to believing Christians and to outsiders.'

Bishop Georg Moser of Rottenburg-Stuttgart to Cardinal Franjo Šeper,
12 December 1979[1]

Despite my years of immense difficulties with Rome, I remain true to my conviction that a Petrine office ('papacy') orientated on the constitution of the New Testament church and the great Catholic tradition of the first millennium with a moral and pastoral rather than a formal and juristic authority can still be an opportunity for Christianity as a whole. In this respect I am certainly perhaps the most radical Catholic critic of a medieval juristic primacy of rule by the Pope, but paradoxically at the same time possibly one of the most effective Catholic advocates for a pastoral primacy in the service of Christian ecumenism. I also get increasing support from the Protestant side. For that I must go back once again to 1975.

An ecumenical or an anti-ecumenical papacy?

In May 1975 I received an enigmatic book from the Catholic publisher Styria of Graz entitled 'The Vision of the Pope'; the author, writing under the pseudonym Sebastian Knecht, was said to be a well-known Protestant theologian. I told the publisher that this vision of an ecumenical Pope 'particularly in the form of a novel, is stimulating and hopeful for someone who has to deal so often with raw reality here' (7 May 1975). I would see many things similarly: the ambivalence of

Vatican II, the role of opportunistic politics, the resistance of the Curia generally. And also the positive side: the unity between the churches, which is greater than their differences; the experience of such unity in worship, which transcends the possibilities of theology; the great opportunities for a Pope who commits himself seriously in ecumenical relations. The only thing I found questionable was the series of stages proposed in the book. But I sent my warmest thanks to the unknown author.

The publisher asked me to write a public commendation for the book but I refused to lend my name for an author who wouldn't reveal his. Only some years later did the author get in touch with me personally – under a seal of secrecy which I have preserved beyond his death. He was no less than Professor Edmund Schlink, a perceptive Lutheran theologian and observer at Vatican II for the Evangelical Church in Germany who taught in Heidelberg. I collaborated intensively with him for our ecumenical memorandum on the reciprocal recognition of Christian ministries and had taken part in his 70th birthday celebrations in Heidelberg on 6 March 1973. This is just one sign of how deep is the longing in the Protestant world, too, for the overcoming of splits in the church and an ecumenical papacy.

Since then I have never ceased to work in this direction. My Catholic and Protestant friends from the university ecumenical institutes – Heinrich Fries, Peter Lengsfeld, Wolfhart Pannenberg, Hans-Heinrich Wolf and (as successor to Edmund Schlink on his retirement) Reinhardt Slenczka – agreed with me to hold a well-prepared conference with competent theologians on 'The Papacy as an Ecumenical Question'. This took place in Heidelberg at the end of October 1977. The papers and summaries of the discussion which followed were published in 1979.[2] In his closing paper Jürgen Moltmann remarks:

> Only a strong ecumenical fellowship and constant service to the freedom of the church prevents national churches (Gallicanism, Anglicanism), state churches with heads of state as so-called 'emergency bishops', racial, caste and class churches, from arising. We must rely on the greater fellowship of the *ecclesia universalis* if we have to become 'strangers in one's own land' for the sake of the gospel. The catholicity of the church creates this freedom in the face of the social, political and ideological pressure in a society. Therefore 'service to the community' is always also service to freedom. An 'ecumenical papacy renewed in the light of the gospel' has this great task: *libertas Ecclesiae!*[3]

At the end of the discussion Wolfhart Pannenberg notes an 'increasing consensus also among Protestants on the need for an office of unity, as a sign and instrument for remaining in the truth that is promised to the church. This is an authority which – as Yves Congar says – can guide our perspectives in the case of an emergency, a *status confessionis*.' It seems important to Pannenberg here 'that the connection between a critical reworking of the absolutist false development of the papacy by Catholic theology itself and the new possibility of accepting the topic of the papacy openly outside the Roman Catholic Church is seen more clearly. The critical reworking of the absolutist false development by Catholic theology has become the presupposition for the possibility of discussing the topic outside the Roman Catholic Church. In the discussion more notice should be taken of H. Küng's positions in particular.'[4]

The prominent theologians gathered in Heidelberg – they include Eberhard Jüngel, Heinrich Ott, Eduard Schweizer and Lukas Vischer – are to be taken as representative of German-language Protestant theology; Josef Blank, Peter Bläser, Yves Congar, August B. Hasler, Heinrich Stirnimann, Wilhelm de Vries and I of Catholic theology.

Was Joseph Ratzinger invited? I don't remember. But certainly the Tübingen missiologist Peter Beyerhaus wasn't. I had taken particular trouble with this Protestant colleague in the first years and, as I reported, in 1968 even held a joint seminar with him. But in 1975 I am asked by Protestant colleagues to warn Cardinal Johannes Willebrands in connection with a planned visit by Beyerhaus to the Secretariat for Unity. Beyerhaus is said to be neglecting scholarly work in the University of Tübingen and to be 'agitating all round the world – against ecumenism. He is hoping to gain support from reactionary Catholic forces such as Bishop Graber of Regensburg, with whom he has arranged an anti-ecumenical meeting. Now he is also behind the counter-event to the Evangelical Kirchentag in Stuttgart, "Community Day under the Word". All in all this seems to be counter-ecumenism organized as internationally as possible against an apocalyptic background (division between believers and evil, the Pope or Marxism as Antichrist), driven by fear and hatred' (2 June 1975). This is an alliance of fundamentalist believers in God, Christ and the Bible, no longer against the Pope but against godless modernity, on the assumption that the end-time is here. Later Beyerhaus will see Islam as the Antichrist.

In his answer of 8 July 1975 Willebrands shows an understanding of this, but accepts an invitation from Bishop Rudolf Graber on 20/21 July. Bishop Graber of Regensburg, propagandist of Fatima, on the extreme right of the German episcopate, is no longer generally taken very seriously. But afterwards many people raise the question what role the Regensburg Professor Ratzinger plays in these efforts.

On 28 May 1975 Ratzinger is consecrated bishop and is created a cardinal on 27 June of the same year. I am horrified, as I have said, when I read in Cardinal Ratzinger's memoirs of 1998 that in Tübingen in the 1960s he 'joined two Lutheran theologians in trying to plan a common course of action; they were the patristic scholar Ulrich Wickert and the missiologist Wolfgang Beyerhaus ... Beyerhaus became the spokesman for the Lutherans, fighting his battles against this background'.[5] I really hadn't noticed anything of this. Perhaps this alliance wasn't quite so personal, since Beyerhaus is now called Peter and not Wolfgang. Evidently the (later) successor of (erring) Peter is in error here.

A year of John Paul II

On Friday 5 October 1979 I take part in a service with Bishop Moser in the Catholic Academy of Hohenheim, Stuttgart, within the framework of a congress of artists; my lecture on art is broadcast on Süddeutscher Rundfunk, slightly abbreviated, in the hour before midnight. The next day Cardinal Joseph-Albert Malula from Kinshasa visits me and we discuss the situation of the church in Zaire and generally. There is great anxiety in Africa and elsewhere that the Polish Pope has stopped the practice of laicization for priests operated generously by Paul VI and in so doing has put countless priests in an emergency situation. Does he seriously think that in this way he can 'solve' the problem of obligatory celibacy which has existed since the eleventh century? Evidently!

On Sunday 7 October 1979 I hear on the media of the closing speech by John Paul II in Washington at the end of his US tour, which is far more polemical than his earlier speeches, in June in Poland or in September in Ireland. A whole series of verdicts is solemnly presented: 'We shall stand up' against married couples who use the pill; against divorced persons who think that they can take part in the sacraments; against homosexuals who call for equal treatment, and so on.

The next day, 8 October, I arrive at our Institute at 9 a.m. and gather my team for a discussion of my proposal. I think that it is no longer enough as before just to respond with barbed remarks, point by point, to the Pope's reactionary policy as expressed not only in the encyclical on celibacy which has appeared in the meantime but also in his numerous public statements and now particularly clearly in the Washington speech. A year of his pontificate is enough to show very clearly the direction in which the ship of the church is to be steered: evidently not accepting the impulses of the Council but backwards. As far as is still possible, this is a restoration of the status quo before the Council.

I argue that someone should take a public stand against this development, which is evidently being pressed forward at breakneck speed by the Vatican. None of the cardinals or bishops can be expected to draw attention to himself in this way. The advocates of renewal have been removed. Many of those who took part in the Council are either dead, or old and infirm, and unfortunately as things now are there is hardly anyone in the church whose warning would be heard all over the world. So since I have the theological competence and more possibilities than others of raising the voice of conciliar renewal in the media, should I keep silent? We have a lengthy discussion. Finally there is agreement that I may write this article as a stocktaking.

I am well prepared. On 9 October I telephone the various papers. And the article 'A Year of John Paul II' appears on Saturday 13 October 1979, on the anniversary of the Pope's election, in the *Frankfurter Allgemeine Zeitung* and almost at the same time in the *New York Times*, *Le Monde* (Paris), *Panorama* (Milan), *Elsevier's Weekblad* (Amsterdam), *El País* (Madrid), *Veja* (São Paulo), *The Age* (Melbourne), and in many Swiss and other papers.

How is it possible to produce a relatively comprehensive and balanced stocktaking in a short time? As a framework I use the declaration that our international group of theologians had published after the death of Paul VI, under the title 'The Pope We Need', which also appeared in numerous major newspapers. Against this background I venture an interim stocktaking with the title 'A Year of John Paul II': 'Will a Catholic theologian in particular be allowed to put critical questions instead of joining in the euphoric applause of so many people? For many traditional Catholics a criticism of the Pope, even if it arises out of loyal commitment to this Catholic Church, is more unforgivable than blasphemy. But we think that the Pope has a right to a response from his own church in critical solidarity.'[6]

Following the six criteria which were formulated in the original article without a particular person in view, I put six questions with reference to Pope Wojtyla: 1. Is he open to the world? 2. Is he a spiritual leader? 3. Is he a true pastor? 4. Is he a collegial fellow bishop? 5. Is he an ecumenical mediator? 6. Is he a real Christian? The stocktaking is split on every question. But in recognition of this, on every point I always say clearly what can be put positively. And I clothe the criticism not just of a few but of many in the form of questions. To give an example of the whole article, here is point 6, 'A real Christian?'

First the positive side:

It is impossible to dispute that:

This Pope, who happily does not claim to be a saint or a genius, wants to be truly a Christian despite all limits, mistakes and defects: orientated in thought, speech and action on the gospel of Jesus Christ as the decisive norm.

He attempts to proclaim the good news convincingly, grounded in a well-tested faith and an unshakable hope.

He wants to preside in a relaxed, patient and confident way over the church, which is not a bureaucratic apparatus, a social enterprise or a political party but the great fellowship of believers.

He wants to act as a moral authority with objectivity, passion and perspective, not only for the interests of the church as an institution but for the realization of the Christian message among men and women.

And he regards commitment to the oppressed and disadvantaged throughout the world as his special obligation.[7]

But then equally honestly there is the negative side:

Nevertheless – and this must now be added – many people inside and outside the Catholic Church are asking:

Is this commitment to the world outside matched by a commitment inside, in the church, in the institutional church itself? Is preaching to convert the world credible unless Pope and church themselves act practically in such a conversion – also and particularly where they themselves are affected?

Can Pope and church convincingly speak to the conscience of men and women today if there is not at the same time a self-critical searching of conscience within the church and its leaders, with consequences that are uncomfortable for them?

Is talk of the fundamental renewal of human society credible unless the reform of the church, head and members, in doctrine and life makes decisive progress and unwelcome questions (such as the population explosion, contraception and church infallibility) are finally taken seriously and answered honestly?

Is the support by the church of human rights in the world honest if at the same time human rights are not fully guaranteed in the church itself: a right to marriage for those in office, as this is granted in the gospel itself and the old Catholic tradition; a right also to leave the priestly ministry with a church dispensation after a thorough examination of conscience (instead of the inhuman bureaucratic ban on dispensations for priests introduced by the present Pope); the right of theologians to free research and expression of opinion; the right of women in religious orders to choose their own form of dress; the ordination of women, which can be argued for in today's changed situation in the light of the gospel; the personal responsibility of spouses for conception and the number of their children? So mustn't the Vatican allow itself to be asked why it signed the Helsinki Final Act but to the present day hasn't signed the Council of Europe's Declaration of Human Rights?

My conclusion is a wish for the new Pope:

Some people doubt whether this Pope, who can present his views so powerfully in public and can give simple answers to many complicated questions, can change and learn. We hope so. A year of his pontificate has gone by, but only a year. Some doors are still open and some that have been prematurely closed could be opened again.[8]

Offence at the truth?

The conclusion is conciliatory but the criticism of the way in which John Paul II has exercised his office so far is massive; however – and in retrospect I would say this with more conviction than ever – every word seems apt. Indeed, in retrospect it seems relatively moderate to me. Many people later have found far more critical, indeed polemical words. But because in 1979, a year after John Paul II's accession, no one has formulated this criticism so directly, so analytically and so fundamentally, the article achieves the shock effect it aimed at: to arouse and warn the Catholic Church and its episcopate. The wider public is also immediately clear how serious it is.

The Op-Ed page editor of the *New York Times*, Howard Goldberg, who to be certain read out the long text in English translation over the Atlantic by telephone twice, with all the punctuation (and 'Roman Catholic' always with the addition 'capital R – capital C'), tells me that no author on the Op-Ed page since Solzhenitsyn has been allowed to over-run the prescribed length by so much. He remarks that at the *New York Times* they have the publicity slogan 'I got my job through the *New York Times*'; I would now probably be the first who could say of himself 'I lost my job through the *New York Times*'.

I am well aware of the risk I run with this article, which is why I end it with a saying of one of John Paul II's great predecessors: 'But if offence is taken at the truth, then it is better for scandal to be caused than for the truth to be abandoned.' Thus Pope Gregory the Great.

The Protestant theologian Wolfhart Pannenberg writes to me after reading the article: 'I hope that in Rome it will be accepted as an expression of solidarity not only with the task of the papal office but also with the person of the present Pope, to whom you devote many very friendly words, and will not be taken as a hostile act' (18 October 1979). However, this particular hope was not to be fulfilled.

The Polish Pope and his theology

The fact is that John Paul II feels personally attacked by this article. A participant in the later conversation between bishops in the Vatican indicates this, whereas the official statement of the German Conference of Bishops later declares that the disciplinary measure against me has nothing to do with the article. That is a deceitful remark which, had it been true, would have been superfluous.

However, already on his first trip to Poland after his election the Pope had said at a secret conference with around two dozen Polish theologians that he regarded the Tübingen theologian Küng as the main obstacle to his planned course of restoration. After the event I think that presumably Karol Wojtyla was affected by my questioning of his theological competence even more than by my assessment of his leadership of the church. But such questioning was unavoidable in the case of a Pope who already differed from his more tolerant predecessor by his authoritarian approach and strict doctrinal measures against theologians such as the renowned French moral theologian Jacques Pohier.

Hence in my stocktaking article the critical question: 'Isn't it clear beyond specialist circles that this Pope from Poland – as is shown by his theological publications and numerous public statements so far – is insufficiently informed about more recent developments in theology (critical exegesis and the history of dogma, more recent developments in moral theology or liberation theology in Latin America, not to mention Protestant theology)?'[9] Pope John XXIII also had his theological limitations, but he was aware of them and had a deep antipathy to any magisterial intervention against theologians, as in the anti-Modernist campaign against his student friend Ernesto Buonaiuti. But Pope John Paul II doesn't know his limitations and again adopts the inquisitorial policy of Pope Pius XII, whose theological education was likewise extremely thin.

However, I was unaware that with my critical questions about Wojtyla's theological limitations I had touched on a sore point in his life story of which he never spoke – unlike Joseph Ratzinger and 'the drama' of his habilitation. Rather, this man who in his youth had devoted himself not to theology but to professional acting can admirably disguise the fact that he studied only lightweight theology. He was turned down as a doctoral student by the Gregorian, Rome's top university – as I already reported in *My Struggle for Freedom* (III: Dogmatics Roman-style), to the disapproval of some Pope venerators – because of a deficient theological background (certainly not deficient intelligence), so that he had to go to the second-ranking Dominican Angelicum University, a bulwark of traditionalist Neo-scholasticism.[10] There he heard above all the lectures of the leading dogmatic theologian Réginald Garrigou-Lagrange. They consisted in nothing but interpretations of the *Summa theologiae* of Thomas Aquinas. My Swiss student friend Josef Fischer and I, as curious visitors in scarlet gowns, had had enough of these lectures after two hours. The same Garrigou, a strictly Thomistic traditionalist, had already instigated vigorous campaigns against the '*nouvelle théologie*' which led to the dismissal of prominent French theologians, above all from the Jesuit Order.

So under Garrigou's direction Wojtyla worked on a doctoral dissertation on the doctrine of faith in the Spanish mystic John of the Cross. He made too many concessions to mysticism for Garrigou, but Garrigou accepted the dissertation. However, because a dissertation had to be printed as it stood, Wojtyla finally sent his to the Jagellonian University of Krakow. Moreover he gained his habilitation there with a work on the German philosopher Max Scheler, though he interpreted and corrected Scheler wholly in accordance with his Neo-scholastic categories. He then became a student pastor in Krakow and shortly afterwards also a lecturer in moral philosophy. At that time with a group of students he also read the Latin *Summa theologiae* of Thomas Aquinas, had some contacts with poets, scientist and philosophers, acted, and wrote poems and plays. But the acting was soon to come to an end. He became a suffragan bishop in 1958 and as such took part in the Second Vatican Council. During the Council he became archbishop in 1964 and in 1967, soon after the Council, a cardinal.

So Karol Wojtyla grows up in the context of a deeply conservative church in which, as one notes even 40 years after the conclusion of the Council, it is still impossible to find a complete and generally accessible edition of the Council documents – in a new translation with a theological and historical commentary. As late as 2005 a stormy discussion is taking place among Catholic theologians and journalists – clergy and laity – in Poland on the question whether Karl Rahner deserved the name of 'Catholic theologian'. The bishops ask why anything in the church should change at all. From the perspective of the Polish church the forms so far had completely proved themselves. In the discussion within the Polish church, the Council thus doesn't represent any essential point of orientation; for example, hardly anyone knows that the Council promulgated a declaration *Nostra aetate* on the world religions. Against this dark background Archbishop and Cardinal Wojtyla appears more as a figure of light.[11]

In 1977 I received a dramatic letter from one of the spiritual inspirers of the renewal movement in Poland: 'The renewal of the church inspired by John XXIII and the Second Vatican Council has collapsed and it is clear to all that the ardent enthusiasm of the rejuvenated church inspired by God has come to grief. The counter-offensive by conservative forces continues and seeks to annul all the results of the last Council.' Here Archbishop Karol Wojtyla is evidently not the new figure of hope. And many problems of the church in Poland in particular are already known at that time (high abortion rates, many problems over celibacy) while others become notorious only later (the collaboration of some bishops and priests with the Communist secret service) and darken the picture of a Polish church which allegedly remained pure, and which claims to be a model for the whole world.

And now as Pope? From the start Karol Wojtyla, who in his Polish homeland has got to know two totalitarian systems but not a functioning democratic system, sets out to achieve an imperial papacy (indeed one that is in some respects totalitarian). Paul VI, who changed from being Council Pope to Pope of the Curia, had prepared the way for him. In a declaration of war an overwhelming majority of the Council fathers had voted for a collegiality of the Pope with the bishops, had prescribed this collegiality in a solemn and binding way in the Constitution on the Church, and in so doing had hoped for something like a Catholic commonwealth (instead of a Roman empire). But as I reported in *My Struggle for Freedom*, on 16 November 1964, over the heads of the Council fathers, Paul VI prefaced the third charter of the Constitution on the Church about the hierarchy with a four-paragraph explanatory '*Nota praevia*', formulated in precise legalistic terms, which again prescribes unrestricted papal primacy along the lines of Vatican I. This *de facto* removes the principle of collegiality in everything, restores the medieval *Imperium Romanum* – of course now limited to the church, or more precisely to its Roman Catholic provinces – and guarantees the ongoing existence of the 'divine grace' of an absolutist Roman monarchy which has not been realized elsewhere since the French Revolution. What Paul VI had then practised after the Council by his authoritarian decrees in encyclicals on celibacy and the pill, without consulting the episcopate, heralded Roman absolutism and a personality cult, again practised completely without inhibitions. In the rising media age this is demonstrated to all the world with increasing brilliance by media-effective imperial mass demonstrations, at which the bishops are mere cardboard figures. Perhaps it can now be understood better that I had to announce my opposition here in the light of the Second Vatican Council, indeed the New Testament constitution of the church. My article 'A Year of John Paul II' is an expression both of deep disappointment and of hope.

A bad signal

The fateful winter semester of 1979/80 begins for me on 15 October. On 16 October, the day on which my Pope article appears, Cardinal Joseph Ratzinger gives an interview of his own on Deutschlandfunk on one year of John Paul II in office. He is critical but quite objective about my criticism of the Pope. On 5–9 November 1979 the plenary assembly of the College of Cardinals takes place in the Vatican. On this occasion the German cardinals are received by Pope John Paul II in a private audience. The withdrawal of my permission to teach must have been discussed at it and a consensus must have been reached.

For immediately after his return Ratzinger suddenly expresses himself in a completely different way. Strikingly he is the first to let drop the previously little-known ominous phrase *missio canonica*. What is meant is the 'church's permission to teach' given officially to professors involved in the university training of theologians. A report by the Catholic news agency KNA of a discussion between Cardinal Ratzinger and young people on the occasion of the St Corbinian pilgrimage in Freising near Munich on Sunday 11 November causes astonishment on all sides.[12] Ratzinger said: 'The reality is that Küng, with whom I have always got on personally very well, "quite simply no longer represents the faith of the Catholic Church". It is "only honest to say that he does not present the faith of the Catholic Church and so cannot speak in its name".' I am completely perplexed: how can my former Tübingen colleague suddenly dismiss me in public as un-Catholic?

And above all, how can he claim that I had disputed 'that the church can give a *missio* (its commission to teach) to a professor of theology, because the professor speaks "on his own account"'. I never said this. What nonsense! Ratzinger goes on to contradict himself: 'At the same time, however, Küng thought it very important that the *missio* should not be withdrawn from him.' To quote Ratzinger literally: 'I cannot be given by the church a commission to say that it cannot give a commission.' At any rate Ratzinger sees a contradiction here. Anyone has the freedom to think what he wants, and 'we hope that that will always remain the case. For example, one can think along the lines of a political party or otherwise, but of course a committed Christian Democrat cannot present himself as a Social Democrat General Secretary or vice versa. He must represent the body whose opinions he can and wants to advocate out of conviction, and it has to be said quite simply that Küng energetically disputes essential doctrines of the Catholic Church and thus does not speak in its name. He should be recommended to speak in his own name or in the name of someone else.'

I am infuriated by such a statement, and have forebodings. A new stage of demarcation and exclusion is becoming visible – presented in an ice-cold way with harsh logic, and at the same time basically false and mendacious. This is more than a slip of the tongue, it has been well considered. My reaction is correspondingly sharp: 'A cardinal should stick to the truth, even if he is being applauded by young people,' I say in a press statement for dpa on 13 November 1997.[13] It is untrue that I have said that the church could not give a theologian its permission to teach (*missio*) because the theologian speaks 'on his own account'. Rather, the truth is that the church's permission to teach has always been important to me and in many cases I have defended it against the whim of the official church. However, Ratzinger hasn't shown himself to be a correct interpreter of my writings. But it is at least to be hoped that under the present pontificate senior church officials will not again lapse into the pre-conciliar customs of heresy-hunting, insinuations and defamations.

There is a little prehistory to Ratzinger's unusually sharp remark. The obviously aroused Archbishop of Munich had been annoyed at the announcement that my lecture 'What One Can Hold On To' was to be given in Regensburg, where he had previously worked. I had also spoken on this topic that same weekend of November 1979 to large audiences in cities of the traditionally Catholic Swabian Oberland, in Biberach (10 November), Ravensburg and Sigmaringen (11 November) and in so doing had discussed the historical relativity of particular Catholic traditions and the concentration on Jesus Christ and his gospel which can give support to the church and the individual Christian. There had been much appreciation everywhere.[14] Why shouldn't I also give the same lecture in Catholic Regensburg?

Bishop Rudolf Graber of Regensburg, of ill repute throughout the Republic and even among bishops as a reactionary 'Fatima bishop', puts pressure on the Catholic colleges who had invited me to withdraw their invitation: he will remove all financial support (DM 120,000 per year) and dismiss two student pastors. They give in. There is great indignation far beyond Regensburg, except of course among the bishop's supporters. Finally, with the agreement of the president of the university, the student committee responsible for inviting speakers invites me to give the planned lecture in the main auditorium of the university. An alumnus of the German College, living in Regensburg, with whom I always had good relations in Rome, pleads with me in a letter to turn down the lecture 'in true humility and without compulsion – for the sake of peace and unity'. But am I now to leave the college community and the many people who want to hear me in Regensburg in the lurch in order to comply with

an authoritarian bishop? I reply: 'I didn't take the decision to come to Regensburg easily and am risking my neck, not yours' (20 November 1979). The lecture
takes place on 17 November in an auditorium packed with more than 2000
people, with ovations before, during and after it.

Now Cardinal Ratzinger, forced into a corner by the young people in the
discussion in Friesing which I mentioned, allows himself to be lured into those
irresponsible comments and takes the side of the Bishop of Regensburg with the
amazing remark that the colleges who invited me are an 'institution of the bishop'
and therefore anyone who speaks in them is a guest of the bishop.[15] He says that
in Rosenheim, where the same theologian is to speak on the same topic, the
lecture is taking place in the Catholic Education Agency; this is a separate body in
law and he doesn't want to intervene, but tells these people that this lecture
(which he hasn't heard) 'does not depict what one can hold on to'.

In my press statement I observe that the justified questions of countless
Catholic lay people and pastors about official church teaching, morality and
discipline cannot simply be resolved by discrediting theologians who discuss these
questions openly. It is well known that Archbishop Ratzinger doesn't like to have
conversations with his pastors and prefers to write letters to them. 'It is horrifying
that a bishop about whom there are many complaints over lack of contact with
his own clergy does not hesitate to belittle the loyalty to the church of committed
Catholic pastors and lay people simply because they venture to invite an allegedly
uncomfortable professor of theology to their community. What does the President of the Bavarian Conference of Bishops really think of the judgement and
spiritual level of Bavarian Catholics? Of course I have never claimed to speak for
the official Catholic Church; that is not my task. But I have claimed and still
claim to speak as a Catholic theologian for the justified concern of countless
Catholics within the Catholic Church. When will the representatives of the
church machine, which is financially so well oiled and perfectly administered,
understand the silent exodus of hundreds of thousands of Catholics – fewer and
fewer churchgoers, baptisms, marriages, parishes with pastors – as an alarm signal
for self-critical reflection? It should really be possible to talk about that in a
friendly way in a spirit of the collegiality.'

At the same time I write a personal letter to Cardinal Ratzinger:

Dear Herr Ratzinger, It has always been my concern that controversies over
issues should not get too personal. I have taken especial trouble not to
introduce your name where this has not been forced on me. I found your
criticism of my interim stocktaking 'A Year of John Paul II' on Deutschlandfunk restrained and without personal sharpness and I accepted it. I have
also warned my friends against associating the events in Regensburg and
Rosenheim with your name.

I was therefore all the more dismayed at the frontal attack on my
Catholicity and intellectual and moral integrity which has been reproduced

today in many German newspapers – among others, at length in the *Frankfurter Allgemeine Zeitung*. Granted, these are remarks that you made answering young people's questions and which presumably should not have reached the press in this form. But you were on the record, have been quoted in the press and also make an impact beyond Germany.

I want to ask you to understand that I had to respond quite clearly to these attacks. At the same time I ask you not to continue the controversies in this personal style, since all this is certainly not good for our church.[16]

Ratzinger replies on 16 November:

Dear Herr Küng, Many thanks for your kind letter of 13 November 1979, which pleased me greatly. I completely agree with you that controversies over issues must not become too personal, therefore I find it encouraging that at the end of your declaration you express the wish for a friendly conversation in a spirit of collegiality. I can only welcome this. I do not want to comment further on the issue itself now. I am concerned to counter the crude statements which I read in the press. From the beginning, contrary to other tendencies and wishes that have been conveyed to me from Rosenheim, I have maintained that your lecture there must not be prevented. I did not intervene either positively or negatively in the case of Regensburg. Nor have I dismissed anyone who invited you to his community – I want to make that clear from the start. I can only hope that the events in Rosenheim as in Regensburg do not take a negative turn as a result of fanaticism on one side or the other. That could help no one.
With friendly greetings,
Yours,
+ Joseph Ratzinger[17]

Isn't it understandable that this letter reassured me? I couldn't have suspected what had been hatched in the Palace of the Holy Office with the highest degree of secrecy and had been discussed immediately beforehand between the Pope and the German Cardinals in the Apostolic Palace. My reply in subsequent days to the question what was going on in Rome was therefore always: 'To my knowledge at the moment there are no proceedings against me.'

The wearisome life of engaging in single combat

Certainly I was not and am not ever alone in my struggle for the truth. Countless people support me from far and near, most of course the men and women in my house and in my Institute. But I alone must be responsible for my articles and statements in the media – and quite particularly my article on John Paul II – and in any case in all the lectures in Germany and abroad I stand alone at the desk in the auditorium. On radio and television people want my personal standpoint, and some who have never read a book of mine judge me solely by brief interviews.

But I don't complain. My life is never boring, that's the good thing about it, so I wouldn't want any other. Theology in the service of fellow men and women is part of my life and I am constantly asked to present my theological message not only in books but in person in local lectures, though I can accept only the most important invitations. However, if one is given a great task one must also take into account the *strapazzi* (to use the Italian term, which means over-exertion) associated with it. I give the last lectures of this year 1979 unhindered and undisputed – including the one in Regensburg. Here too the church isn't 'split', but the enormous audiences and the tremendous applause signal to the bishop and his followers that he should go more by the *sensus fidelium*, the 'sense of the faith' of his Catholics.

Most of my lectures take place at the weekend or at the beginning of the week. In the middle of the week I give my dogmatics lectures on the Apostles' Creed and (together with my assistant Urs Baumann) the seminar on 'What theology can hold on to'. In addition there is my English-language group on *On Being a Christian* and the doctoral and habilitation colloquium. I hold the latter right at the beginning of the semester (19-21 October) in the compact form of a three-day colloquium with my Protestant colleague Eberhard Jüngel, with evening social gatherings in my new house. I had invited my Catholic colleagues in the same week after the session of the faculty (26 October). Then there is the ever-increasing correspondence on which I have already reported.

1979 was very strenuous in every respect.[18] Lectures had already been in full swing in the summer semester. My main series of lectures introduced my hearers to the mysteries of the doctrine of the Trinity, my seminar was on 'What Should Theology Hold On To?' Between 27 and 29 April our Institute had a symposium with Edward Schillebeeckx, which resulted in a happy agreement in approach, method and results. In addition there were my obligations abroad, as I reported, in May 1979 in Israel, Italy and Spain. On 22 May immediately after the lectures I went by car for a weekend with Karl-Josef Kuschel to the GDR, where over the following three days I gave lectures in the Leipzig student community ('What One Can Hold On To') and the universities of Leipzig, Halle and Dresden ('How to Advance in Ecumenism'). Over the night of Saturday/Sunday – after impressive Vespers by the Kreuzchor – we drove back from Dresden to Tübingen, where we arrived about 2 a.m.[19]

Of course I sense that tremendous physical and psychological efforts will be required of me every day; I don't sleep much but always have a short siesta. In addition to the teaching and lectures and the discussions associated with them in larger or smaller groups there are car drives, often of hundreds of kilometres. Before big public appearances I am sometimes asked how I feel; do I enjoy appearing before hundreds, sometimes thousands, of people? No, I reply honestly, enjoyment isn't the word I would use. Fortunately I have no stage fright, that tension before public appearances which can bring speakers out in a sweat or make them stutter.

Nor, though, do I sense any euphoria, any state of heightened feeling or drive which might lead me to fail to assess the concrete situation precisely. As a result of many personal experiences I have less an expectation of failure than an expectation of success, which provides motivation. But I am always aware that success is never guaranteed, that much can go wrong, from the loudspeaker system and bad acoustics, through a long introduction which anticipates the lecture, to aggressive questions in the discussion which can spoil the mood.

Therefore my basic state before lectures, which are never on harmless topics but always involve taking a stand, is heightened responsibility. I must always present myself to my public as being in 'single combat'. I must attempt to convince and find the right tone, which rings bells, not being monotonous, boring or aggressive but with disciplined passion or passionate objectivity. After all, I am not making an appearance as a populist politician, as a pious guide of souls or a psychotherapeutic guru, far less as an American teleevangelist, but simply as a university professor and recognized specialist in the sphere of theology and religion. I work primarily with reasons and arguments and not with feelings and emotions. As a 'theo-logian' I am an advocate of responsible talk (*logos*) of God (*theos*) but at the same time I am also the advocate of thinking, questioning, doubting and suffering men and women. My friend Edward Schillebeeckx performs a similar function in the Netherlands and in Belgium. However, during our symposium with him in Tübingen at the end of April 1979 he had no idea of what would await him in Rome in December of the same year.

Fiction of a 'colloquium': Schillebeeckx

The Dominican Edward Schillebeeckx, Professor of Dogmatics at the Catholic University of Nijmegen, is closely associated with me through the *Concilium* Foundation. He holds similar positions to me in the church, theology and politics. And for a long time he has already been subjected to inquisitorial proceedings. His first publications were mostly written in Dutch and so could hardly be read in the original in the Vatican. But doubtless in the Netherlands, as in other countries, even in Tübingen, there are numerous informers to denounce him to Rome – usually with press reports and tendentious quotations – and to set the alarm bells of the mistrustful guardians of the faith ringing in the Doctrinal Congregation. Schillebeeckx, too, is denounced time and again. In the old Holy Office numerous texts are being collected which 'reek of heresy' (*haeresim sapiunt*).

However, as I hear only subsequently, it is in connection with my case that Schillebeeckx is summoned at relatively short notice for a colloquium at the

Congregation for the Doctrine of the Faith on 13-15 December 1979 in long-drawn-out Inquisition proceedings. Certainly there is a desire to settle the 'Schillebeeckx case' for tactical reasons, so as not to become involved in a war on two fronts, before tackling the considerably more difficult 'Küng case'. The Vatican thinks that sufficient patience has been shown over Schillebeeckx, and that everything should be cleared up before Christmas. Then in the northern ('Protestantizing') countries the criticism of the uncomfortable theologians and their followers will in any case finally be silenced in the snow of Christmas and 'Silent Night, Holy Night'. In this way the 'Holy Father' can wish 'peace to men on earth' to everyone undisturbed.

But in the Doctrinal Congregation 'colloquium' isn't – as it is understood to be in general parlance – a 'conversation with someone' so to speak among brothers in the faith. As the Congregation understands it, a colloquium is in fact – and of course I have also spoken with Schillebeeckx about this – an interrogation by the Vatican judges of someone who has already been condemned, for its own confirmation and public justification – should he not recant his errors. Such a 'colloquium' can easily become a last meal before execution for a Catholic theologian, after which the accused is declared guilty and leaves the Palazzo del Sant'Uffizio no longer the Catholic theologian he was when he entered it. That happened a couple of years previously to Stephan Pfürtner, also a Dominican and professor of moral theology at the University of Fribourg, Switzerland, for certain remarks on sexual morality. And it also happened to the clever French Dominican Jacques Pohier, professor of moral theology in Paris and with me on the editorial board of *Concilium*, for certain theses in his book *Quand je dis Dieu*. Both were removed from their posts after the 'conversation' when they didn't publicly recant their theses.

On the basis of such experiences, after my trip to China I try to dissuade Schillebeeckx at the last minute from going to Rome. I tell him:

> I think that this is a serious mistake which should and could now be corrected. First there must be a guarantee of just and fair proceedings. Otherwise you should certainly not submit to them; in any case they can only be to your disadvantage. What they want from you is only a particular record of the investigation which will then be the basis for the Congregation to judge you and possibly condemn you in your absence, without your advocate. Another way is to send a well-grounded refusal, make it accessible to the public at the same time and appeal on television to the Pope, if he still thinks human rights are of any importance in the church, to stop these measures which have already led to the condemnation of our Dominican friend Pohier. I am convinced that public resistance needs courage, intelligence and wisdom, but you have all these. Things can't be any worse. In this way you will be able to help yourself and presumably also others (3 October 1979).

In my insistence on fair conditions of course I am not concerned solely with Schillebeeckx and myself. Rather, we are to set a precedent, so that in future other less known theologians who are complained against are granted fair conditions. A week later I write to Johann Baptist Metz about the need for a public protest from the editorial committee of *Concilium* (after my stocktaking article on the first year of the pontificate there can be no question of a formal memorandum).

> The Pope made such an impact in North America that we need to issue a public statement. But I've already written my own. You'll see it soon, but it won't be the end of the matter. Our memorandum to the Pope decided on in Nijmegen shouldn't follow too long after our protest in the Pohier cause – as you know, Edward is also threatened and has to go to Rome in December, as does Charlie Curran (in confidence) and another well-known moral theologian – otherwise we will miss all the buses in Rome. I don't think resistance to the Pope's populist course hopeless – as long as some people remain who do not bow the knee to Baal (10 October 1979).

Despite all his reservations Edward Schillebeeckx goes to Rome and attends the 'colloquium' with representatives of the Doctrinal Congregation. Reports can then be read in the press that the 'colloquium' took place in a 'friendly atmosphere'. Of course comparisons are made – not only by Cardinal Höffner – between 'Schillebeeckx's readiness to converse' and 'Küng's refusal to converse'. But in fact the course of Schillebeeckx's colloquium confirms all the reservations I had expressed against the Roman proceedings. This 'colloquium', too, clearly had the character of an inquisitorial interrogation. That emerges from the report by the Dean of the Theological Faculty of the Catholic University of Nijmegen, Professor Bas van Iersel,[20] who went to Rome as adviser to Schillebeeckx. He wasn't allowed to enter the negotiating room but could only be available for consultation in a neighbouring room. Witnesses are a burden to the Inquisition. The secret Inquisition proceedings finally continue in the Doctrinal Congregation without Schillebeeckx's participation. The outcome is completely uncertain and is probably not unconnected with the outcome of the Küng 'major operation', which that same 15 December becomes official with the signature of John Paul II under a document to be published on 18 December. The same charges are made against Schillebeeckx in connection with his theologically well-founded article on 'The Christian Community and its Office-Bearers' as have been made against me since my *Structures of the Church* and *The Church*. One learns nothing more in Rome. The Catholicity of the views of Edward Schillebeeckx, one of the great representatives of the Catholic Church in the Netherlands, is disputed, as is his Catholicity as a theologian.

But in the Catholic Church with its centralistic and authoritarian leadership may one assume the role that Schillebeeckx and I hold? May one assume it as a

Catholic theologian? That depends on the answer to the question 'Who is Catholic?'

Again: who is Catholic?

It isn't surprising that especially after Ratzinger's attack on my Catholicity time and again I have to defend myself: that I am Catholic and intend to remain Catholic. So at this time I also give a major interview in *Die Welt*.[21]

'What has also shocked many Catholics is that this disparagement of my Catholic orthodoxy and theological and moral integrity has sparked off a campaign of defamation which has been expressed not least in countless letters from readers to every possible newspaper and to me personally.' Even a professor of my own alma mater, the Gregorian, the ultra-conservative theologian Jean Galot, SJ, is allowed with impunity to attack Schillebeeckx's and my understanding of the person of Jesus on Vatican Radio and denigrate us both as 'heretical' and 'Arian'.

For the umpteenth time I reply to the question of my Catholicity:

The person who agrees with the Catholic hierarchy on every single point isn't the only Catholic. Such total identification is an unjustified and excessive demand. There are countless good Catholics throughout the world who have very justified questions about official teaching, morality and discipline, which are not settled by discrediting those who put them forward.

A Catholic is someone who understands himself or herself to be a member of the *Ecclesia catholica*, for whom the 'catholic', i.e. the 'whole, universal, comprehensive, total', church is particularly important. In this sense I have been concerned as a theologian to teach the Christian faith in catholic breadth and depth. So I have been concerned for the continuity of faith and fellowship in faith which lasts through all the breaks: catholicity in time (tradition) and likewise the universality of faith and the fellowship of faith which embraces all groups: catholicity in space.

As for the errors of the church:

Errors are possible – we should be self-critical here – not just among theologians, but also in the Catholic hierarchy, as is shown not just by the Galileo case – after 350 years for the first time openly conceded by a Pope to be an error. In the spirit of catholicity I also continue as a Catholic theologian in the Catholic Church to represent the Catholic concerns of countless Catholics and to perform my *missio canonica* in this sense. Here I know myself to be at one with countless theologians, pastors, teachers of religion and lay people in our church.[22]

445

Where I was deceived

On the basis of the conciliatory letter from Cardinal Ratzinger and finally unimpeded lecturing in south Germany, Austria and Switzerland I can assume that the waves have subsided. As a lover of Latin and admirer of Roman law I have always put forward the view that while the members of the Roman Curia are legalists who overestimate the law and use it to consolidate their own power, they would observe their own laws. But I was deceived, particularly about this.

Of course I am mistrustful in view of the fact that neither in Germany nor in Rome did it prove possible to complete doctrinal proceedings against *The Church, Infallible?* or *On Being a Christian* in an orderly way: all proceedings always came to grief on the lack of fair legal conditions, especially on a refusal to allow me to see the records. Nevertheless, Rome and the German bishops issued one declaration after another against my theology. May I not therefore assume that they have said clearly enough what they had to say against me, often repeating it and propagating it all over the world?

On Tuesday 11 December I give my last lecture of 1979 in the great hall of the Siemens Foundation in Munich before an invited audience with many academic and other prominent figures on the question 'Should Managers Believe in God?' I am introduced by the knowledgeable and shrewd Protestant Munich theologian Wolfhart Pannenberg, with whom I have ecumenical ties: an impressive plea of almost half an hour arguing on the basis of all my publications so far that despite all the criticism I am a good Catholic theologian.

I sit next to him in full view of the audience and the whole film of my life passes before my eyes: everything that I have experienced, worked on, fought for and suffered in the past 25 years since my doctoral dissertation *Justification* in 1957 through the books of the 1960s and 1970s, *The Church, The Incarnation of God, On Being a Christian* up to *Does God Exist?*, books which with translations into many other languages have been a real help for countless people. However, unfortu-nately they have been no cause for joy for leading bishops of my church, but rather for suspicion and slandering of their author. Over all the decades there has hardly ever been an honest word of recognition, but time and again new letters, admonitions, complaints and finally official decrees, declarations, threats. Now in Munich it suddenly flashes through my mind: you've got to the point as a Catholic theologian when a Protestant theologian has to explain at great length to a predominantly Catholic public that – despite everything – you are a Catholic theologian.

But now I have to go up to the desk. With a still fairly firm voice, in my first sentence I thank my colleague Pannenberg very warmly for his support for my Catholicity. But then suddenly emotion overwhelms me. I lose the composure that I usually always preserve, my voice fails me – there is a psychologically infinitely long pause which is a terrible memory for me. Before the whole audience, which unwillingly suffers with me, I attempt to regain my composure

446

and finally can calmly give my lecture with a firm voice. Is my unconscious here indicating an intimation that I just didn't want to perceive?

I am glad that I can complete the lecture. In the *Süddeutsche Zeitung* I find a positive review by the well-known journalist Albert von Schirnding, which ends with the words: 'Belief in God cannot be argued for, but it can be presented in public – and with what conviction was once again shown very impressively by this theologian who is unjustly controversial' (13 December 1979). Didn't perhaps at least one German bishop – generally they are notable for their absence from my lectures – read this?

A secret meeting abroad

I cannot know that on the day before my Munich lecture, 10 December 1979, the Secretary of the German Conference of Bishops, Prelate Josef Homeyer, had sent the Bishop of Rottenburg-Stuttgart, Dr Georg Moser, the *Declaratio de quibusdam capitibus doctrinae theologicae Professoris Ioannis Küng* worked out by the Congregation for the Doctrine of the Faith with the indication that 'this declaration already (11 December 1979) approved by the Holy Father and intended for publication is to be issued to the public on 18 December 1979'. Content: 'Withdrawal of the church's permission to teach.'

Unfortunately in this case Bishop Moser doesn't, as I had so urgently asked him, make contact with me as the one concerned and also someone experienced in Roman politics. Thus instead of a common defensive front from Rottenburg and Tübingen there is confidential mediation through the bishop between Tübingen and Rome. On Wednesday 12 December 1979 'as the *ordinarius loci* immediately affected' he writes a letter to the Prefect of the Congregation for the Doctrine of the Faith, Cardinal Franjo Šeper, which covers three points, the first of which is put at the head of this chapter, beginning with the words: 'The publication of this declaration will certainly provoke stormy reactions from the public.' I get to know the wording of Moser's letter only after his death.

This letter honours Bishop Moser. It shows that he is clear about the seriousness of the situation and wants to do all he can to avert or at least postpone the worst. And Rome's answer? As if the Vatican were threatened with a terrorist attack, the very next day the Bishop of Rottenburg-Stuttgart is ordered at short notice to Brussels, to a secret meeting of top Roman and German churchmen. And for the sake of secrecy it will be held abroad. The Inquisition shuns the light.

On Friday 14 December the following representatives of the hierarchy meet in Brussels: Archbishop Jérôme Hamer, Secretary of the Roman Congregation for the Doctrine of the Faith, representing its prefect Cardinal Šeper, along with Archbishop Guido del Mestri, Apostolic Nuncio in Bonn; Cardinal Joseph Höffner, President of the German Conference of Bishops; Prelate Josef Homeyer, Secretary of the German Conference of Bishops; and Bishop Georg Moser of

Rottenburg-Stuttgart, accompanied by his own personal adviser, Hubert Bour. The main purpose of the meeting is to co-ordinate the various actions for the imminent removal of the *missio* of the theologian Hans Küng. A tremendous storm rages outside, Cardinal Höffner is late, the mood is nervous: they can't begin without the cardinal.

Bishop Georg Moser in dire straits

Bishop Georg Moser is not only, as he writes to Cardinal Šeper, the '*ordinarius loci* immediately concerned' but also, according to the Concordat, the local bishop who alone is responsible for withdrawing the *missio*. According to the Concordat only he can state that the church's permission to teach has been withdrawn. Rome needs him. So do I. I had examined him for his theological doctorate and to begin with he seems to me to be an ally. I thoroughly like the bishop's personal temperament, with his Swabian directness and sometimes also emotional commitment. With his intelligence and humanity he has the makings of a great bishop. Like me he is deeply stamped by the spirit of the Second Vatican Council and entered his episcopate in 1975 as a renewer and reformer. Despite all the concessions, to the end he is in principle one of the more open members of the German episcopate, which, as is well known, from a world perspective had clearly moved to the right after the Council.

So from the beginning we had good relations. And when once again complaints from Rome had come to Rottenburg we discussed them all in an open and friendly way and sought common solutions. Here we are by no means talking just about personal matters; we are united in a concern for the development of our church after the Council, not least the catastrophic state of the clergy, which is already becoming evident at his accession – with all its consequences for pastoral care. I recall his self-critical comment to me immediately after his consecration: 'To be honest, I don't know how things will turn out.'

There were never personal differences between us; on the contrary, we are on the same wavelength. Even after his return from a trip to China during a press conference on 15 November 1979 Bishop Moser, when asked about the controversy between Cardinal Ratzinger and me, said that 'the Tübingen professor is provocative and sometimes excessive in his approach so he needn't be surprised at harsh criticism'. But at the same time he emphasized that 'objective criticism and questioning is possible, even of the Pope; someone who asks questions is no less Catholic than others. One needn't be anxious about freedom in the church. No one, certainly not Cardinal Ratzinger, will be able to deny Küng personally his Catholic faith.'[23] And now?

Now in Brussels the Bishop of Rottenburg is confronted with a curial 'heavyweight' in the person of the Dominican and Archbishop Jérôme Hamer, the Secretary of the Congregation of the Doctrine of Faith, and with the dogmatically and legally ice-cold but theologically relatively uneducated President of the German Conference of Bishops, Cardinal Joseph Höffner. Evidently these are the two action men who in quite unnecessary haste resolutely insist on a final 'resolution of the Küng case' before Christmas 1979. For the secret can't be kept longer, and in January the explosive Pastoral Council is beginning in the Netherlands. When Bishop Moser objects, 'Does it all really have to be before Christmas?', Höffner replies, 'Küng doesn't believe in Christmas, in the virgin birth.'

Bishop Moser is put under a special obligation to silence, the seal of the Congregation for the Doctrine of the Faith (*secretum Sancti Officii*). Later he will tell a delegation from the Tübingen faculty of Catholic theology that perhaps it had been a mistake from the beginning to allow himself to be bound by the '*sigillum*', the seal of confidence. According to canon law (CIC c.1623 §1) a violation of this command to silence *ipso facto* carries with it excommunication '*specialissimo modo reservata*'. That means that lifting it is reserved to the Pope in person (c.2245 §3) 'because except in mortal danger and in urgent cases no one – not even the great penitentiary – has the authority to absolve from these censures' (Heribert Jone, *Gesetzbuch der Lateinischen Kirche*, Vol. III, p. 510). Isn't it understandable that so many bishops are afraid of speaking openly? They live in a totalitarian system which expects total identification with the Pope from them.

But Bishop Moser in particular is well aware that according to Catholic moral teaching no command to silence, however solemn, can be a reason for covering up injustice and disguising lovelessness. The second point in his letter to the Prefect of the Congregation for the Doctrine of the Faith dated 12 December is: 'In view of the sense of justice in today's world and in view of the post-conciliar procedural ordinances for resolving conflict in the church, I think it appropriate and necessary that Professor Küng should be once again informed personally before the announcement of the measures envisaged against him, or at least once again be called on to recant the doctrinal views objected to within an appropriate period with an indication of the possible consequences. Such a compromise would be appropriate to avoid the charge that is to be expected of loveless and unbrotherly treatment of an "uncomfortable" theologian. At the same time it would show that the very last effort has been made over dialogue in the church.'

The moment of truth

Bishop Moser is very well aware that he has to join in the action that Rome and its German helpers will now take. In a letter to the faculty of Catholic theology he later describes the course of events: 'When the decision of the Congregation for the Doctrine of the Faith was handed to me, I sent a letter to Cardinal Šeper. In it I pointed out to him that the planned proceedings against Professor Küng had to avoid any appearance of unjust or illegitimate harshness. I also asked urgently that Professor Küng should once again be given a personal hearing before the announcement of the measure envisaged against him or that he should be given the opportunity to make a written statement. Finally I pointed out that I thought that the publication of the declaration immediately before Christmas was unacceptable and at the worst possible time.' And, according to Bishop Moser, what was the result of the secret Brussels conference? 'I defended myself against the attempt to reject this objection and during the negotiations managed to speak to Cardinal Šeper on the telephone and explain my arguments. Cardinal Šeper noted them but insisted that the measures decided on should be implemented at the time planned.'[24] And so because of the secret agreements at top level the bishop had to accept everything.

It emerges clearly from all this (and this is of the utmost relevance for an assessment in terms of the Concordat) that the local bishop, who in my case has sole responsibility, will pronounce the withdrawal of the permission to teach, against his inner convictions. That is why he will also never publish his letter to Cardinal Šeper; as I said, I saw it only after his death. Contrary to his conviction, publicly expressed earlier, that no one, not even Cardinal Ratzinger, would deny Professor Küng his Catholic faith, under extreme pressure in the end Moser declares himself ready to allow and carry through the measures against me. This is a catastrophic mistake on the part of the bishop, which will cost me, and also him, dear.

But did he have an alternative? Certainly, had Bishop Moser from the beginning indicated that while he understood the Roman objections to my teaching, as a responsible pastor of this diocese and in accordance with the Concordat the only competent person, he could in no circumstances be responsible for withdrawing permission to teach for theological, legal and pastoral reasons, what would have happened? Of course he would have provoked annoyance, anger, vigorous protests from his episcopal colleagues. He had to do it! He had to obey! But he could have said that it wasn't possible to do it. He would have been told that the Holy Father very personally wanted it. But, he could have objected, according to Catholic moral teaching he might not in any way act against his conscience. And he would certainly have had the Lord Jesus himself at his side in his pleas for justice and love to the 'representative'.

Some people will say, wouldn't they simply have deposed such a bishop? That is improbable: to depose both the prominent theologian and the popular bishop at the same time would have been too high a price for the coldly-calculating Romans. The authoritarian gentlemen of the Vatican would have thought it too risky to proceed in this way against democratic Germany, Catholic, Protestant and secular. For they know from many historical experiences what can result from the condemnation of a bishop (as in the case of Archbishop Lefebvre). Therefore I am and remain convinced that in this case, too, at the last moment the Roman action would have been stopped – as it was once earlier under Cardinal Döpfner and later in the case of individual Latin American liberation theologians. Certainly, the whole matter would have been extremely unpleasant for Bishop Moser, but understandably would have gained stature in Germany and far beyond if at this moment he had stood by his man 'in apostolic boldness'. For Bishop Moser this was the moment of truth, and also for me.

But what is the moment of truth? I've reflected a great deal about that. The moment of truth is not when one has to write a difficult letter or stand firm in a difficult conversation or resist pressure from above. No, the moment of truth is when one risks one's own neck, when one is ready to accept painful hurts and wounds, indeed to risk career and life.

There is no question that the issue for Bishop Moser is his existence as a bishop, and for me my existence as a theologian, as a university teacher. And what happens? In this decisive situation, which really is the moment of truth, this bishop doesn't risk his own neck but hands me over to the Inquisition. Bowing to pressure from the Roman Curia, he fails at the decisive moment. What a disaster! This bishop, aware of the problems and ready for renewal, has given way in the decisive controversy, not ready to offer resistance if need be even at his own expense and for the sake of the Christian cause, in circumstances like those of Paul resisting Peter 'face to face' (Galatians 2.11-14). But I hear of all this only later. How did the Roman enterprise, which in the view of the bishops, too, would necessarily lead to a great confrontation, turn out? First of all it was carried on in the utmost secrecy. At any rate Bishop Moser refused to give me the verdict personally. So the Bonn nuncio was brought in.

Dark deeds before Christmas

For me, too, the difficult year 1979 is coming to an end. I have the impression that in past months I have done my church not inconsiderable services. While I wouldn't expect a papal order or the title of prelate, which in any case wouldn't have been welcome, or even an episcopal word of thanks, which would have delighted me, I would have liked just finally to be left in peace. I think back: to the lecture in the Academy of Social Sciences in Peking in favour of religion, then the speech at the European Congress of Radiologists in Hamburg in favour of humanity in medicine, and finally the ceremonial lecture on art and the question of meaning to the German Federation of Artists in Stuttgart – not to mention the teaching and all the lectures in Germany, Austria, Switzerland and France. I think that I've done my theological duty. I had virtually no summer holidays; I'm tired and long for a little rest and refreshment.

So I leave my last lecture before Christmas to our academic counsellor Dr Hermann Häring and the last seminar to my assistant Dr Urs Baumann, who in any case runs it with me. After the last meeting of the faculty on 15 December I can be glad that everything is behind me and travel to Lech am Arlberg. Lech, a three-hour drive from Tübingen, is a hospitable Austrian mountain village which has happily remained simple, in the midst of a beautiful and perfectly developed ski area, closer than the ski slopes of central Switzerland, the Grisons or the Valais, which I also know. Our familiar quartet meets again: my sister Rita, my brother-in-law Bruno and Marianne Saur. Here I hope for a pause in my hectic life and a breathing space. What a delight to be above the clouds in pure, clear cold air, to go down the slopes over the snow, with the mountains around me and the valley far below me – no time and need to think of theology, church, bishop and Pope.

On Tuesday 18 December as usual I am on the ski piste early: at almost 2000 metres, around 10.30, I show my ski pass in a ski lift: 'Professor Küng? You're being called at all the stations. You must return to the valley immediately.' Normally one is summoned only in the case of a death or similar misfortune. What's up? Have Rita and Bruno, who are in another group, perhaps crashed into something? Is it my mother, my father? Or ...? I speed down to Lech as quickly as possible. On skis one can cover in minutes stretches which take an hour on foot.

The hotel is waiting for my arrival: 'Telephone Tübingen immediately, it's a matter of life and death.' I immediately know it can only be Rome. And it is. In a muted, faltering voice Dr Häring says that he's terribly sorry to have to tell me, 'They've withdrawn your permission to teach!' And this immediately before Christmas. Who could have suspected such an insidious surprise attack, and from one's own church government at that? It's a real shock, but it doesn't throw me. I am immediately resolved to fight. Still on the telephone I tell Dr Häring to ask Bishop Moser urgently not to make any legally binding statement on the matter until he has had a conversation with me.

No capitulation to the Inquisition!

I am later told that Bishop Moser was too cowardly to speak to me on the telephone. He had organized the campaign against me locally in complete secrecy with his whole staff. There must have been some officials in his chancery who had to put in unwelcome night shifts to prepare for it immediately before Christmas. Under seal of silence they had to place the official declarations by Rome and the bishops in thick packets for express delivery to hundreds of parishes throughout the diocese for 18 December. A rebellion by the clergy in favour of their former professor, who is not unpopular, had to be nipped in the bud. Catholic press agencies and church papers work at top speed. Many people in church circles, where I have always had many friends, asked whether this was a preparation for the feast of love.

Moreover this is precisely what Bishop Moser had foretold in the third point of his letter to Cardinal Šeper on 12 December: 'At all events the time chosen for the publication of the declaration immediately before Christmas seems to be the most unpropitious conceivable. Despite a far-reaching secularization of public life in our country the Christmas season is regarded as a time of humanity and peace. Even tax offices and courts at this season feel morally obliged to protect dilatory or indebted citizens where possible from unwelcome and burdensome revelations. People certainly won't understand why the church in particular, as the bearer of the good news of Christmas, sets itself above these customs.'

'The church as the bearer of the good news of Christmas': despite the warning by the local bishop who alone has the competence, the Doctrinal Congregation, in any case not known for the spirit of love, has insisted on the proclamation of the threatening un-Christmaslike message. And unfortunately the bishop goes along with it – against his better judgement. I now need to act fast. Rita and Bruno remain in Lech with the luggage and all the books I had taken. After a quick snack, I leave with Marianne in the car. A thousand thoughts go through my mind as I wind round the Alberg, then go along the Bodensee and finally over the Swabian Alb, where we pick up our faithful housekeeper Martha Walz and quickly drive on to Tübingen.

I speak one thought aloud: 'Things won't be the same.' Anyone who has thus been publicly branded by Rome world-wide won't have the same status in church and university. The calculation of the Curia is clear: they want finally to finish me off as a Catholic theologian. I am to remain a Catholic and a Catholic priest, but without the church's permission to teach, so I shall have no students, doctoral students or habilitation candidates and finally no faculty. 'Without the church's permission to teach,' one of my Catholic colleagues remarks, 'Küng will be out of it in fourteen days, and he knows it!' However, I'm not so certain about this. But the situation is serious. I am not only to be put out of the way academically but also to be neutralized in the church.

A second thing is equally clear to me: 'No capitulation to the Inquisition!' but rather resistance with all legitimate means. In the end no regular proceedings have been carried through against any of my books. I was never offered a sight of the record or a fair chance to justify myself, just the possibility of humble submission. But are we in the Federal Republic of Germany living in a totalitarian system? This republic isn't yet a church state but a democratic constitutional state. Three years earlier in the Communist GDR the highly popular actor Armin Mueller-Stahl (who later portrayed Thomas Mann) was banned from acting and declared an enemy of the state because he had signed a protest petition when the satirical singer Wolf Biermann was deprived of his citizenship. He coined the phrase 'Better a kink in one's career than in one's backbone'. For me that means that whatever happens now, I will never let it break my back; I will continue to walk upright, I will fight.

So in the late afternoon of this black 18 December I return home, where the press, radio and television are already waiting for a statement. Television and radio are on the ground floor and Second German Television on the first floor; on the second floor, with Marianne Saur, a small 'crisis management group' is forming, consisting of Urs Baumann, Norbert Greinacher, Hermann Häring,

Inge and Walter Jens and Karl-Josef Kuschel. Before I make a statement I must look at the most important documents. There are so many that I can't read the whole dossier in a moment. For all this is not, as it used to be, just another document disapproving of my theology. It is an action against my person as a professor of theology and a Christian who is to be made a non-person in the church and in public.

The general attack: disturbing complicity

This much is clear: this is manifestly an attack by the Curia and episcopate, planned on a grand scale and prepared for all over the world, in order to break at last, after various vain attempts, a theologian who has long been burdensome. The day after the secret meetings in Brussels, a brief summary in coded form goes to all the nunciatures around the world. In Germany the media are mobilized against me on a broad front, and again tons of paper are produced against me at the expense of those who pay church tax. And who is the man behind the complex theological logistics? To my great sadness, by his own confession, it is Karl Lehmann.

After his move from *Concilium* to *Communio* Lehmann has increasingly fallen in with the official church line. He is evidently aiming at a bishopric, and like others who expect to become bishops he doesn't begin any major scholarly work but contents himself with articles and lesser occasional writings. After he was passed over for the diocese of Freiburg which he had wanted, in a circular letter to the nuncio and his friends he said that he was no longer available for being made a bishop. He continues to maintain friendly relations with me but in no way informs me about the operations which have been planned against me and are now in progress. Rather, he works with Cardinal Döpfner, very much in line with the hierarchy.

The 2002 Lehmann biography by the *Frankfurter Allgemeine Zeitung* editor Daniel Deckers significantly puts the whole life of this theologian under the title 'The Cardinal'[25] (which he receives only shortly beforehand, after difficulties). It first reveals to me how deeply Lehmann was involved in the machinations against me. So here for the sake of historical truth they must be reported.

To appreciate the embarrassingly petty manner in which Lehmann/Deckers treat me in the chapter of the biography entitled 'The Hans Küng Case', it is important to note the shameful, self-serving way in which Lehmann presents himself at the expense of his great teacher Karl Rahner (who died in 1984). Rahner is depicted as a time-consuming, restless and uncomprehending boss (cf. 'Holiday with Karl Rahner' and 'Trip to a Roman Hell'). Like me, Rahner is accused of 'provocative formulations, painful unmasking, scandalizing, all the media-effective tools for the public staging of conflicts and controversies' (p. 212). For as the first winner of the Romano Guardini Prize, at the presentation on 18 March 1970 Rahner had dared to describe the 'institutionalized mentality' of the bishops (with two exceptions they hadn't even bothered to acknowledge the confidential 'memorandum on the celibacy discussion' which he had composed and which had also been signed by other theologians) as 'feudalistic, discourteous and paternalistic'. Cardinals Döpfner and Volk and other bishops present are furious and insulted. And Karl Lehmann? For him, 'on this day it becomes clear that his way in the church cannot be that of his theological teacher Karl Rahner' (p. 212). Moreover, since then the questions of compulsory celibacy and the lack of priests have been taboo in the German Conference of Bishops and remain so to the present day under Lehmann's presidency – regardless of the collapse of an ordered pastoral care which has been built up over the centuries.

In this biography, in which Lehmann is constantly described as 'the cardinal', there is much wrong and perverse information about me and some things are invented (that Cardinal Döpfner had summoned me to Munich in 1976 and had 'shaken' me there – as if I allowed anyone to shake me). It becomes clear from the whole report that Lehmann hadn't explained to Döpfner the precarious foundations of the doctrine of infallibility which he had already recognized in the Tübingen seminar, but rather had acted as his ghost writer, totally neglecting the question of truth and concentrating only on forcing me to compromise and submit.

Lehmann proudly discloses to his biographer how he came to be involved in the dark deeds against me: what an honour to be allowed to receive in Freiburg at 2 a.m. on a Sunday morning Josef Homeyer, Secretary of the German Conference of Bishops, direct from the secret meeting in Brussels, to compile a press dossier by 4 a.m. and to plan the strategy against me. Without a word about the arguments pro and con the gentlemen agree on just one thing: 'Küng is to be hit with his own weapons' (p. 223). It is to be made clear to the press with such comments that the hierarchy is completely in the right and that the now proud, stubborn and incomprehending Küng is wrong.

Still by night, Homeyer returns to the Secretariat of the Conference of Bishops in Bonn and on Monday 17 December summons the leading media people familiar with church reporting to a confidential briefing. All are given a chronological table of the conflict going back to 1968 and a one-sided documentation of my correspondence with the conference of bishops and Rome. The shadowy men triumph: 'It is the hour of reckoning. For the first time the Tübingen theologian has not succeeded in winning over public opinion by targeted "information"' (p. 224). But Lehmann's and Homeyer's weapons are not Holy Scripture and exegetical consensus, nor the old Catholic tradition and the evidence of church history, nor the arguments of reason, but more recent documents from the conference of bishops and Rome which often have nothing to do with my name. However, these gentlemen rejoice like forgers who have finally succeeded in passing counterfeit currency: 'Hans Küng is not a theologian who soberly struggles for the truth, but one who provokes and schemes.' That was still being printed in 2002.

On 18 December 1979 Professor Lehmann spreads the word: 'Küng has undoubtedly overtaxed the church authorities.' Is that a mortal sin? But after New Year 1980 a handwritten letter reaches me from him with the remarkably precise date, '28 December 1979, 18.00'. It begins solemnly. 'At this hour the representatives of the German Conference of Bishops are with the Pope to decide on your case.' At 18.00? At this hour the conference in Castel Gandolfo is already over. And isn't it to be assumed that Lehmann, who is keenly interested in the outcome, has immediately learned the result on his direct line to the conference of bishops? At all events it is certain that had the outcome been positive his letter would have been composed quite differently. Lehmann compares himself with the old man at the end of Ernest Hemingway's story 'The Old Man and the Sea': 'Sadness and vanity, bitterness and disappointment. It could have turned out differently.' But now he 'does not want to reprove' me and goes on to make one accusation after another: that I had 'started such provocation', 'flagrantly destroying the basis of the laborious 1975 peace', 'despite the courageous acts of mediation on the part of Bishop Moser and others has shown no desire for compromise', indeed that 'a change from resolution to a lack of insight' has come about in me. That he already knows the negative result is confirmed by his closing request to me for 'moderate reactions and reflection'. 'As I have done much for you and risked a good deal, I beg you to collaborate at the last minute.'

In this way the accomplice makes himself the victim and the victim the perpetrator. In reality the mediator Lehmann is on the side of Rome and the bishops from the start and will remain so over the decades, whereas I am to 'make concessions', show 'insight', 'reflection', 'collaboration': in short, I am to capitulate. He is concerned with politics and diplomacy, I am concerned with the truth. 'Even today for Lehmann the "Küng case" is not a dispute over dogmatic truths but the failure of an attempt to keep theology and the magisterium in tension in a dialogue.' And because I cannot accept this betrayal of the truth and the untruthfulness that is practised, my 'recalcitrance' is made 'responsible for a possible deterioration of climate between theology and the magisterium' (p. 224). At any rate, at the end of his letter of 28 December 1979 he says: 'I want to remain in touch with you and wish you God's blessing with all my heart.' I can fully reciprocate this wish: I remain interested in good relations with him.

The verdict

For fear of premature publication and a rapid reaction on my part, everything takes place at the last moment. As Bishop Moser has been pledged by Cardinal Höffner to discretion up to the beginning of the press conference on 18 December, he informs his chapter only on the morning of the ominous day: there is general consternation. Only then does a courier bring the relevant documents to the dean of the faculty of Catholic theology in Tübingen, though in fact he isn't informed until later. Moser sends his suffragan bishop Franz Josef Kuhnle with the same documents to the Wilhelmstift, to 'inform' the head of the house and the Catholic students there. The whole church machine is running in top gear – and all this for the sake of a single professor of theology.

The Secretariat of the German Conference of Bishops has issued invitations at short notice for a press conference on this Tuesday, 18 December 1979, at 11.30 a.m. in Cologne under the chairmanship of Cardinal Joseph Homeyer – without indicating the topic. Very shortly beforehand, around 10 a.m., so that I can't react immediately in Tübingen, in my absence a courier from the Bonn nunciature delivers to my house the Latin text of the declaration with a covering letter from Cardinal Franjo Šeper. One could feel honoured, weren't this a Job's message. But on this day I am bombarded publicly with the following documents, some of which have many pages:

- Declaration by the Congregation for the Doctrine of the Faith on some main points of the theological teaching of Professor Hans Küng.
- Opening letter from Cardinal Šeper on the declaration by the Congregation for the Doctrine of the Faith.
- Statement by the President of the German Conference of Bishops, Cardinal Höffner, on the removal of Professor Hans Kung's permission from the church to teach.
- Declaration by Bishop Moser.
- Statement by the Swiss Conference of Bishops.
- Commentary by the Congregation for the Doctrine of the Faith on its declaration on some main points of the theological teaching of Professor Hans Küng.
- Observations of the chancery of Rottenburg on the declaration by the Congregation for the Doctrine of the Faith.

In the covering letter from Cardinal Šeper, the Prefect of the Congregation for the Doctrine of the Faith, sent out on 15 December with the reference number 288/57/i, which has been attached to me since my doctoral dissertation in 1957 (i = division of the Index of Prohibited Books), I read: 'The Congregation for the Doctrine of the Faith has to note with great displeasure the publication of your two new writings on the infallibility question, namely *The Church – Maintained in Truth?* and the introduction to A. B. Hasler's book *How the Pope Became Infallible.*'[26] The Congregation says that it had already warned Küng in its declaration of 15 February 1975 not to teach such opinions further. 'By the publication of your two above-mentioned writings this Congregation must regard the condition laid down in the *monitum* cited as not having been fulfilled. It therefore sees itself compelled to take account of the situation changed by you and issue a new public declaration, of which we enclose a copy for you.'[27]

For the moment it may be asked: what is there in my introduction to the new state of the infallibility debate that is so bad? Basically nothing that could not already have been read in my 1973 stocktaking of the infallibility debate. Rome deliberately didn't take note of this and so in this introduction six years later I sum it up compactly and precisely. My introductory sentence is: 'Can a great public question be settled before it has found an answer?' Then very briefly: 1. The justification for the enquiry; 2. The present Catholic consensus; 3. The decisive question. 4. The unexpected confirmations. And what new contribution does Hasler's book make to matters connected with infallibility? I also sum this up briefly: Hasler's book gives a vivid account of the history of how the infallibility definition came about and secondly sharpens the question how well founded it is. Was Vatican I a really free, really ecumenical council? And were the sacrifices worth while? Finally, should Pius IX be beatified? Aren't there good reasons for asking all these questions?

The declaration by the Doctrinal Congregation, though several pages long, doesn't answer these questions. Instead it begins in pompous curial style, refers to God and identifies itself with Jesus Christ, who is commandeered uninhibitedly by the 'magisterium' for its action:

> The church of Christ has received from God the mandate to preserve and protect the deposit of faith so that all the faithful, under the guidance of the magisterium through which the person of Christ himself exercises his role as teacher in the church, may unfailingly hold fast to the faith once delivered to the saints, penetrate more and more deeply into it with right judgement, and apply it more fully in everyday life. In order to perform this important task, which is entrusted to it alone, the magisterium avails itself of the work of theologians, especially those who have officially received permission to teach in the church and so for their part have in a certain way become teachers of the truth.[28]

Are theologians the lackeys of a magisterium acting in a monopolistic way? What would Jesus of Nazareth, who got into conflict with the high priests and scribes of the then religious establishment, have said to this infallible and unteachable 'magisterium' which in this case appropriates for itself the authority of the 'person of Christ', indeed of God himself? What is this 'church of Christ', which has 'received the commission from God', with the help of a 'magisterium' with sole competence officially to liquidate a teacher whom it finds is uncomfortable?

So this is to be the theological foundation on which the penal measures are based, since 'some doctrinal opinions of Professor Küng are opposed in different degrees to the teaching of the church which is binding on all believers ... namely the dogma of infallibility in the church and the task of authentically interpreting the one, holy, deposit of the word of God which has been entrusted only to the living magisterium of the church and – finally – those views which relate to the valid consecration of the eucharist'.

This 'magisterium' requires unconditional submission to doctrine which even many Catholics cannot understand with the best will in the world:

> In the aforementioned document, in 1975 the Congregation refrained for the moment from further proceedings against the doctrinal views of Professor Küng cited above, presuming that Professor Küng would dissociate himself from them. As this presumption no longer holds, in duty bound the Congregation sees itself constrained to make the following declaration: in his writings Professor Hans Küng has departed from the complete truth of the Catholic faith. Therefore he cannot be regarded as a Catholic theologian or teach as such.
>
> This declaration, which has been resolved on at an ordinary meeting of the Congregation, has been approved and ordered for publication by Pope John Paul II on 15 December 1979 in an audience which he granted to the Prefect of the Congregation mentioned below.
>
> Given in Rome, Congregation for the Doctrine of the Faith, 15 December 1979.
>
> Signed: Franciscus Cardinal Šeper, Prefect   Jérôme Hamer, Secretary[29]

As President of the German Conference of Bishops, of course Cardinal Höffner unreservedly identifies himself with the Doctrinal Congregation and presents his own long declaration, which is in tune with the Curia down to the very word. In it among other things one can read the marching orders for the diocesan bishop Dr Georg Moser, who according to the Concordat is alone (!) responsible:

> The Congregation for the Doctrine of the Faith has stated in a 'declaration' of 15 December that in his writings Professor Hans Küng has departed from the complete truth of the Catholic faith. Therefore he cannot be regarded as a Catholic theologian and cannot teach as such. Accordingly the diocesan bishop responsible, Dr Georg Moser, will inform the Minister of Science and Art for the state of Baden-Württemberg that the conditions for the *nihil obstat* no longer exist and that the *missio canonica* which was given 19 years previously on his call to the University of Tübingen has been withdrawn from Professor Küng. Here the inevitable conclusions are being drawn after efforts over almost ten years to clarify theological foundations which are being put in doubt by Professor Küng. The German Conference of Bishops regrets that it had to come to this painful decision. It stands unreservedly behind the decision of the Congregation for the Doctrine of the Faith and the steps taken by Bishop Moser as a result. Given the whole development there was no other way out.[30]

Really? The 'regret' and 'pain' must be limited.

For at the same time Cardinal Höffner infamously shifts the emphasis: the question of the divine sonship of Jesus is vividly emphasized in his statement and subsequently – especially in view of the Protestant part of the German population – this question becomes the main point of attack against me, far more than the doctrine of infallibility, which isn't very popular even among Catholics. Moreover, while my critical preface to Hasler's book *How the Pope Became Infallible* is printed in the episcopal documentation, my positively formulated 'Theological Meditation' *The Church – Maintained in Truth?* is unfortunately withheld from readers.

Then comes the pronunciation of guilt in the name of the 'church': 'By the withdrawal of the church's permission to teach Professor Küng loses his commission to teach in the name of the church and as a teacher of Catholic theology recognized by the church. He is not excluded from the church and remains a priest.'[31] What 'church' here is speaking to the 'church'? Only the official church – to the church community, to the people of God?

A statement by the conference of bishops of my Swiss homeland, again tuned to the very word, is also part of the precisely prepared general offensive. It too completely identifies itself in substance with the declaration by the Roman Inquisition. It is said afterwards that it couldn't have been done differently. I bitterly note that even my school friend of many years from Sursee and student friend from Rome, Otto Wüst, now suffragan bishop of the diocese of Basle, didn't dare to refuse to put his signature under my condemnation. In an authoritarian system the office of bishop seems to corrupt the character even of the best.

Only later does it become known that Bishop Georg Moser hadn't yet sent the decisive letter to the minister and had deliberately written the imminent public declaration in the future tense ('I will') without giving a date:

1. I will inform the Minister of Education of the state of Baden-Württemberg that there are serious objections to the teaching of Professor Küng along the lines of the Concordat and ask for the provision of a substitute, in agreement with me, for one of the teaching needs of the Tübingen faculty of Catholic theology.
2. I will report to Professor Dr Hans Küng that on the basis of the declaration handed to him by the highest church office he can no longer be active on behalf of the church as a theological teacher and that I therefore see myself caused to withdraw the church's permission to teach (*missio canonica*) from him.[32]

And as the letter hadn't yet been sent, Moser, as we shall see, still had scope for action. At any rate, he believed that he had.

I am ashamed of my church

That same 18 December the faculty of Catholic theology of the University of Tübingen meets for a crisis session. In welcome unanimity – in any case the last semester in the faculty had been very harmonious – it expresses its dismay at the completely surprising action by Rome and the bishops:

> We have learned from the radio that on the basis of simultaneous declarations by the nunciature and the papal Congregation for the Doctrine of the Faith of 15 December 1979 the church's permission to teach has been withdrawn by the Bishop of Rottenburg from our colleague Professor Dr Hans Küng. We are deeply disturbed by this drastic step by the Congregation for the Doctrine of the Faith and the way in which it has proceeded in concerted action. We fear the consequences, which are as yet unforeseeable. We see serious dangers for the credibility of the church in today's society and for the freedom of theology in research and teaching.
>
> Dean Professor Dr Wolfgang Bartholomäus, Pro-Dean Professor Dr Gerhard Lohfink and Professors Alfons Auer, Norbert Greinacher, Bernhard Lang, Rudolf Reinhardt, Max Seckler, Professors Hermann Josef Vogt, Ludger Oeing-Hanhoff, Walter Kasper, Herbert Haag.[33]

In all the excitement I take the trouble to study at least the most important documents. For I am prepared to make a first statement for the television evening news, in which I do not hide my indignation:

> I am ashamed of my church that secret Inquisition proceedings are still being carried out in the twentieth century. For many men and women it is a scandal that in a church which appeals to Jesus Christ and more recently wants to defend human rights, its own theologians are defamed and discredited with such methods.

And what about the substance of the matter? I explain that in the new short writing on the problem of infallibility to which objection is being made I had only repeated the old and still unanswered question and at the same time asked the Pope to appoint a commission of internationally recognized specialists to clarify it. The objections to *On Being a Christian* had never been the subject of Roman proceedings. Finally, in my last book *Does God Exist?* I had made precise statements about christology to which so far no church office had objected. All the charges were evidently only excuses for silencing an uncomfortable critic. And whereas the Dutch Cardinal Willebrands had defended his theologian Edward Schillebeeckx by a personal intervention with the Pope, quite specific German cardinals and bishops had collaborated with the Roman Inquisition to discredit one of their own theologians in his own church by dark deeds before

Christmas. Now that the Pope himself after 350 years had finally conceded that the Roman Congregation for the Doctrine of the Faith had made a fundamental mistake over Galileo, the Roman Inquisition authority was continuing to act not only against me but also against countless other theologians.

For all my protest against the Roman Inquisition I leave no doubt in this statement about my loyalty to the Catholic church community and end with the words:

> But I continue to think that as a Catholic theologian in the Catholic Church I represent the Catholic concern of countless Catholics and I know that here I am at one with numberless theologians, pastors, teachers of religion and lay people in our church. At the same time I will fight in our church for this disciplinary measure to be formally reversed, just as at the time John XXIII reversed the condemnation of prominent French theologians such as Teilhard de Chardin, Congar, de Lubac and others. Here I hope for support in and outside the Catholic Church. I am certain that the fight of so many people for a more Christian church will not remain without result in the long run.[34]

A wave of protests

The state organs adopt cautious tactics, but civil society rebels. In the Vatican, which as so often is badly attuned to the mood in the different churches and states because its information is one-sided, people think that with the well-prepared general attack the Küng case has definitively been settled before Christmas. Quite the opposite: large parts of the German public passionately take part in the controversy between the overpowering church machine and a single theologian. The situation deteriorates. The next day Cardinal Joseph Höffner attempts to calm the public with a further press statement, but in vain. This Wednesday, 19 December, is marked by a flood of protests and the first steps towards mediation in the conflict. On the evening of 18 December Walter Jens had stated: 'The Pope, Congregation and Conference of Bishops have now been disfigured out of all recognition. Human rights are a lip service.'[35]

Wolfgang Bartholomäus, Dean of the Faculty of Catholic Theology, says that in view of what has happened Bishop Moser's urgent and heartfelt request to all the faithful to respect the decision of the Holy Father and refrain from over-hasty and unfavourable reactions in this connection seems almost to be cynical and that the bishop's summons to prayer for unity and peace in the church is embarrassing. The Dean of Stuttgart, Erich Sommer, who is generally respected among the clergy, resigns his mandate in the Diocesan Priests' Council and his office as spokesman of this body in protest against the decision by the Vatican and the episcopate.

In the afternoon of 19 December I go to give my regular lecture on the

Apostles' Creed at the university. Around 2000 students in the packed Festsaal demonstrate with applause. Right at the beginning I am given an enormous bunch of red carnations. My audience passes a resolution that it feels the arguments of the Doctrinal Congregation to be a mere pretext 'to silence a committed theologian'.

When quiet has been restored I speak at length on the charges laid against me. Against the main charge of the Congregation that I have expressed myself 'anew and even more explicitly' on the topic of infallibility, I quote the end of my incriminated writing *The Church – Maintained in Truth?* This, as I have already reported, concludes with a proposal to appoint an ecumenical commission of internationally recognized specialists from different disciplines to clarify the situation.

On my legal position at the university I state:

1. The last word has not yet been said on the proceedings, the final validity and the consequences of the removal of the church's permission to teach, since there is all too much unclarity about the whole proceedings, not least the legal issues.

2. On my position as professor at the University of Tübingen I say that I still understand myself to be a professor of Catholic theology. This I am and this I will remain. The church authorities may want to deny me the church's permission to teach, but by a legal contract with the state of Baden-Württemberg I have the Chair of Dogmatic and Ecumenical Theology and am Director of the Institute for Ecumenical Research within the faculty of Catholic theology. Performing the tasks of teaching and research connected with this is meaningful and purposeful for me as a Catholic theologian only within the faculty of Catholic theology and therefore I reject any suggestion that I should move to another faculty, no matter by whom it is made. The solidarity shown to me by colleagues in both the Catholic and the Protestant faculties confirms me in this attitude. I reckon that in the state sphere I shall find that legal protection which has continually been denied me in the church sphere, and that the state authorities, who alone are responsible for the organization of the university, will resist any church pressure.

3. My work is always subject to the demands of scholarly honesty and responsible freedom. I will insist that at least in the state sphere I continue to have the possibility to research and teach as a Catholic theologian. I will strive for that with every legitimate means.

4. I firmly trust that not only colleagues and students in the two theological faculties but also colleagues from other faculties, the Senate and the President will support me with all their power in the interest of the reputation of the whole university in this matter.[36]

There is a report in the *Schwäbisches Tagblatt*:

> Yesterday afternoon Küng received the minutes-long ovation in the packed Uni-Festsaal coolly and without the slightest trace of messianic pressure to be a martyr. On the contrary, he seemed touchingly modest, and spoke compellingly but without aggression while presenting his case firmly and clearly; indeed he even found sympathetic words for the Bishop of Rottenburg, who is evidently under higher pressure (and had dropped him overnight). In contrast to his opponents, Küng declares himself ready to carry on a conversation – he wants to be heard, but not interrogated.

Overwhelming solidarity

The Catholic institutes of tertiary education react very quickly on the same day. They call for a torchlight procession from the university through the old town to the Holzmarkt. Around 1000 students take part. Their banners and shouts are understandably less 'cool': '*Errare Romanum est!*', 'The Pope Doesn't Have a Monopoly of Christ – Solidarity with Küng', 'Against the Inquisition in the Church,' 'One, Two, Three, Four, the Middle Ages are at the Door', 'The Pope is Fallible, Küng Must Stay'. In his speech, Professor Norbert Greinacher, my colleague in pastoral theology, says that if we compare the liberating message of Jesus Christ with the Vatican proceedings, we are dismayed to see a scandal. Those who argue from the church side for the implementation of human rights in society but trample them down within the church have lost all credibility. Despite all the criticism of Küng's position on individual questions it mustn't be forgotten 'what a tremendously important role Küng has played in recent years in communicating the message of Christ in our society'. 'Küng has awakened a readiness to believe to a degree that the bishops have not been able to achieve with their pastoral letters.' In an 'act of self-destruction' the church has let go of 'one of its best missionaries'. But to lapse into understandable resignation is the 'worst service that we can do Hans Küng'. 'We will not let anyone force us out of the church. We too are the church!'[37]

I hadn't joined in the march. As with the mass protest in Switzerland in 1974, I don't want to be a tribune of the people but to remain a professor.

Following Greinacher's statement, a whole series of declarations of solidarity are read out: from the Tübingen Catholic institutions of tertiary education, from the Catholic theological hall of residence the Wilhelmstift, from the Evangelischer Stift, from the professional group of Catholic theologians and from a group of teachers of religion. My friends Eberhard Jüngel and Jürgen Moltmann organize a statement by the faculty of Protestant theology in my defence and take it at midnight to the *Schwäbisches Tagblatt*.

The next day the paper's chief editor, Christoph Müller, comments:

Hans Küng is more than a Catholic dissident, reformer, rebel or heretic; thanks to the momentous verdict of the holy Roman Catholic Church he has now become a symbolic figure for justified contradiction and resistance. In the twentieth century it is no longer possible to maltreat those whose thoughts are uncomfortably different, especially if these are demonstrably true to the same faith and are only arguing that within the framework of the official confession the most urgent questions of the time should not be persistently excluded and ecumenical efforts should not remain merely lip service. A church which no longer puts question about its (self-)understanding nor allows them to be put can abdicate.

The professors of the faculty of Catholic theology write a letter to Bishop Moser in which they repeat and endorse the first part of their declaration:

> We have learned from the radio that on the basis of simultaneous declarations by the nunciature and the Pontifical Congregation for the Doctrine of the Faith of 15 December 1979 the church's permission to teach has been withdrawn by the Bishop of Rottenburg from our colleague Professor Dr Hans Küng. We are deeply disturbed by this drastic step by the Congregation for the Doctrine of the Faith and the way in which it has proceeded in concerted action. We made a statement on this yesterday, 18 December 1979.[38]

They say it is strange that by a public press statement about his intentions the bishop has created almost a *fait accompli* without previously notifying the faculty in an appropriate way:

> The secret proceedings, precisely timed, and immediately before Christmas, are outrageous. It is incomprehensible that the accused has not once been given a hearing before the final statement and its publication. All in all the whole proceedings are riddled with defects which go against the present-day sense of law and Christian ethics.[39]

They concede that it is well known that some of Hans Küng's theological views on doctrine and the style of his controversy within the church are not endorsed by all his colleagues, but they have 'no doubt that he wanted to and wants to stand in the Catholic faith and the Catholic Church. You too (the bishop) also recently confirmed this in public. Herr Küng has reached many people whom we do not reach. The proceedings against him are disheartening. We see serious dangers for the credibility of the church in present-day society.'[40]

The letter ends with an invitation to the bishop:

> In view of the consequences for the church, for relations between church

and state and especially for our faculty which are to be expected, we urgently request you not to take the step envisaged despite the public announcement that has already been made.

Professor Dr Wolfgang Bartholomäus, Dean

Professor Dr Gerhard Lohfink, Pro-Dean

Professor Dr Herbert Haag, spokesman for the professors[41]

Statement for John Paul II

Bishop Georg Moser finds practically no public support for his action against me. On the previous day he had refused to answer the telephone, but in view of the protest demonstrations and declarations of solidarity he decides to call me that same Wednesday, 19 December. Only now does he propose that we should meet for a conversation as soon as possible. Of course I agree. This meeting takes place that same evening in my house. Bishop Moser is accompanied by the Vicar General, Dr Karl Knaupp, and Dean Alfred Weitmann. I had invited my two colleagues Professors Norbert Greinacher and Walter Kasper.

The conversation lasts around three hours. Bishop Moser offers to mediate personally with the Pope if I clarify my position on the disputed questions once again in a letter to be delivered to the Pope. He proposes that he should do this in connection with a declaration by the German Conference of Bishops on *Infallible?* of 4 February 1971 which had avoided the term infallibility. I think it is asking too much for me once again to compose a declaration on the other declarations. But I don't want to refuse.

The next day I telephone the bishop promising to write such a letter but on one condition that is very important to me. In the event of its being published, the bishop's letter to Cardinal Šeper of 12 December, which expresses his reservations about the whole proceedings, should be published simultaneously; the bishop agrees, but later doesn't want to show me his letter. Be this as it may, late in the evening of 19 December at the end of the conversation a sober press release can be agreed on which reports this meeting in Tübingen: 'An attempt has been made in view of the difficult situation once again to arrive at an understanding.'[42]

For the whole of Thursday 20 December I work with my team on this letter for the Pope. I also consult my colleague Walter Kasper, who represents something like a guarantee of orthodoxy for Bishop Moser, and after several telephone conversations Kasper is fully in agreement with the text. Others have heard him: 'You can't go further,' he says. The team is relieved. If even Kasper can agree, then perhaps there is still hope. Towards midnight the letter, which has been often revised and passionately discussed, is finally ready, and is taken to the bishop in Rottenburg that night.

In my covering letter to the bishop I say that with this statement I want to make a contribution 'towards finding a way out of a situation which seems almost hopeless. It is extraordinarily difficult for me at a time when I am so heavily burdened on top of all my other duties to produce a text for which I can be theologically responsible at such short notice. But I hope with all my heart that my declaration can serve to ward off unforeseeable damage from our church. May the Spirit of God and Jesus Christ guide you on your difficult way to Rome.'[43]

In this statement for the Pope on the most recent declaration by the Doctrinal Congregation I first describe how I understand myself as a Catholic theologian and then correct some wrong statements in the declaration:

> I was not and am not concerned with accusations but enquiries; I am ready to have my views tested by a new investigation ... It is not 'contempt for the church's magisterium' – I must energetically reject this charge – but concern for a new credibility of the church's magisterium in the church and the world that has determined my whole theological work so far. I have in no way 'presented my own judgement as a norm of truth' – certainly not in opposition to the 'sense of faith in the church' – but in scholarly honesty and loyalty to the church I have orientated all my theological work on the gospel of Jesus Christ and the Catholic tradition.[44]

I again express serious reservations about the ordering and manner of the proceedings of the Doctrinal Congregation, above all that in its declaration it also makes serious accusations against my view of 'some main points of Catholic faith' (christology, Mariology), although these questions were never the subject of Roman proceedings against me. I then follow the general remarks with the central substantive question, my view of the magisterium and infallibility, which is looked on one-sidedly and negatively in the declaration.

> As far as the First Vatican Council is concerned, it was never my intention to deny its definition of faith, to put in question the authority of the Petrine office or to make my own opinion the criterion for theology and unsettle Catholic men and women in their faith. Quite the contrary. I have merely enquired how in the face of the well-known theological difficulties the possibility of infallibly true statements in the sense of Vatican I can be based on scripture and tradition. For me this is not a pretext but a real question, and the debate on infallibility which followed and was carried on in a wide international framework had at least one result: a great many theologians, including Catholic theologians whose Catholicity is undisputed, have conceded the necessity and justification for this enquiry.

I end with a request:

> I therefore seriously beg you to believe me when I say that in this way – very well aware of my personal risk – I wanted to do a service to our church in order to lead to a clarification of this question which is so burdensome to

many people within and outside the Catholic Church in the spirit of Christian responsibility. The question is of central importance especially for an understanding with the Eastern churches, towards which Pope John Paul II has provided a new hopeful impulse by founding a separate commission. A reorientation of the question is also called for from an ecumenical perspective. This declaration is backed by the trust that the present serious controversy, the consequences of which cannot be foreseen, can be brought to a positive solution in the spirit of true Catholicity.

Dr Hans Küng, Professor of Dogmatics and Ecumenical Theology at the Catholic Faculty of Theology and Director of the Institute for Ecumenical Research of the University of Tübingen[45]

Bishop Georg Moser fully accepts this statement, as did Professor Walter Kasper before him. He too recognizes that I have shown extreme readiness to compromise on the substantive theological questions. All in all this is an exposition which at this time seems quite sufficient even to conservative colleagues in the faculty of Catholic theology in Tübingen. At the same time I several times express the wish to Moser for him to bring about the clarificatory conversation between me and the Pope which has hitherto been refused me. I ask for this not out of vanity but because in a crisis situation which occupies the whole Catholic Church and also many people outside it, a personal encounter can help and should really be taken for granted between Christians.

The university makes a stand

On Thursday morning, 20 December 1979, a delegation of professors from the faculty (Dean Bartholomäus, Pro-Dean Lohfink and the professors' spokesman Dr Haag) talks with Bishop Moser in the bishop's house in Rottenburg. The dean, standing at a formal distance, as is later reported, reads out the professors' letter of 19 December, which he then hands to the bishop. The bishop explains the unfortunate circumstances as a result of which the dean had received the letter from him too late and how he was put under pressure in Brussels.

The bishop sums all this up the next day in a letter to Dean Bartholomäus and then makes the following statement on the faculty's urgent request that he should not withdraw Professor Küng's *missio*:

As things stand at the moment I cannot respond to this request either positively or negatively. I took the trouble on 19 December to have a personal conversation with Professor Küng. On the basis of the results achieved in it I am approaching the Apostolic See and attempting to obtain the possibility of another hearing, a conversation or even a statement for Professor Küng. Throughout these difficult and delicate negotiations I need

room for negotiation on all sides. I have personally taken the risk of pro-
visionally postponing the measures expected of me. I must therefore ask the
faculty for understanding if I do not undertake a further statement in
addition.

Finally, I would like to ask the members of the faculty once again, like
me, to continue to maintain a basis of trust. That is the only way in which
the conflict which has now arisen can be directed into a course which will
lead to a solution.[46]

Now the university too joins in. On 21 December, in agreement with the
professors of the faculty of Catholic theology the President of the University of
Tübingen, Adolf Theis, along with the other members of the Presidium, makes a
lengthy statement: 'The University of Tübingen affirms that Herr Professor Hans
Küng is still *Ordinarius* Professor of Dogmatic and Ecumenical Theology in the
Faculty of Catholic Theology of the University and in this capacity has unrestricted permission to teach.'[47] The statement goes on to quote precisely the
regulations in Concordat law for a withdrawal of permission to teach: this is
possible, but as far as the university is concerned it has not yet taken place.

Even the withdrawal of the church's permission to teach does not do away
with the professor's right to free research and teaching:

The University does not fail to recognize that there is a real tension
between the regulations of the Reich Concordat in connection with Article
4, 140 of the Basic Law and the basic right to freedom of research and
teaching. Nevertheless it starts from the fact that the right of the diocesan
bishop to withdraw the church's permission to teach does not affect the
status of a professor in corporate law, so that Professor Hans Küng can
continue to teach and research at the University, even if his teaching
activities are no longer recognized by the church as a requirement for the
attainment of the priesthood or a teaching office in the church.[48]

The Presidium of the University of Tübingen ends by noting a general deterioration of the relations between the faculty and the church authorities:

The University observes with great concern the increasing conflict between
members of the faculty of Catholic theology and the church authorities. By
virtue of its claim to a secure status as an unlimited autonomous corporation, it stands by its teacher Hans Küng, without thereby wishing in the face
of the church or the public to influence or object to church proceedings as
such. It will also firmly present this standpoint to the state government of
Baden-Württemberg.[49]

Mediating conversations in the Vatican and in Tübingen

In possession of my letter of 20 December 1979, Bishop Moser flies to Rome on Friday, 21 December 1979. He has the promise of an audience with the Pope. However – and this doesn't surprise insiders – the Vatican doesn't keep its word: Bishop Moser isn't received by the Pope. He must content himself with again talking with Cardinal Šeper, the Prefect of the Congregation for the Doctrine of the Faith, who lacks insight, and also with the cautious Cardinal Secretary of State Casaroli. What comes out of all this? He is merely promised that my letter will be delivered to the Pope; of course the bishop has no possibility of checking this. Was the trip to Rome worth while? At any rate he receives news that the Pope will invite representatives of the German episcopate to Rome for a conversation before the New Year. Is this a good or a bad sign?

After his return from Rome on Saturday 22 December the bishop first tells me the outcome on the telephone. At the same time we arrange a personal discussion between him and me in my house for Sunday 23 December. This conversation too lasts almost three hours. As well as giving information about the visit to Rome it centres on the further efforts at mediation.

I make clear to the bishop that it would be asking too much and be irresponsible, under pressure, for me to issue the next day, 24 December, a further statement on my statement of 20 December. So he asks me to collect theological material from my writings on the disputed questions: this could be a help to him in his arguments in the pending negotiations. This material is prepared in our house and sent to the bishop on 24 December.

In these circumstances I think that I have done all I can in Tübingen. It is agreed with the bishop that on Christmas Eve I should therefore return to Lech, where I had left my belongings, to spend the days of Christmas there in peace and at the same time contribute towards calming the public. The press is given the following report: 'After the conversation between Bishop Dr Georg Moser and Professor Dr Hans Küng on 19 December 1979, which was regarded as an attempt at an understanding, in Rome on 21/22 December Bishop Moser was able to present his view on the current situation. He also presented a statement by Professor Küng. Pope John Paul II will have a conversation on this matter with representatives of the German Conference of Bishops after Christmas. Bishop Moser is invited.'[50] Everything seems settled, but what happens?

A letter from Bishop Moser on Christmas Eve

Although it had been agreed in my conversation with Bishop Moser on 23 December that I would not make any further theological declaration, and he knows of my departure, contrary to all agreements on 24 December, literally on Christmas Eve, he writes a letter to me which in content and tone differs markedly from our previous conversations. Possibly Moser sees himself compelled by other church pressures (Rome, Höffner, German complications) to wring yet more concessions out of me. Perhaps it is thought that a bishop who has shown himself capable of being pressed can be pressed further.

It's a fine Christmas present. Since I am no longer in Tübingen, on Christmas Eve Dr Hermann Häring, my deputy in the Institute for Ecumenical Research and father of three children, is telephoned personally by Bishop Moser. Häring goes to Rottenburg and receives the letter on my behalf; he is allowed to open it and tell me the content on the telephone. It makes little sense to repeat Moser's highly inquisitorial 'Christmas questions' here. In substance they are nothing new: time and again the same problems, infallibility and christology. It seems to us to be sheer contempt when at the end of the letter the Bishop writes in a threatening way.

In the light of the Christmas festival I ask you once again with all my heart finally to make your long awaited contribution to the resolution of this conflict. Otherwise – to use Cardinal Döpfner's words of 6 May 1975 – I 'hardly know how to help further'. I can help effectively at the conversation planned to take place in Rome on 28 December only if I am in possession of a written retraction from you by Thursday, 27 December 1979, by 20.00 at the latest. I cannot avoid asking for your reply despite the festal season.[51]

Moser tells Häring that he would be quite content if Haring replied to his letter in Küng's name. He does. The letter which is agreed with me over the telephone is delivered personally to the bishop on the second day of Christmas, 26 December, by Professor Norbert Greinacher, and explained. The letter once again makes some fundamental statements more precise, but without going into detail. It presents to the bishop 'the urgent request on the way to Rome that the Pope, with his capacity to take an extraordinary number of matters into his own hand, will also find time to speak at this critical moment with the theologian of our church who now for decades has attempted with the best will and conscience to work for the cause of the Christian faith inside and outside the church'.[52] Will this request be granted?

After Christmas the composition of the delegation of German bishops is announced: in addition to Bishop Moser and his metropolitan Archbishop Saier of Freiburg the three German cardinals, Höffner, Ratzinger and Volk. Not a single spokesman for me; on the contrary, immediately before his departure, in a long interview with the Catholic news agency Cardinal Joseph Höffner once again vividly manifests his prejudice.[53] Since the delegation is composed in this way, there can be little doubt about the outcome of the 'mediation'. Or can Bishop Moser perhaps achieve something?

Back in the pure cold Alpine air of Lech am Arlberg, I attempt to distance myself from the oppressive events of past weeks and get some relief from the troubles of the months that lie behind me by skiing. The 'Küng case' is at the centre of media interest for the whole time before and after Christmas. A small encouraging episode at about 2000 metres in light snow is symptomatic. Three of us are sitting in the ski lift. A boy of perhaps twelve, when asked by my companion where he comes from, cheerfully replies: 'From Würzburg, and you?' 'From Tübingen, you know, by the river Neckar.' 'I don't know, but isn't that where Küng lives, who has something on with the Pope.' 'Where did you hear that from, your parents?' – 'Oh no, they talk only about oil.' 'Where from, then?' 'From the paper!' 'Look, that's Küng sitting on your right.' 'You're joking!' When I take off my snow goggles and give him a friendly look, he is visibly terrified: 'It really is!!!' We're at the summit – and excited, he speeds down to his parents.

'Oil.' The media interest in the Roman demonstration of power against me is exceeded only by the brutal invasion of Afghanistan by the Soviet Union, threatening Western oil interests, which likewise takes no heed of the Christmas period. On 26 December the USSR sends its paratroops and columns of tanks into this land in the Hindu Kush, thereby involving itself in an ongoing guerrilla war until years later its troops ignominiously have to return. It's a Pyrrhic victory.

On Friday 28 December 1979 I return from Lech. Our crisis staff meets at 6 p.m., for that same Friday Pope John Paul II is receiving the German delegation together with the heads of the Congregation for the Doctrine of the Faith in the better protected papal summer residence of Castel Gandolfo. The conversation lasts five hours. I wait anxiously for news from Bishop Moser. Around 7 p.m. I hear from press people who are following the bishop's every step in Rome that the conversation with the German bishops has ended. When will the bishop get in touch? I assume at any moment. Surely he can put himself in my position?

36 anxious hours: the papal decision is negative

Having discussed and agreed everything constantly and fairly with Bishop Moser in the days before Christmas, I may legitimately expect him to inform me of the outcome of the decisive conversation with the Pope on Friday 28 December, once it has ended. I wait hour after hour with my friends for the telephone call we long for. After all, it's about my fate as a Catholic theologian, university professor and Christian. At the latest – I think – the bishop will inform me on his return to Rottenburg. So I wait alone until deep into the night. But nothing, absolutely nothing, happens.

On Saturday 29 December I learn of Moser's return and several times try to reach him by telephone in Rottenburg. But now again there are the same nasty tactics as there were immediately before the Roman intervention: the bishop is constantly unavailable and even his vicar general cannot or may not give me any information. Bishop Moser keeps me uncertain of my fate and after 36 hours, when the news comes, it comes from elsewhere.

Only on Sunday morning, 30 December 1979, am I finally informed of the outcome of the 'mediating conversation'. The telephone call isn't from Bishop Moser or one of the venerable gentlemen of Rottenburg, but from some Italian monsignor in the Bonn nunciature who communicates the result to me in a restrained voice: the Pope's decision is negative. No personal conversation with the Pope is possible. The removal of the church's permission to teach remains.

I will never forget what are perhaps the most oppressive hours of my life. Nor will the bishop from his perspective. He will never again seek contact with me and never again show himself at the University of Tübingen. Over the next ten years, more than once I indicate my readiness for a conversation with him, but there is no response. I have to be quite clear that the mediation has not failed by my unreadiness for reconciliation. On the contrary, Bishop Moser, having been given my full support, has failed in Rome with his mediation.

After the event, forced on to the defensive on all sides, he foists the blame on me. Indeed with every journalistic means he spreads the rumour that I am to blame for everything. And many have followed him in believing that with my 'pride' and my 'obduracy' I am the real transgressor. The assailed is declared to be the assailant. To say that someone lacks 'humility' has always been a good slogan among the clergy. Of course I never get an opportunity to reply in a diocesan organ. On the contrary, I am also deleted from the chancery mailing list on all clergy matters and am banned from entering the Catholic Academy of Stuttgart, along with all other educational agencies of the diocese, where even atheists and all kinds of people alienated from the church are welcome. To the present day in some clerical circles the rumour stubbornly persists that Küng went skiing while poor Bishop Moser was tirelessly labouring for a compromise. So the truth is stood on its head.

Beyond doubt Georg Moser did much good and boldly took my part as long as it didn't cost him anything personally; enough has been written in the church press about his services. But with many in Tübingen, in the diocese of Rottenburg and the whole of Germany I regret that this well-meaning, highly competent bishop, ready for reform, who had begun so well, is no longer the person he was after the events I have described. His church career suffered a setback and he did not become, as expected, Ratzinger's successor as Archbishop of Munich and cardinal. With his liberal image he had lost all credibility, and having become assimilated to Rome he made no progress with his proposals for reform. The whole conflict was a great psychological burden on him until in 1988 he died all too early of kidney disease.

'With sadness and incomprehension'

I reply with the following statement (slightly abbreviated here) to the withdrawal of the *missio* which has now been made legal:

> With sadness and incomprehension I have heard the outcome of the Roman negotiations. The Pope is condemning a man whom he has not heard. The Roman motto 'audiatur et altera pars' (the other party should also be heard) does not apply in papal Rome. Although I have written to the Pope several times and most recently have urgently asked for a conversation with him through the Bishop of Rottenburg, the Pope did not think it necessary to give a personal hearing to a Catholic theologian who has attempted to serve his church to the best of his ability and conscience for a quarter of a century. An uncomfortable critic is to be silenced with all possible spiritual force. John XXIII and the Second Vatican Council are forgotten. Rome evidently will not tolerate any 'correctio fraterna', any loyal criticism, any brotherly exchanges, any questions arising from the spirit of solidarity. Human rights and Christian love are preached outside the church, but within it despite many fair words they are scorned ... [54]

I say that Roman authorities and German church leaders have failed to recognize that this controversy is not just about a Küng case but about the church, which is in the process of forfeiting the opportunities for reconstruction after the Second Vatican Council. It is:

not only about the case of an individual theologian but about all those, known or unknown, who are disciplined by the church authorities in the past and in the future;

not only about the case of an individual believer but about the unity of the whole church and the credibility of its leaders;

not only about the infallibility of the Pope but about his moral authority inside and outside the church;

not only about a controversy within Catholicism but about the success of ecumenical understanding.

I conclude:

> Despite these disciplinary measures, for the removal of which I will continue to fight, I remain not only a member and priest of the Catholic Church but also Ordinarius Professor of Dogmatics and Ecumenical Theology. I will pursue my central concern of making the message of Jesus Christ understandable to the men and women of today as resolutely as before: ready to converse and learn where there is partnership and brotherly discussion. In this I know that I am not alone. I will fight against all resignation alongside the many who have supported me so far and to whom I am grateful with all my heart. Together we will continue to work for a truly Christian church.

But how will things go on? Evidently no one knows. But one thing is certain: the case is by no means settled, as Rome expects.

XII

ಐಐ൬ಐ൬

Roma Locuta – Causa non Finita: *Rome has Spoken, but the Case is Not Over*

> *'Further let me ask of my reader,*
> *wherever, like myself, he is certain, to go on with me;*
> *wherever, like myself, he hesitates, to enquire of me;*
> *wherever he recognizes himself to be in error, to keep with me;*
> *wherever he recognizes an error in me, to call me back.'*
>
> Augustine, On the Trinity I, 3, 5

This self-critical remark by Bishop Aurelius Augustine (354–430) has been in my mind since *Infallible?* It comes at the beginning of his brilliant treatise on the Trinity because instead of repeating dogmas he is venturing a completely new approach. It goes without saying that I correct myself wherever I am shown to be in error. But the other much-quoted remark of Augustine – '*Roma locuta, causa finita* – Rome has spoken, the matter is settled,' which he is alleged to have made in a sermon in his support during his dispute with Pelagius, wasn't true at that time. The original quotation (*Sermo* 131, 10, 10) shows that the remark is an abbreviated version which gives a false impression. For Augustine it wasn't Rome that had the decisive say but the two African synods, for whose condemnation of Pelagius the church of Rome simply gave him welcome endorsement. Nor does this abbreviated saying apply to the time after the Second Vatican Council.

In 1967 Rome publishes the encyclical on celibacy, and provokes even more discussion of the medieval church law;

In 1968 Rome publishes the encyclical against contraception and with all the means of propaganda and pressure does not succeed in this teaching being accepted by the people of the Catholic Church;

In 1979 my permission to teach is withdrawn, but with all the means of inquisition and denunciation Rome cannot eliminate me or marginalize me as a Catholic theologian.

The fight goes on

On 30 December 1979 the University publishes a declaration. It regrets the Roman decision, thanks Bishop Moser for his mediation and hopes that the dialogue will be resumed in the foreseeable future:

> The University offers once again to mediate. It hopes that both sides will enter into further conversations with the will to reach an agreement. They must always be aware of tension in the relationship between freedom of religion and freedom of research and teaching ... As the University has already emphasized in its declaration of 21 December 1979, the test of the legal consequences of withdrawing the church's permission to teach will take a considerable amount of time. During that time at any rate the status of Professor Küng under corporate law is not changed.[1]

But the same day Cardinal Höffner and Bishop Moser adopt their own standpoint in separate statements on the Declaration by the Holy See. Many episcopal aides and writers will have again been annoyed at the heavy un-Christmaslike additional burdens; it is well known that many church workers, even in the chanceries, church papers and associations, sympathize with my views. If the cause of the magisterium was really clear, would it need so many declarations and explanations of the declarations?

It makes little sense here to report the statements repeated time and again. I have already made it clear that Cardinal Höffner is wrong in referring to the Schillebeeckx case; it is equally false that I am interested only in a direct conversation with the Pope. The very first sentence of Höffner's doesn't sound straight: 'Professor Küng's assertion that "an uncomfortable critic is to be silenced" is dishonest.'[2] What is dishonest is to keep quiet about the demands for reform which were censured in the first statement by the conference of bishops on *On Being a Christian* but now, since they are backed by large majorities among church people, are no longer mentioned and have been replaced by 'dogmatic' accusations about 'christology', which many believers couldn't judge.

Be this as it may, the die is cast. At the end of my fateful year 1979, on 31 December, when humankind celebrates the beginning of a new decade, Bishop Georg Moser finally sends to the Baden-Württemberg Minister of Science and Art, Professor Helmut Engler, the letter which he has so far held back:

> I have made my own the decision of the Congregation for the Doctrine of the Faith which has been approved by the Pope. By virtue of my episcopal responsibility I am therefore making a serious complaint against the teaching of Professor Hans Küng and am withdrawing the *nihil obstat*. At the same time I request that in accordance with Article 29 of the Reich Concordat – in association with Article 3 of the Bavarian Concordat,

Article 12 of the Prussian Concordat and Article 10 of the Baden Concordat (each with their concluding protocols) – the appropriate steps are
taken and that a due replacement is sought for the teaching needs of the
Tübingen faculty of Catholic theology ... Should he [Professor Küng] not
resign of his own accord from the legal position which he occupies as a
member of the faculty of Catholic theology I must request that his dismissal
from this faculty is implemented.[3]

One might now have been able to assume that the bombardment of solemn
Roman and episcopal declarations, so well prepared by the Homeyer–Lehmann
duo with all the commentaries, would have been enough to settle once and for all
the man who had often been disowned in public as a 'Catholic theologian'. But
that isn't the case. The lack of understanding and displeasure in Germany are
great. In panic, Cardinal Höffner and the bishops therefore decide at short notice
on a further unusual major action all over the country. It is to be assumed that in
the new media offensive, launched at top speed, the same proven duo were active
as co-ordinators and possibly ghost writers.

3.5 million words from the pulpit

The final withdrawal of my permission to teach has provoked negative and
sometimes vigorous reactions at all levels of the population – whether Catholic or
not – and also among the clergy. One hears that the majority of the thousands of
letters sent to Cardinal Höffner and the bishops are either critical of the official
measures or against them. All too many people in Germany know who over the
past years has worked indefatigably for their concerns against a church hierarchy
which is fossilized and alienated from the people. Their assumption that this
powerful action of a giant machine against an individual theologian isn't right is
all too well founded.

But since all the proclamations and actions of the 'magisterium' so far evidently
haven't borne fruit, the German Conference of Bishops now resorts to a weapon
that it didn't even have the courage to use against the criminal Hitler and the
National Socialists. Now, against one of their own critical theologians, where no
courage is required, they dare it: a joint pastoral letter, again hastily signed
without discussion by all the German bishops by name, a 'word from the pulpit'
with a further 'explanation' is printed in an edition of 3.5 million copies. On
Sunday 7 January 1980, on which the 'Appearance of the Lord' is being celebrated, the by no means good news is to be read out to the faithful in all the
Catholic churches from Flensburg to the Bodensee.

Chancellor Konrad Adenauer was convinced that the German bishops should
have protested in a pastoral letter at the notorious crimes of Hitler and the
National Socialists: 'I believe that if on a particular day the bishops had all taken a

public stand against it from the pulpits, they could have prevented a great deal. That didn't happen and there is no excuse for it.'[4] Of course I don't want to compare two completely different situations and identify my situation over against the Roman hierarchy with that of those persecuted in the Nazi regime. But I do want to raise the question: can the German Conference of Bishops be excused before history for having had read out in all the churches of Germany on 7 January 1980 a pastoral letter against an individual theologian who has always been committed to his church 'in season and out of season'?

Many pastors refuse to read out the 'bishops' word' against me at their worship on 7 January 1980 and to distribute it. Others read out only part of it and many others make critical comments on it. Often one hears that my books have helped more in pastoral care, in religious instruction and in adult education than all the pastoral words of the German Conference of Bishops. Be this as it may, the way in which the German Conference of Bishops is proceeding is felt to be unjust, indeed un-Christian. Cardinal Joseph Ratzinger is so annoyed at the resistance of his clergy that many weeks later, at Easter 1980, he strictly admonishes his clergy in a circular letter that his pastoral words must be read out if a pastor 'does not want to commit a clear offence against the promise of obedience which is of the essence of the priesthood'.[5] Lofty words, but misguided ones.

Here one can see what is to be served by 'obedience' – not to God or one's own conscience, but to the 'Lord' bishop – in the Catholic Church. In a session of the Pastoral Council of the Diocese of Munich in February 1981 respected priests are still defending to Cardinal Ratzinger their refusal to read out the pastoral letter against Hans Küng. They say that it is a lie that the church's permission to teach has to be withdrawn from him because he doesn't believe in the divinity of Christ. The true reason is his questioning of 'infallibility' and the encyclical Humanae vitae. Ratzinger's predecessor, Archbishop Gregor Scherr, had already fought against infallibility at the First Vatican Council but had then been compelled by Rome to assent, and to expel the great Munich church historian Ignaz von Döllinger, the main theological opponent of the infallibility definition.

Now, more than 100 years after the infallibility definition, the bishops could have had an easy time. They could just have given a short convincing reply to the clergy and people about the 'enquiry' into infallibility which was occupying everyone, stating how they explained from Holy Scripture and the great Catholic tradition that the definition of the First Vatican Council in 1870, prior to which most of the German bishops had departed in protest, was true: that God himself gives Pope and bishops that support of the Holy Spirit which in particular questions of faith or morality – for example in the question of contraception – a priori excludes any error. But even in the long 'word from the pulpit' and the attached explanation this particular elementary question of infallibility isn't answered. As throughout the whole controversy, it is always only asserted and veiled in 'christology'.

478

Basically, all Catholics are to accept that Vatican I was right because it said it was right. In its definition of infallibility the Council has the Holy Spirit behind it because it has claimed this Spirit. So too the proceedings against a theologian are just because no proceedings of the magisterium can be unjust. By this I simply want to indicate that the argument always goes in a vicious circle and presupposes what needs to be proved. With good reason the churches of the Reformation and the Orthodox churches of the East have rejected this doctrine of infallibility from the start. No wonder that the longer this dispute goes on and the episcopal pseudo-arguments are repeated, the fewer are the Catholics who believe in this truth of faith.

Against falsifications and lies

Three days after this national campaign by the bishops, on 11 January 1980, I reply with a short statement for the press.

> I can only regret that the dispute has now been moved to the pulpits. With money from church tax running into hundreds of thousands and editions of millions the whole church machine is being mobilized against one indivi-dual: documentations, brochures, pastoral letters from individual bishops, a pulpit statement from the episcopate as a whole – all conveying incomplete information and one-sided interpretation. Justice and Christian brotherli-ness demand that the person being attacked in this way should have been given the possibility of presenting his own theological position to German Catholics.

But nowhere am I given an opportunity to defend myself in the church press. I therefore correct all the false assertions in the secular media:

> 1. I have always been prepared for conversation and correction and have had countless conversations with the local bishop, representatives of the German Conference of Bishops and personally with the head of the Roman Congregation for the Doctrine of the Faith and have even sought a con-versation with the Pope.
> 2. I have rejected only an inquisitorial procedure in which investigator, prosecutor and judge are identical, in which I am not allowed to look at the records, in which I am not allowed to nominate a defender, negotiations are carried on in my absence and there is no possibility of appeal. This goes against Article 6 of the Council of Europe's Declaration of Human Rights.[6]
> 3. There have been no proceedings either in Germany or in Rome against my publications which have recently come under discussion. This applies both to *On Being a Christian* and the more recent publications on the

479

question of infallibility. The documentation relating to this by the German Conference of Bishops is incomplete. In particular I felt that the descriptions of my christology by the magisterium are deeply inappropriate.

4. I appeal once again to all bodies of the Catholic Church, especially at parish level, to discuss the most recent developments openly and to form their own opinion on the basis of comprehensive information.[7]

Many people, including clergy, saw through and see through the official perplexity and suffer under it. In 2006 I get a letter from relatives of a Munich priest who died a decade previously, which he had written to Archbishop Joseph Ratzinger shortly before his death, a 'cry of complaint and accusation which has built up in me over many years'. Over several pages the pastor and dean writes about the frustrations that he has experienced with his archbishop. The letter culminates in the following accusation:

> In 1938 our class teacher and German teacher Braun threatened me with expulsion from the grammar school in Rosenheim. This was because in a German essay on 'my ideal profession' I had written: 'At a time when everything is dominated by propaganda and lies, my ideal profession is to be able to bear witness to the truth as a priest in the church of Christ.' I never dreamed that my church would behave even more badly. It throttles all questions about a way of truth and truthfulness with the delusion of infallibility. Even people like *you* challenge the orthodoxy of their brothers in episcopal office who together with the Würzburg synod aren't content with the exclusion of remarried divorced people and seek ways out of this. Who doesn't remember here the word of Christ to the hierarchy of his time, 'Woe to you, scribes and Pharisees, hypocrites'? This lie, clothed in the vanity of infallibility, is the main evil in the church of our days. This is what cries out to heaven. I don't know whether one can make the current Pope John Paul II, Karol Wojtyla, the main culprit, because I know him only as a presenter on television. But I make you responsible and accuse you of this deceit.

This accusation is only one of many – I have heard of hundreds of similar ones – which is why I quote it. On his deathbed, the only reply that the pastor received from his former archbishop was a standard Christmas card with best wishes for the coming year. Two weeks after his letter he was dead.

A chair in Zurich?

Immediately after the 'word' from the pulpit produced by the German Conference of Bishops I receive an important letter from Switzerland dated 8 January

1980. The writer introduces himself as the 'President of the Swiss People's Party of the Canton of Zurich, National Councillor and Protestant'. He is in fact the influential and wealthy Zurich politician and pastor's son Dr Christoph Blocher, who is to play a central role in Swiss politics and from 2004 serves as Swiss Minister of Justice. That Blocher now represents an extreme right-wing policy on some points which is not mine (against the United Nations and the EU) shouldn't prevent me from reporting on a letter which still does him honour.

He knows me merely from my books and from the press: 'What I have read of you has impressed me greatly. The controversies in the Catholic Church are far more important than the current attempts at improvement in the Protestant Church.'

He sees my situation realistically: 'The withdrawal of your permission to teach could mean that in future your message will not go out from any theological faculty. That would be disastrous. Therefore I have considered what we could do in this situation – also because we are both Swiss. I have come to the conclusion that it might possibly make sense for a personal chair to be created for you in the theological faculty of the University of Zurich.' But before he undertakes anything he wants to ask for my opinion: 'Perhaps such an offer (from a Swiss Reformed theological faculty) might do more harm than good.'

Dr Blocher doesn't want to be misunderstood: 'I have no political concern; that cannot count in this controversy. Nor am I concerned to get you from Tübingen to Zurich now (even if that would be a great enrichment for us in Zurich). I simply want to create the possibility for your "search for the truth" to go on from an important place in the churches and the world. For the difficult time to come I wish you the strength to make the right decisions and send friendly greetings, Christoph Blocher.'

Here I am quietly offered an alternative: emigration – to my own homeland. The signal is important to me at this time. If I couldn't continue to work in Tübingen in complete freedom to teach and research, then I could in Zurich, the largest Swiss city, with an acknowledged high quality of life. The model for this is another Swiss theologian, Karl Barth, who inspired the resistance of the Confessing Church against the Nazis and had to give up his professorship in Bonn. He was offered a personal chair in Switzerland in the University of Basle and accepted it. Switzerland – as for many emigrants – is a stronghold of freedom.

In my reply, not sent until 28 January 1980 because of the thousands of letters I receive, I thank Dr Blocher for his 'active involvement in my cause': 'Happily here in Tübingen the state and university organs are democratic and I have time and again been assured that they are ready for a solution which must be viable for all sides.' But I keep open this option, of which the public knows nothing: 'Should some extraordinary developments take place, I will gladly let you know.'

International echo

The day before my response to the pastoral letter from the conference of bishops, on 10 January 1980, in my absence my faculty in a secret vote with only one vote against and one abstention asks me and the bishops to contribute to a revision of the decisions: 'The Faculty asks the Senate of the University to exhaust all the legal possibilities for Professor Küng to continue to be a member of the Faculty of Catholic Theology.'[8] On 18 January the weekly *Die Zeit* publishes in a dossier two major articles by Professor Herbert Haag ('Hans Küng and his Church. A Chronology of the Inquisition')[9] and by me ('Why I Remain a Catholic').[10] Again I make it clear that I still want to exercise my teaching office within the faculty of Catholic theology.

The Roman intervention of 18 December sparks off reactions all round the world. It is impossible to count the newspaper comments world-wide. I get to see some of them. Over the weeks around 10,000 letters are sent to me, only 10 per cent of them negative. The records of the events from 18 December 1979 to the middle of April 1980, now in the archives of the University of Tübingen, comprise around 40 boxes.

The new documentation 'The Küng Case', edited by Norbert Greinacher and Herbert Haag, cites 50 statements by important groups and organizations.[11] I am particularly delighted at the indications of solidarity from theologians: a telegram from 70 North American theologians; a declaration by 50 Spanish theologians; a letter from 145 professors of Catholic theology in the Federal Republic to Cardinal Höffner; a declaration by 50 Catholic professors from Switzerland and another declaration by Protestant university theologians; resolutions by the Society of Christian Ethics and many more.

The Catholic youth organizations also make clear statements. There is an open letter from the federal leadership of the Catholic Young Community, a statement by the working group of Catholic students and institutions of further education and a statement by the Main Committee of the Federation of German Catholic Youth.

Special mention should be made of the clear statements from Switzerland. In Lucerne there is a big protest meeting in front of the Hofkirche, where I used to be assistant pastor. Around 25 banners are displayed, for example 'Dialogue not Power', 'This is how the Church becomes a Sect', 'Human Rights YES – Inquisition NO', 'Institutional Church or Küng – Which is Uncertain?', 'Conversation not Orders', 'Pohier, Schillebeeckx, Bishop Iniesta, Küng – Who Next?' 'Believing or Subservient?', 'After the Age of the Council, the Ice Age', 'After the Council, Exile'.

An open letter from Action for Human Rights in the Church, signed by 15,500 people, goes to the Swiss bishops. It is followed by a long letter to the bishops with concrete proposals.[12] Not only do the Swiss Catholic students of theology send an open letter to John Paul II,[13] but the Swiss Writers

Association[14] and the Swiss Artists[15] also make a statement. This shows how the whole event involves people far beyond church circles.

By contrast the reactions from the ecumenical world are more restrained and cautious. The World Council of Churches issues a 'statement on the action against Professor Hans Küng' as early as 19 December 1979 and on 18 Febuary 1980 the General Secretary of the World Council of Churches, Dr Philip Potter, makes a statement to the Executive Committee in Strasbourg. A statement from the Old Catholic Church of Germany also follows. Strikingly there is no official statement from the Council of the Evangelical Church in Germany (EKD), which otherwise is fond of speaking on every possible question; this confirms my criticism of the politically-motivated Protestant pussyfooting and its opportunistic alignment with the Catholic hierarchy.

However, the honour of German Protestantism is saved above all by the faculty of Protestant theology of the University of Tübingen, which on 19 December issues a declaration of solidarity and appeals to the minister responsible, in agreement with the bishop, to ensure that Professor Küng of the University of Tübingen continues to remain within the faculty of Catholic theology. This declaration is signed among others by Otto Betz, Klaus Scholder, Luise Abramowski, Martin Hengel, Oswald Beyer, Peter Stuhlmacher, Dietrich Rössler, Heiko Oberman, Jürgen Moltmann, Karl Ernst Nipkow, Ernst Käsemann and Eberhard Jüngel.[16] Significantly the signature of Ratzinger's friend and leader of the evangelicals, Peter Beyerhaus, is absent.

That same evening Professors Martin Hengel and Eberhard Jüngel visit me as delegates of the Protestant faculty; they express their sympathy and their solidarity and make it clear that I will be welcome at any time in their faculty should there be no other solution. That is an honour to the Protestant faculty. But my colleagues also understand that my Roman Catholic opponents would regard this as capitulation and going over to the Protestant faith – since it would not be just for a guest semester but would be a permanent post. The faculties of Protestant theology in Marburg, Hamburg and Strasbourg and the Harvard Divinity School also express their solidarity, as do the faculties of Catholic theology in Nijmegen, Münster, Mainz and Paderborn, whereas those of Bonn, Freiburg and Munich hesitate over a statement.[17]

I'm also grateful that almost all the Catholic organizations in the diocese of Rottenburg-Stuttgart have also made statements in my support: of course the institutions of tertiary education in Tübingen, along with the candidates for priesthood and alumni of the priests' seminary, the Priests' Working Group of Rottenburg, the teachers of religion in the diocese, the Catholic Youth and finally also the Diocesan Council, which meets under the chairmanship of the bishop. There are hardly any statements supporting the bishop. But in the German state system (with its church tax) the bishop hardly needs to take any account of people and clergy – to the annoyance of many who faithfully pay church tax and note the lack of efficient democratic control and influence.

The colleague in the faculty whom I have already cited – the moral theologian Alfons Auer, who with six other colleagues will soon turn against me – was wrong. He is the one who said to a friend, a professor of German studies, that without the church's *missio* Hans Küng would be 'out in fourteen days'. The view of the Roman Congregation for the Doctrine of the Faith that with the withdrawal of the *missio* before Christmas 1979 the Küng case was settled was even more wrong. On the contrary, this affair constantly occupies the national and international press[18] and doesn't bring Rome many friendly greetings for Christmas and the New Year.

The solidarity of theologians

There is hardly a significant theologian who doesn't say something in this controversy: around 40 statements are printed in the documentation.[19] It is to be expected that colleagues who had written against me earlier and had made Roman careers – Hans Urs von Balthasar, Walter Kasper, Karl Lehmann and Joseph Ratzinger – will support the Doctrinal Congregation. However, these are also joined by the constitutional lawyer Alexander Hollerbach and Axel von Campenhausen (but not Ernst Gottfried Mahrenholz and Klaus Scholder). But amazingly Karl Rahner, who had launched the smear campaign against me as a 'liberal Protestant' within Catholicism, doesn't find any absolute affront in my work, at least in christology. 'I really have read Hans Küng's book *On Being a Christian* from beginning to end – perhaps there aren't so very many people who have done that (here he is deceiving himself enormously!) – and have to concede that I could not discover any absolute affront against a defined dogma in christology.'[20] There are qualifications in what he writes, but nevertheless!

Particular attention is paid to the statement by Professor Heinrich Fries of Munich under the title 'Hans Küng – A Witness to Christian Faith', which ends with the words 'Has the Catholic Church in 1979 become so narrow and anxious that it can no longer accept Hans Küng as a theologian – despite much justified criticism? And is the same church so wastefully rich in gifts and theologians whose voices are heard all over the world that it can dispense with Hans Küng without further ado?'[21]

Of course my colleagues and friends from Tübingen make positive statements: the Catholics Norbert Greinacher, Hermann Häring, Karl-Josef Kuschel, Hans Nagel and Johannes Neumann.[22] So do the prominent Protestant theologians Eberhard Jüngel ('How Free Must Theology Be?') and Jürgen Moltmann ('Hans Küng, Rome and the Gospel'). Other Protestant theologians join in: Heinrich Ott ('Danger to an Ecumenical Hope'), Wolfhart Pannenberg ('Asking Too Much'), Heinz Zahrnt ('Thirtieth December 1979, Nothing New from Rome') and Peter Højen ('Thorns on the Way to Unity. An Infallible Decision in Ecumenical Perspective').

The Catholic theologian and sociologist Andrew Greeley of Chicago speaks out as clearly as ever from the US:

> The violation of human rights which is involved in the case of the theologians Schillebeeckx and Küng has brought these two men great sympathy and popularity and the Pope hostility. One hears no sound of protest from the faithful when cartoonists depict John Paul II as a Catholic Ayatollah. The Pope is certainly not an Ayatollah, but he has done great damage to himself and the church in surrendering to the vengeful German hierarchy in the case of Küng and the resentful Congregation for the Doctrine of the Faith in the case of Schillebeeckx.[23]

On 20 December 1979 a Committee for the Defence of Christian Rights in the Church had been founded, in which Inge and Walter Jens and Norbert Greinacher play an important role. They are shocked at 'how much these inquisitorial measures contradict Jesus' commandment of love and reconciliation. Instead of implementing in an exemplary way as Christian rights the basic rights of all human beings which were achieved in the French Revolution, in accordance with its commission, the church today is far from guaranteeing in its own sphere the rights which it often itself proclaims. We therefore demand that there shall be no going back on the basic democratic rights of all human beings created by the Enlightenment, especially no obstacles to freedom of opinion and conscience; no disciplining of those who think critically; no toleration of proceedings in which the prosecutor has all the rights and the accused virtually none; no promotion of dependent relationships which rest on authority, discipline and obedience instead of collegiality and brotherliness; and therefore no offending against the commands of tolerance and mutual respect.'[24] The other signatories are: Heinrich Albertz (Berlin), Josef Blank (Saarbrücken), Walter Dirks (Freiburg), Otto Herbert Hajek (Stuttgart), Ernst Käsemann (Tübingen), Johann Baptist Metz (Münster), Jürgen Moltmann (Tübingen) and Rolf-Michael Schulze on behalf of the support group associated with *Publik-Forum*. In the end more than 7000 people sign this declaration.

But what moves me most is what Yves Congar writes at the end of his long article in *Le Monde*:

> In 1964 or 1965 a cardinal told me what Paul VI had said to him: 'I'm looking,' said the Holy Father, 'for young theologians who one day can succeed the older ones. I've thought of Hans Küng, but it seems that he has too little love.' I would not say that he lacks love for either Christ or the church; indeed he loves them passionately, but not in the same way as Paul VI and not – if I may be allowed to say so – in the same way as I do. Küng's love of the church and Christ is expressed in his concern for absolute honesty to history and the needs of the time. That is behind his study. It

moves him to formulate the expectation and hopes of the grass roots and then take up the painful questions of the Reformation and modern criticism.

Church of God, my mother, what are you doing with this difficult child, my brother?[25]

A case for politics: consensus of the parties

Whereas the Christian Democrat Federal President Helmut Kohl, with whom I had had such friendly conversations, shrouds himself in diplomatic silence, the Federal President of the Free Democrats and Foreign Minister, Hans-Dietrich Genscher, speaks out quite plainly at his party's top-level meeting in Stuttgart: 'The Education Minister of this state – the homeland of Schiller, Hegel, Kepler, Melanchthon and Hölderlin – could bring clarity with one remark; he could say that whatever the Vatican decides in its responsibility for the training of priests, Professor Küng will remain in Tübingen. The Federal Republic of Germany is a liberal state. Here freedom of scholarship and not the domination of dogma prevails. We are not talking about a dispute but about mutual respect in questions of faith.' With all due respect to the right of the church to set its own criteria for its servants and for its members, the state cannot and may not 'allow the criteria of the Catholic Church alone to be forced on it in dealing with its professors'.[26]

And whereas the Prime Minister of the state of Baden-Württemberg, Lothar Späth, at first in an ill-informed and unthinking way adopts the bishop's position, the Christian Democrat Party leader in the Baden-Württemberg parliament, Erwin Teufel, a theologically well-educated Catholic in the spirit of Vatican II, is critical of the Roman decision from the start. On 18 January 1980 he visits me in Tübingen with his press spokesman Hans Georg Koch. During a working lunch we discuss the theological, legal and political aspects of the case thoroughly. As it ends he assures me that as representative of the majority party in the parliament he will ensure that there isn't a 'political' but a constitutional solution here. Only now does it become clear to me what connotations the word 'political' can have. The previous day, 17 January 1980, my conversation with the Minister of Science and Art of the state of Baden-Württemberg, Professor Helmut Engler, which he had long wanted and which was now safeguarded by the university, took place in Stuttgart, though I wasn't sure whether he himself wasn't aspiring to a 'political solution'. It did me good afterwards to drink a glass of wine with the Catholic dean of Stuttgart, Erwin Sommer, who had taken such a bold public stand on my behalf.

At the instigation of the Social Democrat party a debate takes place in the Baden-Württemberg parliament on 30 January 1980 because, as the party argues, the delicate balance of church and state is being endangered by the Roman intervention. The Social Democrat spokesman, Roland Hahn, states: 'To part with Hans Küng would not only be an irreplaceable loss for teaching bodies, students and scholarship in this faculty, it would also be complete submission on the part of the state to the claim of the Holy See to have not only the first word in the occupation of professorial posts – on appointment – but also the last – on dismissal.'[27] Catholic faculties would then be reduced to the function of being outposts of priests' seminaries. The twofold task of the faculty of being an official church institution and a scholarly theological institution would be lost. Teaching at the faculty of Catholic theology must go on – with Hans Küng.

The chairman of the Christian Democrats, Erwin Teufel, emphasizes that both the principle of religious freedom (Article 4 of the Basic Law) and the ideological neutrality of the state and the principle of freedom of research and teaching (Article 5 of the Basic Law) need to be observed: 'It is a matter of dispute whether according to the Concordat law the exclusion of Professor Küng from the faculty is necessary or whether it is possible for him to remain with a special status. We support the Social Democrat motion to request the state government in good time to inform the standing committee of its assessment of the legal situation and the regulations intended.'[28] The spokesman of the Free Democrats, Heinrich Enderlein, speaks in the same vein, so it becomes clear that there is an amazing consensus between the parties in my case.

Ecclesiastical constitutional lawyers

Science Minister Engler assures me that after conversations with me, Bishop Moser and the University President Adolf Theis he will commission an external constitutional lawyer to work out a legal opinion which all concerned could acknowledge. That sounds convincing. But the Achilles heel of the legal opinion soon becomes clear to me: the external lawyer is the well-known constitutional lawyer Professor Ulrich Scheuner, who is unquestionably a specialist in church and state law, but is known to have served the Nazis faithfully in the Third Reich. As early as 1934, in a major article he had justified the legitimacy and legality of the Nazi seizure of power and their departure from the principles of the liberal constitutional state. As a loyal Nazi party member he defended the overcoming of individualism by the notion of community and people. After the war he had every reason to offer himself to the churches, which he helped with various opinions. I am told that I can't expect any opinion in my favour from him. Moreover the opinion wouldn't in fact be worked out by the professor himself, who retired in 1972, but by a Jesuit with the telling name of Fr Listl, who has often undertaken such commissions in the service of the nunciature and the conference of bishops. So I can't count on any unpartisan opinion.

Because I am well aware that the Roman Catholic hierarchy can employ whatever advocates, financial and legal means it wishes, at an early stage I have already looked for my own adviser specializing in Concordat and university law. I find him in Dr Dietrich Bahls of Heidelberg, who subsequently advises me on all legal steps and drafts the important letter to the ministry. I gladly accept that my survival at the University of Tübingen will cost me a sum running into five figures in Deutschemarks. We meet in Tübingen on various occasions and telephone each other.

I also make a special journey to Speyer, where Professor Helmut Quaritsch teaches at the highly-respected German College for Administrative Sciences; he is almost the only really critical specialist on questions of state–church law. He draws my attention to my precarious situation. There are only a few specialists in the discipline. Just as the few advocates in energy law usually have to write legal opinions for electricity companies, so most advocates in state–church law have to write legal opinions for church institutions. Therefore I can't expect that colleagues who mostly work for the church hierarchy and constantly support it with opinions will be in favour of a theologian who has been blackened by the hierarchy as 'rebellious'.

This description of the situation in the discipline is evidently so black that when my case is discussed in the Greater Senate of the University the Tübingen state–church lawyer bellows in fury: how dare I make this comment? However, this involuntarily confirms that not a single state–church lawyer supports me. That the same state–church lawyer doesn't mind defaming Professor Quaritsch personally (he lives on the edge of the forest and is guarded by dogs) shows me the 'legal' means with which lawyers can argue in cases of injustice.

Before the debate in the state parliament I had presented my view of the legal situation to the Minister of Science and Art in a long letter.[29] With many references to documents I was able to demonstrate:

- that the Roman decree of 14 December 1979 had not been preceded by any orderly procedure;
- that I had been given no opportunity to express myself on the most recent proceedings;
- that Bishop Moser had drawn the attention of the Prefect of the Congregation for the Doctrine of the Faith to the serious error in proceedings both on the telephone and in writing from Brussels but had withheld this letter from the public and continued to do so;
- that in the end Bishop Moser did not withdraw the *missio* of his own free will but only on instructions from Rome.

From all this I conclude than it is an 'abuse of the stipulations of the Concordat that in the case pending the bishop acted as the executive organ of the Roman Curia. The basis of Concordat law is that the bishops have to act by virtue of their own responsibility and their own law.'[30] Therefore I ask the minister to examine the legitimacy of the proceedings: 'A clarification seems to me to be the prerequisite for seeing whether the state must accede to the request of the Bishop of Rottenburg-Stuttgart at all.'[31] What the Roman Catholic hierarchy regards as legitimate for the sphere of the church can by no means be the criterion for state law. A brief version of this letter to the minister, without mentioning all the legal details, also goes to all the delegates of the Baden-Württemberg parliament.[32] I am content with the debate there. But an ominous development awaits me in Tübingen.

Betrayal by the Seven

So far the unanimous solidarity of the faculty with me, already demonstrated impressively on 18 December 1979 and confirmed by a further resolution on 10 January 1980, has held despite all church pressures. However, I don't know what has been going on behind the scenes between Rottenburg and Tübingen. Be this as it may, on the morning of 1 February 1980, two days after the Württemberg parliament debate, Professors Auer, Lohfink and Reinhardt present themselves to me and disclose the intention of some colleagues to make their own statement to the public. In view of the ongoing negotiations and the long letter to Bishop Moser which is being worked out I beg them urgently to dissociate themselves from it.

In the afternoon of 1 February 1980 there is a faculty meeting and afterwards – Herbert Haag's retirement is imminent – a 'farewell supper' in the Haag house. The mood is very tense. I detect coolness, animosity, indeed hostility towards me in some colleagues. People feel strong and make me, the 'star' of the faculty, whom for a long time they couldn't touch, aware of my weaknesses. After all, they know that they have the bishop, 'Rome', the 'church' behind them. Most shameless is a question from one particular colleague who, although he has been ordained priest, as professor has never performed the least priestly function, preached or presided at the eucharist. Why do I attach such great importance to being a Catholic theologian, he asks me. Shaking with anger, I say to him that it is because I had been working as a Catholic theologian in the Catholic faculty long before him. A deeply depressing evening.

This meeting doesn't bode well, but it doesn't prevent me from going to Ulm next morning. I am given an enthusiastic welcome at a big meeting of several hundred teachers of religion. They zealously use my books for teaching religion, which isn't easy today, when only thorough, honest and understandable information helps. If only they, the teachers of religion, their pupils and the people in the parishes, had the vote! But in the hierarchy, which again presents itself as 'the church', there is hardly any talk of the 'people of God' in the sense of Vatican II.

The farewell lecture by my colleague and friend Herbert Haag, *Ordinarius* Professor of Old Testament Exegesis, who is now 65, had long been planned for 4 February 1980 on the topic 'The Distinctive Value of the Old Testament'. Immediately before the ceremonial occasion I receive a telephone message from the President of the University, Adolf Theis, asking me to look in at the

Rectorate on my way, as he has an important message to give me. Professor Walter Kasper and two other faculty colleagues have just paid him a visit.

When I enter the Rector's room the President tells me without beating about the bush that he has sad information to give me. The next morning an extended statement from seven of my colleagues in the faculty will appear in the *Frankfurter Allgemeine Zeitung* and the *Schwäbisches Tagblatt*; in it, in a disguised but clear way, they will argue that I should be excluded from the faculty of Catholic Theology.[33] This is a betrayal which shakes me deeply. All seven were once called to the faculty with my vote. Unfortunately they now form a majority in the twelve-member faculty. The photograph taken in the Festsaal immediately after the lecture shows me beside Professor Haag, my face marked with deep disappointment. Professor Greinacher, who with Dean Bartholomäus, Professors Haag and Lang, and me forms the minority of five against the Seven, had wagered only a couple of weeks beforehand that if it came to the crunch all eleven colleagues would back me.

And indeed why shouldn't I rely on these seven colleagues (to suppress their names would provoke false speculations):

the New Testament scholar Gerhard Lohfink, also an advocate of historical–critical exegesis, who could always speak so convincingly about Jesus and his message of the kingdom of God;

the *Ordinarius* Professor of Early Church History Hermann Josef Vogt, to whom so many cases of 'heretics' falsely accused are known;

the *Ordinarius* Professor of Modern Church History Rudolf Reinhart, who remarkably had given a precise description of the shift of power in the nineteenth-century faculty from the enlightened 'Tübingen school' to the school more orientated on Rome;

the philosopher Ludger Oeing-Hanhoff, who had so often spoken solemnly about the modern history of freedom;

the fundamental theologian Max Seckler, who had written his own short work on the Tübingen dogmatic theologian Wilhelm Koch, unjustly disciplined at the beginning of the twentieth century;

the theological ethicist Alfons Auer, who had argued in a pioneering way against traditional moral theology and for an autonomous ethic;

the dogmatic theologian Walter Kasper, who had been my assistant. I had been a key figure in collaborating in his habilitation and call to Tübingen and had worked well with him for so many years.

Why might I not have expected that these seven colleagues would also stand at my side in the hour of need?

But 'a friend in need is a friend indeed', says the proverb. And evidently the pressure from the church hierarchy – four of the seven belong to the diocese of Rottenburg and are on familiar terms with the bishop – has become so strong that they have resolved on this fatal step. How far personal resentment, above all envy, played a part in the case of individual members can only be guessed. Once the bishop had definitively withdrawn the *missio* on 30 December, there was an unexpected change of mind among these Catholic theologians, which is now documented in the press. And what a document!

'Grovelling, obsequiousness, slimy covering up'

Hardly ever has a declaration by professors at my University of Tübingen sparked off so much indignation. This convoluted and involved text, dressed up with many compliments, seems to me to be deeply mendacious from beginning to end. Of course the Seven, too, don't present any proof of the infallibility of Pope and bishops. The sub-headings of their declaration could all have been in support of me, but are now directed against me, their colleague, and sound scornful: 'How Christians deal with one another' – 'The question of truth alone gives the dispute its value and its seriousness' – 'It is concerned throughout with the freedom of theology' – 'The theological faculties in danger' ... As if I and not the Roman intervention and its episcopal instruments – to take up only the last sub-heading – were bringing the theological faculties at state universities into disrepute.

Be this as it may; there is no sign among these colleagues now of the substantive reservations they had expressed earlier. On the contrary, the Roman penal measure is interpreted as 'the magisterium's call to the cause'. The accusation of the Roman Congregation for the Doctrine of the Faith is taken over word for word, thus insinuating that I am a theologian who 'presents his own judgement and not the church's sense of the faith as the norm of the truth (cf. *Declaratio* of 15 December 1979)' and who thus 'arrogates to himself the supreme teaching authority in the church'. This is a lie of the first order.

I find this adoption of the attitudes and statements imputed to me in the Roman declaration deeply depressing in its untruth. But what is politically and legally fatal is that the Seven decide in the negative what had still been deliberately left open in the faculty resolution of 10 January 1980: 'Anyone who allows or wishes a theologian without a *missio canonica* to belong to a theological faculty in the long term,' it is now said, 'undermines its scholarly status and its guarantee under constitutional and concordat law.' Who is 'undermining' what here?

It is immediately clear to me that this public declaration by the Catholic professors has destroyed any basis for my remaining in this faculty.[34] The investigative process of *missio*-free status for me within the faculty has been nipped in the bud. The Seven have throttled it without giving it a chance. To the present day in Catholic circles the assertion of the Seven is bandied around that had I remained, the faculty would have been 'closed' or 'dissolved' by Rome; the Seven have 'saved' it. That's nonsense. As if the Vatican had such power over a German state university faculty and had embarked on a trial of strength between state and church!

491

The public immediately sees through the manoeuvre. The *Schwäbisches Tagblatt* of the same day, 5 February 1980, writes: 'Küng's defence in the university crumbles. No *missio*, not in the faculty. Predominant majority for the exclusion of the theologian.' And the *Südwestpresse* of 6 February writes: 'Seven of Küng's colleagues organize a theological ostracism. Deep rift in the faculty – Dean passed over – negotiations with the state destroyed.' Under the headline 'Stabbed in the Back' the *Schwäbisches Tagblatt* of 6 February comments: 'It is impossible to understand how it is the task of a majority of the *ordinarius* professors of a faculty – a "qualified majority", one would say in another context – to stab a colleague in the back with a lengthy declaration. The text of the statement makes it clear that their job is dealing with words. The seven *ordinarius* professors are scribes enough to formulate clear statements in an ambiguous way. As could be read yesterday in this paper these statements are made in general terms (or rather in a tortuous explanation) and for the sake of balance the other side is treated decently; infamous thrusts are wrapped up in such a way that it can be said afterwards that this wasn't what was meant. Banalities are formulated which any reasonable person could subscribe to, the content of which has little to do with the concrete case and occasion – but in the specific context quite deliberate positions can be recognized. When the institutional Catholic Church withdrew the *missio* from Küng it was often pointed out that one should not confuse the official church with the church. There is now occasion to point out that the faculty must not be confused with seven *ordinarius* professors, even if the seven seem to do this in their malicious trick.'[35]

What next? The Dean recalls the joint faculty resolution of 10 January and complains that he and the rest of his colleagues hadn't even been consulted. A letter from the students, academic counsellors and assistants of the faculty of Catholic theology opposes the Seven. On 7 February 1980 the Senate of the University of Tübingen passes a resolution in which it requests the Presidium to take all possible and legitimate steps to make possible a compromise between the sides involved in the 'Küng case' and allow 'Professor Küng to remain a full member of the faculty of Catholic theology for the long term ... The Senate asks the members of the university and all those involved not to make any more public statements on the case (unless these are needed for an immediate refutation of public statements by a third party) in order not to endanger the possible success of the efforts.'[36]

So as not to have to discuss with my colleagues at this level, I drop my last lecture in this eventful winter semester of 1979/80. I've had enough. But the historian Professor Christoph Weber of Düsseldorf speaks to my heart. The *Ordinarius* Professor of Modern Church History, now one of the Seven, had proposed that he should be invited to give a guest lecture at the faculty of Catholic theology of the University of Tübingen. However, on 6 February 1980 Weber sends the following telegram to the dean of the faculty: 'Of all the documents of nineteenth- and twentieth-century church history that I know, today's declaration by the seven Tübingen professors is the most shameful. The grovelling, obsequiousness, slimy covering up here is unprecedented in its form. The tortuous manoeuvring with its fussy concern bears witness to only one thing: cowardice and hypocrisy. So of course I cannot give my lecture now.'[37]

The student commitment is encouraging in all these disappointments. The theological tutors under Norbert Kunze produce an extensive documentation under the title 'Ideas, Information, Suggestions for an Objective Discussion' and on 11 February 1980 send it to the Secretary of the Conference of Bishops, Dr Josef Homeyer, in Bonn. Homeyer doesn't reply until 14 April, countering the charges very sharply and going over to vigorous attacks. But he does invite a delegation of the group for a conversation to Bonn, even though that doesn't take place until 11 June 1980 and produces no positive results. The negative consequence is that subsequently only one of the student members of this team is accepted into church service; the others are rejected for threadbare reasons.[38]

Pressure on the press

The Roman Catholic hierarchy of the Federal Republic of Germany has tremendous power in three respects: 1. legally, on the basis of the Concordat with Hitler which continues to apply and is constantly interpreted in favour of the church; 2. financially, on the basis of the billions in tax contributed every year by the state; 3. politically, on the basis of the countless relations with personalities of the state, the parties, business. Can an individual do anything against this?

Those concerned wisely keep silent about what pressure the Bishop of Rottenburg puts on individual members of the Tübingen faculty, above all on members of his diocese of Rottenburg and his friends. But I am well aware of the pressure which for example he put on the local Tübingen and Rottenburg paper *Schwäbisches Tagblatt*. In January 1980 I am struck by the change in tone and tendency of this paper. So far, as has been evident, in all evaluations of the bishop's statements it has taken the side of my academic freedom to teach and research. Now it is clearly guarding against taking sides with me directly and instead is disseminating the episcopal version. What has happened? Only about two decades later does the publisher and chief editor of the *Schwäbisches Tagblatt*, the notorious non-conformist Christoph Müller, tells me how at that time the Bishop of Rottenburg telephoned him and brutally threatened that he would call for a public boycott of the paper unless the tendency of the reporting changed. That helped; it changed.

To give another example, I have never discovered why the then Tübingen dpa correspondent (who lived near Rottenburg) was initially for a long time grateful for the slightest news from me, and indeed often came to my house, but suddenly wasn't seen again and hardly ever heard. Even complaints from the editorial headquarters in Hamburg about a lack of reporting produced no change. I can only presume that the arm of the 'sacred rule', the 'hierarchy', is long.

The attitude of the *Frankfurter Allgemeine Zeitung*, which was well-disposed to me for so long, and for which on various occasions I had written whole-page articles, changes markedly. In the decisive week I have the doubtful satisfaction of reading all four papers with a circulation beyond the region in connection with my affair: the *Frankfurter Allgemeine Zeitung*, the *Süddeutsche Zeitung*, *Die Welt* and the *Frankfurter Rundschau*. It soon strikes me how the attitude of the *Frankfurter Allgemeine Zeitung* towards me has become negative. It begins with the formulation of headlines to my disadvantage and the placing of the articles, goes on to the space given to statements by the hierarchy, and ends with verdicts which uncritically adopt the bishops' position.

I will probably never learn what a scholar will one day investigate, namely what went on behind the scenes of the *Frankfurter Allgemeine Zeitung*; what episcopal or Roman authorities influence the publishers or editors, what editors (there is talk of a 'Catholic trio' which makes this originally thoroughly liberal paper increasingly a Catholic paper in disguise) cut back Protestant influence and in later years make the features section virtually a nest for Opus Dei sympathizers. In the future people will attack my contributions with malice or polemic, ignore me wherever possible and in any case minimize me to my disadvantage. Will *Der Spiegel* also follow suit?

Not on the side of the avalanche

Public interest in the outcome of the struggle has by no means died down after the discussion in the Stuttgart parliament. I hear from the editors of *Der Spiegel* that they are planning a 'personality story' on Hans Küng which, since the editor envisaged for it has already devoted a malicious and tendentious article to me in connection with *Does God Exist?*, could be a somewhat ambiguous affair. I could have done without it!

On the spur of the moment, on 7 February 1980 I telephone the *Spiegel* publisher Rudolf Augstein. He is now definitely no longer a Roman Catholic. As an ex-Catholic, in the earlier stages of the controversy he had adopted a very simple standpoint in a *Spiegel* article – in practice self-justification: either one remains in this church, in which case one must also subscribe to all that it prescribes and practises, or one doesn't go along with all this and leaves. In so doing he is calling not only for me to leave the church, but also all the millions of Catholics who all over the world don't agree with present Roman teaching and politics and yet don't want to give up their church. Rudolf Augstein didn't emigrate from the Federal Republic of Germany simply because he didn't agree with the Adenauer government, but engaged in loyal opposition. However, he could object that the Federal Republic was a democratic country with regular elections, whereas the Catholic Church is a quasi-totalitarian system without any possibility of democratic correction.

But I don't want to argue with Augstein about that now. Rather, I tell him on the telephone that I am already having enough difficulties with the Roman colossus and I don't think it right that *Der Spiegel*, which in other respects stands for liberalism, should also attack me from the rear. Augstein shows understanding and says: 'When an avalanche descends on someone, one shouldn't really be on the side of the avalanche.' In short, he cancels the 'personality story'. It was thanks to him that this weekly had supported my efforts at reform in the Catholic Church for a long time, but (like me) was disappointed by certain reactionary developments in Vatican II under Paul VI, and then resumed a strictly anti-Catholic orientation. Without the support of the *Frankfurter Allgemeine Zeitung* on the right and *Der Spiegel* on the left I will have a difficult time in the German press landscape.

A 'true novel'?

Things are quite different with a 'personality story' of another kind. The Australian best-selling author Morris West, whose novel about the Pope, *In the Shoes of the Fisherman* (1963), has found countless enthusiastic readers in many languages and has been filmed with Anthony Quinn, telephones me from Australia on 6 February. He wants to visit me in Tübingen to discuss a project with me. At dinner at the Krone Hotel he explains to me that in this controversy I have reached the point where I have said all that can be said in my defence and I can no longer defend myself. He is ready to do this by writing a 'true novel'.

It's a noble offer. I thank Morris West warmly for his sympathy and readiness to help. I have to confess to him that I am finding it increasingly difficult to defend myself and keep repeating the same argument. The dispute is now being carried on at very different levels and with very different weapons.

At the theological level: how am I to keep repeating my questions about Vatican I and at the same time emphasize that I am and want to remain a Catholic theologian?

At the legal level: I have already demonstrated often enough the undeniable defects in the Roman proceedings.

At the political level: haven't I already mobilized all the forces that can be mobilized in my cause, and isn't the institutional church increasingly using its diverse possibilities to exert pressure along with its media opportunities?

On the other hand, how is an Australian, however intelligent and gifted, to study and understand all the involved theological and legal documents written not in English but in Latin and German, even if he has many of them translated, as he intends? And it isn't easy even for a theologian to see through all the problems. Despite a degree of attractiveness, a 'true novel' of the kind that Morris West plans doesn't seem to me the right way to defend me and my standpoint. I don't want to go down in church history as a character in a novel. Of course Morris

West is disappointed that I can't agree to his plan; later he will write a novel in which a Tübingen theologian plays a role in another context. But who can help me in this wretched situation? Do I still have friends in the hierarchy?

Weak episcopal friends

One expects more from some than from others. And there was something that pained me more than the signatures of all the other Swiss bishops. As suffragan bishop of the diocese of Basle, Otto Wüst, my boyhood friend from Sursee, with whom I first worked for years in the Jungwacht and with whom I had studied for seven years in the German College, for whose return to Rome after a stay in a Swiss hospital I had fought with the Rector, and with whom I had planned to set out on my second world trip, sealed my condemnation with his signature. Just as the German generals swore a solemn oath to the Führer, so on his consecration every bishop to the present day swears a solemn oath to the Pope – in both cases without any reservations and even against his better judgement and conscience. Refusal to obey is a serious matter.

So what am I to do when our common mentor Pastor Franz Xaver Kaufmann telephones from Switzerland and says that he and Otto Wüst would like to visit me in Tübingen? Of course I say yes, and the two of them come on Saturday 12 January 1980. Otto asks for my forgiveness and attempts to explain his betrayal of our friendship. But I can't listen to such explanations for long; they don't convince me and are extremely embarrassing. I quickly say, 'All right, Otto. Everything's back to normal.' Forgiving isn't a matter of psychological understanding, which of course I have for a bishop who so conforms to the system. Nor does forgiveness consist in forgetting; one can never forget anything like this. In good biblical terms, forgiveness consists in 'not imputing guilt', drawing a line so that all is well again. We are once again good friends and remain so until the last phase of his life. Otto Wüst becomes Bishop of Basle and as *episcopus emeritus*, with severely impaired health and psychologically often depressed (especially before visits to Rome), returns to our birthplace of Sursee. We meet in my lake house, as we have done so often, for a good fish meal with good Swiss wine and talk of past times – until finally on 19 August 2002 he dies quietly of his last illness in the hospital, almost in sight of my house.

Another case is Cardinal Johannes Willebrands, President of the Roman Secretariat for Unity. He had invited me as a young doctor of theology at the end of the 1950s in Warmond in the Netherlands to address him in the familiar second person and accepted me into the 'Ecumenical Conference' which he had initiated. There, as I report in *My Struggle for Freedom*, I got to know all the important ecumenical theologians of the Catholic Church. Most of the members and advisers of the Vatican Secretariat for Unity are taken from this circle. I didn't for a moment hold it against my friend that he passed me over. No one doubted my competence. But at that time the Swiss member of the Secretariat, Johannes Feiner, a good theologian and an equally good diplomat, had thought that I could disrupt any commission. He then himself left the new Pontifical Theological Commission with Karl Rahner when they saw that it was being manipulated by the Doctrinal Congregation.

I too can be a diplomat when it comes to strategy and tactics, but when it's a matter of the truth I am undiplomatically direct. And certainly I had campaigned energetically with the Secretariat for Unity for the ecumenical problems finally to be tackled and for the recognition of non-Catholic ministries and eucharistic celebrations to be put on the Council agenda. Would that have 'disrupted' the Commission? At that time, when I was invited to dinner with Johannes Willebrands in Rome, I told him that I understood very well that he could no longer do what he wanted, and he gratefully accepted this. One can't expect everything of everyone.

Now in my distress I consider which of my friends among the cardinals I should ask to intervene on my behalf. There can be no question of Cardinal Volk, who has already gone over to the other side; Döpfner of the German College is dead and Höffner is one of my main opponents, as no less is my colleague Ratzinger. Should it be Cardinal König, also formerly of the German College, who once said, 'Pius XII has our respect, John XXIII our love, Paul VI needs our understanding', and now John Paul II perhaps our obedience? But he tends to avoid direct controversy with the Pope. Should it be Cardinal Suenens, who in his famous interview ten years previously had lamented the 'long *via crucis* of our best theologians' (Rahner, Congar, Murray, de Lubac), who 'have been suspect or even condemned' under a former Pope 'so that yesterday's mistakes aren't made tomorrow's'? But he's now 'dropped' church reform and with it the 'reform theologians'.

Then perhaps my old friend Johannes Willebrands? None of my friends in the College of Cardinals or in the episcopate has been in touch. Presumably most of them think that I alone am to blame or don't dare to quarrel with the Pope and Curia. In any case it isn't easy for me simply to plead for help on the telephone. Finally I decide on Willebrands, who as a Curial cardinal is in any case closest to the Pope and is also involved as President of the Secretariat for Unity. I ask him to intervene for me personally with the Pope.

But what does he do? He doesn't have the courage (or the opportunity?) to telephone the Pope or to go to him. Instead he telephones my opponent, the Bishop of Rottenburg, and tells him that a 'former friend', Hans Küng, has telephoned him and asked for his help. But what can he do? Küng must help himself. Bishop Moser, highly delighted, immediately releases this sensational news to the papers: even a 'former friend' such as Cardinal Willebrands has abandoned Küng. This is a victory for the bishop. Deeply disturbed, I can't bring myself to telephone another cardinal. They're all the same, I think, literally 'creatures' of the Roman system. In any case none of the bishops who had studied with me in Rome or with whom I had been at the Council gets in touch with me of his own accord, or any of the cardinals whom I know.

When it's all over, Johannes Willebrands writes to me that he would very much like to visit me in Tübingen. Of course I agree and offer him a room in my house for the night. The cardinal comes and asks his friend for understanding and forgiveness. In a long evening conversation he attempts to make clear to me that the expression 'former friend' was a misunderstanding. But since our very first meeting in 1957 I've known enough Dutch to understand the essential difference between a 'former friend' and an 'old friend'. The first means that a friendship has ended, the second means loyal friendship. But what am I to do? In this case, too, I can't bear to listen to long excuses and explanations: 'All right, Johannes, we remain friends!' We never see each other again.

Willebrands will remain President of the Secretariat for Unity until 1989, but at the same time also function as Archbishop of Utrecht so that a reactionary successor to Cardinal Alfrink isn't appointed. In Rome his main achievement has been the appointment of the papal Commission for Religious Relations with the Jews (1974). Of course I can write to him if I have a small wish, for example a papal audience for my friend and colleague Jürgen Moltmann. But our friendship now consists only in mutual reminiscences. One of his former students tells the cardinal, who is now 93, that he has read *My Struggle for Freedom*, to which the cardinal replies: 'Küng is not only a good acquaintance but also a good friend; I was at his home in Switzerland' (20 April 2004). He dies at the age of 96 as senior member of the College of Cardinals in a monastery in Denekamp in the Netherlands on 2 August 2006.

I have the best memories of Willebrands' great achievements in ecumenical matters and above all in achieving a different relationship between the Catholic Church and Judaism before and after the Second Vatican Council. But I am deeply worried. Think what this calm and friendly man, full of goodwill and energy, even as a cardinal (since 1969), could still have done for ecumenical progress had he not been prevented by the Vatican hardliners, above all in the Doctrinal Congregation. In his case it is evident how little even the best man can do once he is caught up in the Roman system. But conversely, it isn't easy to refuse the honours and constraints of the system.

Good Friday mood

I was always more relaxed about the great, quasi-historic controversy with the Vatican than those around me, say in my own faculty. Since after his retirement Herbert Haag will no longer be making his house available for drinks after a faculty meeting, I decide to provide refreshments if they're wanted, and when my house is rebuilt I buy twelve comfortable dining-room chairs, one for each member of our faculty. That they are no longer used for this purpose is only one of the signs of the sad breaking off of collegial relations which have lasted for decades.

It's all hard for me, though from the start I've been blessed with strong physical and psychological health. The constant conversations and negotiations, the wretched study of all the documents and articles against me, all the telephone conversations and all the uncertainty are getting to me. True, the crisis staff at first meets round the table cheerfully almost every day and we drink together the 'Beaujolais primeur' of which I had ordered three dozen bottles when before Christmas my wine merchant in Neckargasse had hinted that perhaps I was forgetting him. Soon I had to order another three dozen. But the meetings, which are increasingly becoming torture for me, get postponed week after week and finally stop altogether.

The controversies in the faculty are visibly a strain. A compromise paper worked out by Walter Jens is rejected by the Seven on 11 February. Then there are again long discussions about a letter to Bishop Moser, which are concluded on 13 February. Another faculty meeting is fixed for the afternoon. Malicious scenes are again to be expected. We four colleagues who remain still have the Seven as a front against us. An hour before the meeting I have unusually severe pains around my heart and have to lie on the sofa. My secretary makes my apologies for missing the meeting, and a doctor friend is called. He wisely and soberly thinks that he should really give me a medical certificate, but in the present political situation that's not on, so I get medication.

And then there are the media, whose support I urgently need against the church machine; truly, I have now spoken to enough journalists, made use of every possible agency, given numerous interviews all over the world. Bishop Moser was right in his prediction of the international repercussions of the Roman action. But when I'm asked, I still don't know what my future will be. Can I stay at the University of Tübingen or must I fight through a hearing before the Constitutional Court in Karlsruhe? Or must I simply emigrate? I can usually get back to work quickly, but given all the uncertainties not even work therapy helps.

I feel so wretched that I don't even want company, to whom I have to talk about the whole wretched affair. So I even avoid Rotary meetings. And when I'm invited by one of my best Tübingen friends, Marianne Saur's brother Dieter, to a fine dinner for six at a restaurant in Bebenhausen near Tübingen, I, who in any situation am hardly lost for words, can't bring myself to utter a single sentence the whole evening. I sit silently throughout the whole meal, shocked at myself.

Evidently I've reached my psychological and physical limits. If I've not been forsaken by everyone, have I perhaps been forsaken by God? I need tablets to sleep. My opponents would be delighted to see me like this. It's finally wiped him out! I can't deny it. I'm exhausted, completely exhausted. I'm incapable of going on repeating the same thing time and again and also incapable of creating anything new. I've done all I could, I've given everything I had. I can't take on anything else. So is my power of resistance defeated?

Chance has it that the last revision of these pages in 2007 falls on Good Friday. I don't want to experience this sorry time of powerlessness and exhaustion again. And I've often thought, 'They know not what they do ...' Or do they? Some years later the moral theologian Alfons Auer, one of the Seven, unexpectedly sends me a postcard of a late medieval window of the Tübingen Stiftskirche, so to speak as an apology. I sometimes seem to him like the man on the wheel depicted here, who after all his limbs have been broken has been put on show on the wheel. Those were truly fearful times. But I don't want to exaggerate; after all, I hadn't been forsaken by my fellow men and women or – as only later becomes clear to me – by God.

Not the end

What helped me to get back on my feet after this manifest failure? What were my spiritual resources? I hadn't forgotten how to pray, but it was comfortless and I felt an inner void. What restored me were the thousands who had visibly, audibly and tangibly taken a stand for me. When with my friends Walter Jens, Herbert Haag, Norbert Greinacher, Hermann Häring and Karl-Josef Kuschel I made the decision to produce a 'documentation' and I then read the hundreds of statements in my favour and all the letters in my support, I again slowly found strength, the more as time went on. No, you can't leave them all in the lurch, you mustn't give up. Pull yourself together, we'll see, a battle may have been lost but not the war. I get to work now on our documentation, in which in well over 500 pages one can read and examine the documents leading up to the crisis and the withdrawal of my permission to teach, the statements by groups and institutions, by theological faculties and specialist groups and important individuals. The excellent editors are Norbert Greinacher and Herbert Haag.[39]

From then on things look up. Moreover, even in total exhaustion I haven't for a moment doubted the truth that I have to represent. On the contrary, while I'm aware of my capacity to be wrong, I also know that my opponents haven't demonstrated any error in me, but only shown their power. And if the historical Peter, too, didn't prove infallible and didn't 'walk in the truth of the gospel', one was allowed, indeed commanded, like Paul in the scene in Antioch which Rome keeps quiet about in liturgy as in life, 'to oppose him to his face' (Galatians 2.11-14). However, there wasn't a Paul in the whole episcopate.

For me, none of these are *ad hoc* tactical considerations but fundamental reflections, which I had already developed as a theologian at the Council and set down in the penultimate chapter of my book *The Church*, under the title 'The Petrine power and the Petrine ministry'. It had struck me at the time that in the Bible, a reproof by Jesus has been added to each of the statements cited by Rome as proof of a 'primacy' of Peter. Matthew 16.18 is followed by Matthew 16.22f., 'Get behind me, Satan! You are an obstacle in my path, because you are thinking not as God thinks but as human beings do.' Luke 22.32 is followed by Luke 22.34, 'I tell you, Peter, by the time the cock crows today you will have denied three times that you know me.' And John 21.15 is followed by John 21.20ff.: 'What does it matter to you? You are to follow me.'

So already at that time I had written what now has become existentially very important to me:

> It is doubtful whether Peter would have recognized himself in the picture that was to be drawn of him. Not only because he was no prince of the apostles, but remained to the end of his life the modest fisherman, now a fisher of men, who wanted to follow and serve his Lord. But much more because he had another side, which all the gospels agree upon, a side which shows us the truly human Peter, misunderstanding, making mistakes, failing his Lord. It is little short of scandalizing that each of the three texts classically used to prove the precedence of Peter are accompanied in counterpoint by three passages, the dark tones of which balance, if not obscure, the bright tones of the three Petrine texts. The three great promises are balanced by three serious failures. Anyone who wishes to base his claims upon the promises cannot avoid applying to himself the three failures, which at least represent three possible temptations. And if the promises in large black letters on a golden background surround the church of St Peter like a frieze, it would be only right, to avoid misunderstandings, to add to them the three contrary incidents in golden letters on a black background. Gregory the Great at least, who is buried in the church, would surely have understood that as well as John XXIII.[40]

The confrontation has now lasted two months, and the outcome is still uncertain. After all that has happened, I am nevertheless able after the end of the semester to go on the trip to Egypt with our faculty which had been planned many months previously for the period between 15 February and 1 March under the leadership of our eminent Egyptologist Helmut Brunner. Before our departure I am asked whether I would prefer not to go because some of the Seven will be going. My answer is clear: if anyone has reason to stay at home it is the Seven and not I. I have a good knowledge of Greco-Roman culture, and for some years I've wanted to make closer acquaintance with the grandiose culture of the country by the Nile which preceded it.

In fact only two of the Seven come. However, when we arrive in Cairo I am able to visit only the pyramids and the rich Cairo museum. Then I have to retire to bed. Unfortunately I have to cry off the flight to Abu Simbel to see the great temple of Ramses II. But I recover for the flight to Asswan and also travel in the bus to Luxor and Thebes, then to Dendera, Abydos and Karnak and finally back to Cairo. These are incomparable experiences which I can't go into here. On 1 March we are back in Tübingen. In the meantime my letter had been sent to the

Bishop of Rottenburg. And again the question arises: how do we get out of this whole mess?

Last attempt at mediation

Even after the change of position by the Seven on 5 February, the efforts at mediation between the University President Adolf Theis, Bishop Moser, Minister Engler and me continue. President Theis has made special efforts to resolve the conflict. He persuades me to write yet another letter to Bishop Moser, who hasn't contacted me in all the weeks since his return from Rome. Understandably I have little desire to do this. But the President thinks that a renewal of contact from my side could serve as the basis for an agreement.

So I change my position and in a 26-page document dated 12 February 1980[41] I declare myself ready to accept a proposal by the Rottenburg diocesan council 'to collaborate in proceedings of the German Conference of Bishops aimed at an objective clarification of my theological position on infallibility and christology, as is provided for by the "Order for proceedings over a complaint about doctrine by the German Conference of Bishops" of 1 January 1973. Until the conclusion of these proceedings the legal consequences of the withdrawal of the *missio* should remain suspended as they have been so far. To promote clarification of the situation and to relax the tension in the university situation I would be prepared to ask the Minister of Science and Art for a research semester.'[42]

Bishop Georg Moser makes positive comments on this letter to President Theis. But between 24 and 28 February 1980 the spring general assembly of the German Conference of Bishops takes place in Vierzehnheiligen. And as I have already experienced more than once, put under pressure by the strong man Cardinal Joseph Höffner and other bishops who appeal to Rome, Moser gives way. Before I receive an answer from the bishop, immediately after the end of the conference on 28 February, Cardinal Höffner tells journalists in Cologne that my letter has not clarified 'the decisive point'. So there is the same obstinate attitude and the observation that the Roman proceedings are 'not so bad', though they could be improved. However, proceedings at the conference of bishops cannot be opened, because the matter will be dealt with in Rome. So all the efforts of the University President, the diocesan bishop and me are in vain.

After our return from Egypt it becomes clear that this last mediating action has also failed. On 1 March Bishop Moser composes a formal letter to me, the content of which largely corresponds with Höffner's statements.[43] One factor in the unwillingness of the German episcopate to give way, as Bishop Moser indicates, is that, as was to be expected, the opinion in state–church law by the former Nazi sympathizer and now pious churchman Professor Scheuner of Bonn, or his minion Listl, called for by the minister, requires my removal from the faculty of Catholic theology and my transfer to another university post. So why should the hierarchy with the 'law' behind it come even a millimetre to meet me? Their law gives them the power to get rid of me.

In a reply to Bishop Moser of 13 May I express my disappointment at his negative response and once again work to answer the theological and legal questions which have been thrown up. But this is really to be the last time I bother about long letters to bishops which don't achieve anything at all. Moreover my seven colleagues, unimpressed by all the efforts at mediation even by Dean Bartholomäus and Professor Greinacher, stand by their declaration of 5 February, so that by now the originally strong common basis for my continued presence in the faculty of Catholic theology has finally crumbled. I can't expect to have the church's permission to teach restored in the foreseeable future. It is imperatively brought home to me that I must change my strategy. What does that mean?

Voluntary departure instead of being thrown out

In several constructive conversations with President Theis and his colleagues a solution internal to the university is worked out: instead of being driven out of my faculty or shifted elsewhere I myself will suggest to the university that my chair and the Institute for Ecumenical Research should be separated from the faculty of Catholic theology. Until my *missio canonica* is possibly restored, the chair and the Institute will be directly under the President and Senate of the university.

This is an unheard-of innovation for the bi-confessional German university system: a chair of Christian theology which isn't connected with either a Catholic or a Protestant faculty. In legal terms it can only be justified as 'provisional'. However, one knows from politics how long provisional can mean. Be this as it may, in this way at least my freedom to research and teach guaranteed by the constitution, along with the functioning of the Institute for Ecumenical Research, is guaranteed by the university.

On 19 March 1980 – which happens to be my fifty-second birthday – President Theis sends me four copies of the agreed letter in which the university solution is described prior to negotiations. Above all to safeguard the possibility of doctorates and habilitations for my pupils and colleagues – which is essential for freedom of research and teaching – on 24 March I send President Theis a lengthy reply,[44] which contains a retrospect on developments within the faculty. The declaration of the Seven on 5 February and the rejection of my compromise proposal of 12 February by the bishop on 11 March have forced on me consequences which I deeply regret but which are unavoidable: 'Publicly I have never left any doubt that I still understand myself to be a Catholic theologian and in this sense will work for the renewal of my Catholic Church. I have assured you, Herr President, that I am ready to make my contribution to an agreed solution within the framework of the university.'[45] However, an indispensable prerequisite is 'that my right to collaborate without hindrance in the doctorates and habilitations of my pupils and colleagues remains guaranteed'.[46] The seminar certificates obtained in the Institute for Ecumenical Research are to continue to be recognized by the faculty as before.

Before the final step by the university it is necessary to discover whether a change in Bishop Moser's attitude is to be expected on the basis of my letter to him of 13 March. However, a letter which is brought to my home the next day by a messenger from the bishop[47] doesn't show even a minimal readiness for compromise. Time and again there are the same accusations, time and again the readiness for 'bridge-building' which has been announced verbally and also bandied around in public, which must seem contemptuous, given the bridges which the bishop himself has demolished.

For precisely twenty years I have belonged to the faculty of Catholic theology of the University of Tübingen and have joined in all the joys and sorrows, all the appointments and nominations of those who are now to decide my fate in this faculty. We are in the period in 1980 between winter and summer semesters which is free of lectures. Time presses, since if there isn't to be a risk of student demonstrations on my behalf a decision has to be made on my status before lectures resume in the middle of April. For this reason the hierarchy, too, is interested in an end to the controversy which has now gone on for three months – the three blackest months of my life. Walter Jens tries to cheer me up: 'Out of the faculty, fresh air in the Schönbuch!' I am to enjoy nature more, and like him and his wife Inge walk in this beautiful forest, which extends along the borders of Tübingen for dozens of kilometres. Indeed they buy me a 'Schönbuch' jacket and I go for trial walks on 15 March with a group of four and then twice more. But I love the sun and nature around me on my terrace; I'm a swimmer and a skier, not a walker.

The extended faculty council (with assistants and student representatives) is called by the Dean for 25 March 1980 at 10.15 a.m. in the President's office. It's a historic setting. The negotiations are carried on in the President's presence and concern only my case. The President describes the legal situation and the situation brought about by the unwillingness of the church hierarchy to give way. To their complete surprise, my seven opponents, who had hoped that they could catapult me out of the faculty by a simple majority decision, now find themselves confronted with my decision to leave the faculty voluntarily for the university – but keep my chair and institute.

The President draws the attention of the faculty to the serious consequences of their decision: the state will certainly create a substitute for the chair of ecumenical theology which has been separated off, but the faculty will lose the highly respected Institute for Ecumenical Research – their only faculty institute. Professor Küng may be excluded from the faculty, but his reputation in the world is such that he will not lack powerful support even outside his faculty (on this point

I think that the President is bluffing, but he will in fact prove right). Taken completely by surprise, around 2 p.m. my seven colleagues call for a break.

Getting rid of me fails

My opponents, who constantly operate as a closed group, have manoeuvred themselves into an impasse; they will be rid of me, as they wanted, yet they won't be rid of me, as they will soon discover. They want me 'out of the window' but are putting me in a showcase. Their intention is to make me a university wall-flower, like all those who have lost their *missio* before me (mostly for violating the law of celibacy), most recently in the 1950s the *ordinarius* professor of Old Testament, the Rottenburg diocesan professor Fridolin Stier, who had to acknowledge an already adult daughter and therefore was shifted to the faculty of philosophy as an honorary professor. But instead of my isolation my opponents now have to reckon with my new sphere of influence. By the withdrawal of the church's permission to teach, my lectures are to become uninteresting and irrelevant for all those who, whether as candidates for the priesthood or lay theologians, are dependent on recognition by the church for their appointment in church or state (as pastors, teachers of religion, etc.). But I hope that I will gain myself a new audience.

Getting rid of me was to be the decisive blow against me, and in this faculty meeting, too, the argument concentrates on this point. Because of the pressures exercised by the church I am prepared to give up my right to lecturing, examining and involvement in appointments. But in no way am I prepared to renounce my right to propose present or future pupils for doctorates and habilitations. This for me is an essential element in the freedom of teaching and research guaranteed by Article 5 of the Basic Law of the Federal Republic of Germany. Without this right, in time I would no longer have any academic colleagues. If this right weren't granted me I would see myself compelled to take legal steps, with the support of the university, which would have to implement this process. This would result in a complaint to the Constitutional Court in Karlsruhe about the violation of my freedom to teach and research.

After five hours of exhausting discussion, despite all reservations on the part of individuals the faculty council unanimously resolves on a change to the university rules: it will guarantee me as Director of the Institute of Ecumenical Research membership of the faculty's doctorate and habilitation committee in connection with my students. But the decision is made on the presupposition that an acceptable solution is arrived at between bishop, minister and me. So this memorable session of the faculty of Catholic theology, which will be my last, is concluded.

Two days later the minister gives his assent. But the bishop needs time to reflect. He has so pitifully allowed himself to be chained by the Roman Curia that in this matter, for which according to the Concordat he alone is responsible, he can't take the least decision without inquiring of the Bonn nunciature, or the Vatican. And there is no question that the Curia will find it extraordinarily difficult after all these controversies not to have achieved my complete academic disempowerment. Again there are days of anxious waiting. What will Rome's answer be?

Rome gives in

I am aware that the legal course to the Constitutional Court in Karlsruhe would take years and would be extremely demanding on me politically, psychologically and financially, and thus would keep me from scholarly research. To tell the truth, I would take this difficult course only in an emergency – and the outcome would be uncertain, given that the church has unlimited financial means, the best advocates and unfortunately even many possibilities of influencing justice. So I hope with all my heart that I am spared the way to Karlruhe and, if the outcome of the proceedings were negative, emigration.

The reply from Rome comes days later: the bishop, or the Vatican, accepts the 'agreed solution' that has been found on condition that I am only an 'advisory' member of the doctorate and habilitation committee and am not appointed as an examiner. *Deo gratias*! Now everything goes ahead quickly. I immediately assent and on 8 April send my application to the University President for my chair and institute to be removed from the faculty of Catholic theology, once again clearly formulating my basic attitude and the concrete conditions.[48] The very next day, 9 April, this resolution receives the force of law by a rapid decision on the part of the President and on 10 April by a letter from the Minister of Science and Art.

Everyone asks why Rome has given way at the last moment on a question which is decisive for my future. No one can know and I can only guess. When talk of the legal course arose I continued to emphasize that if there were legal proceedings I would raise for public discussion not only Article 19 of the Reich Concordat which grants the bishop (and not Rome) the right to give the church's permission to teach but also – with all available means – the whole of the Reich Concordat concluded with Hitler. As is well known, after the war it was taken all too much for granted – and many competent jurists hold this view – that this Concordat continued to remain legal and in a highly artificial way it was combined with various previous state concordats and judicial decisions to provide a legal consolidation of 'holy rule' within the state legal order. In giving the reasons to the minister for his withdrawal of my permission to teach (31 December 1979) Bishop Moser had to appeal not only to Article 19 of the Reich Concordat but at the same time to 'Article 3 of the Bavarian Concordat, Article 12 of the Prussian Concordat and Article 10 of the Baden Concordat (each with their concluding protocols)'. Even with this reinforcement, in my view the argument from concordats constructed in a roundabout way wouldn't stand up to legal examination.[49]

In any case both Rome and the German episcopate had a bad conscience about this treaty in international law made between Nuncio Eugenio Pacelli (later Pius XII) and the Third Reich immediately after Hitler's 'seizure of power' on 20 July 1933. For the sake of problematic advantages to the church the Vatican was the first foreign power to give the Nazi regime respect and prestige. At the same time, until 1945 it had refrained from an explicit condemnation of National Socialism and even avoided any public protest against the Holocaust, the worst crime in human history. Moreover, after the conclusion of the Concordat in 1933 the German episcopate had signalled to German Catholics that it was now capitulating to National Socialism, although it had previously fought vigorously against it, despite the regime's well-known nationalist and racist programme and despite all the acts of terror it had perpetrated. The church had come to terms with this totalitarian regime and thus broken the backbone of the resistance of the Catholic clergy and people. Throughout the time of National Socialism the German episcopate ventured no public statement on behalf of the Jews (and virtually none on behalf of the considerable number of Catholic priests and laity who had been arrested). And on Hitler's last birthday in 1945, immediately before the end of the war, the compliant President of the German Conference of Bishops, Cardinal Bertram, sent the 'Führer' a warm congratulatory letter.[50]

So Rome and the episcopate are afraid of a new discussion of the Concordat. Church tax, likewise guaranteed by the Concordat, which in my view would be better paid direct (as in Switzerland) to the congregations or urban communities than into the bishop's fund, thus giving him undue power over the pastors and parishes dependent on him, would likewise be drawn into the discussion. God forbid, they presumably said in Cologne, where the archbishop has almost a billion Deutschemarks in tax at his disposal and after torpedoing *Publik* bought the conservative weekly *Rheinische Merkur*. They preferred not to have another discussion on church tax and all the other privileges worth millions (financial contributions to bishops and church institutions). The hierarchy fears such a discussion as the devil fears holy water. So gnashing their teeth they acceded to my *conditio sine qua non*. And this in particular helps an apparent loser in reality to become a winner. Thank God, and I mean that literally!

Redeemed Easter laughter

Thanks, too, to the state of Baden-Württemberg. Granted, contrary to the Concordat certain state authorities accepted the Vatican decision over the withdrawal of my *missio* and didn't have the courage to attack its legitimacy. But on the other hand the state authorities protected my person as a professor at the university against the demands of the church, in a way which would have happened in few other countries. My professional income remained intact and my scholarly activity could continue – though in some respects it was restricted, at the same time unexpected new possibilities opened up.

I never saw the Bishop of Rottenburg, Georg Moser, again; he avoided any encounter with me and no longer appeared at university occasions. Granted, over the next year he attempted once again, with the help of a diocesan synod, to improve the situation somewhat in his own diocese. But despite the tremendous dedication of many clergy and laity of goodwill, despite all the financial and material expenditure, despite countless speeches and papers, nothing essential emerged which decisively improved the pastoral situation in the diocese. Every year there were more parishes without pastors and pseudo-reform by fusion (liquidation) of parishes into 'pastoral units'. There were no married pastors. And how can a single priest be a genuine pastor for five parishes? Whenever the decisive structural questions of church reform arose, Bishop Moser had either to avoid or block the discussion from the start or appeal to Rome, which was known to provide no help over these questions. I would truly have wanted a better end for the bishop. But this wasn't to be.

In my dealings with the seven colleagues who were immediately responsible for my departure from the faculty of Catholic theology I have observed the rules of academic courtesy. Even the colleague who had sent me the card with the man on the wheel didn't want to excuse himself privately or in public, and the others certainly didn't. By 2007 three of them have died, two have left Tübingen, one lives in retirement in Tübingen and one has made a career in the church. Eight years after the great confrontation Bishop Moser died of kidney disease; he was only 65. I asked his suffragan bishop Kuhnle to visit him on his death bed to offer reconciliation with him, and also with the philosopher Oeing-Hanhoff, one of the Seven, who was also terminally ill, but I received no reply.

I know that some readers will find it physically difficult to read these last two chapters. How can an institution which constantly appeals to love do all this to an individual? It has also been difficult for me to describe scene after scene. But for the sake of the truth all this had to be set down as it took place from the perspective of the one at the centre, even if it is painful. I very much hope that this chapter doesn't read like a contemptuous settling of accounts but conveys disappointment and sorrow. I have tried to avoid all personal attacks and vengeful reckonings while clearly distancing myself from the machinations of certain gentlemen and identifying those responsible.

I am very glad that the revision of this section in 2007 takes place at Easter. For me all this in 1980 was not the end. On the contrary, it was a new beginning. Good Friday is followed by Easter. What I mean isn't the banal 'He who laughs last laughs longest', because only at the end does it become evident who has won. Rather, the 'redeemed laughter' of Easter was given to me, grounded in a joyful faith and accompanied by hope. Medieval preachers who delighted their hearers with jokes after the strict time of Lent and Passiontide provoked 'Easter laughter'.[51] Laughter was given to me again when I hadn't laughed for a long time. From now on things look up.

ဢၵၼဢၵၼ

Prospect

*'I am especially grateful to you for emphasizing what we have continued
to have in common and the mutual human respect despite all the
controversies, which must always remain a matter of course for
Christians. Of course I am prepared to have a conversation with you.'*

Pope Benedict XVI in his reply to Hans Küng, 15 June 2005

For me 1980 begins – and who could have expected it? – a new and extremely
hopeful period of my life, at the centre of which will be the Global Ethic project.
However, it is a long time until that happens. After a dark three months,
immediately before the 1980 summer semester light dawns. The students
returning for the beginning of the semester in the middle of April put pressure on
the hesitant church authorities in Rome and Germany to act. On the Friday of
Easter week there is a press conference in the Südwestkundfunk studio in
Tübingen with the University President, Adolf Theis, and Professor Walter Jens:
the 'Tübingen compromise' achieved with the official church, which is my
deliverance, is announced. I can keep my position, but the questions remain.

Roman retrogression and ecumenical confrontation

On the 'provisional' resolution of the conflict which has arisen between me and
the institutional church I am the first to say: 'In future, as Professor of Ecumenical
Theology and Director of the Institute for Ecumenical Research I shall continue
to give lectures and seminars, research, teach and publish. As a Catholic theologian I shall continue to fight for a Christianity orientated more on the message
of Jesus, ecumenical understanding and the renewal of my Catholic Church, to
which I still feel bound as priest, pastor and scholar.' But at the same time I make
a second point: 'I shall continue to work for the revision of inquisitorial "proceedings" which from beginning to end have gone against all legality and
Christian brotherliness; I am grateful to all the many people who have supported
me in this and will continue to support me in the future.'[1]

Then I sketch out and comment on the compromise achieved and announce
the publication the next month by Piper Verlag of a book of extensive documentation by my colleagues Norbert Greinacher and Herbert Haag, which is

already at proof stage. It describes the background and fall-out of the 'Küng case' and those responsible for it, since the Küng case is truly the 'case of the institutional church'.

I conclude by saying that regardless of the solution within the university the fundamental questions remain:

> There remains the question of the infallibility of Rome and the bishops, which has still not been answered. There remains the question of a Christian proclamation in church and schools which is credible today. There remains the question of understanding between the confessions and the mutual recognition of ministries and eucharistic celebrations. There remains the question of the urgent tasks of reform, from birth control through marriage between those of different confessions and divorce to the ordination of women, mandatory celibacy and the resultant catastrophic lack of priests. There remains above all the question of the leadership of our Catholic Church: where is it taking our church? On the way of John XXIII and the Second Vatican Council into greater Catholic breadth, humanity and Christianity? Or on the way of the First Vatican Council and the Pius Popes back into an authoritarian ghetto? I would still like to hope that in the end the spirit of true evangelical catholicity will triumph over the pernicious ideology of a legalistically narrow, doctrinally fossilized dogmatic and triumphalistically fear-filled Catholicism.[2]

All in all there is no doubt that for the Catholic Church these proceedings against one of their theologians whose concerns stand for so many is a retrograde step. The editors of the documentation spell this out in their conclusion when they describe the 1. pastoral, 2. theological, 3. ecumenical, 4. political, 5. church–historical and 6. procedural dimensions of the 'Küng case'.

In the last 25 years the world has been able to observe the negative consequences for both the Catholic Church and the Christian ecumenical world generally of the retrogression in Roman Catholic church policy which began in 1979.[3] There is no need once again to point out the lamentable state of the church and clergy behind the glittering façade of papal demonstrations. Everywhere the criticism of theologians is stifled by sanctions and refusals to give them jobs, constraints and fear. Consequently only men who conform to the system are chosen for the episcopate or for the College of Cardinals. This leads to the election of the head of the Congregation for the Doctrine of the Faith as Pope in 2005.

When Joseph Ratzinger was unexpectedly elected Pope I argued that he should be given a chance. And it was regarded by many as a sign of hope that in contrast to his predecessor, soon after his election he invited me to an open and friendly four-hour conversation in Castel Gandolfo; for that I was and am honestly grateful to him. But the hope that he would take a constructive initiative in the dialogue of religions (of which we talked in our conversation) and that he would at least identify with one or another demand for reform (which were deliberately excluded from our conversation) has not been fulfilled in the first years of his pontificate. On the contrary, Benedict XVI's 2006 Regensburg speech, in which he disseminated errors about Islam, about the Reformation and about the Enlightenment as the de-Hellenization of his own (Hellenistic–Roman) Christianity, unfortunately wasn't just a slip. Nor was it fortuitous that he condemned the liberation theologian Jon Sobrino, whose Jesus book, unlike his own, cannot be discussed freely in public.

In July 2007 the Doctrinal Congregation published for no apparent reason a brusque declaration which again demands a total identification of the church of Christ with the Roman Catholic Church as it currently is, contrary to the explicit desire of the Second Vatican Council. In its five 'Responsa' (answers), the questions which weren't settled in the conflict with me are taken up again and once more the absolute primacy of jurisdiction of the Bishop of Rome over the whole church is asserted in an anachronistic way. The Roman Catholic Church is the only true church of Jesus Christ, the Orthodox churches of the East are defective churches and the Reformation churches aren't churches at all. Such Roman glorification and alienation of the world which sees Christians separated rather than united was greeted with relaxed repudiation by Orthodoxy, indignation by Protestantism and incomprehension at the Catholic grass roots. The same month saw the announcement of permission to reintroduce the pre-conciliar Tridentine Latin celebration of the mass. That too could split congregations. Readers will hardly be surprised at the new Roman document in the light of the Pope's career and of the Roman system. Many in the Catholic Church and beyond are asking: what are we to do about such disastrous Roman leadership of the church which makes our congregations bleed to death, often saddles the dioceses with incompetent bishops and highlights and isolates the Catholic Church at the expense of the wider ecumenical world? This newest development emphatically confirms the continuing urgency of my concern, for which I was fighting even before the great confrontation in 1979/80.

Victory despite defeat

The confrontations didn't set me back personally, but drove me forwards more than I could have suspected at the moment of the Tübingen compromise. In 1980 I could look back on twenty years as a theologian; I still had almost twenty years before my retirement – *Deo bene volente*, if God wills, as I always add. I have lived an extraordinarily rich life – rich in conflicts and successes, as is already attested by this book and *My Struggle for Freedom*. Mine has been the life of a theologian in which all that I have done has aimed to serve the truth in freedom. It was in this disputed service of the truth that I became involved in a controversy which I hadn't wanted but which, if forced on me, I didn't want to avoid. It demanded all my strength – to the point of complete psychological and physical exhaustion. All that I had laboriously built up seemed lost. To that point I had felt supported, but then I felt abandoned. Certainly I never doubted God, but my reasonable trust in him no longer seemed to have any support in experience.

Didn't I live a 'life guided by God', as other theologians somewhat pompously say? I couldn't make such a pious claim. In my spiritual training in Rome I was always concerned 'to do the will of God' and in difficult decisions to discover by mature consideration what God wanted of me. My later exegetical efforts over the figure of Jesus and being a Christian showed me that according to Jesus' message God's will always aims at human well-being. But that didn't allow me simply to answer that in all my actions and passions I was 'guided by God', so that even a book such as *Infallible?*, which caused me so much trouble, could so to speak be set to God's account?

I had to content myself with the trust that in everything I had been 'accompanied and supported by God'. And in the situation it was difficult enough to put my trust in that. Was I really accompanied and supported? I am reminded of the story of someone who dreams that he is walking along by a lake with a mysterious companion. Images from his life flit past his eyes. After the last one has disappeared, he looks back at the way they have taken and notes that in the most difficult times of his life only a single track can be seen in the sand. Confused, he turns to his companion: 'When I turned to you, you said that you would always be with me. Why did you forsake me when I needed you so desperately?' 'I never left you alone,' was his answer, 'not even in times of fear and distress. Where you see only one pair of tracks in the sand, I was carrying you.'[4]

Indeed I could now see what I couldn't see in the hours of darkness; God had supported me in a hidden way. And in the midst of the crisis, without my noticing it, he gave me what I needed to seek the greater truth in a new freedom. For a long time I had dreamed in my overburdened university work of something like a Max Planck Institute for ecumenical theology where I could give lectures and shape and co-ordinate my lecturing and teaching programme freely without being forced into a rigid cycle, but all down the years I thought that this would have to remain a beautiful dream. I didn't even notice when such an institute was actually given to me. But when my opponents thought that they had got the better of me, in the hours of deepest defeat and darkness – *hominum confusione dei providentia* – I was given a university institute independent of the faculty, which would make possible for me a new quest for the truth in new freedom. Only very much later would I be able to recognize and understand that without this painful defeat for me there would have been

- no interdisciplinary work with scholars of literature and religion, with physicists, psychologists, political theorists and economists;
- no serious practice of the dialogue of religions and cultures;

- no discovery of an elementary ethic of humankind, a global ethic.

The new freedom

Over the next two decades I kept the freedom which, as I described in *My Struggle for Freedom*, I had to fight for in the first four decades, as will be clear from this book. The outcome of this conflict freed me of a great deal of baggage. Very soon, one of the Seven who had spoken out against my remaining in the faculty of Catholic theology enviously pointed out to the other six my enormous new freedom: 'Küng's kept all that a professor needs and has got rid of all that a professor doesn't need.' How could I regret the faculty and commission meetings at which one wastes so much time and at which those who have least to say as scholars and in public talk the most? How could I long for examining when I could see the students at my lectures and seminars voluntarily, with no pressure towards examinations?

Now, since I no longer needed to give perhaps boring series of lectures on dogmatics or to take account of the different sensibilities of faculty colleagues, quite other intellectual adventures became possible. Professor Klaus Scholder, *Ordinarius* Professor of Church Order in the Tübingen Faculty of Protestant Theology, perceived the positive aspect of the new freedom earlier than others: '... and anyone who knows Hans Küng knows that he also knows how to use this freedom'.[5] I relate this, not to give the Inquisition a trace of justification, but after the event to make it clear that its calculations don't always work out.

It was good that I didn't accept the proposal of my Protestant colleagues and friends Eberhard Jüngel and Jürgen Moltmann to extend my teaching of dogmatic theology. I had been ostracized publicly from the church, to the point that the hierarchs and the second professor of dogmatics in the faculty, Walter Kasper, did all they could to make my chair no longer responsible for 'dogmatic and ecumenical theology'. Why should Catholic students listen to my lectures if they had to listen to the 'orthodox' lectures of my quasi-successor? *Tant mieux*, I was delighted no longer to have to be a 'dogmatic theologian'. The term has fallen into disrepute since Kant and even according to the dictionary 'teacher of dogmatics' is secondary to the definition 'rigid uncritical defender of an ideology'. I certainly didn't want that role.

However, I did take up with enthusiasm a grand proposal by my colleague and friend Walter Jens. After some unpleasant controversies he had turned down the Lessing professorship in Hamburg which had been offered him and decided to stay in Tübingen. He was now interested in a revival by the two of us of the *studium generale*, more general lectures, which had gone into decline. Here I could develop a more comprehensive ecumenical theology in a broader context, which would incorporate not only other Christian confessions but also the world religions.

This was in fact to be the programme of my first major series of *studium generale* lectures in the winter semester of 1980/81 to a packed Festsaal of the University of Tübingen. I was already thinking in bigger terms: in future shouldn't I be able to carry on quite practical dialogues at a higher scholarly level with representatives of Judaism and Islam and also Hinduism and Buddhism, and finally also Chinese religion, Confucianism and Daoism? And shouldn't it be possible with Walter Jens to bring in world literature and talk about great figures such as Pascal, Lessing, Hölderlin, Kierkegaard, Dostoievsky and Kafka, Thomas Mann, Hermann Hesse and Heinrich Böll, of whom I am fond? The first such joint lectures by Walter Jens and me on world literature and religion took place in the summer semester of 1981 and attracted around 1000 listeners every Monday evening from 8 p.m. to 10 p.m.

So I was as delighted as a professor can be with academic freedom. I could even spend every fourth semester in America and get to know the whole world, its cultures and its religions better.

'You're doing well!'

Bad Adelhozen by the Chiemsee in July 1983; for our first meeting after long years Cardinal Joseph Ratzinger, now Prefect of the Congregation for the Doctrine of the Faith, successor to Cardinal Šeper, clad in a simple black gown, comes down the broad steps of a large convent, smiling: 'You're doing well, Herr Küng!' I smile back. 'Yes, I'm doing well, Herr Ratzinger, but that's not what the Congregation for the Doctrine of the Faith intended.' He is evasive in a friendly way: 'I don't know what my predecessor had in mind.'

Indeed, unexpectedly my situation has developed in a pleasant way with my new freedom in the university, church and world; I certainly don't long for my previous position in the Catholic faculty. My Protestant friends Eberhard Jüngel and Jürgen Moltmann, concerned to achieve some understanding, have urged our former colleague Walter Kasper, who has now likewise emigrated into the Roman Curia, to arrange a meeting between me and Cardinal Ratzinger. I'm happy with this, though as things are I can hardly expect anything positive under the Polish Pope.

On this Saturday, 30 July 1983 – the withdrawal of my *missio* is now three and a half years behind me – Joseph Ratzinger has invited me for lunch at a large convent in his Bavarian holiday residence. At 8 a.m. I drive off in my BMW (the Alfa which has continued to excite the imagination of some journalists had long since been traded in). But in Bavaria, of all places, this product of the Bayerische Motoren Werke shamefully lets me down. On the Munich–Salzburg autobahn in the traffic jam of holiday travellers and the summer heat the fuel injection system packs up. I have to go to a garage and report the breakdown to Bad Adelhozen.

I finally arrive an hour and a half late. Of course I'm given lunch, but what I couldn't have expected is that the cardinal, knowing my Roman custom, offers me his bed for a siesta. I gladly accept this kindness. At any rate it's a sign that despite the sharp controversies our human relations haven't completely broken down.

But the conversation which follows quickly shows that we live in two different worlds, in two different paradigms. By chance, right at the beginning of our discussion, because I have recently been in Canada, we get on to the subject of the large number of women religious who have left their order in Quebec. I think that they should have been given more freedom in dress and lifestyle. He accuses me of having contributed to the loosening of discipline with my talk of the church and freedom. And so it goes on. We differ over every problem of the church as much as a Ptolemaean and a Copernican differed over the heavens in the transition from the Middle Ages to modern times. I'm amazed that he avoids even the slightest criticism of the Pope – for example his excessive travel and his media presence. We don't talk at all about central problems such as that of infallibility.

So we don't reach any agreement. We both observe the courtesies, talk sensibly and part in a friendly way. I'm glad to be driving direct from Upper Bavaria to my Sempachersee in Switzerland. It is to be 22 years before we meet again – by Lake Albano at Castel Gandolfo. But what is my role in church and society? That isn't easy to define.

Mission and betrayal of the intellectuals

In September 2005, I am put on the list of the '100 most important intellectuals in the world' by the two journals *Foreign Policy* (US) and *The Spectator* (UK), with Jürgen Habermas and Joseph Ratzinger the only German-speaking representatives. Rightly so? Like Ratzinger, I've always understood myself more as a theologian and scholar than as an 'intellectual'. I'm certainly an intellectual if by that one understands someone with a scholarly education engaged in intellectual work, but not if one understands it as someone who is opinionated and remote. But perhaps for most people intellectual means an educated person who in some way criticizes society and investigates existing institutions, not a free-ranging intelligence but at best something like a moral authority.

But can I compare my enquiry *Infallible?* with Emile Zola's *J'accuse* (1898) in the Dreyfus affair, which in another way was an affair of the truth, by which the birth of the modern intellectual is dated? Unlike this French writer, I didn't write a manifesto but a controversial book using historical, philosophical and theological arguments, though it is backed by a critical moral attitude, if not towards the hypocritical power of the state, then against uncontrolled church power. In the Dreyfus affair, at first sight Zola, Clemenceau and Jaurès couldn't gain much, since the wider public was against Dreyfus; in the circumstances the fight had to be for the truth, if need be over years. But such commitment, in which one is involved incorruptibly for truth and humanity and takes the consequences of one's action, can nevertheless be worth while, even if one has perhaps to wait years for rehabilitation.

Nor have I ever, like the English intellectual Bertrand Russell in the 1960s, organized a 'tribunal' (against the US crimes in Vietnam) or, like the French philosopher Jean-Paul Sartre, drawn attention to myself by spectacular actions and perplexing intellectual shifts (from existentialism to Marxism). I would therefore prefer to see myself close to the Iranian jurist and Nobel Peace Prize winner Shirin Ebadi (he gave the fifth Global Ethic Address in Tübingen in 2005), who is also on this list of 100, or my immediate contemporary Noam Chomsky (an opponent of the Vietnam war), who with me received an honorary doctorate in Chicago in 1970. Or even (with me a member of the Academia Europea of Yuste in Spain) the cellist, conductor and fighter for human rights in the Soviet Union Mstislav Rostropovich (died 17 April 2007), who was deprived of his citizenship in 1978 for inviting Solzhenitsyn to his dacha: 'Never in my life have I done anything better than support Solzhenitsyn in this situation,' he declared when he was later rehabilitated.

Nor should I forget that American intellectual who died in December 2005 at the age of 89 and whose guest I had been on my first lecture tour through the United States, Senator Eugene McCarthy, a Catholic Democrat from Minnesota. He led the political revolt against the Vietnam war and compelled President Lyndon B. Johnson, who had previously been elected with the biggest majority in the history of the United States, not to seek re-election. Unfortunately McCarthy himself lost the contest for the Democrat presidential candidature to Hubert Humphrey, who then lost the election to Richard Nixon. This cost the United States and Vietnam another seven years of war with tens of thousands of dead. One remark by Eugene McCarthy could easily be applied to Pope and church: 'We do not need presidents who are bigger than the country, but rather ones who speak for it and support it.'

But at this time the United States hardly at all attempted to neutralize intellectuals critical of the regime by disciplinary measures. And President Charles de Gaulle, when called on during the student unrests of 1968 to arrest the 'student seducer' Jean-Paul Sartre, gave the classical answer: 'One doesn't lock up a Voltaire.' The Vatican would certainly have locked him up had they got hold of him.

Of course there are also intellectuals who betray their mission. Julien Bendan demonstrated this in his stimulating culture–critical investigation 'The Betrayal of the Intellectuals' (*La trahison des clercs*, Paris 1927), which proved prophetic for the period after 1933. Indeed there are intellectuals who instead of defending spiritual and humane values against the prevailing powers put themselves at the service of these powers, as in the Catholic sphere for example the nationalist 'Action Française', or those Catholics who supported Italian and Spanish Fascism, or the anti-democratic right-wing radicals in Germany, or theologians and journalists who put themselves at the service of Opus Dei or 'Wojtylismo'. But there were and are also many others, known and unknown, who do not betray truth and freedom intellectually, but resist and stand fast in public.

'A public intellectual'

It was the Chinese scholar of religions Professor Tu Wei-Ming, Director of the Harvard Yenching Institute, who introduced the concept of the 'public intellectual' into the discussions of our 'Group of Eminent Persons' convened by the UN Secretary-General Kofi Annan to work out a manifesto on the 'Dialogue of Civilizations'.[6] According to Tu Wei-Ming, public individuals have three characteristics: they are culturally sensitive, politically concerned and socially committed. By virtue of their professional competence they tackle questions of the common good in public and spark off debates by pointing to abuses – all on the basis of particular convictions, values and criteria.

This is also how I understand myself. I am not an ivory-tower scholar who researches and lives without any connection to life and actual practice. Nor am I a conformist who avoids commitment and makes life comfortable for himself. Nor am I a maverick. I am a scholar who investigates thoroughly and may stir things up with his words, and to this degree belong among the movers and shakers. I don't just raise problems but where possible solve them; my mind isn't just analytic but also synthetic. I'm not a one-issue person captivated by a single problem (the emancipation of women, the environment, peace), important though this may be, but attempt to see beyond my specialism and my personal field.

A public intellectual in this sense would be more than a 'committed observer', the ideal of Rolf Dahrendorf, my former Tübingen colleague, whom I respect highly: Dahrendorf became Director of the London School of Economics and head of St Anthony's College, Oxford, and is now a member of the British House of Lords. Certainly I have every respect for critical liberal thinkers such as Karl Popper, Isaiah Berlin, Raymond Aron and Norberto Bobbio, all portrayed by Lord Dahrendorf, who in the age of totalitarianisms and faced with the 'temptations of unfreedom' didn't go over to either the Fascist camp (like Heidegger or Jünger) or the Communist camp (like Sartre or Louis Aragon), but none of whom offered active resistance.[7] This is truly a question of a political ethic.

More than an 'involved onlooker'

Dahrendorf's key figure is Erasmus of Rotterdam, prototype of that intellectual whom Dahrendorf calls 'Erasmian'. By that he means those liberal intellectuals who in the face of totalitarianisms choose neither to retreat into themselves nor to resist, but become 'involved onlookers': in prudence using the wisdom of passionate reason as an inner compass. For me that is good, but not enough.

For me the position of Erasmus – in the dispute between Rome and Luther – has long been more than a theoretical or historical question; rather, it is an existential question to which I devoted a study two decades ago.[8] Perhaps, I asked myself seriously at that time, the humanist reformer Erasmus showed the right way between the Medici Pope Leo X, who was unwilling for reform, and the revolutionary Martin Luther? Long before Luther, Erasmus had called for better biblical scholarship, theology and popular piety, another clergy and another hierarchy.

Of course prudence is always called for. However, for Erasmus Martin Luther with his radical demands for reform which appeal to the gospel was the test case. Erasmus wanted to remain an 'involved observer'; he didn't want either to judge Luther or to identify with him, at any rate to risk his neck. This scholar, always reflecting, differentiating, criticizing, demonstrably makes tactical and strategic mistakes. He is unwilling to follow up his words with deeds and so loses the opportunity to bring his unique European authority to bear (for example at the meeting of the three monarchs at Calais in 1520 or a year later at the Reichstag in Worms) in order, with all those who at that time formed a third force, to prevent the schism between Rome and Wittenberg by reform within Catholicism. In this moment of truth one misses in Erasmus a clear public protest at and resistance to the un-Christian character of the authoritarian Roman system which at the same time could also have identified one-sidednesses and premature conclusions in the person and theology of Martin Luther. But the *casus disputationis* has long since become the *status confessionis*: one cannot remain neutral. Scholarship in particular is challenged to practical involvement. In such a situation of decisions, words must become deeds.

The attitude of the English cardinal Reginald Pole, cousin of King Henry VIII and friend of Erasmus, who had a humanistic education, is unfortunately typical of the Erasmians of that time. In the Roman conclave on 3/4 December 1539 – three years after Luther's death – by his indecision he missed the opportunity to ascend the throne of Peter as an Erasmian reformer with a vote of acclamation from the College of Cardinals. This opened the way for his opponent, the arrogant and lofty Gian Pietro Carafa, exponent of the conservative restorative 'zealots', who in 1542 had founded the central Roman Inquisition ('*Sacrum Officium Santissimae Inquisitionis*') and was finally elected at the age of 80 as Paul IV, soon feared with his minions as a dictator. He published an anti-Jewish bull and the first Index of Prohibited Books, but showed no interest in the continuation of the reforming Council of Trent. That finished the Erasmian third force, and the Counter-Reformation was established in Rome.

For me 1979 was a time of testing. In the face of the 'temptations of unfreedom' and the threat of a test to destruction, it was clear to me that the

Roman conformity which is required and which capitulates despite the clear evidence of scripture and one's own conscience was no more a possibility for me than it was for Luther. Nor was that Lutheran aggression, often understandable, which, if engaged in without restraint and quickly escalated, can lead so easily to revolution and a split in the church. So perhaps between the two one should adopt the Erasmian withdrawal which limits itself to 'committed observation' and in oneself as in others leads to resignation and perhaps again ends up in conformism? Certainly as a 'committed observer' one can introduce it into the College of Cardinals (which Erasmus rejected), the British upper house, the Académie Française or the Prussian order 'Pour le mérite'. However, one cannot want to achieve subtle distinction, skilful reporting and academic balance where resistance, defence and steadfastness are called for.

What then? As a Christian theologian I prefer to take the apostle Paul rather than Erasmus as a model. When Peter, whom some (wrongly) call the 'first Pope', 'was not true to the gospel', Paul publicly opposed him 'to the face'. 'How can ...?' (Galatians 2.11-14). In short, resist and stand firm. Stand up, don't leave. This can perhaps finally lead to change and renewal from within without breaking the church community but going beyond temporary loyal opposition.

Those who are given the role of the 'public conscience' usually make themselves unpopular and have to reckon with reactions and sanctions. I admire the intellectuals of resistance more than the great 'liberal observers': in National Socialism, for example, the theologians Karl Barth, Dietrich Bonhoeffer and Alfred Delp, or in Communism Alexander Solzhenitsyn, Lev Kopelev, Mstislav Rostropovich or Andrei Sakharov. They all want to create validity for the truth and show up the inhumanity of systems and are ready to risk their necks for this.

They and many others like me have had the experience that the apostle Paul formulates in his Second Letter to the Church of Corinth and that I emphasized (quite unsuspecting at the time) in *On Being a Christian*:

> We are harassed on all sides, but not crushed;
> plunged in doubt, but not despairing;
> persecuted, but not forsaken;
> struck down, but not destroyed;
> as dying, but see we live;
> as punished, but not put to death;
> as poor, yet making many rich;
> as having nothing and yet possessing everything
> (2 Corinthians 4.8f.; 6.9f.).

A passion for truth

Kung in Conflict: under this title Professor Leonard Swidler of Temple University, Philadelphia, with whom I have been friends since my first US lecture tour, has taken enormous trouble to select all the important documents from the three documentations available in German, to translate the German-language documents into English and to publish 137 documents on 627 pages in chronological order.[9] At the end he draws some conclusions as a historian of theology. I emphasize only two of them: 'Probably the most important reason why Küng does get into difficulties with Church authorities is that he takes the historical–critical method seriously and carries its results over into his theological reflections … Another reason for Kung's difficulties is his total honesty. For him that is a virtue that cannot be displaced by other considerations – he says as much in the whole book entitled *Truthfulness: The Future of the Church*. A number of other Catholic theologians are aware of the results of historical studies, but at certain critical points "fudge" their application to Christian doctrine' (p. 610).

A Passion for Truth: this is the fine and appropriate title that the English Catholic writer Robert Nowell has given to his well-documented book with the subtitle *Hans Küng: A Biography*. It is published in London in 1981, soon after the great confrontation. In it Nowell has not only illuminated my Swiss, Roman, German background and analysed individual works. He has also discovered the deepest motivation in the intellectual adventure of this life with all the studies and controversies as 'a passion for truth'.[10] His final conclusion under the title 'What is at Stake' is:

> If the Church has no room for someone like Hans Küng among its accredited theologians, someone who is fired by a passion for truth and a love for the Church such that he finds it difficult to accord its defects the tolerant welcome others do, then there will be many humbler people, people to whom his books and writings and lectures have given new heart and new hope in the daily struggle of trying to be a Christian, who will conclude that there is no room for them either. The Church would then court the danger of allowing itself to be narrowed down to a sect, the congregation of those with a particular antiquarian and romantic appreciation of the gospel, rather than as the universal assembly of believers that finds room for all genuine expressions of the human spirit within its fellowship.

'Hans in luck?' Joseph Ratzinger ended his Tübingen *Introduction to Christianity* with this folk tale by the brothers Grimm, but has protested several times that he didn't mean it to be an allusion to me. In fact I am the opposite of a lucky fool who simply and cheaply surrenders the Christian truth and thinks that he is gaining by that. Rather, I work and struggle for the Christian truth, have constantly learned down the decades, but also engage in conflicts when a 'truth of faith' seems to me to be unfounded. Robert Nowell's comparison with Andersen's tale of the emperor's (or Pope's) new clothes is more appropriate:

In all this Küng's position has been rather like that of the small boy in Hans Christian Andersen's story. As readers will recall, the ostensible virtue of the emperor's new clothes was that they were invisible to anyone who was either unfit for his job or unforgivably stupid. It took the small boy to blurt out the truth that everyone privately was uncomfortably aware of; and the first reaction of his elders and betters was to tell him to shut up (p. 361).

Indeed, I have fought not only for my freedom but at the same time for the truth, and hope that I haven't betrayed them. How easy it would have been to ignore the question of the truth of the Roman doctrine of infallibility, to suppress it or no longer raise it, and to have a career. How easy, too, in christology just to pronounce the traditional formulas instead of looking deeper into the truth of the Christian message for men and women today.

Neither 'dictatorship of relativism nor dictatorship of absolutism'

With what truth am I concerned? As a scholar I have always been concerned with the truth in a general sense, the accord of our thought with reality, with the thing (*adaequatio rei et intellectus*), in other words with a thoroughgoing intellectual truthfulness and critical rationality. But as a theologian I have been concerned with the divine truth, the truth of the one infallible God, indeed God as the truth: we can only touch on it and never finally grasp it. And as a Christian I have been concerned quite specifically with God's truth as it has been revealed in Christ Jesus, his message, his conduct and his faith: for believers he is 'the way, the truth and the life' (John 14.6).

Today a Christian theologian has to find the way between a relativism of truth for which there is no abiding truth and an absolutism of truth which identifies itself and its position with the truth. There is not just the 'dictatorship of relativism' of which Cardinal Ratzinger spoke in his speech before his election as Pope. There is also the 'dictatorship of absolutism', for many people embodied in the personality cult of the papacy. Neither dictatorship corresponds to the Christian truth.

'Truth' in the Hebrew Bible (*emet*) and in the New Testament (*aletheia*) means decidedly more than true (or correct) propositions. Truth in the biblical sense means faithfulness, constancy, reliability, the faithfulness of God to his words and his promises as they have been shown anew in Jesus Christ, and to this degree is also the truth of Jesus Christ.

The church remains in the truth wherever Jesus himself remains 'the truth' (= the Christ) for the individual or the community. But Jesus does not remain the truth simply by being confessed as the truth ('Say Lord, Lord'). As 'the truth' he is also 'the way' and 'the life'. That means that one lives out the truth that he is, so that this Jesus – his message, his conduct, his fate, his spirit – remains ultimately decisive in the concrete life of the individual and the community of faith for relations both with fellow men and women and with God himself. 'For there is only one God, and there is only one mediator between God and humanity, himself a human being, Christ Jesus' (1 Timothy 2.5).

I would have sold my soul

Even less than in 1965 – after my private audience with Paul VI – do I now regret, 15 years later, that like the theologians and later cardinals Dulles, Lehmann, Mejía, Kasper, Ratzinger, Tucci and other friends from the time of the Council I haven't entered the service of the Roman system which calls itself simply 'church'. It is even clearer to me now than then what infallible and fallible, true and untrue things I would have had to accept, against my conscience having to say yes and amen ('let it be') to everything possible. Here I would like to repeat the sentence from my Tübingen farewell lecture at my retirement in 1996 which I quoted at the end of *My Struggle for Freedom*: 'I could not have gone another way, not just for the sake for freedom, which has always been dear to me, but for the sake of the truth. I saw then, as I see now, that had I gone another way I would have sold my soul for power in the church' (p. 461).

Of course that doesn't mean that I do theology in a free-floating way, responsible only to myself. To take up a famous distinction by my colleague and friend David Tracy of the University of Chicago,[11] I still feel obligated to a threefold sphere of activity:

- the university, where freedom for research and teaching is guaranteed and I may seek and teach the truth according to all the rules of honest scholarship;
- the church, which for me as a theologian is the community of faith that, despite all errors and wrong ways, is maintained in the truth of the gospel on the basis of its testimonies of faith;
- society, for which here and now I may reflect on and formulate the truth about God and the world.

So I have to stand before the public of the university, the churches and society as a systematic and practical theologian who can bring together both Old and New Testament exegesis and church history and the history of dogma. I can do this with some effort; but it involves considerable tensions. In the future the accents will shift, but my basic attitude will remain: scholarship, being a member of the church and worldliness are not incompatible for me.

Life goes on

I had firmly reckoned on being able to describe the whole second half of my life (1968–2007) in this second volume. But this has proved so complex and full of tensions that I didn't want to make any cuts which might be at the expense of precision and concreteness. So I am making a break at the year 1980.

A life can only be understood in retrospect, but has to be lived in a forward direction. A coherence, an inner connection, has become evident in my life which allows me to recognize a meaning. Thank God! My life goes on. In 1980 I am 52 years old, and Joseph Ratzinger, from whose parallel career I began in my prologue, is 53. A year later he will be Prefect of the Congregation for the Doctrine of the Faith in Rome. But remarkably he breaks off his 1998 memoirs in 1977, when he becomes a bishop, with words that are difficult to understand: 'What else could I say in detail about my years as a bishop?' He could certainly say a good deal more – and what prevents him? It is disturbing that Ratzinger leaves out of his memoirs the very years in which he was the second most powerful man in the Catholic Church, years in which dozens of theologians and countless Catholic men and women at the grass roots suffered under his regime. Perhaps we would understand some things better had he said more. One would have particularly liked to hear more about his 24 years as Prefect of the Congregation for the Doctrine of the Faith.

How will things turn out for me? I will continue to resist for the sake of the truth, to prize freedom, advance my research and fight: for a church which doesn't regard itself as infallible and which in order to defend its stance often conceals the truth, makes mistakes, betrays. I will fight for a church which despite all possible errors bears witness to the truth of the gospel, open to the honest debate of disputed questions and well prepared to enter into truthful dialogue with the various religions, philosophers and cultures.

In the years to come I shall not walk like the Curial cardinal 'in the streets of the eternal city', but on every conceivable street of the world. Nothing prevents me from writing; I have nothing to hide, no skeleton in the cupboard. So I hope, God willing, to be allowed to live a little longer and to be able to give an account of the third part of my life, which has broadened out in a totally unexpected way, supported by the reality of this Wholly Other: 'Until your old age I shall be the same, until your hair is grey I will carry you' (Isaiah 46.4).

Notes

Abbreviations

Conflict	Leonard Swidler (ed.), *Küng in Conflict*, New York 1981 (unfortunately the translation of this book is often clumsy and inaccurate; references are given to it in the notes, but the material has almost always been retranslated)
Dokumentation I	H. Häring and J. Nolte (eds), *Diskussion um Hans Küng 'Die Kirche'*, Freiburg im Breisgau 1971
Dokumentation II	W. Jens (ed.), *Um nichts als die Wahrheit. Deutsche Bischofs-konferenz contra Hans Küng*, Munich 1978
Dokumentation III	N. Greinacher and H. Haag (eds), *Der Fall Küng. Eine Dokumentation*, Munich 1980

Prologue

1. J. Ratzinger, *Milestones. Memoirs 1927-1977*, San Francisco 1998, p. 135.
2. Cf. ibid. Also id., *Salt of the Earth: The Church at the End of the Millennium: An Interview with Peter Seewald*, San Francisco 1997.
3. Id., *Milestones* (n. 1), p. 103. Further Ratzinger quotations in this chapter come from this book.
4. If Joseph Ratzinger thinks that revelation is 'always greater than what is merely written' and that the truth 'discloses itself in stages', every possible (apocryphal) Gnostic revelation hitherto concealed can be discovered and invented. Thus in practice the primacy of canonized Holy Scripture is abandoned and tradition is put above scripture. Indeed the 'understanding church' (in practice Roman officials) is given the possibility and power, with a reference to the Holy Spirit, to 'develop' or 'sanction' every possible new revelation, even if it was completely unknown in the church for many centuries: thus Mary's immaculate conception (1854) or her assumption to heaven (1950), which had originally been rejected in the Munich faculty. As a Council theologian Joseph Ratzinger, with Karl Rahner, attempts to introduce his view of the 'overlap of revelation over scripture' rejected by the Munich faculty into the Constitution on Divine Revelation with the help of his own scheme, but he comes up against 'bitter reactions' which finally are also to result in the 'parting of ways' between him and Rahner (*Milestones*, pp. 128f.).

I. Roman Provocations

1. Cf. L.-J. Suenens, *Théologie de l'apostolat: Commentaire doctrinal de la Promesse Legionnaire,* Paris 1951.
2. Id., *La coresponsibilité dans l'Église d'aujourd'hui,* Paris 1968.
3. Cf. id., 'L'unité de l'Église dans la logique de Vatican II', in *Informations Catholiques Internationales,* 25 April 1969.
4. Cf. J. de Broucker, *Le dossier Suenens. Diagnostic d'une crise,* Paris 1970.
5. In connection with this interview I sketch a 'Portrait d'un pape', which is published in *Le Monde,* 12 August 1969 and *Publik,* 15 August 1969.
6. Cf. the interview with Suenens on the bishops and the question of celibacy in *Le Monde,* 12 May 1970.
7. Cf. C. Davis, *A Question of Conscience,* London 1967, and on it my *Truthfulness. The Future of the Church,* New York 1968, chapter B1: A Challenge to the Church.
8. For the record it should be noted that the further places where I give lectures are Kansas City, Northwestern University in Chicago, University of Michigan in Ann Arbor, University of Philadelphia in Pennsylvania and finally Boston College again, where I gave my very first lecture on American soil in 1963. At that time the Catholic Fordham University in New York, the University of California and finally the University of Hawaii in Honolulu are new to me.
9. In the new (37th) edition of the 'Denziger' documents of the church, edited by P. Hünermann, the encyclicals on celibacy are simply – for whatever reason – suppressed.
10. Text in *Herder Korrespondenz* 22, 1968, pp. 368-70.
11. *Dokumentation* I, p. 302.

II. 1968: Year of Decisions

1. Cf. the new publications by Ingrid Gilcher-Holtey, Eberhard Rathgeb, Alfred Schmid, Michael Schmidtke and Uwe Wesel.
2. H. Gollwitzer, *Krummes Holz – aufrechter Gang. Zur Frage nach dem Sinn des Lebens,* Munich 1970.
3. For the course of events and the following quotations see *Dokumentation* I, pp. 293f.
4. Ibid., pp. 294-7.
5. Ibid., p. 26; *Conflict,* p. 10.
6. Ibid.
7. Ibid., pp. 27-30; *Conflict,* pp. 11-14.
8. H. Küng, *That the World May Believe. Letters to Young People,* London and New York 1963.
9. Cf. G. A. Wetter, *Dialektischer Materialismus,* Vienna 1952, pp. 574-80.
10. Cf. O. Šik, *Prager Frühlingserwachen. Erinnerungen,* Herford 1988.
11. Cf. B. van Onna and M. Stankowski (eds), *Kritischer Katholizismus. Argument gegen die Kirchen-Gesellschaft,* Frankfurt am Main 1969.
12. 'Kardinal Suenens las während seines Referates folgenden Brief von Professor Küng vor', *Publik* 29, 1969, p. 23.
13. *Publik* 33, 1969, p. 22.

14. G. N. Schuster, 'What Caused Today's Turbulent Waters?', *The Catholic News*, 10 October 1968.
15. Cf. his extremely competent sociological analysis: W. Goddijn, *The Deferred Revolution. A Social Experiment in Church Innovation in Holland 1960-1970*, Amsterdam 1975.
16. K. Barth, *Offene Briefe 1945-68*, ed. Dieter Koch, Zurich 1984, p. 540.

III. Tübingen in Restless Times

1. J. Ratzinger, *Milestones. Memoirs 1927-1977*, San Francisco 1998, p. 137.
2. *Theologie im Wandel. Festschrift zum 150jährigen Bestehen der Katholisch-Theologischen Fakultät an der Universität Tübingen 1817 bis 1967*, Munich and Freiburg im Breisgau 1967.
3. *Die Zeit*, 26 December 1967.
4. Cf. T. Eschenburg, *Letzten Endes meine ich doch. Errinerungen 1933-1999*, Berlin 2000, pp. 221-7: 'In view of my many critics he gave me a saying from Goethe (*Zahme Xenien*, Book 5): "If your hinges aren't to creak, your head mustn't be on the church tower."'
5. H. Häring, *Theologie und Ideologie bei Joseph Ratzinger*, Düsseldorf 2001, pp. 25f.
6. At my request Dr Achim Battke, at that time a member of the Political Working Group of the Catholic Institutions of Tertiary Education in Tübingen and later student pastor and lecturer in the Academy of the Diocese of Rottenburg-Stuttgart, looked through the minutes of the discussion on the articles of association of the Catholic colleges in Tübingen 1968-69 and on 23 March 2004 gave me a precise report to which I refer. Unfortunately this congenial pastor died a year later of a serious illness.
7. Ratzinger, *Milestones* (n. 1), p. 138.
8. Ibid., p. 135.
9. Häring, *Theologie und Ideologie bei Joseph Ratzinger* (n. 5), pp. 22f.
10. Cf. ibid.
11. By contrast, another student of Friedrich Wilhelm Maier, Pastor Johannes Kurka, in whose parish of St Laurentius in Berlin-Moabit I spent several weeks engaged in practical pastoral work in 1953, was sympathetic (the church, which was at that time brand new, had to be sold on 1 January 2007 to Christ Embassy, a Protestant group from Nigeria). It encouraged me that he wrote to me on 13 December 1977, telling me how 'our dear Professor Maier' was 'inwardly broken' by being put on the Index in 1934. He went on to say how 'loveless' he thought it that the Old Testament scholar Schmidtke had also been put on the Index of Prohibited Books in the same meeting of the 'Holy'(!) Office for his book on the creation stories as was the Nazi ideologist Alfred Rosenberg's *The Myth of the Twentieth Century* (Rosenberg was condemned to death at Nuremberg), as though they were both 'opponents of the church' in the same way.
12. J. Ratzinger, 'Schriftauslegung im Widerstreit: Zur Frage nach Grundlagen und Weg der Exegese heute', in *Schriftauslegung im Widerstreit*, ed. Joseph Ratzinger, Quaestiones disputatae 117, Freiburg im Breisgau 1989, pp. 82-97.

13. R. E. Brown, 'Der Beitrag der historischen Bibelkritik zum ökumenischen Austausch zwischen den Kirchen', in J. Ratzinger (ed.), *Schriftauslegung im Widerstreit* (n. 12), pp. 15-44: pp. 16, 20, 24-34, 36, 40.

14. J. Ratzinger, *Salt of the Earth: The Church at the End of the Millennium: An Interview with Peter Seewald*, San Francisco 1997, p. 50.

15. J. Ratzinger, *Das neue Volk Gottes. Entwürfe zur Ekklesiologie*, Düsseldorf 1969, p. 141.

16. Id., 'Die ökumenische Situation – Orthodoxie, Katholizismus und Reformation', in id (ed.), *Theologische Prinzipienlehre. Bausteine zum Fundamentaltheologie*, Munich 1982, pp. 203–14: p. 209.

17. Cf. H. Häring, *Hans Küng: Breaking Through*, London and New York 1998; id., *Theologie und Ideologie bei Joseph Ratzinger* (n. 5), especially Part A: Joseph Ratzinger – zu Stein gewordene Theologie.

18. In 2007 all three volumes were published by Piper Verlag as a special edition.

IV. Infallible?

1. Cf. First Vatican Council, *Constitutio dogmatica de Ecclesia Christi I*, chapter IV (in Denziger, *Enchiridion*, nos 1839f.)

2. Hans Küng, *Infallible? An Enquiry*, London and New York 1971.

3. H. Küng (ed.), *Fehlbar? Eine Bilanz*, Zurich 1973, p. 38.

4. In fact, as I have reported (*My Struggle for Freedom*, IV), Heinrich Schlier, beyond question a highly-gifted Bultmann pupil, was converted to the Catholic Church during my time at the German College in 1953 as he told us then as a result of his New Testament research into ministry and church. However, by careful studies in the meantime I have discovered that while Schlier rightly took seriously the 'early catholic' witnesses of the New Testament about ministry in Acts and the Pastoral Letters to Titus and Timothy, he did not understand them exclusively at the expense of the authentically Pauline letters, in which there is no talk of laying on of hands but rather of other charismatic ways in the ministry of the church. Like the New Testament, authentic catholicity embraces both.

5. K. Rahner (ed.), *Zum Problem Unfehlbarkeit. Antwort auf die Anfrage von Hans Küng*, Freiburg im Breisgau 1971, pp. 102f.

6. J. Ratzinger, 'Die Bedeutung der Väter für die gegenwärtige Theologie', *Theologische Quartalschrift* 148, 1968, pp. 257-82.

7. Y. Congar, H. Küng and D. O'Hanlon (eds), *Konzilsreden*, Einsiedeln 1964, p. 57.

8. W. von Loewenich, 'Ist Küng noch katholisch?', in Küng (ed.), *Fehlbar?* (n. 3), pp. 17f.

9. Cf. B. Tierney, 'Ursprünge der päpstlichen Unfehlbarkeit', in Küng (ed.), *Fehlbar?* (n. 3), pp. 121-45.

10. Cf. H.-J. Sieben, 'Zur Entwicklung der Konzilsidee, I-II', *Theologie und Philosophie* 45, 1970, pp. 353-89 and 46, 1971, pp. 40-70.

11. More details in Küng (ed.), *Fehlbar?* (n. 3), 'Die neue Petrusfrage', pp. 405-14.

V. Global Trip and Global Theology

1. O.Karrer, 'Friedvolle Bemerkungen zu einer theologischen Fehde', *Vaterland* (Zurich), 15 January 1971.

2. Thus on 4 November at the University of Santa Clara in Silicon Valley, the day afterwards a long flight north and a lecture in Fargo, North Dakota, where it is already quite cold at the beginning of November and snows lightly – a marked contrast to the tropical temperature of the past weeks. Then at Marquette University in Milwaukee and on 8 November two lectures in River Forest, Chicago (Rosary College). So I am grateful to be invited by Andrew Greeley with other American friends for a day at his villa in Grand Beach on Lake Michigan before I have to speak the same evening (9 November) at Notre Dame University. Again in Detroit (10 November) and then immediately south to Columbia, capital of South Carolina (11 November), where it is so hot that I leave my raincoat in the plane – I never see it again. I could have used it, since the same week I had to talk on the east coast: Philadelphia (12 November), Boston (13 November), New York (14 November) and finally Toronto (15 November).

3. J. Moltmann, *A Broad Place,* Minneapolis 2007, p. 251.

4. An example: Pentecost week 1972, the annual gathering in Brescia, the home of the publisher of the Italian edition of *Concilium*, splendidly organized by Rosino Gibellini, who was on the same course at the Gregorian University and became my friend. First on 25 May 1972 I drive from Tübingen through St Moritz and over the Alps to Brescia. Then there are three days of intensive discussions on the coming issues of the journal, elections and organizational questions, usually with conversations deep into the night. On 28 May, after the final morning session at 11 a.m., I take part in the episcopal pontifical mass, and after noon leave Brescia for Milan through Ticino and, because of the traffic jams before the tunnel, drive over the St Gotthard Pass to Zurich. I have an hour's rest there in the clergy house of the Grossmünster, where at 8 p.m. I give a lecture to a packed church on 'What Must Remain in the Church'. I have a snack after it and at 11.30 p.m. I leave again in my own car from Zurich, arriving in Tübingen around 1.30 a.m.

VI. Battle for the Truth – or a Struggle for Power?

1. Letter of the Congregation for the Doctrine of the Faith dated 12 July together with the 'Quaestiones de libro: H. Küng, *Unfehlbar?*', reprinted in H. Küng (ed.), *Fehlbar? Eine Bilanz*, Zurich 1973, F: Dokumentation, pp. 497-500.

2. Cf. B. Jaspert, '*Roma locuta, causa non finita est.* Dokumente zum Küng-Prozess in Rom 1973-98', in id., *Theologie und Geschichte, Gesammelte Aufsätze*, vol. 3, Frankfurt am Main 1999, pp. 493-534.

3. Letter to the Congregation for the Doctrine of the Faith dated 24 January 1972 (with copies to Cardinal Julius Döpfner, Bishop Carl-Joseph Leiprecht, the University Rector Johannes Neumann and Dean Walter Kasper), printed in *Fehlbar?* (n. 1), pp. 501-9.

4. *Der Spiegel*, no. 12, 1972, p. 73.

5. W. Kasper, 'Das Wesen des Christlichen', *Theologische Revue* 65, 1969, pp. 182-8: p. 186.

6. J. Moltmann, 'Gott in der Revolution', *Evangelische Kommentare* 1, 1968, pp. 565-71.
7. *What Must Remain in the Church*, London 1977.
8. Reprinted in H. Küng, *Reforming the Church Today. Keeping Hope Alive*, New York 1990, pp. 177-80.
9. *L'Osservatore Romano*, 29 March 1972.
10. *L'Osservatore Romano*, 25 April 1972.
11. *Kathpress Wien,* 27 March 1972.
12. Cf. the major work by A. Riklin, *Machtteilung. Geschichte der Mischverfassung*, Darmstadt 2006. This monograph by a political theorist provides the first history of representative ideas and constitutions of the mixed form of the state from antiquity to the present.
13. J. Ratzinger, *Milestones. Memoirs 1927-1977*, San Francisco 1998, p. 138.
14. *Reform und Anerkennung kirchlicher Ämter. Ein Memorandum der Arbeitsgemeinschaft ökumenischer Universitätsinstitute*, Munich and Mainz 1973.
15. Ibid., p. 17.
16. J. Laubach, *Soviel Glück im Leben. Streiflichter 1917-1997*, Mainz 1997, pp. 106f.

VII. The Demand for Capitulation

1. Cf. L.-J. Suénens, *Souvenirs et espérances*, Paris 1991.
2. J. Grootaers, 'Le cardinal L.-J. Suenens, Un apostolat qui a traversé le siècle', *Revue théologique de Louvain* 27, 1996, pp. 425-31.
3. Ibid.
4. Cf. N. Trippen, *Josef Kardinal Frings (1887-1978)*, vol. II, Paderborn 2005, p. 384.
5. Cf. *Unser Kirche. Evangelische Sonntagsblat für Westfalen-Lippe*, 23 April 1972, German translation of the letter from A. Solzhenytsin by Professor Robert Stupperich of Münster, Westphalia.
6. W. Jens (ed.), *Um nichts als die Wahrheit. Deutsche Bischofskonferenz contra Hans Küng. Ein Dokumentation*, edited with an introduction by Walter Jens, Munich 1978, Phase I, no. 3.
7. Cf. *Dokumentation* II, Phase I, no. 1.
8. *Dokumentation* II, Phase I, no. 2. The last edition of Denziger (1991), edited by P. Hünermann of Tübingen, conceals the fact that with this document an intervention was made in unfinished proceedings and the withdrawal of permission to teach was anticipated. This is a prime example of the arbitrariness of Roman law.
9. *Dokumentation* II, Phase I, no. 4.
10. *Dokumentation* II, Phase I, no. 10.
11. *Dokumentation* II, Phase I, no. 6; *Conflict*, pp. 85-91.
12. *Dokumentation* II, Phase I, no. 7.
13. *Dokumentation* II, Phase I, no. 10.
14. *Dokumentation* II, Phase I, no. 11; *Conflict*, pp. 92-8.
15. Ibid.; *Conflict*, pp. 96-7.
16. Ibid.; *Conflict*, pp. 97-8.
17. *Dokumentation* II, Phase I, no. 2, cf. no. 7.
18. *Dokumentation* II, Phase I, no. 13.
19. *Dokumentation* II, Phase I, no. 14; *Conflict*, pp. 98-101.

20. Ibid.; *Conflict*, p. 99.
21. Ibid.; *Conflict*, pp. 99-100.
22. Cf. *Publik-Forum*, 2 November 1973, p. 19. On p. 27 there is also an accurate account of the 'Painful events behind the scenes of a nuncio controversy'.
23. Cf. *Dokumentation* II, Phase I, no. 19; *Conflict*, pp. 104-18.
24. Ibid.; *Conflict*, p. 110.
25. Ibid.; *Conflict*, p. 109.
26. *Dokumentation* II, Phase I, no. 21.
27. *Dokumentation* II, Phase I, no. 20.
28. Cf. S. H. Pfürtner, 'Freiheit in der Kirche? Skizze eigener Erfahrungen, Ansprache zur Preisverleihung durch die Herbert-Haag-Stiftung "Fur Freiheit in der Kirche" am 21.August 2003 in Luzern', *Offener Kirche. Ein ökumenischer Forum*, 35.1, April 2004. There is further information here about the whole inquisitorial proceedings.
29. Cf. the correspondence with Dr Homeyer, Secretary of the Conference of Bishops, in *Dokumentation* II, Phase I, no. 1, nos 22-4.
30. *Dokumentation* II, Phase I, no. 25; *Conflict*, pp. 118-28.
31. *Publik-Forum*, 28 June 1974.
32. *Dokumentation* II, Phase I, no. 29.
33. Ibid.
34. *Dokumentation* II, Phase I, nos 32-3; *Conflict*, pp. 140-41.

VIII. The Adventure of a Book

1. H. Küng, *On Being a Christian*, London and New York 1974, p. 602.
2. *Dokumentation* II, Phase I, nos 27, 28, 30, 31; *Conflict*, pp. 151-61.
3. *Dokumentation* II, Phase I, no. 34.
4. *Dokumentation* II, Phase I, no. 35.
5. *Dokumentation* II, Phase I, no. 36; *Conflict*, p. 156.
6. Ibid.; *Conflict*, p. 156.
7. *Dokumentation* II, Phase I, no. 37; *Conflict*, p. 157.
8. *Dokumentation* II, Phase II, nos 1-3; *Conflict*, pp. 162-4.
9. *Dokumentation* II, Phase II, no. 4; *Conflict*, pp. 165-72.
10. *Dokumentation* II, Phase II, no. 5.
11. *Dokumentation* II, Phase II, no. 6; *Conflict*, pp. 172-3.
12. *Dokumentation* II, Phase II, no. 7; *Conflict*, pp. 173-4.
13. Ibid.; *Conflict*, p. 174.
14. *Dokumentation* II, Phase II, no. 8.
15. *Dokumentation* II, Phase II, nos 10-11.
16. R. Augstein, *Jesus Menschensohn*, Gütersloh 1972.
17. *Dokumentation* II, Phase III, no. 6; *Conflict*, pp. 188-206.
18. Cf. e.g. the composite volume *'Jesus von Nazareth' kontrovers. Rückfragen an Joseph Ratzinger*, Münster 2007.
19. *Dokumentation* II, Phase III, nos 1 and 2.

IX. Problems of the Hierarchy and Problems of the World

1. *Dokumentation* II, Phase IV, no. 1; *Conflict*, pp. 213f.
2. *Dokumentation* II, Phase IV, no. 2; *Conflict*, p. 215.
3. *Dokumentation* II, Phase IV, no. 3.
4. *Dokumentation* II, Phase IV, no. 4.
5. *Dokumentation* II, Phase IV, no. 5.
6. *Dokumentation* II, Phase IV, no. 4.
7. *Dokumentation* II, Phase IV, no. 5.
8. On 6 November, I gave a benefit lecture 'Why Sunday Worship?' for the Thomas More Association and its journal *The Critic* at Rosary College, Chicago; on 7 November in New York I was invited by my publisher to the musical *Godspell*. The next day there was a press conference for *On Being a Christian* at the Overseas Club, combined with several radio and television interviews. In my experience, what the special adviser for religious broadcasts of the Canadian Broadcasting Corporation (CBC) said is true of many readers of my book: 'It helped me to clarify my own thinking and proved a life raft for several friends.'
9. *Dokumentation* II, Phase IV, no. 7; *Conflict*, pp. 216-307.
10. *Dokumentation* II, Phase IV, nos 10 and 12.
11. *Dokumentation* II, Phase IV, no. 13; *Conflict*, p. 320.
12. *Dokumentation* II, Phase IV, no. 15.
13. Cf. R. Dallek, *An Unfinished Life. John F. Kennedy 1917-1963*, Boston 2003.
14. Cf. D. Tracy, H. Küng and J. B. Metz (eds), *Towards Vatican III. The Work That Needs To Be Done*, New York 1978.
15. *Dokumentation* II, Phase V, no. 1; *Conflict*, pp. 322-8.
16. *Dokumentation* II, Phase V, no. 2; *Conflict*, p. 328.
17. *Dokumentation* II, Phase V, no. 3.
18. *Dokumentation* II, Phase V, no. 4.
19. *Dokumentation* II, Phase V, no. 5; *Conflict*, p. 329.
20. *Dokumentation* II, Phase V, no. 6; *Conflict*, p. 331.
21. *Dokumentation* II, Phase IV, no .7.
22. *Dokumentation* II, Phase V, no. 7.
23. *Dokumentation* II, Phase V, no. 10; *Conflict*, pp. 334-47.
24. *Dokumentation* II, Introduction by Walter Jens, p. 19.
25. Cf. 1 Corinthians 12.28f.
26. *Dokumentation* II, Hans Küng: Ein Appell zur Verständigung, pp. 388f.; *Conflict*, pp. 347-64: p. 363.
27. 1 Peter 3.15.
28. H. Häring and K.-J. Kuschel (eds), *Hans Küng: His Work and His Way*, London 1979, p. 8. An expanded and updated German version was published in Munich in 1981.
29. N. Greinacher and H. Haag (eds), *Der Fall Küng. Eine Dokumentation*, Munich 1980 (= *Dokumentation* III), 1. 2.
30. *Dokumentation* III, 1. 3.
31. *Dokumentation* III, 1. 4.
32. *Dokumentation* III, 1. 5.
33. H. Küng, *Does God Exist? An Answer for Today*, London and New York 1978, pp. 680-88: p. 686, quoted in *Dokumentation* III, 1, 4.

34. *Dokumentation* III, 1. 7 (Bishop Moser); 1. 8 (Cardinal Höffner).
35. Hans Küng, *Great Christian Thinkers*, London and New York 1994.
36. As early as 1956, in Paris, immediately after completing my theological dissertation on Karl Barth, I had devoted myself closely to the more difficult works of the philosopher Hegel: his youth in Stuttgart, his studies in Tübingen and his time as a tutor in Berlin. As I describe in *My Struggle for Freedom*, I continued to work on them, first in the Biblioteca Nacional in Madrid, then in the British Museum Reading Room in London and finally again in my Swiss home in Sursee, so that before becoming assistant priest in Lucerne I had produced a handsome manuscript of 200 pages. I then worked over this in Münster in 1959/60 for a habilitation thesis, but after my call to Tübingen in 1960 this became as superfluous as the doctorate *ès-lettres* at the Sorbonne which I had planned. Only after the Council could I work over the whole manuscript thoroughly a second time: from the diaries Hegel kept at school through the great published works to the notes of his lectures on the philosophy of history.
37. Interview in KNA, 10 January 1979.

X. 1978: The Year of the Three Popes

1. Thus on 9 October at the Catholic Academy in Munich (the Director likes the title so much that without consulting me he makes it the title of a series of lectures in which my notorious opponents Hans Urs von Balthasar and Robert Spaemann then speak against me) and on 10 October in Karlsruhe. After my return from the US and Latin America I work on this lecture and give it in Frankfurt (27 November 1978), Mönchengladbach (28 November), Wuppertal (29 November) and Koblenz (30 November) On 1 December I pay a visit to the Schönstatt Centre in Vallendar and in the evening speak at the University of Bonn. On 2 December I visit the big Parler exhibition ('Fine Arts around 1400') in Cologne and in the evening speak in Düsseldorf. But I am back in time for a conversation with Bishop Moser on 6 December about lay theologians and the ultra-conservative parish priest of Tübingen.
2. J. Moltmann, *A Broad Place*, Minneapolis 2007, pp. 356f.
3. *Die Zeit*, 11 August 1978.
4. *Dokumentation* III, 1. 9.
5. G. Andreotti, *A ogni morte di Papa*, Milan 1980 (the German title is *Meine sieben Päpste*).
6. J. Cornwell, 'Marcinkus, The man I knew', *The Tablet*, 25 February 2006.
7. For more than three decades Peter Hertel has been critically concerned with Opus Dei. See *Geheimnisse des Opus Dei. Verschlusssachen – Hintergründe – Strategien*, Freiburg [3]1995; *Schleichende Übernahme. Josemaría Escrivá, sein Opus Dei und die Macht im Vatikan*, Oberürsel [5]2005; id., *Benedikts Stosstrupp. Das Opus Dei und der deutsche Papst*, Hörscheiben CD 1, 2007.
8. John Paul II, *Rise, Let Us Be on Our Way*, London and New York 2004, p. 88.
9. *Dokumentation* III, 1. 10; *Conflict*, pp. 370-71.
10. Ibid.; *Conflict*, p. 372.

11. Lectures at the University of Ulm (16 May 1979), Hohenheim, Stuttgart (18 May) and Ludwigshafen (11 June), and also at Bregenz in Austria (25 June) and Strasbourg in France (23 June).
12. I was allowed to give lectures at the Karl Marx University in Leipzig on 'The Christian Message and the Ecumene' (23/24 May 1979), and on the next day in the great hall of the University of Halle and to workers in the Lutheran Church of Saxony in Dresden (25 May 1979).
13. H. Küng, 'Neuen Thesen über Religion und Wissenschaft', *Die Zeit*, 19 October 1979, p. 72.
14. Ibid.

XI. The Great Confrontation

1. So far, this letter by Bishop Moser has not been published and is not contained in any documentation. I received it only after his death.
2. Cf. *Papsttum als ökumenische Frage*, edited by the Arbeitsgemeinschaft ökumenischer Universitätsinstitute, Mainz 1979.
3. J. Moltmann, 'Ein ökumenische Papsttum?', in ibid., pp. 260.
4. W. Pannenberg, in ibid., pp. 325f.
5. J. Ratzinger, *Milestones. Memoirs 1927-1977*, San Francisco 1998, pp. 138f.
6. *Dokumentation* III, 1. 10.
7. Ibid.
8. Ibid.
9. Ibid.
10. It is significant that the question why Karol Wojtyla did not study at the Gregorian but at the Angelicum is not investigated even by biographers such as G. Weigel, *The Witness of Hope. The Biography of John Paul II*, New York 1999, even though elsewhere he painstakingly describes the smallest details about His Holiness; of his 991 pages he devotes only one and a half to the connection between Wojtyla and Opus Dei and just one to the *'cause célèbre'* of the 'Küng affair', which is treated in a thoroughly partisan way.
11. Cf. M. Zajac, 'Die Konzilslehre in Polen: Eine unvollendete (R)evolution', *Zur Debatte* (Katholische Akademie in Bayern) 7, 2005, pp. 14-16.
12. *Dokumentation* III, 1. 14.
13. *Dokumentation* III, 1. 15
14. I have given similar lectures previously in Pforzheim (18 October) and Urach (22 October), in Mühlheim (11 October) and Stuttgart (23 October) on 'Managers and Belief in God'. Then I give my lecture on 'What One Can Hold On To' also in Protestant Erlangen (19 November), in Rosenheim (21 November), Linz (22 November) and Graz (23 November).
15. *Dokumentation* III, 1. 14.
16. *Dokumentation* III, 1. 16.
17. *Dokumentation* III, 1. 18.
18. Now and then I also preach sermons, for example at student worship (22 January 1979), 'Against Parties in the Church' (1 Corinthians 1.10-13), or at parish worship (21 January), 'Towards the Active Participation of Everyone in the Eucharist' (1 Corinthians 11). From 1 to 9 February 1979 I am at the World

Economic Forum in Davos where I give the major lecture 'Should Managers Believe in God?' For 10 to 19 March I accept an invitation from Marianne Saur's old friend Heinrich Schmid, head of a nationwide firm of painters, to go to Cannes on a small art trip to prepare my lecture to the German Federation of Artists towards the end of the year: Ronchamps, Audincourt, Châlons sur Saône, Autun, Beaune and then the famous museums of Chagall, Picasso, Matisse and others on the Côte d'Azur.

19. The annual meeting of *Concilium* traditionally takes place in Pentecost week, this time in Nordwijkerhout, the Netherlands. Then follow lectures in Ludwigshafen (11 June), Bregenz (25 June) and the annual meeting of our Institute (16 June) on 'How Do We Speak of God Today?'. Later I give lectures at the University of Ulm (16 July) and for creative artists at the Catholic Academy in Hohenheim, Stuttgart (18 July). On 3/4 December I again speak in Strasbourg (on 'La Science et le problème de Dieu') and in Luxembourg.

20. B. van Iersel, 'Wie fair war das Kolloquium mit Schillebeeckx?', *Orientierung* 44, 1980, pp. 42-5.
21. *Dokumentation* III, 1. 19 (*Die Welt,* 15 December 1979).
22. *Die Welt,* 15 December 1979.
23. *Dokumentation* III, 1. 17.
24. *Dokumentation* III, 2. 16.
25. D. Deckers, *Der Kardinal. Karl Lehmann. Eine Biographie*, Munich 2002.
26. *Dokumentation* III, 2. 2.
27. Ibid.
28. *Dokumentation* III, 2. 1.
29. Ibid.
30. *Dokumentation* III, 2. 3; *Conflict*, pp. 390-92.
31. Ibid.
32. *Dokumentation* III, 2. 4.
33. *Dokumentation* III, 2. 6; *Conflict*, pp. 392-3.
34. *Dokumentation* III, 2. 7; *Conflict*, pp. 393-4.
35. *Südwestpresse*, 20 December 1979.
36. *Dokumentation* III, 2. 11.
37. *Schwäbisches Tagblatt*, 20 December 1979.
38. *Dokumentation* III, 2. 12.
39. Ibid.
40. Ibid.
41. Ibid.
42. *Dokumentation* III, 2. 13.
43. *Dokumentation* III, 2. 14; *Conflict*, p. 399.
44. *Dokumentation* III, 2. 15; *Conflict*, pp. 400-01.
45. Ibid.; *Conflict*, p. 404.
46. *Dokumentation* III, 2 .16; *Conflict*, p. 405.
47. *Dokumentation* III, 2. 17; *Conflict*, p. 406.
48. Ibid.; *Conflict*, p. 407.
49. Ibid.
50. *Dokumentation* III, 2. 18.
51. *Dokumentation* III, 2. 19.
52. *Dokumentation* III, 2. 10.
53. Cf. *Dokumentation* III, 2. 21.

54. *Dokumentation* III, 2. 25.

XII. Roma Locuta – Causa non Finita: *Rome has Spoken, but the Case is Not Over*

1. *Dokumentation* III, 2. 26; *Conflict*, pp. 422-3.
2. *Dokumentation* III, 2. 27.
3. *Dokumentation* III, 2. 28; *Conflict*, pp. 423-5: p. 424.
4. K. Adenauer, letter to the Bonn pastor Dr Bernard Custodis, 23 February 1946, quoted in G. Denzer and V. Fabricius, *Die Kirchen im Dritten Reich*, vol. II, Frankfurt 1984, p. 255.
5. Cf. *Süddeutsche Zeitung*, 5/6 April 1980.
6. Even now it has not proved possible for the Vatican, otherwise highly skilled in international influence and participation, to sign this because it would involve numerous changes in the medieval–modern canon law.
7. *Dokumentation* III, 2. 31; *Conflict*, pp. 438-9.
8. *Dokumentation* III, 2. 32.
9. *Dokumentation* III, 2. 32.
10. *Dokumentation* III, 2. 33.
11. Cf. *Dokumentation* III, 3.1-50.
12. *Dokumentation* III, 3. 38.
13. *Dokumentation* III, 3. 42.
14. *Dokumentation* III, 3. 40.
15. *Dokumentation* III, 3. 41.
16. Cf. *Dokumentation* III, 4. 2.
17. *Dokumentation* III, 4. 1-9.
18. Cf. *Dokumentation* III, 5. 41.
19. *Dokumentation* III, 5. 1-40.
20. *Dokumentation* III, 5. 24.
21. *Dokumentation* III, 5. 5.
22. The headlines also indicate the line taken by many other Catholic theologians: Dietrich Wiederkehr: 'Küng Case or the Case of the Congregation for the Doctrine of the Faith?'; Peter Stockmeier, 'In Conversation with Other Confessions does Küng want to Demolish what Separates Them?'; Ludwig Kaufmann, 'Pohier, Schillebeeckx, Küng and the Right of the Faithful'; Josef Blank, 'The Noose round the Neck'; Stephan Pfürtner, 'In Search of Heresies'; Gerhard Dautzenberg, 'Inappropriate for the Cause of the Faith'; Wolfgang Seibel. 'The Consequences of Doctrinal Proceedings'. Finally also the Catholic historian Friedrich Heer, 'Hans Küng: a Royal Sacrifice'.
23. *Dokumentation* III, 5. 33; *Conflict*, pp. 536-8.
24. *Dokumentation* III, 3. 8.
25. *Dokumentation* III, 5. 7.
26. *Dokumentation* III, 3. 50.
27. *Dokumentation* III, 3. 49.
28. Ibid.
29. *Dokumentation* III, 6. 1.
30. Ibid.

31. Ibid.
32. *Dokumentation* III, 6. 2.
33. Cf. *Dokumentation* III, 3. 31.
34. *Dokumentation* III, 6. 6; *Conflict*, pp. 440-45.
35. *Dokumentation* III, 3. 31; *Conflict*, pp. 446-7.
36. *Dokumentation* III, 2. 35.
37. *Dokumentation* III, 3. 31; *Conflict*, p. 448.
38. I owe this information to a committed student representative of the Tubingen Solidarity Movement, Jutta Flatters.
39. I have been helped in surveying the comprehensive and complex material and in the laborious work of editing and correcting and translating documents in foreign languages by Dr Urs Baumann, Dr Margret Gentner, Eleonore Henn, Dr Karl-Josef Kuschel and Michael Stemmeler.
40. H. Küng, *The Church*, London 1968, pp. 474f.
41. *Dokumentation* III, 6 3; *Conflict*, pp. 454-80.
42. Ibid.; *Conflict*, p. 479.
43. *Dokumentation* III, 6. 4; *Conflict*, pp. 481-6.
44. *Dokumentation* III, 6. 6; *Conflict*, pp. 498-502.
45. Ibid.; *Conflict*, p. 501.
46. Ibid.; *Conflict*, p. 501.
47. *Dokumentation* III, 6. 7.
48. *Dokumentation* III, 6. 8.
49. The Constitutional Court judge Ernst Gottfried Mahrenholz proved an outstanding advocate of my standpoint (against U. Scheuner): 'Staat und staatliches katholisch-theologischen Lehramt', *Die Staat* 26, 1986, vol. 1, pp. 79-103.
50. For the facts cf. H. Küng, *Judaism*, London and New York 1992, Part Two, Chapter A II 5: A pope who kept silent: Pius XII; A II 7: An episcopate which capitulated: the German bishops.
51. Details in K.-J. Kuschel, *Laughter. A Theological Reflection*, London 1994.

Prospect

1. *Dokumentation* III, 6. 9; *Conflict*, pp. 507-10: p. 510.
2. Ibid.; *Conflict*, pp. 509-10.
3. M. Drobinski, *Oh Gott, die Kirche*, Düsseldorf 2006, depicts the current state of the Catholic Church realistically and precisely from a German perspective and R. Blair Kaiser, *A Church in Search of Itself*, New York 2006, from an American perspective.
4. The parable comes from the German Canadian Margaret Fishback Powers (1964).
5. *Dokumentation* III, 5. 12.
6. G. Picco, H. Küng, R. von Weizsäcker et al., *Crossing the Divide. Dialogue among Civilizations*, South Orange, NJ 2001.
7. Cf. R. Dahrendorf, *Versuchungen der Unfreiheit. Die Intellektuellen in Zeiten der Prüfung*, Munich 2006.
8. Cf. H. Küng, 'Ökumenische Theologie zwischen den Fronten. Konsequenzen aus dem Streit zwischen Rom, Luther und Erasmus', in *Theologie im Aufbruch. Eine ökumenische Grundlegung*, Munich 1987, pp. 31-66.
9. L. Swidler (ed.), *Küng in Conflict*, New York 1981.

10. R. Nowell, *A Passion for Truth. Hans Küng: A Biography*, London 1981.
11. Cf. D. Tracy, *The Analogical Imagination. Christian Theology and the Culture of Pluralism*, London and New York 1981, chapter I, 1: A Social Portrait of the Theologian.

Select Bibliography

Books by Hans Küng
(The date of the German publication is given in brackets)

Justification. The Doctrine of Karl Barth and a Catholic Reflection (1957), New York: Thomas Nelson and Sons 1964 and London: Burns and Oates 1965

The Council and Reunion (1960), London: Sheed and Ward 1961; American edition *The Council, Reform and Reunion*, New York: Sheed and Ward 1961

That the World May Believe. Letters to Young People (1962), London and New York: Sheed and Ward 1963

Structures of the Church (1962), New York: Thomas Nelson and Sons 1964 and London: Burns and Oates 1965

The Theologian in the Church (1964), London: Sheed and Ward 1965

The Church (1967), London: Burns and Oates and New York: Sheed and Ward 1967

Truthfulness. The Future of the Church (1968), London and New York: Sheed and Ward 1968

The Incarnation of God. An Introduction to Hegel's Theological Thought as Prolegomena to a Future Christology (1970), Edinburgh: T&T Clark 1987

Infallible? An Enquiry (1970), London: Collins and New York: Doubleday 1971

Why Priests? A Proposal for a New Church Ministry (1971), London: Collins and New York: Doubleday 1972

What Must Remain in the Church (1973), London: Collins 1977

On Being a Christian (1974), London: Collins and New York: Doubleday 1977

Brother or Lord? A Jew and a Christian Talk Together About Jesus (1976, with Pinchas Lapide), London: Collins 1977

Signposts for the Future (1980), New York: Doubleday 1978 (contains '20 Theses on Being a Christian')

Freud and the Problem of God, New Haven: Yale University Press 1979

The Christian Challenge: A Shortened Version of On Being a Christian (1980), London: Collins 1979

Does God Exist? An Answer for Today (1978), London: Collins and New York: Doubleday 1980

The Church – Maintained in Truth? (1979), London: SCM Press and New York: Seabury Press 1980

539

Art and the Question of Meaning (1980), London: SCM Press and New York: Crossroad 1981

Eternal Life? (1982), London: Collins and New York: Doubleday 1984

Global Responsibility (1990), London: SCM Press and New York: Crossroad 1991

Judaism (1991), London: SCM Press and New York: Crossroad 1992

Christianity: Its Essence and History (1994), London: SCM Press and New York: Crossroad 1995

Reforming the Church Today. Keeping Hope Alive (1990), New York: Crossroad 1996

The Catholic Church: A Short History (2001), London: Weidenfeld & Nicolson and New York: Random House 2001

Tracing the Way: Spiritual Dimensions of the World Religions (1999), London and New York: Continuum 2002

Women in Christianity (2001), London and New York: Continuum 2002

My Struggle for Freedom (2002), London: Continuum and Grand Rapids, MI: Eerdmans 2003

Islam (2004), Oxford: Oneworld 2007

The Beginning of All Things. Science and Religion (2005), Grand Rapids, MI: Eerdmans 2007

Books about Hans Küng and the Controversies
(also including important documentation in German referred to in the text by the English title between quotation marks)

H. U. von Balthasar (ed.), *Diskussion über Hans Küngs 'Christ Sein'*, Mainz: Matthias Grünewald 1976

N. Greinacher and H. Haag (eds), *Der Fall Küng. Eine Dokumentation*, Munich: Piper 1980

H. Häring, *Hans Küng: Breaking Through*, London: SCM Press 1998

H. Häring and K.-J. Kuschel, *Hans Küng: His Work and His Way*, London: Collins 1979

H. Häring and J. Nolte (eds), *Diskussion um Hans Küng 'Die Kirche'*, Freiburg im Breisgau: Herder 1971

W. Jens (ed.), *Um nichts als die Wahrheit. Deutsche Bishofskonferenz contra Hans Küng*, Munich: Piper 1978

H. Küng (ed.), *Fehlbar? Eine Bilanz*, Zurich: Benziger 1973

K. Rahner (ed.), *Zum Problem Unfehlbarkeit. Antwort auf die Anfrage von Hans Küng*, Freiburg im Breisgau: Herder 1971

L. Swidler (ed.), *Küng in Conflict*, New York: Doubleday 1981

A Word of Thanks

Almost a thousand people are named in this book, many of whom I have got to know personally, members of my family, friends, colleagues, collaborators, fellow theologians, politicians, fellow Christians. I would like to thank them for all the stimulation, support and collaboration they have provided for many years. I have always been aware just how much I owe to others: 'What have you got that was not given to you?' (1 Corinthians 4.7).

Here I must limit myself to naming those who have helped with this second volume of memoirs. First I want to thank my two colleagues who put on the computer and then checked the many pages that I had written out twice by hand, dictated and then corrected again. Anette Stuber-Rousselle was tireless, often working on my manuscript late into the night and incorporating my endless corrections to almost every sentence. Likewise, day by day Dr Günther Gebhardt kept looking through the manuscript in addition to his work as Academic Co-ordinator of the Global Ethic Foundation. Both were spared distractions by my chief secretary of many years, Inge Baumann, and more recently her successor, Ute Wanner.

Then I want to thank all those who took the trouble to read critically a manuscript which was by no means short – I know how deep their commitment has been. From beginning to end it was assessed: at home by two people who lived through the events in my house, Marianne Saur and Professor Dr Karl-Josef Kuschel, who for decades has kept a keen eye on my literary style. Extremely well-informed contemporaries also read the manuscript: my friend from the German College, Fr Wolfgang Seibel SJ, formerly chief editor of *Stimmen der Zeit*, and my assistant and academic counsellor in the 1960s and 1970s, Professor Dr Hermann Häring. Katharina Elliger corrected first an early and then the last version of the book, supported by my former chief secretary Eleonore Henn. Parts of the manuscript were read by Professor Dr Walter and Dr Inge Jens, Chancellor of the University Emeritus Professor Dr Georg Sandberger and Dr Thomas Riplinger.

This whole gigantic work was brought to a successful conclusion after four years by Dr Stephan Schlensog, who in addition to all his duties as General Secretary of the Global Ethic Foundation also read the proofs and supervised the layout, format and index of names; this made it possible for me to make improvements up to the last moment.

I am grateful to all these individuals for numerous improvements to style and content. Collaboration with Piper Verlag (Ulrich Wank in the editorial department, Hanns Polanetz in production, Eva Brenndörfer in publicity and Ingrid Ullrich in sales) has been as smooth and professional as ever.

I must make one important correction to *My Struggle for Freedom*. In it I said that 'the second (and last) English edition of my biography' would follow. That was careless. There will be, I hope, a third volume. But whether I shall be able to complete it in my ninth decade is in the hands of Another.

Tübingen, 1 August 2007 *Hans Küng*

Translator's note

I would like to thank John Wilkins, former Editor of *The Tablet*, and my long-standing colleague Margaret Lydamore, former Associate Editor of SCM Press Ltd, for their painstaking checking of the translation and their many creative suggestions. The book would have been markedly less good without their help.

Highgate, 1 December 2007 *John Bowden*